CONTENTS

xii CONTENTS

PREFACE

My intention is to make this book both original and derivative. Those familiar with the existing literature on risk management will note that the book differs substantially from its predecessors. It offers little descriptive detail of insurance policies and procedures, it has little on the technology of loss reduction and little of the organizational/managerial discussion familiar in existing texts. It may not look like a risk management book at all. Those approaching the book from a background in financial management may find the book somewhat derivative. It represents an application of the analytical framework of financial management to that set of issues addressed by the risk manager.

Those involved in risk management (practically or educationally) will probably be aware of immediate linkages with finance. Most risk managers are responsible, directly or indirectly, to the finance director. In colleges, most risk management courses are offered by, or in collaboration with, the finance department. Despite these ties, there has been little past effort to ensure the compatibility of risk management and other financial decisions. The risk management literature has all but ignored the radical developments that have transformed the way in which financial decisions are formulated and analyzed. Indeed, my immediate motivation for writing this book stems from my joint function to teach finance and insurance at the University of Illinois. To master standard materials for the afternoon risk management class, students were often required to ignore, or even forget, the basic principles of financial economics learned in the morning!

The imposition of a financial economic framework on the risk management function is not an empty academic exercise. Though some theory is needed to develop and to understand the basic ideas, the application of finance to risk management provides a practical decision framework.

The book is aimed primarily at students in higher level undergraduate classes and at graduate students. A prerequisite is a basic course in statistics and probability. A prior introduction to financial management and to capital market theory is also a distinct advantage. However, relevant concepts are introduced to the new reader and the material has been tested on actuarial students without a background in finance as well as upon mainstream finance majors. I am somewhat hesitant to anticipate the reaction of practicing risk managers. To those with no background in the concepts of finance, the material will be very new and many of the concepts will be surprising and at variance with accepted wisdom. But these ideas are having a big impact on corporate decision making. The risk manager wishing to talk the same language as his or her finance colleagues may well find the investment to be worthwhile.

My thanks are due to a number of people who have provided explicit feedback. Others have debated patiently, and at length, the rapid evolution of risk management and its isolation from the mainstream subject areas. On the dubious principle that omission from a longer list is a greater slight than omission from a shorter list, I will mention just a few: Robert Mehr, Bob Witt, Mike Smith, James Garven, Harris Schlesinger and George Head. Carol Carillo did the bulk of the typing with touching good cheer. Helpful comments and reviews were provided by: Charles A. D'Ambrosio, University of Washington at Seattle; J. D. Hammond, The Pennsylvania State University; and C. Arthur Williams, University of Minnesota.

Finally, I wish to thank my family—Ann, Simon, Timothy, and Kathryn—for their good cheer during the writing of this book.

Neil A. Doherty

CORPORATE RISK MANAGEMENT

A FINANCIAL EXPOSITION

CHAPTER 1

INTRODUCTION TO RISK MANAGEMENT

RISK AND CORPORATE ACTIVITY

The term *risk management* does not yield to simple definition. The terms *risk* and *management* offer some clues on content, although without prior knowledge, few would accurately guess the subject matter from the title. Certainly *risk management* is more specific than the title would have us believe; only some risks will be managed under our subject umbrella. The class of risks does have distinguishing characteristics that set it apart from other forms of corporate risk, although in trying to achieve tight definitions, we find many cases that behave badly. Despite these difficulties in formalizing a definition for our subject matter, it is not difficult to capture its general flavor.

To set discussion underway, let us adopt a temporary definition of *risk*. Many activities undertaken by an individual or a firm do not have a predictable outcome, e.g., the return from investing in a stock, the wages resulting from labor contract negotiations, the outcome of an auction for a government contract, the future demand for a newly marketed product, the outcome of research in new products, etc. At best, we can identify a range of outcomes for such events and give some indication of the likelihood or probability of each possible outcome. At worst, we just do not know what the prospects are. The lack of predictability of outcomes may be termed *risk*. Risk, in this sense, does not imply that outcomes are adverse, only that they are not known in advance. Thus risk includes the possibility that the result may provide a pleasant surprise; e.g., an investment may yield a higher than expected return.

From such a working definition of risk, it is apparent that corporate activity is replete with risk and that risky activity can be classified. For example, one such classification might be:

1 *Marketing risk*. The demand for a firm's products depends on many factors that may or may not be within the control of the firm, e.g., product design, promotion, general income levels, price, price of competing and complementary products, consumer tastes, changes in government regulation of trade in the firm's products, etc. Such influences combine to cast a thick veil of uncertainty about a firm's future demand.

2 *Financial risk*. The cost of providing and maintaining capital for a firm is subject to capital market fluctuations. In recent years, both debt and equity costs have been subject to considerable fluctuation. Financial risk may be modified by particular corporate decisions; for example, an increase in corporate debt will often increase the default risk on old debt and enhance the variability of stockholders' returns.

3 *Resource management risk*. In the production process, the firm brings together specific resources. The productivity of these resources is subject to risks of varying nature. The cost of resources is subject to changes in price, resources may be withdrawn from the production process (as in strikes), resources may be subject to sudden physical impairment or destruction (such as fire, explosion, etc.), and resource use may be beneficially or adversely affected by technological change, etc.

4 *Environmental risk*. Risk may arise from the incidental interactions between a firm and its environment. For example, corporate operations, such as ownership of property and operation of vehicles, may expose the public to certain dangers for which the firm has a statutory or common-law liability. Also, government regulation other than that having a specific product or industry basis, such as zoning laws, may impose contingent costs on the firm or result in unexpected benefits, etc.

This classification of risk is, perhaps, arbitrary,[1] and the types of risk defined are neither mutually exclusive nor exhaustive. It serves merely to suggest that typically a firm is subjected to a wide variety of risks.

In monitoring the total performance of a firm, the collective effect of these various risks is important. In its continuing activity, the firm hopefully earns a profit for its owners. The level, growth, and variability of these profits will depend on the interaction of the various sources of risk. Each single risk will usually have an effect on total corporate risk, although risk aggregation is a subtle and complex process. We will seek to define a subset of corporate risks, and this will become the focus of this book. However, the analysis of these "risk management" risks can only properly be understood in the context of the wider set of risky activities undertaken by a firm in the course of its business.

---

[1]An alternative classification presented many years ago by Hardy (1923) is often used to introduce risk management:

1 Risk of destruction of property through physical hazard
2 Uncertainties in the production process
3 Risk resulting from market processes, such as price changes
4 Risk caused by "abnormal" social conduct
5 Risk arising from the failure to utilize available knowledge

PURE RISK AND RISK MANAGEMENT

Against the backdrop of diverse corporate risks, risk management writers have sought to isolate a particular class of risks that is the object of their attention. Perhaps the most enduring classification was given by Mowbray (1930):

Speculative risks are those that offer the firm a chance of gain or loss. Such activities are usually undertaken in the hope of gain, although the range of possible outcomes includes those that will register to the owner an economic loss. Investment in business activity is invariably risky in the speculative sense; other examples of speculative risk arise with the holding of currency, stocks, real estate, etc., where price fluctuation can either benefit or deprive the owner.

Pure risks are those that offer only the prospect of loss. Thus the possible outcomes from activities or events exhibiting pure risk range from zero to negative.

From the examples of corporate risk given earlier, risks can be identified as either of a *speculative* or of a *pure* nature. Marketing risks are usually speculative. The marketing of products or services is an indispensable ingredient in the entrepreneurial process, since the firm is in business to make a profit. Demand changes can either decrease or increase corporate earnings. Similarly, changes in the regulatory posture adopted by the government can either increase corporate earnings (by shielding the firm from competition) or decrease them (by removing impediments to competition). Another example of speculative risk is the capital gains or losses the firm experiences on its holdings of physical or financial assets.

Contrast these examples with the following: A firm is exposed to the possibility of fire loss to its plant and equipment; corporate assets may be stolen; defective products might induce liability suits against the firm; or corporate officers or others with access to corporate finances might defraud the firm. Events of this nature threaten the firm with financial loss. They are unfavorable by-products of the firm's main profit-seeking activities and hold only the prospect of reducing profit. Risk management is concerned with such *pure* risks.

The terminology *pure risk* is quite unfortunate because it does have normative overtones: Indeed, one might reflect on the curious paradox that such purity of risk often leads to moral hazard. No doubt, the intended connotation is that risk is generally understood to be adverse in quality and that pure risks concentrate on adverse events. While the definition of pure risk does capture the "flavor" of risk management risks, the definition is not very tight. Two borderline examples have been noted by Dennenberg and Ferrari (1966). *Credit risk* refers to the prospect of bad debts on the firm's credit accounts. Certainly, a bad debt is a loss to the firm. However, if the activity giving rise to the risk of bad debts is defined to be the extension of credit, such activity may be said to exhibit speculative risk. The extension of credit is used as a marketing device to stimulate product demand. Thus liberal credit may lead both to higher sales and more bad debts. A second borderline example is the prospect of a *strike*. Although a strike usually results in financial loss to the firm, this may not always be the case. During a period of excess capacity, a firm can possibly achieve more effective cost savings through a strike than through layoffs. Furthermore, strikes result from labor negotiations, which carry the prospect of improved productivity and thus economic gain for the firm.

Not surprisingly, these two borderline cases are on the fringes of risk management. Management of credit risks sometimes falls within the risk manager's sphere of responsibility; other times it does not. Similarly, the risk manager may or may not have a role to play in contingency planning for potential strikes. In contrast, the risk manager typically does have well-defined responsibilities in the following areas:

1 The protection of corporate property
2 The financing of losses arising from destruction or damage to corporate property
3 The safety of employees, customers, contractors, and third parties
4 The financing of losses arising from injury to these groups
5 The security of other assets, such as money, corporate records, industrial or commercial "secrets," etc.
6 Other contingent liabilities imposed on the firm by the activities of its employees or agents

Clearly, such responsibilities refer to "no win" situations, prompting the thought that risk management might upstage economics as the "dismal science." Often, risk management is also defined to include

7 Pensions
8 Other employee benefits, such as life insurance and health insurance

These latter activities relate to pure risks to which employees are exposed. However, it is by no means clear that the firm's involvement in the administration of such activities imposes only the prospect of loss.

The concept of pure risk gives a rough guide to the content of risk management. Our feeling for the subject matter might be enhanced by briefly describing the rapid evolution of the subject.

THE EVOLUTION OF RISK MANAGEMENT

A professional society for risk managers exists in the United States, and other countries have parallel organizations. The U.S. society is the Risk and Insurance Management Society, Inc. (RIMS). The functions of this society are similar to those of other professional societies. RIMS provides appropriate forums for the interchange of ideas and information of common professional interest, including local chapter meetings, an annual conference, and the publication of a magazine. RIMS also has an educational function, the purpose of which is to enhance the level of professional skill of its members and to establish standards for new risk managers. Most of the members of RIMS are practicing risk and insurance managers who exercise comparable risk-management functions for their respective employers. An insight into the nature of these functions can be obtained by looking at the previous title of the RIMS. In 1975, the American Society of Insurance Management changed its title to the Risk and Insurance Management Society, Inc. In so doing, the society recognized the changing nature of its members' corporate functions—from insurance management to the more general risk management.[2]

Many medium- and large-sized firms have long employed specialists to administer the firm's insurance portfolio. Identification of insurable risks and purchase of appropriate insurance calls for a particular set of skills: knowledge of insurance coverage and insurance law, familiarity with insurance markets, and technical skills to identify prospective hazards are needed. Such skills can be obtained by the firm on a consultancy basis (employing an insurance broker), or they may be lodged in house by maintaining a suitably qualified individual or group of people on the payroll. These insurance managers are charged with the administration of the firm's insurance portfolio. The risks administered by insurance managers are those typically underwritten by the insurance market, and insurance managers are typically recruited from the various segments of this market.

The responsibilities of an insurance manager are not the same in all firms, however. For example, some insurance managers have the added responsibility of administering the firm's pension program and other employee benefit programs, such as health and life insurance. Some are responsible for maintaining programs for safety and loss prevention. However, these functions are ancillary to the firm's insurance portfolio. Life insurance, pensions, and health insurance are often marketed simultaneously with property, casualty, and liability insurance (e.g., by multiline insurers, agents, and brokers), so it would appear natural for an insurance manager to assume responsibility for company programs in these fields. Furthermore, loss prevention and safety may be seen as ancillary to the provision of insurance, so again the assignment of these responsibilities to an insurance manager is a natural development. Consequently, insurance management is simply the subject "insurance," studied from the corporate buyer's perspective.

A term that captures some of the traditional attitude to corporate insurance is "sleep insurance." If a firm buys insurance on all insurable perils, managers are free to go home for a "good night's sleep." Upon waking, duly refreshed, they are free to consider the "real" business decisions and tackle the "real" business risks. This attitude is partly reflected by Mehr and Hedges (1963), who, in the introduction to their risk-management text, describe one of the corporate objectives as a "good night's sleep."

The role of insurance managers has changed as, in many cases, has the job title. Alternatives to insurance are being explored with increasing vigor. Various surveys of risk management activity have revealed a progressive trend toward higher risk retention.[3] The most visible part of this trend has been growth in the number and size of "captive" insurance companies. A *captive* is a subsidiary of a noninsurance firm that handles all or part of the parent's insurance needs. In this framework, risk retention is still undertaken in a formal manner using underwriting techniques, but the losses still fall deadweight on the parent's shareholders. Accompanying these new techniques has been a developing risk-management literature. Although it is uncertain whether

---

[2]A brief history of RIMS is given by Mehr and Cammack (1980; pp. 35–37). Other statements on the evolution of insurance are given by Crockford (1982) and Head (1982).

[3]See Hogue and Olson (1976) and various surveys published in the RIMS publication *Risk Management*.

the literature has led or followed developments in the field, many of the new ideas have now been formalized into an accepted field of study.[4]

The purpose here is not to give a scholarly history of risk management, but simply to make the point that risk management today is a product of risk management in the past. In attempting to define the subject matter by means of the concept of pure risk, we ran into rather foggy boundaries. By stressing the evolution of risk management from insurance management, we at least have another handle on the subject matter: *Risk management is predominantly concerned with insurable risks.*

Insurable risks are risks that are typically underwritten by insurers. It is fairly usual for insurers to write corporate risks of the following nature:

1 Property risks for such perils as fire, weather damage, collision, acts of violence, etc.

2 Liability risks, such as workers' compensation, employer's liability, vehicle collision, product liability, malpractice, etc.

3 Transport insurance for land, sea, or air travel covering both property and liability risks

4 Surety and guarantee bonding

In addition, however, insurers typically carry personal risks, such as life and injury insurance, and administer pension plans. The association of these types of activity with the insurance sector explains why they are often embraced within the scope of risk management, even though their inclusion is somewhat dubious on the basis of the definition of pure risk. (In fact, we will pay little attention to employee benefits in the book, concentrating instead on those events which directly impose loss on the firm.)

The use of *insurable risk* to describe the subject matter of risk management does not imply that such risks should be insured. Indeed, the development of risk management is seen as the pursuit of alternatives to insurance. The decision criteria developed here place insurance somewhat insignificantly within a framework designed to maximize the firm's value.

THE STRUCTURE OF RISK MANAGEMENT

During the rapid evolution of risk management, a decision structure has emerged that has gained widespread acceptance. This structure is understandable once we accept the fact that risk management has arisen from and is defined around the insurance function. Under this traditional structure, decision making proceeds along the following lines[5]:

1 Risks should be identified.
2 Risks should be measured.

---

[4]See Crockford (1982).
[5]See, for example, Williams and Heins (1964; Ch. 1), Greene and Serbein (1983; Ch. 2), and Mehr and Hedges (1963; Ch. 1).

3 Risks should be "handled"
  a by insuring the risk.
  b by retention of the risk.
  c by transfer to a party other than the insurer, e.g., a subcontractor.
  d by reducing the probability or magnitude of loss.
  e by avoiding the activity that gives rise to loss.

This structure serves well to break away from the rigidity of insurance management because it identifies alternatives to insurance. However, it still seems that the alternatives are defined around the insurance function. Respectively, alternatives (*b*) to (*e*) may be seen as

  b Not insuring
  c Quasi-insuring by finding another party to underwrite the risk
  d and **e** Reducing or removing the need for insurance by reducing the underlying peril

Later we will be somewhat critical of this traditional approach. For now, we will attempt to derive a structure for risk-management decisions that ensures compatibility with other types of financial decision making by a firm. To do this, we will add into the preceding structure a further risk-management function that calls for the risk manager to measure the impact of loss against whatever financial objective may be used to measure corporate performance. Furthermore, the handling devices just listed may be subdivided into two very different types of financial functions: investment and financing. To properly identify and evaluate alternative risk-management strategies, we must pay attention to this distinction.

The broad framework for financial risk management is as follows:

1 Identify pure risk exposures.
2 Measure risks in terms of direct costs.
3 Measure the impact of risk on financial performance measures.
4 Develop a risk-management strategy.

The formation of a risk-management strategy entails

  a Investment decisions on loss reduction and/or prevention projects.
  b Investment decisions on replacement of resources destroyed by pure risk events
  c Selection of sources of finance if the preceding investments are to be undertaken

This framework is designed to emphasize that risk-management decisions must be consistent with other corporate decisions. Risk management, like other corporate activities, requires that decisions be made on the use of costly resources and on the sources of finance for such resources. It is not enough that such decision making permits us to select the better of two competing risk-management strategies; it must also permit us to compare risk-management decisions with other corporate decisions. Suppose, for example, that a firm must make one of three mutually exclusive choices:

Choice 1 involves spending $100,000 on a safety program.

Choice 2 involves putting $100,000 into a reserve fund from which to pay future losses.

Choice 3 involves investing $100,000 in new machinery to increase the firm's output of widgets.

To make such a choice, a consistent procedure is required to evaluate the three alternatives. Since all are essentially investment decisions, the obvious way to achieve consistency is to set a financial goal and determine which alternative scores highest against that goal. For example, which course of action adds most to corporate profitability, or which scores highest in terms of the value of the owner's equity, etc.

This approach to risk management emphasizes that decisions must be made in a consistent manner. Since risk management decisions are a subset of a firm's total set of financial decisions, a fruitful way of achieving such consistency is to use financial management techniques.

DEFINITION OF RISK

At this stage it is useful to be more precise in defining risk. Confusion arises because risk management overlaps with other subject areas, and these subjects have not used *risk* in a consistent manner. For example, in insurance, the word *risk* is used to describe

1 The subject of the policy, i.e., the property or liability that is insured. An example of such usage would be: "The insurer's records reveal that it covers 20 risks all in close proximity to each other, thereby constituting a fire conflagration hazard: The potential for catastrophic claims payments is clear."

2 The peril that is insured under the policy. For example, "This policy covers all risks to the insured property except those arising from war."

3 The average of long-run value of loss, the probability of loss, or the expected value of loss. An example of such usage is: "The insurer declined to renew the automobile policy since the claims record indicated that the policyholder was a bad risk."

In an actuarial context, risk is usually given a statistical interpretation. Actuaries are often concerned with the statistical properties of the insurer's underwriting portfolio: What "average" value of total loss payment is expected, and what is the level of variability about this average level? The degree or range of variability is known as the *riskiness* of the portfolio. This interpretation of risk is also used in finance and will be adopted in this text.

Consider a simple game in which a coin is flipped. If the coin lands heads, you win $10; if it lands tails, you lose $10. On average, you might decide that this is a "breakeven" or "even odds" gamble, and this feature may well influence your decision to play the game. However, the game has another feature: The outcome is not predictable. There is more than one possible outcome, but only one outcome will prevail. The potential outcomes are spread over a range and have associated probabilities. The lack of predictability, or spread of outcomes, indicates that the game is risky. There are various conventions for measuring this spread, and accordingly, these are known as *measures of risk*.

Other examples of risk can be found quite easily, although not all of them are quite as straightforward. Consider the potential profitability to the National Aeronautics and Space Administration (NASA) of commercial space shuttle cargoes. So many uncertainties—technical, political, and economic—surround such a value that the number of dollars of profit must be viewed as a random value. Subjectively, one may impose a range on the possible magnitude of this value. The inability to predict future profit suggests that the value is risky. However, this example differs from the previous one in that probabilities attaching to possible outcomes are not known objectively. Risk is present, but it cannot be measured so conveniently.

In both examples, the outcome was surrounded by uncertainty, but the term *uncertainty* is used here in an everyday sense. Both *risk* and *uncertainty* have been subjected to more precise interpretations.

At the turn of the century, A. H. Willet (1901) sought to offer a distinction between risk and uncertainty in his important work *The Economic Theory of Risk and Insurance:*

> My only reason for mentioning it here is to show why it seems necessary to define risk with reference to the degree of uncertainty about the occurrence of a loss, and not with reference to the degree of probability that it will occur. Risk in this sense is the objective correlative of the subjective uncertainty. It is the uncertainty considered as embodied in the course of events in the external world, of which subjective uncertainty is a more or less faithful interpretation [p. 8].

And again,

> Risk and uncertainty are the objective and subjective aspects of apparent variability in the course of natural events [p. 24].

In his more widely known classic, *Risk, Uncertainty, and Profit,* F. H. Knight (1933) offered an interpretation that rested on a similar objective-subjective distinction. Knight distinguished between measurable and immeasurable risk. In the gambling example given earlier, possible outcomes and associated probabilities are known; therefore, the spread of values can be subjected to mathematical measurement. Knight defines such variability as *risk.* In the space shuttle example, the distribution of possible values and probabilities is not known; this is a situation of *uncertainty.* The similarities between Knight's and Willett's definitions may be more important than their differences, especially since modern finance theory has not become involved in the semantics of the issue.

The convention in finance is to interpret *risk* as the absence of certainty. This is entirely in the spirit of Willett and Knight, although *uncertainty* has more or less been dropped from the technical lexicon. A *risky outcome* is one that can assume a number of values, the particular value not being known in advance. Thus risk, in this sense, corresponds to Willett's generalized concept of uncertainty. Yet the great leap forward that finance achieved, both as an academic and an applied discipline, in the 1960s and 1970s was based on both the application of economic analysis and quantification. In its central role in this development, risk has been subjected to intensive measurement. Thus standard deviation, variance, and more theoretically derived concepts such as beta are measures of risk. Such constructs are mathematical conventions, and as such, they are somewhat arbitrary; they may serve well or serve poorly according to how much relevant and accurate information they convey about the spread in outcomes. Thus risk relates to the underlying variability in some relevant value; measures of risk are mathematical conventions to summarize the pattern and extent of such spread.

Risk management concerns the management of events that cannot be predicted. The contemplated events usually are adverse, but it is not this feature that makes risk management an interesting and difficult subject.[6] Rather, it is the quality of unpredictability in the events contemplated. This quality calls for a particular decision framework that will apply equivalently to pure and speculative risk. Risk managers have, for the most part, been slow to recognize the need for such consistency in the application of decision criteria, and the bulk of risk-management literature has developed in untroubled isolation from the somewhat revolutionary advances in financial management.

THE SIGNIFICANCE OF RISK MANAGEMENT

Risk management is big business. A somewhat surprising fact quoted by Mayers and Smith (1982) is that aggregate annual insurance premiums paid by U.S. corporations are of a similar order of magnitude to the aggregate dividend disbursements of these corporations. Dividends have been the object of considerable research; risk management has not. Yet even this comparison understates the importance and size of risk-management activity. As we have seen, insurance represents only one of a number of ways of handling pure risk, and the costs of insurance represent only part of total risk-management costs. Adding in the cost of loss reduction, retained loss, etc. will no doubt inflate the relative importance of risk management.

Recent annual surveys by RIMS have attempted to estimate the aggregate size of corporate risk-management costs (see Blinn and Brown, 1982). The survey of society members attempts to establish the cost of corporate insurance purchases, the costs of loss prevention or reduction, the costs of retained risks, and the administrative costs of risk-management activity. For various reasons, these estimates are probably on the low side, although the degree of underestimation is unclear. Some reasons for probable underestimation include

1 Many activities have safety or loss-reduction costs built in without direct reference to the risk manager. Consequently, they may never be recorded.

2 Similarly, provision for retained losses may be built into the cash-management plan and are also unrecorded.

These and other qualifications noted in the survey results necessitate some caution in interpretation of the RIMS costs. However, the RIMS survey, summarizing the responses of 445 of their members (a response rate of 13%), reveals that risk-management costs probably average a little under 1% of corporate revenues. While this figure seems

---

[6]Contrast this with the view of Houston (1964), who argued that the distinction between *pure* and *speculative* separated a loss-gain pattern rather than a risk pattern. Leading on from this observation, Dennenberg and Ferrari (1966) speculate on whether the risk manager might be better viewed as a loss manager.

rather small at first sight, it should be noted that these costs probably represent something approaching 10% of net income. Consequently, the potential for increasing income and shareholder earnings from a reduction in risk-management costs is significant.

Naturally, risk management costs can be expected to vary considerably across industries. A bank or insurance office is probably not a mansion of lurking hazards, but a construction site is. Table 1-1, reproduced from the previously mentioned survey, shows the spread of costs. Some comparisons are not surprising, but others are. The high risk cost for hospitals is largely due to the alarming trend in malpractice suits. (I hope the fairly high cost for education does not suggest a similar threat; otherwise, I may be forced to try to earn my living from these ideas.)

Table 1-2 gives some indication of the composition of total risk management costs with comparative data for prior years. Of significance is that insurance premiums comprise more than half of total risk management costs, although this proportion does appear to be declining. There is a distinct upward trend in the proportion of expenditure on risk control, which embraces safety, loss prevention, and loss reduction. The

TABLE 1-1
RISK MANAGEMENT COSTS AS A PERCENTAGE OF CORPORATE REVENUES

Industry	Number of sample	Percentage
1. Agriculture, paper	15	0.63
2. Mining	4	0.77
3. Construction	17	1.51
4. Food, tobacco, etc.	28	0.50
5. Textiles, apparel	10	0.47
6. Printing, publishing	7	0.47
7. Chemical allied products	18	0.81
8. Petroleum	26	0.81
9. Rubber, plastic	7	1.02
10. Metals	17	0.71
11. Machinery	37	0.51
12. Transportation equipment	11	0.78
13. Communication utilities, etc.	40	0.59
14. Wholesale, retail	24	0.38
15. Finance—banks	37	0.31
16. Finance—other	20	0.12
17. Real estate	5	1.19
18. Services	15	1.24
19. Government	41	0.44
20. Hospitals	12	1.45
21. Educational institution	14	1.10
22. Conglomeration	30	0.75
23. Other	10	0.80

Source: Reprinted from J. D. Blinn and B. M. Brown, "The Cost of Risk: A Summary of the 1981 Survey," *Risk Management,* November 1982, with the kind permission of the Risk and Insurance Management Society.

TABLE 1-2
COMPOSITION OF RISK MANAGEMENT COSTS

	1977	1978	1979	1980
Property insurance premiums	22.1%	20.8%	20.0%	18.3%
Unreimbursed property loss	7.3	8.0	6.6	7.3
Liability insurance premiums	43.1	42.7	37.1	34.2
Unreimbursed liability losses	12.5	13.1	15.9	15.0
Captive insurance costs	(3.1)	(2.2)	(2.7)	(2.5)
Risk control	15.7	15.5	20.4	24.9
Outside services	0.4	0.4	0.6	0.6
Departmental costs	1.9	1.9	2.1	2.1
	100%	100%	100%	100%

Source: Reprinted from J. D. Blinn and B. M. Brown, "The Cost of Risk: A Summary of the 1981 Survey," *Risk Management,* November 1982, with the kind permission of the Risk and Insurance Management Society.

treatment of captives here is somewhat obscure, so we appeal to outside data to obtain ideas of the relative magnitude of this new market institution.

As mentioned earlier, *captives* are insurance companies that are owned and operated by a noninsurance parent firm to underwrite the latter's pure risk exposures. Thus captives represents a formalization of the process of retaining risk. Recently, it was estimated that there are upwards of 1800 captive insurance companies (most owned by U.S. parents) controlling some 6% of world insurance premium volume (see Kloman and Rosenbaum, 1982). Growth in the number and size of captives suggests that the 6% figure could easily double in the next 2 to 3 years. Among their number, the captives include some very large firms. For example, Exxon's captive subsidiary Ancon has assets already approaching $1 billion and would rank as the second largest U.S. reinsurer (Kloman and Rosenbaum, 1982).

The importance of risk management cannot be gleaned solely from an examination of the size of its cash flows. The events that are under study here may determine the success, or even the survival, of a firm. Destruction of corporate assets can impose a serious, or even fatal, financial burden on a firm, even if the assets are insured. For example, a somewhat dated study by the National Retail Credit Association reported that of a group of firms suffering serious fire loss, 83% subsequently failed or suffered a severe increase in their cost of capital (see Whelan and Gregory, 1960, p. 8). Similarly, liability settlements can easily wipe out a firm's assets. The rapid escalation in awards for injury claims, the spread of class action suits, and legal developments that impose liability for hazardous exposure over long periods of time (e.g., asbestos) have all contributed to the mammoth contingent liabilities for defective products, industrial injuries or disease, and the like that firms typically face today.

IS RISK MANAGEMENT PROPERLY VIEWED AS AN INDEPENDENT FIELD OF STUDY?

Economics is a social science that is concerned with the study of the production, exchange, distribution, and consumption of goods and services. It is widely recognized as an independent field of scientific enquiry, its status gaining recognition in 1969 with the establishment of a Nobel prize. For some purposes, it is useful to subdivide the subject matter of economics according to the market that is under study. For example, one market is that for products, another is for labor services, and another is for capital. Capital market behavior encompasses the activities of those offering, and those demanding, the use of capital (money) for investment purposes. The activities of the capital market are closely interrelated with those of other markets, and study of the capital market makes use of the common methodology of economics. However, the study of capital markets has come to be recognized as an independent field. Although the methodology is common to other branches of economics, its application requires detailed knowledge of the institutions that operate in the capital market and the contracts that are traded, as well as command of particular mathematical and statistical techniques. Thus while finance can still be considered a subset of economics, it is useful to organize the study of capital markets on a separate (but not isolated) basis.

This hierarchical structure can be extended downward to establish a relationship between finance and risk management that is similar to that currently existing between economics and finance. The study of capital markets encompasses the activity of investors, of firms seeking funds for investment purposes, and of the financial intermediaries that complete the market. Risk management defines those particular investment activities undertaken by firms in anticipation of or following contingent losses and the selection of appropriate financing. Defined in this way, risk management is a specialized application of financial management. Both are concerned with decisions concerning the sources and uses of funds, the risk-management decisions simply being a subset of the financial management decisions. If a firm is to maximize its welfare, however defined, it must be consistent in its use of decision criteria, and these criteria should embody the accepted paradigms of finance and, therefore, of economics.

To address the question raised in the title to this section: Can risk management be spawned off from such a hierarchial structure as a separate field of study? Certainly, the described structure implies that decision rules, such as those used in capital budgeting, apply with equal force to investment decisions that fall under the title of risk management, as well as to any other investment decisions. Similarly, in financing risk-management investments, sources of finance may be compared using the same guidelines as those used for the wider set of financing decisions. However, the *application* of these criteria requires specialist knowledge. First, the identification of investment opportunities calls for specialized knowledge of hazardous processes and appropriate safety feature; such is the province of the risk manager. Second, the estimation of the appropriate cash flows to be fed into the financial decision requires specialized knowledge and skills, notably the ability to estimate appropriate loss probability distributions. Third, some specialized forms of financing may be available for risk management investments, such as insurance and contingency loans. Operation with these forms of financing again requires specialized skills and knowledge of the marketplace for these services. Thus the subject area of risk management may be separated on the ground that its application necessitates the acquisition of highly specialized skills.

This characterization of the place of risk management in the framework of subject disciplines and field applications does not correspond with the evolution of risk management, nor would all risk managers subscribe to this description of their function. Some would undoubtedly see themselves essentially as safety engineers, others as managers responsible for the administration of several disparate functions, and still others as insurance specialists. Yet all would claim responsibility for the administration of corporate resources that are costly to the firm. Like the marketing manager, the production manager, the research manager, etc., the risk manager will be required to show that departmental projects add value to the firm. If resources are scarce, it will be necessary for the risk manager to show that risk-management projects create more value than competing bids. Such comparisons require the application of consistent corporate financial criteria. It is the task of this book to show how such criteria apply to the risk management process.

REFERENCES

Blinn, J. D., and B. M. Brown: "The Cost of Risk: A Summary of the 1981 Survey," *Risk Management,* November 1982.

Crockford, G. N.: "The Bibliography and History of Risk Management: Some Preliminary Observations," *The Geneva Papers in Risk and Insurance,* vol. 7, no. 23, 1982, pp. 169–179.

Dennenberg, H. S., and J. R. Ferrari: "New Perspectives on Risk Management: The Search for Principles," *Journal of Risk and Insurance,* vol. 33, 1966, pp. 647–661.

Greene, M., and O. Serbein: *Risk Management: Text and Cases,* 2d ed., Reston Publishing Company, Reston, Virginia, 1983.

Hardy, C. O.: *Risk and Risk Bearing,* The University of Chicago Press, Chicago, 1923, pp. 2–3.

Head, G. L.: "Continuing Evolution of the Risk Management Function and Education in the United States," *The Geneva Papers in Risk and Insurance,* vol. 7, no. 23, 1982, pp. 180–186.

Hogue, M. E., and D. G. Olson: *Business Attitudes Towards Risk Management, Insurance and Related Social Issues,* Wharton School, University of Pennsylvania, Philadelphia, 1976.

Houston, D. B.: "Risk, Insurance and Sampling," *Journal of Risk and Insurance,* vol. 31, 1964, pp. 511–538.

Kloman, H. F., and D. H. Rosenbaum: "The Captive Insurance Phenomenon: A Cautionary Tale," *The Geneva Papers in Risk and Insurance,* vol. 7, no. 23, 1982, pp. 129–151.

Knight, F. H.: *Risk, Uncertainty and Profit,* London School of Economics, Reprints of Scarce Tracts, No. 16, 1933.

Mayers, D., and C. W. Smith: "On the Corporate Demand for Insurance," *Journal of Business,* vol. 55, no. 2, 1982, pp. 281–296.

Mehr, R. I., and B. Hedges: *Risk Management in the Business Enterprise.* Irwin, Homewood, Illinois, 1963.

———and B. Hedges: *Risk Management: Concepts and Applications,* Irwin, Homewood, Illinois, 1974.

———and E. Cammack: *Principles of Insurance,* 7th ed., Irwin, Homewood, Illinois, 1980.

Mowbray, A. H.: *Insurance: Its Theory and Practice in the United States,* McGraw-Hill, New York, 1930.

Whelan, J. D., and J. R. Gregory: *Business Interruption Primer,* The Rough Notes Company, Indianapolis, Indiana, 1960.

Willett, A. H.: *The Economic Theory of Risk and Insurance,* 1901; reprinted by Irwin, Homewood, Illinois, 1951.

Williams, C. A., and R. M. Heins: *Risk Management and Insurance,* McGraw-Hill, New York, 1964.

CHAPTER 2

A FINANCIAL FRAMEWORK FOR RISK MANAGEMENT

The practical application of risk management usually calls into play various subject disciplines. In Chapter 1, the financial nature of the decision process was stressed, and furthermore, some claim was made that *risk management* might find a natural home under the umbrella of *financial management.* Such "financial imperialism" can be challenged by those who adopt a behavioral view of the firm and stress the "management" role in risk management. The role of the risk manager may indeed be one of "managing" the diverse resources under his or her control. This role is not challenged by imposing a finance structure on risk management. *Financial management* is simply a decision framework directed at maximizing the value of a firm. The inputs into the decision process will be influenced by the quality of management: Good management may well influence the relationship between the cost and benefits of corporate activities.

An alternative view of risk management stresses its technological nature. Losses are by-products of the technological processes adopted by a firm. Control of these losses requires knowledge of the processes involved; thus risk management may be seen as loss reduction or safety engineering. Again, this view does not challenge the use of a financial decision framework; rather it is complementary. Knowledge of technological processes and their propensity to produce losses is essential to identify potential risk-management projects and to measure their respective costs and benefits. However, the projects must be appraised against corporate objectives. Financial management offers such a decision framework. The financial perspective does not compete with alternative subject areas in its claims on risk management. Rather, each has its own place and its own role to play.

CORPORATE OBJECTIVES AND RISK MANAGEMENT

Value Maximization

The recent development of financial management has been linked to a very specific corporate objective. The firm is assumed to be a profit-seeking organization that is owned by the holders of its equity. These equity interests are usually, although not always, represented by shares of stock, and the value of each share is equivalent to the value of each ownership claim. Except with owner-managed or family businesses, the operating decisions of a firm are made by paid managers who are charged with advancing the welfare of the owners. Owners' welfare is assumed to be measured by the value of ownership claims; thus the appropriate corporate objective is assumed to be the maximization of the share value. In some, although not all, circumstances, this is equivalent to maximizing the total value of the firm. Thus the explicit objective assumed for financial management is to promote the economic welfare of the firm's shareholders by maximizing the value of their shares. Qualifying this statement, managerial concern is with existing shareholders. For example, we might assume that the objective is to increase the total value of the firm's equity, but this may be achieved by raising new equity and investing in marginal projects. If this leaves the share price unchanged, existing shareholders will be no better off. Thus the objective is taken to be the maximization of the wealth of existing shareholders, which is equivalent to the maximization of the value of each share.

The use of value maximization as a corporate objective is broadly consistent with the agency relationship that exists between the shareholders and managers of a firm. The management is appointed by the shareholders, and the task of management is to maximize the value of the shares. Furthermore, management is accountable to the shareholders and can be removed if dissatisfied shareholders can muster sufficient voting power. Thus paid managers do have an incentive to satisfy the wealth aspirations of shareholders, even though the managers may have other personal objectives that pull in other directions. This qualification will be addressed presently.

Delving deeper into the value-maximization objective shows that it provides a measure of performance. The share price represents the capital market's assessment of the expected future earnings of a firm given available information. The value of equity is the risk-adjusted capitalized value of the firm's expected-earnings stream. Thus use of value maximization implies that corporate decision makers will seek to maximize the size of the firm's future-earnings stream and/or minimize its level of risk. Since share values respond to relevant financial decisions, capital markets thereby impose a discipline on the firm and a continuous monitor of its financial performance.

If risk management is to be encompassed within a financial management decision structure, it appears that a similar objective must be adopted for risk management. We will now discuss whether such a straightforward objective is appropriate.

Value Maximization and Profit Maximization

Earlier, financial management was presented as the study of economic relationships in a particular market: the capital market. The methodology used to study financial management is that of economics, and financial management may be seen simply as a particular application of economic study. Financial management focuses on a particular set of operating decisions made by a firm, i.e., those concerned with the sources and uses of funds. Alternative uses of funds, together with competing forms of financing, are appraised in terms of their contribution to share value. However, elsewhere in economics the firm is studied from different perspectives.

The *theory of the firm* is the title given to the study of the microeconomic behavior of a firm. This area of study relates to the production, pricing, resource usage, and marketing decisions of a firm. It is necessary to impose some economic rationality on the firm in order to model its behavior. In particular, the firm typically is assumed to be a profit-maximizer. From this objective are derived the familiar marginalist decision rules. If a particular action contributes more to the revenue of the firm than to its costs, that action will, by definition, increase profit and should be undertaken. Consequently, the optimal level of activity is that at which marginal cost equals marginal revenue.

At first sight, there appears to be a conflict of objectives between the theory of the firm and financial management; the former seeks to maximize profit and the latter seeks to maximize equity value. *Profit*, as defined in microeconomics, is the difference between the firm's revenues and costs. Costs include what is known as *normal profit*, which is a normal (i.e., competitive) return to those supplying capital to the firm as a reward for its use. The normal return includes interest payments to bondholders as well as a competitive yield to shareholders, both of which are deducted from revenue, leaving profit as a residual or surplus return to equityholders. For the most part, microeconomic analysis has been static (i.e., concerned only with maximizing profit over a single period) and has been free of considerations of risk.

From this comparison of share-value maximization and profit maximization, it may be concluded that *value maximization* is a multiperiod, risk-adjusted analogue of single-period profit maximization. *Economic profit* includes any excess in the return to shareholders, but it does not include the normal return that currently prevails for investments with similar risk characteristics. Insofar as this excess return accrues to current shareholders, maximizing the capitalized value of future economic profits is tantamount to maximizing share value. Any increase in the capitalized value of future economic profits, as perceived by investors, will be reflected in a capital gain to the stock.

Some complications do arise in the comparison of profit maximization and share-value maximization if existing shareholders are not able to capture all the surplus profit. Further coordination between the assumptions and objectives used in finance and economics (as well as in accounting) is also desirable. In the meantime, however, it may be noted that the economic concept of profit maximization is broadly compatible with share maximization.

Value Maximization and Managerial Decision Making

A second challenge to the adoption of value maximization as the appropriate corporate objective arises with the observation that it is paid managers, not shareholders, who typically make most financial decisions, including risk management decisions. Managers will have their own objectives that need not necessarily coincide with those of shareholders. A very pertinent example in the current risk-management context lies in differences in attitude toward individual risk. The prospect of pure losses imposes risk on the firm. For shareholders, the effect of this risk may be lost within their investment portfolios. If shareholders hold fairly diversified investment portfolios, the effect of pure risk on a particular stock in the portfolio will probably have an insignificant effect on the riskiness of the whole portfolio. However, managers cannot diversify away their employment risk so easily. Consequently, they may adopt more risk-averse postures in making corporate decisions (see Elliott, 1972).

Two related aspects of the separation of ownership and control were discussed by Simon (1959) and by Jensen and Meckling (1976). Simon's "satisficing" model envisions a firm whose managers provide satisfactory, not maximizing, results for the owners while simultaneously pursuing policies that ensure their own survival. Jensen and Meckling derive an "agency model" of the firm that analyzes the costs imposed on shareholders by managers (i.e., the agents of shareholders) who pursue their own objectives. These ideas suggest that actual decisions may not always be in the best interests of a firm's shareholders.

Any divergence between value-maximizing behavior and actual managerial behavior is likely to be constrained by the market process:

1 Managerial compensation systems often incorporate incentives for value-maximizing behavior; examples are share ownership plans and bonuses related to corporate profitability.

2 Firms that do not fully exploit opportunities for value creation for their shareholders are clear targets for takeover, with the accompanying substitution of new management.

3 The reputation of senior managers, and therefore their ability to command attractive alternative employment, is often linked with the financial success of their previous employer.

4 In a competitive environment, profitability may be driven so low that failure to pursue value maximization may lead to insolvency.

These points concern the determination of actual behavior. Our adoption of value maximization represents a normative goal. Even if managerial behavior does depart from value-maximizing behavior, it does not follow that satisficing behavior or agency costs should be built into the statement of objectives. Rather, such costs represent constraints on the fulfillment of a firm's goals.

Value Maximization and Social Responsibility

The separation of ownership interest and decision making permits a coalition view of a firm. A firm may be regarded as a conglomerate of different interests, each having recognizable claims on the firm's output. In addition to shareholders and managers, others, such as employees, bondholders, creditors, and customers, not to mention the Internal Revenue Service, have enforceable claims on a firm's output. Each group will have its own objectives, and often, interests conflict. For example, shareholders may prefer more risky investments than bondholders if they can pass on to bondholders most of the potential bankruptcy costs (see, for example, Myers, 1977). Employees, like managers, may be more nervous about corporate risk taking than shareholders or bondholders, because the riskiness of employment is much more difficult to diversify away than the riskiness of a single financial asset (stock or bond) in an investment portfolio. Those purchasing the firm's products may have little interest in its survival and financial performance unless they maintain a financial stake in the firm after purchase. For example, the issue of a guarantee with the product or the provision of after-sales service will constitute such a continuing financial interest. Creditors may be classed with bondholders; since they have prior claim to shareholders on the firm's revenues, they maintain an interest in the level and stability of those revenues.

These differences in risk attitudes between claimholders of the firm are of particular interest in examining the firm's handling of pure risks. By their very nature, these risks may upset the stability of the firm, and consequently, different claimholders will seek quite different risk management strategies. Sometimes the effect of risk-management strategy will be particularly acute if the costs of a loss are borne disproportionately by the different claimholders. For example, the prospect of industrial injury affects each employee in two ways: First, the financial strain on the firm from paying damages to other injured employees might affect the security of his or her employment. Second, there is the prospect that he or she might be the one who is injured and that compensation will not be adequate. Another example might be the operation of a nuclear power plant within a particular local community. Local residents have an interest in survival of the plant because it brings employment and trade to the community. However, they might lobby for severe safety controls because they bear the risk of radiation leakage but do not bear the costs of its prevention. In both examples, the interests of shareholders lie simply in the value of their assets. The disproportionate sharing of the effects of loss by the shareholders and the employees and local residents will no doubt condition their respective views on risk-management decisions.

How should such diverse claims be embodied in the risk-management decision process? One approach that is frequently adopted in risk management textbooks is to treat the protection of each interest group implicitly as part of the firm's objectives. This approach is made explicit by some writers. For example, Mehr and Hedges (1974) make the following statement of corporate objectives (p. 3):

1 "Performance of the function for which the Organization was created." The adoption of value maximization is compatible with this statement in the case of business firms.

2 "Satisfactory performance of the unit in meeting societal goals."

3 "Satisfaction of the personal tastes and preferences of those members of the organization having direct influence on its policy."

From the preceding discussion it would appear that these stated objectives are in some conflict with each other. If a decision structure was to be based on these objectives, some method of resolving the conflict, or of determining appropriate tradeoffs between objectives, would be required. Furthermore, it does appear that a simple statement of value maximization is incomplete alongside Mehr and Hedges' more general statements. Value maximization appears to concentrate only on the interests of shareholders to the neglect of other interests. Value maximization appears to be too narrow. *However, we will now argue that the value-maximization objective does take into account the risk costs imposed on other corporate claimholders. Furthermore, by impounding the risk costs of various claimholders in a single value, the value of equity, the value-maximizing objective does provide a resolution of these conflicting claims.* To pursue these ideas, we must understand the nature of market forces facing the firm.

RESOLUTION OF THE COSTS OF RISK THROUGH MARKET MECHANISMS

The various claims on a firm's output are traded in different markets. Financial claims, such as stocks and bonds, are traded in the capital market, and prices that reflect the relative strength of supply and demand will prevail. The claims of employees and managers arise from contracts negotiated in the labor market. Similarly, the firm buys and sells goods and services in the product market. In both the labor and product markets, prices also will result from the interaction of supply and demand forces. The various economic markets do not operate in isolation from each other; they simply are convenient classifications for analyzing economic behavior. Thus the demand for capital depends on the demand for the firm's products (product market) and on the firm's costs, which include labor costs (the labor market). Similarly, the supply of capital depends on individual decisions concerning the allocation of income between savings and consumption, which in turn depends on product market forces. The firm finds itself at the center of a web of economic relationships contracted in a set of distinct but interrelated markets.

Let us focus on one such relationship: the employment contract. The contract price, or wage, will depend on supply and demand pressures. But in determining supply and demand, each party will decide what factors are important, with the employee, *ceteris paribus,* wanting more pay and the firm wanting to pay less. The firm will be interested in the productivity of labor, and the employee will be interested in the quality of work. The resolution of these conflicting claims occurs as a result of some market process, such as collective bargaining. However, another factor of importance to both parties is risk. If the employee perceives employment to be risky in terms of security of employment or, perhaps, in terms of suffering uncompensated industrial injury, he or she will require higher compensation to be induced to work in the particular job. Risk is also important for the owners of a firm. If the firm is easily able to dismiss workers following poor financial performance, or if it can avoid compensation costs for industrial injury, it will be able to stabilize the earnings it delivers to its shareholders. Thus employment risks may be absorbed by one or the other party or perhaps shared. Since risk imposes costs on both employer and employee, it will likely become an issue in wage determination. Other things being equal, those employed in occupations that, for one reason or another, exhibit high levels of risk will demand higher wages than others in low-risk employment. Alternatively, the same wage might prevail but employers absorb the risk by various contractual devices, e.g., layoff compensation, sick pay, etc. If a high-risk firm fails to compensate its employees by extra wages or compensating benefits, then it will tend to be unsuccessful in competition for labor with other firms.

Similar considerations apply in other markets. High-risk corporate bonds offer higher yields than low-risk bonds. Individuals are less likely to do business with an insurance company with a high risk of bankruptcy unless premiums are correspondingly cheaper (which might explain the high risk of bankruptcy). Similarly, automobile purchasers appear to have responded adversely to the financial problems of Chrysler Corporation around the late 1970s and early 1980s when it appeared that after-sale service facilities were in jeopardy from impending bankruptcy. Thus the prices of a firm's contracts will tend to adjust for risk. The extent of risk aversion and the degree of risk involved, together with the relative bargaining strength of the parties, will determine the price adjustment. For example, if the shareholders are indifferent to risk and the employees are highly risk averse, the firm will prefer to absorb risk rather than offer some price compensation to employees for the uncertainty they face.

The adjustment to the price of a contract to compensate for its riskiness is known as the *risk premium*. An example is now given to show that share prices do impound the risk premiums extracted by other claimholders. Furthermore, since the risk premiums result from supply and demand forces, the share-maximization criterion offers a market-determined resolution of the conflicting claims of the various interest groups that constitute the firm.

Consider a firm whose simplified annual income statement is depicted in Table 2-1. The firm expects to earn a revenue of $1000 per year, but this is an average, or expected, annual value. In any given year, revenue could be much higher or much lower; thus earnings are risky. This risk has an adverse effect on

1 the firm's customers, who fear that the firm could go into liquidation and therefore default on service contracts.

2 employees, who feel that the risk of being laid off due to possible poor financial performance is significant.

3 bondholders, who, for similar reasons, fear default on repayment of principal or interest on the debt.

TABLE 2-1
ANNUAL INCOME STATEMENT: BEFORE PROGRAM OF
RISK REDUCTION

	Expected values, $
Revenue	1,000
Wage costs	(800)
Earnings	200
Interest payments	(100)
Earnings available to shareholders*	100

*Capitalized equity value: $\dfrac{\$100}{0.1} = \$1000$

However, for simplicity, we assume that shareholders can diversify away earnings risk and do not demand a risk premium.

The various claims on the firm are shown in Table 2-1, and each reflects an appropriate risk premium. Customers pay less for the product than they would in a risk-free environment, employees demand higher wages, and bondholders require higher interest payments. Taxation is ignored in this example. The final earnings available to shareholders have an expected annual value of $100, although the riskiness of earnings will flow through to this value. Shareholders are assumed to require an expected rate of return of 10% on their investment. Therefore, corporate equity will be priced such that expected annual earnings of $100 represent a 10% rate of return, that is,

$$\frac{\$100}{E} = 0.1$$

where E is the expected value of earnings. Therefore,

$$E = \frac{\$100}{0.1} = \$1000$$

Now suppose that the firm is able to reduce the riskiness of its revenue stream. For example, it might purchase an insurance policy. Insurance is usually expensive, in the sense that the insurance premium exceeds the expected value of the insurer's claim payments. Therefore, insurance increases the expected value of the firm's cost, in this case, by $40, as shown in Table 2-2. However, there are compensating benefits:

1 Customers are impressed by the added security, and the firm is able to pass on part of the insurance cost as a price rise. Thus revenues are increased (assuming inelastic demand) by $20.

2 The firm is also able to negotiate more favorable labor contracts, thereby reducing its wage bill from $800 to $760.

TABLE 2-2
ANNUAL INCOME STATEMENT: AFTER PROGRAM OF
RISK REDUCTION

	Expected values, $
Revenue	1,020
Wage costs	(760)
Cost of risk-reduction program	(40)
Earnings	220
Interest payments	(95)
Earnings available to shareholders*	125

*Capitalized equity value: $\dfrac{\$125}{0.1} = \$1250$

3 The firm is able to renegotiate its debt, adding an insurance clause i[n the] deed that binds the firm to purchase insurance. The renegotiated debt [has an] annual interest cost of $95 compared with the previous $100.

The resulting earnings to shareholders are $125, which, when capitalized at the same rate of 10%, gives an equity value of

$$E = \frac{\$125}{0.1} = \$1250$$

The value of the firm's equity has risen by $250. However, notice that none of this increase arises because the shareholders benefit from the added security. The discount rate used by shareholders has not changed. Rather, all the increase arises because the reduction in riskiness brings benefits to other claimholders. Since the various contract prices and risk premiums result from market negotiations, the price change provides a market valuation of the benefit of risk reduction. In this way, the market value of equity impounds the risk costs imposed on all those having contractual claims on the firm and resolves conflicting claims through the process of price determination in each market.

The same ideas can be considered in reverse. An increase in risk cost (e.g., by acceptance of a new and risky investment project) will lead to a deterioration in the firm's bargaining position when negotiating contracts with risk-averse agents. Consequently, the firm will tend to pay risk premiums in the contract prices, thereby increasing its costs.

The market mechanism permits each claimholder to negotiate with the firm for suitable contracts that reflect the respective cost and benefits of the parties. It is often thought that, if the markets in which these contracts are negotiated are very efficient, the resulting distribution of the costs of risk will be optimal in an economic welfare sense. However, markets are not perfect and we may expect some distortion in the allocation of the costs of risk. For example, workers are unlikely to have full information about the firm's risk management policies, and these policies may not be fully considered in the wage bargaining process.

Another issue concerning the use of value maximization as a corporative objective involves the imposition of costs on outsiders having no contractual relationship with the firm. One resolution adopted by some writers is to attribute to the firm the subsidiary objective of assuming a social responsibility. If the fulfillment of such social responsibility imposes costs upon the firm (e.g., the cost of pollution controls) it will lose earnings and therefore lose value. Consequently, social responsibility might well be the prerogative of monopolistic firms that earn excess profits. In a highly competitive environment, a firm adopting costly social goals will be at a cost disadvantage vis-à-vis its competitors and, ultimately, may fail to survive. A more convenient characterization is to charge management with a responsibility for the welfare of its shareholders and to charge the State with a responsibility for the creation of a regulatory environment in which a firm acts within broad social welfare guidelines. Thus actual regulation, or the threat of impending regulation, may constrain the firm to act in accordance with broad social goals, even though these goals do not appear in the firm's objectives.

Despite these problems of imperfect markets and social responsibility, the value-maximization criterion is probably the best available yardstick for appraising diverse corporate decisions in a consistent manner. While it focuses directly on the economic welfare of the shareholders, it impounds the risk effects of each decision on those claimholders contracting with the firm.

A CHARACTERIZATION OF THE RISK MANAGEMENT PROCESS

The risk-management process can be represented in terms of the responses to two questions: (1) What is the problem? and (2) How can the problem be handled? It is convenient to consider a spinoff from the first question in order to highlight the importance of measurement. Thus the following three questions are posed:

1 What is the problem? (Identification)
2 What is the magnitude of the problem? (Measurement)
3 What can be done about the problem? (Decision)

These three questions form the skeleton of the decision framework that we will use. This is laid out in Figure 2-1. The structure is not unique to risk management problems, but it does provide a convenient starting point. This type of decision structure is also used in other risk management texts. However, in putting flesh on the skeleton, we will differ from those texts. For comparison, the appendix to this chapter provides a representation of the more traditional risk management structure and provides a discussion of why it does not lead to effective financial decision making. In the meantime, our purpose will be to address each of the steps in Figure 2-1 in sequence and elaborate on the decision choices, presented. This will lead to a more complete decision chart.

IDENTIFICATION

The first step calls for the identification of those risky events which impose contingent losses on the firm. Examples can be given immediately, but it may be more useful to structure the search by a finer classification of the types of losses. Pure risks may be

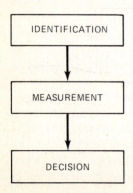

FIGURE 2-1

subdivided into (1) those which threaten the productive assets of the firm, and (2) those relating to contingent pecuniary claims against the firm (Table 2-3). Under the first heading we can group those events which involve the destruction or impairment of the firm's productive assets or those events which deny the firm effective use of its productive assets. Examples are straightforward, including fire and related damage, weather-related destruction of buildings or other property, collision damage to vehicles, and theft of property. *Productive assets* include financial assets that can result in an investment yield and money that is used as working capital. *Liquid assets* can be productive in the same sense as *physical assets,* such as plant and equipment. The loss of productive assets directly interferes with the business operations of the firm. If the loss is large enough, or if it hits some strategic process, it will bring the firm to a halt, cutting off its ability to offer income to its owners. Without some corrective action, the firm will fail to survive. However, we must not fall into the trap of assuming that survival is an overriding objective of a firm. We will address this issue later.

Contingent pecuniary claims against a firm are of a different nature. In the course of operations, a firm may incur liabilities from those actions of its officers and agents which result in damage or injury to third parties and/or property. The third parties may be contractually related to the firm, such as injured employees or customers, or they may not, such as motorists involved in a collision with a firm's vehicle. Events that create such liabilities are usually sudden and accidental. Examples are an injury to a worker caused by falling materials or the failure of an electrical product causing an electric shock to a customer. However, examples can be found that are not so sudden in their occurrence and may not even be accidental. Continuous inhalation of asbestos fibers can result in severe, and perhaps fatal, respiratory disease. Knowing of such danger, employees have sometimes chosen levels of pollution that are (by decree or otherwise) considered to be "safe." In practice, such "safe" levels do not guarantee the absence of danger, but merely confine it to a level that is "acceptably" low. However, even when the occurrence is not sudden or accidental, the financial claim levied against the firm often is. The claim comes in the form of litigation, or threatened litigation, after the injury or damage or after responsibility for the damage has been established.

TABLE 2-3
IDENTIFICATION

	Losses to productive assets		
	Destruction of or damage to productive assets	Denial of access to productive assets	Contingent pecuniary claims
Physical assets	Fire and related damage	Theft, strikes	Liabilities for injury to or damage of property of employees, customers, and/or public agents
Liquid assets	Fire and related damage	Theft, fraud, strikes	

Financial claims of this kind do not directly impede a firm's productive operation, but the firm must raise funds to meet the damages. If the firm uses existing assets for this purpose, selling off physical assets or depleting liquid assets, the effect is the same as if these assets were destroyed. However, the firm can seek new funding to pay the damages, but the burden of new funding may, in severe cases, be so onerous that survival is not feasible or desirable. Thus, ultimately, contingent financial claims have an effect that is similar to that of risks involving the physical destruction of property.

MEASUREMENT

Some losses are either so remote or so routinely small that they are of minor concern. The probability of corporate property being destroyed by the impact of a comet is so small that it would be futile to devote costly managerial resources to contemplating such an event. Certainly, if such an event occurred, the result could be catastrophic. A probable impact by a comet recorded in Tunguska, Siberia, in 1908 revealed immense destructive power, although the effect was confined to a forested area. At the other extreme, we may encounter losses with very high probability but with insignificant consequences. For example, few large firms are concerned with routine broken windows, other than to make a general allocation in the cash plan for such minor contingencies. Between the ends of this spectrum lurk some risks with sufficient probability and severity to impose significant threat and conspicuous uncertainty. These are the losses that give rise to managerial concern. They are not so improbable that odds are astronomical (sorry about the pun); they are not so probable that their occurrence is routine; nor are they so small that the burden on the firm is insignificant.[1] To set the stage for any decision, the extent of risk requires measurement.

The significance of potential losses to a firm depends on the combined effect of the possible values and associated probabilities. Such information may be presented in the form of a probability distribution. For example, consider a game in which drawing an ace from a shuffled pack of cards results in a prize of $10, drawing a face card results in a prize of $5, and no prize is given at all for any other card. The probability distribution is

Outcome	Probability
$10	4/52 or 0.076923
$ 5	12/52 or 0.23079
$ 0	36/52 or 0.692308
	1.0 1.0

For risk-management issues, we usually do not have objective probabilities; therefore, probability estimates must be made, perhaps from past data on the incidence of losses

---

[1]Willett (1901) argued at the turn of the century that "the uncertainty is greatest when the chances are even, that is, when the degree of probability is represented by the fraction $1/2$" (p. 5). For a more recent view on uncertainty and intermediate probabilities, see Mehr and Hedges (1974).

and/or subjective judgment. Thus we may have a probability distribution as follows:

Size of loss	Probability
$ 2,000,000	0.0001
1,000,000	0.0005
500,000	0.001
100,000	0.005
20,000	0.0934
10,000	0.5
0	0.4
	1.0

The combined effect of loss values and associated probabilities will determine the degree of riskiness of the risk-management exposure. Later, the severity of exposure will, in part, determine the type of risk management decision to be taken. Thus we wish to determine how risk management exposure affects the firm. Traditionally, the degree of risk has been estimated using the direct cost of making good the loss. In the preceding probability distribution, the "size of loss" might be represented in terms of the replacement costs of the assets if destroyed, the repair cost if damaged, or the actual cost of settling liability suits. However, the replacement and related values only represent costs to the firm if the firm actually chooses to make good the damage or replace the destroyed resources. The use of replacement value begs the question of whether replacement should be undertaken. Since our concern is to protect the value of the firm's equity, which is the capitalized value of its future earnings, a more satisfactory way of measuring loss is to derive the *capitalized loss of earnings*.

To make the point by way of example, consider two firms, one operating with five machines at full capacity and the other operating with only three machines, although five are actually owned. If the first firm loses a machine by, say, a fire, it will lose the earnings that the machine would have generated. If the second firm loses a machine, it will suffer no direct loss of earnings, foregoing only the ability to sell the machine for its secondhand value. The extent of loss of earnings differs widely for the two firms, and this difference will be recorded in the respective market values of each firm's equity.

To record the effect of pure risk exposure on the value of a firm's equity requires probability estimates of the value of resources that may be affected and the productivity of those resources in generating earnings. In the preceding example, the productivity of the marginal machine to the respective firms differed widely, thereby accounting for the different effects on equity value following loss. However, lurking behind this issue of productivity lies a decision that must be addressed. Should the destroyed resources be replaced? The answer depends on the productivity of those resources.

DECISION MAKING

Once the nature of the risk-management exposure is identified and its severity and extent are measured, the firm faces a decision: What, if anything, should be done?

Various choices are available. Some are interdependent with others, and some are contingent on others. To structure the decision-making process, consider that the choices involve the use of funds to generate or preserve shareholder wealth and the sources of those funds. Choices involving the sources of funds are contingent on the identification of uses for those funds. We will refer to decisions involving the uses of funds as *investment decisions* and those concerning the sources of funds as *financing decisions*.

Investment Decisions

The criteria for making investment decisions are well known and have been widely analyzed. Widespread acceptance has been gained for the class of techniques known as *discounted cash flow* (DCF) over other, more primitive, capital-budgeting techniques, such as payback period or accounting rate of return. Under DCF, the cash flows emanating from a project (both positive and negative and including capital costs) are capitalized at an appropriate discount rate. This process will reveal the market value created for the firm if it accepts the project. If the capitalized value is positive, acceptance of the project will increase the value of the ownership claims, i.e., the share price. However, acceptance of a project with a negative capitalized value causes the share price to fall. DCF criteria are not specific to any class of investment decisions and have equal validity for risk management decisions, for marketing decisions, research and development decisions, decisions concerning the replacement of old equipment, etc.

Application of DCF (or, indeed, simpler capital-budgeting techniques) requires that the costs and benefits of projects be quantified. This is not always easy, especially in risk management, where decisions are probabilistic. However, risk managers partly earn their keep by their skill in making such probability estimates. No doubt, these estimates will be partly subjective. Indeed, this may be inevitable, since perfect data are never available, but such difficulties do not constitute an argument against quantification. On the contrary, the discipline of making quantitative estimates exposes subjective judgments to scrutiny and discussion and ensures consistency of application over different decisions. Furthermore, such difficulties in quantification are not unique to risk management.

The investment decisions facing the risk manager are broadly of two types. The first is investment in the replacement of destroyed resources. Consider again the example raised in the prior section on measurement. The two firms in question reaped very different levels of productivity from the marginal machine. The first firm, working at full capacity, would suffer loss of output and, consequently, revenue and profits if a machine were to be destroyed. The second firm, working with surplus capacity, would not suffer such a loss of earnings. Consequently, the two firms may well make different decisions on the replacement of a destroyed machine.

The reinvestment decision is ignored in most risk-management texts. This omission may be explained by the use of survival and continuity of operations as a corporate objective (see Mehr and Hedges, 1974, Ch. 2). However, even when continuity is not assumed explicitly, a high emphasis on insurance to finance losses has a similar effect. Nevertheless, the goals of survival and continuity are not necessarily compatible with value maximization, and the decision to reinvest is not necessarily a rational economic one.

It may be thought that the decision to reinvest is trivial. After all, if it was profitable for the firm to be in operation at the time of the loss, it is obviously profitable to restore operations to their preloss basis. However, such reasoning is fallacious. The decision to continue before loss is based on the exit value of the business; the decision to continue after loss is based on the replacement costs of the destroyed resources, which may be very different from the exit value. Furthermore, the loss itself may affect the earning capacity of the firm, especially if the firm is unable to reestablish production and trading immediately. The decision to reinvest is not a trivial one; it must be addressed if the firm is to derive a value-maximizing risk-management strategy.

The second type of investment decision involves investments in safety, loss prevention, and loss reduction. By way of example, the firm can reduce the probability of fire loss through the installation of sprinklers, fire alarms, fireproof doors, etc.; injury loss to employees may be reduced by guarding machinery and implementing safety education; improved quality control can protect against hazardous product defects; antijackknifing devices can reduce the probability of accident to articulated vehicles; etc. These loss-reduction investments have identifiable cash flows comparable with those arising from the installation of a new machine or the replacement of an old one. With loss reduction, the payoff takes the form of a reduction in the costs of contingent losses. This reduction is a positive cash flow, and if its capitalized value exceeds the capitalized cost of the project, the project will create value for the shareholders.

If investment decisions are positive, sources of finance will be required (in fact, the investment decision is not independent of the financing decision, since a positive investment decision requires that the project deliver a return in excess of the cost of capital).

Liability losses do not relate to the destruction of, or damage to, resources owned by the firm. Rather, damage is suffered by third parties, but the firm acquires an obligation to pay compensation. Contingent liabilities for such events evoke investment decisions that are similar to those involving damage to corporately owned resources. First, investments may be made to reduce the expected burden of such losses. The payback to such investments lies in a reduction in the expected costs of financing liability payments. For example, if losses are insured, the payback will take the form of a premium reduction (assuming that the premium is sensitive to the expected value of the claim payment).

A more complex issue is whether a liability loss evokes a decision concerning the continued operation of the firm analogous to the reinvestment decision that arises when productive resources are lost. A liability suit is an enforceable claim against a firm. Even though the claim does not directly affect the earnings of the firm, it can affect the willingness and ability of a firm to survive. To pay damages, the firm must secure a source of financing. If retained earnings, which otherwise would have represented owners' equity, are used, the value of ownership claims will fall by the value of the liability costs. If new external funds are used, the cost of servicing these new funds will similarly reduce the value of ownership claims. Either way, the cost of meeting the claim will be borne ultimately by the owners. However, suppose that the damages awarded exceed the value of the firm's equity. The share price will not assume a negative value, for under such circumstances, it will be rational to liquidate the firm and allow the shares to expire worthless. Thus, under limited liability, it may not be worthwhile for the firm to survive in the event that liability damages exceed the value of ownership equity.[2]

There are additional reasons why a liability suit may cause a firm to reconsider the continuation of all or part of its economic activity. Side effects from the event, apart from damages, may disturb profitability. For example, if employees are injured, employee consciousness of work hazards may be raised and may be reflected in higher compensatory wage rates. If customers are damaged (e.g., by a design defect in an automobile or through side effects of a drug), demand for the firm's products might wane. If a local community is harmed, say, by release of a toxic substance from a factory, local political pressure might force closure or induced safety regulations might increase operating costs. Such effects might tip the economic balance sufficiently that although production was profitable before the event, this state does not continue after the loss.

Continued production after a liability loss should not be taken for granted simply because the firm's productive facilities are left intact. The loss may upset the economic calculus, and a decision to cease operation could result. As with the destruction of physical resources, liability losses also should cause a firm to question the continuation of its operations.

 ## Financing Decisions

Various sources of financing are routinely available to firms to meet their investment requirements, including new issues of debt or equity, term loans or lines of credit from lending institutions, supplier credit, and internally generated sources. Each of these sources is potentially available for risk-management investment, although other tailor-made sources of funds are also available, notably for the purpose of postloss reinvestment. It is convenient to discuss these financing decisions in conjunction with the corresponding investment decisions.

Financing Postloss Reinvestment   The need to secure funds arises when the firm wishes to repair damage, replace destroyed resources, or pay a liability claim. At such a time, the firm may try to secure funds in a conventional way, e.g., retaining earnings or raising new debt or equity. This procedure is termed *postloss financing* because the arrangement is set in place after the loss. Furthermore, the burden of meeting the financing costs, such as payment of interest, debt, principal, or dividends, is also borne after the loss. Contrast this with the purchase of insurance. Here, the loss-financing arrangement is set in place in anticipation of a possible loss, and the financing

---

[2]An interesting case that has not currently been resolved concerns the Manville Corporation. Faced with an accumulation of liabilities for asbestos-related disease of substantial, but as yet unknown, value, Manville filed for Chapter 11 bankruptcy. The process is seen as a device to contain the value of liability claims and to preserve the operation of the firm as a continuing productive unit. See *Wall Street Journal*, January 27, 1983.

burden, the premium payment, is also incurred before the loss. Accordingly, insurance is termed *preloss financing*. Another example of preloss financing is the establishment of an internal reserve fund from which the reinvestment costs of potential future losses can be met.

Some financing arrangements fall between preloss and postloss financing, exhibiting some characteristics of each. A firm may set up a line of credit in anticipation of uncertain future investment demands, including postloss reinvestment needs. The line of credit may be restricted solely to risk-management needs; i.e., it can be drawn on only in the event of a defined loss. This arrangement is known as a *contingency,* or *contingent, loan.* Both the specific contingency loan and the more general line of credit are set up in anticipation of loss, and some securement fee is usually paid to establish the facility. In this sense, these arrangements resemble preloss financing. However, the loan is drawn at the time reinvestment funds are needed, and it is repaid subsequently. In this sense, these arrangements resemble postloss forms of financing. Correct filing of these forms of financing is not critically important. It is more important that we use this classification to explore alternative financing sources, including conventional debt and equity sources that have received little or no attention in risk management.

Financing Loss-Reduction Programs Investment in safety, loss prevention, or loss reduction shares common financing requirements with other corporate investment decisions. Usually, the main demand for funds is "up front," i.e., at the inception of the project, although subsequent costs for maintenance, continuing safety education, etc. may be required. Such projects create no special financing problems, and the usual sources may be evoked, i.e., debt, new equity, retained earnings, etc.

As with investment appraisal, well-developed criteria for comparing competing sources of financing exist. Our principal objective is to maximize the firm's share value, and this yardstick accordingly serves to compare competing sources of financing. Greater focus can be gained by reducing this general objective to an operational objective—notably, that the source of financing which leads to the lowest cost of capital is preferred. This does not always mean that the cheapest source of financing is preferred. For example, debt may be cheaper than insurance, but it may introduce new leverage risk that bids up the cost of equity. The cost-of-capital concept must take into account such risk effects and spillover effects on the cost of other funds.

THE DECISION STRUCTURE AND PLAN OF THE BOOK

The discussion in the preceding sections can be summarized by a decision chart. This chart is given in Figure 2-2. The stages of the decision procedure identified in Figure 2-1 have been filled out, showing broad decision alternatives and how these alternatives are interrelated.

This structure is stamped upon this book. Chapters 3 to 6 deal with preliminary concepts, which will be explained presently. Chapters 7 and 8 are concerned with the impact of losses on corporate value. If a loss arises, productive resources may be destroyed, thereby depleting the expected future earnings of the firm. Alternatively,

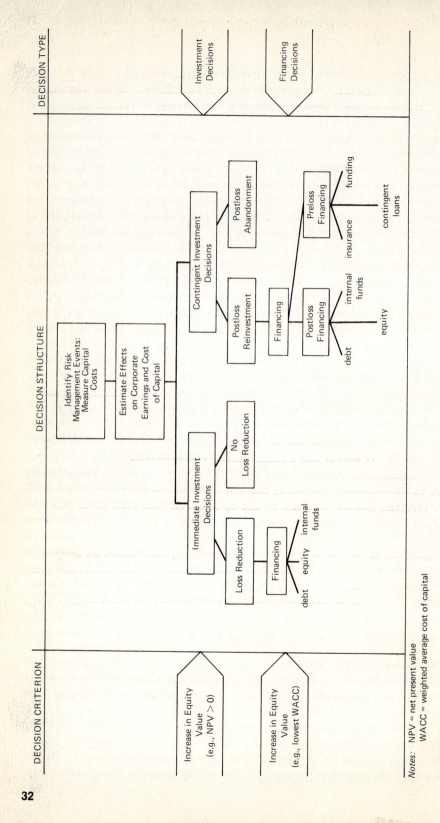

FIGURE 2-2
Decision framework for financial risk management.

Notes: NPV = net present value
WACC = weighted average cost of capital

32

if a liability loss arises, the cost of financing the payment of damages will absorb part of the firm's earnings stream. Either way, the firm's owners will be left with smaller residual earnings and the value of the firm will fall. Chapter 7 examines these effects and, in so doing, establishes the role of share price as an appropriate criterion for appraising risk-management decisions. Chapter 8 is concerned with contingent investment decisions, i.e., the decision to reinvest after a loss. A loss will reduce the value of a firm's equity. Part of this loss of value will be recaptured if the firm is able to reinvest and if such reinvestment creates value in excess of the investment costs. However, reinvestment will compound the fall in equity value if the productivity of the resources committed in the reinvestment is not high enough to cover the costs of capital. Chapter 8 uses capital-budgeting criteria to examine the reinvestment decision.

The reinvestment decision determines the need for reinvestment financing. The examination and comparison of sources of finance is conducted in Chapters 9 through 12. Following Figure 2-2, sources of finance are divided according to postloss (Chapter 9) and preloss (Chapters 10 and 11). The analysis of sources of financing is guided by the value-maximization criterion. Chapter 12 examines possible financing solutions that combine various individual sources into a financing package. The use of the value-maximization criterion is somewhat unusual, especially when applied to insurance. Normally, insurance is considered to be of benefit because of its facility for reducing risk, and the optimal level of insurance is that which achieves a marginal balance between the costs and benefits of risk reduction. The value-maximization approach is not at variance with risk aversion: The risk cost imposed on equityholders by risk management exposures are impounded in the value.

The arm of Figure 2-2 that lists loss-reduction decisions is dealt with in Chapter 13. Condensing this subject into a single chapter is not intended to diminish its role in risk management. Rather, the financial issues are fairly straightforward, following standard capital-budgeting procedures that will be familiar to those with some knowledge of corporate finance. Chapters 14 and 15 round off with other issues that arise at various junctures throughout the book; it serves little purpose to elaborate on these at this stage.

The treatment of risk management that is sketched out here requires the integration of ideas and skills that are borrowed from other disciplines, most particularly from economics, finance, and statistics. The purpose of Chapters 3 to 6 is to present and adapt such material. In the first place, any treatment of risky decisions requires some treatment of why risk is considered to be costly and how risk affects economic behavior. These ideas have been analyzed by economists using utility theory, and some basic analyses, applied to simple risk-management issues, are presented in Chapter 3. However, development of the subject also requires some command of basic statistical concepts that enable us to measure risk and to describe and summarize risky prospects. Such concepts are presented in Chapter 4. Chapter 5 extends our perspective from individual risky prospects to whole portfolios of such risks. The typical firm does not have a single source of risk, but rather has many such sources. Some of these fall within the web of risk management; others do not. The combined effect of multiple risks on the firm's owners is of concern, and some knowledge of portfolio theory is required. Portfolio ideas serve two purposes here. First, they permit us to examine ways in which the risk manager can "spread" or "diversify" risk across several exposures. In addition, diversification is at the heart of any modern explanation of how investors behave. We adopt the objective that a firm will seek to maximize the value of its owners' equity. The owners are investors, and a study of their market behavior is essential in determining how the equity of a firm is priced. These ideas are presented in Chapter 6. At this juncture, the reader should be well positioned to tackle the impact of pure risk losses on the value of a firm and the risk-management decisions that flow from such prospects.

SUMMARY

The derivation of a decision framework from which to derive and appraise risk management strategy requires a clear statement of corporate objectives. This book follows the mainstream of financial economics in assuming that a firm wishes to maximize the value of the existing owners' equity, which, for publicly traded companies, means the maximization of share price. This objective is referred to, somewhat loosely, as *value maximization*.

At first sight, the value-maximization objective appears to be very narrow and may conflict with objectives attributed to a firm in other subject areas. We argue that value maximization is roughly comparable with the microeconomist's assumption that a firm wishes to maximize profit, value maximization being roughly a multiperiod, risk-adjusted analogue of the single-period, profit-maximization concept. A further problem with value maximization is that it ignores that decisions are made by managers. However, we argue that although monitoring of managerial performance may not be perfect, managers do have strong incentives to maximize share value, for against this yardstick their performance and, in part, their income are determined.

Despite appearances to the contrary, the value-maximization objective does not ignore the risk costs that risk management decisions might impose on other claimholders, such as employees, agents, and customers of the firm. These claimholders establish a contractual relationship with the firm, and in a reasonably competitive market, contracts will be negotiated on the basis of the costs and benefits imposed on each party. Such costs may include the effects of risk management exposure, and if so, these costs will be reflected in the contract prices. The value of the owners' equity is derived from expected earnings after negotiation of contracts. Consequently, share value will impound the risk premiums negotiated with the firm's various contractees. While value maximization focuses directly on the welfare of the firm's shareholders, it is sensitive to those risk costs absorbed by other groups having claims on the firm.

From the value-maximization objective, a risk management decision structure was derived. The three processes in a risk management decision relate to the identification of risk management exposures, the measurement of their impact on the firm, and the actual decision. Once risk exposures are identified, their potential for destroying share value must be measured. This calls for measurement of the value of the resources affected and their productivity in generating earnings, together with appropriate loss probabilities. The decision process may be divided into those decisions concerning the use of funds (investment decisions) and those concerning the source of funds (financing decisions).

Investment decisions fall under two headings: those concerning the commitment of resources to replace those destroyed in a loss event (reinvestment decision) and those concerning the commitment of new resources to reduce the probability of, or contingent costs resulting from, such loss events. Both decisions can be appraised using conventional capital-budgeting techniques, and neither decision should be taken for granted.

Financing for investment decisions may come from general or specialized sources. For reinvestment decisions, insurance has absorbed much attention, although other sources are also available, such as new debt and equity, contingency loans, and internal reserve funds. These sources are subdivided according to when they are set up and when the burden of financing is met. Preloss financing includes insurance, since a contingent financing arrangement is set up in anticipation of loss and the premium is paid in advance. Postloss financing includes new debt that is secured after the loss and is serviced by subsequent repayment of principal and interest. Financing for loss-reduction investments is more straightforward, and conventional sources of finances such as debt, equity, and retained earnings may be used.

This framework is presented in a formal chart (Figure 2-2) and is used to structure the remainder of this book.

APPENDIX: A Critique of the Traditional Risk-Management Structure

The decision framework used in this book differs from that traditionally presented. The purpose of this appendix is to summarize the conventional risk-management structure and to show why it is not well suited to the pursuit of a value-maximization goal. The reader who is new to risk management should ignore this appendix. Those familiar with other views of risk management might wish to use this appendix as a point of reference and contact with preceding literature. Some of the books mentioned here are the pioneering works of risk management, whose major achievement was to map out and stake a claim on the risk-management subject. Having consolidated this claim, risk-management attention is now turning outward again to establish its relationship with other disciplines—in particular, with such disciplines as statistics, economics, and finance, which can provide the powerful analytical tools that risk management currently lacks. This secondary stage will inevitably expose many of the original risk-management concepts to serious scrutiny, with the prospect that previous ideas may need to be modified or replaced. Here, we provide critiques of the decision framework conventionally adopted in risk management and the decision alternatives it identifies.

Classification is important in the development of a new subject area. In risk management, considerable attention has been given to the classification of the stages of the decision process and to the types of decisions available. The sequence presented in Figure 2-1 forms the basic structure for the risk management process. That is, issues should be *identified*—then *measured*—and then *handled*. However, a set of handling devices has been grafted onto this structure, and it comprises

1 Reduction in the cost of contingent losses. This may be achieved by reducing the size, or probability, of such losses or by avoiding those activities which result in exposure to loss.

2 Risk transfer. The costs of contingent losses are transferred to another party. The most conspicuous device for achieving transfer is insurance, although other possibilities also exist, such as the incorporation of liability clauses into business contracts.

3 Retention of risk. The financial burden of loss is left as a deadweight cost to the firm. The firm may or may not choose to manage such retention by establishment of a reserve fund from which future losses are to be paid.

This structure is shown in Figure 2-A1.

This system of classification is not right or wrong in any absolute sense. The relevant issue is whether it is useful in pursuing a particular goal. Does this system address questions that are relevant to the pursuit of that goal? Does the system provide information in a suitable form? Does the system identify available choices? The answers to these questions clearly depend on the objective that is chosen. For our purposes, we have assumed that a firm wishes to maximize the value of its equity, and we have argued that this value will impound the risk costs imposed on those holding a contractual relationship with the firm. The traditional decision structure, and the analyses that it has spawned, does not well serve the value-maximization objective for the following reasons:

1 The traditional risk-management structure supports an inappropriate measure of the costs of loss events. The cost is assumed to be the replacement cost of making good the damage, although incidental costs may be added in. However, the value of a firm is derived from its projected earnings stream. Accordingly, the valuation objective requires that the impact of the loss on the firm's earnings stream be identified. The capitalized value of this projected earnings displacement provides a measure of the loss of equity value. Special cases may arise where the loss of equity is equal to the replacement costs of the destroyed resources. However, in general, this is not so. Thus the appropriate measure of loss is the capitalized value of earnings lost, not the value of the resources destroyed or damaged.

2 The traditional structure ignores the productivity of resources employed by a firm. The productivity of resources is central to a new investment decision, but it is also important in deciding whether to replace resources that have already been destroyed. As argued in this

FIGURE 2-A1

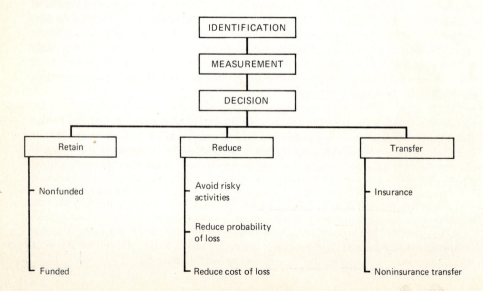

chapter, the decision is not trivial, and there is an a priori reason to believe that many firms currently utilize resources whose replacement cannot be justified on economic criteria. However, this issue is assumed away in existing texts, which place heavy emphasis on corporate risk aversion and the supposed desire for continuity of production.

3 The traditional view fails to distinguish between those decisions which involve the commitment of resources to productive use (i.e., investment decisions) and those decisions concerning the funding of such investments (i.e., financing decisions). Thus a large emphasis is placed on insurance purchase, which is as a source of finance, without discussion of whether this financing is ever needed to support postloss reinvestment. Further, the failure to identify the nature of financing and investment decisions might explain why the risk-management literature ignores conventional sources of funds for risk-management projects, such as debt, retained earnings, and new equity.

4 The existing structure encourages a piecemeal approach to the handling of risk rather than an integrative approach. Risk is identified, measured, and handled on the implicit assumption that the degree of risk measured for an individual exposure unit translates into an equivalent degree of risk to be absorbed by the firm's owners. However, risk does not follow a simple additive process. Possibilities for diversification exist at various levels. For example, risks can be "spread" over various risk management exposure units, risks can be spread between risk management and business exposure, and further diversification can be achieved by the firm's owners in the management of their personal investment portfolios. While the first possibility for diversification is often recognized, the latter two are not.

These related issues cast doubt on whether the existing decision structure can be used to generate effective financial decisions. The decision structure in Figure 2-A1 appears to serve a different master, but it is not entirely clear what this master is. Existing risk-management texts appear to agree on the decision structure to be used, but they do not reach consensus on identifying the corporate goals that motivate the structure.

Some examples will illustrate this issue. Williams and Heins (1964) assert that "risk management may be defined as the minimization of the adverse effects of risk at minimum cost through its identification, measurement, and control" (p. 11). In the discussion surrounding this definition, Williams and Heins appear to argue that the objective of risk management is to balance the benefit from the removal or reduction of risk with the costs of such action. The more recent work of Greene and Serbein (1983) opens with a more deliberate statement of risk-management objectives that appears to reflect a similar cost/benefit tradeoff: "In the top level management of the firm, there is often a conflict between optimization of return on capital and the increasing demand that waste of human, natural, and financial resources cease. Risk managers can help in the resolution of the conflict through their activities in risk and cost control" (p. 4, with quotation from E. S. Clark). In neither case is the statement of objectives clear enough to support precise decision criteria, although in the subsequent development of both texts, the guiding principle appears to be corporate aversion to risk.

A somewhat different and more precise objective for risk management is provided by Rosenbloom (1972): "Stated another way, the risk manager's basic job is to assure the financial solvency of the firm against the consequences of pure risk at the lowest possible cost" (p. 5). It is not clear how this operating objective is derived from more general corporate goals, but it does appear to imply an extreme form of risk aversion. Certainly, such a strong emphasis on survival may be at variance with the value-maximization objective outlined earlier.

A more specific statement of corporate objectives and of derived operating objectives for risk management is presented by Mehr and Hedges (1974). The objectives of a corporation are taken to be

1 Survival.

2 Efficiency and growth. "Efficiency may relate to a primary objective stated in terms of market share, sales volume, continuity of performance, nature and quantity of resources controlled or other items which are expected to produce desired long run results" (p. 2).

3 A "quiet night's sleep."

4 Good citizenship.

Such a statement is certainly comprehensive and can encompass each of the prior statements of goals and more. However, such an embracing statement of objectives leaves much room for conflict of goals, and the subsequent text provides a rich discussion of issues without clear guidance on how such conflicts can be resolved.

Such tentative statements of corporate objectives do, somewhat surprisingly, support a consensus on the form of the decision structure, as shown by Figure 2-A1.[3] For the most part, the same methods of handling risks are identified. Perhaps the common denominator that gives rise to this decision structure is not an agreement on objectives, but rather, that most risk-management writing and thinking have emerged from an insurance background. Certainly, the central role in the traditional structure is given to insurance as a method of handling risk. If this is not apparent from the structure shown in Figure 2-A1, little doubt over the role of insurance is left in risk-management texts, which typically concentrate heavily on the analysis of insurance contracts and insurance markets.

REFERENCES

DeAngelo, H.: "Competition and Unanimity," *American Economic Review,* vol. 7, 1981, pp. 17–27.

Elliott, J. W.: "Control, Size, Growth and Financial Performance in the Firm," *Journal of Financial and Quantitative Analysis,* vol. 7, 1972, pp. 1309–1320.

Greene, M., and O. Serbein: *Risk Management: Text and Cases,* 2d ed., Reston Publishing Company, Reston, Virginia, 1983.

Jensen, M. C., and W. H. Meckling: "Theory of the Firm: Managerial Behavior, Agency Costs and Ownership Structure," *Journal of Financial Economics,* vol. 3, 1976, pp. 305–360.

Mehr, R. I., and B. A. Hedges: *Risk Management: Concepts and Applications,* Irwin, Homewood, Illinois, 1974.

Myers, S. C.: "Determinants of Corporate Borrowing," *Journal of Financial Economics,* vol. 4, 1977, pp. 147–175.

Olson, D. G., and J. A. Simkiss: "An Overview of Risk Management," *The Geneva Papers on Risk and Insurance,* vol. 23, 1982, pp. 114–128.

Rosenbloom, J. S.: *A Case Study in Risk Management,* Meredith Corporation, New York, 1972.

Simon, H. A.: "Theories of Decision Making in Economics and Behavioral Sciences," *American Economic Review,* vol. 49, 1959, pp. 253–283.

Willett, A. H.: *The Economic Theory of Risk and Insurance,* 1901; reprinted by Irwin, Homewood, Illinois.

Williams, C. A., and R. M. Heins: *Risk Management and Insurance,* McGraw-Hill, New York, 1964.

---

[3]A curious exception to the preceding literature is provided by Olson and Simkiss in a recent (1982) article. These writers start with the premise adopted for this text—that risk management is a specialized form of financial management. Accordingly, the motivating objective for risk-management activity is to maximize share value. However, their subsequent identification and classification of risk-management strategies follows risk-management convention rather than incorporating the sources and uses of funds concepts of financial management.

CHAPTER 3

RISK AND UTILITY: ECONOMIC CONCEPTS AND SIMPLE DECISION RULES

Risk is present when the outcome of some defined activity is not known. Given the financial or economic approach of this text, the outcomes with which we are concerned can be directly or indirectly measured in money terms. *Risk* refers to the quality of variation in the range of possible outcomes; the greater the potential variation, the greater the risk. In the economic sense, risk does not refer to the adverse quality of some outcomes (losses instead of profits), but rather to the lack of knowledge about which of several outcomes may prevail. Risk is implied by our inability to predict the future. If risk was not present, many of our decisions would be trivial: We would simply choose that course of action which has the highest certain payoff. Under such circumstances, risk management would be a simple clerical task and this book would serve no purpose. However, when chance intervenes in the selection of outcomes, decision making becomes simultaneously more complex and more personal. Even though we may reasonably assume that everyone prefers more money to less, people differ in how they respond to risk. The differences in personal preferences to risk may relate to our personalities and to our economic circumstances. Accordingly, if economics is to provide us with a useful framework for making decisions under conditions of risk, it must help us to process and compare the potential outcomes on terms dictated by our personal preferences and circumstances.

Our task in this chapter is to specify simple decision rules that will help us to come to terms with the nature of risk and its effect on decision making. The so-called expected-utility hypothesis will be used to analyze simple risk management decisions—notably insurance decisions. In addition, the basic ideas will be useful in making preliminary statements concerning loss prevention and in analyzing certain features of the insurance market. The concepts to be discussed in this chapter are preliminary.

At first approximation, we may think of the simple risk-management decisions discussed here as being faced by an individual rather than by a corporation. The individual must make decisions on financing or take steps to prevent events that might prove catastrophic to him or her. When we come to look at corporations later, the separation of ownership and control will call for considerable modification of the decision procedure. Ownership of a corporation is represented by financial claims (shares of stock). We must then determine how the risky prospects facing a firm affect the ownership claims and how risk-management decisions can best protect the welfare of a firm's owners. This will require some development of statistical measures of risk, an understanding of the process of diversification, and some rudimentary awareness of how capital markets function. These are the subjects of the following chapters. For now, we will concentrate on an individual who must make decisions concerning risky events that may profoundly affect his or her personal welfare.

DERIVATION OF DECISION RULES

Simple Risky Prospects

A convenient starting place for our exploration of risky decision rules is an analysis of choices in which no risk is present. The decisions to be made in this uncomplex and safe world turn out to be trivially simple if we assume that outcomes can be specified in money terms. Of course, some events bring payoffs that are not directly specified in money values, but we assume that money equivalents can be assigned by the decision maker. For example, consider a choice between action A and action B. Action A is simply "do nothing" and has a zero payoff. Action B involves working for 10 hours for a fee of $200. To make a comparison, the decision maker must place a money-equivalent value for the labor involved in action B. If he decides that he is indifferent between each hour's work and receiving $18, then 10 hours' effort has a negative money value of $180. The comparison between actions A and B is now presented in the following terms:

Action		Payoff ($)
A (Do nothing)		$ 0
B (Work 10 hours)	Fee	$200
	Value of effort	− 180
	Net value	$ 20

As long as the decision maker is confident that he has correctly valued his time and effort at $18 per hour, the decision is quite mechanical. Action B has a higher payoff than action A and should be preferred.

To stretch our assumption of a certain world, consider a "gamble" between two people who have the unnerving facility to predict the future. The "gamble" involves the flip of a coin, the outcome of which, for us mortals, is certainly a risky activity, but which, for our prophets, is never in doubt. Prophet A will pay prophet B $10 if the coin turns up heads; otherwise prophet B will pay prophet A $10. Since both know that the coin will turn up tails, a meaningful transaction will never take place; prophet B will never agree. Possibly prophet A might be willing to pay prophet B $10 to induce him to make the "bet," but the activity is pointless because both break even. If we descend from Mount Olympus, the transaction will have quite different implications, since the outcome from tossing a coin is quite risky. Neither party will, in reality, know the outcome in advance, and the gamble therefore exposes both parties to a risky future. The payoff to the parties depends on chance, as follows:

Decision	Payoff
A's Decision:	
1. Gamble	$10 or −10
2. Do not gamble	$0
B's Decision:	
1. Gamble	$10 or − 10
2. Do not gamble	$0

To help A and B decide whether to gamble with each other, they might each make use of further information they have at their disposal. Neither knows whether the coin will land heads or tails, but each, believing the coin to be unbiased, assumes that the coin is equally likely to land on heads and tails. In other words, A and B believe that the probabilities of heads and tails are each one-half. We will represent this information, together with the payoffs, in the following format (the alternatives available to each decision maker are prospects V, that is, gamble, and W, that is, do not gamble):

$$V \text{ (gamble)} = \begin{cases} \$10 & 0.5 \text{ probability} \\ -\$10 & 0.5 \text{ probability} \end{cases}$$

$$W \text{ (do not gamble)} = \begin{cases} \$0 & 0.5 \text{ probability} \\ \$0 & 0.5 \text{ probability} \end{cases}$$

The dollar value on each line represents the payoff, and the associated probability follows.

In this choice, risk is present in the spread of values for the first alternative, but it is absent from the second alternative. With the gamble, the outcome cannot be predicted; it can take a range of values. Risk is inherent in this range or spread. If no gamble is selected, the outcome is the same, regardless of some chance event such as the toss of a coin. However, risk is a relative term. Consider the preceding gamble V along with the following:

$$X = \begin{cases} \$10 & 0.99 \text{ probability} \\ -\$10 & 0.01 \text{ probability} \end{cases} \qquad Y = \begin{cases} \$10 & 0.01 \text{ probability} \\ -\$10 & 0.99 \text{ probability} \end{cases}$$

$$Z = \begin{cases} \$20 & 0.5 \text{ probability} \\ -\$20 & 0.5 \text{ probability} \end{cases}$$

X has the same range of outcomes as V, but the probabilities have changed. Certainly, the odds have been altered in favor of the gambler, but the degree of predictability has also changed. Winning comes close to being a "sure thing." Thus chance has less opportunity to be capricious. Although the range of possible outcomes remains unchanged, the degree of "variability" has changed significantly. Y simply reverses the probabilities from X. Now the odds are biased against winning, and undoubtedly, this reduces the attractiveness of gambling. However, the degree of "predictability," or variation in outcomes, remains similar to that for X. Our concept of risk will take account of probabilities. Comparing Z with V, the probabilities are the same, but the range of outcomes has increased. The increase in the range of outcomes contributes to an increase in risk. Thus *risk*, in the economic sense, is a quality that reflects both the range of possible outcomes and the distribution of respective probabilities for each of the outcomes.

The Expected-Value Rule

Let us now set up a decision rule that can help us to choose between risky alternatives. Consider, for example, a choice between the following (outcomes in dollar values, followed by probability):

$$A = \begin{cases} 10 & 0.5 \\ 10 & 0.5 \end{cases} \quad D = \begin{cases} 0 & 0.4 \\ 20 & 0.6 \end{cases}$$

$$B = \begin{cases} 0 & 0.5 \\ 20 & 0.5 \end{cases} \quad E = \begin{cases} 0 & 0.6 \\ 20 & 0.4 \end{cases}$$

$$C = \begin{cases} 5 & 0.5 \\ 15 & 0.5 \end{cases} \quad F = \begin{cases} 1 & 0.5 \\ 21 & 0.5 \end{cases}$$

Each alternative will be called a *prospect;* outcomes B, C, D, E, and F may be further described as "risky" prospects. Outcome A is clearly a nonrisky prospect.

The decision rule will focus on the outcome that may be expected to prevail "on average." More precisely, we will select the alternative with the highest expected value EV, defined as follows:

$$EV_j = \sum_i P_i X_i \tag{3-1}$$

where EV_j = expected value of the prospect j
 P_i = probability of outcome X_i
 X_i = outcome in money value

Thus, for alternative B, the expected value is

$$EV_B = 0.5(\$0) + 0.5(\$20) = \$10$$

One interpretation of this value is as follows. If an individual accepted a large number of such risky prospects, he or she would win $20 on some and nothing on others. The average outcome would be very close to $10 per prospect if the number of prospects was sufficiently large.[1] Thus $10 is the long-run average value for the risky prospect. If the individual paid $10 for each bet of type B, he or she would break even in the long run.

Using this expected-value rule, a single value can be assigned to each prospect, and this, hopefully, will aid in decision making. The respective values are

$$EV_A = EV_B = EV_C = \$10$$
$$EV_D = \$12$$
$$EV_E = \$ 8$$
$$EV_F = \$11.5$$

Consequently, our ranking should be

$$D > F > (A \text{ or } B \text{ or } C) > E$$

If this rule works successfully, testing a group of decision makers should confirm the ranking. Testing on a class of graduate and undergraduate students reveals some problems. Preference of D over E appears to be virtually unanimous for all subjects. So far so good; this is exactly what the rule predicts. However, preferences tend to appear between A, B, and C, and according to the rule, they should rank equally. Most students prefer A to B (or C) and C to B. One stubborn approach to such problems is to assert that students do not know what is good for them and that we should continue to believe the rule. However, the rule must *serve* preferences, not be a master to them. Other problem rankings tend to arise. The expected-value rule asserts that F should be preferred to A, but many students (not all) prefer A. Several other choices do not correspond with the expected-value rule. Such experiments are not laboratory-controlled, and differences between group responses appear. However, such simple tests do reveal that individuals have strong preferences that cannot obediently be classified by such a simple rule. Having preferences different from those predicted by the expected-value rule does not imply irrationality.

The St. Petersburg Paradox

A more dramatic illustration of how such a rule may break down was formulated some two centuries ago by Daniel Bernoulli. Bernoulli was an eighteenth-century Swiss mathematician and physicist and one-time professor of mathematics at the Russian

---

[1] This also assumes that successive outcomes are independent. This will be discussed in detail later.

Academy in Saint Petersburg. Bernoulli posed the following problem, which has come to be known as the *St. Petersburg paradox:*

Consider a game in which one player flips a fair coin. If the coin reveals heads, the player will pay the other player 2 dollars (or ducats or whatever), and the game is over. If the coin lands on tails, it is tossed again. If the second toss lands heads, the first player pays ($2)^2 dollars to the second, and the game is over. If the second toss lands tails, the coin is flipped again. Thus the game continues until the first heads appears, and then the first player pays the second ($2)^n, where n signifies the number of tosses required to reveal the first heads. Since a head will turn up eventually, the second player wants a long preceding run of tails. The problem is: How much will the second player be willing to pay to enter the game? Of course, individuals vary in their responses, but seldom will anyone be willing to pay more than $10 to enter such a game.

The nature of the paradox can be seen by considering the expected value of such a game. We will represent the risky prospect in the following form, showing the sequence of tails and heads required to produce each outcome:

	Outcome	Probability	Sequence required to produce outcome
	$2	$1/2$	H
	2^2	$1/2^2$	TH
	2^3	$1/2^3$	TTH
St. Petersburg Paradox =	.	.	.
	.	.	.
	.	.	.
	2^n	$1/2^n$	TT $\cdots$ [$(n-1$ times)] $\cdots$ H

The expected value of the game is

$$\sum P_i X_i = 2(1/2) + 2^2(1/2)^2 + 2^3(1/2)^3 + \cdots + 2^n(1/2)^n + \cdots$$
$$= 1 + 1 + 1 + \cdots$$
$$= \infty$$

Why is it that people will typically only pay a few dollars to participate in a game that has an infinite value? Clearly, the expected-value rule has broken down dramatically.

What causes the expected-value rule to fail in the simple-choice experiments given to the class and in the St. Petersburg paradox? The answer is that risk is ignored. Returning to the simple prospects, $10 with certainty (prospect A) is clearly very different from a fifty-fifty gamble for $20 or nothing (prospect B). The general preference for A over B and the small entry price to the St. Petersburg game indicate that the quality of variability in outcomes is an adverse factor for the decision maker given equality in expected values. Most people prefer choices with less risk rather than more. This does not mean that people will never choose risk when it can be avoided. The expected value of one prospect may be so advantageous in comparison with a competing prospect that aversion to risk is overcome. It is easy to construct such choices. Consider the following:

$$G = \begin{cases} \$10 & 0.5 \text{ probability} \\ \$10 & 0.5 \text{ probability} \end{cases} \qquad H = \begin{cases} \$9 & 0.5 \text{ probability} \\ \$20 & 0.5 \text{ probability} \end{cases}$$

G may be seen as the entry price to gamble H; by not gambling, the individual retains $10 with certainty. If I were to make an offer of accepting such gambles, I imagine that I would be killed in the rush. I hasten to add that idle speculation does not constitute such an offer. The next question therefore is: How can attitudes toward risk be considered in an appropriate decision rule? One useful answer lies with the concept of utility.

The Expected-Utility Rule

There are two related ways of trying to resolve the St. Petersburg paradox. One approach, suggested by Bernoulli, is to place some weighting on money outcomes; later, this approach led to the concept of utility of income or wealth. A second approach is to recognize explicitly that risk per se has a cost and to embody this cost as a parameter in the decision. This second approach will be examined later when we discuss the mean-variance rule. We will now present the utility approach and show that this embodies a welfare measurement of risk.

Utility is a scale of measurement of the satisfaction derived from some economic good, particularly income or wealth. To represent utility, let us make some fairly innocuous assumptions. First, we will order levels of satisfaction with the statement that "more wealth is preferred to less wealth." Second, we will make a further statement that has the effect of ordering differences in wealth. The incremental utility, or satisfaction, from unit increases in wealth decreases as wealth increases. Thus, if I am poor, an addition of $1000 to my wealth will make a considerable impact on my level of welfare. If I am rich, the extra $1000 will still increase my satisfaction, but only marginally. These concepts are known in economics as the *law of diminishing marginal utility*, and the law is represented by utility function *OA* shown in Figure 3-1. Of course, different individuals will scale different levels of wealth in different ways. Thus two other utility functions, *OB* and *OC*, are also shown in the figure. The positions of these functions have little significance, because they apply to different people. We are unable to make direct comparisons of different individuals' capacities for enjoying wealth. However, some forms of comparison can be made. The function *OB* seems to be less concave than *OA*, whereas *OC* appears to change its slope more rapidly than *OA* as wealth increases. In other words, individual B (with curve *OB*) appears to value increases in wealth almost as highly at high levels of wealth as at low levels of wealth. In contrast, the satisfaction curve *OC* of individual C flattens out very quickly, indicating that individual C's capacity for enjoying additional wealth tails off quickly as wealth increases. These features, as we shall see, reveal differences in attitudes toward risk.

What is the connection between utility and risk? Consider a simple gamble. The

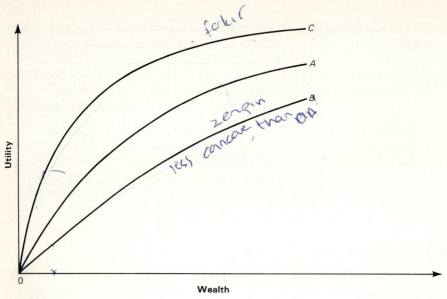

fokus

zergin

less concae thar ɒ,ɒ

FIGURE 3-1

choices are (1) to keep our current wealth and not gamble or (2) to enter an "equal odds" gamble in which we win or lose $10. Put another way, the gamble substitutes for our current wealth of $10, a fifty-fifty chance of wealth $0 or wealth $20. Should we enter the gamble? Let us represent the choices on the wealth scale of Figure 3-2, which also shows a utility function conforming to the preceding assumptions. If the gamble is not undertaken, wealth is $10, which has a utility value shown on the vertical axis as $U(\$10)$. For an income of $10, the slope of the utility curve is neither very steep nor very flat, showing an intermediate value on changes in wealth. Now consider a very small gamble in which we either win or lose $1. If we win, wealth increases to $11, which, naturally, has a higher utility than $10. If we lose, our wealth falls to $9, which has a lower utility than $10. However, notice the respective sizes of these prospective changes in utility. Because the utility curve becomes flatter as wealth increases, the loss of utility from the fall in wealth exceeds the increase in utility from an equal gain in wealth. This differential valuation of the gain or loss from the gamble causes a bias against taking such a risky decision. Now consider the larger gamble. Losing reduces wealth drastically to position $0, where marginal dollars have a very high value, as indicated by the steep slope of the utility curve at this level of wealth. However, winning takes us to $20, where the utility curve is pretty flat, showing that marginal dollars have relatively low utility value. If the utility curve is of the form shown, gambles represent a trade in which the individual sacrifices dollars that are highly valued (because they coincide with low wealth) in exchange for contingent dollars that have a low utility value (because winning will transport the individual to a higher wealth level, where the marginal utility of wealth is low). At face value, this prospect does not appear very attractive. Diminishing marginal utility creates a bias against gambling.

The relationship between utility and risk is now presented in a more precise fashion. The *expected-utility rule* represents a revised decision rule that substitutes utility values for money values in risky prospects in order to select among risky alternatives. The rule was developed by John von Neumann and Oskar Morgenstern (1944) and has proved to be a very powerful technique for analyzing risky choices. The rule is based on a set of formal axioms that will not be examined here; however, we will show that it can be used to provide some very useful preliminary insights into risk-management problems.

An expected utility *EU* is assigned to a risky prospect in accordance with the following expression:

$$EU_j = \sum_i P_i U(X_i) \qquad\qquad (3\text{-}2)$$

where EU_j = expected utility of prospect j
P_i = probability of outcome X_i
$U(X_i)$ = utility value of outcome X_i derived from the individual's
 utility function

FIGURE 3-2

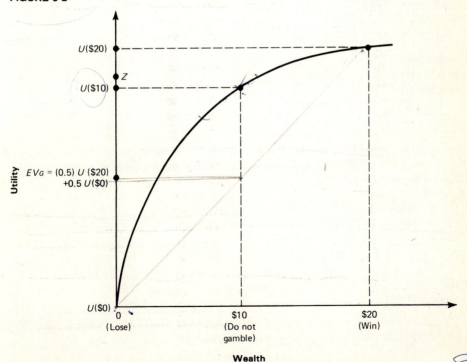

Notice how similar this rule is to the expected-value rule. Whereas *expected value* is the weighted average of the money outcomes, *expected utility* is the weighted average of outcomes when those outcomes are expressed in utility values.

The application of the rule is illustrated in Figure 3-2. The utility values of winning and losing are shown on the vertical axis as $U(\$20)$ and $U(\$0)$, respectively. Since the odds on winning and losing are each 0.5, the weighted average of the two utility values is the halfway point; that is, the expected utility of the gamble EU_G is

$$EU_G = 0.5U(\$20) + 0.5U(\$0)$$

The position is shown on the vertical axis. Now consider the alternative choice, which is to avoid the gamble and keep current wealth with certainty (i.e., a probability of unity). Writing the expected utility from not gambling as EU_{NG}, we have

$$EU_{NG} = 1.0U(\$10) = U(\$10)$$

Clearly, the expected utility from not gambling is higher than that from gambling. Therefore, according to the decision rule, the gamble should be avoided.

There is no indication from this analysis that one should never gamble, but it does imply that gambling should not be undertaken at such odds. The preceding example reveals fair odds; that is, the entry price is equal to the expected payoff. There is an entry price for the gamble of zero and the expected payoff is also zero, as shown:

$$EV = 0.5(-\$10) + 0.5(\$10) = 0$$

It is possible to play with the odds until the gamble becomes attractive. For example, at 0.9 probability of winning, the expected utility is recalculated at point Z on the vertical axis. This is higher than the utility of not gambling.

From these results, we can make some general statements that apply to an individual who has a utility curve of the concave shape shown in Figures 3-1 and 3-2:

1 These individuals would not rationally gamble at fair odds.
2 The odds would have to be loaded in the individual's favor in order to induce him or her to gamble.

Accordingly, we will state a very important conclusion. If an individual has a concave utility function of the form shown in Figures 3-1 and 3-2, that individual is averse to risk by definition. As we shall soon see, aversion to risk implies the willingness to pay a premium to avoid risk. Before proceeding, the interested reader may try constructing a utility function that is convex, i.e., slopes upward at an increasing rather than a decreasing rate. The same gamble can be represented and the expected utilities recalculated. From such an exercise, it should be concluded that an individual with a convex utility function derives positive value from risk and would gamble at fair odds. Such a person may be described as a "risk lover."

INSURANCE AND THE EXPECTED-UTILITY RULE

An insurance policy has the opposite risk effect to a gamble. A gamble involves the sacrifice of certain wealth in order to acquire the possibility of an increase in wealth. An insurance policy involves the sacrifice of certain wealth in order to avoid the possibility of a loss of wealth. With a gamble, one pays to acquire risk; with an insurance policy, one pays to avoid risk. The insurance strategy can be valued using the expected-utility rule in an identical manner as the gamble.

Suppose you wish to insure your home. To simplify the issue, your total wealth is $120, of which $100 is the value of your home. The house may or may not burn down, but assuming any loss to be a total loss, a fire would reduce your wealth from $120 to $20. The probability of a fire is 0.25 (this does not reflect pathologic tendencies in your children; it is simply a convenient value for purposes of illustration). Since your final wealth will be either $120 or $20, with respective probabilities of 0.75 and 0.25, you can represent your utility in contemplating this insecure prospect as

$$EU_{NI} = 0.75U(\$120) + 0.25U(\$20)$$

where the subscript *NI* indicates that no insurance has been purchased. What if insurance is available? The expected value of the loss is

$$EV = 0.25(100) = \$25$$

Ignoring transaction costs, an insurer charging such a premium would break even if it held a large portfolio of such policies. This premium could be called a *fair premium* or an *actuarially fair premium,* denoting that the premium is equal to the expected value of loss (sometimes called the *actuarial value* of the policy). The term *fair* is not construed in a normative sense, rather it is simply a reference point.

If you are offered insurance at a fair premium, in this case $25, should you insure? Consider Figure 3-3, which shows a utility curve revealing aversion to risk. The horizontal axis shows possible values of terminal wealth. The positions $20 and $120 represent possible wealth positions if you do not insure, and the respective utility values are revealed on the vertical axis. Insurance at a premium of $25 will remove the financial impact of a chance fire, but you must sacrifice $25 of certain wealth to pay the premium. Thus, with insurance, my wealth position will be $120 - $25 = $95 with a corresponding probability of unity. The expected-utility values for insurance EU_I and no insurance EU_{NI} are constructed as follows:

$$EU_I = 1.0U(\$95) = U(\$95)$$
$$EU_{NI} = 0.25U(\$20) + 0.75U(\$120)$$

Both positions are clearly shown on the vertical axis of Figure 3-3. As shown, EU_I is greater than EU_{NI}, suggesting that insurance should be purchased. Is this ranking accidental? In fact, it is not.

A geometric technique to find the expected utility of two wealth levels is shown in Figure 3-3. A chord *AB* is drawn from the two positions on the utility curve corresponding to the alternative wealth levels. The position at which this chord intercepts the expected money value of wealth (position *C*) traces out expected utility. The reason this trick works is that the same probability weights are used for expected value and expected utility. Clearly, if the utility curve is concave from below, point *C*, which traces out the expected utility of not insuring, will always be below point *D*, which identifies the expected utility of insuring. Thus we can state the following preliminary ideas:

1 A concave utility curve implies aversion to risk, in confirmation of our earlier result.

2 A rational, risk-averse individual will choose to insure if the premium is equal to the expected value of loss.

This second statement is very important. It is often known as the *Bernoulli principle,* and it provides a powerful rationale for insurance and will help condition our thinking for more complex corporate risk-management problems.

Before introducing more realistic problems, let us dwell for a little while longer on risk aversion and stress the equivalence between the shape of the utility function

FIGURE 3-3

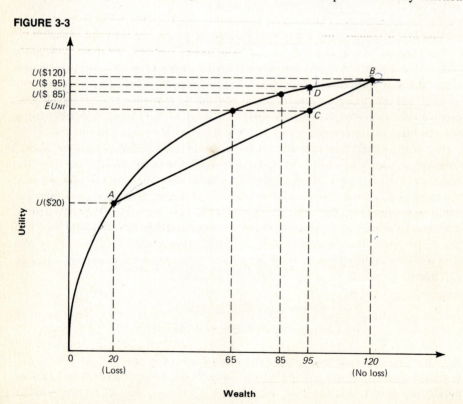

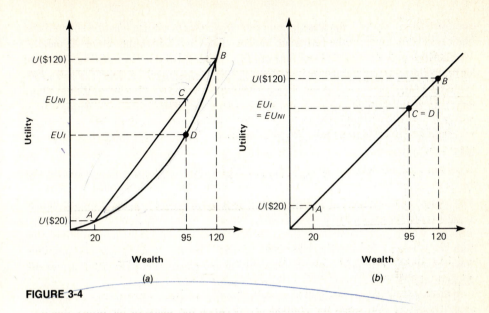

FIGURE 3-4

and attitude toward risk by considering exceptional cases. Figure 3-4(*a*) shows a utility function that is convex, implying that, for this individual, the marginal valuation of wealth increases as wealth increases (the more money she gets, the more money she wants). The attitude toward insurance is quite different from that revealed by a concave utility function. Since the marginal valuation of wealth is high when we pay the premium but low when we receive a loss settlement, insurance is unattractive. The same geometric construction is undertaken, using the same notation as in Figure 3-3, to show the respective positions of EU_I and EU_{NI}. Notice that EU_{NI}, derived from position C, is now higher than EU_I, from position D, showing that insurance should not be purchased. It takes little imagination to show that if the utility curve is linear, as shown in Figure 3-4(*b*), the individual is neither averse to risk nor does she like risk; she is risk-neutral. Now the expected utility from insuring is exactly equal to that from not insuring. The risk-neutral individual will choose purely on the basis of expected values of alternative risky prospects; the risk per se has no value.

SOME RISK-MANAGEMENT PROPOSITIONS FOR INDIVIDUALS

Insurance with Premium Loadings

The Bernoulli principle provides a useful starting point for a treatment of risky decision making. It reveals that risk has a cost and that this cost is neglected in a decision rule that uses expected value alone. However, for practical risk management, the Bernoulli principle addresses a problem that is not very interesting. Seldom, if ever, is an insurance premium equal to the expected or actuarial value of the policy payment. Even if the insurance market is highly competitive, such that all surplus profit is removed from insurers, the transaction costs of writing insurance must be covered and the capital employed in the insurance industry must make a normal return. Typically, transaction costs of writing insurance are high, both for the insurer and for the agent or broker. Consequently, the insurance premium usually ranges between 125 and 175% or more of the expected value of losses. Can we use the expected-utility rule to say anything about optimal insurance decisions with these, more realistic, premium structures?

Consider Figure 3-3 again, but suppose that the premium charged by the insurer is $35 instead of $25. The effect of purchasing insurance would be to give the insured a certain wealth of $85 (that is, $120 − $35 = $85). The utility from insuring can be ascertained by using the utility curve to plot the corresponding value, U($85), on the vertical axis. Clearly, this value lies between U($95) and EU_{NI}; therefore, insurance is still preferred to no insurance. If the premium were $55, it would turn out that insuring would give the same utility, U($65), as not insuring. At this premium, the individual would be indifferent between insuring and not insuring. At any premium lower than $55, insurance would be desirable; at any greater premium, insurance would be undesirable.

This example reveals that a risk-averse individual would be willing to pay a premium above the expected value of loss in order to remove risk by purchasing an insurance policy. The maximum an individual is willing to pay above the expected value of loss is known as the *risk premium* (not to be confused with the *insurance premium,* which is simply the price of the insurance policy). The fact that an individual is willing to pay a risk premium to remove risk indicates that the individual is risk-averse. The more risk averse the individual is, the greater the risk premium that he or she will pay. Thus the risk premium provides a measure of an individual's attitude toward risk.

Risk premiums will differ among individuals, and it is not possible to offer a general theorem that states precisely the conditions under which insurance will be purchased. The most general statement that can be made at this point is that *a risk-averse individual is willing to incur a risk premium to remove the riskiness of his or her wealth prospect by means of an insurance policy*. In reality, the insurance premiums charged by an insurance company may or may not be too high to induce any given individual to purchase insurance. Conceptually, we can state that if the insurance premium satisfies the following condition, individual i will purchase insurance:

$$P - E(L) < RP_i$$

where P = the insurance premium
$E(L)$ = the expected value of loss
RP_i = the risk premium for individual i

The left-hand side of the inequality represents the portion of the insurance premium allocated to transaction costs and insurer's profit. This is known as the *premium loading* or *markup*. If we know the loss distribution and the insurance premium, we can calculate the left-hand side of this condition, but the right-hand side is a subjective value that will differ among individuals. At any given premium loading, some people will purchase insurance and others will not. The best we can say is that, other things being equal, the higher the premium loading, the smaller the number of people who will wish to buy insurance.

From this discussion it seems that the expected-utility rule can help to discipline and organize our thinking about the purchase of insurance or similar risky decisions. We can use the rule to make general statements about the decision process and the tradeoffs an individual has to make. However, to correctly predict the actual decision made by an individual requires knowledge of that individual's utility function—not just its general shape (such as concave), but its exact form. We can never look inside people's heads, nor are people usually able to articulate and quantify a concept as abstract as utility. Despite these operational limitations, the rule does yield important insights. It focuses attention on the types of costs and benefits that are involved in the decision, and it will often enable us to narrow down the set of alternative choices so that we focus only on those solutions which are compatible with our general attitude toward risk. Some further general propositions are now appropriate.

Gambling at Unfair Odds

The preceding proposition asserted that a risk averter would be willing to pay a risk premium (i.e., pay an insurance premium in excess of the expected value of loss) in order to purchase an insurance policy. The risk premium is really the price to the insured for converting a risky wealth prospect into a riskless wealth prospect. With this reasoning, it would appear that a risk averter would want to be paid a risk premium in order to induce him or her to voluntarily accept risk. Put another way, a risk-averse individual would have to be offered odds that were in his or her favor in order to induce him or her to gamble. First, we will demonstrate this proposition; then we will try to resolve the difficulty it creates for us in explaining why people actually gamble at *unfair* odds.

Figure 3-5 depicts a gamble that is, initially, identical to that shown in Figure 3-2. The individual starts with a wealth level of $10. The individual can choose to keep the $10 or gamble. The gamble might involve rolling a die. If the resulting number is even, the gambler wins $10; if the resulting number is odd, the gambler loses $10. Assuming the die is unbiased, the odds of winning and losing are each 0.5 and the expected value of the gamble is

$$0.5(-\$10) + 0.5(\$10) = 0$$

The expected wealth is the same for both the gamble and the no gamble alternatives, that is, $10. The expected utilities differ significantly. Respectively, the expected utilities of not gambling EU_{NG} and EU_G are as follows:

$$EU_{NG} = U(\$10)$$
$$EU_G = 0.5U(\$0) + 0.5U(\$20)$$

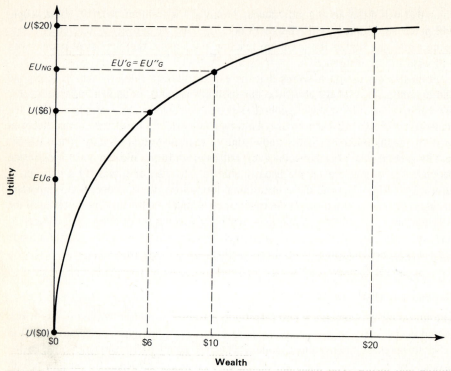

FIGURE 3-5

The respective positions are shown on the vertical axis, revealing that the individual will prefer not to gamble.

What will induce this risk-averse person to gamble? Two possibilities spring to mind: (1) keep the stakes the same, but change the odds in the gambler's favor or (2) keep the fifty-fifty odds, but change the stakes in the gambler's favor. For solution 1, consider the probability of

a Winning = 0.85
b Losing = 0.15

Therefore,

$$EU'_G = 0.45U(\$0) + 0.85U(\$20)$$

These odds have been engineered such that $EU_{NG} = EU'_G$, revealing that the individual is indifferent between not gambling and gambling at these favorable odds. If the odds are further improved in the gambler's favor, she would definitely prefer to gamble.

Much the same result can be achieved by changing the stakes instead of the odds, i.e., solution (2). Consider the gamble to involve a win of $10 with a probability of

0.5 and a loss of $4 with a probability of 0.5. The expected utility of gambling is now

$$EU_G'' = 0.5U(\$6) + 0.5U(\$20)$$

which, again, has been engineered to give the same utility value as not gambling, as shown on the vertical axis of Figure 3-5.

In each of these cases, the expected value of the gamble has been increased in order to make the gamble more attractive relative to the no gamble choice. Expected wealth without gambling is $10. In contrast, the expected values, respectively, of (*1*) and (*2*) are

$$EV_{(1)} = 0.15(\$0) + 0.85(\$20) = \$17$$
$$EV_{(2)} = 0.5(\$6) + 0.5(\$20) = \$13$$

This increase in expected value is necessary in order to induce a risk averter to gamble, and as such, it is analogous to the risk premium discussed in connection with insurance.

Resolution of the Insurance and Gambling Paradox

This analysis of gambling leaves us with a problem in explaining why people, in reality, choose to gamble. Even more puzzling is the fact that the same people often gamble and insure. The weekend visitor to Las Vegas or Atlantic City will return home and promptly pay the insurance premium for his or her home or life policy. Let us first address the simpler issue of why an individual might choose to gamble. The difficulty in explaining gambling is enhanced when we consider that most gambling is undertaken at unfair odds; after all, the bookmaker and the casino must come out ahead to stay in business.

1 One explanation of gambling is simply that gamblers are not risk-averse; their utility curves are convex rather than concave. For such individuals, gambling is rational behavior. However, we observe many people who gamble but otherwise appear to behave in a risk-averse manner. Some possible explanations of gambling that do not upset the notion of risk aversion are as follows:

2 Gamblers act on subjective rather than objective probabilities. Gamblers often believe they have a system or that they can read the cards or have a superstitious belief in "Lady Luck."

3 The attraction of gambling is not confined to the money outcomes; other forms of consumption also arise. A weekend in Las Vegas may be considered to be good entertainment, and any loss in gambling is the "price" of that entertainment. The unfair odds are comparable with the price of a theater ticket or the cost of a football game.

4 Another explanation, associated with the British economist G. L. S. Shackle, (1938) is that individuals do not respond mathematically to the odds, but instead focus their attention on particular outcomes that exert an undue influence on their decision.

For example, with gambling, we might be blinded by the thought of winning; with insurance, we might be consumed by the image of our house reduced to ashes.

5 The previous explanation offered a possible resolution of why people might simultaneously gamble and insure. A more direct attack on this paradox was undertaken by Friedman and Savage (1948) and by Markowitz (1952), who suggested that the utility function may not be uniformly concave. A brief examination of the Friedman-Savage analysis follows.

Figure 3-6 shows a utility curve that is concave over most of its length, but it also exhibits a convex section over part of its range. It is important that the point at which the curve changes its curvature from concave to convex is current wealth W_O. Thus, for any reduction in wealth, the relevant section of the curve is concave (i.e., in the range $0-W_O$). Insurance relates to events that will reduce wealth from W_O, and since this range is concave, the individual responds in a rational risk-averse manner by purchasing insurance. For wealth increases (i.e., above W_O), the relevant section of the curve is convex. Since gambling offers us the prospect of wealth increases, this section of the utility curve is relevant in analyzing such decisions. The curve reveals risk preference in this range, and accordingly, it predicts that gambling will be undertaken at fair or even unfair odds. Subsequent debate on this issue has centered on whether the curve will eventually return to the concave form at very high wealth levels and on what form of gambling would appear to be rational from this model (high odds and high stakes or low odds and small stakes).

Some recent experimental evidence by Shoemaker and Hershey (1980) suggests

FIGURE 3-6
The Friedman-Savage hypothesis.

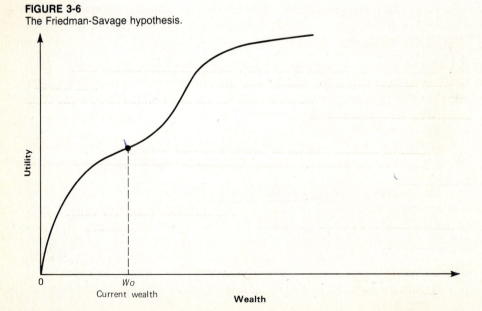

that the context in which a decision is presented may affect the decision. For example, consider the following choices:

$$A = \$100 \text{ with certainty} \qquad B = \begin{cases} \$120 & 0.8 \text{ probability} \\ \$0 & 0.2 \text{ probability} \end{cases}$$

The selection might represent the choice about purchasing insurance. Current wealth is $120, but there is a 20% chance that it will be totally destroyed. For a premium of $20, insurance can be purchased that gives the individual $100 with certainty. The same prospects could be presented as a speculative business opportunity. The individual can invest $100. There is an 80% chance that this will earn a return of $20, giving the investor a final wealth of $120, but there is a 20% chance that the investor will lose everything. Although these two stories are very different, the mathematical descriptions of the two problems are identical. Laboratory evidence reveals that subjects often respond differently when the context of the decision is changed.

The ideas discussed here reveal that actual decisions may be a little more complex and may have other dimensions than revealed by simple application of the expected-utility rule. Nevertheless, many of these ideas represent attempts to describe actual behavior, which may not always be rational or which may reflect unusual risk preferences, rather than attempts to identify rational optimizing behaviors. Our task is to prescribe a decision rule that will assist in identifying rational risk management decisions, and for this purpose, the expected-utility rule provides keen insights. Thus our main interest lies in the prescriptive value of the rule rather than its descriptive value.

Partial Insurance

In the insurance decisions presented earlier, the choice was of an "all or nothing" nature. Insurance was purchased or it was not. More useful is a consideration of intermediate solutions. Various devices are currently available through which risk can be shared between insurer and insured. One common practice is to write an insurance policy with a deductible that assigns liability for the first k dollars of each loss to the insured, the insurer picking up the residual. Alternatively, the insurer may cover an agreed proportion of each loss, leaving the residual proportion to the insured. Other policies place an absolute limit on the insurer's liability. With such devices, the risk may be shared by the parties to the insurance contract, and the appropriate decision is one of degree. The question: How much insurance should be purchased? replaces the question: Whether insurance should be purchased?

Consider here that the risk is divided on a proportionate basis. The individual has an initial wealth of $120, of which $20 is nonrisky and $100 represents some asset that is subject to possible destruction with a probability of 0.25. Only total loss is assumed in this example. The reader will recognize this example (see Figure 3-3). In the earlier discussion, only full insurance was available, and it could be purchased at a premium of $35, the expected value of loss being $25. Let us view full insurance as the purchase of $100 of compensation in the event of (total) loss. However, we might have insured half the loss [i.e., purchased $50 compensation in the event of (total) loss] or a quarter of the loss (purchased $25 of compensation), etc. We may think of the degree of coverage as variable, the relevant issue being: How many dollars of protection should we purchase for the contingent $100 loss?

To promote this example, the premium is scaled according to the number of dollars of protection purchased. If the premium is scaled according to the expected value of the insurer's claim payment, it will be 25 cents per dollar of compensation purchased, reflecting the 25% probability of loss. Full coverage would cost $100 × 0.25 = $25; 50% coverage would cost $50 × 0.25 = $12.50, etc. However, in the example given earlier, there was a premium of $35 for full coverage, reflecting a premium rate of 35 cents per dollar of insurance purchased. What is the optimal level of insurance to be purchased?

This problem will be tackled using a rather different diagram. Figure 3-7 shows individual wealth in the event of a loss and in the event of no loss. Each possible event is called a *state of the world*. State 0 refers to loss, and state 1 refers to no loss. The respective axes show the respective wealth levels, and the initial contingent wealth position with no insurance is shown at position A. If the actuarially fair premium is charged, full insurance can be purchased for $25. With such full insurance, the in-

FIGURE 3-7

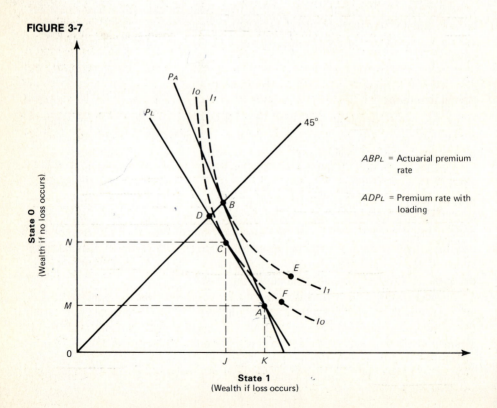

ABP_L = Actuarial premium rate

ADP_L = Premium rate with loading

State 0 (Wealth if no loss occurs)

State 1 (Wealth if loss occurs)

dividual will have $95 regardless of whether a loss occurs or not. This position is represented at position B. The 45° line shows equal wealth in both states and, as such, plots out full-insurance positions. Only by purchasing full insurance will wealth be independent of which state arises. However, the actual premium is 35 cents per dollar of insurance purchased. Thus starting at position A, each 35 cents of income sacrificed in state 1 in insurance premium will purchase $1 of compensation in state 0 (loss payment from the insurer). The insurance possibilities are shown on the line ADP_L. Full insurance is shown at position D (in which case, wealth would be $85 with certainty), but the individual can select partial insurance along segment AD. Position C represents a partial-insurance solution because it reveals greater wealth in the event of no loss than in the event of loss. In other words, compensation would be insufficient to provide full indemnity for the loss.

Now let us establish what level of insurance would be optimal at different premium rates. The solution of this problem requires some knowledge of the individual's risk preferences. These are represented by a set of curves such as I_0 and I_1, which are indifference curves. To understand these curves, consider two points such as B and E. These are on the same curve, indicating that our subject is indifferent between the wealth combinations represented by these points. Notice the tradeoff involved in a move such as that from position E to position B. Maintaining the same level of utility (i.e., indifference) requires that loss of income in the contingent state 1 be compensated by increased income in the contingent state 0. Despite such tradeoffs at a constant utility level, more wealth in both states is preferred to less wealth in both states; thus position E is clearly preferred to position F. Therefore, position F must offer a lower satisfaction level than position E, and consequently, it is on a lower indifference curve, that is, I_0. Summarizing, all positions on a given indifference curve represent the same level of utility, but any point on an indifference curve such as I_1 is preferred to any point on a lower indifference curve such as I_0. Indifference curves denote increased satisfaction as they move away from the origin. The convexity of the curves to the origin indicates aversion to risk. Thus a set of indifference curves can represent the same concepts as a utility function.

We know from the Bernoulli principle that a risk averter will choose to fully insure at an actuarially fair premium. Thus at premium rate ABP_A, the subject chooses position B over partial-insurance solutions on the segment AB. The preference for position B is shown by the fact that it is on the highest possible indifference curve that can be obtained given the opportunities along AB. The higher premium rate of 35 cents per dollar is shown by the line from ADP_L. However, the subject can no longer achieve the satisfaction level denoted by indifference curve I_1. The best that can be achieved is to just reach curve I_0, which offers lower satisfaction than I_1. This is the highest indifference curve that can be reached, as indicated by the tangency point C. Thus point C is the optimal position. Notice that point C is below the 45° line, indicating that less than full insurance is purchased. In fact, the insured pays JK dollars in premiums to receive MN dollars in compensation should the loss occur. Notice that the subject could have chosen not to insure (position A) or to fully insure at this premium rate (position D). However, both these positions are below indifference curve I_0, indicating lower utility than position C.

This diagrammatic approach illustrates an idea that was proved mathematically some years ago by both Mossin (1968) and Smith (1968): *that a risk averter will normally choose to partially insure if the insurance premium includes a loading factor that is positively related to the expected claim payment.* Since premiums are usually structured in this way, we would expect that most rational people will not choose to insure everything in sight, but will retain part of the risk themselves. As with most other goods, it appears that as price increases, we choose to purchase less.

The Design of an Insurance Policy

The utility concept predicts that, in the face of premium loading, a rational risk-management strategy for an individual is to partially insure rather than to fully insure. We can use the same ideas to say something about how such a partial-insurance arrangement may be constructed.

As mentioned earlier, various devices are commonly used to structure a risk-sharing strategy between an insured and an insurer. A *deductible policy* covers only the surplus above a stated value. Losses below this value are not covered, and the value of the deductible is subtracted from the insurer's payment if the loss exceeds the deductible. A *proportionate coinsurance policy* simply pays a stated proportion of all losses. With an *upper-limit policy,* the insurer's claim payment is limited to an upper value; i.e., the insurer pays the value of loss or the policy limit, whichever is the lower. Each of these policies will be illustrated in the following example, and we will show that the risk-averse insured will have definite preferences for the different types of policies. The preferences are demonstrated in the example using the expected-utility rule. (A more general proof of these rankings can be derived mathematically, although this goes a little beyond the current text; see Arrow, 1963; Raviv, 1979; and Doherty, 1981.)

Consider an individual with an initial level of wealth of $200 (we can denominate this in thousands of dollars or millions of dollars if this is more appealing), which is tied up in physical assets, such as a home, furniture, etc. In addition, he or she has $60 in cash. The physical assets are subject to the possibility of damage or destruction, the appropriate information being given in the first two columns of Table 3-1. Thus, there is a

50% chance of no loss
10% chance of a loss of $20
20% chance of a loss of $40, etc.

The expected value of loss is $40. If the subject were fully insured, at a premium of $60, he or she would receive an insurance payment equal to the value of loss, as shown in the third column. The final wealth (i.e., after any loss has occurred and the insurance payment is made) is shown in the fourth column. Final wealth is calculated as the initial wealth ($260) minus the premium ($60) minus the loss plus an insurance payment. Since the subject is fully compensated, the final wealth does not vary from $200. However, our problem here is to choose between the different partial-insurance strategies shown in the remaining columns of the table. Respectively,

1 The *deductible policy* pays the value of loss minus $20, or $0, whichever is higher. Thus with a loss of $20, nothing is paid; with a loss of $40, the policy pays $20. The expected policy payment is $30, and the final wealth shown has an expected value of $205.

2 The *proportionate coinsurance policy* simply pays 75% of loss, irrespective of size. The insurance payments and final wealth are shown accordingly. Notice that this policy has been designed so that the expected value of the policy payment is again $30, and accordingly, the expected value of final wealth is again $205.

3 The *upper-limit policy* pays the value of loss or $100, whichever is lower. Again, the respective values of policy payment and final wealth are $30 and $205.

For each policy, the premium is $45, which is 150% of the expected policy payment. Which of these policies is preferred? On the face of it, they appear to give equal value for money, since the policies have the same actuarial value and the same premiums have been charged. (If the insurer had a well-diversified portfolio of such policies, then the same premium could be charged for each type, since long-run claim costs are identical.) The expected-utility rule will now be evoked to arrive at a ranking. To undertake this task, we will assume a particular form for the utility function that

TABLE 3-1
EXAMPLES OF PARTIAL INSURANCE POLICIES

Probability	Loss	Full insurance		$20 deductible	
		Insurance payment	Final wealth	Insurance payment	Wealth
0.5	0	0	200	0	215
0.1	20	20	200	0	195
0.2	40	40	200	20	195
0.1	100	100	200	80	195
0.1	200	200	200	180	195
Expected value:	40	40	200	30	205

Probability	Loss	75% coinsurance		$45 upper limit	
		Insurance payment	Wealth	Insurance payment	Wealth
0.5	0	0	215	0	215
0.1	20	15	210	20	215
0.2	40	30	205	40	215
0.1	100	75	190	100	215
0.1	200	150	165	100	115
Expected value:	40	30	205	30	205

Note: Final wealth is calculated as: Initial wealth − insurance premium − loss + policy payment

ensures that the shape concurs with the risk-averse, concave form illustrated earlier. The form chosen is[2]

$$U(X) = X^{0.8}$$

To calculate expected utility of wealth EU, we see that

$$EU = \sum_i P_i U(X_i)$$

The calculations are as follows:

1 Deductible:

$$EU_D = 0.5(215)^{0.8} + 0.1(195)^{0.8} + 0.2(195)^{0.8} + 0.1(195)^{0.8} + 0.1(195)^{0.8}$$
$$= 70.68$$

2 Coinsurance:

$$EU_C = 0.5(215)^{0.8} + 0.1(210)^{0.8} + 0.2(205)^{0.8} + 0.1(190)^{0.8} + 0.1(165)^{0.8}$$
$$= 70.66$$

3 Upper-Limit:

$$EU_{UL} = 0.5(215)^{0.8} + 0.1(215)^{0.8} + 0.2(215)^{0.8} + 0.1(215)^{0.8} + 0.1(115)^{0.8}$$
$$= 70.55$$

A definite ranking appears. The deductible policy is preferred to a coinsurance policy having an equal expected policy payment. In turn, the coinsurance policy is preferred to an upper-limit policy having the same expected policy payment. This preference reveals that the deductible policy is a more effective instrument for containing the riskiness in the insured's final wealth. Certainly, the deductible exposes the insured to some risk, but an upper value is placed on his or her loss. However, the upper-limit policy limits the insurer's payment, leaving the insured's potential loss quite open-ended. Thus, if we compare the final-wealth columns under the respective policies, the final wealth under the deductible policy exhibits the lowest degree of risk and the final wealth under the upper-limit policy is the most risky. A cautionary note is given: The expected utilities are rather close in value. It should not be concluded that differences in utility are marginal. The expected-utility rule is a ranking device only.

---

[2]The reader may wish to experiment with other types of functions that also exhibit the concave property, for example,

$$U(X) = X^{0.5} \quad \text{or} \quad U(X) = \log X$$

This example may also be used to illustrate that partial coverage is often preferred to full coverage. In the previous section we demonstrated that if the premium loading is positively related to the expected value of claim payment, some degree of partial coverage is optimal. We have not tried to ascertain what level of risk sharing is optimal; thus the $20 deductible may be inferior to a $30 deductible. However, it is of interest to see whether the various forms of partial coverage are preferred to the full-insurance policy. The respective premiums for each of the policies are set at 150% of the expected policy payment; thus in each case the loading is 50% of the expected payment. This satisfies our premium criterion, since the loading is positively related to the expected payout. The utility index for full coverage is established easily, since final wealth is $200 with certainty. Expected utility is

$$EU_{FC} = 200^{0.8} = 69.31$$

Clearly, each of the partial-insurance strategies is preferred to full insurance. This is quite compatible with our previous result, although it is still possible that some other levels of partial insurance may prove even better.

ALTERNATIVE DECISION RULES

Problems with the Expected-Utility Rule

The expected-utility rule is a very useful device for helping to condition our thinking about risky decisions, because it focuses attention on the types of tradeoffs that have to be made. Furthermore, the results it generates are useful as first approximations in the search for risk-management solutions. Certainly, it makes sense to transfer risk if there is no sacrifice in terms of expected return. When the transfer of risk is costly in terms of expected return, somewhat lower insurance purchases appear to be justified. And so on! However, the expected-utility rule and the literature it has spawned do have several limitations that reduce their relevance for risk-management purposes:

1 To calculate expected utility, we need to know the precise form and shape of the individual's utility function. Typically, we do not have such information. Usually, the best we can hope for is to identify a general feature, such as risk aversion, and to use the rule to identify broad types of choices that might be appropriate.

2 The rule cannot be applied separately to each of several sets of risky choices facing an individual. For example, consider three choices:

Choice 1: Purchase automobile insurance *or* do not purchase automobile insurance.

Choice 2: Purchase home insurance *or* do not purchase home insurance.

Choice 3: Purchase risky shares of stock *or* put money in riskless bank account.

Decisions such as these are interdependent, as we shall see in the bulk of this book. However, the expected-utility rule has normally been applied to each choice as though it were independent of others.

3 The third problem is really a composite of the first two. For corporate risk management, it may not be possible to consider a utility function for a firm as though the firm were an individual. Much of risk management has been developed on the simplistic, and possible erroneous, assumption that a firm can be treated as a risk-averse individual. However, a firm is a coalition of interest groups, each having claims on the firm: shareholders, bondholders, managers, employees, customers, agents, etc. The decision process must reflect the mechanisms with which these claims are resolved and how this resolution affects the value of the firm. Furthermore, the risk-management costs facing a firm may be only one of a number of risky prospects affecting the firm's owners and other claimholders. The expected-utility rule is not an efficient mechanism for modeling the interdependence of these sources of risk.

We will briefly outline alternative decision rules that can be used for risky choices. The first of these rules, the *mean variance rule,* will occupy a central role in much of this book. The second rule, *stochastic dominance,* is more sophisticated, but is presented in sketchy form only because it is more difficult to apply. Some readers may choose to skip the stochastic dominance section, and this will not destroy continuity. Stochastic dominance uses cumulative probability distributions, so the reader who is unfamiliar with this concept may wish to defer or omit this treatment.

The Mean-Variance Rule

The *mean* in the name given to this rule relates to expected value. Expected value already has been used as a simple decision rule. Its drawback is that it ignores the riskiness of the different alternatives, as dramatically illustrated by the St. Petersburg paradox. Instead of developing the subtle and indirect treatment of risk implied by expected utility, we could instead find a direct measure of risk and then make our choice on the basis of *both* expected value and risk.

Consider the alternatives shown in Table 3-2. Assume that people are risk-averse, but prefer a higher expected value to a lower expected value. Under such conditions, which probably apply to most of us, clearly choice A is better than choices B, C, or D; choice C is better than choice B; and choice D is better than choice B. In each of these rankings, the preferred alternative scores higher on at least one of the two criteria, but it does not score lower on either criteria. For example, choice A is preferred to choice D on expected value, but they score equally on risk. Notice, however, that the risk/expected-value rule does not rank all alternatives. Choices C and D cannot be

TABLE 3-2

Choice	Risk	Expected value
A	Low	High
B	High	Low
C	High	High
D	Low	Low

ranked. Choice D is preferred to choice C on the risk criterion, but on the basis of expected value, choice C has a better result. Thus the risk/expected-value rule will not always work.

In order to make this approach operational, we need to be able to measure risk. From reading introductory statistics textbooks, the reader will recall that various measures of risk are available. Consider a risky prospect such as

$$A = \begin{cases} \$10 & {}^1/_3 \text{ probability} \\ \$20 & {}^1/_3 \text{ probability} \\ \$30 & {}^1/_3 \text{ probability} \end{cases}$$

The risk is implicit in the spread of possible values. One easy measure is simply the *range* of values, i.e., from $10 to $30. The range is the highest possible value minus the lowest possible value. Clearly, this gives some idea of spread, but it ignores probabilities. Among the various alternative contenders for a risk measure, the one with the most convenient properties is standard deviation (or its square, variance). Standard deviation σ is defined as

$$\sigma = \left[\sum_i P_i (X_i - \bar{X})^2 \right]^{1/2}$$

where P_i = probability of outcome X_i
$\bar{X}$ = expected value, which equals $\sum_i P_i X_i$

The expected value EV of prospect A is

$$EV_A = {}^1/_3(\$10) + {}^1/_3(\$20) + {}^1/_3(\$30) = \$20$$

and the standard deviation is

$$\sigma_A = [{}^1/_3(\$10 - \$20)^2 + {}^1/_3(\$20 - \$20)^2 + {}^1/_3(\$30 - \$20)^2]^{1/2}$$
$$= 8.165$$

The variance is

$$\sigma_A^2 = 8.165^2 = 66.67$$

This measure will be used extensively in later chapters. For the moment, we will simply examine one or two general properties of the mean-variance rule. Consider the choices outlined in Table 3-2. We can represent each of these as a probability distribution, showing the range of possible values on the horizontal axis and the associated probabilities on the vertical axis. The four choices are represented in this way in Figure 3-8. Choices A and D have the same shape or spread, indicating a low level of risk;

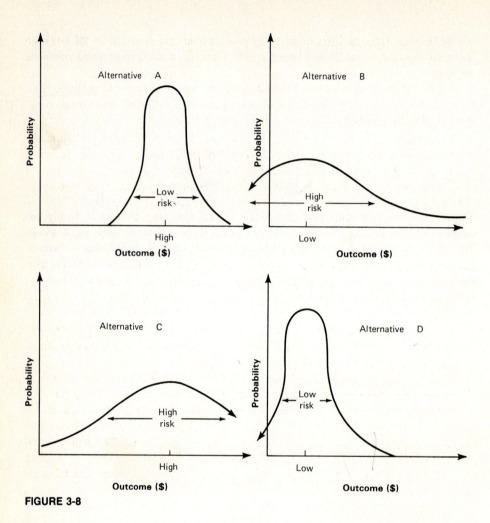

FIGURE 3-8

in each case, the possible values are closely clustered around a central value. The central, or expected, values of the two distributions are different. The expected value of choice A is high, whereas the expected value of choice B is low. Alternatives B and C have the same shape, the wide spread indicating high risk. However, whereas choice B is centered on a low expected value, choice C centers on a high expected value. Comparison of different pairs of these alternatives will confirm the rankings we derived earlier.

Both the expected-utility rule and the mean-variance rule require the decision maker to be able to estimate the possible outcomes and their respective probabilities. Such measures are feasible in principle and often in practice. However, this is the only input required for the mean-variance rule, in contrast with the expected-utility rule, which also requires specification of the utility functions. This operational advantage is achieved at some cost, since we find that not all risky choices can be ranked. We derive only a limited ranking that applies to all risk-averse individuals. This rule has proved very useful in analyzing investor behavior and, in consequence, in valuing the firm.

Stochastic Dominance

Like the mean-variance rule, stochastic dominance describes a decision procedure that is applicable for risk averters and does not require specification of the individual utility function. As with mean variance, it can rank some, but not all, choices. However, it has one particular advantage over mean variance. Expected value and standard deviation or variance are arbitrary values for the central tendency and riskiness of a prospect. Furthermore, they describe only certain features of a prospect. Often a risky prospect cannot be represented by a smooth or symmetric curve, such as those shown in Figure 3-8, but rather the curve will be irregular and asymmetric. Such features may be relevant to an individual's choice, but they are ignored by the mean-variance rule. Stochastic dominance is designed to overcome such problems, although it is more difficult to use and may sometimes fail to produce clear rankings, even where mean variance succeeds.

Stochastic dominance is really a set of decision rules that applies to progressively more restrictive groups. A full mathematical specification is beyond our scope. However, an intuitive understanding is easily presented.

Consider distributions A and D shown earlier in Figure 3-8. These are represented in Figure 3-9 on the same diagram, and immediately below, the respective cumulative distributions are presented. The cumulative probability distribution shows the probability that any given outcome will be equal to or less than a given value. Examples of probability and cumulative probability distributions are developed in Chapter 4, and the reader who is unfamiliar with these distributions may wish to defer discussion. The preference of A over D is pretty clear. Both have the same shape, indicating the same level of risk, but A clearly centers around a higher expected outcome. The cumulative probability distributions reveal that distribution A is always equal to or below distribution D. In essence, prospect D exhausts "probabilities" at low levels of wealth. In prospect A, the probability is allocated at higher wealth levels; thus the distribution appears to be shifted to the right. This reveals the *first rule for stochastic dominance:*

> If the cumulative distribution of A is equal to or below that for D for every level of wealth, then prospect A dominates (is preferred to) prospect D.

This rule is not restricted to those who are averse to risk, but it does apply to all who prefer greater wealth to lesser wealth. This probably describes us all, and the rule is quite general.

Now look at the right-hand side of Figure 3-9. Distributions for A and C are extracted from Figure 3-8 and are presented on a single graph. The distributions have the same expected value, but choice C exhibits considerably more risk. Choice A should be preferred to choice C. The appropriate stochastic dominance rule is developed from the cumulative distribution. It will be seen that the cumulative distribution for choice

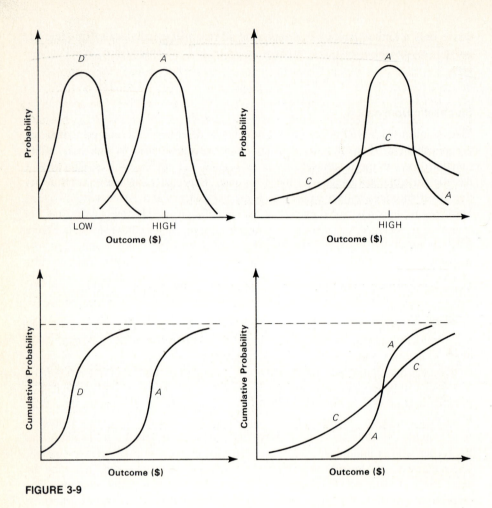

FIGURE 3-9

A starts below that for choice C, the distributions intercept, and then at higher wealth levels, choice C is lower than choice A. The lower level of risk in choice A is revealed by the much steeper slope in the cumulative distribution. This is anticipated in the *second stochastic dominance rule,* which applies only to risk-averse decision makers:

> If the cumulative distributions of A and C intercept one or a greater number of times, A is preferred to C if

$$\int_{-\infty}^{x} [C(X) - A(X)] \, dx \qquad x \geq 0 \text{ for all } x \text{ with inequality for some } x$$

where $C(X)$ and $A(X)$ are the cumulative distributions for prospects C and A

The application of this rule is a little complex, although in Figure 3-10 we give an example of how it might apply to a simple risk management problem. If full insurance is purchased, the resulting distribution of wealth for an individual will exhibit no risk; wealth level W_0 will be achieved with certainty. An appropriate cumulative distribution is shown as I in Figure 3-10. If no insurance is purchased, wealth will be risky, and an appropriate distribution is shown as N. The distributions intersect just once. Under such circumstances, second-degree stochastic dominance will apply if the premium for insurance is actuarially fair. The full-insurance distribution is preferred to the no-insurance distribution. This is compatible with the Bernoulli principle.

Our treatment of stochastic dominance is sketchy and will not be developed further. The interested reader might consult the literature review provided by Bawa (1982) for further applications, including insurance applications.

PROBLEMS IN INSURANCE MARKETS

Moral Hazard

Economic analyses have been used to address the risky choices that often face individuals, particularly the risk management choices that are of interest here. However, similar analyses have been used to enrich our understanding of how insurance markets function. Two unusual and possibly disturbing issues are examined: moral hazard and adverse selection.

The term *moral hazard* is emotionally loaded. This is quite unfortunate, since many activities that fall under such a label are neither improper nor illegal. Any ethical connotations placed on this term will serve only as a barrier that clouds our understanding of the real issues.

Moral hazard relates to the behavioral effect that insurance might have on the level

FIGURE 3-10

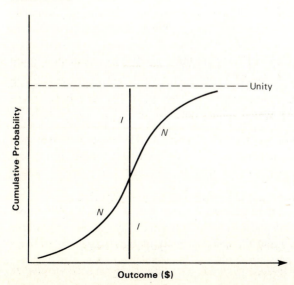

of effort or expenditure devoted to loss-reducing activities. If an individual or a corporation owns property, the ultimate value of that ownership claim depends on the value of the property. The property value might be reduced by the risky events we consider here, such as fires, explosions, etc. The value of individual or corporate wealth is similarly affected by claims by employees, agents, and third parties for defective products, industrial injuries, and other torts and statutory liabilities. Any expenditure allocated to reduce the probability of such loss, or the size of any loss that might occur, will benefit the owner and increase the value of his or her ownership rights. Thus ownership of a sprinklered building is more valuable than ownership of an otherwise identical, unsprinklered building.

The owner has an incentive to protect his or her ownership rights, and it makes sense to undertake those forms of protection which yield benefits in excess of costs. To understand moral hazard, it is useful to see how this incentive is affected by the purchase of insurance:

1 The insurance policy transfers the cost of losses from the owner to the insurer. Any reduction in this cost will accrue to the insurer, who will thereby derive benefit from loss-reduction efforts. With full insurance, the owner will be indifferent as to whether the loss occurs or not (unless, of course, there are nonfinancial dimensions to the loss that cannot be compensated, such as pain and suffering and sentimental value). For the owner, the payoff to any expenditure on loss reduction is reduced possibly to zero by the insurance policy. Accordingly, there is a reduced or zero incentive for the owner to protect the property or other rights that are insured. The transfer of the cost of loss under an insurance policy reduces or removes incentives for loss reduction.

2 This effect may be modified by the pricing structure or the contractual conditions of the insurance policy. If the insurer is able to monitor any loss-prevention efforts, it may structure the premium to restore loss-reduction incentives. Premium reductions may be allowed for installation of preventative devices and better safety practices, and premium increases may be included for adverse features. For example, fire insurance schedules usually specify premium adjustment for sprinklers, fire alarms, construction standards, storage of hazardous materials, etc. Even if the insurer cannot directly observe safety practices, it may indirectly reward good practice by calculating future premiums with respect to past loss records. Experience rating and retroactive rating have this effect.

3 Much the same effects can be achieved by imposing conditions in the insurance policy that make insurance coverage conditional on certain safety practices. Possibly this practice is less flexible than direct premium adjustment. The incorporation of both policy conditions and premium adjustments will serve to restore incentives for loss reduction that had been removed by the transfer of loss costs under the insurance policy.

The problem of moral hazard arises from an inequality in the information on loss reduction available to the insured and insurer. An insurer may be able to observe whether a building is sprinklered and the combustibility of the materials used in its construction, but it may not be possible to observe the standards of housekeeping and everyday work practices that may give rise to fire, explosion, and other hazards. Those practices which cannot be observed cannot be controlled by the insurer by pricing incentives or by policy conditions. The essential problem for the insurer is that it may not be able to charge the correct premium. As a consequence, insurers may be reluctant to offer insurance protection when they suspect moral hazard will be a problem.

Moral hazard has other dimensions, however. From the risk manager's viewpoint, moral hazard is simply rational economic behavior. This is not to say that risk managers should be sloppy about safety practices or try to deceive the insurer about loss expectancy. Rather it is simply an assertion that the rational risk manager would take account of any premium incentives in constructing a loss-prevention program. For example, in deciding on the type and form of fire prevention for a building, the premium savings offered by an insurer may represent a major part of the expected benefit to the insured. If the insurer does not offer substantial premium reductions, the effect may be to kill the fire safety program, even though such a program might well have been undertaken without insurance.

Much attention has been given in insurance literature to the adverse effects that insurance may have on the allocation of resources for loss reduction and preventative activities. The role of premium incentives has received relatively little attention. If premiums are sensitive to changes in the expected value of loss, they will serve the valuable purpose of conveying information to the insured on the effectiveness of different forms of loss reduction. Insurers essentially serve as a clearing house for loss-reduction information. By classifying loss data according to the identifiable features of different risks, insurers may compile information on the contributions of those features to the expected value of loss. This information may then be reflected in premium differentials, thereby providing information to the insured on the effectiveness of different forms of loss prevention. Several features of insurance market lend support to the view that insurers disseminate appropriate safety information:

1 Competition in insurance markets tends to lead to premium structures that adequately discriminate among risks according to loss expectancies.

2 Insurers often pool information to refine their data base.

3 Regulation of insurance markets usually aims toward supporting the concept of fair discrimination.

4 Insurers typically employ technical experts to survey risks in order to convey information to underwriters and to insureds.

If markets are reasonably efficient in disseminating loss-prevention information, then it would seem prudent for risk managers to look to the conditions of insurance protection to guide them in loss-prevention decisions. What may be labeled *moral hazard* may sometimes lead to an efficient allocation of loss-reduction resources.

Adverse Selection

Like moral hazard, *adverse selection* may have the effect of reducing the supply of insurance services. Furthermore, it may prevent the insurance market from reaching a set of stable equilibrium prices. Adverse selection plays an important role in the functioning of insurance markets, and an introductory understanding is useful for risk managers.

Both adverse selection and moral hazard arise from information asymmetry between the insurer and insured. Consider an insurer that writes a portfolio of policies. Insureds may be grouped into two classes: those with a high expected value of loss and those with low loss expectancy. If the insurer can distinguish insureds according to their respective loss characteristics, each can be charged a premium that reflects his or her expected value of loss. Thus insurers may use observable characteristics, such as automobile type, location, or age, to distinguish different risk groups of automobile policies. However, the insurer cannot always separate risk groups and will be forced, by lack of information, to charge the same premium. This results in an effective subsidy from low-risk insureds to high-risk insureds. The effects of this subsidy may destabilize the insurance market and reduce underwriting capacity, as shown below.

In Figure 3-11 we consider a portfolio of two groups of insureds: high risk and low risk. Each insured starts with a wealth level of $125, but a loss (total loss only) may reduce the wealth to $25. The groups differ in the probability of such a loss. For the high-risk group, the probability of loss is 0.75, resulting in an expected value of loss of $75. For the low-risk group, the probability loss is 0.25, resulting in an expected

FIGURE 3-11

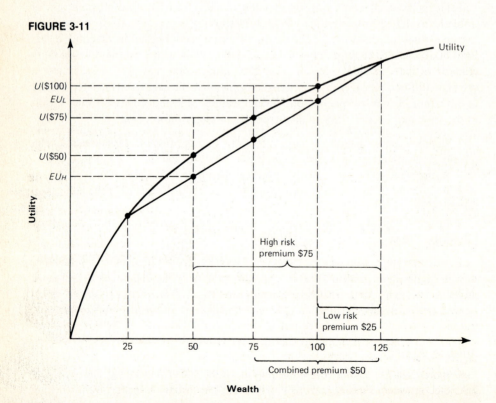

loss of $25. If the insurer can distinguish between the two groups, respective competitive premiums of $75 and $25 may be charged (ignoring transaction costs). With premiums set at the expected value of loss for each insured, the Bernoulli principle asserts that each would fully insure. Thus, for the low-risk group, the utility of insuring and having wealth of $100 with certainty, that is, $U(\$100)$, is higher than the expected utility of not insuring EU_L. Thus,

$$U(\$100) > EU_L = 0.75U(\$125) + 0.25U(\$25)$$

and for the high-risk group,

$$U(\$50) > EU_H = 0.25U(\$125) + 0.75U(\$25)$$

The respective positions are shown on the vertical axis of Figure 3-11.

Now suppose that the insurer is unable to distinguish between high- and low-risk insureds. If there are equal numbers in each group, the breakeven premium will be $50. However, at this premium we see that the low-risk group will not insure because the utility of not insuring EU_L is greater than the utility of insuring and having a wealth level of $75 for certain, that is,

$$EL_L > U(\$75)$$

Conversely, the high-risk group will find insurance to be a bargain and will rationally choose to insure, that is,

$$EU_H < U(\$75)$$

Thus the portfolio composition will change as low-risk insureds cancel their policies, leaving a portfolio of high-risk insureds (each having an expected cost of $75) and an inadequate premium.

In practice, the process will be somewhat smoother. There may be several risk groups, and coverage may be arranged on a partial basis. The insurer that averages premiums over a number of risk groups will find that it tends to lose the good risks as they cancel or reduce their coverage. The resulting change in the composition of the portfolio will cause the average premium to be inadequate, forcing the insurer to raise the premium. This serves merely to aggravate the flight of low-risk insureds, and so the process continues until only bad risks are left. This process is usually attributed to information deficiency on the part of the insurer, but the same effect may result from regulation designed to prevent insurers from using classification variables that are politically sensitive, such as sex or race. Indeed, one of the rare pieces of empirical evidence documenting this process relates to regulation-induced adverse selection (see Dahlby, 1983).

Competition between insurers may help reduce problems of adverse selection. Information on loss expectancies of individual insureds is of economic value to an insurer. Armed with such information, an insurer can selectively attract low-risk insureds from a rival insurer that is unable to discriminate simply by offering a lower price and admitting only low-risk insureds. Thus competition will induce insurers to seek and compile information that will enable them to operate premium structures that adequately discriminate between risk groups. Of course, information will never be perfect, and adverse selection will never disappear. But in an actively competitive market, adverse selection will be reduced to a level that is compatible with the costs of information.

SUMMARY AND CONCLUSION

The task of this chapter has been to present decision rules that can be used to rank competing risky choices. From these rules we have derived a set of preliminary risk-management strategies for individuals that will help focus our thoughts when we tackle the more complex corporate risk-management decisions.

The simplest decision rule considered is to choose that alternative which has the highest expected value. There is some long-run virtue in this rule. Its repeated use in many separate decisions will ultimately lead to wealth maximization. However, the rule fails to account for differences in the riskiness of competing prospects, as dramatically illustrated by Bernoulli's St. Petersburg paradox.

The expected-utility rule requires that the decision maker select that prospect with the highest expected utility. Under this rule, the possible outcomes are weighted according to their respective probabilities and according to the utility scale of the decision maker. The substitution of outcomes measured in utility terms for money outcomes ensures that individual risk preferences can be impressed on the decision process. This rule has been widely used in the economics literature, and it is used here to compare some simple risk-management choices.

The expected-utility rule can be used in conjunction with the assumption of aversion to risk to reveal a propensity to insure at fair prices (premiums are equal to the expected value of loss) or even at unfair prices. There is an equivalent aversion to gambling. This is not to assert that people will never gamble and will always insure, for both activities can be priced to encourage or deter demand. Under realistic pricing assumptions, partial-insurance solutions often appear more attractive than "all or nothing" attitudes toward insurance purchase. For insureds, deductibles appear to provide a more attractive mechanism for risk sharing than other devices, such as coinsurance or policy limits.

Despite its generality, the expected-utility rule does have the serious shortcoming that it requires the decision maker to specify his or her utility function. Thus while the rule establishes generalized patterns of behavior that are useful in guiding individual decisions, it lacks operational value for corporate risk-management purposes. An alternative is to use mean and variance to characterize risky prospects. This approach is introduced and will be used extensively in later chapters.

To set the background for later analysis, the economic concepts introduced in this chapter were used to illustrate two important issues that arise in insurance markets and which constrain the supply of insurance services. *Moral hazard* refers to the adverse incentives that insurance may convey to the insured to reduce the prospect of future loss. The problem may be severe if the insurer is unable to monitor the insured's behavior. Similar information problems may lead to *adverse selection*. If the insurer is unable to correctly discriminate between insureds in its pricing structure, it will effectively subsidize the higher risks. This will lead to disproportionately high demand from high-risk groups, causing a deterioration in the risk composition of the insurer's portfolio and escalating loss experience. The prospect of adverse selection again acts as a constraint on insurance supply or capacity.

We will turn our attention in the ensuing chapters to the identification and measurement of those risks which form the subject matter of risk management.

QUESTIONS

1 Consider the following game. Peter is to turn over one card from a deck. If the card is a face card (ace, jack, queen, or king), Peter will win $100. If any other card is selected, Peter will win nothing. To play this game, Peter must pay an entry price of $25.
   a What is the expected value of the game
   b If Peter's utility function is

$$U = W^{0.5}$$

   where U = utility and W = wealth, should Peter enter the game? Assume Peter's starting level of wealth is $200.
2 Construct utility diagrams to display the following:
   a A risk averter will insure when faced with an actuarially fair insurance premium.
   b The risk premium (the difference between the insurance premium that a risk averse person is willing to pay and the expected value of the loss).
   c A risk preferrer will choose to gamble when the expected value of the gamble is equal to the entry price.
   d A person who may rationally choose to gamble and insure when he knows all probabilities.
3 Donne faces the following loss distribution:

Loss	Probability
$ 250	0.4
500	0.4
1,000	0.2

An insurance policy can be purchased that
a has a $250 deductible for a premium of $300.
b covers 50% of all losses for a premium of $350.
c fully covers all losses for a premium of $550.
Donne's initial wealth is $2000 and his utility can be described by the function

$$U = \log W$$

where W is final wealth. Which, if any, policy should Donne purchase?

REFERENCES

Arrow, K. J.: "Uncertainty and the Welfare Economics of Medical Care," *American Economic Review,* vol. 53, 1963, pp. 941–973.

Bawa, V. J.: "Stochastic Dominance: A Research Bibliography," *Management Science,* vol. 28, 1982, pp. 698–712.

Borch, K.: *The Economics of Uncertainty,* Princeton Studies in Mathematical Economics, Princeton University Press, New Jersey, 1968.

Dahlby, G. G.: "Adverse Selection and Statistical Discrimination," *Journal of Public Economics,* vol. 20, 1983, pp. 121–130.

Doherty, N. A.: *Insurance Pricing and Loss Prevention,* D. C. Heath, Lexington, Mass., 1976.

————: "Stochastic Ordering of Risk Insurance Exchanges," *Scandinavian Actuarial Journal,* no. 4, 1981, pp. 302–308.

Friedman, M., and L. J. Savage: "The Utility Analysis of Choices Involving Risk," *Journal of Political Economy,* vol. 56, 1948, pp. 279–304.

Hirshleifer, J., and J. G. Riley: "The Analytics of Uncertainty and Information—An Expository Survey," *Journal of Economic Literature,* vol. 17, 1979, pp. 1375–1421.

Markowitz, H.: "The Utility of Wealth," *Journal of Political Economy,* vol. 60, 1952, pp. 151–158.

Marshall, J. M.: "Moral Hazard," *American Economic Review,* vol. 66, 1976, pp. 880–890.

Mossin, J.: "Aspects of Rational Insurance Purchasing," *Journal of Political Economy,* vol. 76, 1968, pp. 553–568.

von Neumann, J., and O. Morgenstern: *Theory of Games and Economic Behavior,* Princeton University Press, Princeton, New Jersey, 1944.

Raviv, A.: "The Design of an Optimal Insurance Policy," *American Economic Review,* vol. 69, 1979, pp. 223–239.

Shackle, G. L. S.: *Expectations Investments and Income,* Oxford University Press, London, 1938.

Shoemaker, P. J. H.: *Experiments on Decisions Under Risk,* Kluwer Nijhoff Publishing, Amsterdam, 1982.

————, and J. C. Hershey: "Risk Taking and Problem Context in the Domain of Losses: An Expected Utility Analysis," *Journal of Risk and Insurance,* vol. 47, 1980, p. 111.

Smith, V.: "Optimal Insurance Coverage," *Journal of Political Economy,* vol. 76, 1968, pp. 68–77.

Zeckhauser, R.: "Medical Insurance—A Case Study of the Tradeoff between Risk Spreading and Appropriate Incentive," *Journal of Economic Theory,* vol. 2, 1970, pp. 10–26.

CHAPTER 4

ESTIMATION OF LOSS DISTRIBUTIONS

The quality of the output of any system depends both on the quality of the inputs to that system and the quality of the process by which the inputs are transformed into an end product. In our case, the end product is the set of risk management decisions made by a firm, and the process is the decision framework. The decision process will occupy the lion's share of the remainder of this book, and we will be at pains to ensure that this framework is compatible with the overall financial decision process for a firm. In the meantime, we will direct our attention to the quality of the inputs. The importance of quality inputs is captured by the phrase "Garbage in, garbage out."

The two most basic inputs into the risk management process are

1 *Data inputs,* which describe prospective losses and their associated probabilities.

2 *Value inputs,* which represent the values of those who make decisions or on whose behalf decisions are made. These values are incorporated in the goals of the decision process. Since the subject is corporate risk management, the main concerns will be ownership values and a decision framework that focuses on owner welfare.

In this chapter we are concerned with data inputs. The quantity and quality of the raw materials of the risk manager, namely, information, are not fixed. Furthermore, the assembly of this information into a form that is usable for making financial decisions is important to the quality of the decisions. The objective of this chapter will be to provide an estimate of the probability distributions for losses of various types that face a firm and to aggregate these distributions in order to estimate the distribution of total-loss costs facing the firm. This aggregate distribution and its components will be of importance in making decisions on the financing and reduction of possible losses. Before examining techniques to estimate a loss distribution, we will first look at the sources of data available to the risk manager.

SOURCES OF DATA

Statistical Data Sources

The most obvious source of data from which to estimate loss probabilities is the past loss experience of the firm and other firms engaged in similar activities. These historical data may be presented as a frequency distribution, and if it is thought that the underlying factors that generate losses are not changing over time, the frequency distribution may be used to estimate the distribution of future loss probabilities. This process is known as *statistical inference*. A very similar process is used by insurers to set premium rates. However, the insurance company usually has at its disposal a much more comprehensive statistical base than the individual noninsurance firm wishing to measure its risk-management exposure. Usually, the insurer will write a portfolio of many policies that will be classified according to the features of the individual risks. A large portfolio will generate a large number of losses, and statistical techniques can be used to correlate loss results with a number of observable characteristics of individual policies. In this way, the insurer can estimate both the distribution of total claims for which it is liable and the loss probabilities for individual risks, which form the basis for rate setting.

In estimating the probability distribution of its risk-management costs, an individual firm typically does not hold a large, diversified portfolio of individual risk units and its historical loss experience is a scant and random selection of events that does not cover the whole gamut of possibilities. The adequacy of an individual firm's loss data will depend on circumstance. A small family-owned grocery store may attempt to measure the probability of fire loss from its loss experience over the last 10 years. However, having not had a loss in that period, the exercise becomes somewhat frustrating. A national chain having hundreds of stores that are geographically spread and all exposed to comparable degrees of hazard will have a credible loss experience with which to estimate loss probabilities for individual stores. The quality of data is related to the size and degree of diversification of the firm. A large, single-plant firm may well generate a reasonable number of losses, but this experience will often be inadequate to estimate the probabilities of large losses.

Whether or not the loss experience of a firm provides a reasonable basis for estimating probabilities depends on the quality of the sample from which that experience is drawn. Consider the concept of an *exposure unit* or a *risk unit*. Suppose we wish to measure the distribution of losses that might arise over a period of 1 year for a single automobile owned by a firm. If the firm looks only at the loss experience for the vehicle in question over the past year, it is not likely to get a good estimate of future loss probability. It may be that the vehicle has not been in an accident, but we cannot project from this a zero-loss probability, nor can we project a 100% loss probability if the vehicle was involved in a crash last year. To improve our estimate of probability, we need more years of experience for the vehicle in question and/or the experience of more (similar) vehicles for the year. Thus if the firm has owned 100 vehicles for a period of 10 years, then we have 1000 vehicle-years of experience from which to estimate probabilities. In this case, there is a sample size of 1000 comprising 100 exposure units, each covered for 10 years. For practical purposes, the exposure units may be considered to be separately exposed to the prospect of loss. The idea of separate, or independent, exposure is not absolute (loss probabilities for two vehicles can simultaneously increase because of bad weather), but a matter of relative judgment. We will discuss this further in the next chapter.

The quality of internal data depends on the number of exposure units and the length of experience. Together these determine the size of the statistical sample from which data are drawn. The size of the sample of internal data is often a given fact for the risk manager, but it may be supplemented by the use of external data. Thus the single-outlet retail grocer may have access to industry data on relevant losses and may use such data to estimate internal loss probabilities. The use of external data requires access and presupposes relevance. Industry loss data are routinely collected by insurers, although this information is usually not publicly available. Other potential data sources include industry publications, safety and loss prevention organizations, and the sharing of information among firms. The issue of relevance of information depends on whether the individual firm is representative of the industry. Some statistical testing may be helpful in addressing this issue. For example, it is possible to test whether the samples of loss experience for two firms can be drawn from the same probability distribution. However, if internal data are scant, such tests are not powerful, leaving the issue of relevance of external data as a matter of subjective judgment.

Subjective Data Sources

Nonstatistical data sources include the technical, organizational, and economic judgments made by a firm about the probabilities that specified events will happen and the economic consequences of these events for the firm. Engineers designing equipment, together with operators using that equipment, have knowledge of potential flaws and may be able to provide some "guesstimates" of failure probabilities. Civil engineers and architects may be able to offer judgments about the vulnerability of a structure to earthquake or weather-related damage or, perhaps, the spread of a fire within a building. Fed with possible scenarios of this kind, production experts can make judgments about the impact of considered events on the production flow, and marketing and finance experts can draw conclusions about trading and financial performance. Such exercises may establish credible bounds on the consequences of prospective events. These "what if such and such happened" exercises resemble Pentagon war games, but they do provide a useful framework for translating technical judgments into subjective probability estimates.

Often, statistical and subjective data can be combined. For example, a firm with few exposure units but a long history of loss experience may query whether losses arising 10 years previously are directly relevant to future loss probabilities given changing technology. Similarly, one may accept that the industry experience bears *some* relationship to the loss probabilities for a single firm, but the firm may be somewhat better, worse, or simply different from other industry firms. Under such circumstances, it may be desirable to temper statistical inference with subjective judgment. This process resembles the use of credibility formulas by insurers. To illustrate, suppose that historical data reveal a mean loss value of $100,000 per year, but due to the small sample size and underlying changes in the technology used, there is reason to suppose that this value underestimates the true expected value of loss. A surveyor inspects the risk and provides an independent estimate of the expected loss, which is $140,000. The underwriter must reconcile the differing expected values of loss. To do so, he or she uses a "credibility" formula, which is simply a weighted average of the statistical estimate $E(L)_{ST}$ and the surveyor's estimate $E(L)_{SU}$. The weight Ω reflects the relative credibility the underwriter attaches to the respective estimates:

$$\Omega E(L)_{ST} + (1 - \Omega)E(L)_{SU} \qquad (4\text{-}1)$$

When $\Omega = 1$, the underwriter accepts only the statistical estimate, and when $\Omega = 0$, the underwriter believes only the surveyor. The decision to be made by the underwriter is to assign a value to Ω that lies within the range $0 \leq \Omega \leq 1$.

For the risk manager, subjective judgment may be used to complement statistical inference. However, the need for subjective judgment depends on the quality of the statistical data. Our purpose here is to examine both the use of statistical data to draw inferences about loss probabilities and the properties of these probability estimates.

DIRECT ESTIMATION OF THE PROBABILITY DISTRIBUTION OF AGGREGATE LOSS

The main focus of attention in this section will be the total cost of losses to a firm within a given period, usually 1 year. There will be a range of possible values for this cost—normally a very wide range—and different possible values will be associated with different probabilities. Thus we may construct a probability distribution for aggregate loss costs. This is called the *probability distribution of aggregate loss*.

Suppose that a firm operates with a large number of independent exposure units. Examples might include a retailing chain owning a large number of stores, a chain of service stations or restaurants, or other less homogeneous firms operating with a large number of plants, outlets, warehouses, etc. that exhibit geographic spread. If the number of exposure units is large and the spread is not dominated by one or two very large exposures, the distribution of aggregate loss can be estimated directly. Consider a chain of retail grocery stores and associated warehouses. The firm has 20 years of loss data for the chain that comprises roughly similar risks which are spread out geographically. For this example, we assume that the number of exposure units has been constant over the period and that all losses are expressed in constant dollar terms. (When these assumptions are not met, the data can be adjusted, as illustrated later, with indirect estimation methods.) The loss data are shown in Table 4-1.

The data in Table 4-1 give a guide to the range of potential loss costs to the firm. Clearly, the precise values are not too important, so we can divide the observations into convenient ranges, as shown in Table 4-2. The *relative frequency* is calculated by counting the number of losses within each range and dividing by the number of observations. Thus the relative frequency for the first class, $0–10,000, is $^3/_{20} = 0.15$. The *cumulative frequency* indicates the proportion of losses lying within the range in question or below that range.

TABLE 4-1
RAW DATA ON AGGREGATE LOSSES

Year	Total fire loss costs, $
1963	260,000
1964	35,000
1965	97,000
1966	425,000
1967	8,000
1968	18,000
1969	90,000
1970	82,000
1971	38,000
1972	35,000
1973	132,000
1974	49,000
1975	280,000
1976	5,000
1977	40,000
1978	10,000
1979	14,000
1980	76,000
1981	62,000
1982	620,000

The frequency values may be used as probability estimates if the sample is sufficiently large and if economic or technical factors have not changed the degree of hazard. In this case, there are 20 annual observations and each reflects the loss experience of a large number of exposure units. This is a respectable sample size, but problems can still arise. For example, if the relative frequencies are used to infer probabilities directly, we must conclude that there is no chance of a loss exceeding $1 million. However, very large losses are rare, and it would not be surprising for a

TABLE 4-2
DISTRIBUTION OF AGGREGATE LOSSES

Range, $	Relative frequency	Cumulative frequency
0–10,000	0.15	0.15
10,001–25,000	0.1	0.25
25,001–50,000	0.25	0.50
50,001–75,000	0.05	0.55
75,001–100,000	0.2	0.75
100,001–250,000	0.05	0.80
250,001–500,000	0.15	0.95
500,001–750,000	0.05	1.0

20-year loss history to not show such an event. We cannot conclude that there is a zero chance of such a loss, particularly if the firm has concentrations of asset values in excess of this amount. We also find that the distribution is rather "jumpy." If the $49,000 loss in 1974 had been just a little larger, it would have fallen into the class boundary $50,001–$75,000, thereby changing the structure of Table 4-2. To avoid such problems, the distribution can be smoothed by fitting a *characteristic curve*. This issue will be discussed in the next section in the context of indirect estimation of the distribution of aggregate loss.

INDIRECT ESTIMATION OF THE PROBABILITY DISTRIBUTION OF AGGREGATE LOSS

Loss Frequency and Loss Severity Distributions

For many firms, it is not possible to obtain a reasonable direct estimate of the distribution of aggregate loss because there is some concentration of risk into a small number of exposure units. In such cases, available information can be put to better use by separating both the number of losses arising within each year and the severity of the losses that do arise. Separate estimates can be made of the distribution of loss frequency and the distribution of loss severity. By a process known as *convolution,* the separate distributions can be assembled to form an estimated probability distribution of aggregate loss. This process is somewhat richer than direct estimation of the distribution of aggregate loss because use is made of the additional information on frequency and severity.

The use of historical loss data to estimate loss probabilities implies that the economic and hazard conditions prevailing in the period over which the data were generated will continue into the future. The firm may have grown in recent years, and even if processes are inherently no less hazardous, the effect of size implies that the firm will generate more losses. Furthermore, the effect of inflation will enhance the cost of given losses. These considerations imply that basic historical data must be standardized such that any probability estimates will correctly reflect present price levels and will relate to the firm's current scale of operations. These standardization processes can be conducted separately on the loss frequency and loss severity distributions. An illustration of a simple standardization process is given in Table 4-3. Columns 1 and 4 show unadjusted data on the number of claims arising each year, and the sizes of the claims are expressed in prevailing dollar values. These data are not directly relevant to present loss probabilities because the firm doubled the size of its productive capacity in 1980, thereby increasing its capacity for generating losses. Some indication of this change is given in column 2, which shows the *real* value of the property at risk. The size of claims has also been affected by change. An inflation index is shown in column 5. This index could be a general price index, such as a retail or wholesale price index. However, events such as industrial fires, liability claims, and vehicle collision costs do not always follow such general price indexes. Special indices have been developed for claims costs by Norton Masterson (1984). The hypothetical index used here is assumed to be specific to the claims under discussion.

TABLE 4-3
UNADJUSTED LOSS FREQUENCY AND LOSS SEVERITY

Years	1 Number iosses	2 Real value of property at risk, $ million	3 Adjusted loss frequency	4 Loss size; current values, $	5 Price index year 8 = 100	6 Adjusted loss size, $
1	1	$1 million	2	500	82	610
2	2	$1 million	4	600; 1,500	84	714; 17,857
3	0	$1 million	0	—	85	—
4	1	$1 million	2	2,500	88	28,409
5	1	$1 million	2	400; 4,000	90	444; 4,444
6	2	$2 million	2	700; 5,000	93	752; 5,376
7	3	$2 million	3	600; 9,000; 16,000	95	631; 9,474; 16,842
8	1	$2 million	1	7,000	100	7,000

An adjustment to loss frequency is made by multiplying by the ratio of the real value currently at risk to the real value at risk in year i

$$f_{a,i} = f_{r,i}\left(\frac{V_c}{V_i}\right) \tag{4-2}$$

where $f_{a,i}$ = the adjusted loss frequency

$f_{r,i}$ = raw frequency for year i

V_c = the real value of the property currently at risk

V_i = the real value of property at risk in year i

This adjustment will provide a basis for estimating the loss frequency distribution given the current size of exposure. Adjusted values are shown in column 3 of Table 4-3.[1] This type of value adjustment to control for changes in risk size may not always be appropriate. Liability claims may not bear a close relationship to the value of the firm's assets, and some other measure may be more suitable, such as the firm's output level, the number of vehicles in the firm's fleet, and so forth. Methods for size adjustment depend very much on the features of the individual risk, but some appropriate form of size standardization is usually necessary.

Adjustment of the loss-severity values is straightforward; the main issue is simply the selection of an appropriate price/cost index. The adjusted severity level for a loss arising in year i is

$$S_{a,i} = S_{r,i}\left(\frac{P_c}{P_i}\right) \tag{4-3}$$

---

[1]This adjustment process may result in fractional values such as 2.6 losses per year, 1.7 losses per year, etc. If curves are to be fitted, as discussed earlier, these fractional values should be used to estimate the distribution.

where $S_{r,i}$ = the raw severity value for loss in year i

$\quad\quad\;\; P_c$ = an index value for current prices

$\quad\quad\;\; P_i$ = an index value for prices in year i

Inflation-adjusted values are given in column 6.

Adjustment of the loss-frequency data for growth in exposure and adjustment of the loss-severity data for inflation will often remove the most serious distortions that arise from the use of historical data. However, some of the underlying trends may not be removed. It may be that the risk has become more hazardous over recent years because of poor maintenance of vehicles and equipment, increasing moral hazard, changes in technology, etc. Tests for these further distortions can be undertaken by searching for trends in the data series. Trend-analysis methods are widely used and are discussed in most basic statistical textbooks.[2] An example using direct estimation of aggregate annual loss data is developed in the appendix to this chapter. However, where separate loss-frequency and loss-severity data are available, each should be tested and adjusted for trend before attempting convolution or curve fitting.

The information from columns 3 and 6 of Table 4-3 may be used to infer probabilities. The derivation of probability distributions requires that we arrange the adjusted losses into size groups and associate the probability of loss in each group with the adjusted relative frequency. A similar process is used to derive the probability of each given loss frequency within a period. The resulting distributions are shown in Table 4-4. Derivation of the probability values is straightforward. Calculation of the probability of loss severity within the range \$0–\$1,000 starts with the relative frequency after adjustment. Five of 12 recorded losses lie within this range, and this ratio is used as a probability estimate, that is, 0.417. Calculations for other categories, and for loss frequency, follow a similar pattern.

One of the problems that arises when using loss-frequency and loss-severity distributions of the form shown in Table 4-4 is that events that have not arisen are ignored

TABLE 4-4
ADJUSTED FREQUENCY AND SEVERITY DISTRIBUTIONS

Loss frequency per year	Probability	Loss severity	Probability
0	0.125	0–1,000	0.417
1	0.125	1,001–5,000	0.083
2	0.5	5,001–10,000	0.25
3	0.125	10,001–20,000	0.167
4	0.125	20,001–30,000	0.083
	1.00		1.00

[2]For example, simple regression techniques are discussed in almost every textbook on business or economic statistics. Other nonparametric methods are discussed by, for example, Connover (1980).

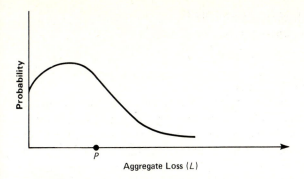

Aggregate Loss (L)

FIGURE 4-1

and events that have arisen are often given too much weight. For example, Tables 4-3 and 4-4 reveal no year in which five losses have arisen (after adjustment), and so the distribution of loss frequency ascribes a zero probability to this outcome. The largest loss shown is $28,409 (after adjustment), and this is placed in a severity interval of $20,001–$30,000 in Table 4-4. Are we to assume that the probability of losses above $30,000 is zero, or does the distribution have a missing tail? These can be severe problems, especially if the loss data are drawn from a small number of exposure units and/or cover only a few years. One method of addressing these issues is to consider that the actual loss data, frequency or severity, constitute a sample that is drawn from an underlying distribution having a definite form. If the form is known, curve-fitting techniques can be used to estimate the parameters of the distribution from the sample data. This procedure will "smooth out" the loss-frequency or loss-severity distribution and often can be used to fill in the missing tail. As an illustration, consider Figure 4-1. The rectangular shape of the probability distribution is replaced by a smooth curve that fills in the missing intermediate severities and the tail. Both missing sections had been neglected simply because losses within these ranges had not occurred over the sample period.

A simple example is now given in which a Poisson distribution is fitted to loss-frequency data.[3] The Poisson distribution is perhaps the easiest distribution to fit, since the shape of the distribution can be specified with just one parameter, the expected or average loss frequency. The form of the distribution is

$$P_k = \frac{e^{-\lambda}\lambda^k}{k!} \tag{4-4}$$

where P_k is the probability that k losses will arise within a year; λ is the expected loss

---

[3]Estimates of expected values from sample data are discussed later.

frequency, and $e = 2.71828$. Suppose that we estimate the expected loss frequency from historical data and the value derived is 2.3. The distribution is

$$P_0 = \frac{(2.71828)^{-2.3}(2.3)^0}{0!} = 0.1003 \qquad (\text{since } 0! = 1)$$

$$P_1 = \frac{(2.71828)^{-2.3}(2.3)^1}{1!} = 0.2306$$

$$P_2 = \frac{(2.71828)^{-2.3}(2.3)^2}{2!} = 0.2652$$

$$P_3 = \frac{(2.71828)^{-2.3}(2.3)^3}{3!} = 0.2033$$

$$P_4 = \frac{(2.71828)^{-2.3}(2.3)^4}{4!} = 0.1169$$

$$P_5 = \frac{(2.71828)^{-2.3}(2.3)^5}{5!} = 0.0538$$

$$P_6 = \frac{(2.71828)^{-2.3}(2.3)^6}{6!} = 0.0206$$

and so on

Since we have no objective way of knowing whether the Poisson distribution correctly describes the underlying data, it is important to know whether the calculated distribution fits the data reasonably well. Testing for "goodness of fit" is discussed in many risk-theory tests, although detailed analysis takes us beyond the mathematical boundaries prescribed for this test.

Other distributions that are widely used include the bimodal distribution for loss frequency and such distributions as the gamma, pareto, and lognormal for severity.[4] We shall see in the next chapter that the distribution of total loss cost will approximate a normal distribution when the firm's portfolio of risk units is highly diversified and the units are independent.

Convolution

The loss-frequency and loss-severity distributions may be combined into the probability distribution of aggregate loss by a process known as *convolution*. Convolution may be undertaken by several methods that are discussed in varying detail here. Conceptually, the most simple method follows a *tabulation* procedure, in which each possible combination of frequency and severity is identified and the resulting combinations are then assembled into a distribution of aggregate loss. A second process involves *simulation,* in which randomly selected values are used to mimic actual loss experience.

---

[4]An easily readable presentation of these issues is given by Cummins and Friefelder (1979).

TABLE 4-5
SAMPLE FREQUENCY AND SEVERITY DISTRIBUTIONS USED FOR TABULATION

Loss frequency per year	Probability	Cumulative probability	Loss severity, $	Midpoint	Probability	Cumulative probability
0	0.5	0.5	0–1,000	500	0.4	0.4
1	0.3	0.8	1,001–5,000	3,000	0.3	0.7
2	0.2	1.0	5,001–20,000	12,500	0.2	0.9
			20,001–50,000	35,000	0.1	1.0

The resulting values for simulated total loss are then treated as raw loss data, and a histogram is constructed. Finally, *numerical analysis* can be used where mathematical skills are available and other methods, such as curve fitting, fail.

Tabulation   The tabulation process is the most simple to understand, although it may be practical only when the frequency and severity distributions have a fairly small number of classes. To illustrate this technique, we will use simpler distributions than those shown in Table 4-4 for reasons that will become apparent. The loss-frequency distribution to be used has just three points, and the loss-severity distribution has just four points. The distributions are shown in Table 4-5. Since loss severities are divided into a range, we identify a representative severity level for losses within that range, and here, the midpoint is used for this purpose.

The next task is to tabulate each possible loss scenario within an annual period. This process is shown in Table 4-6, with losses within each class represented by the class midpoint. There is a 0.5 probability that no loss will arise, as shown in the first row of Table 4-6. If one loss arises, it can take any one of four different values, as shown in the next 4 rows. For example, one loss of $3000 may arise, giving total loss cost for the year of $3000. The probability of this total cost is given by the product of the probability of one loss (0.3) and the probability of a severity of $3000 (0.3). Many combinations of two losses may arise, as shown by the next 16 rows. All possible combinations are recorded, showing the loss sequence and the joint probability. Notice that two losses can be of the same value or different values. Also notice that losses of different values can arise in different sequences. For example, losses of $500 and $12,500 may arise in a single year, but this combination may arise in two different ways: The first loss may be $500 and the second $12,500, or the first may be $12,500 and the second $500. Both possibilities must be recorded. In total, there are 21 possible sequences.

The information from Table 4-6 may be assembled into a more convenient form, with the total-loss costs arranged in ascending order and different sequences resulting in the same total-loss cost combined by adding the probabilities. The streamlined distribution of aggregate loss is shown in Table 4-7.

In using the tabulation method for this example, 21 possible loss sequences were identified. In general, we can easily identify the number of such sequences for any loss-frequency and loss-severity distribution. Suppose the maximum frequency shown in the frequency distribution is p (in this case, $p = 2$) and the number of severity classes is q (here $q = 4$). The number of possible loss sequences is

$$S = \sum_{i=0}^{p} q^i \qquad (4\text{-}5)$$

which gives 21 for this example. Notice that with the information shown in Table 4-4, $p = 4$ and $q = 5$, giving 781. This explains why we did not continue with the Table 4-4 material to illustrate tabulation. Without too much difficulty, one can imagine how quickly tabulation can become unmanageable. For a large firm, it may not be unusual to have up to, say, 20 losses in a single year (it does not take a very large fleet of road vehicles to reach this figure). Combine this with a severity distribution that has, say, 20 classes, to give some precision to defining loss values, and we are left with over *one hundred million, billion, billion* sequences. Clearly, this is unmanageable, and for such problems, we require an alternative method. Simulation overcomes such problems.

Simulation   Small simulations can be tackled by hand, although computer programs can easily be written to provide synthetic loss experience. Simulation can be used to "expose" a firm to the hazards summarized by the loss frequency and severity

TABLE 4-6
TABULATION—LOSS PERMUTATIONS

Number of losses	First loss	Second loss	Total loss cost	Probability
0	—	—	0	(0.5) = 0.5
1	500	—	500	(0.3)(0.4) = 0.12
1	3,000	—	3,000	(0.3)(0.3) = 0.09
1	12,500	—	12,500	(0.3)(0.2) = 0.06
1	35,000	—	35,000	(0.3)(0.1) = 0.03
2	500	500	1,000	(0.2)(0.4)(0.4) = 0.032
2	3,000	3,000	6,000	(0.2)(0.3)(0.3) = 0.018
2	12,500	12,500	25,000	(0.2)(0.2)(0.2) = 0.008
2	35,000	35,000	70,000	(0.2)(0.1)(0.1) = 0.002
2	500	3,000	3,500	(0.2)(0.4)(0.3) = 0.024
2	500	12,500	13,000	(0.2)(0.4)(0.2) = 0.016
2	500	35,000	35,500	(0.2)(0.4)(0.1) = 0.008
2	3,000	500	3,500	(0.2)(0.3)(0.4) = 0.024
2	3,000	12,500	15,500	(0.2)(0.3)(0.2) = 0.012
2	3,000	35,000	38,000	(0.2)(0.3)(0.1) = 0.006
2	12,500	500	13,000	(0.2)(0.2)(0.4) = 0.016
2	12,500	3,000	15,500	(0.2)(0.2)(0.3) = 0.012
2	12,500	35,000	47,500	(0.2)(0.2)(0.1) = 0.004
2	35,000	500	35,500	(0.2)(0.1)(0.4) = 0.008
2	35,000	3,000	38,000	(0.2)(0.1)(0.3) = 0.006
2	35,000	12,500	47,500	(0.2)(0.1)(0.2) = 0.004

TABLE 4-7
DISTRIBUTION OF AGGREGATE
LOSS FROM TABULATION
EXERCISE

Total loss cost	Probability
0	0.5
500	0.12
1,000	0.032
3,000	0.09
3,500	0.048
6,000	0.018
12,500	0.06
13,000	0.032
15,500	0.024
25,000	0.008
35,000	0.03
35,500	0.016
38,000	0.012
47,500	0.008
70,000	0.002
	1.0

distributions over and over again. Each replication represents the simulated loss experience for a period of 1 year, with the occurrence of loss determined by a random process. This is illustrated with the data shown in Table 4-5. For the first replication, we wish to consider one possible loss sequence the firm may suffer and to calculate the total cost of losses. Such a sequence will represent 1 year's loss experience. To do this, we first select a random number between zero and unity that will be used to determine how many losses arise in the year. Bearing in mind that loss experience will be guided by the loss probability distributions, we will compare the random number with the cumulative probabilities shown for the loss frequency in Table 4-5. If the random number lies in the range 0–0.5, we will determine that no loss has arisen in the replication. If the random number is in the range 0.5–0.8, one loss is assumed to have arisen. Finally, if the random number lies within 0.8–1.0, two losses are assumed. This process ensures that the chances of 0, 1, or 2 losses reflect the loss probabilities.

The next step is to select the loss severities. This is undertaken by a similar procedure. The value of the first loss (assuming that the frequency equals 1 or 2) is chosen by selecting *another* random number between zero and unity and comparing that number with the cumulative probabilities for loss severity. Similarly, a second loss is chosen, if appropriate, by making *another* random number selection and comparing it with the cumulative probability for severity. This procedure will generate the simulated loss experience for that replication.

The whole process is repeated for a second replication, taking care that different random numbers are used, to give a second year's simulated loss experience. The procedure is repeated as many times as required. In this way, we can simulate loss experience for tens, hundreds, or thousands of years with a total cost for each year. The total costs for each year then can be compiled into a distribution in the direct manner described for actual data on total costs in the section Direct Estimation of the Probability Distribution of Aggregate Loss.

To illustrate the process of simulation, a small program was written and results were generated using the loss-severity and loss-frequency data presented in Table 4-5. We have suggested that simulation is most attractive when complex distributions are present and convolution is too costly. However, we choose the same example to show that simulation results tend to converge on the distribution derived with convolution as the number of replications is increased. The larger the number of replications, the more reliable the results. Table 4-8 reproduces the tabulation results from Table 4-7. In addition, the distribution of aggregate loss is derived using simulations with 10, 100, 1000, and 10,000 replications. The results do show a pattern of convergence with the tabulation results. With 10 replications, the probability of zero loss turns out, by fortune, to be exactly 0.5. However, the rest of the distribution is very poorly defined, with zero probability alongside most loss values. In this particular replication, the firm is unfortunate enough to "suffer" two fairly large losses, but this is a product of the random numbers selected. Increasing the number of replications to 100 produces a dramatic improvement, with loss probabilities for most values that bear a reasonable resemblance to the tabulation results. Increasing the replication to 1000 and then to 10,000 shows further convergence toward the tabulation values.

TABLE 4-8
CONVOLUTION BY SIMULATION

		Probabilities			
		Simulation with:			
Total cost	Tabulation	10 Replications	100 Replications	1,000 Replications	10,000 Replications
0	0.5	0.5	0.54	0.5040	0.5045
500	0.12	0.2	0.13	0.1390	0.1193
1,000	0.032	0	0.04	0.029	0.0306
3,000	0.09	0.1	0.09	0.079	0.0894
3,500	0.048	0	0.02	0.05	0.045
6,000	0.018	0	0	0.016	0.0186
12,500	0.06	0	0.07	0.07	0.0598
13,000	0.037	0	0.06	0.034	0.032
15,500	0.024	0	0.01	0.018	0.0238
25,000	0.008	0	0	0.003	0.0095
35,000	0.03	0.1	0.04	0.025	0.0302
35,500	0.016	0	0	0.015	0.0147
38,000	0.012	0.1	0.01	0.01	0.0129
47,500	0.008	0	0.01	0.006	0.0081
70,000	0.002	0	0	0.002	0.0015

Indeed, the results generated with 10,000 replications may be considered to be a good approximation of the "true" values.

The number of replications necessary to obtain good results cannot be decided by any golden rule. As the number of replications increases, the quality of the results improves, but there are diminishing returns. In Table 4-8, the increase from 10 to 100 replications makes a dramatic improvement, but the increase from 1000 to 10,000 replications makes only a modest improvement. In this case, the distribution of aggregate loss may be considered to be reasonably well defined with 1000 replications and very well defined with 10,000 replications. Different component severity and frequency distributions require more or less replications to achieve comparable degrees of accuracy. If the severity and/or frequency distributions have long tails with very small probabilities, a large number of replications will be needed to achieve a reasonable definition of the aggregate distribution. In practice, severity and frequency distributions often have many more points than the simple distributions shown in Table 4-5, and many more replications will be needed. As always, the need for greater accuracy should be balanced against the computing costs, although a large number of replications can usually be accomplished at modest costs. Simulation is a relatively simple procedure with modern, high-speed computers, and it offers an attractive fallback when tabulation becomes impractical.

Numerical Analysis   When curves are fitted to the loss-frequency and loss-severity distributions, it is occasionally possible to derive a precise mathematical form for the distribution of aggregate loss. This is so if the loss-frequency distribution is Poisson and the loss-severity distribution is gamma. However, in most circumstances, the distributions do not combine in this way. In such circumstances, a mathematical technique known as *numerical analysis* can be used to "integrate" the component distributions. Examples, such as the compound Poisson process, are to be found in risk-theory texts, although development of such processes requires some mathematical sophistication.

PROPERTIES OF THE DISTRIBUTION OF AGGREGATE LOSS

The prospect of future loss events imposes a cost on a firm that can be summarized in terms of the expected, or average, cost and in terms of the riskiness, or variability, of the periodic cost. Measures of risk vary. One commonly used measure records the mean level of dispersion about the expected value of the distribution; this is the *variance,* or *standard deviation.* Another measure that is useful for risk management purposes is the probability that losses will exceed some defined critical value. To explore these risk measures, we must first define some statistical properties of the distribution of aggregate loss.

Consider the distribution shown in Figure 4-2. The distribution may be described as positioned about some value P, although prospective losses do seem to spread around this central value. Furthermore, the spread is not symmetric; rather, it exhibits a long right tail (i.e., it is skewed to the right). The measures commonly used to describe these properties are the expected value $E(L)$, the variance $\sigma^2(L)$ [or its standard

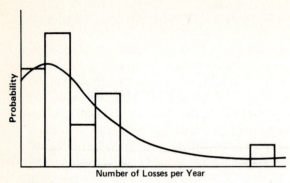

FIGURE 4-2

deviation $\sigma(L)$, which is the square root of variance], and a skewness measure denoted as $\alpha_3(L)$. These are defined as follows:

$$E(L) = \sum_i P_i L_i \qquad (4\text{-}6)$$

where P_i is the probability that the loss will assume a value L_i.

$$\sigma^2(L) = \sum_i P_i [L_i - E(L)]^2 \qquad (4\text{-}7)$$

$$\sigma(L) = [\sigma^2(L)]^{1/2} \qquad (4\text{-}8)$$

$$\alpha_3(L) = \frac{\sum_i P_i [L_i - E(L)]^3}{[\sigma(L)]^3} \qquad (4\text{-}9)$$

In practice, we rarely will be able to calculate the values $E(L)$, $\sigma^2(L)$, $\sigma(L)$, and $\alpha_3(L)$ because we do not have access to the underlying probability distribution. However, we do have historical data that may be treated as a sample of observation drawn from the underlying distribution. The characteristics of this sample may be used to provide estimates of the population characteristics. The quality of these estimates depends on the size of the sample. Suppose that we must estimate the expected value, standard deviation, and skewness for the distribution of aggregate loss when this distribution is constructed with the direct method described earlier in this chapter. The distribution is derived from a set of n observations, each of which is the total cost of losses for a particular year. The respective estimates are

$$\bar{L} = \frac{1}{n}\sum_{j=1}^{n} L_j \rightarrow \text{estimate of } E(L) \qquad (4\text{-}10)$$

$$S(L) = \left[\frac{1}{n-1}\sum_{j=1}^{n}(L_j - \bar{L})^2\right]^{1/2} \rightarrow \text{estimate of } \sigma(L) \qquad (4\text{-}11)$$

$$a_3(L) = \frac{\dfrac{n}{(n-1)(n-2)}\displaystyle\sum_{j=1}^{n}(L_j - \bar{L})^3}{[S(L)]^3} \rightarrow \text{estimate of } \alpha_3(L) \qquad (4\text{-}12)$$

To illustrate the application of these formulas, consider the aggregate-loss data shown in Table 4-1. Since the table contains sample data, equations (4-10), (4-11), and (4-12) must be used to adjust for sample bias. Straightforward application gives the values

$$\bar{L} = \$118,800$$
$$S(L) = \$160,360$$
$$a_3(L) = \$2.162$$

Even though most of the losses are well below $100,000, the few outliers, such as 1963, 1966, 1975, and 1982, pull up the mean loss to over $100,000. These outliers have two more effects. First, they give rise to a fairly wide spread of values, which is revealed by the standard deviation. In this case, the standard deviation is approximately 1.33 times the mean. Second, they provide a skewed form for the distribution. The positive sign for $a_3(L)$ reveals that the skewness is positive, resulting in the long right tail shown in Figure 4-1.

The application of equations (4-10), (4-11), and (4-12) was illustrated using the directly observed values for aggregate total loss. However, the formulas are quite general and can be used to estimate the relevant parameters of the loss-frequency and loss-severity distributions.

SUMMARY AND CONCLUSION

The proper estimation of loss distributions precedes the efficient handling of risk. Each firm faces a set of loss exposures that may be thought of as contingent costs for the firm. Each of these exposures may be represented as a probability distribution, and collectively, these distributions determine the total contingent costs for the firm. This aggregate cost is itself represented as a probability distribution and is labeled the *distribution of aggregate loss*. The task set for this chapter was to present methods for estimating this distribution from available loss data. The principal source of such data is likely to be historical observations of the claim frequency, claim severity, or total cost of losses arising within past years. However, such data may be supplemented by subjective judgment based on a technical and organizational understanding of the firm's operations.

This chapter was mainly concerned with the methods for using historical data, largely because such data are usually more reliable than purely subjective data, but also because the interpretation of historical data lends itself to analytical techniques. The form in which the data are available is important. Data may be available in the form of annual records of the total cost of losses arising within, or paid within, each year. The distribution of such annual values can be used to estimate future loss probability, although the data set will be much richer if separate records are available for loss frequency and loss severity. By combining frequency and severity data (a process known as *convolution*), risk managers can avail themselves of additional information and can achieve greater definition in the distribution of aggregate loss.

Data on loss frequency and loss severity rarely can be used in their raw state. The data are affected by such disturbances as inflation and changes in the number or value of exposure units at risk. Adjustments for these disturbances can be made by relatively straightforward indexing techniques. However, the adjusted data may still accommodate temporal trends that need to be removed in order to yield reliable probability estimates. Simple techniques for trend removal are discussed in the appendix. The adjusted and "detrended" data may be seen as sample observations that are randomly selected from the underlying probability distributions for loss frequency and loss severity.

The combination of frequency and severity, that is, convolution, may be undertaken by such processes as tabulation, simulation, or numerical analysis. *Tabulation* requires that every possible permutation of loss frequency and loss severity be identified from the estimated component severity and frequency distributions. The probabilities associated with each of these permutations, together with the total annual costs, form the distribution of aggregate loss. This technique is satisfactory if the number of permutations is reasonably small. To achieve a reasonable definition of the component distributions requires that they be broken down into a fairly large number of class sizes. However, such a process explodes the number of permutations of severity and frequency into astronomical numbers. For such cases, *simulation* can be used. A random process is used to generate a large number of synthetic values for aggregate loss. Each such value represents a sample loss cost randomly selected from the estimated frequency and severity distributions; therefore, the simulated values can be used to directly estimate the distribution of aggregate loss. The third method, *numerical analysis,* is only briefly mentioned, and it involves the use of sophisticated mathematical techniques to give precise mathematical form to the combined distribution.

The distribution of aggregate loss describes a set of possible values for aggregate-loss cost together with the associated probabilities. For this material to be useful for decision making, summary statistics are required. Three such statistics are presented, and together they provide a good deal of information about the distribution of aggregate loss. These summary statistics are the *expected value,* the *standard deviation* (or *variance*), and the *skewness*. These measures, particularly the first two, become extremely important in the next chapter. The set of individual risk units within a firm may be thought of as a risk portfolio. The distribution of aggregate loss describes the properties of this risk portfolio. However, these properties depend on the characteristics of the component risk exposures in a fascinating manner. Our task now is to examine these portfolio relationships.

QUESTIONS

1 A firm has recorded its workers' compensation losses for the past 10 years. These are presented below together with relevant background data.

Year	Total loss costs	Number of losses	Number of workers at risk	Price index (year 10 = 100)
1	50,000	5	8,000	84
2	40,000	1	8,000	86
3	100,000	6	8,000	87
4	250,000	9	10,000	89
5	35,000	6	10,000	89
6	10,000	1	9,000	90
7	30,000	10	12,000	91
8	220,000	12	14,000	96
9	300,000	6	14,000	98
10	400,000	10	14,000	100

Making appropriate adjustments for changes in the number of workers at risk, calculate the loss frequency distribution. Making adjustment for changes in the price level, calculate the loss severity distribution. In each case compress the distributions into four class intervals using your judgment to determine the class boundaries.

2 Using the distributions below derive the convolution of the severity and frequency distributions using tabulation.

Loss frequency	Probability	Loss severity	Probability
0	0.5	0–10	0.2
1	0.4	10–20	0.4
2	0.1	20–30	0.4

3 You are given the following distribution for the frequency of losses experienced by a firm.

Relative frequency	Loss frequency per year
0.5	0
0.4	1
0.1	2

These losses are assumed to be generated from a Poisson distribution. Construct the smoothed Poisson distribution of loss frequency per year.

4 Compute the expected value, standard deviation, and skewness of the following distribution.

Loss	Probability
0	0.3
100	0.3
500	0.2
1,000	0.15
10,000	0.05

APPENDIX: Tests and Adjustments for Trends in Loss Data

Historical loss data reflect the capricious, random process that generates the loss events. Not surprisingly, the successive observed values for frequency, severity, or aggregate annual loss will jump about widely, often exhibiting a large variance. Yet we have observed that these data may reveal underlying trends. Certainly, growth in the number of risk units or in the real value of exposure will affect loss values, and inflation will also have an impact on loss data. Adjustments for these disturbances were proposed in this chapter, but there remains a possibility that even the adjusted data may reveal residual trends. In such circumstances, derivation of loss probability statistics in the usual way will lead to incorrect inferences. In this appendix, we will illustrate how further adjustments can be made for the effects of underlying trends.

Table 4-A1 presents a series of loss data. The values represent aggregate annual loss. These are not the raw observed data; they have been adjusted for inflation and for growth in the size and value of the exposure. In many cases, these adjustments may be sufficient, and the remaining data may reveal no trend. However, this will not always be so. Changing technology, improved safety control, changing standards and quality of supervision, changes in the quality of the work force, etc. may all lead to changes in the level of underlying risk that are not removed by the preceding adjustment factors. If such trends remain, any estimates of expected loss made from the inflation- and exposure-adjusted data will be less than the true expected loss if the trend is positive or will be excessive if the trend is negative.

The data from column 2 are illustrated in Figure 4-A1. Although varying widely from year to year, there does seem to be an upward movement in the loss series. This should put us on alert. However, "eyeballing" the series is not a strong method of testing for trend, and we require a more formal device. Several statistical methods are available, and two are presented here. The first method is simply a test for trend; it does not provide any factor for detrending the series. However, since the test is nonparametric, it has a more general application than the second test. The second test provides an adjustment factor. However, to apply this technique, one must make certain assumptions concerning the error terms.

The nonparametric test illustrated here is the Daniel-Spearman's rank correlation test. This test is based on the order rankings of the data. The sequencing of observations is shown in column 2 of Table 4-A1. These rankings are denoted $R(Y_i)$, and they correspond directly with the successive years for which observations are available. Column 4 presents the rank order of the observations in column 3 in terms of size. The highest value (that is, 120) is ranked 1, the

TABLE 4-A1
TRENDING LOSS DATA

1 Year	2 Rank, $R(Y_i)$	3 Aggregate value of loss adjusted for inflation and growth in the size and value of exposure, L_i	4 Rank, $R(X_i)$	5 Estimated aggregate annual loss (least squares), $\hat{L}_i$
1961	1	2	18	10.18
1962	2	28	8	12.59
1963	3	3	17	15.01
1964	4	19	12	17.42
1965	5	56	5	19.83
1966	6	8	16	22.24
1967	7	0	19.5	24.66
1968	8	24	11	27.07
1969	9	25	10	29.48
1970	10	17	14	31.89
1971	11	120	1	34.30
1972	12	13	15	36.72
1973	13	35	6	39.13
1974	14	0	19.5	41.54
1975	15	72	3	43.95
1976	16	18	13	46.36
1977	17	32	7	48.78
1978	18	26	9	51.19
1979	19	94	2	53.60
1980	20	70	4	56.01
	Mean:	33.1	Projected (1981):	58.42

next highest value (that is, 94) is ranked 2, and so on. These rankings are denoted $R(X_i)$. The test statistic is

$$R = \sum_{i=1}^{n}[R(X_i) - R(Y_i)]^2$$

and this is calculated as

$$R = (1 - 18)^2 + (2 - 8)^2 + (3 - 17)^2 + \cdots + (20 - 4)^2$$
$$= 2158.5$$

If there is a negative trend, the order of magnitude of the observations will look very like the order of sequence (i.e., high-magnitude orders will be at the top of the sequence), and the value for R will be small. With a positive trend, the reverse is true, and R will assume a high value. Thus significant trends will be indicated by high or low values, with intermediate values indicating that no significant evidence of trend is present. To find the critical upper and lower

values we use Table B at the back of this book. Suppose that we wish to test at the 0.01 significance level. Since the test is two-tailed, we may associate probabilities of 0.005 in each tail. To
find the lower limit, we simply select the appropriate significance level for the lower tail,
which is 0.005, and for $n = 20$ observations, the value is 574. The upper limit is determined by

$$W_{1-p} = \frac{1}{3}\, n(n^2 - 1) - W_p$$

where $W_{1-p} =$ the upper limit

$W_p =$ the lower limit

$n =$ the number of observations

Therefore,

$$W_{1-p} = \frac{1}{3}(20)(20^2 - 1) - 574 = 2086 \qquad \text{and} \qquad W_p = 574$$

The calculated value for R lies above the upper limit; therefore, we must reject the hypothesis
that no trend exists at the 0.01 level. Had the value for R been within the upper and lower
limits for the test, we would not reject the hypothesis that no trend exists at the appropriate
confidence level. Since the test for trend was conducted at the 0.01 level, the confidence of a
positive trend for loss costs is substantial. However, the test gives no indication as to how the
data might be detrended.

The second test does provide an appropriate adjustment factor. We describe a simple linear
regression. Let us suppose that the data on losses L_i represent random deviations from some
linear relationship on time, i.e.:

$$L_T = \beta_0 + \beta_1 T + \varepsilon$$

where L_T is the loss observation for year T and ε is a random error. Regression techniques
enable us to calculate this underlying relationship, thereby fitting a trend line to the data. The
technique is to fit a straight line that minimizes the sum of the squared deviations of the actual
observations from the fitted values. The technique is widely described in basic statistics texts
along with the important assumptions that are not discussed here. Programs for computing values
for the coefficients β_0 and β_1 are readily available, and many pocket calculators are prepro-
grammed to calculate these values. For a simple regression, such as the one required for Table
4-A1, the basic calculation can be performed manually. The appropriate formulas are given
below, and the calculations are performed using values 1, 2, 3, 4, etc. for the successive years:

$$\beta_1 = \left[\frac{\sum_T L_T - \dfrac{\sum_T L_T \sum_T T}{n}}{\sum_T L_T^2 - \dfrac{\left(\sum_T L_T\right)^2}{n}} \right] = \frac{8555 - \dfrac{620(210)}{20}}{2870 - \dfrac{44,100}{20}} = 2.412$$

Therefore, $L = 7.77 + 2.412T$. The estimated values, using this equation, are shown in column
5. These values are calculated simply by fitting in the appropriate value for T (that is, 1 for
1961, 2 for 1962, etc.). In this manner, we can also project a value for a future year. Thus for

1981 the projected value is $(7.77) + 2.412(21) = 58.42$, and for 1982 the value is $(7.77) + 2.412(22) = 60.83$.

Suppose that we have simply tried to estimate expected loss for 1982 using the mean of loss data. The mean is 33.1, but allowing for trend, we can project a value of almost double this value. This example illustrates the importance of trend factors.

In interpreting the results of simple regressions, other statistics are useful. Two of particular value are the *correlation coefficient* and the *student's t value* for the trend coefficient. The correlation coefficient is defined as

$$r = \sqrt{\frac{\sum \hat{L}_T^2}{\sum L_T^2}} = \sqrt{\frac{25,778}{42,586}} = 0.778$$

where $\hat{L}_T$ is the estimated value of loss for year T shown in column 5 of Table 4-A1. The usefulness of the correlation coefficient lies in the fact that its square r^2 reveals the proportion of variation in L that is explained by the estimated equation. In this example, approximately 60% of the variation is so explained. An r^2 of unity suggests a perfect fit. The r^2 is graphically, but ungrammatically, described as the "goodness of fit."

Finally, we wish to determine whether the trend detected is statistically significant. Only if the trend is significant should any adjustment be made. Often the calculated value for β_1 assumes high absolute values, but the relationship is not statistically significant. Under such circumstances, one cannot reject the hypothesis that no trend exists. It would be mistaken to try to detrend when no trend exists. To test for significance of β_1, the student's t statistic is used. The t value is defined as the ratio of the estimated coefficient for β and its standard error. In this case, the value is 5.25. The equation has $(n - 2)$ degrees of freedom, since n data points are used to estimate two coefficients. The appropriate value for t at, say, the 0.01 level of significance $(1 - \alpha = 0.99)$ and for $V = 18$ degrees of freedom is 2.552. The calculated t value is 5.25; therefore, we can reject the null hypothesis that there is no trend. The trend adjustment made earlier is therefore appropriate.

This example merely scratches the surface of regression and trend analysis. The techniques are readily accessible to those having little training in statistics. However, herein lies its weakness and its strength. We have hinted at various assumptions concerning the error terms in the regression. These assumptions are extremely important and should be studied by anyone using the technique. Failure to satisfy these assumptions may lead to biased and misleading estimations.

The example developed here was based on observed values for annual aggregate loss payments. The advantages of separation of loss-frequency and loss-severity data were stressed in the chapter, and there is no intention to negate that contention. When separate distributions are to be estimated, the frequency and severity data each should be tested for evidence of trend. If such trends exist, then detrending is necessary to derive appropriate probability estimates.

REFERENCES

Beard, R. E., T. Pentikainen, and E. Personen: *Risk Theory*, Methuen, London, 1969.

Brieman, L.: *Probability*, Addison Wesley, Reading, Mass., 1968.

Connover, W. J.: *Basic Non-Parametric Statistics*. Wiley, New York, 1980.

Cummins, J. D., and L. R. Friefelder: "A Comparative Analysis of Alternative Maximum Probable Yearly Aggregate Loss Estimators," *Journal of Risk and Insurance*, vol. 45, 1978, pp. 27–52.

———— and ————: "Statistical Analysis in Risk Management," *Risk Management,* September 1978–April 1979.

————, and L. Wiltbank: "Estimating the Total Claims Distribution Using Multivariate Frequency and Severity Distributions," *Journal of Risk and Insurance,* vol. 50, 1983, pp. 377–403.

Feller, W.: *An Introduction to Probability and Its Applications,* Wiley, New York, 1966.

Gerber, H.: *An Introduction to Mathematical Risk Theory,* Huebner Monograph No. 8, Irwin, Homewood, Illinois, 1979.

Masterson, N.: "Economic Factors in Property Insurance Claims Costs," *Bests Review,* vol. 85, #2, 1984, pp. 68–70.

CHAPTER 5

PORTFOLIO THEORY AND RISK MANAGEMENT

The essence of portfolio theory is captured in such well-known sayings as "Don't put all your eggs in one basket" or "You will gain on the swings what you lose on the roundabouts." The intuitive logic of these statements warns us not to bet all our money on one horse, nor to purchase a single stock with all our capital. It tells us that single-engined aircraft are inherently more dangerous than multiengined aircraft and informs us that we should take a large (random) sample if we wish to measure popular support for competing presidential nominees. Diversification, it seems, helps us to avoid, or at least minimize, the probability of extreme outcomes. The same mechanisms help to explain how insurance functions and can be put to work to help us identify strategies for corporate risk management. More formally, these mechanisms have been analyzed under the heading of *portfolio theory*.

The growth and evolution of portfolio theory have occurred mainly in three subject areas. In statistics, the properties of samples and their relationship to the population from which they were drawn have been intensively studied. The properties of the sample, which constitute simply a portfolio of observations drawn from a parent population, enable us to make statements about the population and to evaluate the degree of confidence we can place in such statements. For example, if we choose a suitable large sample of female Americans in a random fashion, not only can we estimate the average height of all female Americans, but we can also place a confidence interval around our estimate. This permits us to make a statement such as "The estimated average height of American females is 5 feet 4 inches plus or minus $1/2$ inch at the 95% confidence level." Subject to proper sampling techniques, the larger the sample, the more we can narrow the range of error at some accepted degree of confidence. More loosely speaking, the larger the portfolio, the more we cut down the risk of being wrong.

A second area in which portfolio theory has been developed and successfully put to work is security analysis. The rate of return on securities of all kinds is rarely, if ever, free of risk. In the case of common shares, the variance of the return is usually fairly large; thus it is not uncommon for a stock to lose or gain a large proportion of its initial value over a short period. The investment risk can be partially controlled simply by holding a number of securities; then, over a certain period, some security prices may fall while others rise. Even this diversified stock portfolio can suffer a large loss in value if there is common movement in stock prices. Most stocks do tend to track movements in a representative price index (e.g., the Dow Jones Index or the Standard & Poors Index) to a greater or lesser degree, and this element of risk is not amenable to simple diversification. The common movement or correlation between such variables as stock prices is of great concern to us and will be considered in some detail presently. Moreover, the analysis of security markets is also important to our treatment of risk management. Investor behavior determines the value of a firm. Since our financial approach to risk management requires that decisions be appraised in terms of their contribution to the value of a firm, we must set our decision criteria with reference to investor behavior.

The third area that has provided a fertile field for the growth of portfolio theory is actuarial science. Its roots lie in the study of mortality rates, typically classified by age and sex groupings of the population. For large samples of individuals, such as the portfolios of insureds underwritten by life insurance companies, the actual mortality rates usually show little deviation from the expected rates calculated from large banks of mortality data. While the insurance company knows little of the time and place the "Lord cometh" for any individual, its prediction of average mortality is fairly accurate. Consequently, it can budget for its claims liabilities with reasonable confidence. The life insurer is diversified and has accordingly reduced risk. More recently, attention has been paid to the portfolio properties of other forms of insurance, and a sophisticated branch of mathematics, *risk theory*, has been developed. The focus of risk theory has been on the probability (or risk) that aggregate claims liability will exceed the insurer's reserves, although this forms part of the wider study of the risk properties of a diversified insurance portfolio.

The study of diversification within an insurance portfolio provides a useful starting point for our analysis of portfolio theory in risk management. However, the terms of reference of risk management go beyond the study of insurance. The same basic relationships that explain risk spreading in an insurance fund can therefore be used to show how the individual exposure units under a corporate umbrella combine to form the aggregate loss distribution for the firm. Knowledge of the properties of the corporate portfolio of exposure units is essential to the formation of proper risk-management strategy.

DESCRIPTION OF AN INSURANCE PORTFOLIO

In an insurance fund, the basic units that are insured are usually called *exposure units*. These are not synonymous with the policies in an insurance portfolio. A policy might provide insurance coverage on several automobiles, but for practical purposes, each automobile is a unit of coverage. Each vehicle is insured along with many other vehicles, and each is assumed to introduce its own risk properties to the portfolio. It would be convenient to define *exposure units* as units that are independently exposed to the prospects of damage or loss by the perils covered. Since each is independent of the other, it may be introduced to the portfolio with predictable and acceptable risk effects. However, the assumption of independence begs too many questions, and we will rely on a judgmental interpretation that roughly approximates independence. Thus individual houses may be considered exposure units within a homeowners' insurance portfolio. However, if two homes are condominiums separated by a nonfireproof party wall, it may be convenient to consider these as a single risk from a fire insurance viewpoint, since a single fire could easily destroy both homes. A home a block or two away may be considered as a different exposure unit, even though common factors could jointly affect the probability of loss in each (examples are a local arsonist, local weather conditions, construction hazards, since both were erected by the same contractor, etc.). The relevant criterion is the degree of independence, although no hard and fast rule can be applied.[1]

Each exposure unit insured by an insurance company represents a liability of the insurer for potential claims that may arise. At the inception of the policy, the value of this liability is not known, but over time, its value will be revealed. For most policies, the eventual liability turns out to be zero, since no loss arises and therefore no claim is filed. However, for some policies, a loss does arise, and the insurer will be faced with a set of claims that will vary in size according to the intensity with which the peril struck, the inherent protection, the value at risk, etc. If we include the "zero" cases, we can represent the final set of outcomes for the insurer having n exposure units as

$$L_1, L_2, L_3, \ldots, L_n \tag{5-1}$$

where $L_i \geq 0$ is the revealed liability of the insurer under exposure unit i. The total liability of the insurer is therefore

$$L = L_1 + L_2 + L_3 + \cdots + L_n = \sum_{i=1}^{n} L_i \tag{5-2}$$

For our purposes, it is useful to think of the insurer's liability on a per risk basis. This is determined by dividing L by the number of exposure units n:

$$\frac{L}{n} = \frac{1}{n}\sum_{i=1}^{n} L_i \tag{5-3}$$

---

[1]An alternative definition of an exposure unit may be formulated by reference to the peril. If two "items" can be destroyed by the same peril or event, they may be considered as the same exposure unit. Thus adjacent condominiums could be destroyed by the same fire and could therefore be reasonably considered as one unit. However, a vehicle owned by a man residing in New York might collide with a vehicle owned by a woman from Los Angeles in Iowa. Does this imply that these vehicles form one exposure unit? To avoid silly problems, we simply allow units to be identified by judgment, and then we ask questions concerning correlations. It does not matter if different people identify units differently, since the relevant information will be conveyed by the correlations.

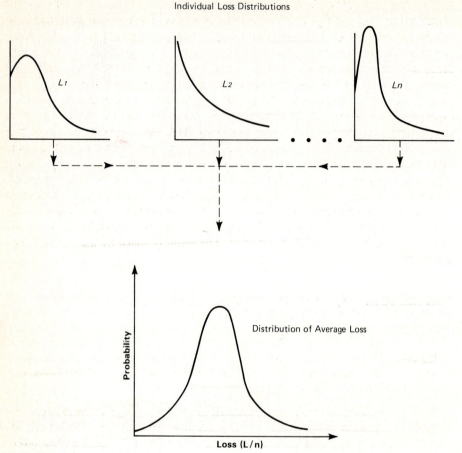

Individual Loss Distributions

FIGURE 5-1

This will be called the *average loss,* and we will refer to the *distribution of average loss*. Most policies run for a year, but the value of L may not be known for some considerable time after the expiration of the policies. Liability claims in particular may take an extremely long time to settle, and it may be many years before final values are known.[2] At the time of writing the policies, the insurer knows none of the outcomes L_i. Each liability is a random variable that may assume one of a range of values.[3]

The professional interest of the insurer focuses on the properties of the variable $L/$

---

[2]Recent litigation on asbestos claims suggests that policies written 30 or more years ago may still carry liabilities for cases of asbestos-related disease that are currently being diagnosed.

[3]An alternative notation is to use tildes to denote random variables ($\tilde{L}_i$). Since most of the discussion in this book relates to random variables, we can conveniently omit the tilde, taking care to point out particular cases in which we refer to a realized value from a random distribution.

n. The component values L_i may be of intense interest to their owners, but the interest of the insurer arises solely from the insurance contract. The financial performance of the insurer rests on the distribution of average claim payments. However, the distribution of L/n is determined by the distributions of L_i. Schematically, this interdependence may be represented as shown in Figure 5-1. The exposure units are represented on the top row by a set of probability distributions from which the values $L_1, L_2, \ldots, L_n$ will eventually be revealed. The probability distribution for losses on individual exposure units will generally be skewed to the right. However, their shapes may differ considerably according to size, value, degree of peril, and related factors. In combination, these distributions form the average distribution L/n, as shown by the arrows. The process of aggregation accomplishes one very interesting and useful result if the right conditions are met, the relevant conditions being that the individual exposure units are statistically independent of each other. Ideally, the units might have been defined as independent; we will assume for the moment that this condition strictly holds. The very useful property that emerges is that the distribution of the mean loss value will approach a *normal distribution*. The result is stated by the Central Limit theorem.

RISK REDUCTION IN AN INSURANCE PORTFOLIO OF INDEPENDENT AND IDENTICAL RISKS

The *Central Limit theorem* states that

> The distribution of the mean value of a set of n independent and identically distributed random variables each having mean μ and variance σ^2 approaches a normal distribution with mean μ and variance σ^2/n as n tends toward infinity.

To apply this theorem to insurance, consider an insurer writing n automobile policies in some homogeneous rating category, e.g., male urban drivers over 25. These policies can be viewed as a sample of the total population of drivers in this category, the others being insured by other companies or self-insuring. We assume that the risks are sufficiently similar that they can be seen as identically distributed, each having the same expected loss $E(L)$ and the same variance σ^2. Our task is to find out what happens to the riskiness of the insurer's portfolio as the insurer increases the number of risks it insures. To undertake this task we consider two different definitions of risk:

1 The first definition consists of the variance of the distribution of

$$\frac{L_1 + L_2 + L_3 + \cdots + L_n}{n}$$

This is a conventional measure of the spread of the distribution.

2 The second definition consists of the probability that

$$\frac{L_1 + L_2 + L_3 + \cdots + L_n}{n}$$

exceeds some critical value. The critical value can be set at the level of the insurer's total reserves plus surplus averaged over all policies. If average losses turn out to be below this value, the insurer is able to discharge its claims liabilities. However, should average losses exceed this value, the firm will fail in its obligations and will become insolvent. The probability that such an eventuality will arise is known as the *probability of ruin,* and this is considered to be an important risk measure for the insurer.

In order to examine how these risk measures are affected by the size of the insurance fund, it is necessary to define the relationships between the individual loss distribution and the average distribution. Consider a portfolio formed just by adding two random variables L_1 and L_2. The average distribution will have the following properties:

$$E(L) = E(L_1) + E(L_2) \tag{5-4}$$

and

$$\sigma^2(L) = \sigma_1^2 + \sigma_2^2 + 2\sigma_{1,2} \tag{5-5}$$

where $\sigma^2(L)$ = the variance of the portfolio L
   σ_i^2 = the variance of L_i
   $\sigma_{i,j}$ = the covariance between L_i and L_j

Although variance is useful, the more useful summary description of risk is *standard deviation,* which is simply the square root of the variance:

$$\sigma(L) = \sqrt{\sigma^2(L)} \tag{5-6}$$

Covariance is a measure of the common variations between L_1 and L_2 and is defined by

$$\sum p_i(L_{1i} - \bar{L}_1)(L_{2i} - \bar{L}_2) \tag{5-7}$$

where p_i is the probability of the joint occurrence of L_{1i} and L_{2i}.

Examination of covariance reveals that it looks very much like the formula for variance, which is

$$\sum p_i(L_{1i} - \bar{L}_1)(L_{1i} - \bar{L}_1) = \sum p_i(L_{1i} - \bar{L}_1)^2$$

In effect, variance is simply covariance of one variable with itself.

If there are more than two variables, the formulas for mean and variance are

$$E(L) = E(L_1) + E(L_2) + E(L_3) + \cdots + E(L_n) \tag{5-8}$$

$$= \sum_{i=1}^{n} E(L_i)$$

and

$$\sigma^2(L) = \sigma_1^2 + \sigma_2^2 + \sigma_3^2 + \cdots + \sigma_n^2 + 2\sigma_{1,2} + 2\sigma_{1,3} + \cdots \quad (5\text{-}9)$$

$$= \sum_{i=1}^{n} \sigma_i^2 + \sum \sum_{i \neq j} \sigma_{i,j}$$

Our task is to calculate the risk in a portfolio of identically distributed independent exposure units. Since the risks are independent, the covariances are, by definition, equal to zero. The variance of the distribution of average loss is therefore

$$\sigma^2\left(\frac{L}{n}\right) = \text{var} \frac{L_1 + L_2 + \cdots + L_n}{n} \quad (5\text{-}10)$$

$$= \text{var} \frac{L_i}{n} + \text{var} \frac{L_2}{n} + \cdots + \text{var} \frac{L_n}{n}$$

since the covariances are zero. Now,

$$\text{var} \frac{L_i}{n} = \sum p_i\left(\frac{1}{n}L_i - \frac{1}{n}\bar{L}\right)^2 \quad (5\text{-}11)$$

$$= \frac{1}{n^2}\sum p_i(L_i - \bar{L})^2$$

$$= \frac{\sigma_i^2}{n^2}$$

Thus,

$$\sigma^2\left(\frac{L}{n}\right) = \frac{1}{n^2}\left(\text{var } L_1 + \text{var } L_2 + \cdots + \text{var } L_n\right) \quad (5\text{-}12)$$

Since all risks are identically distributed, they all have the same variance, that is, $\sigma_i^2 = \sigma_1^2 = \sigma_2^2 = \cdots = \sigma_n^2$

or

$$\sigma^2\left(\frac{L}{n}\right) = \frac{1}{n^2}(n\sigma_i^2) = \frac{\sigma_i^2}{n} \quad (5\text{-}13)$$

This is the result stated by the Central Limit theorem.

To put some meat on these bones, let our automobile portfolio with male urban drivers over 25 comprise exposure units that each have an expected loss of $500 and a standard deviation of $800. The variance of each unit is $\sigma_i^2 = (\$800)^2 = \$640,000$. The variances and standard deviations of the insurer's liability per exposure unit are given in Table 5-1.

TABLE 5-1
RISK REDUCTION IN PORTFOLIOS OF
INDEPENDENT RISKS

n	$\sigma^2\left(\dfrac{L}{n}\right) = \dfrac{\sigma_i^2}{n}$	$\sigma\left(\dfrac{L}{n}\right) = \dfrac{\sigma_i}{\sqrt{n}}$
1	640,000	800
10	64,000	253
100	6,400	80
1,000	640	25
10,000	64	8
∞	0	0

In general, the effect of portfolio size on portfolio risk is traced as shown in Figure 5-2.

Diversification does benefit the insurer because it reduces risk. However, a word of caution is needed. It is the measure of risk *per policy* that is reduced. The standard deviation of the *absolute dollar liability* of the insurer increases. As a simple exercise, consider an increase in size from 100 to 1000 exposure units. The standard deviations of *absolute dollar liability* before and after the increase in portfolio size are, respectively,

$$\sigma_p = \sqrt{100(800)^2} = 8000 \qquad \text{when } n = 100$$

and
$$\sigma_p = \sqrt{1000(800)^2} = 25{,}298 \qquad \text{when } n = 1000$$

However, it will be noticed that the standard deviation has increased at a much smaller proportionate rate (just over 3 times) than has the portfolio size (10 times). This less than proportionate increase in aggregate *total* risk explains why the riskiness per policy falls.

FIGURE 5-2

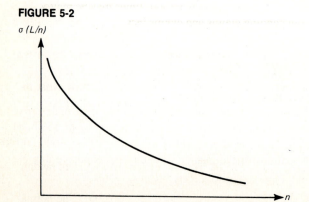

$\sigma\,(L/n)$

n

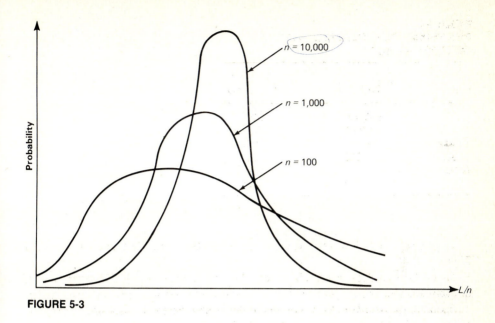

FIGURE 5-3

Our result on diversification can be summarized graphically. Figure 5-3 shows possible distributions of L/n at different portfolio sizes. An n increases, not only does the distribution exhibit a smaller standard deviation, but it becomes more symmetrical, approaching a normal distribution. This last feature becomes important for our examination of the probability of ruin. Figure 5-3 reveals that as n increases, the distribution of L/n huddles closer and closer around the mean value μ. This property is known as the *law of large numbers*.

The second measure of riskiness we wish to examine is the probability that the distribution of the average loss will exceed that critical value which defines the solvency of the insurer. This is the so-called *probability of ruin*. When the insurer receives the premium on a policy, it is allocated to a reserve fund for unearned premiums (after deduction of expenses). Funds in this reserve are held to match liabilities developing on the maturing policies. At the end of the accounting period, funds may be reallocated to other reserve funds, such as outstanding claims and claims incurred but not reported. Procedures also govern the allocation of any residual values to surplus, which can be either distributed or retained. Thus an insurer can meet aggregate claims up to the total value of its reserves plus retained surplus. If this total value is denoted L^*, the insurer will be able to pay on average L^*/n per policy. We wish to know what the probability is that the average claims liability will exceed L^*/n per policy. This is the *probability of ruin*. Figure 5-3 depicts such a critical value. The probability of ruin is depicted by the area of the tail to the right of L^*/n. Apparently, this is systematically related to the size of the portfolio, although it behooves us to demonstrate this effect.

As a rule of thumb, when a portfolio is formed of more than 30 independent random variables, the distribution of the mean value is considered to be sufficiently close to normal that statistical tests based on the normal distribution can be used. The normal

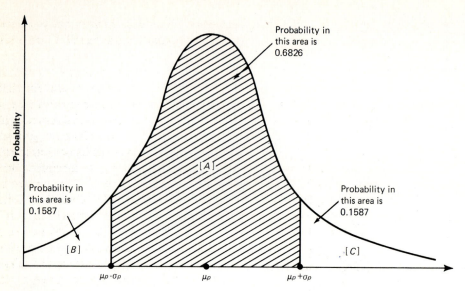

FIGURE 5-4

distribution has the convenient property that the total probability (or area under the curve) can be segmented symmetrically if we know the mean and the standard deviation. We know, for example, that the probability that a randomly selected value will be above $\mu + \sigma_p$ (that is, one standard deviation above the mean) is 0.1587, as shown in Figure 5-4. Similarly, the probability that a randomly selected value will be below $\mu - \sigma_p$ is also 0.1587, since the distribution is symmetric. Consequently, there is a $1 - 0.1587 - 0.1587 = 0.6826$ chance that a randomly selected value will lie within the range of one standard deviation on either side of the mean. We can work out the probabilities in any other segments, and they are described in terms of multiples of standard deviations from the mean. Thus the probability that a randomly selected value is greater than or less than μ minus the same multiple of σ is as follows:

$$\mu_p + 1.5\sigma_p = 0.0668$$
$$\mu_p + 1.96\sigma_p = 0.025$$
$$\mu_p + 2.33\sigma_p = 0.01$$

and so forth

These and other values are conveniently tabulated in z tables, which are available in many statistics textbooks. A segment of such a table is reproduced at the end of this text. Given this facility, and the tendency of the portfolio toward a normal distribution, we can easily calculate the probability that the insurer's average claim liability exceeds the ruin value L^*/n simply by defining this value as a multiple of standard deviations from the mean. The value L^*/n will be defined to be z standard deviations above the mean:

$$\frac{L^*}{n} = \mu_p + z\sigma_p \qquad (5\text{-}14)$$

Rearranging gives

$$z = \frac{\left(\frac{L^*}{n}\right) - \mu_p}{\sigma_p} \qquad (5\text{-}15)$$

Values can now be calculated using the automobile portfolio considered earlier. Recall that each exposure unit had an expected value of $500 and a standard deviation of $800. The expected loss per policy is calculated from equation (5-4). Therefore,

$$\mu_p = E\left(\frac{L}{n}\right) = \frac{E(L_1) + E(L_2) + \cdots + E(L_n)}{n}$$

$$= \frac{n(500)}{n} = 500$$

The portfolio standard deviation has already been calculated from the variance, that is, equation (5-13):

$$\sigma_p = \sigma\left(\frac{L}{n}\right) = \frac{\sqrt{\sigma_i^2}}{n} = \frac{800}{\sqrt{n}}$$

Substituting these values into equation (5-15) gives

$$z = \frac{(L^*/n) - 500}{800/\sqrt{n}}$$

Now suppose that the insurer's reserves and surplus permit it to pay up to a maximum of $660 per policy. We have

$$z = \frac{660 - 500}{800/\sqrt{n}} = 0.2\sqrt{n}$$

Thus if $n = 9$, $z = 0.6$. Reading from the table of z values, the probability that $L/n > L^*/n$ is 0.2743. This value is recorded in Table 5-2 alongside values calculated for other n.

The results in Table 5-1 and Table 5-2 confirm the pattern in Figure 5-3 that diversification reduces risk, both in the sense of reducing variance and by reducing the probability of ruin. We will now try to apply these ideas to more complex portfolios.

TABLE 5-2
RUIN PROBABILITIES IN PORTFOLIOS OF
INDEPENDENT RISKS

n	z	Probability that $\frac{L}{n} > \frac{L^*}{n}$
1[a]	0.2	0.4207
9[a]	0.6	0.2743
50	1,41	0.0793
500	2.0	0.0228
1,000	6.3	Negligible
10,000	20.0	Negligible
∞	∞	0

[a]These values are too small for reasonable approximation with the normal distribution.

RISK REDUCTION IN AN INSURANCE PORTFOLIO OF INDEPENDENT, HETEROGENEOUS RISKS

The second type of portfolio preserves the assumption that risks are independent of each other, but relaxes the restriction that all units are homogeneous in the sense of having identical probability distributions. The heterogeneous portfolios we have in mind here could comprise policies of different types, such as a mixture of fire, automobile, and liability policies, or they could comprise policies of the same type but having different risk levels, such as a fire portfolio that comprises different types of risks drawn from different industries. In order to measure the effects of size on this type of portfolio, it is important to distinguish between two possibilities, one relating solely to the size of the portfolio and the other combining both size and composition effects:

1 Growth of a portfolio might arise without change in the mix of the various types of exposure units. The firm might simply write different types of new policies in the proportions that those policy types represent in the existing portfolio.

2 Conversely, growth may arise if the insurer deliberately targets its acquisition effort at a limited range of policy or insured types. For example, an insurer with a heavy automobile portfolio might acquire another company with a predominantly fire portfolio.

Our main concern is with the effect of size on portfolio risk; thus we will consider size changes that preserve composition. The combined size and mix effects will be examined presently.

Insurers typically subdivide their liability portfolio into risk classes that are fairly homogeneous internally. Fire, automobile, marine, and liability policies are primary subdivisions. In turn, these lines are subclassified by insured characteristics relating to hazard level (e.g., by age and sex in life insurance, by industry, and protection location in fire insurance, or by vehicle type, driver age and sex, location, etc. in automobile insurance). The number of homogeneous categories may be very large, but the purpose is to group units that are a priori similar in order to aid the rating and underwriting decision process. For our purposes, let us suppose that there are three categories, labeled R, S, and T. Within each group, units are identically distributed, having the same mean and variance, and they are subscripted by the group code, for example, $E(L_R)$, $E(L_T)$, σ_S, etc. The total number of policies is n, where $n = r + s + t$, and r, s, and t are the number of R, S, and T policies, respectively. Let us combine the policies to examine the risk-return characteristics of the portfolio (L/n).

Recalling the calculations of expected value and variance of the distribution of mean loss, we have

$$\mu_p = E\left(\frac{L}{n}\right) = \sum_{i=1}^{n} E(L_i) \tag{5-17}$$

$$= \frac{rE(L_R) + sE(L_S) + tE(L_T)}{n}$$

and since the covariances are zero,

$$\sigma_p^2 = \sigma^2\left(\frac{L}{n}\right) = \sum_{i=1}^{n} \sigma_i^2 + \sum \sum_{i \neq j} \sigma\sigma_{i,j} \tag{5-18}$$

$$= \frac{1}{n^2} (r\sigma_R^2 + s\sigma_S^2 + t\sigma_T^2)$$

To put flesh on this skeleton, consider the following portfolio:

R refers to fire policies each with $E(L_R) = 300$ and $\sigma_R = 400$
S refers to automobile policies each with $E(L_S) = 400$ and $\sigma_S = 350$
T refers to liability policies each with $E(L_T) = 200$ and $\sigma_T = 300$

The portfolio comprises

$$r = 0.5n \qquad s = 0.3n \qquad t = 0.2n$$

This permits us to examine the effect of growth in n without change in the composition of the component units. Now,

$$\mu_p = E\left(\frac{L}{n}\right) = \frac{0.5n(300) + 0.3n(400) + 0.2n(200)}{n}$$

$$= 310$$

and

$$\sigma_p^2 = \sigma^2\left(\frac{L}{n}\right) = \frac{1}{n^2}[0.5n(400)^2 + 0.3n(350)^2 + 0.2n(300)^2]$$

$$= \frac{0.5(400)^2 + 0.3(350)^2 + 0.2(300)^2}{n}$$

$$= \frac{134,750}{n}$$

giving

$$\sigma_p = \sqrt{\frac{134,750}{n}} = \frac{367}{\sqrt{n}}$$

The forms of the variance and standard deviation clearly reveal that riskiness of the portfolio will fall in the pattern depicted in Figure 5-2 for the portfolio of homogeneous risks. Furthermore, the standard deviation will tend toward zero as the number of exposure units tends toward infinity. Some values for n and the corresponding variances and standard deviations are shown in Table 5-3.

The reader might experiment with other portfolios that show different initial compositions. However, caution must be exercised to ensure that the proportionate mixture of units does not change. This will reveal that the *law of large numbers* continues to apply for all portfolios of independent risk units, regardless of proportionate mix, as long as diversification does not affect the composition.

The second measure of risk was the *probability of ruin*. We can apply this in an identical manner to that shown for homogeneous portfolios. The reason is that the normal approximation continues in view of the independence of the risk units. To illustrate the process, let us assume that the insurer's reserves and surplus permit it to meet claim liabilities up to a limit of $400 per policy. We now have sufficient information to calculate ruin probabilities for different portfolio sizes. From equation (5-15) and the previously calculated values for μ_p and σ_p, we have

$$z = \frac{(L^*/n) - \mu_p}{\sigma_p} = \frac{400 - 310}{367/\sqrt{n}} = 0.245\sqrt{n}$$

Values for ruin probabilities at different levels of n are given in Table 5-4.

The ruin probability behaves in fashion similar to that for the portfolio of independent and homogeneous risks; it diminishes with increases in n, approaching zero when n approaches infinity. Combining this with the result for the behavior of standard de-

TABLE 5-3
RISK REDUCTION: INDEPENDENT
HETEROGENEOUS RISKS

n	$\sigma^2\left(\dfrac{L}{n}\right)$	$\sigma\left(\dfrac{L}{n}\right)$
1	134,750	367
10	13,475	116
100	1,348	36.7
1,000	135	11.6
10,000	14	3.7
∞	0	0

TABLE 5-4
RUIN PROBABILITIES: INDEPENDENT
HETEROGENEOUS RISKS

n	z	Probability that $\dfrac{L}{n} > \dfrac{L^*}{n}$
1	0.25	0.4013
9	0.74	0.2296
50	1.73	0.0418
100	2.45	0.0071
1,000	5.48	Negligible
10,000	24.5	Negligible
∞	∞	0

viation, diversification achieved by increasing the size of the insurance portfolio reduces portfolio risk. This result is valid if exposure units are independent, regardless of whether the units are identical or not, as long as the portfolio composition remains unchanged. To see how important this last assumption is, we will consider an example in which the portfolio size grows but the composition also changes. Independence is retained in this example.

EXAMPLE: CHANGING PORTFOLIO COMPOSITION

Consider an initial portfolio of, say, 10,000 automobile policies, each with a standard deviation of $300 and an expected loss of $300. To calculate the ruin probability, assume the insurer can pay claims up to $400 per policy. The mean, standard deviation, and ruin probability of the insurer's portfolio are

$$\mu_p = E\left(\frac{L}{n}\right) = \sum_{i=1}^{n}\frac{E(L_i)}{n} = \frac{n(300)}{n} = \$300$$

$$\sigma_p = \sqrt{\left[\sigma\left(\frac{L}{n}\right)\right]^2} = \left[\frac{1}{n^2}\left(\sum_{i=1}^{n}\sigma_i^2 + \sum_{i \neq j}\sum\sigma_{i,j}\right)\right]^{1/2}$$

$$= \left[\frac{1}{(10,000)^2}\,10,000(300)^2\right]^{1/2} = \$3$$

and $\quad z = \dfrac{L^*/n - \mu_p}{\sigma_p} = \dfrac{400 - 300}{3} = 33.33 \quad \left(\text{probability that }\dfrac{L}{n} > \dfrac{L^*}{n}\right)$

Hence, the probability of ruin is negligible (less than 0.001).

Now suppose that this insurer writes a set of fire insurance policies in order to diversify its line base. The firm writes 1000 fire policies each covering fairly large industrial risks. Each risk has an expected loss of $10,000 and a standard deviation of $15,000. Now the firm estimates that its reserves and surplus permit it to meet claims up to $1300 per policy. Now the portfolio mean, standard deviation, and ruin probability are

$$\mu_p = \frac{10,000(300) + 1000(10,000)}{11,000} = \$1181.8$$

$$\sigma_p = \left\{ \frac{1}{11,000^2} \left[10,000(300)^2 + 1000(15,000)^2 \right] \right\}^{1/2}$$

$$= \$43.21$$

and $z = \dfrac{1300 - 1181.8}{43.21} = 2.74$ $\left(\text{probability that } \dfrac{L}{n} > \dfrac{L^*}{n} \right)$

Hence, the probability of ruin is 0.0031.

Diversification in this case has increased the portfolio risk both in terms of the standard deviation averaged on a per policy basis and in terms of the ruin probability. A little reflection will reveal what has gone wrong. Originally, the insurer had written a book of automobile risks that each had a small expected value and a small level of risk. In diversifying, the insurer changed the composition of the portfolio to include a significant number of high-value, high-risk policies. The impact is to "swamp out" the already diversified risks of the automobile portfolio. The mean and variance of the subportfolio of fire policies alone is

$$\mu_{p(\text{fire})} = \$10,000 \quad \text{and} \quad \sigma_{p(\text{fire})} = \$474.3$$

Thus diversification means that a portfolio having a standard deviation of \$4 per policy is combined with one having a standard deviation of \$474.3 per policy. Not surprisingly, the fire policy risks dominate the portfolio, increasing overall portfolio risk.

MEASURING CORRELATION BETWEEN RISK UNITS

With independence, the covariance terms between risk units are defined to be zero. Now we consider portfolios in which there is some nonzero correlation between the exposure units. To give some descriptive context to the concept of covariance, consider some examples:

1 Close proximity of buildings implies that a fire in one immediately increases the probability of a fire in each of the remaining buildings, since the natural progression of the fire or the blowing of burning embers may cause the fire to spread. Thus the probabilities of loss in each are interdependent.

2 Bad weather conditions increase the probability that any one vehicle may crash, but the same conditions increase the accident probability for every other vehicle in the same meteorological region. Thus the probabilities are interdependent.

3 Many types of losses, e.g., fires, industrial accidents, collisions, burglaries, etc., may bear some relation to the economic cycle. For example, arson increases during recession; people drive more miles during peak periods in the cycle, increasing exposure to loss; etc. These sorts of effects may lead to relationships between the loss probabilities in different types of portfolios. For example, fire losses might be correlated with automobile losses.

Whether such relationships do exist or not is an empirical matter.

To illustrate the operation of covariance, consider the loss experience on two fire policies for industrial risks. The historical record for a 16-year period is given in Table 5-5. The data are expressed in real terms to remove the effect of inflation.

The formula for covariance was given by equation (5-7), but the following form will make the computation somewhat simpler:

$$\sigma_{1,2} = \sum p_i (L_{1i} - \bar{L})(L_{2i} - \bar{L}) \qquad (5\text{-}19)$$
$$= E(L_1 L_2) - E(L_1)E(L_2)$$
$$= 19,373,125 - 6550(1569)$$
$$= 9,096,175$$

The positive sign for this relationship carries the information that the relationship is positive. Large losses on exposure unit 1 tend to arise at the same time as large losses on exposure unit 2; small losses similarly coincide. Intuitively, we might expect that if all units in a portfolio exhibited such positive relationships, the portfolio risk would tend to be high. Bad weather or depressed economic conditions would bring a flood of claims. "It never rains but it pours." However, good weather or a strong

TABLE 5-5
SAMPLE FIRE LOSS DATA

Year	Total losses for exposure unit, $	
	1	2
1965	5,000	500
1966	300	600
1967	6,200	3,200
1968	7,000	2,900
1969	—	1,500
1970	500	—
1971	5,300	—
1972	25,000	5,600
1973	5,000	2,000
1974	7,000	1,800
1975	200	—
1976	—	—
1977	1,000	500
1978	8,000	—
1979	32,000	3,000
1980	2,300	3,500
μ	6,550	1,569
σ	8,831	1,625

economy might reverse the flow of claims. This could cause large fluctuations in the insurer's total claims experience, even if the insurer holds a large number of policies. The impact of covariance on portfolio risk depends on the relative strength of the covariance. Unfortunately, the measure $\sigma_{i,j}$ does not directly reveal the strength of the relationship; it is an absolute number that is not placed on any scale. Certainly, the number 9,096,175 seems a large number, but a casual inspection of Table 5-5 shows the relationship to be less than perfect. If covariance were very strong, we would always find that above-average losses on unit 1 are associated with above-average losses on unit 2. This is clearly not so; witness 1967, 1973, 1978, and 1980. The good news is that a convenient measure of the strength of the relationship is available. This is the *correlation coefficient,* which is defined as

$$r_{i,j} = \frac{\sigma_{i,j}}{\sigma_i \sigma_j} \tag{5-20}$$

Thus for the information in Table 5-5, the correlation coefficient is

$$r_{i,j} = \frac{9,096,175}{8831(1625)} = 0.634$$

The correlation coefficient is defined on a scale of minus unity to plus unity. Negative values denote a negative relationship, with -1 suggesting a "perfect negative correlation." A "perfect" relationship of this form means that there is a directly proportionate relationship between the variables of an inverse nature; if one falls to half its previous value, the other variable doubles in value. A correlation coefficient of zero indicates that there is no association between the variables. Positive values denote a positive relationship, with $+1$ indicating a "perfect correlation." A "perfect" relationship of this form is a directly proportionate relationship between the two series. Thus, on this scale, the example in Table 5-5 reveals a reasonably strong positive relationship. In insurance terms, this relationship would be very strong and would suggest that there might be a serious conflagration hazard (assuming fire insurance) encompassing the two risk units. In a diversified portfolio, it would be expected that correlations would average much lower values.

Using the correlation coefficient instead of covariance, the variance of a portfolio is established by combining equations (5-9) and (5-20) to give

$$\sigma^2(L) = \sum_{i=1}^{n} \sigma_i^2 + \sum\sum_{i \neq j} \sigma_{i,j} \tag{5-21}$$

$$= \sum_{i=1}^{n} \sigma_i^2 + \sum\sum_{i \neq j} r_{i,j} \sigma_i \sigma_j$$

Thus the standard deviation of the mean loss is

$$\sigma\left(\frac{L}{n}\right) = \left[\frac{1}{n^2} \left(\sum_{i=1}^{n} \sigma_i^2 + \sum\sum_{i \neq j} r_{i,j} \sigma_i \sigma_j \right) \right]^{1/2} \tag{5-22}$$

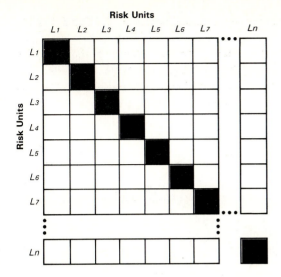

FIGURE 5-5

This is the expression we must now use to calculate the variance of the insurance portfolio. This task will be more complex in view of all the correlation terms that had previously dropped out. In order to perform such calculations, it is helpful to know how many terms there will be in this expression and, in particular, how many covariances or correlations.

The variances and covariances in a portfolio can be represented schematically, as shown in Figure 5-5. All the shaded terms in the leading diagonal are the variances, for example, the pair L_4, L_4. The remaining expressions represent all the possible covariances, for example, L_3 and L_7. In total, the matrix must have n times n elements, since it is square. Of these elements, there are n variances, leaving

$$n^2 - n = n(n - 1)$$

covariances. Thus the double summation sign in equation (5-22) contains $n(n - 1)$ terms. This will be very convenient to remember.

The behavior of a portfolio having correlated exposure units can now be examined.

RISK REDUCTION IN AN INSURANCE PORTFOLIO OF INTERDEPENDENT RISKS

For a portfolio of n identically distributed exposure units in which the correlation coefficient between any pair i and j is $r_{i,j}$, the mean and standard deviation are

$$\mu_p = E\left(\frac{L}{n}\right) = \sum_{i=1}^{n}\frac{E(L_i)}{n} = E(L_i)$$

$$\sigma_p = \sigma\left(\frac{L}{n}\right) = \left[\frac{1}{n^2}\left(\sum_{i=1}^{n}\sigma_i^2 + \sum\sum_{i\neq j}r_{i,j}\sigma_i\sigma_v\right)\right]^{1/2}$$

$$= \left[\frac{1}{n^2}\left(n\sigma_i^2 + n(n-1)r_{i,j}\sigma_i\sigma_j\right)\right]^{1/2}$$

$$= \left[\frac{\sigma_i^2}{n} + \left(\frac{n-1}{n}\right)r_{i,j}\sigma_i\sigma_j\right]^{1/2}$$

If $r_{i,j} > 0$, then portfolio risk will not converge on zero when n approaches infinity because the term $(n-1)/n$ approaches unity as n approaches infinity. Thus the second term in the bracket will approach the positive constant $r_{i,j}\sigma_i\sigma_j$ as n approaches infinity. This can easily be seen in the following example.

Consider a portfolio with n policies that each have

$$\mu_i = 500 \qquad \sigma_i = 650 \qquad r_{i,j} = 0.1$$

Now,

$$E\left(\frac{L}{n}\right) = 500$$

and

$$\sigma_p = \left[\frac{650^2}{n} + \frac{n-1}{n}0.1(650)(650)\right]^{1/2}$$

$$= \left[\frac{380,250}{n} + 42,250\right]^{1/2}$$

Values of σ_p are shown in Table 5-6 for different portfolio sizes.

Consequently, the portfolio is seen to converge on some positive value, that is, 205.5, as n approaches infinity. Diversification brings some risk reduction, but there is a limit to this process. This limit is determined by the size of the correlation coefficient. The higher the correlation coefficient, the higher the lower limit on portfolio risk. In Figure 5-6 we show how the correlation coefficient affects diversification. We assume the same portfolio of units that each have $\sigma_i = 650$, but we allow the correlation coefficient to assume the values $0.1, 0.2, 0.5$, and 1.0. The calculation follows the previous case. For each correlation coefficient, the portfolio standard deviation asymptotically approaches the value shown. There is a clear scope for risk reduction as long as units are not perfectly correlated. However, the risk-reducing benefits become more pronounced as the correlations get lower.

TABLE 5-6
RISK REDUCTION:
INTERDEPENDENT RISKS

n	$\sigma^2\left(\dfrac{L}{n}\right)$	$\sigma\left(\dfrac{L}{n}\right)$
1	422,500	650
10	80,275	283
100	46,052	214.6
1,000	42,630	206.5
10,000	42,288	205.6
∞	42,250	205.5

The second aspect of risk that has been explored is the *ruin probability*. When risks are independent, the combined distribution approaches normal as the number of risks approach infinity. The distribution cannot be assumed to be exactly normal, but the approximation is sufficiently close for reasonable estimation when n exceeds, say, 30. The assumption that the portfolio distribution approaches normal does not hold when the exposure units are correlated. This means that use of the normal distribution to estimate ruin probability is not appropriate even when n is very large. The degree of error in using the normal approximation for such cases depends on the degree of correlation. If the correlation coefficient is close to zero, the normal approximation may be reasonable if n is fairly large. However, when the correlation coefficient diverges widely from zero, the error may be very substantial. Our purpose here is not to give accurate estimates of ruin probabilities; rather, it is to show how diversification reduces the risk of ruin. This will be illustrated on a portfolio with fairly low correlations, and we will use the normal distribution as a crude approximation. However, we recognize that the results may contain a significant error factor, and we will therefore supplement with alternative calculations based on Chebyshev's inequality. The Chebyshev method enables us to establish an upper bound for the ruin probability without actually providing a direct calculation.

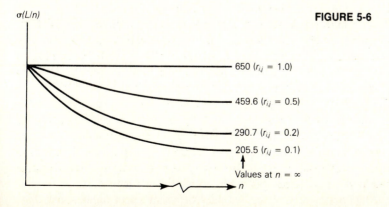

$\sigma(L/n)$

FIGURE 5-6

650 ($r_{i,j} = 1.0$)

459.6 ($r_{i,j} = 0.5$)

290.7 ($r_{i,j} = 0.2$)

205.5 ($r_{i,j} = 0.1$)

Values at $n = \infty$

n

The normal approximation is calculated as before, recognizing the additional error:

$$z = \frac{L^*/n - \mu_p}{\sigma_p} \qquad \left(\text{probability that } \frac{L}{n} > \frac{L^*}{n}\right)$$

Chebyshev's inequality states that

For any random variable x, the probability of realizing an outcome beyond k standard deviations from the mean is at most $1/k^2$.

This implies that an *upper limit* can be set on the ruin probability for any critical value L^*/n. The actual ruin probability will be lower than this value. However, unlike the calculation from the normal approximation, the upper-limit calculation is valid for any distribution. Given this generality, the upper limit calculated by the Chebyshev method tends to be conservatively high. Nevertheless, we will observe how the estimated ruin probabilities behave as the number of items in the portfolio increase. To simplify the calculation, we will specify the Chebyshev inequality in the following terms:

$$\text{Probability} \left(\left|\frac{L^*}{n}\right| > \mu_p + k\sigma_p\right) \le \frac{1}{k^2}$$

Verbally, the probability that L^*/n is greater than $\mu_p + k\sigma_p$ is at most $1/k^2$. Therefore, an upper limit on the ruin probability, given some maximum payout L^*/n, is given by α in the following expression:

$$\frac{L^*}{n} = \mu_p + \sqrt{\frac{1}{\alpha}}\,\sigma_p$$

Rearranging gives

$$\alpha = \frac{1}{\left(\dfrac{L^*/n - \mu_p}{\sigma_p}\right)^2} = \frac{1}{z^2} \tag{5-23}$$

where z is defined as earlier for the normal distribution. The Chebyshev method will only provide meaningful answers (probabilities below unity) if $k > 1$.

Now consider the portfolio discussed earlier with $\mu_i = 500$, $\sigma_i = 650$, and $r_{i,j} = 0.1$, to which we will add the information that the insurer can pay losses up to a maximum of \$800 per policy. Calculating rough ruin probabilities with the normal approximation gives

$$z = \frac{800 - 500}{\sqrt{380{,}250/n + 42{,}250}}$$

Table 5-7 shows sample calculations using this expression and the z tables.

Both the normal-approximation values and the Chebyshev upper limits reveal that

TABLE 5-7
RUIN PROBABILITIES: INTERDEPENDENT RISKS

n	z	(a) Normal approximation	(b) Chebyshev upper limit ($1/z^2$)
		Probability that $\frac{L}{n} > \frac{L^*}{n}$	
1	0.462	0.3228	—[a]
10	1.059	0.1446	0.892
100	1.398	0.0808	0.512
1,000	1.453	0.0735	0.474
10,000	1.458	0.0721	0.470
∞	1.460	0.0721	0.469

[a]Value exceeds unity.

ruin probabilities decline as the number of exposure units increase. Furthermore, both the normal-approximation values and the Chebyshev upper limit converge on positive values, revealing no tendency for the ruin probability to approach zero as n approaches infinity. This may be contrasted with the portfolio of independent units that does converge to zero risk.[4] In view of the latent error in the normal approximation and the severe conservatism of the Chebyshev method, these results are not as strong as we would like here. However, they may be interpreted as providing weak support for the claim that diversification will provide limited benefits in the form of risk reduction even when exposure units are positively correlated. The reduction in risk arises in all cases in which the correlation coefficient is less than unity.

For completeness, we should show that limited risk reduction can be achieved in heterogeneous portfolios of positively correlated risk units as long as the correlation coefficients are less than unity. The method of tackling this should be well established by now, and we will content ourselves with a quick example showing the calculation of portfolio standard deviation.

Let us consider a mixed portfolio of fire and automobile policies in which there are s fire policies and t automobile policies. To preserve the portfolio mix, we assume that s and t bear a constant ratio to each other. The total number of policies is $s + t = n$. In order to calculate the portfolio standard deviation, we need to know how many terms will be present in the formula. Clearly, there are $s + t$ variance terms for individual policies. In addition, there will be

$s(s - 1)$ correlations between different fire risks
$t(t - 1)$ correlations between different automobile risks
$2st$ correlations between fire and automobile risks

[4]For independent exposures, it is easily verified that the Chebyshev upper limit on ruin probability also approaches zero. Tables 5-2 and 5-4 showed that for such portfolios $z \to \infty$ as $n \to \infty$. Since the Chebyshev value α equals $1/z^2$, then clearly $\alpha \to 0$ as $n \to \infty$.

The respective correlation coefficients for these groups are

$$r_{F,i,j} = 0.1 \qquad \text{for fire policies}$$
$$r_{A,i,j} = 0.1 \qquad \text{for auto policies}$$
$$r_{A,F} = 0.05 \qquad \text{for fire and auto policies}$$

Further information for the portfolio is

$s = 20,000$	$\mu_F = 500$	$\sigma_F = 700$	for all fire risks
$t = 10,000$	$\mu_A = 300$	$\sigma_A = 400$	for all auto risks

The standard deviation of the distribution of mean loss can now be calculated in the usual manner:

$$\sigma_p = \sigma\left(\frac{L}{n}\right) = \left[\frac{1}{n^2}\left(\sum_{i=1}^{n}\sigma_i^2 + \sum\sum_{i \neq j}r_{i,j}\sigma_i\sigma_j\right)\right]^{1/2}$$

$$= \left\{\frac{1}{(30,000)^2}\left[20,000(700)^2 + 10,000(400)^2\right.\right.$$

$$+ \ (20,000)(19,999)(0.1)(700)(700)$$

$$+ \ (10,000)(9,999)(0.1)(400)(400)$$

$$+ \ 2(20,000)(10,000)(0.05)(700)(400)\left.\left.\right]\right\}^{1/2}$$

$$= 26,678^{1/2}$$

$$= 173$$

The interested reader might experiment with different values of s and t (but retaining the ratio of $s = 2t$) to confirm that risk does indeed fall as n increases and that it converges on a positive value as n approaches infinity.

Our final word in this section concerns negative correlations. Within a real insurance portfolio there may be a large degree of heterogeneity between risks and a wide diversity in the correlations between individual pairs of risks. Some of these correlations might be negative. The incremental effect of including a policy that is negatively correlated with other policies already in the portfolio is to reduce risk substantially. Therefore, such negative correlations should be valued by the insurer. Negative correlations may be fairly unusual. One possibility arises when the insurer writes two or more lines of business. Loss statistics in one line may show a cyclic pattern with economic activity, whereas the other line may reveal a countercyclic pattern. Although such patterns are often hinted at, they are not usually strikingly apparent. However, the benefits to the insurer in terms of risk reduction imply that efforts to investigate such possibilities may be well rewarded.

THREE APPLICATIONS

To highlight the process of diversification, three examples are now given below in which common risk-management types of activities take advantage of diversification.

EXAMPLE 1: MERGERS AND ACQUISITIONS

An insurer with some 80,000 industrial fire policies acquires a second firm writing 20,000 automobile policies. The respective policies will be subscripted F and A, and details of individual policies are given as follows:

Fire policies: Each policy has mean $\mu_F = 1000$ and standard deviation $\sigma_F = 1500$. The correlation between any pair is $r_{F,i,j} = 0.1$.

Automobile policies: Each policy has mean $\mu_A = 500$ and standard deviation $\sigma_A = 700$. The correlation between any pair is $r_{A,i,j} = 0.1$.

Fire and auto policies are uncorrelated.

The standard deviation of the distribution of mean loss of each insurer before acquisition is

$$
\begin{aligned}
\sigma_{pF} &= \left[\frac{1}{n^2} \left(\sum_{i=1}^{n} \sigma_i^2 + \sum\sum_{i \neq j} r_{i,j}\sigma_i\sigma_j \right) \right]^{1/2} \\
&= \left\{ \frac{1}{(80,000)^2} \left[80,000(1500)^2 \right.\right. \\
&\qquad \left.\left. + (80,000)(79,999)(0.1)(1500)(1500) \right] \right\}^{1/2} \\
&= \sqrt{225,025} \\
&= 474
\end{aligned}
$$

and

$$
\begin{aligned}
\sigma_{pA} &= \left\{ \frac{1}{(20,000)^2} \left[20,000(700)^2 \right.\right. \\
&\qquad \left.\left. + (20,000)(19,999)(0.1)(700)(700) \right] \right\}^{1/2} \\
&= \sqrt{49,022} \\
&= 221
\end{aligned}
$$

And after the merger, the acquiring insurer will have a portfolio with standard deviation

$$
\begin{aligned}
\sigma_{p(F+A)} &= \left\{ \frac{1}{(100,000)^2} \left[80,000(1500)^2 + 20,000(700)^2 \right.\right. \\
&\qquad + (80,000)(79,999)(0.1)(1500)(1500) \\
&\qquad \left.\left. + (20,000)(19,999)(0.1)(700)(700) \right] \right\}^{1/2}
\end{aligned}
$$

$$= \sqrt{145{,}977}$$

$$= 382$$

This reduction in risk has been accomplished by two effects. First, the acquiring company has obtained a group of policies with significantly lower risk (standard deviation) per policy. Second, the initial fire portfolio and the acquired automobile portfolio are uncorrelated; thus diversification is achieved simply by combining two uncorrelated portfolios.

It might be objected that the reduction in risk calculated on a per policy base is misleading. The original portfolio consisted only of fire policies, but the combined portfolio averages over the "chalk and cheese" of fire and automobile policies. To avoid this problem, consider what happens to total risks (that is, not averaged over policies). This is calculated in a similar fashion to σ_p except that we do not divide by $1/n^2$. The before and after values are

$$\sigma_{pF(\text{TOTAL})} = 37{,}949{,}466$$

$$\sigma_{pA(\text{TOTAL})} = 4{,}428{,}184$$

$$\sigma_{p(F + A)(\text{TOTAL})} = 38{,}206{,}947$$

Not surprisingly, total risk increases. However, the combined value is significantly less than the sum of the parts. In fact, total risk hardly increases at all, despite the fact that insurer F has increased its portfolio by some 20,000 policies.

EXAMPLE 2:   REINSURANCE

Two insurers have identical portfolios that each comprise 10,000 identical policies with $\sigma = 400$ and $r_{i,j} = 0.1$, for any i and j. The correlation between a policy of insurer A and any policy of insurer B is also 0.1. The insurers establish a reciprocal reinsurance treaty in which A receives half the premium on each policy written by B. In return, A pays B half the cost of each and every claim suffered by B, and vice versa. That is, each pays half its premiums to the other in return for reimbursement on half of each claim. Before the treaty, each insurer had a level of portfolio risk of

$$\sigma_p = \left[\frac{1}{n^2} \left(\sum_{i=1}^{n} \sigma_i^2 + \sum\sum_{i \neq j} r_{i,j}\sigma_i\sigma_j \right) \right]^{1/2}$$

$$= \left\{ \frac{1}{(10{,}000)^2} \left[10{,}000(400)^2 \right.\right.$$

$$\left.\left. + (10{,}000)(9{,}999)(0.1)(400)(400) \right] \right\}^{1/2}$$

$$= 126.5$$

To calculate standard deviation after the treaty, consider that the agreement has produced two relevant effects. Whereas each insurer previously had an interest in only 10,000 risk units, it now has an interest in 20,000. Second, it will pay only half the loss on each policy; thus the standard deviation per risk unit will be smaller. Both effects should reduce the portfolio standard deviation. The standard deviation per exposure unit can be calculated as follows:

Before reinsurance:

$$\sigma_i = \left[\sum_i p_i (L_i - \bar{L}^2) \right]^{1/2} = 400$$

After reinsurance:

$$\sigma_i = \left[\sum_i p_i \left(\frac{L_i}{2} - \frac{\bar{L}}{2} \right)^2 \right]^{1/2}$$

$$= \left[{}^1\!/_4 \sum_i p_i (L_i - \bar{L})^2 \right]^{1/2}$$

$$= {}^1\!/_2 \left[\sum_i p_i (L_i - \bar{L})^2 \right]^{1/2}$$

$$= 200$$

Then the portfolio standard deviation for each insurer after the treaty is

$$\sigma_p = \left\{ \frac{1}{(20,000)^2} \left[20,000(200)^2 \right. \right.$$
$$\left. \left. + (20,000)(19,999)(0.1)(200)(200) \right] \right\}^{1/2}$$
$$= 63.26$$

The fact that it turns out to be almost exactly half is a coincidence. However, the reduction in risk is dramatic. Generally, the smaller the correlation coefficients between the portfolios of the participating insurers, the greater the risk reduction achieved by reciprocal reinsurance arrangements of this nature.

EXAMPLE 3:   RUIN IN A SELF-INSURANCE FUND

A grocery retailer has 100 stores that are located in several states. In view of the geographic separation and similar size and risk of the stores, the firm decides to self-insure. The administration of this program involves the establishment of a fund into which "premiums" are paid and from which losses are financed. Each store has an expected loss of $1000 and a standard deviation of $1500. The risks are assumed to be independent. Ignoring any administrative expenses, how much should the firm contribute to the fund for each store in order to restrict the probability to 10% that the fund's resources will be inadequate to meet losses.

Since there are 100 units and they are independent, we can assume that the normal approximation applies. Recall that z tables record the probability that any revealed value from a normal distribution will be more than z standard deviations from the mean. The z value corresponding to a 10% probability is 1.28. Thus,

$$z_{10} = \frac{p - \mu_p}{\sigma_p} = 1.28$$

where p is the cutoff contribution that leaves a 10% chance of ruin. Therefore,

$$1.28 = \frac{p - 1000}{\sqrt{(1500)^2/100}}$$

giving $p = 1192$.

Since the assumptions for the use of the normal approximation are met in this particular case, the result is fairly accurate (not strictly accurate, since the portfolio distribution only approaches normal as n approaches infinity). Had there been significant correlations, this method would not have produced reliable answers. However, we would generally expect that the required contribution to maintain any given ruin probability would be higher with positive correlation because the portfolio distribution would exhibit higher risk.

DIVERSIFICATION AND THE DISTRIBUTION OF AGGREGATE LOSSES FOR THE (NONINSURANCE) FIRM

Example 3 provides a bridge between the use of portfolio theory to explain risk reduction in an insurance fund and its application to risk management in other types of corporate organiazations. All firms face a variety of risks, and each type of risk can affect the firm's financial performance and indeed its valuation. For some purposes it may be useful to identify and treat these risk units individually. A narrow focus on individual units provides a starting point in estimating an aggregate loss distribution or at least summary measures. Furthermore, attention to individual units may reveal possibilities for reducing loss costs by safety and preventive activities. However, in determining the financial performance of a firm, it is the aggregate impact of these risk units on the earnings and value of the firm that is of importance. Since the properties of a portfolio are somewhat different from the sum of its parts, we must derive risk-management strategies with reference to these aggregate effects. Later we will show how risk-management strategies derived for individual risk units can produce results that may be damaging for a firm. In the meantime, we consider the properties of the portfolio of exposure units that is owned or controlled by a firm.

All firms are exposed to multiple risks. In addition to the risks inherent in business activity, there are multiple pure risks, such as fires, liability suits, weather-related perils, etc. Even a very small single-plant firm can therefore consider itself to have a portfolio of risk-management exposure units, and each unit pertains to a different type of loss. Just how diversified such a portfolio will be depends on how the risks units are defined and the correlations that exist between them. We have already argued that the identification of separate exposure units is a matter of judgment relating to the degree of correlation between risks. However, it should be clear from the preceding discussion that we cannot usefully define exposure units as statistically independent. (This may lead us to accept that a fire risk in Pennsylvania and a liability risk in California for an entirely separate firm constitute one exposure unit if the loss probabilities are both related to some common indicator, such as the weather or the level of economic activity.) Thus for a one-plant firm, the risk of fire to the plant may exhibit a "small" correlation with the probability that the firm's truck will collide, leading to the common-sense judgment that they are separate exposure units.

For larger, more diversified firms, the portfolio of risk units is more obvious. Firms such as Safeway, Ford, IBM, etc. own many plants, stores, warehouses, offices, etc., and each may be considered to be a separate exposure unit, even when contemplating a single peril such as fire. Again, we are not asserting independence. It may be that due to the quality of management, corporate protection policies, the effect of economic cycles on corporate activity, etc., there is interdependence between the loss distributions for separate exposure units. Nevertheless, these firms do achieve some degree of diversification, since the correlations between units will fall far short of unity. The same general principles of diversification apply to the risk-management issues facing a firm and to the formation of an insurance portfolio. Therefore, it is important to examine the properties of a firm's portfolio of exposure units in order to properly measure risk-management costs and derive appropriate risk-management strategies.

Although the general principles of portfolio theory can be transferred to risk-management problems for industrial, commercial, and service firms, the resulting portfolio may not display such convenient properties as those for the insurance portfolio. The main differences that do arise are

1 Many firms comprise only a small number of risk units. Consequently, portfolio risk will not substantially disappear even if risk units are not correlated.

2 However, the last condition may not apply. Risk units within a firm may be exposed to common influences that imply statistical dependence. For example, losses in various exposure units may be commonly related to the level of business activity for the firm. Common management strategies, labor relations, and safety programs may give rise to interdependence. Physical proximity of some units may give rise to conflagration hazard (although at some stage conflagration hazard may be so severe that risks may be combined into a single exposure unit).

3 A third difference is that exposure units may differ vastly in terms of value and expected loss. Insurance portfolios are usually far from homogeneous, although insurers do try to group exposures into fairly homogeneous classes. The device of "averaging" risk over exposure units was useful in illustrating the nature of risk spreading. For risk-management purposes, the main focus of attention is on the distribution of aggregate losses. It is this distribution that measures the risk costs to the firm, and it is this distribution that becomes a primary focus in formulating risk-management strategy. We have already seen how this distribution might be estimated from loss data. We will now show how the distribution can be affected by diversification within the firm's portfolio of exposure units.

These conditions (if present) imply that the degree to which risk is reduced by diversification is limited. Nonetheless, risk can always be reduced to some extent if exposure units are not perfectly correlated. To illustrate the range of possibilities, consider three firms that differ with respect to the degree of diversification. Details of assets held by the firms and summary measures of the fire-loss distributions are as follows:

Firm A: Operates 30 fast-food restaurants. The restaurants are constructed in a similar style and have equivalent value and fire-risk characteristics:

Value of each restaurant	$300,000
Total value	$9,000,000
Expected loss, each restaurant	$1,500
Total expected loss	$45,000
Standard deviation, each restaurant	$2,500
Exposure units are independent	

Firm B: Manufactures plastic goods. Its business premises are constructed on a fairly large site with sufficient physical separation of buildings to limit fire conflagration hazard. The building values and summary loss measures are:

	Value	Expected loss	Standard deviation
Factory	$5 million	$30,000	$50,000
Warehouse	$2 million	$10,000	$16,667
Distribution	$1 million	$ 3,000	$ 5,000
Office	$1 million	$ 2,000	$ 3,333
Total	$9 million	$45,000	

The correlation coefficient between exposure units is $r_{i,j} = 0.1$.

Firm C: Also manufactures plastic goods. Manufacture, storage, and related office works are all housed in a single building, which is considered a single exposure unit from a fire viewpoint.

Value of premises	$9,000,000
Expected loss	$45,000
Standard deviation	$75,000

The three firms described are comparable in terms of the value at risk and the risk characteristics. Each firm has assets at risk valued at $9 million. The total expected loss in each case is $45,000, indicating comparable degrees of hazard. Furthermore, the variability of risk for each exposure unit, measured as the ratio of standard deviation to expected loss, assumes the same value (≈ 1.67). Thus the three firms differ only with respect to the degree of diversification on the riskiness of the firm's *aggregate* loss distribution. Using the standard deviation formula,

$$\sigma(L) = \left[\sum_{i=1}^{n} \sigma_i^2 + \sum\sum_{i \neq j} r_{i,j}\sigma_i\sigma_j \right]^{1/2}$$

For firm A:

$$\sigma_A(L) = [30(2500)^2]^{1/2}$$
$$= \$13,693$$

For firm B:

$$\sigma_B(L) = [(50,000)^2 + (16,667)^2 + (5000)^2 + (3333)^2$$
$$+ 2(0.1)(50,000)(16,667) + 2(0.1)(50,000)(5000)$$
$$+ 2(0.1)(50,000)(3333) + 2(0.1)(16,667)(5000)$$
$$+ 2(0.1)(16,667)(3333) + 2(0.1)(5000)(3333)]^{1/2}$$
$$= \$55,633$$

And *for firm C,* the standard deviation of aggregate losses is already given, since there is only one exposure unit:

$$\sigma_p(L) = \$75,000$$

Although the expected loss is the same, the variability in losses differs considerably. This difference may substantially affect the type of risk-management strategy adopted by each firm. Consider, for example, whether the firms should purchase insurance. The need for insurance is normally considered to arise from the variability of the loss distribution. Insurance certainly does not reduce expected-loss cost (in view of transaction costs and insurer's markups, the expected cost of an insurance policy usually exceeds the expected value of the loss). However, insurance does reduce, or ideally eliminate, variability. One might therefore suppose that firm A has the least to gain from insurance and firm C has the most to gain. Thus we should not be surprised to find firms with a wide spread of exposure units choosing not to purchase insurance and firms with a high concentration of value in a small number of exposure units choosing extensive insurance protection.

FURTHER DIVERSIFICATION: BUSINESS RISK AND RISK MANAGEMENT

The level of riskiness of the aggregate loss distribution is usually determined initially by the business decisions taken by a firm. Such decisions as basic as the choice of industry the firm elects to be in, its aggressiveness and success in exploiting growth opportunities, choices over location, centralization or decentralization of production, etc. all determine the structure of the portfolio of exposure units upon which risk-management decisions must be made. For most purposes, the risk manager must simply work with, and make the best of, the portfolio that exists. However, sometimes risk-management considerations have an influence on other business decisions. For example, the choice of a method of work that is safer than an alternative proposed on efficiency grounds and the relative location of construction on a site might be influenced by risk management considerations. We will argue that effective decision making is often promoted by simultaneous considerations of business and risk-management factors.

A central proposition of this text is that financial decisions can be assessed in terms of their contribution to the value of a firm. A theme still to be developed is that the ownership interests in a firm are best served if the value of the claims that represent those interests (e.g., shares of common stock) is maximized. The value of ownership is derived from expected future earnings. Such earnings will be determined jointly by operating and risk-management factors. In essence, the total earnings may be considered to represent a portfolio that is assembled, in turn, from a portfolio of business factors and a portfolio of risk-management exposure units. From our study of the properties of portfolios thus far, it is apparent that interactions are important and that decisions made without reference to these interactions are suboptimal. Most risk-management literature points to the distribution of aggregate losses as the basic information requirement for risk-management decisions. We argue that risk-management decisions are properly formulated by reference to their effect on a firm's earnings. In light of the risk-reducing effects of forming portfolios, it should be clear that aggregate risk (business risk and pure risk) differs from the sum of the parts. Unless there is perfect correlation, the riskiness of the aggregate loss distribution overestimates the contribution of the component exposure units to the riskiness of the firm's earnings. Consequently, decisions formulated purely with reference to the distribution of aggregate losses will be too conservative. We will now briefly examine the interaction between the two sources of risk. This will serve as an introduction to a more extensive examination of corporate financial decisions and how diversification *beyond the confines of the firm* has an impact on risk-management decisions.

The variable X is used to denote the earnings of a firm exclusive of any risk management losses that might arise. Loss events are distributed as L; thus net earnings N are

$$N = X - L \tag{5-24}$$

which has an expected value and standard deviation of

$$E(N) = E(X) - E(L) \tag{5-25}$$

and

$$\sigma_N = (\sigma_X^2 + \sigma_L^2 + 2r_{X,L}\sigma_X\sigma_L)^{1/2} \tag{5-26}$$

The risk properties of net earnings are clearly comparable with the portfolios of risk exposure units considered earlier. To give some range to the possible features of this portfolio, values for means and variances are selected together with a range of possible correlation coefficients:

$$E(X) = 20 \qquad \sigma_X = 10$$
$$E(L) = 1 \qquad \sigma_L = 2$$

$$\sigma_N = 12 \qquad \text{when} \qquad r_{X,L} = 1.0$$
$$= 11.14 \qquad \text{when} \qquad = 0.5$$
$$= 10.19 \qquad \text{when} \qquad = 0$$
$$= 9.17 \qquad \text{when} \qquad = -0.5$$
$$= 8.0 \qquad \text{when} \qquad = -1.0$$

SUMMARY AND CONCLUSION

This chapter examines the pooling process that permits insurance companies to diversify much of the risk in their portfolios. Current interest in the insurance process arises, first, because insurance is an important risk-management device and, second, because a similar pooling process arises within the portfolio of risk units held by the noninsurance firm. The interaction between these risk units is important in determining the total level of risk facing a firm. An insurance portfolio is a collection of insurance policies, each of which represents a separate contract with an external party. Whether claims arise under each policy and the size of such claims are random processes. These random processes are represented by the frequency and severity distribution described in the previous chapter. The insurer's interest lies in the aggregate claims to be paid under the portfolio, for it is upon this aggregate that the insurer's financial performance depends. Aggregate claims also follow a random process that is determined by the risk and return characteristics of the individual policies. However, as we see in this chapter, the insurer's risk is not equal to the sum of the individual policy risks.

When insurance contracts in a portfolio are independently and identically distributed, the riskiness of the portfolio, as measured by the standard deviation of the average loss, tends toward zero as the number of policies in the portfolio tends toward infinity. Furthermore, by the Central Limit theorem, the distribution of average loss tends toward a normal distribution as the number of policies increases. This last tendency makes possible the use of the normal-approximation method to estimate the probability of ruin. The probability that the average loss for the portfolio will exceed some critical value (determined by the insurer's reserves) in excess of the mean falls as the number of policies increases. As n approaches infinity, the ruin probability approaches zero. Thus both risk measures, the standard deviation and the ruin probability, reveal that portfolio risk is related inversely to size in a portfolio of independent and identical policies.

Broadly similar results prevail when the insurer's portfolio comprises heterogeneous but independent policies. Risk tends to disappear as the number of policies becomes very large. However, this conclusion is qualified, since it assumes that the relative composition of the portfolio is independent of its size.

When policies are not independent, the conclusions on portfolio diversification require substantial modification. First, with correlated policies, the distribution of average loss does not tend toward normal as the number of policies increases. This implies that use of the normal approximation to estimate ruin probability is not strictly appropriate. Even more significant, the riskiness of the distribution of average loss does not tend toward zero as the number of policies approaches infinity. Such portfolios exhibit an irreducible minimum level of risk that cannot be diversified away. The size of the remaining risk depends positively on the correlations between the policies. An example of this problem is earthquake insurance. It is not so much the high expected value of loss that makes insurers nervous about insuring this risk, but rather the high degree of geographic interdependence between individual policies.

The same process of diversification arises with the portfolio of exposure units possessed by a noninsurance firm. The riskiness of the firm's distribution of aggregate loss is derived from the characteristics of individual exposure units. But risk does not add up in a simple way. The aggregate risk is less than the sum of its parts. Thus, as part of the firm's risk-management strategy, it might well consider the natural risk pooling that arises within the firm. A good example of such pooling is an oil company that owns several hundred service stations. The aggregate loss from, say, fire might be fairly predictable, even though the loss to any individual station is highly uncertain. Further opportunities for internal pooling arise when it is considered that the business risk of a firm often exhibits low correlation with risk-management risk.

The process of diversification is also important in understanding how investors behave and in determining the value of a firm. Similar concepts will now be put to use to help derive sensible financial criteria for evaluating risk-management strategies.

QUESTIONS

1 Consider an insurance portfolio comprising 10,000 independent and identically distributed automobile policies each having an expected loss of 2000 and a variance of $(4000)^2$. Calculate the expected value of the insurer's average loss per policy, and the corresponding standard deviation. If the insurer has a total aggregate reserve fund of \$20,000 what, approximately, is the ruin probability of the fund? The premium paid (net of expenses) is \$2100 per policy.

2 Demonstrate why portfolio risk does not disappear in a very large portfolio of positively correlated policies even if the losses for each policy are identically distributed.

3 An insurer holds a portfolio of 77 identically distributed automobile policies each having

$$E(L) = 200$$
$$\sigma_L = 200$$
$$\sigma_{i,j} = 4000 \text{ (covariance for any pair of policies)}$$

For values of n (10, 100, 1000, 10,000, ∞) show the effects of diversification on the portfolio standard deviation. Using Chebyshev's inequality, provide an upper bound on the ruin probability assuming the maximum the insurer can pay in losses is \$300 per policy. Is the upper bound on ruin calculated in this way of much value? Could you use the normal approximation to estimate ruin probability?

4 The Ace Fire and Auto Insurance Company merges with the Acme Liability Insurance Company. Details of the portfolios of the two companies before merger are:

Ace   10,000 identical fire policies with

$$E(L_F) = \$300$$
$$\sigma_F = 500$$
$$F_{i,j} = 0.1 \text{ (correlation between any pair)}$$

20,000 identical auto policies with

$$E(L_A) = 500$$
$$\sigma_L = 500$$
$$r_{A,i,j} = 0.2 \text{ (correlation between any pair)}$$

Acme   20,000 identical liability policies with

$$E(L_L) = 200$$
$$\sigma_L = 300$$
$$r_{L,i,j} = 0.05$$

The correlation between any auto and any liability policy is 0.1 but fire and liability policies are independent.

Calculate the standard deviation of average loss for

(a) Ace
(b) Acme
(c) The merged firm of Ace and Acme

REFERENCES

Beard, R. E.: *Risk Theory: The Stochastic Basis of Insurance,* Halstead Press, New York, 1977.
———, T. Pentikainen, and E. Pesonen: *Risk Theory,* Methuen, London, 1969.
Breiman, L.: *Probability,* Addison-Wesley, Reading, Mass., 1968.
Cramer, H.: *Mathematical Methods in Statistics,* Princeton University Press, Princeton, N.J., 1946.
Feller, W.: *An Introduction to Probability and Its Applications,* vol. 2, Wiley, New York, 1966.
Friefelder, L. R.: *A Decision Theoretic Approach to Insurance Ratemaking,* Huebner Foundation Monograph no. 4, Irwin, Homewood, Ill., 1976.
Gerber, H.: *An Introduction to Mathematical Risk Theory,* Huebner Foundation Monograph no. 8, Irwin, Homewood, Ill., 1979.
Houston, D. B.: "Risk, Insurance and Sampling," *Journal of Risk and Insurance,* vol. 31, 1964, pp. 511–538.
Markowitz, H.: *Portfolio Selection: Efficient Diversification of Investments,* Wiley, New York, 1959.
Spurr, W. A., and C. P. Bonini: *Statistical Analysis for Business Decisions,* Irwin, Homewood, Ill., 1973.

CHAPTER 6

CAPITAL MARKET THEORY

The corporate objective assumed for this book is that a firm wishes to maximize the value of its owners' equity. In effect, this is equivalent to maximizing the value of the firm's shares. To derive risk management strategies in pursuit of this objective requires some knowledge of how stock prices are determined. In particular, we must examine how the capital market functions and what motivates investors in their decisions to purchase securities. In the conclusion of the previous chapter, we summarized the possibility for diversification across the various risky activities undertaken by a firm. The effect of pooling the various risk management and nonrisk management risky cash flows is to reduce the total level of risk in a firm's earnings. These earnings accrue to the owners of the firm, and the owners must absorb any remaining risk. How does this remaining risk affect the welfare of the shareholders? Presumably, the shareholders' main concern is with the value of their shares. So we may restate the last question: How does the remaining risk in the firm's earnings affect the share values? It is tempting to reply that shareholders are risk-averse, and therefore, risk will simply reduce share value. Therefore, any reduction in risk, perhaps by risk management strategy, will increase share value. This straightforward total-risk approach is widespread in risk management literature. However, we will see that it is an oversimplification that results in misleading and sometimes incorrect conclusions. The possibilities for diversification have not yet been exhausted.

A CAPITAL MARKET IN WHICH INVESTORS HOLD ONLY ONE SECURITY

It is common, and probably not unreasonable, to assume that most people are averse to risk and that this attitude is reflected in many forms of economic behavior. The most obvious *prima facie* evidence in support of this assumption lies in the widespread demand for personal insurance protection. Most of us appear willing to convert the uncertain prospect of a large loss of wealth through the destruction of our home or our life into a regular payment of an insurance premium, even though insurance is costlier in the long run, since premiums typically exceed the expected value of loss. There is considerable evidence that investors (if indeed they form a separate group from homeowners) typically are averse to risk and that this attitude influences their investment strategies and thereby helps to determine the prices of securities.

Investors prefer higher returns on their investment holdings to lower returns, other things being equal. A slightly stronger assumption is that investors prefer less to more risk, other things being equal. Together, these assumptions are broadly acceptable as a general statement of investor motivation. It is conventional to measure return and risk as the expected value of the rate of return and its standard deviation. The rate of return yielded on an investment in a share of stock is the sum of the dividend payment and the capital gain expressed as a ratio with the price initially paid for the stock. Thus the actual rate of return is

$$r_t = \frac{d_{t+1} + (P_{t+1} - P_t)}{P_t}$$

where r_t = the return from time t to $t + 1$
   d_{t+1} = the dividend payable at $t + 1$
    P_t = the share price at t
   P_{t+1} = the share price at $t + 1$

The expected rate of return for any period t is denoted

$$E(r_t) = \sum_i p_i r_{i,t}$$

where p_i is the probability of return $r_{i,t}$. The *standard deviation* is

$$\sigma(r_t) = \{E[r_{it} - E(r_t)]^2\}^{1/2}$$

Now consider an investor who is faced with a choice between alternative investments and who seeks to base his or her decision on expected return and standard deviation. For our example, we will consider just three possible stocks from which to choose, and to keep things simple, we will further assume that the expected return and its standard deviation can be estimated from recent past experience. More specifically, the mean annual rate of return over the recent 10 time periods and its standard error are used as estimators for future returns.

As shown in Table 6-1, an examination of the three stocks reveals that stock C has the highest mean return and, therefore, is estimated to have the highest expected return. Stock B has the lowest expected return, with stock A having an expected return roughly halfway between stocks B and C. In terms of risk, stock B clearly performs badly,

TABLE 6-1
ACTUAL RATES OF RETURN

Period	Stock		
	A	B	C
1	0.06	0.03	0.13
2	−0.03	0.33	−0.07
3	0.00	0.23	0.05
4	0.06	−0.12	0.13
5	0.20	−0.22	0.18
6	0.13	−0.15	0.13
7	0.10	0.19	0.08
8	−0.06	0.24	−0.10
9	0.05	0.16	0.10
10	0.23	0.00	0.18
Mean return			
[= $E(r)$]	0.074	0.069	0.081
Standard error	0.089	0.179	0.091

having a much higher standard deviation than stocks A and C. Stock C is a little riskier than stock A.

Our intrepid investor must now make his or her choice. If the investor has to choose one stock, he or she will clearly avoid stock B because it has the lowest return and highest risk. So the choice is between stocks A and C. Stock C exhibits higher return and higher risk than stock A. If the individual is highly risk averse, he or she will probably choose stock A, being more impressed by its lower risk and being willing to sacrifice a little in terms of expected return. However, if the investor is not so intensively averse to risk (although still risk-averse), he or she may decide that stock C offers a distinct improvement in expected return over stock A with only a small increase in risk. Under such circumstances, stock C is preferred to stock A. Thus the ranking of the three stocks, using the symbol > to denote preference, is

A > C > B   for highly risk averse
C > A > B   for less risk averse

There is no doubt about the first two choices, only about which is first and which is second. Figure 6-1 shows the risk-return characteristics of the stocks. Stock C has the highest return and stock B the lowest. Stock B has the highest risk and stock A the lowest. In the space shown in the figure, the investor wishes to be as far in a "northwesterly" direction as possible, since movement in this direction signifies increasing return and falling risk. On this criterion, stock B is clearly dominated by both stocks A and C, but stocks A and C cannot be ranked because they fall in a "southwest-northeast" array with respect to each other.

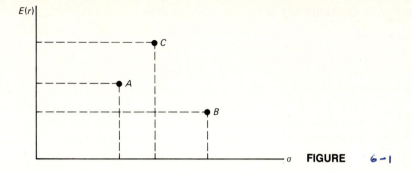

FIGURE   6-1

Let's now see how the capital market would function to determine the price of securities. If investors were only allowed to hold one stock, then it is clear that nobody would wish to hold stock B and all investors would seek stocks A and C. Those already holding stock B would try to sell, thereby driving down its price. Simultaneously, investors would seek to purchase stocks A and C, thereby driving up the price. Since the rate of return for a security is based on its price, a fall in price will push up the expected rate of return, assuming no change in the firm's expected earnings. Conversely, an increase in price will lead to a fall in expected return, *ceteris paribus*. This supply-demand pressure will restructure the risk-return characteristics of the three stocks, perhaps until each of the stocks matches the preferences of some subgroup of investors. The final position might look like that shown in Figure 6-2, which reveals that expected return is positively related to standard deviation.

Some of the older theories of capital markets did indeed produce results like those displayed by Figure 6-2. This pricing structure certainly is based on risk aversion, but modern capital market theory recognizes that the assumption of risk aversion also leads the investor to hold a portfolio rather than a single security, and this radically affects the capital market equilibrium.

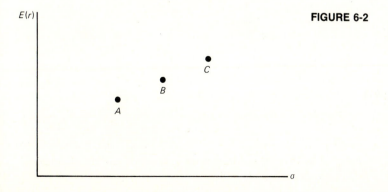

FIGURE 6-2

CAPITAL MARKET EQUILIBRIUM WITH DIVERSIFICATION

Simple Diversification

Table 6-2 reproduces the information concerning stocks A, B, and C, but it also includes a fourth asset D. It is seen immediately that D dominates stocks A and B in terms of risk and return and that it compares favorably with stock C. In fact, asset D delivers an expected return that is only slightly lower than that for stock C, but asset D has a much lower standard deviation. Therefore, most moderately risk averse or highly risk averse investors probably would prefer asset D to stock C. Where did asset D come from? Asset D is a portfolio comprising securities C and B.

Let us return to the problem of selecting from securities A, B, and C without the constraint that the investor hold only one security. Suppose two securities can be held, thereby forming a portfolio. It is tempting to return to the ranking derived earlier, which showed stocks A and C to be superior to stock B, although the ranking between stocks A and C was unclear. From this ranking, it appears that no rational investor would ever choose stock B.

However, this view ignores one important dimension. When risky cash flows are combined into a portfolio, the riskiness of the portfolio depends not only on the individual variances or standard deviations of the component stocks, but also on their

TABLE 6-2
ACTUAL RATES OF RETURN

Period	A	B	C	D
1	0.06	0.03	0.13	0.097
2	−0.03	0.33	−0.07	0.063
3	0.00	0.23	0.05	0.11
4	0.06	−0.12	0.13	0.047
5	0.20	−0.22	0.18	0.047
6	0.13	−0.15	0.13	0.037
7	0.10	0.19	0.08	0.116
8	−0.06	0.24	−0.10	0.013
9	0.05	0.16	0.10	0.120
10	0.23	0.00	0.18	0.120
Expected return	0.074	0.069	0.081	0.077
Standard error (σ_n)	0.089	0.179	0.091	0.038
σ_{N-1}	(0.093)	(0.188)	(0.096)	(0.040)
Covariances	$\sigma_{A,B} = -0.0117$	$\sigma_{A,C} = 0.007$	$\sigma_{B,C} = -0.0131$	
Correlation coefficients	$r_{A,B} = -0.8$	$r_{A,C} = 0.86$	$r_{B,C} = -0.73$	

Note: D = 0.33 B + 0.67 C

covariances or correlations. Negative covariances can have a dramatic effect by reducing portfolio risk, even if the items concerned each exhibit a high level of risk. Reexamination of stocks A, B, and C reveals that stock B has the attractive property that it appears to vary inversely with both stocks A and C. When stocks A and C deliver high returns, stock B tends to deliver low returns, and vice versa. However, stocks A and C appear to vary in the same direction, suggesting positive correlation. Although stocks A and C appear to be attractive when each is considered in isolation, a portfolio comprising these two securities would not be effective in reducing portfolio risk. A portfolio comprising stocks B and C would contain securities whose returns tended to vary in opposition, thereby producing a fairly stable portfolio return. Asset D is such a portfolio, and it is formed by permitting the investor to invest one-third of his or her capital in stock B and two-thirds in stock C. The resulting portfolio has an expected return between that of stocks B and C, but a standard deviation that is much lower than that of either stock B or stock C.

The behavior of security portfolios closely parallels the portfolio behavior identified in the previous chapter. It is necessary to modify the formulas used there to calculate the portfolio mean and variance, for here we are not dealing with dollar values but with rates of return. Thus analogous to equations (5-8) and (5-9), we state the expected return, the variance of that rate of return, and its standard deviation for a portfolio of n securities as follows:

$$E(r) = \sum_{i=1}^{n} w_i E(r_i) \tag{6-1}$$

$$\sigma^2(r) = \sum_{i=1}^{n} w_i^2 \sigma_i^2 + \sum_{i \neq j} \sum w_i w_j \sigma_{i,j} \tag{6-2}$$

$$\sigma(r) = [\sigma^2(r)]^{1/2} \tag{6-3}$$

where w_i = the weight of security i in the investor's portfolio

r_i = the rate of return on security i

σ_i = the standard deviation of the rate of return on security i

$\sigma_{i,j}$ = the covariance between the returns on i and j

Often, it is more useful to use the correlation coefficient instead of the covariance. This is easily accomplished by noting that the correlation coefficient $r_{i,j}$ is defined by

$$r_{i,j} = \frac{\sigma_{i,j}}{\sigma_i \sigma_j}$$

Substitution into equation (6-2) is straightforward.

The means, standard deviations, covariances, and correlation coefficients are shown at the bottom of Table 6-2. Consider portfolio D, comprised of one-third of capital invested in stock B and the two-thirds invested in stock C. The expected return and standard deviation can be confirmed by equations (6-1) and (6-3):

$$E(r_D) = 0.33(0.069) + 0.67(0.081)$$
$$\approx 0.077$$
$$\sigma(r_D) = [(0.33)^2(0.179)^2 + (0.67)^2(0.091)^2$$
$$+ 2(0.33)(0.67)(-0.0131)]^{1/2}$$
$$\approx 0.038$$

The means and standard deviations of stocks B and C are now plotted in Figure 6-3(a). By forming the portfolio from stocks B and C, the investor can also choose the risk-return combination shown as D on the graph. However, these possibilities do not exhaust the investor's choice. The investor could have invested 50% in each of stocks

FIGURE 6-3

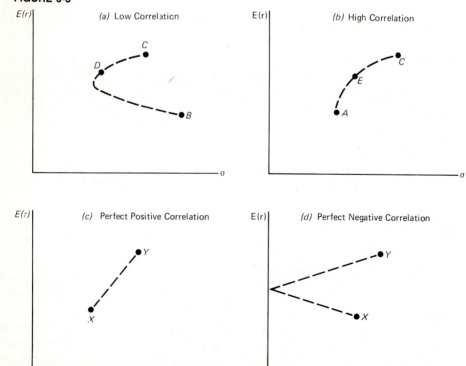

B and C, or perhaps 75% in stock B and 25% in stock C, and so on. The various options are plotted along the broken line traveling through B and C but which is convex to the vertical axis. The fact that the line is convex clearly illustrates possibilities for reducing risk by forming a portfolio.

From earlier analysis, it should be clear that the facility for reducing risk depends on the covariance between the securities. Suppose a portfolio, labeled E, was formed by combining stocks A and C. Since these stocks are positively correlated, there should be no dramatic reduction in risk. Figure 6-3(b) shows, on a similar diagram to Figure 6-3(a), a broken line giving the risk-return combinations for portfolios of stocks A and C. Position E shows weights of 0.5 on each of stock A and stock C, with $E(r_E)$ and $\sigma(r_E)$ calculated as follows:

$$E(r_E) = 0.5(0.074) + 0.5(0.081)$$
$$= 0.0775$$
$$\sigma(r_E) = [(0.5)^2(0.089)^2 + (0.5)^2 (0.091)^2$$
$$+ 2(0.5)(0.5)(0.007)]^{1/2}$$
$$\approx 0.087$$

Figure 6-3(a) and (b) illustrates the effect of correlation on the potential for risk reduction through portfolio formation. The more pronounced convexity in part (a) indicates much greater risk reduction than that shown in part (b). The limiting cases are given by perfect positive correlation (the correlation coefficient is unity) and perfect negative correlation (the correlation coefficient is minus unity). Although none of the pairs of securities in our example meets these criteria, Figure 6-3(c) and (d) shows what the portfolio possibilities would be. Notice that with perfect positive correlation there is no curvature in the portfolio line at all. This is consistent with the analysis in the previous chapter, which revealed no prospect for diversification under these circumstances. With perfect negative correlation, the portfolio line actually touches the vertical axis, showing that one portfolio exists that will remove all risk. (It might be pointed out that with securities such as stocks, this very attractive perfect correlation is rarely, if ever, found.)

Derivation of the Efficient Frontier

So far, the portfolios have only been formed using pairs of securities. Relatively little imagination is needed to realize that further possibilities for diversification might exist by combining three or more securities into a portfolio. The equations given for calculating expected return and variance are not restricted to any number of securities, and we could search through the wide selection of stocks and other finanical assets available to us until we found our preferred risk-return combination. This may prove to be a long search, but it is quite simple to represent what might happen.

In Figure 6-4, a set of stocks is represented, each by its expected return and standard

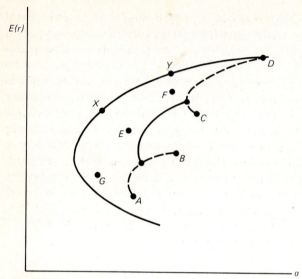

FIGURE 6-4

deviation. For any pair of stocks, we could construct portfolio lines such as those shown in Figure 6-3, and the shape of each line would depend on the correlation coefficient. Only two such portfolio lines are shown to avoid congestion. However, portfolios could be formed with three or more stocks. These can be represented as "portfolios of portfolios." Thus the thin solid line joining the broken lines *AB* and *CD* represents some of the portfolios that can be formed by combining securities A, B, C, and D. It is clear that portfolios along this line would not be attractive, since there are still other securities offering higher return and lower risk, such as stocks E and F. However, even further prospects for improvement arise from combining stocks E and F into a portfolio and perhaps including stock C and/or stock D. When all such possibilities are exhausted, the resulting *envelope curve,* i.e., the curve enclosing all the portfolio lines, will look like the thick solid line. The upper left portion of this envelope is known as the *efficient frontier* because it represents the most efficient portfolios that can be formed. The portfolios represented along this line deliver the minimum level of risk for each given level of expected return.

The various positions along the "northwest" segment of the efficient frontier represent portfolio choices that are efficient in mean-variance terms. Apparently, there is no optimal portfolio along this line (a statement that will be revised in due course). The more risk averse investors presumably would choose portfolios, such as X, that exhibit relatively little risk but have a corresponding low level of expected return. More speculative investors would accept more risk to deliver higher expected return, such as portfolio Y. According to individual preference, each investor would locate at a position reflecting his or her degree of risk aversion.

To derive the efficient frontier in practice would appear to be an enormous task. There are hundreds of securities to choose from, and we have to consider every possible combination. Bearing in mind that the number of securities to be assembled into portfolios is not fixed and that the weights for each security can assume any value (subject to their summing to unity), the number of possible portfolios is infinite. This implies a pretty long game of trial and error; in fact, the proverbial three monkeys might well randomly type out the complete works of Shakespeare earlier than trial and error would lead to complete specification of the efficient frontier. However, there are easier methods. One possibility is to use quadratic programming, since its application is straightforward and quite cheap with modern computers. Another possibility is to solve mathematically, since an analytical solution has been derived by Merton (1972). Thus the technology to solve the efficient frontier is now routinely available.

The efficient-frontier solution to the problem of portfolio selection was presented in 1952 by Markowitz. This work represented an important turning point in capital market theory, because it offered a usable quantitative solution to the issue of portfolio selection. Its implications have proved to be far-reaching, leading to a "revolution" in the way we view the workings of the capital market.

The Market Portfolio

The efficient frontier turns out to be a misnomer, for there may be ways of improving investment performance as measured by risk and expected return. Let us suppose that in addition to the various risky securities that are used to derive the efficient frontier, there is also a riskless security. This may be represented as debt that is free of default

FIGURE 6-5

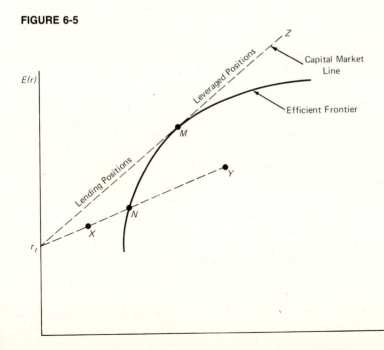

risk and has a fixed yield. As a rough approximation, a Federal Treasury Bill may be considered to be risk-free. Given the absence of risk, we would expect such a security to bear a fairly low yield, which is denoted r_f in Figure 6-5. The diagram also reproduces the efficient frontier.

The rate r_f is the risk-free rate, and we will assume that unlimited borrowing and lending take place at this rate. The reader should not get nervous about simplifying assumptions here. Indeed, several more simplifying assumptions will soon be made to proceed with the analysis. These assumptions are necessary to construct a predictive model, and this model should be appraised on its predictive power rather than on the accuracy of its assumptions. The assumptions can be relaxed, causing some modification of the model; however, the basic insights of the simple model are still preserved.

With borrowing and lending available at r_f, the investor may chose not to invest all his or her capital in risky securities. Instead, he or she may choose some portfolio, such as N, and invest half of the capital in N and the remainder in the risk-free security yielding r_f. This composite position will yield an expected return and standard deviation shown as X on the straight line connecting r_f and N. Indeed, any other position on the line is also available by varying the proportions of capital invested in N and r_f. A more aggressive investor may choose to borrow money at r_f, thereby permitting him or her to invest more than the initial capital in portfolio N. This leveraged investor will achieve some position on the broken line such as Y.

These two investment strategies are illustrated quite easily by considering a lending investor who lends half his or her capital at the risk-free rate and a leveraged investor who borrows an amount equal to half his or her initial capital to invest in a risky portfolio. In this example, the risk-free rate is 0.1; the expected return on the risky portfolio is 0.15 with a standard deviation of 0.2 The covariance between r_f and the risky portfolio must be zero, since the former has no risk.

Lending Investor

The expected return and standard deviation are

$$E(r) = 0.5(0.1) + 0.5(0.15) = 0.125$$
$$\sigma(r) = [(0.5)^2(0)^2 + (0.5)^2(0.2)^2$$
$$+ 2(0.5)(0.5)(0)]^{1/2} = 0.1$$

Leveraged Investor

$$E(r) = -0.5(0.1) + 1.5(0.15) = 0.175$$
$$\sigma(r) = [(-0.5)^2(0)^2 + (1.5)^2(0.2)^2$$
$$+ 2(-0.5)(1.5)(0)]^{1/2} = 0.3$$

In this example, the investor generated new opportunities not available with the efficient frontier. Portfolios along the segment r_fN may well be chosen over positions on the efficient fronter. However, a leveraged position such as Y clearly is suboptimal, since there are positions on the frontier offering higher expected return for the same level of risk.

By choosing another risky portfolio on the efficient frontier and then lending or leveraging, the investor can do even better. This portfolio is defined by a point of tangency between the efficient frontier and a straight line going through r_f. The tangency point defines a risky portfolio that is denoted M. Lending positions are defined along the segment r_fM, and leveraged positions are defined along the segment MZ. The line r_fMZ is known as the *capital market line*. Notice that the capital market line dominates the lending/leveraged positions that could be attained holding portfolio N. For every position on r_fNY, there are corresponding positions on r_fMZ offering higher returns for the same risk or, equivalently, offering lower risk for the same level of expected return. It is also fairly obvious that the tangency portfolio M is optimal in the sense that it offers lending/leverage opportunities that dominate those offered by any other risky portfolio on the efficient frontier.

This analysis leads to the conclusion that there is a single portfolio of risky securities that is optimal for all investors regardless of personal attitude toward risk. This portfolio is M. Investors who are risk-averse are better served by holding part of their capital in M and lending at the risk-free rate to achieve a position on the lending portion of the capital market line than by holding a portfolio such as N that is fairly low in risk. Similarly, investors who are more speculative are better off borrowing at r_f and investing the proceeds, together with initial capital, in risky portfolio M. This leads to a position on the leveraged part of the capital market line that is superior to holding a risky high-return portfolio such as Y. Consequently, all investors, regardless of risk preference, would choose the same portfolio of risky assets, but they would differ in their financing decisions. On the latter decisions, some investors will achieve lending positions and others will achieve leveraged positions to match their individual risk preferences. This conclusion can be given as a separation theorem:

The selection of a portfolio of risky stocks is independent both of the financing decision and of individual risk preference given the assumptions of the analysis

If all investors are to choose the same portfolio, it is of obvious advantage to be able to identify the portfolio in question. This task is straightforward. If all investors are predicted to hold the same portfolio of risky stocks, then all stocks represented on the market must find their way into the portfolio. The portfolio can be none other than the *market portfolio,* which includes all traded stocks, with each stock being held in the proportion its market value bears in relation to the total market value of all stocks. This is quite a dramatic conclusion, and it leads to interesting conclusions about the way in which securities are priced. This pricing process will now occupy our attention.

Systematic and Unsystematic Risk

Some assumptions have been necessary to get this far in the examination of capital markets. Further assumptions are necessary in order to continue. These assumptions are now collected together, and from these, a model of asset pricing will be constructed:

1 Unlimited borrowing and lending can take place at a single risk-free interest rate. The Federal Treasury Bill rate usually is used as a proxy for this rate.

2 All assets can be bought and sold immediately in any quantity at the prevailing market price.

3 All assets are perfectly divisible; the investor can buy or sell any quantity, including fractions, of assets and short sales.

4 There are no taxes or transaction costs.

5 All investors base decisions only on the expected return and its variance (or standard deviation) and seek the minimum variance for any given level of return.

6 The planning horizon for investment decisions is one period. Note that the return during this period includes the terminal value of the asset.

7 Investors share identical expectations concerning the probability distributions of available assets.

These assumptions clearly do not accurately describe the real world. The relevant question, however is whether the predictions of the model correspond with the actual performance of the capital market. We will comment on the relaxation of these assumptions later.

These assumptions describe a frictionless market in which rational economic men and women conduct their business. In this market, investors would indeed hold the market portfolio, as described earlier, and the market would reach equilibrium when all investors reached the market portfolio position. Let us now enquire how assets would be priced in such a market.

The rational investor in our assumed world is concerned with the expected return and variance (or standard deviation) of his or her investment portfolio. Any individual security that is purchased will affect the return and risk of the investor's portfolio, and the attractiveness of that asset to the investor therefore depends on these portfolio effects. Since the equilibrium portfolio is the market portfolio, each asset will be priced according to its contribution to the risk and return of the market portfolio. The expected return of an asset and its effect on the market portfolio cause no problems. Since the expected return of a portfolio is simply the weighted average of its component securities, an individual asset will increase the portfolio expected return if that asset has a higher expected return than the portfolio. A lower expected return will pull down the portfolio return. However, the incremental risk the asset brings to the portfolio rests not so much on the riskiness of the asset as on its covariance with the portfolio. This leads to the partitioning of risk into *systematic* and *unsystematic* risk.

Consider two securities that have comparable expected returns and, according to past experience, have displayed similar levels of risk. However, the securities have exhibited very different correlations with returns on the market portfolio. As seen in

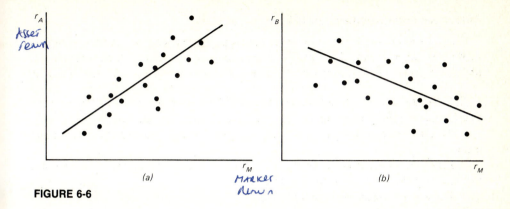

FIGURE 6-6

Figure 6-6(*a*), security A has tended to deliver high returns during periods when returns on the market portfolio were high and correspondingly low returns when returns on the market portfolio were low. Each dot in the diagram represents the pair of returns for the security r_A and the market portfolio r_M during a given period. There is not a perfect correlation, which suggests that there is a random, or unexplained, component to the return of stock A. Nevertheless, there is a strong correlation, and the relationship is represented by a straight line. This line is constructed by fitting a simple regression as follows:

$$r_{A,t} = \alpha + \beta r_{M,t} + e_{A,t} \qquad (6\text{-}4)$$

where $r_{A,t}$ = the return on A in period t

$r_{M,t}$ = the return on the market portfolio in period t

α and β = estimated regression coefficients

$e_{A,t}$ = the residual error in period t

The term β shows the sign and sensitivity of the relationship that exists between A and M. In the case illustrated in Figure 6-6(*a*), r_A moves upward on average as r_M moves upward; thus β has a positive slope. However, the slope is rather less than 45°, indicating that a percentage movement in r_M would be associated with rather less than a 1% movement in r_A. Thus β would have a value of something less than +1. In Figure 6-6(*b*), a negative β security is shown. With this security, rates of return have tended to move in the opposite direction to the return on the market portfolio.

It is clear that β is really measuring a similar relationship to that represented by the covariance. In fact, β is nothing more than a scaled version of covariance:

$$\beta_A = \frac{\text{cov}\,(r_A r_M)}{\sigma^2(r_M)} \qquad (6\text{-}5)$$

where cov $(r_A r_M)$ = the covariance between r_A and r_M

$\sigma^2(r_M)$ = the variance of the return on the market portfolio

Examination of equation (6-4) and Figure 6-6(*a*) and (*b*) reveals that the riskiness of the security is divided into two components. Part of the risk is explained by the relationship between the security's returns and the return on the market index. This risk is transmitted through the sensitivity coefficient β (or covariance). Thus, as the market moves up or down, there are sympathetic movements in the individual stock's returns. For stock A, the explained movement is the same direction as the movement in returns on the market portfolio; for stock B, the movement is in the opposite direction. This explained component of risk is labeled *systematic risk* (otherwise known as *market risk*) because it is systematically related to movement in the market portfolio. The higher β, the more sensitive the stock's returns are to changes in the market portfolio.

The second component of risk also is apparent from examination of equation (6-4) and Figure 6-6. The distribution of security returns in Figure 6-6(*a*) and 6(*b*) is not fully explained by movement in the market portfolio. The various dots in the diagrams show some random variation about the correlation line, revealing that there is an unexplained variation in security returns. The unexplained variation in security returns is also shown by the error term $e_{A,t}$ in equation (6-4), and the unexplained component of risk is known as *unsystematic, or nonmarket, risk.*[1]

The Security Market Line and the Capital Asset Pricing Model

The market portfolio is, by definition, highly diversified. Consequently, the unsystematic component of risk will be almost "diversified out." The unsystematic risk of each security will have little or no effect on the overall riskiness of such a diversified portfolio. As a result, the investor should be indifferent to the degree of unsystematic risk exhibited by an individual security, and this will have no effect on the price of the security.

---

[1]The partition of risk can also be seen as follows:

$$\sigma(r_A) = \sigma(\alpha + \beta r_{M,t} + e_{A,t}) \quad \text{from equation (6-4)}$$

However, the expected return on security A is

$$E(r_A) = \alpha + \beta E(r_M)$$

Therefore,

$$\begin{aligned}\sigma(r_A) &= E[r_A - E(r_A)]^2 \\ &= E\{(\alpha + \beta r_{M,t} + e_{A,t}) - [\alpha - \beta E(r_M)]\}^2 \\ &= E\{\beta[r_{M,t} - E(r_M)] + e_{A,t}\}^2 \\ &= E\{\beta^2[r_{M,t} E(r_M)]^2 + 2e_{A,t}[r_{M,t} - E(r_M)\beta] + e_{A,t}^2\} \\ &= \beta^2 \text{ var } r_M + \text{ var } e_A \quad \text{since } E(e_{A,t}) = 0\end{aligned}$$

or

$$\sigma(r_A) = \text{systematic risk} + \text{unsystematic risk}$$

Systematic risk is an entirely different matter. If the covariance with the market portfolio is high (that is, β is high), the addition of the security to the investor's diversified portfolio will have an adverse effect on the portfolio risk. Conversely, if β is low, the addition of the security will have a beneficial effect on portfolio risk. In the somewhat unusual case that the covariance (and therefore, β) is negative, the inclusion of the security can bring a big reduction in portfolio risk. Thus it is the covariance with the market portfolio, or β, that determines the incremental contribution of each security to the riskiness of the portfolio, and consequently, β exerts an important influence on the security price.

The *capital asset pricing model* (CAPM) embodies a linear relationship, in equilibrium, between the expected return of a security and the security's β value. This relationship is known as the *security market line* (SML) and is shown in Figure 6-7. The security market line reveals that price is determined by systematic risk alone. Unsystematic risk does not affect price, and thereby expected return, because this element of risk is substantially eliminated by simple diversification.

In Figure 6-7, two stocks are represented that do not lie on the SML. For stock X, the expected return is high relative to its β value. If the expected return represents a consensus market view based on the firm's expected earnings, stock X will be viewed as being underpriced. Investors will seek to purchase this security, thereby bidding up its price. The price rise will result in capital gain to existing holders, but for those buying at the higher price, the expected return (based on that purchase price) will be correspondingly lower. In this manner, the expected return will fall until the equilibrium relationship is restored. Conversely, security Y is overpriced according to market

FIGURE 6-7

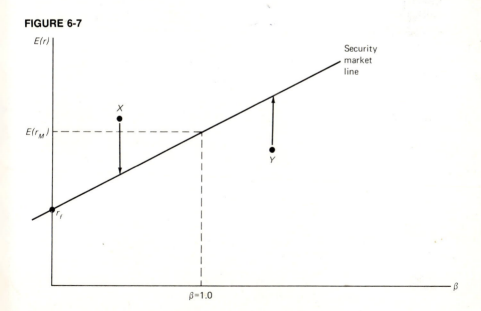

expectation. Excessive selling pressure will drive the price down, causing expected return to be restored to its equilibrium level.

Two positions on the SML may be pointed out. The market portfolio must have a β value of unity, since β measures the correlation with itself. The expected return on the market portfolio is therefore illustrated at β = 1.0. The intercept on the vertical axis shows the expected return for a security that is uncorrelated with the market portfolio. Such a security will have a return of r_f (i.e., the risk-free rate), bearing in mind that a risk-free security also must have no systematic risk.[2] Comparing these two rates reveals that the market portfolio commands an additional return for systematic risk of

$$E(r_M) - r_f = market\ risk\ premium$$

Securities with β values in excess of unity will command higher returns, and thus a higher risk premium, than the market portfolio. When β is lower than unity, the risk premium will be less than that for the market portfolio. Some securities may even have negative β values. These securities would be in high demand because of their facility for counteracting portfolio risk. Consequently, expected return would be very low, even lower than the risk-free rate. The risk premium on securities with negative β values is negative.

The capital asset pricing model (CAPM) was derived independently in the mid-1960s by Sharpe (1964), Lintner (1965), and Mossin (1966) and represented a natural evolution from Markowitz's portfolio theory of the 1950s. We now present the Sharpe-Lintner-Mossin CAPM more formally to reveal the structure of security returns. The security market line is stated by the following equation:

$$E(r_j) = r_f + \beta_j[E(r_M) - r_f] \tag{6-6}$$

where r_j = the return on security j

β_j = the β value for j

The first component of any security's return is simply the riskless interest rate. The second component is the risk premium, which is the β value times the market risk premium. Notice that equation (6-6) shows the expected return in equilibrium to be a linear function of the security's β value. Consistent with the earlier analysis, the equation does not contain any reward for unsystematic risk because this is irrelevant to the security price.

Relaxing the Assumptions of the Model

Clearly, the assumptions used to develop the capital asset pricing model represent an oversimplification of reality. Again, we emphasize that it is not appropriate to reject

---

[2] A risky security with β = 0 and a nonrisky security both have an expected return of r_f.

the model on the basis of its assumptions; rather, we should test whether its predictions correspond with observed behavior. However, we will illustrate how changes in the assumptions affect the predictions. The treatment is illustrative rather than exhaustive, since this is peripheral to our main purpose and an extensive literature already exists on the subject.

One assumption that clearly does not hold up is that there exists a single risk-free interest rate for borrowing and lending. Clearly, intermediaries have transaction costs and wish to make some profit; therefore, borrowing rates typically are higher than lending rates. This implies that there is not one tangency portfolio on the capital market line, but two—one corresponding to the borrowing rate and one corresponding to the lending rate. Labeling these portfolios M_B and M_L, respectively, yields two expressions for the security market line:

$$E(r_B) = r_{f,B} + \beta[E(r_{M,B}) - r_{f,B}]$$
$$E(r_L) = r_{f,L} + \beta[E(r_{M,L}) - r_{f,L}]$$

(6-7)

where $r_{f,b}$ and $r_{f,L}$ are the respective borrowing and lending rates. These security market lines are shown in Figure 6-8(a). The result is that there is no unique equilibrium price for each security. For some investors, trade in a given security will be in the context of a lending portfolio; for others, trade will be supported by a borrowing portfolio.

Consider another assumption—that there are no transaction costs. Without this assumption, investors may observe small differences in expected returns (and therefore prices) from their estimated equilibrium values without being induced to trade. Divergence from equilibrium must be sufficient to cover transaction costs before trading occurs. This suggests that the SML may not be a single line but a band, as shown in Figure 6-8(b). The width of the band will depend on the size of transaction costs: The smaller the transaction costs, the narrower the band.

Differences in expectations among investors may also produce a range of expected returns for a given β value, also producing a band rather than a unique security market line. The resulting band is shown in Figure 6-8(c). Changes such as these produce a pricing relationship that is not as sharp as that shown in the simple model but still has the same general properties. Thus in Figure 6-8(d), a fuzzy upward sloping area is shown in place of a well-defined equilibrium pricing line. The fuzziness reveals some range of uncertainty in the equilibrium price, but this is insufficient to destroy the main insight of the model—that expected returns in equilibrium bear a positive relationship to systematic risk.

Relaxing the assumptions of a unique borrowing/lending rate and no transaction costs implies that investors may hold different portfolios. However, this does not destroy the valuable insight of the model that much risk reduction can be achieved by diversification. The extent of risk reduction depends on the covariances of the securities in an individual's portfolio. Strictly speaking, the use of β values to measure these covariances is appropriate only if investors actually hold the market portfolio. However, if individuals hold portfolios that are highly correlated with the market portfolio, β serves as a useful proxy for these covariances. Most diversified portfolios are highly

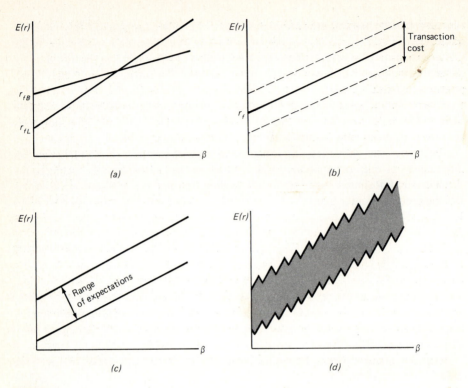

FIGURE 6-8

correlated with the market portfolio, and consequently, β serves as a useful measure of systematic risk.

Some modifications of the capital asset pricing model (CAPM) have been formulated in response to some of its stronger assumptions. For example, Merton (1973) formulated a multiperiod asset pricing model, Gonedes (1976) formulated a capital asset pricing model with heterogeneous expectations, and Mayers (1972) formulated a model with some nonmarketable assets. Perhaps one of the more interesting developments has been the introduction by Ross (1974) of the arbitrage pricing model, which, *ceteris paribus*, measures systematic risk in relation to multiple factors. These developments do represent improvements in our understanding of capital markets. However, they have not displaced the CAPM because its predictions have proved to be remarkably robust even when the assumptions are relaxed. We will now see whether the predictions of the CAPM have empirical support.

TESTING THE CAPITAL ASSET PRICING MODEL

Many tests have been conducted on the capital asset pricing model and its various derivatives. It is difficult to summarize this literature and to arrive at an unqualified conclusion as to whether the CAPM is supported or rejected by the evidence. I will hazard the opinion that the majority of finance professors and, indeed, informed practitioners would accept that the evidence provides substantial support for one form or another of the CAPM, although it must be noted that these tests are not free of problems. Contrary evidence does exist (e.g., Levy, 1978), but it is dominated by the more pervasive evidence that expected return is linearly related to β and is uncorrelated with unsystematic risk. To illustrate this evidence, we will briefly describe the results of a study by Fama and MacBeth (1973) that is widely quoted.

The Fama-MacBeth study was designed to avoid the statistical problems that had plagued earlier studies and which had been pointed out by Miller and Scholes (1972). Fama and MacBeth calculated the β values of stocks traded on the New York Stock Exchange for each successive and overlapping 5-year period between the 1930s and 1960s. Stocks were ranked according to β value and then divided into 20 portfolios, the top 5% forming one portfolio, the second 5% forming the second portfolio, and so forth. The portfolios were re-formed each year on the basis of the revised ranking of β values. The procedure was to use data from years 1 to 5 to produce portfolios for the sixth year, use data from years 2 to 6 to derive portfolios for the seventh year, and so forth. Since the portfolios were ranked according to the β values of their component stocks, the β values of the portfolios should differ, as should their delivered returns. Indeed, there should be a linear relationship between returns and β values for the portfolios.

Fama and MacBeth tested for such a linear relationship using the following model:

$$r_i = a_0 + a_1\beta_i + \varepsilon_i \qquad (6\text{-}8)$$

where r_i = the return on portfolio i

β_i = the β value of portfolio i

ε_i = a random error that is normally distributed

a_0 and a_1 = estimated coefficients[3]

If the CAPM is correct, we should find that when this model is estimated using regression techniques, a_1 should not differ significantly from the term $(r_M - r_f)$.[4] Estimating with data from 1935 to 1968 revealed that this was the case. [In fact, the results are rather more compatible with a slightly modified version of the CAPM developed by Black (1972), in which the rate that is estimated to prevail for a β = 0 portfolio is substituted for the risk-free rate.]

---

[3]Notice that the model tests for a relationship between actual returns and β whereas the CAPM is formulated in expected returns. The test assumes that actual returns for each period are randomly displaced from their expected equilibrium relationship.

[4]The reader not familiar with these statistical techniques may wish to skip the description of this test, although it is useful to pay attention to the broad result.

Fama and MacBeth also tested to see whether unsystematic risk might exert a significant influence on portfolio returns and whether the relationship between returns and β value was nonlinear. In each case, the results were negative, thereby supporting the (modified) CAPM.

Similar results have been generated by other researchers, one notable exception being a study by Levy (1978) that did find unsystematic risk to be significant. Although the general consensus is that results are broadly compatible with one form or another of the CAPM, the studies are not free of statistical problems and problems of interpretation (see, for example, Roll, 1977).

IMPLICATIONS FOR FINANCIAL MANAGEMENT

It is now time to draw attention inward to the decisions made within a firm to see how these are influenced by activity within the capital market. The obvious connection is that financial management is assumed to be directed toward the goal of value maximization, and the value of a firm's securities is determined by investor preferences, as expressed in their trading activity. The equilibrium rate of return given by the CAPM for a stock with a given β value is the return required by investors to compensate for the systematic risk of that stock. This required rate of return provides a guide for the firm's capital-budgeting decisions.

The expected rate of return delivered by a stock depends on the expected future earnings of the firm. Indeed, the equilibrium price of the stock is otherwise defined as the expected value of future earnings of the firm discounted at the equilibrium rate appropriate to the β value. This price implies that the expected return is at its equilibrium rate. With this in mind, consider a new company that has just been floated with a particular investment program in mind. The criterion commonly used to decide whether such a project should be accepted is that the expected cash flows should yield a positive present value when discounted at an appropriate rate. The appropriate rate is simply the equilibrium rate corresponding to the level of systematic risk in the cash flows. This requires calculation of a β value for the cash flows by estimating their correlation with the market portfolio. If the net present-value criterion is satisfied, the firm will yield an expected return to the stockholders that exceeds the equilibrium return. Consequently, the stock of the firm will acquire a value in excess of the capital raised by the original flotation. In this way, value is created in satisfaction of the assumed corporate goal.

The preceding paragraph describes the capital-budgeting framework that will be familiar to many readers. The capital-budgeting criteria apply to the decision to float a new firm, but they also can be used to evaluate new projects contemplated by an existing firm. The rules can be applied separately to individual projects as long as the correct risk-adjusted discount rate is used. The expected return and β value for a firm can be represented as the weighted average of the expected returns and β values of the various component activities of the firm, that is,

$$E(r) = \sum_i w_i E(r_i) \tag{6-9}$$

$$\beta = \sum_i w_i \beta_i \qquad \text{(6-10)}$$

where $E(r)$ = the expected return from all the firm's
  activities

$E(r_i)$ = the expected incremental return on component
  activity i

β_i = the systematic risk for r_i

w_i = the weighting of activity i

The implication of this weighting procedure is as follows: Consider a firm that is currently offering an expected return of, say, 15% to its shareholders, which is the equilibrium rate given the estimated β of 0.8. The equilibrium is illustrated at position A in Figure 6-9. A new project is contemplated for which the expected cash flows represent a 20% return on new capital to be raised. The β value for these cash flows is estimated at 1.4, and the equilibrium return for this β value is 18%. Clearly, the expected return on this new project, position B, is above the equilibrium return shown by position D. If the new activity accounts for 50% of total activity (that is, w_i = 0.5),

FIGURE 6-9

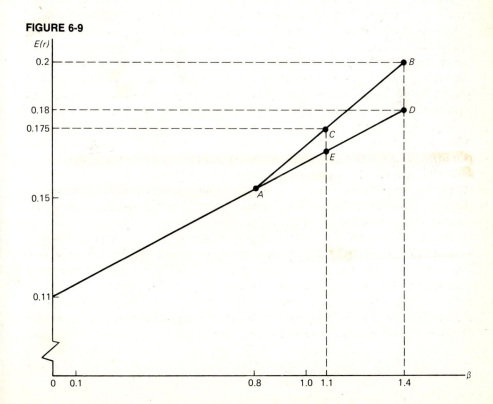

equations (6-9) and (6-10) show that the firm should have an expected return and β value of

$$E(r) = 0.5(0.15) + 0.5(0.2) = 0.175$$
$$\beta = 0.5(0.8) + 0.5(1.4) = 1.1$$

This position, C, is definitely above the equilibrium value shown by position E. This excessive return will cause investors to seek to purchase the stock, thereby bidding up its price. In this way, acceptance of the project will increase the share price in satisfaction of the assumed corporate objective.

The relationship between capital market theory and financial management can be summarized as follows: The equilibrium rate of return is the return required by investors given the level of systematic risk. Since this rate is required by investors to supply capital to the firm, it may be considered to represent the cost of equity capital to the firm. This rate reflects the effect of risk on investors' personal portfolios given that they have the facility for diversification. The rate does contain a risk adjustment, but this only relates to systematic risk. Since the corporate objective is assumed to be value maximization, it follows that any investment project accepted by a firm that delivers an incremental return above its equilibrium rate will add value to the firm's stock. This condition will be satisfied if the estimated incremental cash flows from the project yield a positive net present value when the equilibrium rate relevant to the project's systematic risk is discounted. Alternatively, the condition for value creation is satisfied if the internal rate of return exceeds the cost of capital. Notice that the new project is not assessed on the basis of its total risk, since part of that risk will disappear when combined with the risk of other activities of the firm and when combined with the risk of other stocks held by the shareholder in his or her investment portfolio. These implications carry over to our consideration of risk management.

IMPLICATIONS FOR RISK MANAGEMENT

The equilibrium rate of return is equally relevant to risk management decisions and includes an appropriate risk premium to compensate for the systematic risk of risk management cash flows. This statement ensures that risk management decisions are made on a value-maximizing basis that is consistent with other financial decisions. The imposition of consistency appears to be sensible enough, but its implications will probably come as a big surprise to many risk managers.

Risk management has developed under the assumption that firms are averse to risk and that this motivation gives rise to various tradeoffs between the costs and benefits of removing risk. In this framework, insurance plays a dominant role, for it can be used to remove risk. However, its use is costly, since premiums typically exceed the expected value of loss by a significant margin. The decision framework focuses attention on individual risk exposures, thereby encouraging the decisionmaker to balance the costs and benefits of risk reduction for each exposure or each identifiable group of exposures. For example, the risk manager may look at the firm's property insurance as the subject of a single decision that is to be made by balancing the riskiness of the distribution of property loss against the cost of insurance. In other cases, the risk manager may decide at the level of the individual plant. At best, risk managers may address the cost-benefit tradeoff for all risk management exposures taken as a group. It would be rare for the decision to consider diversification between the pure and speculative components of risk in the company's earnings, let alone to consider the dilution of risk within the shareholder's portfolio of financial assets. Clearly, the isolation of decisions will tend to produce an overly cautious attitude toward risk and may well result in an excessive purchase of insurance.

Now consider the other extreme by looking only at systematic risk. There is little reason to expect that "pure" risk events will bear any close relationship to the returns generated on a stock market index such as the Dow Jones Index. Indeed, we will summarize evidence later that suggests that no significant relationship can be detected. Thus the β value for "pure" risk exposures may well be zero. Although potential losses from liability suits, property damage, and so forth, are extremely risky prospects, this risk is of little or no concern to shareholders *ex ante* because it is easily diversified away by the firm's shareholders in their personal portfolio management strategy. Under such circumstances, the purchase of insurance brings no direct benefit to the firm's owners. Insurance would simply diversify risk across a group of firms similarly exposed to risk. The insurance process works because exposures in the insurance company's portfolio have little correlation. However, without insurance, investors typically hold portfolios comprised of several securities. The risk management exposures of the firms represented in the investors' portfolios have little or no correlation, and the risk is diversified away in exactly the same way as with insurance. Thus insurance of corporate risk simply reproduces the "homemade insurance" achieved by investors' investment strategies. Viewed in this light, insurance is redundant.

The argument in the previous paragraph is a little extreme for two reasons. First, we must admit the possibility that the systematic risk of risk management exposures is not zero. In this case, risk reduction by such devices as insurance does bring direct benefits to the shareholders insofar as systematic risk is reduced. However, this is the only component of risk reduction that is costly to shareholders, and the discount rate used in decision making should reflect only the systematic risk. Second, insurance may bring indirect benefits. For example, risk reduction may be extremely valuable to other groups having an interest in the firm. Employees cannot diversify away their financial stake in the firm as easily as shareholders, since employment income typically is the dominant source of income for most workers. In reducing risk by devices such as insurance, the firm will be able to negotiate more favorable employment contracts that may enhance the firm's earnings. However, notice that this type of reasoning is very different from that traditionally used and will lead to quite different risk management strategies. The traditional approach focuses directly on such issues as stability of earnings and survival without regard for the final incidence of risk on the firm's owners. The valuation approach also embraces a general assumption of risk aversion on the part of a firm's owners. However, this approach relies on the market valuation process to inform the firm's decisionmakers of the burden of risk borne by the shareholders, having due regard for both their attitudes toward risk and the effect of accommodating such risk in their investment portfolios.

The financial management and risk management implications of the capital asset pricing model that are drawn here apply to firms whose ownership is traded. By contrast, consider a family-owned firm whose owners are not solely concerned with value maximization, but with other objectives, such as maintenance of family control. Furthermore, family members may work in the business, thereby combining their ownership interest and their employment interest. For such firms, total risk, not just systematic risk, may be especially important. Family owners probably have not diversified away the joint risk of ownership and employment in the family business. Under such circumstances, ownership interest cannot be separated from employment interest. Indeed, cross-subsidization may arise between these separate interests. The value of ownership claims may not be maximized in order to protect family control and to promote the employment interests of family members. For this firm, financial management and risk management will be differently motivated, and concentration on systematic risk is inappropriate. Investment projects and risk management proposals may be assessed according to their impact on the total risk of corporate earnings. Although we will concentrate on the more widely held firm in the remainder of this book, we do admit the occasional example in which concentrated ownership dictates the use of more substantial risk premiums.

SUMMARY AND CONCLUSION

If the value of a firm's equity is to be used to guide risk management decisions, the process by which the capital market values securities merits examination. For risk management in particular, the examination of capital markets is essential, since risk and the potential for reducing risk through diversification are at the heart of the valuation process.

In a very simple capital market in which investors hold only one security, the valuation process would be correspondingly simple. If investors were risk-averse, then risky securities would be less attractive than alternative securities delivering equivalent rates of return but having lower risk. Excessive demand for low-risk securities would soon drive up their prices, with opposite price movements for high-risk securities. Such price movements would cause the expected return to fall for low-risk securities and to rise for high-risk securities. Eventually, an equilibrium would be reached in which high-risk securities would offer a higher expected return, thereby compensating their holders for the additional risk.

The "one-security world" is not very realistic and probably does not describe rational investor behavior. Investors typically form portfolios, and under simplifying assumptions, it is shown that the optimal portfolio for all investors is, in fact, the market portfolio. Investors can adjust to their individual risk preferences by choosing how much to lend or borrow. The advantage of forming a portfolio lies in its facility for reducing risk. If security returns are not perfectly positively correlated, risk is reduced, often dramatically, by holding a portfolio.

The capital asset pricing model rests on the propensity for an investor to hold a portfolio. The risk of a security may be divided into systematic and unsystematic components. Systematic risk is that which is explained by the correlation of the security returns with returns on the market portfolio. The unexplained, or residual risk, is labeled unsystematic risk. The systematic risk measures the incremental contribution of a security to the riskiness of the market portfolio. Since investors are predicted to hold the market portfolio, it is this measure of risk that is relevant to the pricing of the security. Unsystematic risk is not relevant for security pricing because it is easily diversified away. This reasoning leads to a model of security pricing that asserts that expected returns are linearly related to the security's β value and are independent of unsystematic risk. This relationship is known as the capital asset pricing model.

The capital asset pricing model is based on several restrictive assumptions, thereby tempting the reader to reject it as being unpractical. However, the main insights of the model do survive relaxation of these assumptions. Furthermore, the acid test of the model is not whether its assumptions are realistic, but whether its predictions are confirmed by real-world behavior. Evidence does lend considerable support for the model in a slightly modified form, although some doubts have been raised about whether the empirical tests are adequate. One interesting derivative of this form of model is the arbitrage pricing model, which currently is attracting much attention, although it is premature to try to summarize its effectiveness.

The capital asset pricing model and its variants have substantive implications for financial and risk management. In assessing investment or risk management projects, the relevant measure of risk is the systematic risk of the project, not its total risk. This conclusion is in conflict with traditional thinking in risk management, which has emphasized total risk and its reduction through such devices as insurance. The emphasis on systematic risk serves the stated corporate objective of value maximization, and now we can turn our attention to corporate value and how it may be affected by loss events.

QUESTIONS

1 A portfolio comprises three securities as follows:

Security	Weight	Expected return	Standard deviation
A	.6	.3	.4
B	.7	.2	.2
C	−.3	.1	.2

Given correlation coefficients:

$$r_{AB} = .2 \qquad r_{BC} = -.5 \qquad r_{AC} = .4$$

a What are the respective covariances?
b What is the portfolio expected return?
c What is the standard deviation of return for the portfolio?
d What does the negative weight to security (C) imply?

2 Draw the security market line and the capital market line and explain the function of each.

3 Calculate the equilibrium rates of return for the following securities:

Security	Beta
A	1.5
B	1.0
C	0.5
D	0
E	−0.5

The risk free rate is 0.1 and the expected rate of return on the market portfolio is 0.18. What adjustments would arise if investors expected a rate of return of 0.17 on security C?

REFERENCES

Black, F.: "Capital Market Equilibrium with Restricted Borrowing," *Journal of Business,* vol. 45, 1972, pp. 444–455.

Fama, E., and J. MacBeth: "Risk Return and Equilibrium: Empirical Tests," *Journal of Political Economy,* vol. 71, 1973, pp. 607–636.

Gonedes, N.: "Capital Market Equilibrium for a Class of Heterogeneous Expectations in a Two Parameter World," *Journal of Finance,* vol. 31, 1976, pp. 1–15.

Levy, H.: "Equilibrium in an Imperfect Market, A Constraint on the Number of Securities in the Portfolio," *American Economic Review,* vol. 68, 1978, pp. 643–658.

Lintner, J.: "Security Prices, Risk and Maximal Gains from Diversification," *Journal of Finance,* vol. 20, 1965, pp. 587–615.

Markowitz, H.: "Portfolio Selection," *Journal of Finance,* vol. 7, 1952, pp. 77–91.

———: *Portfolio Selection* (Cowles Monograph No. 16), Wiley, New York, 1959.

Mayers, D.: "Nonmarketable Assets and Capital Market Equilibrium under Uncertainty," in M. C. Jensen (ed.), *Studies in the Theory of Capital Markets,* Praeger, New York, 1972.

Merton, R. C.: "An Analytic Derivation of the Efficient Portfolio Frontier," *Journal of Financial and Quantitative Analysis,* vol. 2, 1972, pp. 1851–1872.

———: "An Intertemporal Capital Asset Pricing Model," *Econometrica,* vol. 41, 1973, pp. 867–888.

Miller, M., and M. Scholes: "Rates of Return in Relation to Risk: A Reexamination of Some Recent Findings," in M. C. Jensen (ed.), *Studies in the Theory of Capital Markets,* Praeger, New York, 1972.

Mossin, J.: "Equilibrium in a Capital Asset Market," *Econometrica,* vol. 34, 1966, pp. 768–783.

Roll, R.: "A Critique of the Asset Pricing Model Theory's Tests: Part 1. On Past and Potential Testability of the Theory," *Journal of Financial Economics,* vol. 4, 1977, pp. 129–176.

Ross, S.: "Risk Return and Arbitrage," in I. Friend and J. S. Bicksler, (eds.), *Risk and Return in Finance,* Lexington Books, Lexington, Mass., 1974.

———: "The Current Status of the Capital Asset Pricing Model," *Journal of Finance,* vol. 33, 1978, pp. 885–901.

Sharpe, W. F.: "Capital Asset Prices: A Theory of Market Equilibrium Under Conditions of Risk," *Journal of Finance,* vol. 19, 1964, pp. 74–80.

CHAPTER 7

VALUATION OF A FIRM AND THE MEASUREMENT OF LOSS

Many problems in risk management have the same dimensions as other problems in corporate finance. Essentially, many risk management problems have an investment content that involves the commitment of current resources against some future payback. This is equally true of the installation of a sprinkler system (where the payback is some savings in the cost of future losses), the use of inventory as a guard against interruption loss following a fire, or the payment of an insurance premium (where the payback takes the form of contingent financing of losses that do arise). As with more familiar investment problems, the purpose is to create wealth for the owners of a firm by increasing the value of the firm. In deciding whether such wealth is created, attention must be paid to the costs of financing the investment, the benefits accruing from the investment and their relationship to the financing costs, and the risks inherent in the alternative sources and uses of funds. Treating the installation of, say, a burglar alarm or a sprinkler system in the same way as, perhaps, additional machinery, equipment, or inventory ensures consistency in decision making. All projects required to clear the same financial hurdles.

This financial approach requires us to be able to measure the wealth created by investment, such as the purchase of insurance or safety devices. Before doing this, we shall step back from risk management to review the process by which the market values investment decisions. In our application to risk management, it will first be necessary to examine how pure losses affect the market value of the firm. This stage is necessary because the benefits derived from risk management take the form of reductions in the probability or severity of such losses. The quality of risk management decisions will depend on how well they preserve the firm's market value. From this viewpoint, we will examine decisions to protect market value made (1) after a loss

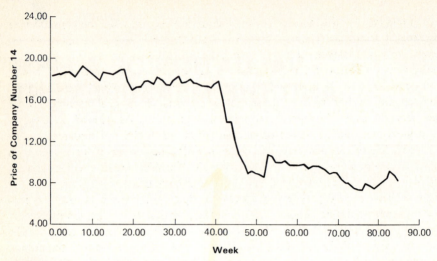

FIGURE 7-1
Price movements of GPU (June 16, 1978 to January 1980).

has arisen and (2) in anticipation of future losses. Our perspective in this chapter will be to value the effect of losses that have already occurred. To illustrate the direction of our financial approach, consider the following incident. On March 28, 1979, an operating failure at the Three Mile Island nuclear power facility at Harrisburg, Pennsylvania, caused damage to the facility and the release of contaminated materials. The facility is owned by General Public Utilities, and the common stock prices for this firm have been traced in Figure 7-1 for the period surrounding the accident. The timing of the incident is in the forty-first week. Although stock prices are responsive to many influences that feed into investor expectations, the effect of the accident is clear and dramatic. The fall in stock price reflects a revision in earnings expectations embodying the effect of protracted delay in earnings, potential liability suits, repair and reconstruction costs, and the cost impact of any new safety standards that might be formulated in response to the incident. The fall in stock value thereby forms an estimate of the impact of the loss on the firm. It also records the loss of wealth suffered by the firm's owners. The value of ownership claims will form the basis of our financial approach to risk management. This value will be used to measure the impact of actual and prospective losses, and it will form the yardstick by which risk management programs are evaluated.

THE CREATION AND DESTRUCTION OF WEALTH

The wealth-creation process arises from the allocation of resources to some productive use. For our initial examination of this process, we will assume that an individual or group owns some valuable resource that either can be sold to yield income for consumption or can be put to some productive use that will yield future income to the owner. Initially, we will ignore risk and assume that we can trace the consequences of our present decisions. The exposition will be made much simpler by assuming that there are only two relevant points in time. At time 1, a decision is made whether to use resources for investment or for consumption. Investment decisions yield income to the owner at time 2, from which he or she can support period 2 consumption. Resources may be thought of either as the market value of physical resources owned by the decision maker (in which case they can be put to immediate productive use or sold to yield their market value) or as cash (from which physical resources can be purchased). Viewed in this way, the decision facing the owner of the resources is whether to use them for current or future consumption. The decision will rest on the productivity of any such investment and the owner's preferences over time.

This problem can be presented graphically. Figure 7-2 has for its axes the consumption available during periods 1 and 2. Investment possibilities are represented by a transformation curve AB. The relevant features of this curve are as follows. The initial resources available are $0A$. One choice is to use these entirely for current consumption, in which case the owner will have the consumption pattern $C(1) = 0A$, $C(2) = 0$. Alternatively, all resources might be invested, yielding $C(1) = 0, C(2) = 0B$. The productivity of investment is represented by the feature $0B > 0A$. Thus, in the long run, roundabout means of production generate greater wealth. Intermediate consumption patterns can be attained by investing only part of the available resources. For example, if $0C$ is used for current consumption, leaving CA for investment, the consumption profile is $C(1) = 0C$, $C(2) = 0D$. The value $0D$ is generated by the investment of CA of current resources. An important feature of this diagram is the concave slope of the transformation curve. This illustrates an important economic phenomenon known as the *diminishing marginal productivity of investment*. Moving

FIGURE 7-2

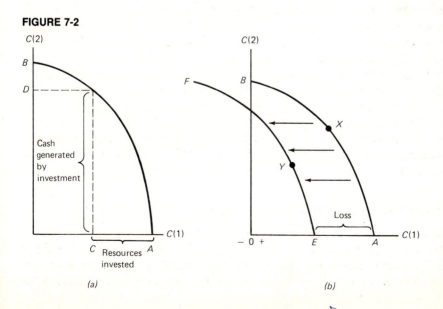

(a)

(b)

backward from position A, we can examine the impact of investing successive dollars. As we move to the left from A on the horizontal axis, the successive dollars invested will each yield somewhat less than the previous dollar invested in terms of time 2 consumption.

In this very simple world, what happens if a fire destroys half the owner's available resources? The possibility of such an event introduces risk into the model and eats at the assumptions we needed to create our simplified model. Accordingly, we must qualify what we mean by risk and be more clear in defining the periods over which the firm is exposed to risky events. The context for the preceding analysis was one in which a decision is made at time 1 and its consequences are traced one period later. The removal of risk means that once a decision is made, the consequences are deterministic. The major part of this book relaxes this assumption. However, for the time being, we merely wish to examine the impact of destruction of wealth just after any initial decision on investment is made. We seek to answer the question: How much wealth has been lost as a result of the fire? Thus our analysis is *ex post* with respect to chance events. For the time being, we also assume that destroyed resources can be replaced immediately. Thus, if financing is available, no loss of production need arise. Later we will look at interruption losses. Further simplification will be achieved by treating all resources as undifferentiated. For example, the resources might comprise n identical sewing machines used for assembling blue jeans rather than different but complementary items of equipment used at different stages in the production process. This simplification relieves us of the burden of stating which particular resources are destroyed.

The effect of a loss is shown in Figure 7-2(*b*) by the shifting of the envelope of consumption possibilities from AB to EF. With undifferentiated resources, the shift is simply a horizontal movement of the original frontier. The loss can be measured in two ways. Most directly, the loss is simply the market value of the resources that have been destroyed, that is, EA. If the loss were insured, this would be the basis for settlement. But this way of viewing the loss is only relevant if it can be established that the owner will consume all resources at time 1. If all resources were to be invested, the loss would be FB. More important to the owner, the real losses are the foregone consumption opportunities in the two periods of time. For example, if the preferred consumption patterns before and after the loss are X and Y, respectively, the loss to the owner is implicit in the movement from X to Y. Since we are debating in a two-period time frame, it seems that this loss cannot be given any single value; it depends on the time preferences of the owner. We shall see presently that with the introduction of a capital market, this loss is measurable. The identification of preferences and the introduction of a capital market are our next tasks.

TIME PREFERENCE

The consumption preferences for individuals over different time periods can be represented by an *indifference map*. This is a construction that displays the rate at which consumption can be transferred between periods of time while maintaining the overall level of satisfaction from the consumption stream at some constant value. If many

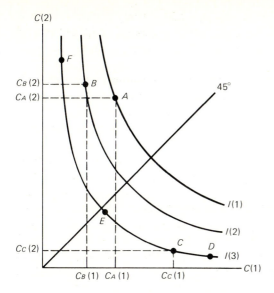

FIGURE 7-3

time periods are involved, the indifference map requires mathematical specification and can become very complex. However, if only two (or at most three) time periods are involved, convention indifference maps can be constructed. Such a map is constructed in Figure 7-3. The features of this map are as follows:

1 The indifference curves do not cross. This implies transitivity such that if the pair $[C_A(1), C_A(2)]$ is preferred to $[C_B(1), C_B(2)]$ and the pair $[C_B(1), C_B(2)]$ is preferred to $[C_C(1), C_C(2)]$, then $[C_A(1), C_A(2)]$ is preferred to $[C_C(1), C_C(2)]$.

2 Indifference curves farther from the origin signify greater utility than those closer to the origin. Essentially, this means that more of both is preferred to less of both. Thus $I(1) > I(2) > I(3)$.

3 The curve is convex toward the origin. This implies diminishing marginal utility from consumption in each time period. Thus if we are at point D, we have high consumption in period 1 and very little in period 2. Consequently, we would be willing to sacrifice a dollar of time 1 consumption for a few cents of time 2 consumption. At point E on the same curve, our consumption is more nearly equal and the rate at which we would be willing to trade time 1 dollars for time 2 dollars is nearer parity. At point F we might only be willing to give up a few cents of time 1 consumption for a dollar of time 2 consumption.

4 The curves are not necessarily symmetrical about the 45° line drawn from the origin. If this were the case, the individual would have neutral time preference. More likely, the lines will be somewhat more elongated than the symmetrical curves, thereby indicating positive time preference. Notice that positive time preference does not imply that $1 at time 1 is preferred to $1 at time 2. This is patently not the case at C, where the slope of $I(3)$ is considerably less than $-45°$. However, the elongation does create a bias in favor of present consumption at most points.

INTRODUCTION OF A CAPITAL MARKET

If we live in a world in which goods cannot be stored and in which there is no borrowing and lending, our consumption possibilities in any time period are constrained by our earnings in that time period. Thus if current income and anticipated income at time 2 are represented by point D in Figure 7-4, we have little choice but to consume at D. In fact, we can consume anywhere within the rectangle D, $Y(2)$, 0, $Y(1)$. However, the interior solutions are clearly wasteful unless greater satisfaction is derived from giving to others. If we can save or store consumption, we can generate a new set of opportunities to the northwest of D. Assuming that such saving attracts no interest, these opportunities are represented by the $-45°$ line DG in Figure 7-4. These opportunities may lead to preferred positions, as illustrated at point F, which is on the higher indifference curve $I(2)$. If so, the owner will benefit by restraint and thrift. So far, however, we have not introduced a capital market. The opportunities generated by moving northwesterly from point D can be grasped simply by storing coins (or tins of beans) under a mattress. Notice that the line is not extended below point D. Thus the individual cannot bring consumption forward in time. To do so would require that he or she be able to borrow to support current consumption, with a corresponding reduction in future consumption when the debt matures.

The simplest conceivable capital market comprises borrowing and lending facilities at a zero rate of interest. In such a world, the lending opportunities would look very much like those depicted on the line DG in Figure 7-4. Instead of postponing consumption by burying money in the ground, one simply lends the money to a third party, who pays back next period. In this riskless world, there is no default. Thus each dollar saved is paid back in period 2 without interest, and the $45°$ slope is maintained. With borrowing possibilities, the line is projected to the horizontal axis, generating consumption possibilities on the segment DH. Again, each dollar borrowed

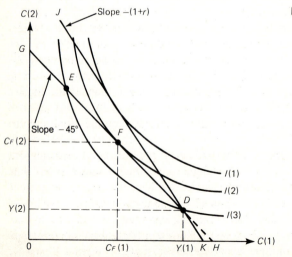

FIGURE 7-4

is repaid without interest next year, thereby reducing next year's consumption by $1. In the situation depicted, the initial income endowment $(Y(1), Y(2))$ and the preferences are such that the individual would be a net saver. Utility would be maximized by consuming $0C_F(1)$ and saving $C_F(1) - Y(1)$ from current income $0Y(1)$. This permits next year's consumption to exceed income by the value $Y(2)$ $C_F(2)$. Had the initial endowment been at point E, the same individual would have been a net borrower.

The 45° slope to GH indicates that each dollar saved (borrowed) increases (decreases) future consumption by $1. With positive rates of interest, this is clearly not the case, and the opportunities generated from any initial income endowment must be represented by a somewhat steeper line. It is easily verified that the slope of the opportunity line is equal to $-(1 + r)$, where r is the rate of interest on borrowing and lending transactions.

Before using these capital market opportunities to examine the process of wealth creation and wealth destruction, it behooves us to be more explicit about the simplified world in which we are operating. Specifically, we will assume that

1 All information relevant to a decision is known to the decision maker. In particular, future case flows can be specified with certainty.

2 There are many agents in the market completing many transactions, and no one agent is large enough to influence prices.

3 All agents have identical knowledge about the terms and prices of all transactions.

4 There are no transaction costs.

In such a world, one interest rate would prevail for all transactions. Contracts offering less advantageous terms would be known to everybody and would be avoided. With a single rate of interest, our two-period analysis can now be developed. Figure 7-4 is overdrawn with the line JDK having a constant slope equal to $-(1 + r)$, where $r > 0$. Since the interest-free circumstances depict a net saver, the rewarding of saving by the payment of interest leads to a preferred utility position on $I(1)$. The reader might verify that had the income endowment required net borrowing, the effect of interest would have been to reduce utility.

The opportunities generated by the capital market can now be used to show how the productive use of resources can generate wealth and how the destruction of such wealth can be measured. In Figure 7-5, we reproduce the transformation curve AB from Figure 7-2. Without borrowing and lending opportunities, the utility-maximizing level of investment would arise when the consumption pattern reached the highest attainable indifference curve. This is shown at point Y, where there is a point of tangency. This indicates that of all the opportunities represented by the transformation curve AB, point Y is preferred. To reach this point, the individual invests AC of current resources, consuming the remaining $0C$. The investment generates future consumption equal to $0E$. A capital market with a positive single interest line is shown as VW with a slope of $-(1 + r)$. It can now be seen that if the individual chooses to invest more (AD rather than AC), he or she will reach point X on the transformation curve. From this position, the individual has available borrowing opportunities that lead to consumption patterns along XW and lending opportunities representing consumption patterns along VX. Clearly, some of these opportunities are superior to point Y, and we

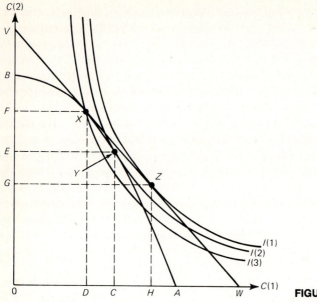

FIGURE 7-5

show utility maximized at point Z. To reach this position, the following transactions have arisen, starting from the initial resource position $0A$:

1 AD has been invested, giving a production pattern at X.

2 Against future income $0F$, an amount DH is borrowed; this permits the individual to maintain current consumption at $0H$ [equal to initial resources ($0A$) minus investment (AD) plus borrowing (DH)].

3 In period 2, borrowing has to be repaid. The repayment is $DH(1 + r) = GF$. Time 2 consumption is therefore $0G$ [which is equal to time 2 income ($0F$) minus repayments (GF)].

The final position Z was determined by individual time preference. We can equally well imagine any position along YW, and the individual may equally well turn out to be a lender rather than a borrower. The point is that all opportunities along VW can be represented in time 1 values by point W, since all these positions can be generated from W by lending at the market rate of interest. Furthermore, W is available from production position X. Thus the wealth of the firm formed by exploiting these investment opportunities is $0W$. From initial resources $0A$, the firm has generated wealth equal to AW. The answer to where this wealth has come from is the first of several fundamental principles of corporate finance that are illustrated by this example:

1 Wealth is generated because the firm is able to exploit an investment opportunity that yields return in excess of the market rate of interest. Consider successive dollars invested starting from point A and moving leftward. The productivity of these investments is depicted by the slope of the transformation curve AB. However, note that this curve is initially much steeper than the slope of the interest curve shown as VW. Thus *even if initial resources were zero,* an individual could generate wealth by borrowing at a 10% interest rate and investing in projects yielding 20%. Investing $100 in this way would produce $120 at time 2. After paying back the debt at time 2 ($100 $\times$ 1.1 = $110), $10 of consumption would be left in time 2. Alternatively, the individual could borrow further against this $10 to yield $10/(1 + 0.1) = $9.01 of current consumption, even though he or she started with no wealth. The market value of such a firm would be $9.01, and since the value of initial resources was zero, the wealth created would also be $9.01. The process of creating wealth by exploiting investment opportunities is reflected in the rules for capital budgeting. Using discounted cash flow (DCF) analysis, projects should be accepted if their internal rates of return (IRR), defined as that rate which when used to discount a project's cash flows yields a zero net present value, exceed the prevailing interest rate. In our simple world, capital can be raised at this interest rate. Since the internal rate of return is reflected in the slope of the transformation curve AB in Figure 7-5, the IRR $> r$ rule is clearly observed by investing up to AD of initial resources.

2 The next two principles are referred to as *separation* principles. The first of these reveals that investment decisions can be made independently of the owners' time preferences. The optimal investment decision is made by reference to the cost of capital (or the interest rate) and the productivity of the investment, as described earlier. The independence of this decision from the utility functions of the owners leads to the use of the standardized evaluation criteria for capital projects described in capital budgeting texts. The second separation theorem is the other side of this coin.

3 The optimal consumption pattern over time for the owner of a firm is constrained by the wealth of the firm, but not by the temporal pattern of cash flows generated by the firm. The wealth of the firm is represented by the discounted value of incremental cash flows generated.

These separation principles are illustrated in Figure 7-6. Suppose the firm is created by individual 1, who starts with resources $0A$. By investing AD, a set of cash flows equal to $0D$ in period 1 and $0E$ in period 2 is created. The intention of the owner 1 is to then borrow DF to support a consumption profile of $C(1) = 0F$, $C(2) = 0G$. However, immediately after the firm has been created by individual 1, individual 2 appears and offers to buy the firm for its current market value. Thus the price for purchase of the firm is $0W$. Note that even though individual 2's utility function is entirely different from that of individual 1, there is no incentive to change the investment decision. Owner 2 is more thrifty, but he or she can most effectively defer consumption by continuing to produce in the profile $0D$, $0E$ and then lending HD at the market rate of interest. Thus owner 2 will reach the preferred position represented by $C(1) = 0H$, $C(2) = 0J$. Notice that the transformation curve AB is somewhat flatter than the interest line to the left of point X. This tells us that deferred consumption achieved by lending at the market interest rate will yield a higher return than that achieved by investment in productive assets. Thus the investment decision is inde-

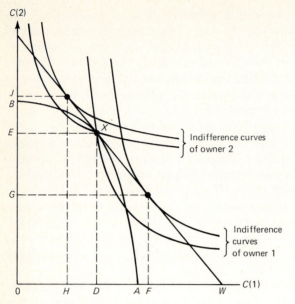

FIGURE 7-6

pendent of the owners' preferences, and the consumption pattern selected is constrained only by the value of the firm, $0W$. Both individuals are able to replicate their preferred consumption pattern from point W just by lending at the rate r. It is of further interest to note that individual 1 has reaped the benefits of the wealth-creation process, securing a real capital gain of $0W - 0A = AW$. However, individual 2 has paid $0W$ for acquisition of the firm, since this is the present value of the firm's incremental cash flows discounted at the rate r. Individual 2 will only secure the market rate of return r on the investment.

AN *EX POST* EVALUATION OF WEALTH DESTRUCTION

It will be recalled that earlier we reversed the process of wealth creation by considering the impact of a random event on the value of a firm. For that analysis, the random event struck immediately after the investment decision, and the task set was to evaluate the loss in terms of foregone wealth. This leads to a method of valuing losses that is distinct from the market value of the resources destroyed or the cost of making good the damage. We will now pursue this issue in a world of time preference and capital markets. However, we will retain our assumptions that the time 2 consequences of decisions made at time 1 are determinate.

In Figure 7-7 we reproduce the now familiar transformation curve AB as shown in Figure 7-2. Some hazard strikes immediately before resources $0A$ are allocated between current consumption and investment. Half the current market value of resources is lost

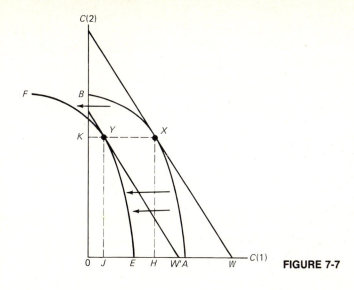

FIGURE 7-7

by this calamity. Now we can compare the wealth the firm would have attained had the event not occurred with the wealth that can now be achieved given that the event has occurred. The market value of the lost resources is simply $0A - 0E = EA$. Had the loss not arisen, the firm could have invested AH to generate the cash flows represented at point X. The wealth of the firm would have been $0W$. Since the loss *has* arisen, initial resources are only $0E$, and the wealth-maximizing strategy is to invest EJ to produce the cash flows represented at point Y. The value of the firm is now W'. *The impact of the loss can be measured in terms of the loss of market value of the ownership claims in the firm,* that is, $W - W'$. Let us now examine the relationship between the competing measures of the loss.

For notational convenience, let us refer to the market value of lost resources as MVLR and to the loss of market value of ownership of the firm (i.e., loss in market value of equity) as LMVE. Casual inspection of Figure 7-7 will reveal that the two measures seem to give the same result, that is, $W - W' = A - E$. Some reflection will reveal that this is indeed the case. The shape of the transformation curve is not affected by the initial level of resources. This is true because these resources can be freely purchased and sold. Thus if physical resources such as buildings, machinery, and inventories are destroyed, they can be replaced at a cost equal to their market value. In effect, all resources are undifferentiated, since they are perfectly interchangeable with cash at their market value and are therefore interchangeable with other physical resources. The transformation curve depends only on the technological aspects of production and on the marketing opportunities presented. Note that AB has simply shifted to the left to form HJ and the optimal level of investment is unchanged, resulting in no change in period 2 production. To press this point further, consider the following example.

EXAMPLE: ABBEY TEXTILES

Abbey Textiles owns 5 cutting machines and 50 sewing machines that are to be used for the manufacture of shirts and dresses. The sewing machines are valued at $500 each, and the cutting machines at $2000 each. Thus initial resources have a market value of $35,000. The firm also has liquid assets valued at $5000. The optimal investment decision is depicted in Figure 7-8 with the transformation curve AB. At an interest rate of 10%, the firm will invest all its machinery in productive use and declare a dividend of $5000 to its owners. The cash flow generated in period 2 is $55,000, and the value of the firm can be calculated as follows:

$$MV = A(1) + B(1) - I(1) + \frac{X(2) - (1 + r)B(1)}{1 + r} \tag{7-1}$$

$$= 40,000 + 0 - 35,000 + \frac{55,000 - (1 + r)0}{1 + r}$$

$$= 55,000$$

where $A(1)$ = initial resources

$B(1)$ = amount borrowed

$I(1)$ = amounted invested

$X(2)$ = cash flow generated in period 2

r = rate of interest

Now, a rented building housing the cutting machines is gutted by fire, totally destroying the machines. The building is insured by the owner, and Abbey has no liability for damage to the structure. Abbey is now left with total resources valued at $30,000 ($25,000 in sewing machines and $5000 cash). At first sight, it would appear that production must cease altogether, since the cutting process is essential to garment manufacture. If this were the case, the transformation curve would lie on the horizontal axis. But Abbey can undertake the following transaction: Borrow $10,000 at the prevailing interest rate of 10% to purchase five replacement cutting machines. These machines, together with the sewing machines, offer identical production opportunities to the original physical capital, and therefore, the transformation curve must have identical shape. However, the *position* of the transformation will have shifted leftward by $10,000 (reflecting initial wealth of $30,000), as shown by CD. The firm thus invests $35,000 ($10,000 in cutting machines and $25,000 in sewing machines, leaving a dividend of $5000 as before). The value of the firm is now derived as follows:

$$MV' = A(1)' + B(1)' - I(1)' + \frac{X(2)' - (1 + r)B(1)'}{1 + r} \tag{7-2}$$

$$= 30,000 + 10,000 - 35,000 + \frac{55,000 - (1.1)\,10,000}{1.1}$$

$$= 45,000$$

Thus the two loss-evaluation methods yield an identical result:

$$MVLR = A(1) - A(1)' = 40,000 - 30,000 = 10,000$$

$$LMVE = MV - MV' = 55,000 - 45,000 = 10,000$$

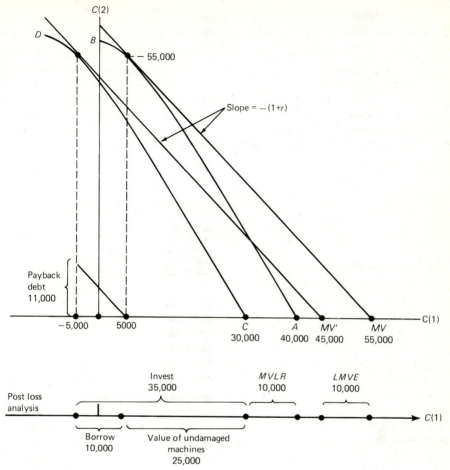

FIGURE 7-8

A quick examination of equations (7-1) and (7-2) reveals that this is inevitable if the firm maintains its investment at the preloss level:

$$
\begin{aligned}
MV - MV' &= \left[A(1) + B(1) - I(1) + \frac{X(2) - (1 + r)B(1)}{1 + r} \right] \\
&\quad - \left[A(1)' + B(1)' - I(1)' + \frac{X(2) - (1 + r)B(1)'}{1 + r} \right] \\
&= A(1) - A(1)' \qquad \text{if } I(1) = I(1)'
\end{aligned}
\tag{7-3}
$$

If Abbey chose *not* to reinvest, the market value of the firm would be the market value of available resources, which is simply the value of the surviving machines plus the cash, $30,000. Clearly, this is a suboptimal decision, since it is lower than the market value achieved from reinvestment. The actual amount borrowed is not critical as long as the reinvestment is undertaken. Suppose that after the fire, Abbey simply borrows $5000. This, together with the $5000 in cash, is sufficient to replace the destroyed cutting machines. The market value is

$$MV = 30,000 + 5000 - 35,000 + \frac{55,000 - 5000\,(1 + 0.1)}{1 + 0.1}$$

$$= 45,000$$

Indeed, inspection of equation (7-2) will reveal that $B(1)'$ cancels out, implying that the value is independent of the financing decision. Either the investment is financed from current cash resources (retained earnings) or from debt. In each case, however, the market rate of interest is the same. This irrelevance proposition is well known in the corporate finance literature, although it does require qualification when taxes, risk, and market imperfections are introduced.

MARKET VALUATION OF LOSSES AND THE USE OF FINANCIAL CRITERIA

The finding that losses to a firm can be valued equally well by using the effect on the market value of the firm or the value of the firm's resources is essential to our exploration of the usefulness of financial theory for risk management. Financial theory has developed a set of criteria for valuing investment projects and for selecting between alternative financing opportunities. These decisions become interdependent because the cost of capital provides a link between the decisions to raise capital and the decisions to use capital. The target return for capital-investment projects is determined by the cost of capital, and projects surpassing this rate will enhance the value of a firm. The use of value creation as a yardstick for financial decisions ensures both consistency in decision making over alternative project choices and that these choices are prudent in relation to the opportunity costs of alternative investment opportunities in the capital market.

The focus in risk management is to undertake activities that reduce the cost of (future) losses or that provide a means to finance such losses. The measurement of such losses can be undertaken by examining the impact on the value of a firm, and indeed, the evaluation of alternative sources of financing may be undertaken with the same value effects in mind. Risk management, therefore, appears to be a study of the sources and uses of funds for a narrowly defined set of purposes; corporate finance is simply the study of the wider set of financial decisions. However, we have shown that the value-creation criterion applies equivalently to the narrow set of risk management decisions and to the wider set of investment and financing decisions. Indeed, our point is somewhat stronger than an apology for using finance criteria for appraising risk management decisions. Since there are competing claims on the available resources of the firm, the most efficient allocation of those resources (that is, the allocation that maximizes the value of the firm) *demands* that the same criteria be used.

VALUATION OF LOSS WITH MULTIPLE TIME PERIODS

Ownership of a firm, or of its stock, bestows a stream of dividends on the owner that will continue for the life of the firm. The life of a firm is theoretically infinite; thus the anticipated dividends continue into the receding future. The value of ownership is derived from this cash stream, or more precisely, the value of the stock is simply the discounted value of dividends generated:

$$V(1) = \sum_{i=1}^{\infty} \frac{d_{i+1}}{(1+r)^i} \tag{7-4}$$

where $V(1)$ = ex dividend value of stock at time 1

d_{i+1} = dividend payable in year $i + 1$ to those stockholders of record at time i

The dividend may not be constant over time, and it is useful to allow for possible growth by including g, the rate of growth dividends. Our world is still riskless; thus the value of g is known:

$$V(1) = \sum_{i=1}^{\infty} \frac{d_2(1+g)^{i-1}}{(1+r)^i} \tag{7-5}$$

Fortunately, this expression reduces as follows, thereby avoiding the summation of an infinite number of terms:

$$V(1) = \frac{d_2}{(1+g)} \sum_{i=1}^{\infty} \left(\frac{1+g}{1+r} \right)^i \tag{7-6}$$

And this reduces to

$$V(1) = \frac{d_2}{1+g} \left[\frac{1}{1-(1+g)/(1+r)} - 1 \right] \tag{7-7}$$

$$= \frac{d_2}{r-g}$$

At this stage, it is convenient to borrow an equivalent result from finance theory. This uses the observation made earlier that the financing decision is irrelevant in our simple world. This is so because the opportunity costs of all forms of financing are identical. Therefore, the dividend policy of the firm does not affect the level of investment, and as a consequence, it does not affect the earnings profile of the firm over time, nor the firm's present value. Thus we can represent value in relation to the earnings stream:

$$V(1) = \sum_{i=1}^{\infty} \frac{X_i - I_i}{(1+r)^{i-1}} \qquad \text{where } X_1 \equiv A(1) \tag{7-8}$$

Now consider a firm that is launched by an investment of $I(1)$ dollars that will yield an earnings stream X_i, where $i = 1, 2, \ldots, n$. The initial resources of the firm are

$A(1)$, as earlier and the firm borrows $B(1)$ to help finance the investment using equation (7-5):

$$V(1) = A(1) + B(1) - I(1) + \sum_{i=2}^{n} \frac{X_i - R_i}{(1 + r)^i} \qquad (7\text{-}9)$$

where R_i is the repayment in year i. Note that the discounted value of the repayment schedule $\Sigma R_i/(1 + r)^i$ should equal $B(1)$, thus confirming the equivalence of equations (7-5) and (7-6). This repayment schedule will likely take the form of an annuity with a present value of $B(1)$. Thus,

$$R_i = \frac{B(1)}{\displaystyle\sum_{i=2}^{n} 1/(1 + r)^i} = \frac{B(1)}{@rn} \qquad (7\text{-}10)$$

where $@rn$ is the present value of an annuity of $1 for n years at $r\%$.

Thus reducing equation (7-9), we have

$$V(1) = A(1) + B(1) - I(1) + \sum_{i=2}^{n} \frac{X_i}{(1 + r)^i} + \left[\frac{B(1)}{\displaystyle\sum_{i=2}^{n} 1/(1 + r)^n} \right] \left[\sum_{i=2}^{n} \frac{1}{(1 + r)^n} \right]$$

$$= A(1) - I(1) + \sum_{i=2}^{n} \frac{X_i}{(1 + r)^i} \qquad (7\text{-}11)$$

Now, if a loss arises prior to the investment decision, reducing resources to $A(1)'$, the market value will be

$$V(1)' = A(1)' - I(1)' + \sum_{i=2}^{n} \frac{X_i'}{(1 + r)^i} \qquad (7\text{-}12)$$

However, since, from prior reasoning, the investment decision is unaffected by the loss, $I(1) = I(1)'$ and $X_i = X_i'$. Thus,

$$V(1) - V(1)' = A(1) - A(1)'$$

This confirms the equivalence of our two evaluation criteria MVLR and LMVE in the multiperiod context.

MARKET VALUE OF EQUITY AND MARKET VALUE OF THE FIRM

The main message to emerge thus far in this chapter is that the impact of loss can be equivalently measured in terms of the market value of the resources (or the market cost of repairing damage) or by the loss in market value of the ownership equity or ownership claims of the firm. Another valuation concept familiar in finance is the market value of the firm, which is defined as the market value of all the securities of the firm, including debt and equity. Recall that the market value of equity (MVE) is defined by

$$MVE_L = A(1) + B(1) - I(1) + \frac{X(2) - (1 + r)B(1)}{1 + r} \qquad (7\text{-}13)$$

for the leveraged firm in a two-period model. The market value of the firm (MVF) is the market value of the debt $B(1)$ plus the market value of equity MVE_L. Distinguishing between the all-equity firm [defined by $B(1) = 0$] and the leveraged firm, we can state the following market values:

$$MVF_E = A_E(1) - I(1) + \frac{X(2)}{1 + r} \qquad \text{(for the all-equity firm)} \qquad (7\text{-}14)$$

$$\begin{aligned} MVF_L &= B(1) + MVE_L \\ &= B(1) + \left[A_L(1) + B(1) - I(1) + \frac{X(2) - (1 + r)B(1)}{1 + r} \right] \qquad (7\text{-}15) \end{aligned}$$
(for the leveraged firm)

Recalling that investment $I(1)$ is independent of the means of financing, it follows that the leveraged firm can reduce the value of initial resources contributed by the owners from $A_E(1)$ to $A_E(1) - B(1)$. Therefore, $A_E(1) = A_L(1) + B(1)$. Straightforward substitution of this equality into equation (7-14) reveals that MVF_E and MVF_L are equal. Thus the market value of the firm is unaffected by the levels of leverage.

Let us now examine the impact of a loss on the market value of a firm. To do this we introduce a further example.

EXAMPLE: ARGOS

Argos Corporation has recently been founded to manufacture sports equipment. Its founder, Mr. R. Ghosh, has supplied the total capital required of $1 million, and he is Argos' sole shareholder. These funds have been used to purchase manufacturing equipment, inventory, etc. Mr. Ghosh estimates that the production transformation curve is linear up to the scale contemplated, such that $C(2) = 1.4I(1)$. $C(2)$ is the cash flow generated in period 2 from an investment of I in period 1. Just before production starts, a fire destroys half the equipment (i.e., the market value of the destroyed equipment is $500,000). The equipment is insured, and the insurance company agrees to pay the market value of the destroyed equipment, that is, $500,000. However, Mr. Ghosh argues that the real loss to him is the reduction in the market value of equity that should be calculated by taking the market values before and after the loss:

Can you use finance theory to resolve this conflict? Make the following assumptions:

a A single interest rate applies to all borrowing and lending. This rate is 10%.

b Argos is able to borrow at this rate to replace the destroyed equipment. Note that Argos had no debt before the fire.

c All equipment can be bought and sold freely. There are no transaction costs on such sales and purchases.

The apparent conflict between the insurance company's criterion and Ghosh's can be resolved simply with the prior analysis. The market value before loss is

$$MVE = A(1) + B(1) - I(1) + \frac{X(2) - (1 + r)B(1)}{1 + r}$$

$$= \$1,000,000 - \$1,000,000 + \frac{\$1,400,000}{1.1} = \$1,272,727$$

since no borrowing is undertaken. Before looking at the value after loss, recall that the optimal level of investment is independent of the method of financing. Thus, if the remaining resources are valued at \$500,000, it will pay Ghosh to borrow a further \$500,000 to restore the investment to \$1 million. (Each dollar borrowed earns 40 cents compared with a 10-cent interest cost.) Thus the market value after loss is

$$MVE' = \$500,000 + \$500,000 - \$1,000,000 + \frac{\$1,400,000 - 1.1(\$500,000)}{1.1}$$

$$= \$772,727$$

Therefore, the loss of market value of equity is \$500,000, which is exactly equal to the market value of the destroyed resources. Thus there is no conflict.

A Fallacious Argument by Ghosh

Ghosh may have been tempted to propose the market-value criterion by using the following calculation. Market value after loss is purported to be

$$[A(1) - L] - [I(1) - L] + \frac{1.4[A(1) - L]}{1 + r}$$

where L is the market value of destroyed resources, and 1.4 refers to the productivity of capital. Using this formula, Ghosh estimates the loss in market value to be

$$\$1,272,727 - \left[(\$1,000,000 - \$500,000) - (\$1,000,000 - \$500,000) \right.$$
$$\left. + \frac{1.4(\$1,000,000 - \$500,000)}{1.1} \right] = \$636,363$$

Check that you understand the fallacy of this argument.

Now look at the impact of loss on the market value of the firm. If the firm borrows $500,000 to replace the equipment, the value of the firm is the market value of equity, which is

$$\frac{\$1,400,000 - 1.1(\$500,000)}{1 + 1}$$

plus the market value of debt, which is

$$\frac{1.1(\$500,000)}{1.1}$$

totaling $1,272,727, which is exactly the same as before the loss. Thus in this world, the market value of the firm is unaffected by the loss.

The intuition behind the assertion that the market value of a firm is unaffected by a loss is as follows: The loss does not affect the optimal level of investment; thus it will pay the firm to replace the destroyed physical resources, financing this by the issue of new debt. However, the new debt is included in the market value of the firm. The economic loss is therefore the destruction in the value of the ownership claims. To maintain the same level of activity, the owners now have to allocate part of the output of the firm to the new debt holders.

RISK AND THE MEASUREMENT OF LOSS

The valuation model that has been developed assumed away the problem of risk. This was convenient because we wished to measure the impact of losses that had already arisen on the value of a firm. In assigning a value to the loss, we simply discounted the value of future cash flows generated by the firm. In a riskless world, these cash flows are known and are discounted at the prevailing risk-free interest rate. In reality, future cash flows will seldom be known with certainty. At best, the firm will only be able to describe its future cash flows in terms of probability distributions with an estimation of the mean values and perhaps the standard deviation. From earlier chapters we know that risk is an undesirable property to most investors, and the cost should therefore be made explicit in the valuation formula.

Since risk is assumed to impose a cost on the owners of a firm, the present value of future risky cash flows will have a lower absolute value than the present value of riskless payments that each have the same expected values. Therefore, risk will reduce the market value of the firm. Risk can be treated in two ways:

1 Use a higher discount rate than that which would be used in the absence of risk. The rate to be used is

$$r = r_f + \pi$$

where r is the risk-adjusted rate, r_f is the risk-free rate, and π is the risk premium.

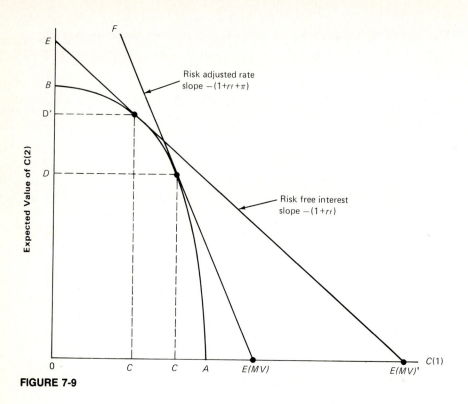

FIGURE 7-9

2 Replace the risky cash flows with certainty equivalents. These are defined as values which, if available with certainty, would convey the same utility as the original risky flows.

Our approach here is to use the risk-adjusted rate, and we will show the impact of risk on the valuation of a firm in both a two-period model and a multiperiod model.

Figure 7-9 reproduces the familiar transformation curve, although with an important difference. The time two values are now uncertain, and the vertical axis is denominated in expected values of $C(2)$ that are estimated to result from different levels of investment in year 1. Thus if AC is invested at time 1, the expected value of $C(2)$ is $0D$. In fact, actual production may turn out to be higher or lower due to chance factors. Notice that time 1 values are not risky because they represent resources that are actually committed to alternative uses by the firm's decisions. If we discount at the same rate used in the risk-free world, the optimal investment decision would be to invest AC', resulting in expected cash flow of $0D'$ in year 2. The value of the equity would then be

$$MV = A(1) + B(1) - I(1) + \frac{E[X(2)] - (1 + r_f)B(1)}{1 + r_f} \qquad (7\text{-}16)$$

$$= 0C' + \frac{0D'}{1 + r_f}$$

where $E(\cdot)$ denotes an expected value and $I(1)$ is determined by the condition

$$E(\text{IRR}) = r_f$$

In this case, the expected-value term signifies that expected cash flows have been used to determine the internal rate of return. In view of the riskiness of the period 2 values, the decision on investment will be made now in the light of the risk-adjusted rate:

$$E(\text{IRR}) = r_f + \pi \tag{7-17}$$

thereby resulting in a lower level of investment AC, as shown in Figure 7-9. The market value is now

$$MV = 0C + \frac{0D}{(1 + r_f + \pi)} \tag{7-18}$$

Risk has influenced the market value in two ways:

1 A higher hurdle rate has been set for investment, i.e., the risk-adjusted rate $r_f + \pi$. Normally, this will reduce the level of investment. The criterion for selecting projects is now

$$E(\text{IRR}) \geq r_f + \pi$$

2 Future cash flows are discounted at the higher risk-adjusted rate.

These ideas can easily be built into the multiperiod model simply by replacing the risk-free rate in equations (7-1) through (7-4) by the risk-adjusted rate. The general form for valuing equity becomes

$$V(1) = \frac{d_2}{(r_f + \pi) - g} \tag{7-19}$$

The analysis of the previous chapter can now be evoked to determine the risk premium π. Recall that the owners of a firm hold the firm's stock. The owners may well be averse to risk, but they do have open to them the facility for diversification by holding a portfolio of financial assets. Unsystematic risk is amenable to such simple diversification, and therefore, it is not costly to the firm's owners. However, investors will be interested in the systematic risk because this will determine the overall risk level of their investment portfolios. Consequently, firms exhibiting a high degree of systematic risk should be assigned a high discount rate, incorporating a high risk premium. High discount rates should also be applied when capitalizing individual projects of a firm that exhibit high systematic risk. Firms or projects with low systematic risk merit a low discount rate.

Using the capital asset pricing model, the form of the risk premium π is stated as follows:

$$\pi_i = \beta_i[E(r_M) - r_f] \tag{7-20}$$

where the subscript i refers to a particular firm or project. The corresponding discount rate is

$$r_i = r_f + \beta_i[E(r_M) - r_f] \tag{7-21}$$

Having allowed for riskiness of cash flows in this manner, the valuation of losses can proceed in a similar fashion to the risk-free case. The impact of actual loss is measured as the difference between the market value of the risky cash flows that would have been available to the owners of the firm had the loss not occurred and the market value of the cash flows that are expected to prevail now that the loss has arisen. This is the criterion LMVE used earlier.

In concluding this chapter, we will introduce some complicating factors that will require our attention in later chapters. Risk was introduced into the valuation model without requiring painful adaptation of the basic model. Losses could still be valued by measuring the loss in the market value of equity. However, risk may give rise to some indirect complications. The LMVE criterion was based on the prospect that a firm suffering loss could seek out sources of finance to replace the destroyed resources, thereby restoring the level of investment to that prevailing before the loss. This possibility for reinvestment permitted the firm to recapture some of the destroyed value and ensured that the two criteria for measuring loss, LMVE and MVLR, gave the same answer. However, risk will also affect the financing costs and may affect different types of financing, debt, equity, etc. to differing degrees. This is a subject of continuing debate in finance, but we may note at this stage that the costs of financing are relevant to a firm in measuring the effects of loss and that any differences between sources may affect the separation principle. That is, investment and financing decisions may affect each other. A second, related complication concerns the transaction costs of financing reinvestment. If a firm calculates that the impact of a loss can be minimized by replacing destroyed resources, then any costs associated with financing the reinvestment are properly considered as part of the effects of the loss. We have in mind transaction costs, such as underwriting costs for new debt and equity issues, together with drafting and legal expenses. These costs would not be picked up by the MVLR criterion, but they do affect the market value of equity. We have also ignored any loss of revenue during the interruption of business following the loss. Again, investors would tend to pick up this effect in valuing the firm, but it is ignored by the MVLR approach. These types of complications will focus our attention firmly on the effects of loss on the market value of equity in the following chapters.

SUMMARY AND CONCLUSION

The choices made by a firm concerning the sources of finance to support investment projects or the selection of competing investment projects will affect the value of the firm and the value of its equity. In corporate finance, the valuation criterion is used as a yardstick for decision making and decision rules, such as those used for capital budgeting have evolved. Risk management decisions are not fundamentally different from other corporate financial decisions, and the principal types of decisions concern (loss) financing and (loss reduction) investment. Compatibility with other financial decisions requires that similar criteria be used. This chapter shows how the value of a firm is determined and how value is affected by loss events.

The firm can use available resources to provide income for its owners or for investments that will yield future income. If no capital market exists, the optimal decision is that which balances the marginal productivity of investment with the time preference of the firm's owners. When a simple capital market is introduced, the production and consumption decisions can be separated, and decision rules can be derived that apply independent of the individual preferences of the firm's owners. The future production or earnings stream of the firm can be reduced to a present value. By borrowing and lending at prevailing interest rates, the owners can support any pattern of income over time that is permitted by the present value of the firm's earnings. The welfare of the owners will therefore be maximized by decisions that maximize the present value of earnings, i.e., that maximize the value of equity. It is also seen that the production decision is independent of the current resources of the firm, since the firm can borrow to reach its optimal position.

Losses can be fitted easily into this framework. Events such as fire and liability suits reduce the value of a firm's current resources. Since an optimal production decision is independent of the current resource value, we can show that it is optimal for a firm to restore the preloss level of production by raising new funds if necessary. Such action will minimize the impact of the loss on the firm's value. Under such simplified market conditions, we show that the market value of lost resources (MVLR) is equal to the reduction in market value of the firm's equity (LMVE). The change in equity value thereby provides a measure of loss. This result is shown to be robust when we look at a multiperiod model and when risk is introduced. However, we shall see that when imperfections are introduced, such as transaction costs and divergent borrowing and lending rates, the MVLR criterion fails to record the total cost of the loss event to a firm. In such circumstances, the market value of equity provides a correct basis for financial risk management decisions.

QUESTIONS

1 Construct a diagram to show why the optimal investment decisions of a firm are independent of its time preferences given perfect market assumptions.
2 Construct a second diagram to show why a loss may be equivalently measured by the loss in the market value of equity and the market value of lost resources. On what assumptions does this result rest?
3 Using algebraic definitions of market value of equity, demonstrate the same result shown diagramatically in question (2) above.

REFERENCES

Bierman, H. J., and S. Smidt: *The Capital Budgeting Decision*, Macmillan, New York, 1970.
Bogue, M. C., and R. Roll: "Capital Budgeting of Risky Projects with 'Imperfect' Markets for Physical Capital," *Journal of Finance*, vol. 29, 1974, pp. 601–613.

Fama, E. F.: "Risk-Adjusted Discount Rates and Capital Budgeting Under Uncertainty," *Journal of Financial Economics,* vol. 5, 1977, pp. 3–24.

Hill, J., and T. Scheeweis: "The Effect of Three Mile Island on Electric Utility Stock Prices: A Note," *Journal of Finance,* vol. 38, 1983, pp. 1285–1292.

Levy, H., and M. Samatt: *Capital Investment and Financing Decisions,* Prentice-Hall, Englewood Cliffs, N.J., 1978.

Litzenberger, R. H., and O. M. Joy: "Decentralized Capital Budgeting Decisions and Shareholder Wealth Maximization." *Journal of Finance,* vol. 30, 1975, pp. 993–1007.

Mao, J. C. T.: "Survey of Capital Budgeting: Theory and Practice," *Journal of Finance,* vol. 25, 1970, pp. 349–360.

Myers, S. C., and S. M. Turnbull: "Capital Budgeting and the Capital Asset Pricing Model: Good News and Bad News," *Journal of Finance,* vol. 32, 1977, pp. 321–336.

Sarnatt, M., and H. Levy: "The Relationship of Rules of Thumb to Internal Rates of Return: A Restatement and Generalization," *Journal of Finance,* vol. 24, 1969, pp. 479–489.

Sprecher, C. R., and M. Pertl: "Large Losses, Risk Management and Stock Prices," *Journal of Risk and Insurance,* vol. 50, 1983, pp. 107–117.

CHAPTER **8**

REINVESTMENT AND ABANDONMENT FOLLOWING LOSS

In the previous chapter we examined the impact of a loss on the value of the owners' equity in a firm. Under perfect market conditions, we were able to show that the loss may be equivalently valued as the reduction in the market value of the equity (similarly, the reduction in net worth) or as the market value of the resources destroyed. The loss could equivalently be valued in the product market or the capital market. To demonstrate this equivalence required, *inter alia,* assumptions that destroyed resources could be replaced immediately without transaction costs and that financing was available, again without transaction costs. Under these conditions, there was no question that the firm would choose to restore its investment to the preloss level by replacing the destroyed resources. In this chapter we will examine this reinvestment decision in more detail, relaxing the somewhat burdensome assumptions that limited the reality of the model. In the next chapter we will examine the financing opportunities available to a firm after a loss.

REINVESTMENT FOLLOWING LOSS: UNDIFFERENTIATED RESOURCES

Recalling Chapter 7, the optimal scale of investment was determined by the equality of the internal rate of return on investment and the interest rate (or cost of capital). By accepting all projects for which the internal rate of return exceeds the cost of capital, down to the marginal project, the value of a firm will be maximized. In order to trace the impact of loss on the value of a firm and its equity, we permitted the firm to replace all destroyed or damaged resources so that production was restored to its preloss level. The logic behind this argument was that given our assumptions, nothing had happened to change the relationship between the productivity of capital and the cost of financing; therefore, the optimal level of investment had not changed. The only thing that had changed was that the need to finance the loss had led the firm to issue new claims in the form of new debt or new equity and that part of the future output of the firm would be allocated to these new claimholders. In this world, the firm would simply reinvest resources to replace those destroyed or damaged and continue production as before.

Two assumptions that were used in the analysis leading to this conclusion were (1) that physical resources were undifferentiated, and (2) that physical resources could be bought and sold freely with no transaction costs. Assumption 1 carries some definite implications for the effect of loss on the shape and position of the production transformation curve. Consider Figure 8-1, in which a preloss transformation curve is shown as AB. Initial resources are, therefore, represented as $0A$. Since resources are undifferentiated, we can view these either in purely liquid form (money) or as physical resources, these being perfect substitutes for each other, as with the sewing machines used by Abbey in Chapter 7. Since all sewing machines are capable of producing exactly the same output, it is a matter of indifference which particular machines happen to be destroyed. The only relevant factor about loss is the *scale* of loss: What proportion of the machines was destroyed in the fire? This will determine the proportion of preloss capacity at which the firm is able to operate. However, if 50% of interchangeable machines are destroyed, this does not imply that 50% of the cash flow $C(2)$ can be generated. The transformation curve is concave, reflecting diminishing productivity of resources at the margin. Since resources are interchangeable, this diminishing productivity cannot be due to physical features of particular resources; it is due to such other factors as organizational diseconomies of scale, the inelastic supply of labor and other resources (which causes the firm to bid up the supply price to increase output), and the downward slope of the demand curve (which requires the firm to

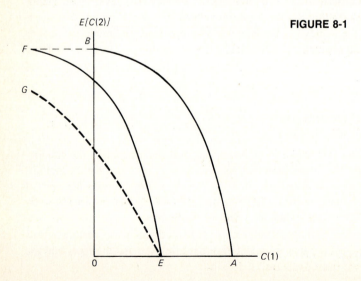

FIGURE 8-1

reduce its supply price to expand output). These considerations imply that a loss will simply shift the transformation curve to the left but will not alter its shape. This is shown in Figure 8-1 by a new curve *EF*. Notice that the effect would be exactly the same if the resources were in purely liquid form and the loss was simply a depletion in value, e.g., through a liability claim. The investment opportunities would not change, nor would the optimal scale of investment. The liability claim does cause the firm to seek alternative financing to sustain this level of investment.

EXAMPLE: LAWN GREEN GARDENING SERVICES

Lawn Green Gardening Services operates a lawn-care service in a large city. Its main equipment is a fleet of vehicles that carry and dispense fertilizers, insecticides, weed-treatment chemicals, etc. The transformation curve for this operation is concave, reflecting the limited size of the urban market and the increasing difficulties of maintaining competing market share from rival firms as Lawn Green grows. The transformation curve is represented mathematically as $10I^{0.6}$, where I is the value of investment in vehicles in thousands of dollars. However, since the vehicles are identical, the loss of one or more does not cause any critical bottlenecks, but merely reduces the overall size of operations. In fact, remaining vehicles can partly make up the loss of business by working overtime, but this entails higher costs both in terms of higher wage rates and increased depreciation and maintenance costs for equipment. Note that the firm could have chosen to restrict the size of its fleet and incur these costs *before* loss. The fact that it had chosen not to do so suggests that the rate of return on additional vehicles exceeded the cost of capital; thus market value would be increased by adding to the fleet. Two vehicles with a combined value of 10 (thousand dollars) are destroyed in a fire while garaged. The cost of capital to the firm is 10%. Should the firm reinvest to restore the equipment destroyed in the loss?

Solution

First, we calculate the optimal level of investment before loss. To calculate this, we simply choose the level of investment that maximizes market value:

$$\left[\max_{I} \frac{C(2)}{(1+r)} - I\right] = \frac{10I^{0.6}}{1.1} - I$$

$$\frac{\partial MV}{\partial I} = \frac{6}{1.1}I^{-0.4} - 1 = 0 \quad \text{or} \quad I^{0.4} = \frac{1.1}{6}$$

Therefore, $I = 69.5$ and $C(2) = 10(69.5)^{0.6} = 127.4$.[1] Thus the internal rate of return is

$$\frac{127.4 - 69.5}{69.5} = 83.3\%$$

Since the equipment is undifferentiated, the postloss transformation curve is identical to the preloss curve, and the firm will find its output reduced as follows:

[1]Note that if the vehicles are valued at 5 (thousand dollars) apiece, the value of I may be roughly considered to be 70 (thousand dollars), representing 14 vehicles.

$$C(2)' = 10(69.5 - 10)^{0.6} = 116.1$$

Now consider whether the firm should replace the vehicles. If one vehicle is replaced for 5 (thousand dollars), production will increase to

$$C(2)'' = 10(69.5 - 10 + 5)^{0.6} = 121.8$$

which represents an additional return of

$$\frac{(121.8 - 116.1) - 5}{5} = 14\%$$

Since this return exceeds the cost of capital of 10%, clearly the firm should replace the vehicle. What about replacing the second vehicle? Production will increase form 121.8 to the preloss level of 127.4, which, on reinvestment of 5 (thousand dollars), represents a return of 12%. Again, this exceeds the cost of capital, so the firm should reinvest. The reader should check that investment in another additional vehicle is unwarranted and reconcile this with the original preloss level of investment.

This example illustrates that when destroyed resources are undifferentiated from those undamaged, and when perfect markets exist for replacing these resources and for financing the replacements, a firm should always reinvest to restore the original level of operations.

REINVESTMENT WITH PRODUCTION INTERDEPENDENCIES

Now suppose that resources are not undifferentiated. For example, Abbey has cutting machines as well as sewing machines, and although this was not included in the previous example, it has a computer that it uses to maintain its accounts for clients, employees, taxes, etc. If a fire does arise, it would probably cause different degrees of damage to the computer, the sewing machines, and the cutting machines. For example, the sewing machine room may be completely gutted, but other operations may be unaffected. In this case, the postloss transformation curve would have a very different shape than the preloss curve. The most extreme outcome would be that all activity ceases completely, since Abbey sells completed garments and the process cannot continue without the sewing machines. In this case, the postloss transformation curve would simply lie on the horizontal axis; that is, remaining resources would yield no production in period 2. Short of this extreme, other possibilities arise. Abbey could employ a contractor to finish garments for delivery to its customers. The fact that subcontracting had not been undertaken previously implies that it is more costly than in-house production, and accordingly, we may construct a postloss transformation curve such as *EG* in Figure 8-1. The vertical distance between *EF* and *EG* represents the additional costs of subcontracting in terms of foregone period 2 cash flow. The destruction of the sewing machines represents an example of the effect of a selective loss on an interdependent production process.

EXAMPLE: BAKER CORPORATION

Baker Corporation manufactures cookies. Its equipment includes dough mixers, ovens, and packaging equipment. Its production possibilities can be summarized by the transformation curve $C(2) = 16I^{0.75}$, where I is the dollar investment in period 1. Since its cost of capital is 20%, Baker has determined that its optimal level of investment is I^* dollars. The risk manager estimates the effect of a total loss of the packaging department due to specified perils. The market value of the packaging equipment is $3600, and the equipment can be replaced immediately for this price should it be destroyed. Because of interdependencies in the production process, the risk manager estimates that $C(2)$ would be reduced to $C(2)' = 16I'^{0.5}$, where I' is the value of resources left after the loss. A fire occurs, destroying all packaging equipment. Calculate the rate of return to the firm from reinvesting in packaging equipment to restore operations to the preloss level.

Solution

First, it is necessary to calculate the optimal level of investment before loss, that is, I^*. Baker will choose to maximize the market value:

$$MV = \frac{C(2)}{1 + r} - I$$

We can establish the maximizing level by taking the derivative with respect to I and setting this to zero:

$$\text{Max}_I \left[\frac{C(2)}{1 + r} - I \right] = \frac{16I^{0.75}}{1.1} - I$$

$$\frac{\partial MV}{\partial I} = \frac{12I^{-0.25}}{1.2} - 1 = 0 \qquad \text{or} \qquad I^{0.25} = 10$$

Therefore, $I^* = 10,000$. In addition,

$$C(2) = 16(10,000)^{0.75} = 16,000$$

Now, after the loss, the remaining value of resources is $6400. Using the postloss transformation function, these resources will produce

$$16(6400)^{0.5} = \$1280$$

Note that because of the interdependencies, a loss of $3600 (36% of the total value of resources) results in a loss of period 2 cash flow of $(16,000 - 1280) = \$14,720$, or 92% of the original cash flow. The dramatic reduction in revenue resulting from the loss arises because the mix of different resources required for efficient operation has been disturbed. Consequently, some equipment will be in such short supply that bottlenecks arise, leaving other equipment idle. Under these conditions, reinvestment to restore the production mix will yield a very high rate of return because it will restore the firm from the (inefficient) postloss transformation curve to the original transformation function. The optimal scale of production is exactly the same as it was before the loss, and the return on postloss reinvestment turns out to be high. Note the internal rate of return (IRR) on the original investment was

$$\text{IRR} = \frac{16,000 - 10,000}{10,000} = 60\%$$

However, the IRR on the reinvestment to restore the investment to its preloss level is

$$\text{IRR}' = \frac{(16,000 - 1280) - 3600}{3600} = 309\%$$

Clearly, postloss reinvestment is highly desirable.

If we compare this example with the previous one, in which products were undifferentiated, there is clearly added force to the argument for reinvestment. On the one hand, reinvestment to make good the damaged resources puts the firm back on its original transformation curve, thereby restoring some appropriate balance in the specialized inputs within the production process. Furthermore, reinvestment restores the scale of operations to a level that has already been determined to be desirable because it represents the level of investment that maximizes the market value of the firm. We will consider a third case, in which the resources destroyed are underproductive, in the sense that the marginal internal rate of return from investment in these inputs is less than the cost of capital. We will describe such resources as *redundant*. However, before doing this, let us collect together our results so far.

REINVESTMENT IN PERFECT MARKETS: SUMMARY

It will be recalled that we started with the assumptions that all products were undifferentiated and that markets (both capital and product markets) were perfect. We retained the assumptions that capital and product markets were perfect and considered the effect of relaxing the assumption that products were undifferentiated. We will now generalize the results beyond the examples chosen.

Consider the original transformation curve before loss to be given as $f_1(I)$, where I is the level of investment. This is shown in Figure 8-2 as curve AB. The optimal level of investment is defined as I^*, shown as AC in the figure. Note that for all $I < I^*$, the internal rate of return on $f_1(I)$ exceeds the cost of capital r. The tangency position is shown where $\text{IRR} = r$. The loss is AE, which will be represented in algebraic notation as I_L. Following the loss, the transformation curve will be EF if resource inputs are undifferentiated. However, recall that the production transformation curve is unaffected by financing considerations and that EF is simply AB shifted horizontally leftward by the value of the loss. Thus $EF = f_1(I)$, and the optimal level of investment with this curve is $EH (= AC)$, which will restore production to the preloss level $C_0(2)$. If resource inputs are specialized, then depending on which particular inputs are destroyed, we will end up with a transformation curve such as EG [or $f_2(I)$], which lies below EF for any level of investment.

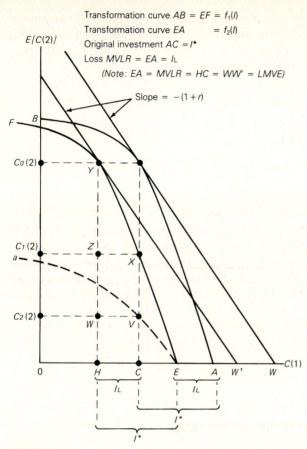

FIGURE 8-2

As a result of loss, the market value of invested resources falls from AC to EC (or I_L), and the loss of period 2 revenue is

$$C_0(2) - C_1(2) = f_1(I^*) - f_1(I^* - I_L) \qquad (8\text{-}1)$$

if resources are undifferentiated, or

$$C_0(2) - C_2(2) = f_1(I^*) - f_2(I^* - I_L) \qquad (8\text{-}2)$$

if resources are specialized and interdependent. Now consider the payback to reinvestment. First, with undifferential resources, the internal rate of return is

$$\text{IRR}_1 = \frac{f_1(I^*) - f_1(I^* - I_L) - I_L}{I_L} = \frac{ZY - HC}{HC} \qquad (8\text{-}3)$$

This reinvestment takes us from point X on EF to point Y to restore the total investment to EH (which is identical to the original investment AC). This segment of the production transformation curve is clearly steeper than the interest time, indicating that $IRR_1 > r$, which confirms that the reinvestment should be undertaken.

With specialized and interdependent resources, the payback to reinvestment is

$$IRR_2 = \frac{f_1(I^*) - f_2(I^* - I_L) - I_L}{I_L} = \frac{WY - HC}{HC} \tag{8-4}$$

However, notice that this can be broken down into the following components:

$$IRR_2 = \frac{[f_1(I^*) - f_1(I^* - I_L)] + [f_1(I^* - I_L) - f_2(I^* - I_L)] - I_L}{I_L}$$

Notice that the first part of this return (in the first set of brackets in the numerator) is exactly the same as we saw in the case of undifferentiated resources. This component alone is sufficient to justify reinvestment. In addition, however, we have a second component: the second set of brackets, which represents the additional return due to restoration of balance in the input mix. This component is positive, although its size depends on the severity of production bottlenecks caused by the loss. Thus we may think of the internal rate of return on reinvestment as comprising:

1 A return from restoring the optimal *scale* of investment.
2 An additional return from restoring the optimal *mix* of resource inputs.

Finally, we draw together the implications in terms of the loss of market value of equity (LMVE), as discussed earlier. The value of the equity before loss is shown in the usual manner as $0W$, and this falls to $0W'$ after the loss. Notice again that

$$LMVE = W'W = HC = MVLR$$

That is, the loss is identical whether measured as the market value of lost resources or as the loss in market value of the firm's equity. Therefore, the following theorem applies:

> LMVE is unaffected by production interdependencies, since these do not affect the decision to restore the level of operations to that prevailing before a loss.

REINVESTMENT AND REDUNDANT ASSETS

Recalling our definition of redundant assets, the marginal internal rate of return generated from investment in these assets is less than the firm's cost of capital. This redundancy might arise either through *scale* or *mix*. If the marginal internal rate of return from a firm's investments exceeds the cost of capital, then investments beyond this point are redundant. However, it is feasible that a firm may be operating within its optimal scale yet still have redundant assets because the input balance is inappropriate. For example, Abbey (which was discussed in Chapter 7) had 50 sewing machines and 5 cutting machines. Suppose that this investment was value-maximizing both in terms of scale and in terms of the ratio of 10:1 sewing-to-cutting machines. With 20 sewing machines and 2 cutting machines, the mix would be fine, but the scale would be too small. Further investment would be warranted to maintain scale, but purchase of another 3 cutting machines might well lead to redundancy.

From the previous discussion, it should be perfectly clear that if assets are redundant and they can be sold without transaction costs, the value of a firm will increase if it sells those assets. This argument has some symmetry. Calling the dollar value of investment in redundant assets I_R, the market value of the firm will fall on the purchase of redundant assets by

$$\frac{I_R(1 + \text{IRR})}{1 + r} \tag{8-5}$$

where IRR = internal rate of return
      r = cost of capital
      $r > \text{IRR}$

However, since our assumption of a perfect product market ensures that disposal of the assets will yield their market value I_R, the value of the firm will increase by the value shown above on their disposal. Accordingly, if such assets are owned, the firm is failing to maximize its market value, and such a position could not exist in equilibrium. However, if such assets were owned and were destroyed by some peril, then reinvestment is not called for on the basis of our financial criterion. The loss provides a suitable opportunity for *abandoning* the investment, and if it were fully insured, the value of the firm would increase on payment of (or in anticipation of) the insurance money.

A common fear of insurers is that policyholders might deliberately induce loss in order to secure payment of the insurance money. Arson, in particular, appears to give rise to special concern. However, in our simple world, such moral hazard should not exist unless the individual is permitted to overinsure. The payback from employing a "torch" to burn a building and claiming the policy money is exactly the same as that from selling the property in a less sinister transaction. In fact, the payback from a sale is higher if one accounts for the prospective costs of civil or criminal proceedings.

In summary, if equilibrium conditions prevail, firms would not own redundant assets. Consequently, the marginal internal return from reinvestment after loss would always exceed the cost of capital and thus firms would always reinvest. However, the real world is not continuously in a state of equilibrium, and firms may have redundant assets. If so, reinvestment to replace these assets will reduce the value of the firm, and the loss should provide the stimulus for abandonment of these assets. In all cases, the appropriate financial criterion for reinvestment is that it should increase the value of a firm. This will normally be the case if the marginal internal rate of return exceeds the cost of capital.[2]

In a world of perfect markets, the only situation in which it will make sense to abandon an investment after loss, rather than reinvest to restore the investment, arises when a firm has failed to achieve a preloss value-maximizing position. When the assumption of perfect markets is relaxed, the circumstances under which investments should be abandoned after loss become more important.

EXAMPLE: LAWN GREEN GARDENING SERVICES

Consider the case of Lawn Green Gardening Services discussed earlier. Suppose that the firm had originally invested 79.5 (thousand dollars) but had lost the same two vehicles in a garage fire. The reinvestment of 10 (thousand dollars) would yield the following cash flow:

$$10(79.5)^{0.6} - 10(69.5)^{0.6} = 10.7$$

The rate of return thus generated on the reinvestment is

$$\frac{10.7 - 10}{10} = 7\%$$

Since the cost of capital is 10%, the reinvestment should not have been undertaken.

MARKET IMPERFECTIONS AND ABANDONMENT

In the cozy world of perfect markets, the firm that chooses not to reinvest after a loss would face the unnerving dilemma that either it was failing to make the correct investment decision after the loss or it had maintained an incorrect level of investment before the loss. Such judgments cannot be made so easily with transaction costs. Before introducing imperfections, let us clarify exactly what we mean by abandonment.

The rules of capital budgeting can be turned on their head to indicate when an existing project, or indeed an existing firm, should be abandoned. Perhaps all investment projects involve some degree of risk, and this is reflected in the uncertainty attaching to estimations of future cash flows. Furthermore, information pertinent to the cash-flow estimates will be revealed progressively over time, although complete information may never be available beforehand. Thus estimates of future cash flows may be revised throughout the lifetime of a project.

---

[2]This statement avoids problems often encountered with the use of IRR, such as the issue of multiple returns. This issue cannot arise in a two-period analysis because cash flows must exhibit more than one sign change. The problem is relevant to multiple time periods, however.

EXAMPLE: PROGRESSIVE GROCERS

Progressive Grocers has located a large grocery store in a new town that has developed around
an important mineral deposit. The decision to go ahead was warranted on estimates of population
growth, which were, in turn, contingent on estimates of future mineral prices. Another important
factor in estimating cash flows was whether any competitors were also located in the town.
However, it was judged that the threat from competition was probably only severe in the first
2 years; after that, a dominant market position would have been reached and new competitors
would have little success encroaching on the market share. After the 2-year period has transpired,
the firm will have monitored *actual* growth together with attempts by competing firms to establish
a foothold in the market. Accordingly, revised estimates of future cash flows can be made. If
mineral prices slump, causing low population growth, or if a competitor is extraordinarily
successful, Progressive may revise its remaining cash flow estimates downward, and this may
cause it to consider whether it should abandon the project.

The decision to undertake an investment project at some time 0 can be appraised
on the basis of the discounted value of the projected cash flows $\tilde{C}_{i,0}$ projected for year
i but estimated at time 0:

$$\text{NPV}_0 = \sum_{i=0}^{n} \frac{\tilde{C}_{i,0}}{(1 + r_0)^i} \tag{8-6}$$

where r_0 is a suitable risk-adjusted discount rate. Since the cash flows are defined to
include the investment costs, a positive value for the term NPV_0 is sufficient to warrant
adoption of the project. For simplicity, we label $C_{0,0}$ as the investment cost $-I_0$ and
$C_{i,0}$ $(i > 0)$ as positive cash flows. Now consider the same project 2 years later,
assuming it has been adopted. The values $C_{0,0}$ and $C_{0,1}$ will already be known, and
the firm will be able to make a new set of estimates $\tilde{C}_{i,2}$ that are, hopefully, improvements on the original estimates made at time 0. Furthermore, these estimates may
have different risk characteristics, warranting a different discount rate r_2. In this period,
and presumably any other, the firm faces a new decision on whether it should continue
with the project or abandon. Calling the abandonment value at time 2, AV_2, the firm
should abandon the project if

$$AV_2 \equiv S_2 - \sum_{i=2}^{n} \frac{\tilde{C}_{i,2}}{(1 + r_2)^i} > 0 \tag{8-7}$$

where S_2 is the value that can be realized from immediate sale. This rule was proposed
by Robichek and Van Horne (1967), although a somewhat modified verison by Joy
(1976) incorporates the possibility that the abandonment value might be increased by
delaying the abandonment decision. For simplicity, we will keep with the simpler rule,
mentally noting the possibility of deferred abandonment.

Now consider what would happen if the project were destroyed by some peril. If the following criterion is satisfied, the firm should be willing to reinvest if

$$\text{NPV}_2 > -I_2 + \sum_{i=2}^{n} \frac{\tilde{C}_{i,2}}{(1 + r_2)^i} \tag{8-8}$$

Comparing NPV_2 and AV_2, it is apparent that with a perfect market, $S_2 = -I_2$. Thus, as we have shown, either

1 Abandonment prior to loss is not warranted, and therefore, postloss reinvestment should be undertaken, *or*
2 Abandonment opportunities should have been realized before loss, but since they were not, postloss reinvestment should not be undertaken.

With market imperfections, $S_2 \neq -I_2$. Normally, the relationship will be $S_2 < I_2$. Consequently, *there may be many cases of firms that are quite rationally maintaining existing operations but which should not replace those operations should they be subject to sudden loss.* This proposition could alternatively refer to a specific project undertaken by a firm or to the firm's entire operations. The latter case raises awkward questions for those texts which assert that survival should be an objective of the risk management process (see, for example, Rosenbloom, 1972; and Mehr and Hedges, 1974).

An examination of the basic NPV formula will reveal the circumstances in which it will be rational for a firm to abandon a project before or after loss. Reproducing the abandonment criterion and setting the current period as 0, the firm should abandon if

$$S_0 - \sum_{i=0} \frac{\tilde{C}_{i,0}}{(1 + r_0)^i} > 0 \tag{8-9}$$

If postloss abandonment is selected, it would appear that important changes have arisen in the economic circumstances of the project. The factors that might have changed since the original investment was undertaken are (1) appreciation of abandonment values, (2) revision of cash-flow estimates, (3) revision of risk costs, or (4) phasing out of an old project. We will consider each in turn.

1 *Appreciation of abandonment values.* London's gentlemen's clubs are part of a middle-class English tradition in which men can take refuge from the hustle and bustle of the city and feminine conversation. Apart from female militancy and contributory causes, the demise of many of the clubs is due to the fact that their premises, acquired in a quieter age in prime central London locations, became valuable sites for alternative city development. Thus abandonment may arise not because of any failure of a project, but simply because it consumes resources that acquire higher value in alternative use.

2 *Revision of cash-flow estimates.* Sharp Dealers operates an automobile showroom. Although the showroom was only established in 1978, it has been severely hit by a slump in automobile sales, due partly to the recent unprecedented levels of interest rates. In trying to reach a decision as to whether to continue with the showroom, Sharp has prepared new estimates of future cash flows that differ considerably from those prepared in 1978, when few believed that interest rates could ever have approached the levels seen in the 1980s.

3 *Revision of the cost of capital.* In revising the expected values of its future cash flows, Sharp has become acutely aware of the potential volatility of future interest rates and their effect on the automobile industry. Thus, in addition to downward revision of the expected cash flows, it has increased the risk premium in its discounting rate. This has led to further downward revision (NPV) of future cash flows. Such a revision in the discounting rate will often accompany a revision in the estimated cash flows, since the expected value of cash flows, the standard deviation, and the correlation with market indices may be simultaneously affected by changing market circumstances.

4 *Phasing out of old projects.* Many old projects using older technologies may still yield positive cash flows even though the equipment used in their production may have no alternative use and therefore little disposal value. If the disposal value is zero, any positive cash flows will add to the market value of the firm. In this case, abandonment before loss would not be called for, although abandonment after loss would be appropriate.

PRELOSS AND POSTLOSS ABANDONMENT

The issue of whether abandonment should arise before or after loss depends on the relationship between the disposal value of the resources used in the project and the cost of reinvesting to replace those resources. The choices and solutions can be summarized quite succinctly as follows:

1 In situations where

$$S_0 > \sum_{i=0}^{n} \frac{\tilde{C}_{i,0}}{(1 + r_0)^i} \tag{8-10}$$

since the discounted value of the cash flows is less than the disposal value, the project should be abandoned without waiting for a loss to arise. A qualification already noted is that the firm may choose to delay abandonment if it expects the abandonment value to rise by more than the cost of capital. If the firm has not grasped the opportunity to abandon (either through deliberate delay or through failure to perceive the opportunity) and a loss arises, the project should be abandoned at the time of loss.

2 In situations where

$$S_0 < \sum_{i=0}^{n} \frac{\tilde{C}_{i,0}}{(1 + r_0)^i} < I_0 \tag{8-11}$$

the firm should not abandon the project as a continuing operation, since the disposal value of assets is lower than their value in continued current use. However, reinvestment should not be undertaken if a loss arises. The larger the differential between S_0 and I_0, the more likely we are to encounter firms that may use the occasion of a fortuitous loss to abandon a project or even to exit from the industry. Furthermore, this can be viewed as a perfectly rational decision, since reinvestment will not generate returns as high as the cost of capital; thus more attractive investment opportunities exist elsewhere. Notice that this conclusion was reached independently of loss financing considerations. If the firm had arranged insurance on a replacement-value basis, the policy would pay the value I_0, but even with this money available, it makes little sense to commit it to unproductive reinvestment, since the opportunity cost of such reinvestment (indicated by the cost of capital) still indicates more attractive alternatives.

3 In situations where

$$I_0 < \sum_{i=0}^{n} \frac{\tilde{C}_{i,0}}{(1 + r_0)^i} \tag{8-12}$$

abandonment is not appropriate, and the firm will add to its value by postloss reinvestment. A qualification we might draw is that if the firm is under capital-rationing constraints and has an alternative project that will yield greater value, the firm might use the loss to switch direction. However, such rationing does not correspond with the assumptions we have made so far.

EXAMPLE: BETTER DAYS MILLINERY

Better Days Millinery makes ladies' and gentlemen's hats. It had been a small but profitable operation, but changing fashions have led to a decline in demand. It still has a small market using old equipment and a small, aging work force of loyal employees. The equipment has little disposal value, although the purchase of new equipment would be expensive. Furthermore, the firm occupies premises in an inner-city area for which property rentals have declined substantially in recent years. The disposal value of the firm is $1 million, considerably less than the book value of assets of $5 million. However, the firm still has market value of $1.5 million, and operations continue. The replacement cost of assets is estimated to be $4 million. Should major loss arise, Better Days' management has determined that it will cease operations. The management is also acutely aware of declining demand, but has determined that, short of catastrophe, it will not close operations during the next 5 years, when it estimates that its key workers will have retired. This loyalty to the work force will be maintained even if the market value should fall below the disposal value of its assets. Thus the firm anticipates the possibility that it may fall under category 1 above, but it will not choose the value-maximizing criterion of abandonment until its noneconomic objectives have been met.

INTERRUPTION LOSS

The impact of a loss on a firm may not be confined to the loss in market value of the resources destroyed or to the loss of value arising directly from the payment of a liability claim. Many losses, especially large losses, cause some interruption of the trading of a firm either because its production flow is disturbed, because depleted inventory is insufficient to meet peak demand, or perhaps because the loss itself has an adverse effect on the demand for the firm's products. Some brief examples will help to clarify:

True Sincerity Greeting Cards sustains serious damages in its warehouse when a sprinkler accidentally discharges. The leak is undetected because the alarm fails, and large stocks of Christmas cards are destroyed. The loss arises in mid-November. The company's production strategy is to produce steadily over the year, building up inventory for the Christmas demand. Even though production is undisturbed, the peak demand cannot be met, resulting in severe loss of earnings.

Fred Bear Carpets manufactures rugs that are sold by a major retailing outlet under its own trading label. A severe fire destroys the plant, and reconstruction takes some 4 months. Fred Bear carried no inventory, since all output was delivered immediately to its customer. The result is a severe interruption in trading with substantial loss of earnings.

A class action liability suit is brought against Michael Finn Pharmaceuticals after it transpires that the tranquilizers it manufactures have produced serious side effects in a number of users; resulting in a state of coma. Even though the case has not been disposed of in the courts, the resulting alarm causes a slump in sales of the company's other products.

In each of these examples, the loss of earnings is independent of any decision to reinvest. True Sincerity will presumably wish to return to its inventory policy for future years, but immediate replacement of the destroyed cards is impossible. Similarly, Fred Bear will reconstruct its plant, but this takes considerable time. With Michael Finn, reinvestment is not really the issue, since production capacity has not been destroyed. The interruption may turn out to be temporary. Consumers may forget Finn's lawsuit, and Fred Bear's outlet may carry itself on its own inventory until production is reestablished. However, some permanent shift in trading may result. When a firm is "out of business" for some time, competitors may steal into the market and capture a market share that may be extremely difficult to win back when production continues. For example, Fred Bear's customer, desperate for supplies of carpets, may sign a long-term supply agreement with a competing supplier.

A more detailed analysis of interruption loss is undertaken in Chapter 14. Here, we note some of the implications for reinvestment. Without business interruption, we have seen that a loss will simply shift the transformation curve to the left, as in Figures 8-1 and 8-2. This implies that the optimal level of investment should not change as we have shown. (We did envision some change in shape where resources were specialized and reinvestment was not undertaken, but the curve bounced back to its original shape with the reinvestment.) With interruption loss, both the shape and the position of the transformation curve will change, implying that restoration of the original level of investment will not be sufficient to generate the original cash flows. Figure 8-3 presents the original transformation curve AB. As a result of a loss and subsequent interruption of business, the production possibilities of the firm are adversely affected, as shown by curve JK. For any level of investment, curve JK shows lower period 2 cash flow than the preloss curve AB. The actual loss in terms of the market value of resources LMVR is AJ. The original level of investment is AM. After loss, the value of remaining invested resources is JM. If the firm wishes to restore the original level of investment, it must reinvest a further MN, restoring the total investment JN to the preloss level ($JN = AM$). However, this investment will only produce a period 2 cash flow of $0S$ compared with original cash flow of $0R$. The difference $0R - 0S$ results from the interruption of business. The interruption loss may be reduced by further reinvestment. For example, marketing expenditures might restore part of the interruption loss. However, in the example illustrated, this does not make good economic sense. The relationship between the return on reinvestment and the cost of capital indicates that it is better to cut the total level of investment from JN to JP. Since undamaged resources equal JM, the optimal level of reinvestment is therefore MP (that is, $JM + MP = JP$).

FIGURE 8-3

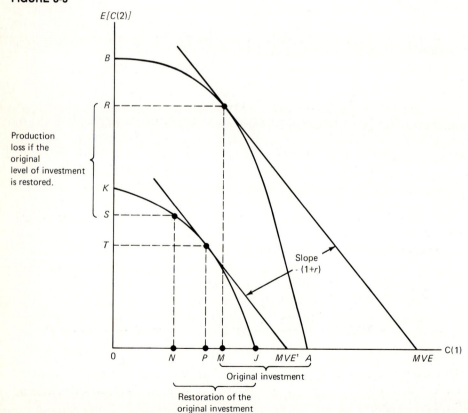

This case also illustrates another important principle. The competing measures of loss were market value of lost resources (MVLR) and loss of market value of equity (LMVE). We introduced the possibility that these might not produce the same values in the discussion at the end of Chapter 7. We now have a further problem that turns our attention more closely to LMVE as the appropriate measure of the financial impact of loss. From Figure 8-3, MVLR is AJ and LMVE is $MVE - MVE'$. The relationship between these two values is as follows:

$$\text{MVE} = 0M + \frac{OR}{1 + r} \quad \text{and} \quad \text{MVE}' = 0P + \frac{OT}{1 + r}$$

We may represent $0R$ as $0T + TS + SR$ and $0P$ as $0M - MN + NP$. Therefore,

$$\text{MVE} - \text{MVE}' = \left(0M + \frac{OT}{1 + r} + \frac{TS}{1 + r} + \frac{SR}{1 + r}\right)$$
$$- \left(0M - MN + NP + \frac{OT}{1 + r}\right)$$

which reduces to

$$\left(MN + \frac{SR}{1 + r}\right) - \left(NP - \frac{TS}{1 + r}\right)$$

or

$$\left(\begin{array}{l}\text{Loss in market} \\ \text{value from} \\ \text{interruption of trading} \\ \text{holding level of investment} \\ \text{constant}\end{array}\right) - \left(\begin{array}{l}\text{partial recapture} \\ \text{of market value} \\ \text{from adjustment} \\ \text{in level of} \\ \text{investment}\end{array}\right)$$

However, it will also be seen that MN is the amount required to restore the investment to its original level. Therefore, $MN = \text{MVLR}$.

Comparing LMVE and MVLR, we have

$$\text{LMVE} = MN + \left(\frac{SR}{1 + r} - NP + \frac{TS}{1 + r}\right)$$
$$= \text{MVLR} + \left(\frac{TR}{1 + r} - NP\right) \qquad \text{since } SR + TS = TR$$

Thus the two criteria differ by the term in parentheses. This term arises because of the interruption loss, and since it is a real loss of value, it should be anticipated by the risk manager.

SALVAGE AND DISPOSAL VALUES

It will be helpful to pause for a moment to clarify what we mean by "total loss." In an earlier example, we referred to a garment manufacturer who lost some machines in a fire. In that case, some, but not all, of the sewing machines and cutting machines owned by the firm were destroyed. In one sense, the loss was partial, since not all the firm's assets were destroyed, but for the equipment affected, the loss was total. *We will refer to total loss in relation to specific assets, and we will define such a loss as arising when the costs of repairing damage is greater than or equal to the cost of replacing those assets.* Otherwise, the loss with respect to those assets is defined to be partial.

Our rule for reinvesting following total loss was summarized earlier and may be restated, with slight rearrangement, as follows:

$$\sum_{i=0}^{n} \frac{\tilde{C}_{i,0}}{(1 + r)^i} - I > 0 \tag{8-13}$$

However, what if the loss generates salvage or if there are disposal costs that must be undertaken by the firm in order to abandon the project? Salvage arises if the remnants of the damaged assets have some market value. In many cases, the loss will be complete, leaving no remains or at least no accessible remains. Examples are a theft or the sinking of a ship in a deep oceanic trench such that recovery of the wreck is not feasible. In other cases, however, there are remains. A crashed vehicle has scrap values for its metal and, perhaps, for a secondhand trade in mechanical or electrical parts. Certainly, such salvage is not precluded by our definition of total loss. In some cases, the salvage values will be realized independently of reinvestment. It makes clear sense to sell damaged machinery for scrap if it is beyond repair, whether or not we choose to replace the machinery. In other cases, reinvestment may require that salvage be utilized, as in the case of a machine that has suffered lesser damage and can be economically repaired. Here, realization of salvage value depends on the reinvestment decision. Salvage is an example of a wider set of disposal values, which may be costs or benefits, and the treatment of these values depends on whether they are "avoidable" or "unavoidable" by making the reinvestment decision.

If a building is damaged beyond economic repair, the owner may well be burdened with further costs to level the site in order to avoid a dangerous or unsightly ruin. A facility using radioactive or other highly toxic substances cannot simply be abandoned in the event of heavy damage. Again, the firm will probably be required to render the facility safe, thereby incurring disposal costs. Disposal costs of a very different nature may arise. If a production facility is to be abandoned following a loss, then workers may have to be laid off. This may entail severance compensation to be paid by the employer. Costs of this nature may or may not affect the reinvestment decision, depending on whether these costs can or cannot be avoided by reinvestment. Severance pay can be avoided if the firm chooses to reinvest. Demolition costs for a fire-damaged building constitute a more thorny case. If the existing shell cannot be used as basis for reconstruction, the disposal costs cannot be avoided, and consequently, it should not affect the decision.[3] However, if the shell can be used for rebuilding, it may still make sense to reconstruct (repair), even though the costs of reconstructing exceed the price of erecting a new building. In reconstructing, the demolition costs are avoided. These considerations imply that our reinvestment rule requires modification. A firm should invest, therefore, if

$$\sum_{i=0}^{n} \frac{C_{i,0}}{(1 + r)^i} + D_A - I > 0 \qquad (8\text{-}14)$$

where D_A refers to avoidable disposal values. Where disposal costs are unavoidable, they have no bearing on the reinvestment decision, and they can be ignored.

EXAMPLE: POLLY U. THANE, INC.

Polly U. Thane, Inc. has its laboratory damaged by fire and subsequent explosion of volatile solvents. The two-story building is severely damaged, with complete collapse of the first floor and roof. The walls are of brick construction and are intact. Laboratory equipment in the building is mostly destroyed, although some salvage can be secured from items in one section that was less severely damaged. The firm's production and financial staff, together with an outside assessor, prepare the following financial estimates to assist the decision on reinvestment:

Building Damage:	
Cost of reconstruction from level site	$25,000,000
Cost of reconstruction from remaining shell	28,000,000
Demolition costs	2,000,000
Site:	
Value of site after leveling	$10,000,000
Equipment:	
Replacement costs	$30,000,000
Salvage (the salvaged equipment could not be reused by the firm because of contamination and lack of precision)	3,000,000
Financial Penalties if No Reinvestment:	
Severance compensation of workers laid off	$ 4,000,000
Nondelivery penalties on existing contracts	2,000,000
Cash Flows from Reinvestment:	
NPV future cash flows	$65,000,000

---

[3]It may be argued that the firm can avoid the disposal costs by walking away from the site, leaving the damaged building in its current state. This may be precluded by building regulations or the terms of a lease on the land. If the land is owned by the firm, its market value would tend to diminish by the value of the disposal cost, and this cost would be internalized to the firm anyway.

If the firm is to reinvest, it is apparent that the site should be leveled and an entirely new building erected. The cost of this option is $27 million against $28 million for rebuilding on the existing shell. The application of our criterion [equation (8-14)] can proceed as follows:

Reinvestment cash flow		65,000,000
Plus avoidable disposal costs*		
Sale of site	(10,000,000)	
Severance compensation	4,000,000	
Nondelivery	2,000,000	(4,000,000)
Minus reinvestment costs		
Reconstruction	25,000,000	
Replace equipment	30,000,000	55,000,000
		$ 6,000,000

*Notice the inclusion of sale of site. This is a cash flow that is avoidable. In this sense, it is a disposal benefit. The inclusion of this item ensures that the use of this resource is properly considered as an opportunity cost of reinvestment. However, notice that demolition costs are not included. If the firm does not reinvest, it will bear these costs. If it does reinvest, it has to level the site before rebuilding, which is cheaper than repair of the original shell. Demolition costs arise regardless of the reinvestment decision.

The correct decision in this case is to reinvest. However, notice that had the site value been $20 million, the decision would be reversed, since the opportunity cost of using the site for reconstruction of the laboratory would be just too high. A further point of interest is that the salvage of equipment did not enter the decision process, the reason being that the equipment was no longer usable by the firm and would be sold for salvage whether or not the reinvestment option was chosen. The benefit was "unavoidable."

The criterion for reinvestment following loss may be summarized in the following terms: *Once a loss has occurred, the cash flows attributable to that loss are sunk* (sorry about the pun) *costs and, as such, are irrelevant to the subsequent decision to reinvest. The only cash flows that are relevant are those which can be attributed to the decision to reinvest.* These flows include direct cash flows, such as the reconstruction and equipment costs in the previous example, and opportunity costs or benefits, such as the foregone sale of the land and the avoidance of severance and nondelivery penalties.

PARTIAL LOSSES

In principle, the criterion for reinvestment following partial loss is identical to that following total loss. The present value of cash flows arising from the decision must be positive. However, a few words of elaboration are in order. To recall our definition, a loss is defined to be *partial* when the cost of repairing the damaged assets is less than the cost of replacing the assets. This definition does not imply that partial loss should be repaired, i.e., that reinvestment should be chosen. This still depends on the respective size of the disposal values, the repair costs, and the cash flows generated. This interaction may still lead to situations in which repair is not warranted.

EXAMPLE: I. BLEARY (LIQUOR), INC.

I. Bleary (Liquor), Inc. distributes beers, liquors, and wines to local clubs and hotels. It still maintains an old bottling plant, and when business is slack, part of the labor force is utilized in bottling beer that is purchased in bulk. The home-bottled beer is slightly cheaper than beer bottled by the suppliers. However, times are rarely slack, and Bleary has only used the equipment on one or two occasions during the last year. The equipment has value only as scrap, and space is not at issue on the premises. Thus Bleary had decided to keep the equipment as a hedge against further slack periods. However, the equipment is hit by a fork lift truck, causing fairly extensive damage. Certainly, the damage would cost less to repair ($25,000) than the replacement cost for similar equipment ($75,000), and the salvage value of the equipment is small ($5000), but Bleary chooses to sell the equipment for scrap because the estimated cash flows generated by repair are, at most, $15,000, and even this sum is highly speculative.

In general, reinvestment decisions following total or partial loss can be evaluated with criteria described in the section entitled Interruption Loss.

SOME COMMENTS ON REINVESTMENT AND SOURCES OF CAPITAL

In order to reinvest, a firm must have access to the necessary sources of finance. Sources may be internal, such as existing liquid funds, or external, such as new issues of debt or equity or an insurance payment. The sources may further be divided into preloss (that is, funds such as insurance payments or internal contingency funds that are set in place in anticipation of future losses and evoked if and when such losses arise) and postloss (in which necessary funds are secured and the terms fixed after the loss). Chapters 9 to 12 will consider these respective sources, although here we will anticipate part of that discussion by showing that the financing decision may not be independent of the source of funds.

Suppose an insurance policy is available that provides full replacement cost compensation for a loss. The financing will be available quickly after loss (especially if the same insurer carries the interruption loss), so that the firm can reinvest quickly and thereby limit any break in production and sales. Compare this situation with one in which contingent funds have not been secured in advance and the firm is exposed to the capital markets for whatever terms it can get. Presumably, the firm would secure some form of financing that complemented its capital structure, and the discount rate to be used in capitalizing the benefits flowing from reinvestment would be determined with this capital structure in mind. However, the decision to reinvest with insurance would also be made on the basis of a cost of capital that reflects the capital structure of the firm. We will explore this issue fully in later chapters, but for now, notice that the use of the same cost of capital would be embodied in the investment decision, and consequently, that decision would be independent of the source of finance.

Now let postloss funding entail transaction costs. If new debt or equity is to be floated, there will be issue and underwriting costs, resources will be consumed within the firm in the search for alternative finances, and loans from financial institutions will entail legal and drafting expenses. These costs are real cash flows that are evoked by the decision to reinvest, and consequently, their presence and magnitude may affect the decision. Normally, with preloss funding, any transaction costs are already incurred at the time of loss (e.g., commissions and mangement expenses written into the insurance premium). These are sunk costs and are irrelevant. Thus preloss financing may create conditions more favorable to reinvestment, since the transaction costs for financing are not conditional on the decision.

Now consider another, related issue. The availability of funds to finance a loss should not preempt any decision to reinvest, even if the funds apparently have been earmarked. For example, it might be supposed that reinvestment is costless if an insurance policy providing full cover is available. This argument is fallacious unless reinvestment is a condition of the policy. Short of such policy conditions, a policy payment simply represents liquid funds that have alternative uses. These uses include investment in alternative projects, redeeming existing debt, share repurchases, and investment in financial assets. Reinvestment is only warranted if it generates a return in excess of the cost of capital, and even then, it may not be warranted if scarcity of capital denies the firm an alternative and more profitable use of funds. Thus reinvestment of insurance money is not costless; there is the opportunity cost of sacrificing alternative uses of those same funds. In short, the case for postloss abandonment is not affected by the availability of insurance money unless that money is contractually tied to reinvestment. Consequently, it would appear to be wasteful for a firm to buy insurance with such a restrictive condition, especially if the firm currently operates with redundant assets.[4]

REINVESTMENT AND q RATIOS: SOME EVIDENCE

The theme of this chapter is that a loss event presents a firm with an investment decision—whether to replace or repair the assets that have been affected. This decision is no different in kind from any other investment decision: If the present value of the incremental cash flows is positive, when discounted at the cost of capital (equivalently, if the internal rate of return exceeds the cost of capital), reinvestment adds value to a firm. If this condition is not satisfied, reinvestment will destroy value and, consequently, is not of benefit of a firm's shareholders. Although neglected in other risk management literature, the reinvestment decision is *not* an academic curiosity, nor can a positive decision be taken as matter of course. We will present *prima facie* evidence to show that a positive reinvestment decision is unlikely for many firms.

The q ratio was derived by Tobin (1969) to analyze the determination of corporate investment. The ratio is simply the market value of a firm divided by the replacement costs of its assets. Our previous analysis suggests that the market value of a firm is the present value of the firm's expected earnings. If the market value exceeds the replacement costs of the assets used to generate the earnings stream, there is a clear incentive to invest in that operation. The investment has created wealth for the firm's

---

[4]Notice that we do not claim that it is wasteful to purchase insurance per se with redundant assets. This is a more complex issue that is considered elsewhere.

owners. If the q ratio for a firm exceeds unity, the firm is earning abnormal profits; thus the ratio provides a measure of monopolistic returns. A ratio of less than unity indicates that the assets in use are redundant. Thus it would seem that the q ratio provides a measure of the incentive to invest. The ratio has been used directly for this purpose, but it has also been used as a measure of monopolistic returns across different firms or industries. The ratio is also well suited to an examination of the reinvestment possibilities following a major loss.

Cross-sectional evidence on the q ratios for firms has been presented by Lindenberg and Ross (1981). The procedures for calculating the ratios are of interest and are described by the authors. The denominator presents the least severe estimation problems, since it is the sum of the estimated market values of the firm's common and preferred shares and its debt. The market values of these securities embody investor expectations of future earnings. Estimation of replacement costs of assets has been possible for large companies since 1976, when the Securities and Exchange Commission required firms to disclose replacement costs in SEC 10-K filings. The methods of calculation vary somewhat among firms, and the cross-sectional results contain corresponding degrees of error. Furthermore, the results presented consider replacement costs estimated from the 1976–1977 period using estimated rates of technical progress, depreciation, and appropriate price indices together with known values for new investments. The quality of these data are discussed by Lindenberg and Ross and should be treated accordingly.

The sample companies are taken from *Compustat* tape, and the appropriate ratios (averaged for 1960–1977) are shown in Table 8-1. The use of average ratios avoids problems of volatility in the ratio due to random fluctuations in security prices from which the denominator is derived. The data reveal q values in excess of unity for most firms, thus indicating that reinvestment following a major loss is appropriate for most firms. For example, Xerox's ratio is 5.52, indicating that reinvestment would be highly desirable. However, there are a significant number of firms with ratios lower than unity. The *a priori* indication is that these firms should not reconstruct their assets following major loss. To do so would destroy value, since the net present value of earnings from such investments is lower than the replacement cost. For these firms, risk management problems have an altogether different flavor. Before writing off these firms, however, or creating false optimism about reinvestment in those with ratios exceeding unity, we need to qualify our conclusions:

1 The quality of data and the methods of calculating replacement costs do vary. Since we are suggesting that this ratio might be used as a risk management tool, the risk manager should assess the quality of data used to derive this estimate. Presumably, he or she will have access to the data used for the SEC filing and will be able to assess its quality.

2 The data are somewhat dated. Further evidence from Lindenberg and Ross reveals that, in general, q ratios for U.S. firms have been falling. Thus up-to-date information might reveal a much greater incidence of redundancy.

3 Market values reveal investor expectations at the date of valuation. These are not "postloss" valuations, but are derived from the then current prices. The firm may not be able to recover these values with complete reinvestment if there is interruption

TABLE 8-1
FIRMS AND AVERAGE q VALUES

Company	1960–1977 Average q Ratio	Company	1960–1977 Average q Ratio
ACF Industries	1.14	Cone Mills Corp.	0.45
AMF, Inc.	1.43	Congoleum Corp.	1.17
Abbott Laboratories	2.35	Continental Group	1.15
Akzona	1.02	Continental Oil Co.	1.69
Alcan Aluminum, Ltd.	0.79	Cooper Industries, Inc.	1.24
Allegheny Ludlum Industries	0.97	Copperweld Corp.	0.69
Allied Chemical Corp.	1.26	Corning Glass Works	3.75
Allied Products	1.07	Crane Co.	0.72
Allied Stores	1.17	Crown Cork & Seal Co., Inc.	1.41
Allis-Chalmers Corp.	0.76	Crown Zellerbach	1.08
Alpha Portland Industries	0.68	Culbro Corp.	1.07
Aluminum Co. of America	0.85	Cummins Engine	1.35
Amcord, Inc.	0.92	Curtiss-Wright Corp.	0.95
American Brands, Inc.	1.23	Cutler-Hammer, Inc.	1.35
American Can Co.	1.09	Dan River, Inc.	0.67
American Cyanamid Co.	1.46	Dart Industries	1.41
American Greetings Corp.	1.94	Diamond International Corp.	1.50
American Telephone and Telegraph	1.09	Diamond Shamrock Corp.	1.55
Ametek, Inc.	1.46	Dome Petroleum, Ltd.	2.94
Anchor Hocking Corp.	1.17	Dow Chemical	1.62
Anheuser-Busch, Inc.	1.95	Du Pont (E. I.) De Nemours	2.47
Armstrong Cork Co.	1.70	Duquesne Light Co.	0.90
Asarco, Inc.	0.91	Eastern Gas & Fuel Assoc.	1.11
Avon Products	8.53	Eaton Corp.	1.17
Bausch and Lomb, Inc.	2.37	Ethyl Corp.	1.48
Beatrice Foods Co.	1.65	Exxon Corp.	1.05
Bell & Howell Co.	1.64	FMC Corp.	1.47
Bethlehem Steel Corp.	0.68	Fairchild Camera & Instrument	2.12
Borden, Inc.	1.26	Federal-Mogul Corp.	1.35
Borg-Warner Corp.	0.97	Federal Paper Board Co.	0.52
Bristol-Myers Co.	3.76	Federated Department Stores, Inc.	2.06
Brunswick Corp.	1.23	Ferro Corp.	0.97
Bucyrus-Erie Co.	1.08	Flintkote Co.	0.86
Carter Hawley Hale Stores	1.28	Foote Mineral Co.	1.07
Caterpillar Tractor Co.	1.52	Foster Wheeler Corp.	0.86
Ceco Corp.	0.84	GAF Corp.	1.27
Celanese Corp.	1.24	GATX Corp.	1.10
Certain-Teed Corp.	0.95	Gamble-Skogmo	0.97
Champion International Corp.	1.35	Gardner-Denver Co.	1.57
Chicago Pneumatic Tool Co.	1.13	General Cable Corp.	1.64
Chrysler Corp.	0.90	General Electric Co.	2.07
Cincinnati Milacron Inc.	1.17	General Foods Corp.	2.10
Cities Service Co.	1.21	General Motors Corp.	1.59
Clark Equipment Co.	1.51	General Portland, Inc.	1.09
Cleveland-Cliffs Iron Co.	1.17	General Refractories Co.	0.70
Cluett, Peabody & Co.	1.12	General Telephone & Electronics	1.32
Coca-Coca Co.	4.21	Georgia-Pacific Corp.	1.63
Colgate-Palmolive Co.	1.34	Gillette Co.	3.92
Collins & Aikman Corp.	1.13	Goodrich (B. F.) Co.	0.89
Combustion Engineering, Inc.	1.14		
Commonwealth Edison	1.01		

Company	1960–1977 Average q Ratio	Company	1960–1977 Average q Ratio
Goodyear Tire & Rubber Co.	1.05	Mead Corp.	0.97
Grace (W. R.) & Co.	1.16	Medusa Corp.	0.60
Graniteville Co.	0.55	Melville Corp.	2.21
Great Northern Nekoosa		Mercantile Stores Co., Inc.	1.27
Corp.	0.79	Midland-Ross Corp.	1.02
Grumman Corp.	1.06	Minnesota Mining &	
Gulf Oil Corp.	1.25	Manufacturing Co.	4.87
Halliburton	1.86	Mobil Corp.	1.20
Hammermill Paper Co.	0.68	Monsanto Co.	1.38
Hercules, Inc.	1.86	Motorola, Inc.	1.97
Hershey Foods Corp.	1.83	NCR Corp.	1.74
Holly Sugar Corp.	0.50	NI Industries	1.56
Honeywell, Inc.	2.28	Naico Chemical Co.	3.69
Ideal Basic Industries, Inc.	1.08	National Distillers &	
Imperial Oil, Ltd.-CL A	1.67	Chemicals	0.94
Ingersoll-Rand Co.	1.76	National Gypsum Co.	0.92
Inland Steel Co.	0.95	National Steel Corp.	0.53
Insilco Corp.	1.39	National Tea Co.	0.97
Interco, Inc.	0.98	Owens-Corning Fiberglass	
Interlake, Inc.	0.75	Corp.	1.71
International Business		Owens-Illinois, Inc.	1.30
Machines Corp.	4.21	PPG Industries, Inc.	1.05
International Paper Co.	1.17	Pabst Brewing Co.	1.31
Iowa-Illinois Gas & Electric	0.85	Pennwalt Corp.	1.36
Iowa Power & Light	0.73	Pepsico, Inc.	2.31
Johns-Manville Corp.	1.24	Pfizer, Inc.	2.49
Johnson & Johnson	3.64	Phelps Dodge Corp.	1.71
K Mart Corp.	1.99	Philip Morris, Inc.	1.45
Kaiser Aluminum & Chemical		Phillips Petroleum Co.	1.74
Corp.	0.80	Pitney-Bowes, Inc.	1.92
Kaiser Cement & Gypsum		Polaroid Corp.	6.42
Corp.	0.96	Potlatch Corp.	0.82
Kaiser Steel Corp.	0.78	Public Service Electric & Gas	1.12
Kellogg Co.	3.20	Publicker Industries, Inc.	0.59
Kimberly-Clark Corp.	1.51	Pullman, Inc.	0.91
Koppers Co.	0.88	Quaker State Oil Refining	1.92
Kraft, Inc.	1.35	RCA Corp.	1.67
Libbey-Owens-Ford Co.	1.47	Revere Copper & Brass, Inc.	1.17
Liggett Group	1.02	Reynolds (R. J.) Industries	1.90
Lilly (Eli) & Co.	4.02	Reynolds Metals Co.	0.81
Lone Star Industries	0.89	Robertshaw Controls	1.11
Long Island Lighting	1.28	Robertson (H. H.) Co.	0.89
Lowenstein (M.) & Sons, Inc.	0.61	Rohm & Haas Co.	2.09
Lucky Stores, Inc.	1.58	Rubbermaid, Inc.	2.03
Lukens Steel Co.	0.74	SPS Technologies, Inc.	0.80
Mallory (P. R.) & Co.	1.22	Safeway Stores, inc.	1.14
Marathon Oil Co.	1.81	St. Joe Minerals Corp.	1.91
Maremont Corp.	1.24	St. Regis Paper Co.	0.98
Marshall Field & Co.	1.14	Schering-Plough	4.30
Maytag Co.	2.71	Scott Paper Co.	1.46
McGraw-Edison Co.	1.28	Scovill Manufacturing Co.	1.05
McLouth Steel Corp.	0.74	Searle (G. D.) & Co.	5.27

TABLE 8-1
(Continued)

Company	1960–1977 Average q Ratio	Company	1960–1977 Average q Ratio
Sears Roebuck & Co.	2.04	Trane Co.	1.82
Shell Oil Co.	1.68	Trans Union Corp.	1.47
Signal Cos.	0.99	UV Industries, Inc.	1.48
Signode Corp.	1.69	Union Camp Corp.	1.43
Simmons Co.	0.90	Union Carbide Corp.	1.67
Singer Co.	1.22	Union Oil Co. of California	1.24
Smithkline Corp.	4.19	Uniroyal, Inc.	0.90
Southern California Edison		United Brands	0.74
Co.	0.81	U.S. Gypsum Co.	1.22
Square D Co.	2.68	U.S. Steel Corp.	0.62
Standard Brands, Inc.	1.87	U.S. Tobacco Co.	1.67
Standard Oil Co. (California)	1.18	United Technologies Corp.	0.94
Standard Oil Co. (Indiana)	1.24	Wallace-Murray Corp.	0.81
Standard Oil Co. (Ohio)	2.09	Warner & Swasey	1.01
Stanley Works	0.96	Western Publishing	1.33
Sterling Drug Inc.	3.46	Western Union Corp.	0.83
Stewart-Warner Corp.	1.20	Westinghouse Electric Corp.	1.48
Sun Co.	1.26	Weyerhaeuser Co.	1.76
Sunbeam Corp.	1.36	White Motor Corp.	1.12
Sundstrand Corp.	1.17	Wickes Corp.	1.60
Super Value Stores, Inc.	1.35	Wisconsin Public Service	0.79
TRW, Inc.	1.32	Woolworth (F. W.) Co.	0.84
Texaco, Inc.	1.86	Wrigley (WM.) Jr. Co.	1.74
Textron, inc.	1.12	Xerox Corp.	5.52
Timken Co.	1.02	Zenith Radio Corp.	2.83

From Lindenberg and Ross (1981). Reproduced with permission of the University of Chicago Press.

loss. For this reason, q ratios probably tend to overestimate the incentive to reinvest following loss.

4 The ratios are calculated at the level of the firm. A firm having a ratio of less than unity may well have some operations that truly create wealth and for which planned reinvestment following a loss is appropriate. Furthermore, even a firm having a single operation for which q is below unity might legitimately contemplate reinvestment following a partial loss. The low q value suggests only that complete reinvestment following total loss is inappropriate. However, because of production interdependencies, it is possible that reinvestment following a small loss may yield an incremental internal rate of return in excess of the cost of capital.

The tabulated values do indicate that reinvestment following loss is not an empty issue. Indeed, our inclination is to rank it among the most important of issues in risk management. This position is reinforced when we consider that declining q ratios and prospects of interruption loss imply that the problem may be more widespread than indicated by the table. However, our role is not to be that of a "Prophet of Doom," rather, it is to suggest that the q ratio can be a useful device for risk management planning because it contains valuable information relevant to the financing needs of a firm following loss. Therefore, there is advantage to be gained from improvement in the quality of the estimate of this value.

SUMMARY AND CONCLUSION

In Chapter 7 we examined production decisions in a perfect capital market and concluded that the optimal level of production was independent of a firm's initial level of resources. If the firm had correctly chosen the value-maximizing level of production before loss, it should restore production to that level after the loss, raising external capital if necessary. We now focus on the reinvestment decision in more detail. We progressively relax the restrictive assumptions of the early model and show when a firm should seek financing to restore production and when it should abandon the activity affected.

Reinvestment is first examined with unspecialized and/or interchangeable resources and perfect capital markets. A loss will affect the scale of operations. Assuming that the preloss scale was value-maximizing, reinvestment to restore that scale will be rewarded by a rate of return in excess of the cost of capital. The case for reinvestment is further strengthened if resources are specialized, giving rise to interdependencies in the production process. Losses may fall indiscriminately on different types of resources, causing bottlenecks in the production process. Assuming that preloss investment was optimal, reinvestment following loss will not only restore the scale of operations to the preloss optimum, but will also restore a sensible mix of specialized resources. Reinvestment will be correspondingly attractive.

These conclusions assume that a firm is producing at its value-maximizing level when a loss strikes. This assumption is strong. The scale and mix of a firm's operations may reflect some inertia in the face of changing economic conditions and transaction costs or in the failure to perceive and correct a suboptimal decision. Thus transaction costs or the absence of an efficient market for the disposal of secondhand goods may cause a firm to retain underproductive assets. These circumstances may prevail in a period of declining secular or cyclical demand. A firm will rationally choose to retain assets if the present value of the cash flows from continued use exceeds the disposal value. However, replacement of those assets will only be warranted if the value in continued use exceeds the replacement cost. Given a differential between disposal values and replacement costs, the value-maximizing criterion may well indicate that reinvestment is not appropriate following loss and the activity should therefore be abandoned.

The issue is further complicated by the prospect of interruption loss. The cash flows from continued productive use of an asset may warrant its retention, but if a loss arises, immediate production may not be possible, nor may the firm be able to restore its preloss position in the market if production has been extensively disturbed. Such interruption may be so severe that future estimated cash flows are insufficient to warrant reinvestment.

The decision to abandon or reinvest will be influenced by salvage and disposal values as well as the cash flows from the respective alternatives. If abandonment generates salvage or incurs disposal costs, these values must be used to balance the respective benefits of reinvestment and abandonment if such effects are conditional on the decision. For example, the demolition of the shell of a severely damaged building may be unavoidable if it is highly dangerous and cannot be used for reconstruction. Therefore, these costs are not relevant to the decision. If the shell can be used for reconstruction, the savings should be credited to the reinvestment alternative.

This chapter was concluded by examining q ratios. Defined as the ratio of the market value of a firm to its replacement cost, such ratios give a *prima facie* indication as to whether major reconstruction is warranted on financial criteria. Values in excess of unity indicate that reinvestment will yield an attractive return and thereby create value for the firm. However, ratios below unity are not uncommon, and in such circumstances, reinvestment following major loss is questionable. Such ratios pose disturbing questions for the traditional risk management objectives of survival and continuity of operations after loss.

QUESTIONS

1 A firm suffers a loss of capital equipment valued at $500,000. The production transformation curve for the firm before the fire was $301^{0.8}$ and $301^{0.78}$ after the fire. What is the optimal level of investment (production) before the loss? What is the internal rate of return on reinvestment assuming that the reinvestment will restore the firm to its preloss transformation curve (students without calculus may ignore this question).

2 Construct a diagram to show how reinvestment may add value by:
  a restoring the scale of operations to that existing preloss (assume preloss scale to be value maximizing).
  b restoring the mix of operations to that existing preloss (assume preloss mix to be value maximizing).

3 Consider the following two decisions facing a laundromat:
  a should it continue to operate?
  b should it anticipate reinvestment in the event of major loss?
The laundromat owns equipment that has a disposal value of $100,000. Replacement by similar secondhand equipment would cost $300,000. The laundromat anticipates expected annual earnings of $25,000 for the next 10 years but does not anticipate any earnings beyond that date. What answers would you provide to the above questions? Should the firm buy insurance?

Assume that the equipment will have no terminal value at the end of 10 years and use a discount rate of 10%.

4 Following a fire, an assessor presents the firm with two tables of costs, one assuming no reinvestment and the other assuming reinvestment.

List A: No reinvestment	
Demolition costs	$ 20,000
Fire extinction and salvage costs	20,000
Non-fulfilment penalties in production contracts	50,000
Sale of salvaged material	(40,000)
Sale of site	(200,000)

List B: Reinvestment	
Demolition costs	$ 20,000
Fire extinction and salvage costs	20,000
Sale of salvage (items that cannot be reused)	(10,000)
Construction costs, new buildings)	250,000
Purchase of new equipment	200,000

The NPV of future cash flows from reinvestment is $600,000. Should the firm reinvest?

REFERENCES

Bierman, H., and S. Smidt: *The Capital Budgeting Decision,* Macmillan, N.Y., 1971.

Bonini, C. P.: "Capital Investment under Uncertainty with Abandonment Options," *Journal of Financial and Quantitative Analysis,* vol. 12, 1977, pp. 39–54.

Ciccolo, J., and G. Fromm: "*Q* and the Theory of Investment," *Journal of Finance,* vol. 34, 1979, pp. 535–547.

Cloninger, D. O.: "Risk Arson and Abandonment," *Journal of Risk and Insurance,* vol. 48, 1981, pp. 494–504.

Jarrett, J. E.: "An Abandonment Decision Model," *Engineering Economist,* vol. 18, 1973, pp. 35–46.

Joy, M. O.: "Abandonment Values and Abandonment Decisions," *Journal of Finance,* vol. 30, 1976, pp. 1225–1228.

Levy, H., and M. Sarnat: *Capital Investment and Financial Decisions,* Prentice-Hall, Englewood Cliffs, N.J., 1978.

Lindenberg, E. B., and S. A. Ross: "Tobin's *q* Ratio and Industrial Organization," *Journal of Business,* vol. 54, 1981, pp. 1–32.

Mehr, R. I., and B. A. Hedges: *Risk Management: Concepts and Applications,* Irwin, Homewood, Ill., 1974.

Pappas, J. L.: "The Role of Abandonment Value in Capital Asset Management," *Engineering Economist,* vol. 22, 1976, pp. 53–61.

Robichek, A., and J. C. Van Horne: "Abandonment Value and Capital Budgeting," *Journal of Finance,* vol. 22, 1967, pp. 577–589.

Rosenbloom, J. S.: *A Case Study in Risk Management,* Meredith Corporation, New York, 1972.

Shillinlaw, G.: "Profit Analysis for Abandonment Decision and Residual Values in Investment Analysis," in E. Solomon (ed.), *The Management of Corporate Capital,* Free Press, New York, 1959.

Tobin J.: "A General Equilibrium Approach to Monetary Theory," *Journal of Money Credit and Banking,* vol. 1, 1969, pp. 15–29.

————: "Monetary Policies and the Economy: The Transmission Mechanism," *Southern Economic Journal,* vol. 37, 1978, pp. 421–431.

Waters, R. C., and R. L. Bullock: "Inflation and Replacement Decisions," *Engineering Economist,* vol. 21, 1976, pp. 244–257.

CHAPTER **9**

POSTLOSS FINANCING

The sources of finance available to a firm may be classified in several ways. Financing may be *short term* in nature (such as available cash or the issue of commercial paper) or *long term* (such as term loans or new issues of debt, preferred shares, or equity). Financing may be *internal* (such as a loss contingency fund or redundant cash) or *external* (such as new issues or insurance policy money). However, the broad categorization we choose is between postloss and preloss financing. *Postloss financing* is defined by the securement of funds after the loss. The financing arrangements are responsive (to the loss) rather than anticipatory. Furthermore, the costs of raising finance are borne after the loss. For example, if the loss is financed by (1) dipping into redundant cash, (2) a term loan, or (3) a new equity issue, the respective costs are (1) foregone investment opportunities for that cash, (2) interest payments, and (3) dividends. All these costs are borne by the firm after the loss. Another characteristic of postloss financing is that the terms and availability of such financing may not be known until after the loss.

In contrast to postloss financing, preloss financing is secured by arrangements made and costs borne in anticipation of loss. The most obvious example is insurance, which is (with a few exceptions) secured by the prior payment of an insurance premium. The opportunity cost for this form of financing is incurred with the payment of the premium, not with the occurrence of loss. A further example is a "self-insurance" fund into which premiums are paid and from which losses are financed. The availability of money from this source depends on the liquidity of the assets in which the fund resources are held. Thus the cost of funding is the difference between the return on fund assets and alternative investment opportunities, a cost that is borne independently of the actual occurrence.

A source of funds that lies somewhere "in between" preloss and postloss financing is a contingency loan. This essentially is a line of credit that becomes available on the occurrence of loss. In one sense, this is a postloss arrangement, since the debt must be serviced after the loss has been incurred. However, the line of credit facility has been set in place before loss and may have been secured by some monetary consideration. For our purposes, it is more convenient to classify this arrangement as postloss, since the principal financing costs are almost certainly postloss. A further reason for classifying contingency loans as postloss will become apparent as this chapter develops. When financing is postloss, the firm will suffer a loss in its net worth on the occurrence of loss. This may not be the case with preloss financing. In fact, complete insurance theoretically will insulate the net worth of the firm from the impact of a loss-producing event.

Our purpose in classifying financing into preloss and postloss is twofold. First, we can present a more fluent flow of ideas by adopting this sequence. Our financial exposition started by measuring the impact of actual losses on the value of a firm, and then we considered whether those losses should be made good by reinvestment. We will now, sequentially, consider the funding possibilities to consolidate positive reinvestment decisions and then the prospect of anticipating both the reinvestment decision and the funding problem. Our second reason is to correct an important omission in earlier risk management texts. Postloss financing is largely ignored, reflecting the prevailing philosophy that efficient risk management is anticipatory and precautionary. Compatible with this philosophy is an absence of discussion on reinvestment. Our view is that risk management planning can only become more efficient by widening the set of alternative strategies. Further, some of the postloss financing strategies may be attractive alternatives to conventional insurance purchases under certain circumstances. Anticipating future discussion, many firms do carry redundant cash. It appears silly to ignore this fact when faced with the prospect of expensive insurance.

The division between preloss and postloss financing is not synonymous with planned and unplanned financing. Postloss financing may be part of a well-formulated risk management strategy in which it is judged that the costs and uncertainties of going to the market following a prospective loss are preferable to incurring the risk premium entailed in the purchase of insurance.

In this chapter we will first consider available liquid resources. Then we will consider "going to the market" for financing and the financial issues (such as the effect on capital structure) that this strategy entails.

SOURCES OF FINANCE AVAILABLE AFTER LOSS

Cash and Marketable Securities

Postloss financing is only at issue if a positive decision on reinvestment is reached, although, as mentioned at the end of Chapter 8, there may be some interdependence between the reinvestment and financing decisions. The opportunity cost of failing to secure funding for reinvestment bears a positive relationship to the internal rate of return that can be generated upon reinvestment. The productivity of reinvestment depends, in turn, on the productivity of the capital employed prior to the loss and on the distortions caused by the loss. These considerations imply that loss financing is most important to those successful firms that have utilized capital productively and, in so doing, have created wealth for their shareholders. Such a sample of firms was the object of a study by William J. Fruhan (1979), and while not directed toward risk management, this study does contain some very pertinent conclusions.

Fruhan's objective was to study the characteristics of firms that have generated investment opportunities that earn returns in excess of their cost of capital and which have sustained such high returns over long periods. Such firms are valued by the market in excess of their book value, and in many cases, they are apparently overvalued. However, another salient characteristic of such firms is that a disproportionate number of these "Hall of Fame" firms carry redundant levels of cash and marketable securities. Thus it would seem that many firms for whom reinvestment is important have available to them existing cash or near-cash resources and that these resources may be available as an immediate and possible low-cost source of financing.

Debt

Lines of Credit   Various forms of debt may potentially be available to a firm following a loss. Perhaps the most convenient form is that debt which can be called upon immediately—notably, lines of credit. In the short term, lines of credit are an immediate substitute for cash and, for many purposes, may be measured as part of the firm's liquidity. Such lines of credit are frequently arranged by firms in order to absorb fluctuations in cash flows generated by trading operations. The advantage of this arrangement is that the loan is confined to the amount required and for the period required. Thus the firm need not maintain large values locked up in cash and low-yield marketable securities. However, a firm may be required to maintain a compensating balance with the financial institution in order to maintain the line of credit.

In view of the frequent requirement for compensatory balances and the fairly low probabilities of major losses, it is probably unwise to contemplate lines of credit merely to finance large "pure" losses. However, the central message of portfolio theory is that different types of risks, that is, commercial and risk management risks, should not be viewed separately. Unless there is a high degree of correlation between commercial and pure losses, the same line of credit would service both needs. Put another way, the combined demand for liquidity for future commercial and future pure losses is somewhat less than the sum of individual demands. From a postloss viewpoint, a firm may view its line of credit as a means of financing, in full or in part, the required reinvestment. However, such use requires that the following questions be addressed:

1 What is the opportunity cost of this form of debt?

2 How does this cost compare with the cost of alternative (debt or otherwise) methods of financing the reinvestment?

3 Will the use of the line of credit deplete the liquidity of the firm? How can this cost be measured?

Lines of credit rarely will be large enough to finance major reinvestment following losses of a catastrophic nature. However, the facility is extremely useful for financing smaller losses that occur with rather less irregularity. Furthermore, the line of credit may be combined with some other form of financing to cope with larger losses. For example, a deductible arrangement on an insurance policy may be set on the basis of available credit.

Contingency Loans   A contingency loan is essentially a line of credit that can be drawn on in the event of some adverse event, such as a large fire or liability suit. It is less flexible than a simple line of credit, which can be used for any purpose. However, if the defined contingencies have low probabilities, contingency loans can be arranged without high compensatory balances and for larger amounts than may be available under ordinary lines of credit. Although our focus here is on postloss financing, a contingency loan is a facility arranged in anticipation of loss with the intention that it will be evoked once loss arises. The terms of such a loan would be the subject of negotiation. For example, there may be a securement fee, the loan may be related to market rates at the time of the loss, it may have a floating rate over its duration, or it may have a rate that is fixed at the time the facility is arranged. Such facilities are not commonplace, and it is not possible to pinpoint standard practice. However, such facilities are sometimes arranged by corporations and/or their brokers. The advantages of contingency loans are as follows:

1 The limits and terms of credit are known in advance of possible losses. This facilitates risk management planning.

2 Contingency credit can be secured for much larger amounts than may be required for other commercial uses.

3 Financing is available quickly after loss, thus minimizing the extent of interruption loss.

As with any other loan, the lending institution will wish to assess the financial risk associated with the facility. In particular, it will wish to ascertain whether the firm's current financial performance and trading prospects are sufficiently attractive to warrant reinvestment following a major loss. Thus if a firm carries much redundant capital, it is unlikely to be viewed as a good credit risk for a contingency-loan facility. Compare this with debt financing arranged *after* a loss. Here the firm's *actual* reinvestment decision is subject to capital market scrutiny. If the firm is unable to arrange debt financing, or if the terms of such financing are particularly onerous, it is likely that the market will judge the reinvestment prospects as unattractive. Either way, the market will impose some financial discipline on the reinvestment decision. We will argue later in this chapter that this financial discipline may be important to the risk management process.

Term Loans   Most commercial banks concentrate on short- to medium-term loans. Loans of this sort, arranged after a loss, will be subject to terms related to current market conditions and to the lender's perceptions of the riskiness of a firm's postloss financial prospects. Thus the reinvestment decision, as mentioned earlier, will be subject to external scrutiny.

If short-term loans are used to finance a major reinvestment following a large loss, the repayment schedule will be burdensome in the year or two following the loss. Unless these loans are confined to fairly small reinvestment programs, particular attention will need to be directed to the postloss cash-flow forecasts or to alternative means of refunding as the debt matures.

Long-Term Debt: Bond Issues For many firms, the most clearly defined market for long-term debt is the bond market. Some form of bond issue may be particularly appropriate when reinvestment requires substantial financing and when a firm does not already have a heavy debt burden. There is considerable variation in the types of bonds that may be issued, and for each general form, the trust deed for the issue usually is adapted to the particular needs of the firm.

It is difficult to make general statements about the suitability of bond issues to finance postloss reinvestments. Clearly, the issue costs render bond issue unsuitable unless financing needs are large. In general, the attractiveness of an issue depends on the terms on which it can be arranged. This depends on the following factors:

1 Market conditions. Fluctuating interest rates expose a firm to the risk that it might need to finance reinvestment at a time of high rates. If postloss financing for future potential losses is embodied in a risk management plan, the risk managers must anticipate this form of market risk. If an issue is made during a period of high rates, suitable call provisions in the issue may permit a refunding of the debt in the event of falling rates. The firm must balance the use of such provisions with the attractiveness of the issue to potential subscribers.

2 The firm's existing level of leverage. Leverage increases the risk for all debt, since the higher the leverage, the higher the default probability. However, the risk will be borne disproportionately by junior debt. The trust deeds for existing debt may severely restrict the freedom of a firm to issue new debt.

3 The firm's credit rating. Agencies such as Moody's and Standard & Poors issue bond ratings that embody judgments about a firm's business and financial risk. Since many institutional and private investors follow these ratings, they determine the terms on which bonds can be issued. For a firm with an attractive rating and little existing debt, postloss financing by a new bond issue may well be attractive.

4 The terms of postloss issue may be affected by the loss itself. In Chapter 8 we saw that postloss reinvestment may prove to be very attractive when it permits a firm to restore a high return on its invested capital. However, we also introduced the possibility of business interruption loss. Bond issues are suited to raising large amounts of money, but if this demand follows a severe loss that threatens to interrupt production and trading for some considerable time, thereby threatening the permanent market position of a firm, its credit risk will plummet. The firm will then find it difficult, or expensive, to raise funds. However, the difficulty in securing debt under such circumstances must itself reflect on the wisdom of reinvesting.

The prospect of interruption loss highlights another possible disadvantage of financing by a bond issue. If interruption loss is to be kept at a minimum, reinvestment should be rapid and not delayed by the search for, and arrangement of, the necessary financing. Bond issues often do take more time to put in place than other forms of debt. In summary, bond issues may become valuable to a firm seeking financing after a loss, but if resort to this form of financing for potential future losses is planned in advance, the firm should recognize the latent uncertainties that it entails.

Equity

The most permanent form of financing entails a new equity issue. The pros and cons of using prospective equity issues to finance potential future losses involve considerations that are similar to those relating to new debt issues. The firm is exposed to the capital market conditions prevailing at the time of loss, the terms of issue will depend on investors' perceptions of the firm's prospects after the loss, and the management of the issue must be handled speedily in view of the urgency of financing needs. Equity differs from debt in that it does not burden a firm with a contractual repayment schedule in the recovery period following loss. However, the earnings of a firm are diluted by the claims of the new shareholders.

The general features of both debt and equity issues suggest they are unsuited to small losses in view of their disproportionately high transaction costs. However, they are also unsuited to financing reinvestment following catastrophic losses that threaten the permanent market position of a firm because interruption loss will be severe. Such conditions will probably be anticipated by investors and will be reflected in the subscriptions to the issue and/or terms on which it can be arranged. This form of financing is therefore most suited to the range of large, but not catastrophic, losses.

EXTERNAL SOURCES AND MARKET DISCIPLINE

In securing external financing after a loss, a firm must expose itself to the scrutiny of the market. The judgment made by the market on the earnings prospects of a firm, given the loss and given the reinvestment plans for which the financing is sought, will be implicit in the terms under which the market will provide funds. For example, with a bond issue, the yield required by investors will reflect their perception of default risk, which is determined by the estimated earnings stream. With equity, the price at which new shares will sell depends directly on the investors' expectation of earnings for the firm, and the relationship between expected earnings and price is cemented by risk. If the price of new securities is too high, the issue will not be fully subscribed. Thus, in order to raise the required funds, the price must be lowered. This will increase the cost of capital to the firm, thereby reducing the value of its original equity.

It is tempting to view this external sanction on reinvestment decisions as a disadvantage of relying on postloss external financing. The terms of financing are determined (apparently at the whim of the market) at the time a firm most needs the funds, i.e., after a large loss. It may be thought that such factors can only introduce unpredictability into the risk management plan and constrain the firm in undertaking a proper postloss recovery program. Another view is that such market "interference" provides a useful external discipline on the reinvestment decision. The terms of postloss financing may be attractive or unattractive, depending on market estimates of the prospects for postloss recovery. It may be tempting for the risk manager to doubt the judgments of the market on the grounds that they are less informed and have been subject to less rigorous analysis than his or her own judgments. This could well be the case, but we must also balance this view with the evidence about the efficiency of capital markets in disseminating information and on the greater objectivity of external analysts in assessing the potential earnings of a firm.

So far as we know, there is little or no evidence to show that the market is able to make efficient and unbiased estimates of the earnings of firms following major loss. However, there is considerable evidence to show that information relevant to the formation of earnings expectations disseminates quickly and effectively throughout the market. The evidence is substantial, although not overwhelming (inside trading, for example, may be associated with some abnormal earnings). Furthermore, there is the so-called agency problem. Decisions made within a firm are made by individuals close to the problem. For those within a firm, attention may be concentrated on the restoration of production following loss rather than on the marketing issues that may determine whether any long-term business interruption is to occur. Even more important, those within a firm are directly affected in an economic sense by the reinvestment decision. For example, if reinvestment determines whether a firm continues to operate or goes into liquidation, then jobs, including the risk manager's, are tied into the decision. The point to be made is not that these factors should be excluded from the reinvestment decision, but rather that the terms of postloss financing convey useful information to the reinvestment decision. Thus if the terms of postloss financing are burdensome, it may well be that the firm is attempting to reinvest in a project that does not satisfy the appropriate financial criteria.

A further point concerning postloss financing should also be made here. It has been mentioned that postloss financing exposes a firm to the capital market conditions prevailing at the time of loss. While this does bring uncertainty into the risk management planning process, it must also be borne in mind that the reinvestment decision is also being made under the same market circumstances. If it turns out, to the chagrin of the risk manager, that reinvestment cannot be justified given current high market rates, then he or she may sit back to reflect on whether such reinvestment is really wise after all. Postloss financing does concentrate attention on whether a reinvestment is currently justified.

A DIGRESSION ON OPTIMAL CAPITAL STRUCTURE

The various sources of finance available to a firm have different costs depending on the level of risk to the investor and to the firm. For example, debt is usually cheaper than equity because it is less risky to the investor (who will therefore accept a lower expected yield) and more risky to the firm in view of the fixed interest and repayment provisions. However, a new issue of debt or equity after a loss will change the capital structure of a firm, which itself affects the financing costs. Before analyzing the choices available to a firm between various sources of finance, we must first summarize the effects of changes in the capital structure on the value of a firm and its cost of capital.

One of the interesting ongoing debates in finance concerns the relevance of capital structure, i.e., the ratio of long-term debt to equity employed by a firm. Much of current thinking is related to the well-known theorem of Modigliani and Miller (1958) that asserts that under perfect market conditions, capital structure does not affect the value of a firm and is therefore irrelevant. The required assumptions for such a proposition (including a later assumption added by Fama and Miller, 1972) are as follows:

1 There are no taxes.
2 Individuals and firms can borrow and lend at the same rate.
3 There are no transaction costs.
4 All investors share homogeneous expectations.
5 Investors protect existing positions in a firm against changes in capital structure by "me first" rules.

A complete exposition of this proposition is beyond our scope, although its main ingredients are necessary to proceed with our examination of postloss financing:

1 Debt is cheaper than equity. Debtholders have a more senior claim on the earnings of a firm than common shareholders, and the value of that claim usually is fixed. This implies that debt is a less risky form of investment for an investor. However, for a firm, debt is more risky, since there is seldom (an exception arises with income bonds) provision for reducing payment of interest and principle in the event of reduced earnings. Debt increases the prospect of insolvency. These relationships imply that investors will accept lower expected returns to hold debt than equity, but firms will be willing to offer higher expected returns to raise equity, which to them is less risky. Notice that debt is cheaper in the sense that the expected yields from debt currently being raised are lower than the expected return from new equity issues. This statement is not invalidated by observations that over certain time periods, the *delivered* yield on debt has been higher than that on equity. Remember that it is *expected* returns which determine the prices for which new issues sell.

2 The costs of both debt and equity increase with the level of leverage (the ratio of debt to equity). As more debt is issued, the new claims either are subordinate to existing claims or rank equally with existing claims. Subordinate claims, by their nature, are lower in the pecking order and are more risky. Alternatively, we may envision a big, rather than a small, issue of bonds that all share equal claims on a firm's earnings. The larger the issue, the larger the probability that a firm will default in servicing the debt and the more risk to all bondholders. Such higher levels of risk require higher yields, and this increases the cost of debt to a firm. However, equity risk also increases with leverage. The earnings of a firm contain some inherent level of risk. The brunt of this risk is borne by the residual claimholders, i.e., the shareholders, since claims of the debtholders are fixed and vary only in the event of default. Greater levels of leverage compress this risk on a smaller expected value of residual claims. This effect is illustrated in Figure 9-1. Consider a firm with earnings that fluctuate over time. The expected level is $0C$, but the range of fluctuation is $0E$ to $0D$. If there is no debt, the relative level of risk may be indicated by the ratio of the range of fluctuation DE to the expected level of earnings of shareholders $0C$, that is $DE/0C$. Roughly consistent with the scale of the figure, this might represent plus or minus 50 cents for each dollar of expected return. Now consider a low level of leverage with interest payments of $0A$. The expected earnings of shareholders is now $0C - 0A = AC$, but the operating risk has not changed. Thus the relative risk is now DE/AC, which is about plus or minus 75 cents for each dollar of expected return. With higher leverage, the interest payment will be $0B$, and the relative risk will be DE/BC perhaps plus or minus $1 for each dollar of expected return. This increase in risk with increased leverage will require compensation to shareholders in the form of higher expected rates of return.

3 The first two points together imply that the *average cost of capital* (which is a weighting of the cost of debt and the cost of equity by their respective proportions in the capital structure) is pulled in opposing directions by increases in leverage. Increases in leverage imply that a greater proportion of capital is in the form of the cheaper source, i.e., debt. This will pull down the weighted average cost of capital (WACC). However, increased leverage will force up the cost of each source of capital, tending to increase the weighted average cost of capital. These relationships are shown in Figure 9-2 in such a way that the opposing effects exactly offset each other, leaving the weighted average cost of capital as a horizontal line, i.e., independent of the level of leverage. So far, a perfectly horizontal shape has not been justified. It could have alternatively assumed the U shape shown by the dotted line. This would show the WACC to be minimized at leverage level X. Level X would be the optimal capital structure. This is so, since the WACC is the rate at which the firm's earnings are capitalized to derive the market value of the firm. The lower the discount rate, the higher the present value of earnings (assuming positive streams). Thus the market value is maximized at leverage level X.

FIGURE 9-1

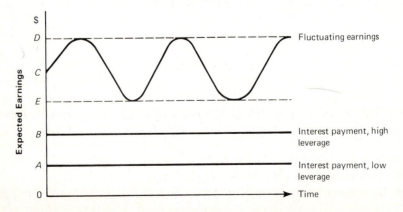

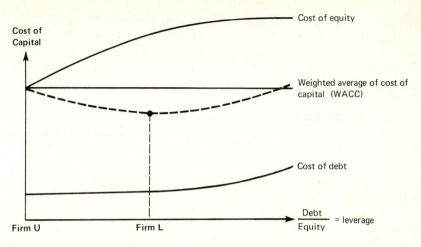

FIGURE 9-2

4 Suppose the effect on leverage is shown by the U-shaped curve in Figure 9-2. This implies that two firms that are identical in every respect, except that one has no leverage (see firm U in the figure) and the other has leverage level X (see firm L in the figure), would have different values. Firm L would have a higher value than firm U. We can illustrate these firms further by assuming that each has a constant annual expected level of earnings of, say, $100. Firm U, by definition, has no debt, but firm L has, say, $500 of debt at a 5% coupon rate of interest. Because of differences in leverage, shareholders capitalize firm U at 10% but firm L at 11% (these are the respective costs of equity). The values of the firms are shown in Table 9-1. Since earnings are constant, we can find the present value simply by dividing by capitalization rate. More important, notice that firm L has a higher market value than firm U, or equivalently, firm L has a lower weighted average cost of capital.

Now consider the position of an investor who owns 100% of firm L. His expected earnings are

$$1.0(100 - 25) = 75$$

Suppose that this investor undertakes the following transactions (which are permitted by our assumption that individuals can borrow at the same rate as firms):

   a He sells his equity in firm L for its market value of $682.
   b He borrows $318 at the market rate of 5%.
   c He now has sufficient funds to purchase all the equity in firm U for $1000.

TABLE 9-1
AN ILLUSTRATION OF CAPITAL STRUCTURE IRRELEVANCE

	Firm U	Firm L	
Expected earnings before interest	100	100	
Interest	—	25	
Earnings available to shareholders	100	75	
Equity capitalization rate	0.1	0.11	(0.15)
Market value of equity	$\frac{100}{0.1} = 1000$	$\frac{75}{0.11} = 682$	(500)
Market value of firm*	$V_E + V_D = 1000 + 0$ $= 1000$	$V_E + V_D = 682 + 500$ $= 1182$	(1000)
Weighted average cost of capital		$W_E k_E + W_D k_D = \frac{682}{682 + 500} 0.11$	

$$W_E k_E = W_D k_D = 0.1 + \frac{500}{682 + 500} 0.05 = 0.085$$

*V_E = market value of equity $\qquad$ W_D = weight of debt in capital structure
V_D = market value of debt $\qquad$ k_E = cost of equity
W_E = weight of equity in capital structure $\qquad$ k_D = cost of debt

Now the earnings of the individual (after deducting the interest payment on personal debt) are

$$1.0(100) - 0.05(318) = 84.1$$

In effect, the individual has substituted his ownership of a leveraged firm for a position in which personal borrowing or leverage permits him to own an unleveraged firm. This is a straight substitution of personal leverage for corporate leverage. In so doing, the individual has increased his earnings. Clearly, this is a rational move. However, the market effects of such moves are as follows: Excessive selling of the equity of a leveraged firm depresses its price. At the depressed price, the expected return would be higher (simultaneously, the price of firm U's equity would be bid up, depressing the rate of return). *This process would go on until there was no longer further advantage to be had from substitution of personal for corporate leverage. At that point, the values of the firms would be equalized, as would their respective WACCs.*

To illustrate the equilibrium position, consider the alternative figures in parentheses in Table 9-1 for firm L (these assume that all the equity price adjustment is borne by firm L). The price of firm L's stock has been depressed such that the capitalization rate increases from 0.11 to 0.15. The market value of equity thereby rises to 75/0.15 = 500, and the market value of the firm increases to $1000, which is identical to that of firm U. Notice also that firm L's WACC is now

$$\frac{500}{500 + 500} 0.15 + \frac{500}{500 + 500} 0.05 = 0.1$$

which is identical to that of firm U.

Now the reader should try the following exercise. Follow through the example of substituting further personal leverage for corporate leverage as shown above. This will confirm that no further advantage can be secured from playing this game. Thus we have an equilibrium situation in which no further price changes will arise. *In equilibrium, the market values of leveraged and unleveraged firms are identical, confirming the irrelevance of capital structure.* The demonstration outlined contains the essence of Modigliani and Miller's *homemade leverage theorem.*

5 The irrelevance proposition also requires that "me first" rules be in place. Detailed discussion is beyond our scope here, and an example will serve to illustrate. If capital structure is to be irrelevant to those owning claims on a firm, then no group must be penalized by any change in capital structure. Consider a firm with an outstanding mortgage bond issue. To finance a new project, a new bond issue is raised, and it is secured by the same assets as the old issue and is ranked equally in priority of claims on those assets. Clearly, the holders of the old bonds would not be indifferent to the increase in leverage from the new issue, since the security for the old debt would now be diluted. The old issue would become more risky and its price would fall. A "me first" rule would protect holders of the old issue by requiring that new issues be subordinate to outstanding claims.

The Modigliani-Miller theorem that capital structure does not affect the value of a firm was a landmark in corporate finance. Since its publication, a steady stream of papers has questioned the effects of relaxing the assumptions. It would be rash to take sides in the ensuing debate over whether irrelevance is of practical importance in a world without such restrictions. Certainly, homemade leverage is a substitute for corporate leverage, although with differences in borrowing costs, transaction costs, and taxes, it is difficult to argue that this will leave the WACC curve entirely flat as in Figure 9-2. Miller (1977) subsequently argued that irrelevance can withstand the introduction of some taxes, but this is a hot issue. Our inclination is to adopt the working premise that the WACC curve is fairly flat, but to stop short of stating that it is horizontal. This is tantamount to accepting that capital structure does affect the value of a firm, but with the proviso that any changes in value are not of large magnitude.

The framework we have outlined can now be used to examine choices between debt and equity to refinance investment after loss. The concepts are introduced graphically and then are developed in the following sections. Figure 9-3 shows the cost of capital of a firm and its component costs of equity and debt at different levels of leverage. Suppose the preloss capital structure is $100 debt and $100 equity, both at market values. The debt equity ratio therefore is unity (shown as 1 in the figure). A loss of $50 arises. The valuation of loss is, equivalently, the cost of replacing destroyed assets or the loss in market value of equity. The postloss debt/equity ratio is 100/ 50 = 2, as shown in the figure. At this higher level of leverage, the cost of equity

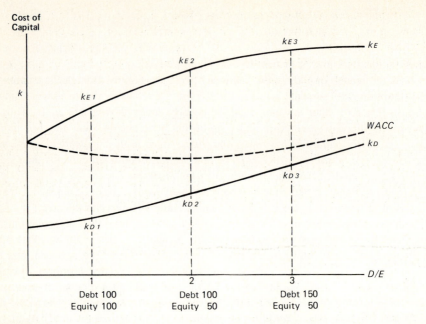

FIGURE 9-3

would increase, reflecting the increased risk to stockholders, as shown by the curve k_E. The cost of servicing existing debt is k_{D1}, but any new debt that needs to be raised will require an expected cost of k_{D2}. The resulting weighted average cost of capital may be higher or lower depending on the shape of the WACC curve. If the loss is financed by an equity issue, the leverage ratio will be restored to $100/100 = 1$, thereby restoring the WACC to the original level. The effect of debt financing is also shown. However, this route will increase the leverage ratio to 3. The new debt will probably be junior to existing debt, and its cost will be greater, as shown by the increasing slope of curve k_D. However, the higher leverage will also bid up the cost of equity in view of the higher potential variability in returns to stockholders. The resulting WACC is shown at leverage level 3. Since the WACC curve can be used to show the capital structure that maximizes the value of a firm, it can also be used to choose between the alternative forms of financing reinvestment. That alternative with the lower WACC will imply the higher market value for the firm and should be preferred. As drawn in Figure 9-3, it appears that equity financing is preferred, but in general, the choice depends on the relative shapes of k_E and k_D. Two special cases should be noted:

1 In the Modigliani-Miller world, the WACC curve is horizontal, and choice between debt and equity would therefore be irrelevant.

2 If the irrelevance proposition does not strictly hold and the WACC curve is U-shaped, and if the firm had adjusted to its optimal capital structure before the loss, then equity financing for the loss would be preferred. In other words, the preloss capital structure (1) would be optimal by definition if it corresponded with the lowest point on the WACC curve. After loss, it would clearly be optimal to return to this position with equity financing.

However, these two cases make strong assumptions about the real world and the efficiency of the financing choices made by firms. To provide generality for our decision, we will not beg the questions that markets are perfect or that effective choices are always made. This more relaxed position can be supported by some recent work that has found capital structure to be relevant in the light of personal and corporate taxes and agency costs (for example, DeAngelo and Masulis, 1980).

ANALYSIS OF POSTLOSS FINANCING WHEN THE EARNINGS STREAM IS CONSTANT

We have tried to guard against a simple view that short-term sources of funds must be used for short-term purposes and long-term sources must be used for long-term purposes. Nevertheless, if the reinvestment calls for substantial funds, then a firm may expose itself to a significant liquidity problem and/or the inherent risks of imminent refunding unless it secures long-term financing. Thus we will focus on financing strategies that affect the capital structure of a firm, and in so doing, we will call into play the issues summarized from the capital structure "irrelevancy" debate. Our examination will develop as follows: In order to concentrate on the structure of a firm's cash flows, we will first consider the effect of postloss financing strategies for a firm whose expected future earnings are constant. This will permit us to present the analysis in the form of a familiar income statement. The assumption of no growth in cash flows is somewhat restrictive, so we will then relax this assumption and incorporate specific growth estimates into the cash flows.

For almost every firm, future earnings cannot be predicted with certainty. The degree of uncertainty attaching to our estimates will depend on how much information we have and will vary according to how far into the future we wish to predict. Strictly speaking, the valuation model requires a prediction of each and every earnings flow from the current year into perpetuity. Such forecasting is for the gods! However, we invariably have some relevant information concerning future earnings. We can monitor the track record of past earnings. This gives us some information about the quality of the incumbent management, the demand for the firm's products, and, perhaps, the dynamics of competition within the industry in which the firm operates. This and similar information give us some yardstick from which to assess future earnings potential. However, the best we are probably likely to do in our earnings forecast is to project some average path about which earnings will fluctuate; the fluctuation perhaps will be due to a combination of random and systematic factors. Thus the earnings forecast may well be of the form

$$\tilde{E}_i = E_0(1 + g)^i \qquad i = 1, 2, 3, \ldots, \infty \tag{9-1}$$

where $\tilde{E}_i$ = earnings estimated for year i

$\quad\ E_0$ = current level of earnings

$\qquad g$ = estimated growth rate

One special case of such a project arises when $g = 0$, that is, when expected earnings are constant. There may well be some random fluctuation in earnings, and depending on the degree of fluctuation and whether it is systematic or unsystematic, an appropriate risk premium is required in the rate at which the earnings stream is discounted to value the firm. Nevertheless, the underlying growth rate is assumed to be zero. However, the underlying growth trend may be positive or even negative. Thus to lighten the formidable task of guessing at each E_i in the future, our judgment is fed into an estimate of the underlying growth trend g. Accordingly, our estimated E_i will take the form of a growth path of expected values and will require a suitable risk adjustment to the discount rate.

The valuation model derived in Chapter 7 discounted estimated earnings in order to value the firm or its equity:

$$\text{MVE} = \sum_{i=0}^{\infty} \frac{E_i}{(1 + k_E)^i} \tag{9-2}$$

where MVE = value of equity

$\qquad E_i$ = estimated earnings for year i

$\qquad k_E$ = cost of equity capital

We can decompose earnings into the current base level of earnings and an expected growth factor; thus $E_i = E_0(1 + g)^i$. Using this, and noting that the summation is to infinity, we can follow previous procedures to reduce MVE as follows:

$$\text{MVE} = \sum_{i=0}^{\infty} \frac{E_0(1 + g)^i}{(1 + k_E)^i} = \frac{E_0}{k_E - g} \tag{9-3}$$

For the time being, we will concentrate on problems in which a firm's expected earnings are not growing; thus our equity valuation model simplifies to E_0/k_E.

Since our intention is to value the equity of a firm, the appropriate earnings stream to discount is that which is available to shareholders. This requires that prior claims of interest and taxation be deducted. Notice that earnings, not dividends, are being discounted, although for reasons analyzed earlier, we have argued that these can be expected to lead to equivalent values. To achieve some familiarity with this approach, consider first the impact of a loss on the value of a firm.

EXAMPLE: H&RD CHEESE

Howard and Roger Davis were dairy farmers who diversified into processing and packaging of their own dairy products. After some years, the brothers perceived a market for synthetic cheeses for use by fast-food restaurants, etc. Investment in this process proved successful, and the firm incorporated under the name H&RD Cheese (lovingly misquoted in the trade as "HARD Cheese"). Expansion was financed by both debt and equity, the firm having $2 million in debt at 10% interest and 500,000 common shares outstanding. Two plants were operated, one for dairy products and one for synthetic cheese. In each case, initial growth has peaked, and earnings having stabilized at an expected annual rate of $1 million. The synthetic cheese plant suffered severe damage from flood and windstorm, a risk that had been retained by the firm because geographic features had rendered flood insurance prohibitively expensive. The loss is virtually total, although some salvage of machinery is possible. The building requires major reconstruction. The loss is estimated by an assessor to be $2 million; that is, a reinvestment of this amount is required in order to reestablish production of synthetic cheese. We will measure the impact of the loss on the value of the firm and establish whether the firm should reinvest in continued production of synthetic cheese. To make the necessary calculations, we will work through the example ignoring corporate tax. The treatment of tax is complex, and we will defer a more complete presentation until Chapter 15. The market capitalization rate of H&RD's equity is 15%. Since dairy products and synthetic cheese have similar levels of market risk, the discount rate will not be affected by the postloss concentration of production in dairy products. However, it will be recalled that the cost of equity is affected by the level of leverage. The effect of loss on leverage can be seen by looking at the debt-to-equity ratio. Debt is contractually determined and is unaffected by the loss. The debt/equity ratio will have increased. To compensate for this additional leverage, shareholders will capitalize the firm's equity at a somewhat higher rate, say, 17%, in view of the increased financial risk. The additional risk may be perceived in the following terms: The firm's earnings will fall as a result of the loss, but its interest commitment will be unaffected. Thus shareholders have to absorb any fluctuations in earnings with a smaller expected residual income.

Table 9-2 summarizes the capital market's response to the loss. The flood has destroyed equity value. The expected earnings of the firm have fallen from an annual $2 million to $1 million. The loss in value of equity results (1) because shareholders now capitalize a reduced earnings stream, and (2) because shareholders now capitalize the stream at a higher rate in view of the increased leverage risk. It may be possible for the firm to recapture some of this lost value by reinvestment. The cost of reconstruction, etc. is $2 million. Ignoring any interruption loss, the firm will be able to restore its level of annual earnings to $2 million. Since the only prior claim on earnings is the fixed interest payment, H&RD will secure an incremental cash flow of $1 million per year on this reinvestment, which is equivalent to an internal rate of return of $1 million/$2 million = 50%. The firm will be able to recapture some of the lost value if the cost of capital is less than 50%.

Another point worth noting at this stage is the effect of loss on the cost of capital. The WACC has increased from 14.29% to 14.9%. This is a combination of two effects:

1 The destruction of equity has resulted in a higher debt-to-equity ratio. Since debt is cheaper than equity, and debt now represents a higher proportion of total capital, the effect is to pull down the WACC.

2 However, increased leverage increases the riskiness of equity capital, which is therefore capitalized at a higher rate by investors.

In this example, the second effect dominates the first; thus the cost of capital rises. Other examples may well reverse this result.

TABLE 9-2
H&RD CHEESE: THE EFFECT OF LOSS ON EQUITY VALUE

	Before loss	After loss
Earnings before interest and taxation (EBIT)	2,000,000	(Estimated) 1,000,000
Interest	200,000	200,000
Taxable earnings	1,800,000	800,000
Taxation (assume zero)	—	—
Earnings available for distribution to shareholders (E)	1,800,000	800,000
Earnings per share (EPS)	$3.6	$1.6
Market capitalization rate (k_E)[†]	0.15	0.17
Price per share (EPS/k_E)	$\dfrac{\$3.6}{0.15} = \$24$	$\dfrac{\$1.6}{0.17} = \$9.41$
Market value of equity (E/k_E)	$\dfrac{\$1.8 \text{ million}}{0.15} = \$12 \text{ million}$	$\dfrac{\$0.8 \text{ million}}{0.17} = \$4.71 \text{ million}$
Market value of firm[‡]	$2 million + $12 million	$2 million + $4.71 million = $6.71 million
Weighted average cost of capital (WACC)[§]	$\dfrac{2}{14}.1 + \dfrac{12}{14}.15 = 0.1429$	$\dfrac{2}{6.71}.1 + \dfrac{4.71}{6.71}.17 = 0.149$

[†]Notice that the ratio of debt to equity rises from 2/12 to 2/4.71. This increase in leverage accounts for the higher capitalization rate after loss.
[‡]Market value of debt plus market value of equity.
[§]$\text{WACC} = W_E k_E + W_D k_D$, where W_E = weighting of equity in capital structure, W_D = weighting of debt in capital structure, k_E = cost of equtiy, and k_D = costs of debt.

The last two issues discussed in relation to H&RD Cheese related to the internal rate of return on reinvestment and to the weighted average cost of capital. The interaction of these two concepts can be used to decide whether reinvestment should be undertaken and, if so, what form of financing should be secured. We will keep with the case of H&RD Cheese, but we will avail the company of two sources of finance; debt or equity.

H&RD Cheese: Refinancing

To finance the reinvestment, H&RD Cheese requires $2 million. This can be arranged by a bond issue, but the terms of this issue are determined both by the current capital market conditions and by the relative seniority of this issue vis-à-vis the $2 million debt issue already outstanding. The terms of the previous issue, which is a mortgage bond issue, require that it cannot be outranked by subsequent issues. Any new issue will be a debenture issue at a coupon rate of 12%. The increased rate reflects the increased riskiness of the junior security. If the reinvestment is undertaken with the debenture issue, the cost is not confined to the 12% coupon payable. The issue will increase the leverage of the firm and will consequently bid up the capitalization rate for equity. The incremental cost of equity is part of the incremental cost of capital. The cost of equity will increase from 15% to 17%.

The alternative to debt is to issue new equity. In this example, there is no interruption loss; thus earnings will be restored to the preloss level. This implies that the original capital structure of the firm will be restored; therefore, the cost of equity will remain at 15%. The restoration of the original capital structure will become apparent with the development of this example.

Table 9-3 reproduces the main elements of Table 9-2 in the first two columns. Column 3 shows the effects of debt financing for the reinvestment. This will increase the total value of

TABLE 9-3
H&RD CHEESE: POSTLOSS FINANCING

	1 Before loss	2 After loss, with no reinvestment	After loss and reinvestment with:	
			3 Debt	4 Equity
Earnings before-interest and taxation (EBIT)	$2,000,000	$1,000,000	$2,000,000	$2,000,000
Interest	200,000	200,000	440,000	200,000
Earnings available for distribution (E)*	1,800,000	800,000	1,560,000	1,800,000
Number of shares†	500,000	500,000	500,000	?
Earnings per share (EPS)†	$3.6	$1.6	$3.12	?
Market capitalization rate (k_E)‡	0.15	0.17	0.17	0.15
Price per share (EPS/k_E)†	$\dfrac{3.6}{0.15} = \$24$	$\dfrac{1.6}{0.17} = \$9.41$	$\dfrac{3.12}{0.17} = \$18.3$	?
Market value of equity (E/k_E)	$\dfrac{1.8 \text{ million}}{0.15} = \$12 \text{ million}$	$\dfrac{0.8 \text{ million}}{0.17} = 4.71 \text{ million}$	$\dfrac{1.56 \text{ million}}{0.17} = 9.18 \text{ million}$	$\dfrac{1.8 \text{ million}}{0.15} = \$12 \text{ million}$
Market value of firm	$\$2 \text{ million} + \$12 \text{ million} = \$14 \text{ million}$	$\$2 \text{ million} + \$4.71 \text{ million} = \$6.71 \text{ million}$	$\$4 \text{ million} + \$9.18 \text{ million} = \$13.18 \text{ million}$	$\$2 \text{ million} + \$12 \text{ million} = \$14 \text{ million}$
Weighted average cost of capital (WACC)§	$\dfrac{2}{14}\,0.1 + \dfrac{12}{14}\,0.15$ $= 0.1429$	$\dfrac{2}{6.71}\,0.1 + \dfrac{4.71}{6.71}\,0.17$ $= 0.149$	$= 0.152$	$\dfrac{2}{14}\,0.1 + \dfrac{12}{14}\,0.15$ $= 0.1429$

*We simply ignore tax here. This example is developed in Chapter 15 with tax.
†See explanation in text for column 4.
‡Note that the leverage ratio in column 3 is 4/9.18 = 0.44, with 2/4.71 = 0.42 in column 2. This similarity explains the equivalent values for k_E in these columns.
§The weighted average cost of capital in column 3 comprises the respective values for mortgage bonds, debentures, and equity, namely

$$\frac{2}{13.18}\,0.1 + \frac{2}{13.18}\,0.12 + \frac{9.18}{13.18}\,0.17 = 0.152$$

outstanding debt to $4 million, of which $2 million is at 10% and $2 million is at 12%, resulting in a total interest payment of $440,000. In the subsequent rows, the price of each share, the market value of equity, and the market value of the firm are calculated. It will be seen that the firm recovers some, but not all, of the lost value of equity. The share price recovers from $9.41 to $18.3 as a result of the reinvestment, thereby confining the capital loss per share to $5.7 ($24 − $18.3) instead of a loss of $14.59 ($24 − $9.41), which would have prevailed had H&RD not reinvested. Turning attention to the loss in total equity, a divergency appears between the destruction in total value of equity (LMVE) and the market value of the destroyed resources (MVLR). In this case, the two criteria for measuring loss do not produce identical results. The reason is that the debt has not been available on the same terms as the original debt. Furthermore, the increased leverage has increased the cost of equity. These two effects have increased the weighted average cost of capital. If debt financing is chosen, then these effects become a relevant cost to the firm, and in measuring the impact of potential losses, the risk manager should include any financing costs of this nature. This consideration argues in favor of the use of LMVE over MVLR. The choice does not matter when capital structure is irrelevant or when there are no transaction costs, since they produce the same answer, but when these conditions are violated, MVLR fails to account for all the consequences of the loss. Had we been in a Modigliani-Miller world in which capital structure is irrelevant, we would have arrived at the same measure of loss. This would occur because increased leverage would produce a neutral effect on WACC (it would be 0.1429 before and after loss). A summary of possible results of refinancing in a simple Modigliani-Miller world is presented in Table 9-4. Readers should review their understanding of these concepts by reproducing the results.

Our attention is now turned to the final column of Table 9-3 to examine the effect of equity financing for the reinvestment. Some (as yet undetermined) number of shares must be issued at a sufficient (again undetermined) price to raise the $2 million required for reinvestment. H&RD Cheese will have suffered some destruction in the value of its original owners' equity. However, it may issue new equity to replace that destroyed value. Thus in terms of capital structure, it will restore the preloss proportions of debt and equity, the only difference being that equity will now be subdivided into the claims of new shareholders and those of old shareholders. Since the old capital structure is restored, the WACC should return to its preloss level, with equity capitalized at 15%, as shown in column 4 of Table 9-3. Discounting the earnings available to shareholders at this rate gives a total market value of equity of $12 million,

TABLE 9-4
DEBT FINANCING IN THE MODIGLIANI-MILLER WORLD

	Before loss	**After loss**
Earnings before deduction of interest	$2,000,000	$2,000,000
WACC	0.1429	0.1429
Market value of firm:	$\dfrac{\$2.0 \text{ million}}{0.1429} = \$14 \text{ million}$	$\dfrac{\$2.0 \text{ million}}{0.1429} = \$14 \text{ million}$
Of which debt is:	$2 million	$4 million
Of which equity is:	$12 million	$10 million

Note: LMVE = $2 million, and MVLR = $2 million.

of which $2 million represents the new issues and the remaining $10 million represents the claims of the old shareholders. In using the criterion LMVE to measure loss, we need to be cautious in making this distinction between old and new shareholders. The LMVE criterion refers exclusively to existing equity, since the loss in value is suffered entirely by the existing shareholders.

Comparing the results in column 4 with the alternative of debt financing shown in column 3 reveals that equity financing is preferable to debt financing. Equity financing will result in a larger market value of the firm, $14 million as compared with the $13.8 million from debt financing. This implies that old equity is also more valuable. Of the total $12 million old and new equity from equity financing, $2 million represents the new equity, leaving old equity valued at $10 million. The value of equity (all old) with debt financing is only $9.18 million. We should also find the advantage of equity financing to be revealed in the new stock price, but this is still to be determined.

If H&RD Cheese is to secure the advantages of equity financing, it must be able to determine how many shares to issue and at what price. Since the capitalization rate is 15%, new shares must be priced such that they offer new shareholders an expected return of 15%. Investors will not subscribe if the return is any less. To calculate the missing values for column 4 of Table 9-3, we know that the price per share must be equal to the total market value of equity divided by the total (old plus new) number of shares, that is,

$$p = \frac{\text{MVE}}{m + n} \tag{9-4}$$

where p = price per share
$\quad$ MVE = market value of equity
$\quad\quad m$ = number of old shares
$\quad\quad n$ = number of new shares

However, we also must raise I = $2 million to finance the reinvestment by issuing n shares at this undetermined price p:

$$I = pn = \left[\frac{\text{MVE}}{m + n}\right]n \tag{9-5}$$

Straightforward manipulation reveals that

$$n = \frac{mI}{\text{MVE} - I} \tag{9-6}$$

Using the values for H&RD Cheese yields

$$n = \frac{\$2 \text{ million}(500,000)}{\$12 \text{ million} - \$2 \text{ million}} = 100,000 \text{ shares}$$

We know that $I = pn$, so

$$p = \frac{I}{n} = \frac{\$2 \text{ million}}{100{,}000} = \$20 \text{ per share}$$

The only other missing value in column 4 of Table 9.3 is the earnings per share (EPS). This is simply calculated as follows:

$$\text{EPS} = \frac{E}{m + n} = \frac{\$18 \text{ million}}{600{,}000} = \$3 \tag{9-7}$$

The reader can now substitute these values back into Table 9-4.

Notice that the share price confirms our predictions. We have already argued that equity financing is preferred, since *old* equity has a higher market value. This is equivalent to saying that the capital loss *per share* is lower under equity financing (that is, $\$4 = \$24 - \$20$) than under debt financing (capital loss $= \$5.7 = \$24 - \$18.3$). Thus the advantage of equity financing is also shown in the higher price.

The development of the H&RD Cheese example has been somewhat lengthy. However, we can streamline the criterion for making choices considerably with a little formalization. The criterion for choosing between competing methods of financing is to select that method which maximizes the market value of old equity (or equivalently the market value of the firm). Using subscripts O and T for old and total equity, we can state the following relationship:

$$\text{MVE}_O = \text{MVE}_T \frac{m}{m + n} \tag{9-8}$$

Or simply, old equity is simply that proportion of total equity which the number of existing shares m bears to the total number of shares (old plus new) $m + n$. We have already shown in equation (9-6) that the required number of new shares is

$$n = \frac{mI}{\text{MVE}_T - I} \tag{9-6}$$

where I is the equity financing required. Therefore, by simple substitution of equation (9-6) into equation (9-8), we have

$$\text{MVE}_O = \text{MVE}_T \frac{1}{1 + I/(\text{MVE}_T - I)} \tag{9-9}$$

We also know that the total market value of equity MVE_T is simply

$$MVE_T = \frac{EBIT - N_1 - N_2}{k_E}$$ (9-10)

where N_1 = interest on outstanding debt
$\quad\quad N_2$ = interest on new debt
$\quad EBIT$ = earnings before interest and taxation

We can therefore apply these formulas to review our analysis for H&RD Cheese:

	With debt	With equity
EBIT	$2,000,000	$2,000,000
N_1	$ 200,000	$ 200,000
N_2	$ 240,000	—
k_e	0.17	0.15
m	500,000	500,000
I	—	$2,000,000

Solution with

Debt	Equity
$MVE_T = \dfrac{\$2 \text{ million} - 0.2 \text{ million} - 0.24 \text{ million}}{0.17}$	$\dfrac{\$2 \text{ million} - 0.2 \text{ million}}{0.15} = \$12 \text{ million}$
$\quad = \$9.18 \text{ million}$	
$MVE_O = 9.18 \left[\dfrac{1}{1 + 0/(9.12 - 0)} \right]$	$MVE_O = 12 \left[\dfrac{1}{1 + 2/(12 - 2)} \right]$
$\quad = \$9.18 \text{ million}$	$\quad = \$10 \text{ million}$
$n = 0$	$n = \dfrac{2 \text{ million}(500,000)}{12 \text{ million} - 2 \text{ million}} = 100,000$

We can now summarize this section and the messages it brings. Our analysis indicated that we should choose that method of financing which maximizes the value of equity of existing shareholders. In fact, we could have used any of the following criteria:

1 Maximize the value of existing owners' equity
2 Maximize the share price
3 Maximize the market value of the firm
4 Minimize the weighted average cost of capital

To show that we can use these criteria interchangeably, consider the following:

Criteria 1 and 2 must give the same result, since the price per share is simply the total value of existing owners' equity divided by the number of shares held by existing owners, which is a constant.

Criteria 3 and 1 must give the same result, since the market value of the firm is simply the market value of existing owners' equity plus the value of new securities. These new securities have just been priced to raise the amount required for reinvestment; therefore, the immediate value of these new securities is the same, regardless of whether they represent debt or equity.

Criteria 4 and 3 are equivalent, since the lower the WACC, the higher will be the discounted value of the firm's earnings (for distribution to both debtholders and shareholders), which, by definition, is the value of the firm.

POSTLOSS FINANCING WHEN THE EARNINGS STREAM IS NOT CONSTANT

We reduced the problem of forecasting the earnings of a firm to manageable terms by estimating only the growth trend. Using current earnings E_0 as a base, we were then able to value the firm's equity by the formula

$$\sum_{i=0}^{\infty} \frac{E_0(1 + g)^i}{(1 + k_E)^i} + \frac{E_0}{k_E - g} \tag{9-11}$$

The analysis in the previous section looked at the special case where growth was zero. We now consider other growth rates. In so doing, we will try to preserve our tabular form of analysis. This requires that forecasts be made of the growth in earnings. Since the value of equity is the capitalized value of the earnings available to common shareholders (E), rather than earnings before interest and taxation (EBIT), the relevant growth rate is that for E. Some complexity is added to this task by the fact that the growth forecast will itself depend on the form of financing chosen for the reinvestment. This issue is discussed in the appendix to this chapter, and the outcome is that separate growth rate estimates will be required for equity and debt financing. These are labeled g_1 and g_2, respectively. The criteria for choosing between the competing forms of financing are now adapted to the growth context and are reproduced in Table 9-5.

TABLE 9-5
FORMULAS FOR SELECTING BETWEEN DEBT AND
EQUITY FINANCING (GROWTH CASE)

$$MVE_O = MVE_T \frac{1}{1 + I/MVE_T - I} \tag{9-9}$$

$$n = \frac{mI}{MVE_T - I} \tag{9-6}$$

$$MVE_T = \frac{EBIT - N_1}{k_E - g_1} \quad \text{with equity financing} \tag{9-12a}$$

$$MVE_T = \frac{EBIT - N_1 - N_2}{k_E - g_2} \quad \text{with debt financing} \tag{9-12b}$$

Equations (9-6) and (9-9) are simply reproduced, although equation (9-10) is now modified to allow for the growth prospects. This is shown as equation (9-12a) and equation (9-12b). The following example is designed to illustrate the growth effects.

EXAMPLE: PLIABLE PLASTICS

Pliable Plastics manufactures assorted plastic products. Earnings (EBIT) for the current year are estimated to be $10 million, although these are projected to grow at an annual rate of 2%. The firm has $20 million debt outstanding at 8% interest, together with 2 million common shares with a current market value of $56 million. The market capitalizes equity at 17%. A fire loss occurs and the assessor estimates the replacement cost of damage to be $20 million. Unless the firm reinvests, earnings are expected to fall to $7 million (current year). Without reinvestment, the market would capitalize equity at 18%, reflecting the increased debt-to-equity ratio.

Two alternative financing plans for reinvestment are proposed:

1 Finance entirely with debt. This could be raised by a second mortgate bond issue at 8.5% coupon rate. The increased leverage of this option implies that investors would discount equity at 18%. Estimated earnings growth is 2.5% with this alternative.

2 Finance entirely with a common share issue, the expected cost of equity being 17%. Estimated earnings growth is 2.0%.

If no reinvestment is undertaken, it is expected that earnings, after interest, would grow at 2.25%.

The alternative financing strategies are presented in Table 9-6. The calculations should now be fairly straightforward. The first two columns present the preloss situation and the impact of loss, assuming no reinvestment. Calculations follow the pattern of the previous table, except that equity values (and prices) are derived taking growth into account, as shown in the equations in Table 9-5. The next two columns show the respective financing strategies. Calculations for column 3 are straightforward. Column 5 requires the calculation of an appropriate number of shares to be issued. This calculation follows equation (9-6). Thus, for example, with equity financing, we require that $I = \$20$ million.

Noting that

$$\text{MVE}_I = \frac{\$10,000,000 - \$1,600,000}{0.17 - 0.02} \tag{9-12a}$$
$$= \$56,000,000$$

we calculate n as follows:

$$n = \frac{mI}{\text{MVE}_T - I} = \frac{2,000,000(\$20,000,000)}{(\$56,000,000) - (\$20,000,000)} = 1,111,111$$

The rest of the calculations are fairly routine.

Now we can examine the result generated by this example:

1 The market value of existing owners' equity is highest with all debt financing, or equivalently,

TABLE 9-6
PLIABLE PLASTICS: DEBT VERSUS EQUITY FINANCING, A GROWTH EXAMPLE

	1 Before loss	2 After loss (no reinvestment)	3 Debt financing ($20 million)	4 Equity financing ($20 million)
EBIT	$10,000,000	$7,000,000	$10,000,000	$10,000,000
Interest:				
Old debt	$1,600,000	$1,600,000	$1,600,000	$1,600,000
New debt	—	—	$1,700,000	—
Earnings available for distribution (E)	$8,400,000	$5,400,000	$6,700,000	$8,400,000
Number of shares				
Old (m)	2,000,000	2,000,000	2,000,000	2,000,000
New (n)	—	—	—	1,111,111
Earnings per share (EPS)	$4.2	$2.7	$3.35	$2.7
Equity capitalization rate (k_E)	0.17	0.18	0.18	0.17
Expected growth of earnings (g)	0.02	0.0225	$g_2 = 0.025$	$g_1 = 0.02$
Price per share $[EPS/(k_E - g)]$	$28	$17.14	$21.61	$18.0
Market value of equity $[E/(k_E - g)]$	$56,000,000	$34,285,714	$43,225,806	$56,000,000
Market value of firm				
Debt	$20,000,000	$20,000,000	$40,000,000	$20,000,000
Old equity (MVE_O)	$56,000,000	$34,285,714	$43,225,806	$36,000,000
New equity (MVE_T)	—	—	—	20,000,000
	$76,000,000	$54,285,714	$83,225,806	$76,000,000
Weighted average cost of capital	0.146	0.143	0.133	0.146

2 The price per share is highest with all debt financing.

3 The total market value of the firm is highest with all debt financing.

4 The WACC is lowest with all debt financing.

Thus, unambiguously, debt financing for the reinvestment is preferred. In this case, the lower cost of debt (new debt being 8.5%) more than outweighs the effect of the risk premium investors impose on outstanding equity given the increased leverage (the price of equity is bid up to 18% with all debt financing and 17.5% with part debt financing from the level of 17% with all equity financing).

SOME COMPLICATIONS: TRANSACTION COSTS
AND INTERRUPTION LOSS

Both interruption loss and transaction costs to the financing arrangements were introduced in the last chapter. Both have a negative effect on the net present value of the reinvestment cash flows, and we will see that they also cause some complications in our analysis of postloss financing. Transaction costs are easier to deal with. These include issue and underwriting costs incurred during the flotation of the issue, together with any internal processing costs, legal expenses, etc. Conceptually, we can treat these as deadweight costs in the accounts for the financial year in question; this approach will fit well with our tax treatment later. However, this implies that our expected cash flow is not constant or does not follow a smooth growth curve. The cash flow will take a sudden dip in the year of loss and then return to a smoother pattern.

Interruption losses (as shown in Figure 9-4) also prove to be inconvenient in destroying the smoothness of the expected cash flows. Our introductory treatment in Chapter 8, together with more detailed analysis to follow in Chapter 14, separates interruption loss into permanent and temporary components. Many losses of any size

FIGURE 9-4

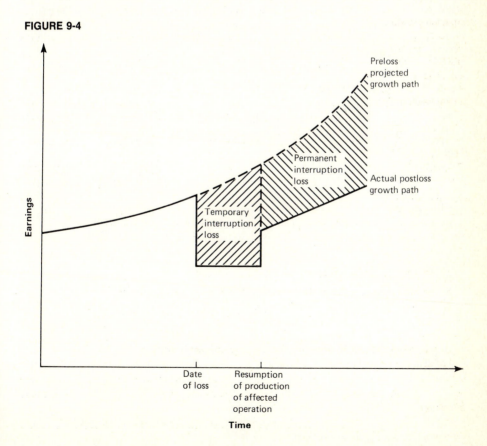

will cause some interruption in trading and consequent loss of earnings. If the firm is able to regain its projected preloss growth path, the interruption loss may be considered to be only temporary. However, if the firm is unable to reach that path, there will be both temporary and permanent effects. We represent these ideas in Figure 9-4.

Conceptually, these ideas are simple, but in practice, estimation of preloss and postloss cash flows may be very difficult, and the results are subject to wide margins of error. Furthermore, the loss itself may increase future earnings uncertainty, since any temporary interruption may result in rival firms posturing to absorb the business of the distressed firm on a permanent basis. These issues will be taken up in Chapter 14. However, notice for the moment that this added uncertainty may force the firm's cost of capital upward. We will combine these effects in an example.

EXAMPLE: DIPSOMANIA BREWERY

Dipsomania Brewery suffered a major fire that apparently started in packaging materials and then spread with the aid of combustible floors and roofing materials to cause severe damage to much of the brewery. The tragedy was complete when the fire department, without adequate water supplies, released the main brewing vats to combat the spreading fire in the lower-level east wing of the brewery. In the aftermath, financial data and forecasts are assembled to determine whether the plant should be rebuilt and, if so, how the reinvestment should be financed. The relevant details are summarized as follows:

Existing capital structure: $20 million debt in a 10% debenture issue; 1 million common shares outstanding, which the market capitalizes at 15%.

Preloss earnings: Earnings for the current year are expected to be $15 million; no growth is forecast.

Postloss earnings (assuming reinvestment): Earnings for the current year are expected to be reduced to $5 million. The firm expects it can recover most of its lost market share by next year, when earnings are expected to stabilize at $14 million. If reinvestment is not undertaken, the firm will have no earnings and will go into liquidation.

Cost of reinvestment: The rebuilding/re-equipment cost is $30 million, although, in addition, a major advertising program will be necessary to reestablish consumer purchasing patterns; the cost will be $5 million.

Financing Alternatives

An insurance policy paying $15 million is available. Reinvestment will require an additional $20 million from either of the following sources:

1 Use all debt. A coupon rate of 12% is expected. Leverage and increased operating risk after the fire increase the capitalization rate on equity to 17%. The issue cost of debt is estimated at $0.2 million.

2 Use all equity. The appropriate capitalization rate is 16%, and the issue costs are $0.3 million.

First, we will address the question of reinvestment; then, if the answer to that issue is positive, we will address the question of financing.

Reinvestment

The cost of reinvestment is $35 million. (Although $15 million in insurance money is available, this money has an opportunity cost, as do all other sources of finance). Reinvestment will generate the following level of earnings before interest and taxation:

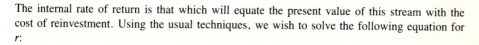

Year:	0	1	2	3	...	infinity
Millions of dollars:	5	14	14	14		

The internal rate of return is that which will equate the present value of this stream with the cost of reinvestment. Using the usual techniques, we wish to solve the following equation for r:

$$0 = -35 + 5 + \left(\frac{1}{1+r}\right)\sum_{i=1}^{\infty}\frac{14}{(1+r)^i}$$

However, the last term can be represented as the sum of an infinite series (NPV $= c/r$) in the following manner:

$$0 = -35 + 5 + \frac{1}{1+r}\frac{14}{r}$$

which gives IRR $= 34\%$. Notice that we have ignored the transaction costs of reinvestment so far, but it seems fairly clear that reinvestment is warranted given the orders of magnitude of the components of the cost of capital.

Choice of Financing

The financing choice is summarized in Table 9-7 shown at the top of p. 244. The tabulation is slightly streamlined to illustrate the application of the appropriate formulas. The calculation simply follows the previous example. We have treated issue costs as expenditures in the year of issue. However, advertising costs have been treated with other capital, since the issue proceeds are used to meet this expense.

SUMMARY AND CONCLUSION

If a firm chooses to reinvest after loss, it will require an appropriate source of funds. Financing may be secured before, and in anticipation of, future losses, e.g., insurance. Alternatively, a firm may seek financing when it is required, i.e., after a loss. This chapter addresses postloss financing.

Postloss financing may take the form of available liquid resources. Firms usually do maintain some level of liquidity. One study suggested that those firms most likely to choose reinvestment tend to be those which maintain the highest levels of liquidity. Cash and marketable securities thus provide a potentially important source of postloss finance. An alternative is to seek external funding, such as new debt or equity. One objection that has been raised is that external financing raised after loss will be more

TABLE 9-7
BREWERY ANALYSIS OF POSTLOSS FINANCING ALTERNATIVES

	Debt		Equity	
	Year of loss (Year 0)	**Subsequent year (Year 1)**	**Year of loss**	**Subsequent year**
EBIT	$5 million	$14 million	$5 million	$14 million
Interest:				
Old	$2 million	$2 million	$2 million	$2 million
new	$2.4 million	$2.4 million	—	—
Financing cost	$0.2 million	—	$0.3 million	—
Earnings for distribution (E)	$0.4 million	$9.6 million	$2.7 million	$12 million
Number of shares				
Old (m)	1,000,000	1,000,000	1,000,000	1,000,000
New $= \dfrac{ml}{MVE_T - I}$				
$= n$	—	—	422,297	422,297
Total	1,000,000	1,000,000	1,422,297	1,422,297
Equity capitalization rate (k_E)	0.17	0.17	0.16	0.16
Market value of equity (MVE_T)		$\dfrac{9.6 \text{ million}}{0.17}$ $= 56.47$ million		$\dfrac{12 \text{ million}}{0.16}$ $= 75$ million
		$0.4 + \dfrac{56.47}{1 + 0.17}$ $= 48.66$ million		$2.7 + \dfrac{75}{1 + 0.16}$ $= 67.36$ million
Price per share $= MVE_T/(n + m)$ $= P$	$48.66		$47.36	
Market value of original equity ($MVE_O = P$)	$48.66 million		$47.36 million	

expensive than funds raised before loss. However, *ex ante,* the increased cost of postloss financing for prospective losses is only a contingent increase, and the *expected* value is small. Furthermore, the increased cost represents project risk and may thereby impose market discipline on the reinvestment decision.

In choosing between alternative postloss financing sources, attention to the issue of optimal capital structure is required. The literature on this subject is inconclusive. While debt usually is cheaper than equity, increased leverage tends to increase the cost of equity. For risk management financing decisions, the issue of leverage is relevant, and these effects require consideration.

This chapter presents a simple decision framework for postloss financing decisions. A set of mutually exclusive postloss decision alternatives is presented, such as not to invest, to reinvest with equity financing, and to reinvest with debt financing. Under each alternative, the expected earnings of the firm to be delivered to the shareholders is estimated and capitalized at a rate appropriate to that decision. The preferred alternative is selected on the basis of the resulting share price or, equivalently, the total value of the existing equity. The valuation process is simple when expected earnings are constant over future years, but potential growth of earnings can be built into the capitalization calculations, as shown in the later examples.

Further complications arise with transaction costs to financing and with business interruption loss. Neither is difficult to incorporate into the decision framework in principle, although interruption loss does pose serious estimation problems that will be considered in Chapter 14.

The choices analyzed in this chapter were exercised after the loss had occurred. Risk management planning may require that postloss choices be anticipated before losses have arisen. Such planning will permit postloss financing sources to be compared with preloss financing sources, such as contingency loans or insurance. This will occupy our attention in the next chapter.

QUESTIONS

1 Respond to the following comment. Postloss financing by external means is not advisable since new debt or equity will be expensive if secured after loss. In contrast, financing arranged before loss will be relatively cheap.

2 A firm suffers a major loss. As a result, its earnings (EBIT) fall from a preloss estimated level of $10 million per year to $8 million. Earnings can be restored to an annual $10 million by reinvestment. The capital cost of reinvestment is $10 million and this can be financed by new debt at 8% or by equity. The firm had no previous debt and its preloss equity capitalization rate was 14%. This rate will increase to 15% without postloss reinvestment. With reinvestment by debt financing the rate also would be 15%, but with equity financing the rate would repair to 14%. The firm has one million shares outstanding.

Should the firm reinvest? If so, should the reinvestment be financed with debt or equity?

3 Compare the effects of postloss financing with debt and equity on the value of the firm's existing equity. You are given the following information

Replacement cost of destroyed resources	$4 million
EBIT, assuming reinvestment	$6 million
Existing debt @ 9% interest	$10 million
Interest on new debt	11%
Growth of earnings for distribution:	
Debt refinancing g_2	3%
Equity refinancing g_1	2%
Equity capitalisation rate:	
Debt refinancing	18%
Equity refinancing	16.5%
Number of shares outstanding before reinvestment	10 million

APPENDIX: Estimating Value with Earnings Growth: Some Complications

With some simplifying assumptions, it was established in Chapter 7 that operating decisions and financing decisions were independent. Although this separation theorem does require modification when market imperfections are introduced, we will assume that the levels of future earnings, before interest and taxation, are independent of the financial structure. Accordingly, one approach to the estimation of future earnings is to forecast earnings before interest and taxation (EBIT) for any future year i as $\text{EBIT}(1 + g)_i^{-1}$. Although this embodies a constant growth rate, the simplification of equation (9-11) [that is, $E_0/(k_E - g)$] cannot be used because the relevant level of earnings for valuing equity is not EBIT, but the earnings available for distribution E. If EBIT grows at a constant annual rate, E will also grow at the same constant rate if the firm has no interest (or tax) obligations. The growth rate, with no interest or tax, for any year i is

$$\frac{\text{EBIT}(1 + g)^i - \text{EBIT}(1 + g)^{i-1}}{\text{EBIT}(1 + g)^{i-1}} = g$$

However, with interest, the growth rate of E is

$$\frac{[\text{EBIT}(1 + g)^i - N] - [\text{EBIT}(1 + g)^{i-1} - N]}{\text{EBIT}(1 + g)^{i-1} - N} = \frac{\text{EBIT}(1 + g)^i - N}{\text{EBIT}(1 + g)^{i-1} - N}$$

where N is the interest payment. This growth rate is not constant across different years, nor will it be the same in any year under different assumptions concerning the capital structure.

In order to make use of the simplified form of equation (9-11), as well as to preserve the income statement form of analysis, we may try to estimate growth in E directly as some equivalent constant value. However, this approach also runs into problems. If growth is constant year after year at one level of leverage, it cannot be constant at some other level of leverage. Consider earnings under two different capital structures.

$$E_1 = \text{EBIT} - N_1 \quad \text{low leverage}$$
$$E_2 = \text{EBIT} - N_2 \quad \text{high leverage}$$

where $N_2 > N_1$.

Assume growth of E_1 for any year i, is a constant value; i.e., where E_{10} refers to E_1 in year 0,

$$\frac{E_{10}^{1+gi} - E_{10}^{1+gi-1}}{E_{10}^{1+gi-1}} = g$$

then E_2 cannot assume the same values as E_1 nor will year to year growth be constant. Growth in E_2 over any year i will be:

$$\frac{E_{2i} - E_{2,i-1}}{E_{2,i-1}} = \frac{[E_{1i} + N_1 - N_2] - [E_{1,i-1} + N_1 - N_2]}{[E_{2,i-1} + N_1 - N_2]}$$

$$= \frac{E_{1i} - E_{1,i-1}}{E_{1,i-1} + N_1 - N_2} > g$$

which must always be greater than g since $N_2 > N_1$. However, this rate will not be constant.

In order to simplify our analysis we will assume that the firm makes separate estimates of constant equivalent growth rates, which are defined by the following equations:

$$\sum_{i=0}^{\infty} \frac{E_{1i}}{(1+k_E)^i} = \frac{E_{10}}{k_E - g_1} \qquad \text{defining } g_1$$

and

$$\sum_{i=0}^{\infty} \frac{E_{2i}}{(1+k_E)^i} = \frac{E_{20}}{k_E - g_2} \qquad \text{defining } g_2$$

We analyzed postloss financing decisions using debt and equity in the Brewery example at the end of this chapter. This required separate estimates of the constant equivalent growth rates of earnings available to common stockholders, and these separate estimates are used in the illustration.

REFERENCES

Chen, A. H., and E. H. Kim: "Theories of Corporate Debt Policy: A Synthesis," *Journal of Finance*, vol. 34, 1979, pp. 371–384.

DeAngelo, H., and R. W. Masulis: "Optimal Capital Structure under Corporate and Personal Taxation," *Journal of Financial Economics*, vol. 8, 1980, pp. 3–29.

Fama, E. F. and M. H. Miller: *"The Theory of Finance,"* 1972, Dryden, Hinsdale, Ill.

Fruhan, W. E.: *"Financial Strategy Studies in the Creation, Transfer and Destruction of Shareholder Wealth,"* 1979, Irwin, Homewood, Ill.

Haugen, R. A., and L. W. Senbett: "The Irrelevance of Bankruptcy Costs of the Theory of Optimal Capital Structure," *Journal of Finance*, vol. 33, 1978, pp. 383–394.

Miller, M.: "Debt and Taxes," *Journal of Finance*, vol. 32, 1977, pp. 261–275.

Modigliani, F.: "Debt, Dividend Policy, Taxes, Inflation and Market Valuation," *Journal of Finance*, vol. 37, 1982, pp. 255–273.

———, and M. Miller: "The Cost of Capital, Corporation Finance and the Theory of Investment," *American Economic Review*, vol. 48, 1958, pp. 261–297.

——— and ———, "Reply," *American Economic Review*, vol. 48, 1958, pp. 655–669.

Myers, S. C.: "Determinants of Corporate Borrowing," *Journal of Financial Economics*, vol. 5, 1977, pp. 147–175.

Stiglitz, J. E.: "A Reexamination of the Modigliani-Miller Theorem," *American Economic Review*, vol. 59, 1969, pp. 784–793.

Turnbull, S. M.: "Debt Capacity," *Journal of Finance*, vol. 34, 1979, pp. 931–940.

PRELOSS FINANCING WITH INSURANCE

Preloss financing probably reaches its purest form with insurance. In exchange for a prepaid fee (the premium), the cost of financing reinvestment after loss is transferred to a financial intermediary (the insurer). The function of the insurer is to diversify the claims of individual insureds over a wide base of policyholders who are commonly exposed to the prospect of loss. The statistical properties of the insurance pool have already been described. The larger the number of independent risks, the smaller the relative variability in aggregate claim payments. However, the aggregate claim payment is never entirely predictable, and the insurer will be able to absorb variations within the limits of net worth or surplus. When claim payments are less than the appropriate premium and claim reserves, the surplus can be increased (or distributed to shareholders and/or policyholders), but the surplus will be run down when claims exceed the reserves. Insurance is only riskless when the surplus and reserves exceed the maximum possible loss. However, within this limit, the risk of default is usually small, and insurance may be considered an efficient (low risk) form of prefinancing for contingent future losses.

With our financial view of risk management in mind, we may view the function of insurance as twofold:

1 Insurance provides funds for financing reinvestment. This function is useful to the risk management process if reinvestment satisfies the appropriate financial criteria. If these criteria are not met, then this function of insurance is redundant. This does not mean that insurance is redundant; insurance may have other functions.

2 Insurance may stabilize a firm's earnings stream. This will add value to a firm if the cost of reducing risk is sufficiently low that the risk-return properties of the returns delivered to the firm's shareholders improve. Insurance achieves this function by restoring (in full or in part) the market value of equity after it has been diminished by loss. Thus the shareholder is protected from random shocks, and if the price is right, the stock should increase in value.

Our task here is to examine the effect of existing insurance protection on the value of equity after a loss has arisen. This will show how insurance is able to protect value for a firm, but it does not provide a complete basis for a decision on whether insurance should be purchased, since the loss might not occur. The decision framework is set up in our preloss analysis that examines the value of a firm given its future risky cash flows and shows how this value is sensitive to insurance protection for future contingent losses. We then consider how insurance might affect the cost of capital and how prospective interruption loss affects the analysis. The analysis of insurance concludes by looking at other related reasons for corporate insurance purchases, which arise largely through the risk-averse behavior of groups other than stockholders (by employees and managers), and then traces the risk-reducing effects of various types of insurance protection.

THE EFFECT OF INSURANCE ON THE MARKET VALUE OF EQUITY: POSTLOSS ANALYSIS

Suppose some event or calamity arises causing loss to a firm. With the assumptions of a perfect market, unlimited borrowing and lending, no taxes, and no interruption loss, we saw that the loss in market value of equity (LMVE) following the event will be equal to the market value of the lost resources (MVLR). If an insurance policy covers these resources, and if the basis for settlement of claims is the market value of the resources, then the policy will indemnify the owners for any fall in value of their equity. The policy payment can be used for reinvestment, thereby restoring projected earnings to preloss levels without issue of further debt or equity. Output will be restored, and the original owners' claims on that output will not have been diluted by the issue of new claims. This implies that (subject to default risk on the insurance policy) the value of equity is protected from the effects of future losses and will not fall if and when such a loss might occur. Thus the insurance policy indemnifies the owners of a firm for any fall in value of their ownership claim following loss.

Now refer to some of the key assumptions used; unlimited borrowing and lending at the same rate, no transaction costs for the replacement of destroyed resources, and no interruption loss. Reinvestment will not be constrained by borrowing opportunities if financing is available from an insurance payment. Thus when looking at insurance, it would seem that this assumption causes little bother. However, a caution is needed; even though policy monies are available, there is an opportunity cost of using the insurance money for reinvestment. The cost of using money for reinvestment is measured by the weighted average cost of capital, since this cost would apply to any foregone opportunities.

What about transaction costs? The market value of resources is a somewhat ambiguous concept. This could, alternatively, refer to the price that could be raised by a firm if it chose to sell those resources or to the price that must be paid to replace those resources given the existing secondhand market. The difference between the "trade-in" and "replacement" prices represents the transaction costs (including traders' profits) of the activity. A third interpretation sometimes used for insurance purposes is the cost of replacement with new resources. If a firm is to protect its market value following loss, then reinvestment may be important. Consequently, transaction costs will be incurred in the repurchase of new property. Unless these transaction costs are covered by the policy, the insurance will be unable to offer complete protection from the loss of market value of equity following loss. Where the policy is on a "new lamps for old" basis, share values might conceivably increase following a loss. The form of protection is a matter of contractual conditions and/or court interpretation. In many cases, policies are contracted on an "actual cash value" basis, under which the insurer will pay an amount not exceeding the repair or replacement cost (property insurance) or the actual settlement reached by negotiation or litigation plus legal costs (liability insurance). These conditions are in the spirit of covering transaction costs, although for risk management purposes, insurance will only be able to compensate for LMVE if all the transaction costs incurred in the reinvestment process are actually covered.

Relaxation of the assumption of no interruption loss leads to more difficult ground. The MVLR criterion does not give a complete measure of loss under these circumstances, and if insurance coverage limits recovery on the basis of this criterion, protection will be incomplete. If only direct-loss policies are available, the value of equity will fall in the event of loss according to the capital market's estimate of the intensity of business interruption loss. However, additional protection for business interruption can be purchased, and in principle, the owners can acquire an insurance package that provides immunity from all effects of a loss. In practice, it may be difficult to ascertain whether a complete indemnity can be established, since this requires the restoration of a firm's earnings to levels that would have prevailed had the loss not arisen. All such earnings forecasts are fraught with major uncertainties, and it will never be known just how much any postloss changes in equity values reflect factors connected with or unconnected with the loss.

Business interruption insurance is available in conjunction with direct property insurance covering the same perils. Policies typically cover fixed charges, such as leases, some wages, interest charges, and profits that would have been earned had the loss not arisen. Also covered are expenses incurred to expedite recovery insofar as they reduce the size of the claim for fixed charges and loss of profits. The basis for claim payment is usually the loss of gross earnings less any charges that do not continue during the period of interruption. Wages may or may not be treated as continuing costs depending on circumstances. Special covers can be arranged for special expenses, such as additional costs of continuing operations to maintain the goodwill of clients. If interruption is temporary, it is probable that carefully arranged cover will indemnify the owners of a firm for any fall in the value of their equity, although since one can never be sure what the levels of earnings would have been had the loss not occurred, this statement is offered with some reservation. The more serious problem arises when interruption loss is extended over a long period or is permanent. Cover is normally available for no longer than 1 year, although, occasionally, cover is arranged for 2 or 3 years. A year's cover may be suitable for small interruptions in which a firm suffers no permanent loss of demand for its product or service or no permanent upward shift in production costs. However, under many market conditions, even a temporary interruption will cause customers to seek out alternative sources of supply, perhaps causing a permanent deterioration in market share. The primary reason that cover is restricted is that it becomes more difficult to measure loss the longer the interruption period contemplated. Given the somewhat random nature of a firm's earnings, it is difficult enough to form a reasonable estimate of earnings loss in the year following loss. However, if we try to estimate earnings loss for longer periods, the confidence intervals surrounding such estimates must widen considerably, permitting wide divergence of opinion between the insured and insurer on the appropriate amount to be paid in settlement of the claim. However, while the loss is difficult to measure, it is no less real. A study undertaken some years ago of firms suffering serious fires revealed that 43% of firms disappeared from the market immediately after the fire and a further 28% did not survive for more than 3 years.[1] The reasons for such a high rate of abandonment after loss may include arson, but these figures nevertheless indicate that firms suffering a major fire are exposed to severe and protracted interruption loss.

The compensatory effects of insurance protection on the market value of equity following a loss are illustrated in the following example.

[1]Quoted from *Face an Risque*, Centre National de Prevention et Protection.

EXAMPLE: NOTIP PITON, INC.

Notip Piton, Inc. recently invested $5 million in the production of mountain climbing equipment. The production facility was damaged by a fire that caused a loss of $2 million, this being the current cost of repairing and/or replacing damaged and destroyed property. The resulting interruption was fairly severe, largely in view of the seasonal nature of demand. It is estimated that roughly half the current year's earnings will be lost, although expectations differ as to the long-term effects of the loss. At one extreme, the firm might suffer no permanent damage to its earnings position, but a "worst outcome" scenario is that the firm will only recover 75% of its preloss expected earnings. This estimate is based on the assumption that rival firms will find it easy to establish a strong position, taking over a greater part of the market. Current earnings are $1 million. The market capitalizes the firm's equity at 10%, and this rate will be unaffected by the loss. The initial investment of $5 million was financed by the issue of 250,000 common shares, there being no debt in the capital structure.

Solution

The analysis is summarized in Table 10-1. It is assumed that all direct loss is fully covered by the insurance policy, including any transaction costs. Consequently, there is no reason for the firm to seek new sources of finance for the reinvestment. Column 2 (*a* and *b*) shows the effect of insurance, including interruption insurance, on the value of equity assuming that interruption loss is only temporary. The loss of earnings is confined to the year following loss (year 1), but this loss is made good from the business interruption policy. It can be seen that the share value,

TABLE 10-1
NOTIP PITON: POSTLOSS ANALYSIS OF INSURANCE

	1	2 After loss (temporary interruption only)		3 After loss (permanent interruption)	
	Before loss	a Year 1	b Years 2 onward	a Year 1	b Years 2 onward
Earnings before interest and taxation (EBIT)	$1 million	$0.5 million	$1 million	$0.5 million	$0.75 million
Insurance payment (business interruption)		$0.5 million	—	$0.5 million	—
Earnings available for distribution (E)	$1 million	$1 million	$1 million	$1 million	$0.75 million
Number of shares (m)	250,000	250,000	250,000	250,000	250,000
Earnings per share (EPS)	$4	$4	$4	$4	$3
Equity capitalization rate (k_E)	0.1	0.1	0.1	0.1	0.1
Price per share (EPS/k_E)	$40	$0.4 + \dfrac{40}{1 + 0.1} = 40$	$40	$4 + \dfrac{30}{1 + 0.1} = \$31$	$30
Market value of equity (MVE = E/k_E)	$10 million	$1\text{ million} + \dfrac{10\text{ million}}{1 + 0.1} = \$10\text{ million}$	$10 million	$1\text{ million} + \dfrac{7.5}{1 + 0.1} = \$7.8\text{ million}$	$7.5 million

252

shown in the final two rows, is restored to the preloss level, i.e., $40 per share with a total value for all equity of $10 million. Column 3 (*a* and *b*) recalculates the impact of loss with the assumption that there is permanent impairment of earnings, but the interruption insurance policy covers no more than 1 year's disturbance. Using similar calculations, it can be seen that share value is not immune from the effects of the loss, the total value of equity falling from the preloss level of $10 million to $7.8 million and the price per share falling from $40 to $31. This fall is equal to the capitalized value of the interruption loss.

This example shows that, in principle, insurance can completely isolate the owners of a firm from any loss of value following a loss. Whether this happens in practice depends on the adequacy of insurance protection and the extent of interruption loss. Serious loss of value will arise when investors estimate that the disturbance to earnings is protracted or permanent. We will now transfer our attention to the effects of insurance on the value of equity at the time of purchase. By doing so, we can analyze whether the decision to purchase insurance will add value and how it compares with alternative methods of financing reinvestments.

PRELOSS ANALYSIS OF INSURANCE

Consider a firm that makes an investment of K dollars, which, in turn, yields an earnings stream of E dollars per year. In order to estimate whether such an investment adds value to the firm, the present value of the earnings stream must be compared with the initial investment K. Thus, according to the usual capital-budgeting criterion, the investment should be undertaken if

$$K < V(1) = \sum_{i=1}^{\infty} \frac{E}{(1 + k)^i} = \frac{E}{k} \qquad (10\text{-}1)$$

where K = the initial investment
V = value
E = earnings
k = cost of capital

In reality, cash flows will be risky, incorporating both speculative and pure risk effects. Thus the values for E will reflect a deduction for pure risk costs. Our task here will be to analyze whether the purchase of insurance will increase the value of the firm or, more specifically, its equity. However, insurance decisions are made annually, and initially, we need only consider whether to buy insurance for the coming year (any number of things may cause us to change our decision next year). If we buy insurance, we will provide ourselves with funds to reinvest should a loss arise over the coming year. Even though we are providing 1 year's cover, the benefits will accrue in future years, since future E will include the return on the reinvestment provided from the insurance proceeds. To get a handle on this problem, let us consider the following possibilities:

1 The expected earnings for all future years i, assuming no loss occurs over the coming year, are

$$E_{N,i} \qquad i = 1, 2, 3, \ldots, \infty$$

where N = no losses.

2 The expected earnings after deduction of the expected value of prospective losses that may arise over the coming year, assuming no reinvestment, are

$$E_i \qquad i = 1, 2, 3, \ldots, \infty$$

In each case, E_i includes the effects of losses that might arise in future years.

Now let us consider the relationship between $E_{N,i}$ and E_i and how this relationship is affected by insurance. The prospect of depletion of the invested resources from some form of loss may be represented by a probability distribution, as shown in Chapter 4. This will be estimated with more or less precision depending on the quality and quantity of data. Among the more important summary statistics is the mean of the distribution, and we will use the expression L_K to refer to the expected value of the loss of capital. Notice that this refers to a capital loss rather than a loss of earnings. The capital loss may be in the form of physical damage to resources or a liability claim; each would result in a similar reduction in the market value of equity. The term L_K refers to the expected loss for the coming year. Now consider the impact of this loss on the earnings of a firm. The earnings loss will depend on the productivity of the destroyed resources and the following relationship may be stated:

$$E_L = r_{FG}L_K \qquad (10\text{-}2)$$

where r_{FG} is the rate of return foregone on the destroyed resources and E_L is the annual expected loss of earnings suffered as a result of prospective loss of capital resources. Notice that a capital loss this year may cause earnings to be lost for many future years. Thus L_K refers to capital loss for the coming year, but E_L refers to the consequent loss of earnings in the following years.

To bring these concepts together clearly, consider that it is January 1, 1985 and the firm is forecasting its expected earnings for the coming 3 years. The forecast might appear as follows:

	1985	1986	1987
Expected earnings assuming no loss occurs during 1985	20	20	20
Expected value of earnings loss from losses that might arise in 1985	1	1	1
Expected earnings	19	19	19

The expected value of earnings loss might be calculated as follows: The possible values of loss of capital resources are $10 million and $40 million, each with a probability of 0.1:

$$
L_K = \begin{cases} \$10 \text{ million} & 0.1 \text{ probability} \\[2ex] \$30 \text{ million} & 0.1 \text{ probability} \end{cases}
$$

resulting in an expected loss of $4 million. The expected value earnings loss E_L depends on the foregone rate of return on these destroyed resources, which is assumed to be 0.25:

$$
E_L = 0.25(4) = \$1 \text{ million}
$$

If we assume that $E_{N,i}$ and E_i are constant annual values, then clearly,

$$
E_L = E_N - E \tag{10-3}
$$

the subscripts being dropped.

With these concepts, we can now start to analyze the insurance decision. Insurance is purchased by the payment of an insurance premium P. The benefit is that finance is provided for reinvestment should a loss arise. Thus the earnings stream is increased from E to E_N. Using a capital-budgeting approach, insurance will add value to a firm if

$$
\sum_{i=1}^{\infty} \frac{E_N - E_L}{(1 + k)^i} < \sum_{i=1}^{\infty} \frac{E_N}{(1 + k)^i} - P \tag{10-4}
$$

where P is the insurance premium.

The left-hand side of the inequality represents the value of the firm if no insurance is purchased and, accordingly, there is no reinvestment. The right-hand side shows the value of the firm if it purchases insurance. Note that the cash flow is restored to its preloss level, since insurance permits the firm to reinvest. However, the premium must be paid, and this is shown as a flat deduction in the current year; thus it is not discounted. Note that with simple manipulation, equation (10-4) is equivalent to

$$
\sum_{i=1}^{\infty} \frac{E_L}{(1 + k)^i} > P \tag{10-5}
$$

which states that insurance will add value if the present value of the lost earnings is greater than the premium. Before developing a simple example, three very important provisos must be drawn:

1 We have ignored any interruption loss in this formulation. Note that the earnings stream is assumed to be restored to its preloss level if reinvestment occurs.

2 We have also assumed that insurance does not affect the discount rate k.

3 We have tied the insurance decision and the reinvestment decision together. It is, of course, possible to reinvest with other sources of finance, such as debt or equity. However, we will see that this presentation helps us to compare alternative sources.

Each of these assumptions will be relaxed shortly, but in the meantime, the basic concepts are illustrated in the following example.

EXAMPLE: MELOMANIA PIANO AND ORGAN COMPANY

The Melomania Piano and Organ Company estimates that its equipment, inventory, buildings, and other assets have a current replacement value of $30 million. From industry statistics, together with previous loss experience for the firm, it is estimated that the expected value of loss from various insurable perils is $0.6 million, and this can be fully insured at an annual premium of $0.75 million. Note that the premium is $P = (1 + \alpha)\overline{L}_K$, where $\alpha = 0.25$ is the premium markup to cover commissions, expenses, and profit for the insurer. Interruption loss is negligible. The anticipated annual level of earnings before loss is $5 million, indicating an average return of 16.7%. The expected value of loss of earnings is

$$E_L = r_{FG}L_K = 0.2(0.6) = \$0.12 \text{ million}$$

(Notice that the rate of return foregone on the destroyed capital is greater than the average rate of return on the investment before the loss, thereby suggesting interdependencies in the production process.) The firm has no debt, but it has 1 million common shares outstanding. The market capitalizes the firm's equity at 10%. The solution shown in Table 10-2 is straightforward following the criterion set down in equation (10-4). Notice that the premium is treated as a "once only" deduction in the current year. The result shows that the market value of equity is higher when insurance is purchased, and this result can be confirmed by applying equation (10-5):

$$1.2 = \sum_{i=1}^{\infty}\frac{E_L}{(1 + k)^i} > P = 0.75$$

This example needs to be interpreted with some caution. We have mentioned three heavily restrictive assumptions, and each of these must be looked at in turn. The first problem is that the insurance decision was tied to the reinvestment decision. Thus we do not know whether the positive signal to buy insurance is really just a signal to reinvest if a loss occurs. Thus the problem should be stated in terms of the relative advantages of insurance versus alternative forms of financing. To illustrate this comparison, reconsider Melomania.

TABLE 10-2
MELOMANIA: PRELOSS ANALYSIS OF INSURANCE

	1 No insurance, no reinvestment	2 Insurance — Year 1	2 Insurance — Subsequent years	Debt
Expected earnings (E_N)	$5 million	$5 million	$5 million	$5 million
Interest	—	—	—	$0.036 million
Expected loss of earnings (E_L)	$0.12 million	—	—	—
Insurance premium (P)	—	$0.75 million	—	—
Earnings available for distribution (E)	$4.88 million	$4.25 million	$5 million	$4.964 million
Number of shares (m)	1 million	1 million	1 million	1 million
Earnings per share (EPS = E/m)	$4.88	$4.25	$5	$4.964
Equity capitalization rate (k_E)	0.1	0.1	0.1	0.1 (0.105)
Price per share (EPS/k_E)	$48.8		$50	$49.64 (47.28)
Market value of equity (E/k_E)	$48.8 million		$50 million	$49.64 million (47.28 million)

Year 1 price per share:

$$4.25 + \frac{50}{1 + 0.1} = \$49.7$$

Year 1 market value of equity:

$$4.25 \text{ million} + \frac{50 \text{ million}}{1 + 0.1} = \$49.7 \text{ million}$$

EXAMPLE: MELOMANIA PIANO AND ORGAN COMPANY

Melomania's risk manager is told by the Vice President (finance) that since the firm has no existing debt, reinvestment following a loss could be financed by borrowing. Since interruption loss is estimated to be negligible, the new debt would probably be raised at little more than prime. Current rates are not expected to change over the coming year, and the cost of debt is estimated at 6%. Since the expected value of loss E_L is $0.6 million, the expected interest burden is 0.06($0.6 million) = $0.036 million. (Notice that this is the *expected* value of the interest burden. If a loss does not occur, the actual burden will be zero. If a loss does arise, the burden would likely be very much higher; e.g., a $10 million loss would require an interest burden of $600,000.)

The solution is shown in the final column of Table 10-2. The assumption that insurance does not affect the equity capitalization rate has been maintained, and we continue to show $k_E = 0.1$. The market value of equity and the price per share have been computed at this rate, revealing values just below those prevailing under the insurance option. Thus it would seem that preloss financing by insurance would add more value to equity than the contingent strategy of seeking out debt financing after the loss arises. In fact, the advantages of insurance would be more pronounced, because the prospect of creating leverage through the issue of postloss debt would bid up the equity capitalization rate. This increase in k_E would probably be fairly small, since it reflects only a prospective increase in leverage rather than an actual debt issue. An alternative solution with a slightly higher k_E is shown in parentheses adjacent to column 4.

INSURANCE AND THE COST OF CAPITAL

The issue of whether insurance affects the cost of capital raises some pretty thorny problems. We are not aware of any direct empirical studies on this issue, and consequently, our discussion relies on indirect evidence and theoretical argument. Much of the reasoning here is based on two recent papers by Mayers and Smith (1982), who analyze the demand for corporate insurance, and Doherty and Tinic (1981), who analyze the demand for reinsurance.

At first sight, the issue appears to be clear-cut. Insurance reduces risk. Therefore, if investors are risk-averse, they would be willing to incur a risk premium to avoid risk. The risk premium would take the form of a lower yield on their investment, which translates into a lower cost of capital for the firm. The insured firm, with its apparently more stable earnings, could sell its equity at a higher price and its debt would also sell at a higher price or a lower coupon rate. However, this explanation ignores modern capital market theory.

The ownership claims on many firms are not bonded in blood but are simply financial assets for which a more or less active market might exist. Since these claims can be traded, it is possible for the investor to diversify away much of the risk of his or her personal portfolio by holding many assets. Just how much risk can be eliminated in this way depends on the degree of common variation in security returns. As we saw in Chapter 6, systematic risk is not amenable to simple diversification techniques, although unsystematic risk can substantially be eliminated in this way. Another method by which the riskiness of a particular ownership claim on a firm can be reduced or eliminated is for the firm to purchase an insurance policy. In this manner, the owner achieves the benefits of diversification, since the insurable risk is spread over the policyholders contributing to the insurance pool. Viewed in this way, "homemade diversification" (achieved by holding a portfolio of securities) and "insurance diversification" produce the same results for the investor and may be regarded as substitutes. From this perspective, we can identify two important ways in which corporate insurance purchases can alter the cost of capital:

1 Insurance can alter the level of systematic risk of a firm's equity. Since stock prices are functionally related to systematic risk, any such change would affect the firm's cost of capital.

2 Both forms of diversification entail transaction costs. If the relative cost of diversification through insurance is lower, the stock of the insured firm will sell at a premium, thereby reducing the cost of equity capital to the firm.

We will consider each of these in more detail.

What little evidence there is on the systematic risk attaching to insurable losses has come from investigations of insurers' claim records rather than from specific risk management studies. The published results include those of Fairly (1979), Biger and Kahane (1978), and Cummins and Nye (1980), each of which assumes the capital asset pricing model (CAPM) and, accordingly, calculates insurance β values. The studies were conducted on insurance underwriting returns using annual data. The results concur in that, with few exceptions, underwriting β values do not differ significantly from zero. The main problem with these studies is that the use of annual data results in very small sample sizes with correspondingly wide confidence intervals and does not permit the detection of covariation with the market over shorter intervals. Further problems concern the allocation of the insurers' expenses over different lines of insurance. If insurable losses truly were uncorrelated with the market portfolio, then insurance would have no effect on the cost of capital. An insurance policy would simply replace one component of the earnings stream that was uncorrelated with the market with a constant premium. This would reduce unsystematic risk but would leave the firm's β value unchanged. Consequently, the price of the firm's stock would record no favorable reaction to the insurance protection, and its cost of capital would remain unchanged. Under this scenario, insurance would only appear to be preferable to alternative forms of financing if the insurance premium were less than the expected present value of the alternative financing cost.

However, there is some reason to doubt that the β values for insurable losses are zero. First, some tentative results by Cummins and Harrington (1984) using quarterly rather than annual data have revealed significantly positive β values for insurers' returns over some time periods. Second, the insurers' returns pick up only those losses which are actually insured. The difficulties in providing adequate long-term insurance protection from interruption loss have already been noted, and undoubtedly, all firms retain much of this risk. The intensity and duration of interruption loss probably depend on the market circumstances in which the firm is trading—factors such as the intensity of competition, the level of demand, the size of inventories, etc. In turn, these factors will be influenced by macroeconomic variables and by capital market conditions such as interest rates. This reasoning is meant only to establish a plausible relationship between insurable losses and the market index. Whether such a linkage does exist is an empirical issue. Our point is simply that such empirical evidence as does exist is fairly weak and the level of systematic risk inherent in insurable losses is an open issue to be investigated for the individual case.

We will now show the mechanism by which systematic risk in the distribution of losses will affect the cost of capital. For simplicity, we shall assume that the firm is "all equity" financed and treat the cost of equity as synonymous with the cost of capital. It is well known that the β value of a firm's stock is equal to the weighted average of the component activities. We will define two components: (1) that relating to returns that would be generated by all business activities but excluding risk management costs, and (2) that relating to risk management costs, that is,

$$\beta_S = \omega_1\beta_B + \omega_2\beta_{RM} \quad \text{(without insurance)} \quad (10\text{-}6)$$

where β_S = beta of stock returns
$\quad \beta_B$ = beta of business activities
$\quad \beta_{RM}$ = beta of risk management costs
$\quad \omega_i$ = the weights attached to the component activities

The weights ω_i reflect the expected contribution of the component activities to the overall rate of return on the firm's equity. These weights can be established easily. Recall the definitions of E_N and E, which, respectively, refer to the earning of a firm exclusive of and inclusive of the expected value of losses arising over the coming year. The difference, $E_N - E = E_L$, is the expected value of loss of earnings from losses arising in the coming year. Since these values define the contributions of the components of a firm's return to overall return, they can be used to define the weights ω_1 and ω_2 as follows:

$$\omega_1 = \frac{E_N}{E} \quad \text{and} \quad \omega_2 = -\frac{E_L}{E} \quad (10\text{-}7)$$

Thus,

$$\omega_1 + \omega_2 = \frac{E_N}{E} - \frac{E_L}{E} = \frac{E + E_L}{E} - \frac{E_L}{E} = 1$$

To derive these weights, we are assuming that the firm has no current debt, so that earnings are available for distribution to shareholders. Substituting these weights into equation (10-6), we have

$$\beta_S = \frac{E_N}{E}\beta_B - \frac{E_L}{E}\beta_{RM} \quad \text{(without insurance)} \quad (10\text{-}8)$$

The weight for the business activity β value is greater than 1, and the weight for risk management activity is negative, since this refers to events that are entirely adverse.

Now let us see what happens when insurance is purchased. The only risky component of the firm's return is E_N. The risk management component is replaced by the premium, which, by definition, has no risk. Consequently, systematic risk can only come from the business activity. Thus,

$$\beta_S = \frac{E_N}{E}\beta_B \qquad \text{(with full insurance)} \tag{10-9}$$

From equations (10-8) and (10-9), the effects of insurance on the stock's β value can be calculated as follows:

$$\Delta\beta_S = \frac{E_N}{E}\beta_B - \left[\frac{E_N}{E}\beta_B - \frac{E_L}{E}\beta_{RM}\right] = \frac{E_L}{E}\beta_{RM} \tag{10-10}$$

The effect on the cost of equity can be traced through the equilibrium asset pricing relationship. Thus, using the capital asset pricing model,

$$E(r_S) = r_f + \beta_S[E(r_m) - r_f] \tag{10-11}$$

where r_S = return on the firm's stock
$\quad r_f$ = risk-free rate
$\quad r_m$ = return on the market index

Consequently, changes in the stock's β value following loss will generate the following change in the cost of equity from equations (10-10) and (10-11):

$$\Delta E(r_S) = \Delta\beta_S[E(r_m) - r_f] = \frac{E_L}{E}\beta_{RM}[E(r_m) - r_f] \tag{10-12}$$

The term on the right-hand side can be given a clear economic interpretation. The expression in the brackets is simply the risk premium on the market portfolio. Multiplying by β_{RM} gives the risk premium allocated by the market on pure risk for the firm, given its covariance with the market portfolio. However, this effect is moderated by the weight of the pure risk costs in the overall return, that is, E_L/E. In most cases, it would be expected that this weight would be fairly small, and consequently, any risk premium from the pure risk costs is likely to produce only a small change in the cost of equity for the firm.

However, there is another implication from equation (10-12) that is also of particular interest. If the β value of the pure risk is positive, the purchase of insurance will increase the β value of the firm's stock. Accordingly, the market will capitalize the firm's equity at a *higher* rate. Thus insurance might conceivably increase the firm's cost of capital. A moment's reflection will show that this unexpected result is not unreasonable. If losses are positively correlated with the market index, then such losses are likely to arise when most other items in the investor's portfolio are performing well. These losses may destabilize the earnings of the firm, but if retained, they may well stabilize the returns to the investor holding the stock in his or her portfolio. The insurance of these losses by the firm will only serve to remove this valuable risk-offsetting effect and will have an adverse effect on the stock price. In general, we find that insurance will reduce the cost of capital to a firm only through its effect on systematic risk if the losses display a negative correlation with the market index. If losses have zero β values, insurance will produce a neutral effect on the cost of capital. The available evidence has suggested that insurer returns have zero or positive β values. Since most of the variations in insurer returns come from losses rather then expenses, and since insurer returns are almost perfectly negatively correlated with losses, this evidence implies that losses probably have zero or negative β values. From this and equation (10-12), our general expectation would be that insurance would either leave the cost of equity unchanged or reduce it slightly. However, we caution that this is based on insurer data that are highly aggregated, and conclusions drawn for a particular case are somewhat perilous.

The second effect of insurance on the cost of capital arises when insurance provides a more efficient mechanism for diversifying away unsystematic risk than the alternative mechanism of "homemade portfolio diversification." Whether this is the case or not depends on the respective costs of the alternative methods of diversification. The costs of diversifying by the investor adjusting his or her personal portfolio depend both on the characteristics of the investor and on those of the firm. The transaction costs of diversification include the brokers' fees and dealers' spreads that are borne in the sale and purchase of securities. These costs will depend *inter alia* on the size of the market for the firm's stock and the frequency of trading. Costs will be relatively high if the market is small and the stock is infrequently traded. However, the qualities of the investor are also important. If the capital of the investor is small, then portfolio diversification may only be achieved by purchasing odd lots of individual stocks, with correspondingly high commissions, or by investing in mutual funds or the like, with the appropriate management fees. At the extreme of this spectrum is the sole proprietorship, which is a business owned and managed by the same individual. In this case, personal diversification is very costly, since it may require that the owner sacrifice his or her employment as well as his or her equity.

The cost of diversification through insurance depends on the relative size of the premium and the expected value of claim payment duly discounted back to the present. For example, consider that the expected value of the claim payment is $100 and that, on average, claims will be paid 1 year after receipt of premiums. This delay will be due to both the time elapsing before any claim might arise and the delays involved in the investigation and settlement of claims. If the premium is $120 and the firm uses a 10% discount rate, the cost of diversification may be represented as

$$\frac{\$120 - (\$100/(1 + 0.1)}{\$120} = 0.24$$

This figure will probably exaggerate the cost of diversification through insurance. The markup in the insurance premium will include the insurer's management expenses, commissions to agents or brokers, and insurer's profit. These are deadweight losses to the insured. However, also included may be some insurer services that have value to the insured and which might be secured independently if insurance is not purchased. Examples are loss-prevention services and claim-settlement services for those liability claims which affect the goodwill of the firm.

Diversification through insurance is likely to be relatively attractive when the ownership of a firm is concentrated and/or where the ownership claims are traded infrequently or not at all. Under these circumstances, the transaction costs from homemade portfolio diversification imply that it may be a poor substitute for insurance. If the transaction costs from diversifying through insurance do turn out to be cheaper, insurance will be attractive to the firm's owners and will, in turn, bid up the value of the firm's equity. The cost of capital would fall accordingly.

The cost-of-diversification effect under discussion depends largely on the particular characteristics of a firm's owners, as well as on the size and activity of the market for its shares. Since the relative costs of diversification through personal portfolio adjustment will differ according to different investor characteristics, we would expect to find that different investors would be prepared to pay differing prices for the shares, even though they might share common information concerning the firm's future earnings. Consequently, there would not be a unique price for the firm's shares, but rather a range of prices. The implication for risk management is that the capitalization rate chosen to discount the firm's earnings under insurance protection might be higher if ownership were concentrated and trade were infrequent than if the stock were widely and actively traded.

Ultimately, both the cost-of-diversification effect and the systematic-risk effect of insurance on the cost of equity require calculation and/or judgment for the individual firm. The size and sign of these effects will be peculiar to the firm and require individual attention. However, we will illustrate how these effects might be handled by returning to the case of Melomania.

EXAMPLE: MELOMANIA PIANO AND ORGAN COMPANY

We will now add some further information for the Melomania Piano and Organ Company. Some 65% of the shares of Melomania are owned by the Morgan family, whose members include the Chairman, President, Vice President (Marketing), and Vice President (Administration). There is an "over the counter" market, and the remaining shares are traded somewhat infrequently. There have been no substantial changes in family ownership over recent years, and it is well known that family control is a major objective of the family members. Accordingly, risk protection through personal portfolio diversification is seen to be a very costly alternative to diversification through insurance. The Vice President (Finance) (not a family member) decides that if insurance is to be purchased, the capitalization rate for equity should fall by 1 percentage point to allow for this effect. This figure reflects a subjective judgment rather than an accurate calculation of these costs.

In addition, the systematic risk attaching to pure losses may have a further effect. To examine whether this is the case, consider the following background information. The equilibrium capitalization rate for the stock (without insurance) was compiled as follows:

$$E(r_S) = r_f + \beta_S[E(r_m) - r_f] \qquad \text{[equation (10-11)]}$$

where $\beta_S = \dfrac{E_N}{E}\beta_B - \dfrac{E_L}{E}\beta_{RM}$ [equation (10-8)]

From previous information, we know that $E_N = \$5$ million, $E_L = \$0.12$ million, and $E = \$4.88$ million. Further information is

$$\beta_B = 0.8$$
$$\beta_{RM} = -0.25$$
$$r_f = 0.06$$
$$E(r_m) = 0.108$$

Therefore,

$$\beta_S = \frac{5}{4.88}(0.8) - \frac{0.12}{4.88}(-0.25) = 0.826$$

and

$$E(r_S) = 0.06 + 0.826(0.108 - 0.06) \approx 0.1$$

The adjustment in this rate to allow for the systematic risk in the pure risk cost that is removed by insurance is

$$\Delta E(r_S) = \frac{E_L}{E}\beta_{RM}[E(r_m) - r_f] \qquad \text{[equation (10-12)]}$$
$$= \frac{-0.12}{4.88}(-0.25)(0.108 - 0.06)$$
$$= -0.0003$$

This effect is so small that it will be ignored.

Summarizing, the equity capitalization rate will be

	0.10	without insurance
less	—	negligible effect for systematic risk
less	0.01	effect for cost of diversification
	0.09	with insurance.

Table 10-2 can now be modified to give Table 10-3 which allows for the effect of insurance on the cost of capital. The only change in Table 10-3 arises from the lower equity capitalization rate due to insurance protection. Previously, the value of equity was $49.7 million, or $49.7 per share. The effect of insurance on the cost of capital has added nearly $6 to the value of each share, resulting in an equity value of $55.56 million, or $55.56 per share. Previously, insurance was only marginally preferred to debt to refinance investments. Now the preference is more pronounced.

TABLE 10-3
MELOMANIA: THE EFFECT OF INSURANCE ON THE COST OF CAPITAL

	1 No insurance, no reinvestment	2 Insurance Year 1	2 Insurance Subsequent years	Debt
Expected earnings (E_N)	$5 million	$5 million	$5 million	$5 million
Interest	$0.12 million	—	—	0.036
Expected loss of earnings (E_L)	—	—	—	—
Insurance premium (P)	—	$0.75 million	—	—
Earnings available for distribution (E)	$4.88 million	$4.25 million	$5 million	$4.964 million
Number of shares (m)	1 million	1 million	1 million	1 million
Earnings per share (EPS = E/m)	$4.88	$4.25	$5	$4.964
Equity capitalization rate (k_E)	0.1	0.9	0.9	0.105
Price per share (EPS/k_E)	$48.8	$4.25 + \dfrac{55.56}{1 + 0.09} = \$55.22$ $\;\leftarrow$ $55.56	$55.56	$47.28
Market value of equity (E/k_E)	$48.8 million	$4.25 + \dfrac{55.56}{1 + 0.09} = \$55.22$ million	$55.56 million	$47.28 million

This discussion of the effect of insurance on the cost of capital has focused on the cost of equity, but there may also be effects on the cost of debt. Bond prices are generally seen as related to the default risk. This is apparent in differences in yields between bonds of differing levels of seniority in a firm's debt structure. Bonds protected by a mortgage on specified assets offer lower yields than debentures. This relationship between prices and yields and the risk of default implies that insurance on a firm's assets is of value to bondholders, since the availability of liquidity at the time of loss increases the possibility of successful reinvestment and will probably decrease the probability of bankruptcy. Such protection is of direct interest to mortgage bondholders to protect the integrity of their collateral. However, it is of more general interest to all bondholders, since it increases the probability that all debt will be fully discharged. We would therefore expect bond prices (and thus capitalization rates) to reflect insurance protection. In fact, this benefit of insurance is often reflected by an insurance condition in the bond indenture deed requiring that property mentioned in the deed be insured against fire and other perils.

The argument that bondholders benefit from insurance protection is given further impetus by Mayers and Smith (1982). An issue that has recently received attention in the finance literature is the transfer of wealth from bondholders who have subscribed to an issue believing the firm to be undertaking low-risk projects (with correspondingly low default risks on the bond), but the firm subsequently undertakes higher-risk projects. The bonds will therefore lose value after their issue. Bondholders, anticipating such switches, will reflect the probability of a change of this sort in the bond price. Nevertheless, if such a switch actually ensues, there will be further adjustment. Partial protection against some types of switches of this kind can be given by an insurance requirement in the bond indenture deed. This will reduce the incentive of the firm (1) to accept a negative present value project that creates wealth for stockholders at the expense of bondholders or (2) to reject projects with positive present value that might subsidize bondholders by reducing risk. "For example, if fire insurance has been purchased, the variance of corporate cash flows . . . does not fall if the firm invests in a safety project such as a sprinkler system, and thus there is no wealth transfer to the firm's fixed claimholders" (Mayers and Smith, 1982, p. 18).

INSURANCE AND INTERRUPTION LOSS

The ability of insurance to protect the equity value of a firm from the effects of loss depends, among other things, on whether the event causes some displacement of earnings. If the interruption of earnings is temporary and the firm reverts to an earnings path that is compatible with preloss expectations, then equity values may well be protected with direct loss and interruption insurance. This was illustrated in Table 10-1. Column 2 (*a* and *b*) showed the effect of business interruption insurance on the value of a firm's equity and on the price per share. On the assumption that the temporary loss of earnings was fully insured, the value of equity was restored to its preloss level. When the interruption was permanent, insurance was unable to provide complete protection, since insurance cover would just not be available. The difficulties in measuring such a loss of earnings would be formidable, since the projection of preloss earnings to estimate what earnings might have been in the absence of loss would involve such large margins of error that it would become impractical to write contracts on this basis. Furthermore, such permanent protection would be extremely expensive (for example, if the preloss projected earnings stream was expected to grow at a rate higher than that used for discounting, the present value of the permanent interruption loss of earnings, and therefore the insurance premium, would be infinite[2]). Although it was possible to separate the postloss effect of insurance according to whether the interruption of earnings was temporary or permanent, such separation is not so tidy when analyzing anticipated losses. There must always be some probability that a prospective future loss would cause permanent depletion of a firm's cash flows or even bankruptcy. Since this contingency cannot be fully insured under currently available insurance contracts, the current equilibrium share value will reflect contingent losses even if an intensive insurance program is undertaken.

The premium charged for interruption insurance will normally be sufficient to provide an adequate reserve from which claim payments can be met, together with an allowance for expenses and profit. Possibilities of adverse selection and concepts of "fairness" to insureds usually require that the premium reflect the loss expectancy of the individual insured, and statistical techniques are used to approximate this value as closely as possible. There will always be some error or shortcomings in this process, and cross-subsidies between different groups of insureds will result. The usual process adopted is to base the business interruption premium rate on the premium rate for direct loss insurance. This has virtue insofar as the direct loss rate is calculated to reflect loss probabilities and such safety features as sprinkler protection. The direct loss probabilities obviously give some indication as to the probability of interruption loss, since direct loss is usually a precondition for interruption loss. However, the relationship between direct and interruption losses is neither simple nor obvious. In some cases, a severe direct damage loss may result in little business interruption, since the production facilities can be quickly reproduced elsewhere. However, a small fire or the like could result in severe interruption loss if it affected the whole production process or the firm's demand curve. For example, a small accident to some process using radioactive materials might be easy to repair, but if toxic substances are released, the facility might have to be quarantined for some considerable time. Alternatively, a hotel fire confined to a single room but causing a death might not be too costly in terms of property damage and the liability claims, but the effect on future room bookings could be disastrous. These factors suggest that rating methods may provide only a crude approximation of the individual expected loss values, even though equitable discrimination in the rating structure remains an objective.

Recall the earlier definitions of E_N, E, and E_L. The term E_L referred to the expected value of future possible earnings losses following the operation of loss events. E_N and E referred respectively to the expected earnings in year i (1) without consideration of possible losses in the coming year and (2) with consideration of such losses. Thus

---

[2]This case is a theoretical curiosity. Such a firm would eventually have its growth constrained when it absorbed all the resources available in the world. Given finite resources, no firm can grow in perpetuity at a rate higher than that used for capitalization.

$E_L = E_N - E$. The term E was defined on the assumption that no reinvestment took place. Consider the earnings forecast for a firm that plans to reinvest should some future loss arise and which has available appropriate contingent financing, such as an insurance policy. If there is no interruption loss, earnings can be completely restored to the levels expected before the loss. The appropriate earnings forecast will simply be E_N. Now suppose that possible future loss events are accompanied by the threat of interrupted earnings, even if the firm fully reinvests. The earnings forecast cannot be made immune from this interruption loss simply by allowing for the opportunity to reinvest. Reinvestment will certainly raise earnings expectations from E, but the expected loss of earnings will not be completely recovered. The expected earnings of the firm will lie between E and E_N. Let us define the interruption loss as the loss of earnings following a loss event that is not made good by reinvestment. The expected value of possible future interruption loss is denoted E_{INT}. Thus we can define the following relationships (with some repetition to bring ideas together):[3]

$$E_N - E = E_L \tag{10-13}$$

This is the expected loss of earnings assuming no reinvestment.

$$E_L/L_K = r_{FG} \tag{10-14}$$

This is the foregone rate of return on destroyed resources.

$$E_N - E_{INT} \tag{10-15}$$

This is the expected level of earnings assuming reinvestment but given the prospect of interruption loss.

$$\frac{(E_N - E_{INT}) - E}{L_K} = r_{RV} \tag{10-16}$$

This is the rate of return or reinvestment. (Note that r_{RV} has not been previously defined.)

---

[3]These relationships do assume that annual values for earnings and expected losses of earnings are constant. If this is not the case, the relationships can be stated somewhat differently using i to subscript future years:

$$E_{N,i} - E_i = E_{L,i}$$

$$\sum_{i=1}^{\infty} \frac{E_{L,i}}{(1 + r_{FG})^i} = L_K \quad \text{(defines } r_{FG})$$

$$E_{N,i} - E_{INT,i} = \text{expected earnings for year } i$$

$$\sum_{i=1}^{\infty} \frac{E_{N,i} - E_{INT,i}}{(1 + r_{RV})^i} - L_K \quad \text{(defines } r_{RV})$$

$$r_{FG} = r_{RV} \qquad (10\text{-}17)$$

if no interruption loss is contemplated on future loss events.

$$r_{FG} > r_{RV} \qquad (10\text{-}18)$$

if interruption loss is contemplated.

If the insurer's rating methods are sufficiently discriminating that premiums reflect the expected value of claim payments, the premium will be functionally related to E_{INT}. For example, if the insurer uses a proportionate markup for commissions, expenses, reserves, and profits, the premium will be

$$P_{\text{INT}} = (1 + \alpha) \sum_{i=1}^{n} \frac{E_{\text{INT},i}}{(1 + k_R)^i} \qquad (10\text{-}19)$$

where P_{INT} = the premium for business interruption insurance
  α = the insurer's loading factor
  n = the number of years of interruption insured
  k_R = the insurer's discount rate.

While recognizing that such perfect discrimination in rating will never be achieved in practice, we will nevertheless illustrate premiums in this way in our example in order to show some sensitivity to the expected value of claim payments.

EXAMPLE: VOLATILITY CHEMICALS

Volatility Chemicals manufactures fertilizers and related organic products at its one plant. The current replacement value of the plant, equipment, buildings, inventory, etc., is $50 million. The firm currently earns $10 million annually, and this is projected to remain constant. The risk manager is asked to prepare a brief for the Board that estimates the prospective costs to the firm of losses due to fire, explosion, storm, and related perils, together with estimates for insurance protection. On the basis of these values, the risk manager is asked to make his recommendation to the Board on an appropriate management program. The summarized information is as follows:

Value of existing capital resources (replacement)	$50 million
Expected value of loss of capital resources (K_L) (derived from industry loss statistics)	$ 1 million
Expected earnings assuming no loss this year (E_N)	$10 million
Expected value of earnings assuming no reinvestment (E)	$ 9.4 million
Expected value of earnings loss assuming no reinvestment (E_L)	$ 0.6 million
Expected value of earnings assuming full reinvestment ($E_N - E_{\text{INT}}$)	$ 9.8 million
Expected value of potential interruption loss (E_{INT})	$ 0.2 million
Internal rate of return on reinvestment $[(E_N - E_{\text{INT}}) - E]/L_K$	0.4

Capital Structure

Existing debt	$10 million at 8% coupon
Existing equity	1.2 million common shares outstanding
Equity capitalization rates:	
No insurance purchased	0.105
Insurance (direct and interruption) purchased	0.10
Planned postloss financing by debt	0.107
Planned postloss financing by equity	0.105

If new debt is raised to finance reinvestment after a loss, it is anticipated that this will cost the firm 9%.

Insurance

Available insurance policies include:

1 Direct loss policy. The premium is calculated as follows:

$(1 + \alpha)L_K = (1.2)\$1$ million $= \$1.2$ million

2 Interruption insurance covering up to 2 years loss of earnings. The premium is

$$(1 + \alpha) \sum_{i=1}^{2} \frac{E_{INT}}{(1 + k_R)^i} = (1.2)\left(0.2 + \frac{0.2}{1.1}\right) = \$0.458 \text{ million}$$

A suggested solution is worked out in Table 10-4. The calculations follow the usual pattern. The comparisons made show current market values of equity under the alternative assumptions:

1 That any loss will not be made good by reinvestment.

2 That preloss financing with direct insurance protection is made available. Also interruption insurance is purchased.

3 That reinvestment will be undertaken, but this will be financed after loss by means of debt.

The results show that reinvestment is clearly desirable whether by means of insurance or debt. This is hardly surprising, since the internal rate of return on reinvestment (r_{RV}) is 40%. Insurance is clearly more desirable than reliance on postloss debt refinancing. The main reason for this advantage is that insurance reduces the equity capitalization rate to 10% compared with a rate of 10.7% with debt financing. The lower capitalization rate with insurance reflects the lower level of prospective leverage and the effects of insurance directly on the cost of equity either through systematic-risk or cost-of-diversification effects.

The "Volatility" example was formulated under the simplifying assumption that future cash flows would deviate only randomly from a constant value or, in other words, that the expected value of these flows was constant. Embodied in this assumption was the requirement that the interruption loss E_{INT} also be constant across all future years. This assumption of constant cash flows was adopted to simplify the presentation. Present values of future constant earnings streams reduce to the convenient form E/k_E. If earnings are not constant or do not follow some conveniently simple growth

TABLE 10-4
VOLATILITY CHEMICALS: INTERRUPTION LOSS AND INSURANCE

	No reinvestment	Insurance financing			Postloss debt financing
		Year 1	Year 2	Subsequent years	
Earnings before interest and taxation (E_{NJ})	$10 million	$10 million	$10 million	$10 million	$10 million
Earnings loss, no reinvestment (E_L)	$0.6 million	—	—	—	—
Earnings loss with reinvestment (E_{INT})	—	$0.2 million	$0.2 million	$0.2 million	$0.2 million
Insurance payment for interruption insurance	—	$0.2 million	$0.2 million	$0.2 million	—
Interest: Existing debt	$0.8 million	$0.8 million	$0.8 million	$0.8 million	$0.8 million
New debt	—	—	—	—	$0.9 million
Insurance premiums	—	$1.658 million	—	—	—
Earnings available for distribution (E)	$8.6 million	$7.542 million	$9.2 million	$9.0 million	$8.91 million
Number of shares (m)	1,200,000	1,200,000	1,200,000	1,200,000	1,200,000
Earnings per share (EPS)	$7.17	$6.29	$7.67	$7.5	$7.43
Equity capitalization rate (k_E)	0.105	0.1	0.1	0.1	0.107
Price per share (EPS/k_E)	$68.29	$6.29 + \dfrac{75.85}{1.1} = \$75.25$	$7.67 + \dfrac{75}{1.1} = \$75.85$	$75	$69.44
Market value of equity	$81.90 million	$7.542 + \dfrac{91.02}{1.1} = \$90.29$ million	$9.2 + \dfrac{90}{1.1} = \$91.02$ million	$90 million	

path, then estimation becomes more cumbersome. The available earnings for distribution each year must be separately calculated and reduced using the usual formulation:

$$V(1) = \sum_{i=1}^{\infty} \frac{E_i}{(1 + k_E)^i}$$

In practice, data limitations will only permit reasonable separate estimates of the cash flows for the first few years; thereafter, some simplifications will be necessary to avoid summation of an infinite number of terms.

OTHER REASONS FOR PURCHASING INSURANCE

In most insurance or risk management texts, the reason given for corporate demand for insurance is that the "firm" is risk-averse. This is sometimes explicit. For example Mehr and Hedges (1974, pp. 4–6) suggest that "survival" and the desire for a "quiet night's sleep" are appropriate objectives. Elsewhere (e.g., Greene and Serbein, 1983, and Williams and Heins, 1964) the assumption of corporate risk aversion is implicit in the presentation. The discussion of concave utility functions early in these texts without serious discussion of the multiple interests under the corporate umbrella, which of these interests is risk averse, and how such aversion enters the decision process implies corporate risk aversion. Our approach so far is based on the welfare of a firm's owners, and such welfare is measured in the value of those equity interests, i.e., through the price at which the firm's shares trade. Insurance does not necessarily increase value even if the shareholders are risk-averse. Shareholders can control risk in their personal portfolio investment strategy. However, insurance may increase value if (1) it reduces the level of systematic risk for a firm's earnings, and (2) if it permits the level of unsystematic risk to be lowered at a cost that is lower than that for personal portfolio readjustment. Neither effect automatically increases value. The critical relationship is between the effectiveness of insurance in reducing earnings risk and the relative cost of the insurance. Furthermore, both effects arise through changes in the cost of capital. We will now examine alternative reasons for insurance purchase that have an effect through the expected level of earnings of the firm. These effects, which will be analyzed in sequence, are

1 Ancillary services
2 Effect on expected earnings
3 Bankruptcy costs
4 Effect on contract prices
5 Agency costs

1 Insurers typically package insurance with other services. Examples are loss-prevention services (such as the surveying of risks and safety education) and claims-handling services. Such services may be purchased in the absence of insurance protection, although if the cost is higher than that built into the insurance premium, the insurance is effectively subsidised. Insurers may be very efficient in providing such

services because they also provide benefit to the insurer. For example, loss-prevention services may reduce expected claim costs for the insurer and are usually provided in conjunction with a survey of the risk, which provides underwriting information to the insurer. Similarly, the insurer can effectively combine its own information-gathering process to settle claims with an objective and efficient claims-handling service that is of independent value to the insured.

  2 In the simple world analyzed at the beginning of Chapter 7, the operating decisions of a firm, and therefore its expected earnings, were independent of the financing decision. In a more complex setting, where firms may suffer interruption of earnings following a loss, insurance protection may alleviate interruption loss. This will be the case if alternative sources of finance are not quickly available so that remedial measures to minimize interruption loss cannot be taken promptly. A crucial factor in determining whether interruption loss arises, as well as its potential severity, is the size of inventories. Trading may continue, despite a cessation of production, purely on the basis of existing inventory. Thus a speedy repair and reconstruction program may permit production to resume before inventories are exhausted. Insurance might aid speedy recovery in two ways. First, if the same carrier writes both the direct loss policy and the interruption policy, an early payment on the former may lead to a reduced payment on the interruption policy. Second, interruption policies typically cover additional expenditure designed to reduce the period or severity of interruption up to the estimated savings in direct charges and loss of profits.

  3 Bankruptcy involves transactions costs. Assets have to be liquidated, and the sale usually involves fees and commissions to agents and dealers. In addition, there may be loss of tax credits and fees for legal and administrative costs arising in the bankruptcy process. If insurance is able to affect the probability of bankruptcy, it will change the probability that bankruptcy transaction costs will actually be incurred. Evidence of the size of these bankruptcy costs is somewhat scant, although a study by Warner (1977) calculated the expected value of bankruptcy costs for railroads as follows:[4]

$$\left(\begin{array}{c} \text{Bankruptcy cost as a} \\ \text{proportion of the value} \\ \text{of the firm} \end{array} \right) \times \left(\begin{array}{c} \text{probability that} \\ \text{the firm will} \\ \text{become bankrupt} \end{array} \right)$$

That is,

$$0.014(0.2) = 0.0028$$

However, even this value is too high, since bankruptcy may occur in the future and the costs need to be discounted. Although these data apply to railroads, they provide a rough order of magnitude when considering other forms of enterprise.

---

[4]These values are quoted from Brealey and Myers (1981, p. 387).

Insurance has the effect of restoring the value of equity after a loss. This reduces the probability that a firm will become insolvent as a result of loss. However, the expected value of bankruptcy costs appears to be of a pretty small order of magnitude, and any reduction in this value will be even smaller. This potential benefit of insurance is probably rather insignificant.

4 A more important effect of insurance is likely to arise through contract prices. For example, consider the set of labor contracts negotiated by a firm. The contract price will usually reflect the bargaining power of the parties, although in the process of negotiation, indirect benefits will usually emerge as a substitute for wage payments. The tradeoff between direct and indirect benefits depends on the respective costs and on the preferences of the parties. Among indirect benefits will be security of employment, and this will be determined, in part, by the ability of the firm to withstand losses without laying off workers. Insurance on direct losses will help restore the value of equity, but interruption insurance may be especially important for this purpose. The interruption policy may or may not treat wage payments as a standing cost to be continued in the event of postloss interruption. The direct beneficiaries of continuing wage payments are, of course, the employees, and if the labor market is reasonably efficient, this benefit should be reflected in the wage rate.

Similar benefits should arise in managerial compensation levels. The benefits of risk reduction are probably of greater importance for managers and other employees than for shareholders. The ownership stake of the shareholder is a financial asset, and its risk is, or can be, controlled by portfolio diversification. However, employment income usually represents the dominant component in the wealth of many workers, and employment risks cannot be eliminated so easily. This is especially true for older workers or for all workers in times of recession, when alternative employment opportunities may be limited.

Other types of contracts may also be affected by insurance. For example, if the product sold by a firm requires after-sales service, the product is likely to be more attractive to customers if the firm is secure from the financial consequences of sudden loss events. A contract of work between a principal contractor and a subcontractor will often allocate liability and/or the responsibility for insurance for specified events between the parties. The presence of an insurance clause usually will be reflected in the contract price.

5 A related reason for corporate insurance purchases may not bring benefit to a firm's owners, but rather it may impose costs. Financial decisions, including risk management decisions, are usually made by paid managers who have their own interests and objectives that may be quite different from those of shareholders. We have already mentioned that managers benefit from the additional security provided by insurance protection. The costs of protection are borne directly by shareholders in the form of reduced earnings; therefore, insurance may be perceived as costless to the managers themselves. In this case, why not buy insurance? Whether insurance is actually costless to the managers depends on the managers' renumeration schedule and the system for monitoring performance. Incentives that relate renumeration to corporate earnings or sanctions based on past performance, such as dismissal, control of promotion, etc., may bring the costs of managerial decisions back to the managers involved. It is very doubtful whether incentive systems can and do lead to a complete equivalence of interests between managers and owners. Even if full costs can be imposed on managers *ex post,* there is still the question of whether they perceive these costs to be internalized at the time of the decision.

The costs imposed on shareholders that arise from managers pursuing their own independent objectives are known as *agency costs*. This subject goes beyond risk management to the wider set of economic decisions, and the problems have been analyzed by writers such as Jensen and Meckling (1976) and Ross (1973). With respect to the insurance problem, it appears likely that managers will place a higher value on the removal of risk than will shareholders, and managers will express this preference by purchasing more insurance than might be required by a firm's owners. If the cost of this excess protection exceeds the (capital) market price of such risk, the firm will lose value. However, if the loading in the insurance premium is small, such excessive protection will not have an adverse effect on expected earnings or on the value of the firm. Thus excessive insurance will bring benefit to managers at no cost to the owners and would presumably survive as a "harmless" activity.

Quantification of these various insurance effects may impose considerable difficulty in practice. The issue of ancillary services is probably the least troublesome, since these can be valued by independent quotation. The remaining effects arise because insurance affects the total (not just systematic) riskiness of a firm and thereby bestows benefits to various parties having claims on a firm's output. The measurement of these effects therefore requires that we measure the effect of insurance on the overall riskiness of a firm and then measure the benefits of this reduction in risk to the parties involved. The second stage of the process calls for judgments in light of the particular circumstances of the firm and of the capital, labor, and product markets in which it operates. Our belief is that such judgments are better made within the financial framework provided. Nevertheless, theory takes us only so far, and decisions require that subjective, but hopefully informed, estimates will be made.

A SIMPLIFICATION USING CAPITAL-BUDGETING TECHNIQUES

The tabular form we have presented for analyzing insurance and related decisions requires that we present all relevant financial data for a firm in order to compare different risk management strategies. The reason that all financial data are presented, rather than just data directly relevant to the risk management decision, is that insurance may affect the cost of capital. If so, the firm's total earnings have to be capitalized at the different rates pertaining to the different risk management strategies that may be adopted. Under some circumstances, we can simplify the decision process by focusing only on risk management data.

If the stock of a firm is widely held, we appeal to asset pricing models, such as the capital asset pricing model, to argue that systematic risk only is relevant for the value of the firm. Under such circumstances, the cost of capital to the firm is affected only by a risk management strategy if the risk management costs exhibit systematic risk. We do not worry about unsystematic risk, since this may be diversified away by the owners' investment portfolio strategies. For such widely held corporations, we use the principle of value additivity to simplify the decision considerably. *Value additivity* refers to the property of corporate valuation that the aggregate value of a firm is the sum of the values of the component activities. If one such activity is risk management, we may simply select the risk management strategy for which the risk management benefits are highest (or the risk management cost is lowest) when capitalized at an appropriate risk-adjusted rate. The concept is presented in more detail in Appendix A. Before developing a simple example, it is worth stressing again that this simplification is appropriate when a firm is valued on the basis of systematic risk only.

EXAMPLE: RATIONALITY, INC.

The risk manager of Rationality, Inc. is asked to evaluate alternative risk management techniques. The stock of the firm is widely held, and the risk manager is instructed to consider only the effects of systematic risk. The expected value of loss is $500,000. This loss can be insured for a premium of $650,000, or alternatively, debt financing may be arranged after loss, should a loss arise. The current risk-free interest rate is 8%, and it is estimated that should postloss financing be required, it would be available at a premium of 1% above the risk-free rate, i.e., 9%. There is no expected interruption loss because the physical plant, equipment, etc. can be replaced with minimal delay. The expected return on the market portfolio is 13%.

To tackle this problem, we must first make some assumptions about the timing of prospective losses. The decision requires us to choose a financing method for losses that may arise this year. Prospective losses may arise any time within the year, although we may reasonably simplify our task by assuming loss to arise halfway through the year. Next, we require an estimate of the systematic risk of losses. From past loss data, the loss β value is estimated to be 0.3.

The risk-adjusted present value (RAPV) of risk management costs under the insurance alternative is simply the premium of $650,000, since this is paid immediately. No further net cash flows are anticipated.

The calculation of the RAPV under the debt alternative is more complex. First, suppose that in 6 months time a loss does arise, and replacement of assets requires debt to be raised in the sum of $500,000. This debt is to be serviced by payment of 9% interest (i.e., $45,000 per year), which, for simplicity, we assume to be paid over a 5-year period, with a balloon repayment of the $500,000 principal at the end of the 5-year period. Once such debt is raised, the repayment schedule is fixed by the contract terms and, therefore, may be considered to be risk-free. Accordingly, the present value of shouldering such a known debt, capitalized at the time the debt is raised, can be calculated as follows:

$$D = \frac{45,000}{1 + 0.8} + \frac{45,000}{(1 + 0.8)^2} + \frac{45,000}{(1 + 0.8)^3} + \frac{45,000}{(1 + 0.8)^4} + \frac{45,000}{(1 + 0.8)^5} + \frac{500,000}{(1 + 0.8)^5}$$

$$= \$519,964$$

However, the problem for the risk manager is a little more involved. She does not know in advance whether such a loss will arise or not, and if it does arise, the value cannot be known in advance. The usual approach in capital-budgeting problems is to treat such risky cash flows by discounting the expected value of the cash flow at a rate that reflects the appropriate risk.

The expected value of the postloss financing costs at the expected time of loss (i.e., 6 months hence) is \$519,964. The risk-adjusted rate is calculated in the usual way:

$$E(r_{RM}) = r_f + \beta_{RM}[E(r_M) - r_f]$$
$$= 0.08 + 0.3(0.13 - 0.08)$$
$$= 0.095$$

However, since the expected loss will arise, on average, in 6 months, we will use only half this rate,[5] that is, 0.0475. Therefore, the RAPV of the postloss debt financing strategy is

$$RAPV_{Debt} = \frac{519,964}{1 + 0.0475} = \$496,386$$

This alternative is considerably cheaper than insurance and is to be preferred.

INSURANCE ON REDUNDANT ASSETS

An a priori case was established at the end of Chapter 9 that stated that if the ratio of the market value of a firm to the replacement cost of its assets, that is, the q ratio, is less than unity, reinvestment following major loss would destroy value and should not be undertaken. This is so because the present value of the cash flow generated by the reinvestment would be less than the cost of the reinvestment. This result was qualified in the case of smaller losses, since interdependencies might still imply positive present values if, for example, the loss causes a bottleneck in production. However, by and large, a negative q ratio usually signifies a declining firm, and reinvestment would retain capital in a fairly unproductive use. This raises the issue of whether such redundant assets should be insured. Our attention focuses only on the insurance of those assets (both direct and interruption insurance). We do not address liability insurance here.

A central theme of our financial approach to risk management is that a loss event may generate a demand for sources of funds, since the loss presents the firm with an investment decision. If the reinvestment decision can be anticipated to be negative, there appears to be no need for financing should a loss arise; therefore, insurance is redundant. However, this negative conclusion on insurance may be a little premature. Insurance may still stabilize equity values because the monetary payment made by the insurer in the event of loss should offset the change in equity value. Thus even though reinvestment is not chosen, the investor has money compensation for the loss in the value of his or her shares. The issues involved in the insurance of redundant assets are rather complex, and we will employ the device of teasing these out by way of an example.

[5]If the rate is compounded within the year, this simplification results in a small error. The appropriate half-year rate $r_{L,1/2}$ can be calculated from the annual rate r_L as follows:

$$(1 + r_{L,1/2})^2 = (1 + r_L) \quad \text{or} \quad r_{L,1/2} = (1 + r_L)^{1/2} - 1 = 0.04642$$

EXAMPLE: PAST GLORIES STEEL CORPORATION

Past Glories Steel Corporation has been severely affected by trends in demand for its products and by international competition. This is evident from the following information: The replacement cost of its assets is $1,200 million, whereas its expected annual earnings are only $100 million. Should the firm need to replace these assets, this would represent a return below the cost of capital, and consequently, replacement would not be justified. However, the disposal value of the firm's assets is only $600 million, and the expected earnings represent a sufficiently attractive rate of return on this value to merit continued operation. We now suppose that the firm faces a 0.002 probability that a *total* loss can arise and that insurance at replacement cost can be purchased for a premium of 0.003 ($1,200 million) = $3.6 million. The firm has $250 million debt outstanding at 8%, and its cost of equity capital for all future years (i.e., ignoring the current year for the time being) is 12%.

Before examining whether Past Glories should purchase insurance, consider the value of the firm's equity *after* a loss occurs. The value will depend on whether the firm reinvests or not and on whether insurance is purchased. We expect to find that reinvestment destroys the value of equity, and if so, we assume that the firm goes into liquidation. In this event, any insurance money must be disposed of by the liquidator settling prior claims, such as debt, before distributing any residual to shareholders. In our example, we assume only debt has a prior claim. We suppose that the loss is settled by the insurer at the end of the current year, and in Table 10-5, we present the value of the firm and its equity under different assumptions.

If the firm insures and uses the proceeds of the policy to reinvest, the firm will restore its preloss EBIT of $100 million, which, after payment of interest, results in an end of year equity value of $667 million. With insurance but without reinvestment, the firm has no earnings. Our scenario is that the firm will go into liquidation, but its only asset is the proceeds of the insurance policy. This is used to discharge debt, which has a more senior claim than common shares, leaving a residual value for equity of $950 million. Comparison with column 1 reveals that reinvestment is unsound. Column 3 shows the postloss value if no insurance is purchased. The firm has no assets and must default on its debt. The firm's equity is without value. Comparison of columns 1 and 2 reveals an interesting feature. If insurance protection is purchased, the proceeds are used to protect the firm's bondholders. If no insurance is purchased, the bondholders must share the burden of the loss in the form of a default in the repayment of debt. In our no-tax world, the insurance premium will be borne entirely by shareholders, since each dollar of premium reduces earnings available for distribution to shareholders by an equal amount. Thus when liquidation follows loss, insurance entails a subsidy (or transfer of wealth) from the stockholders to bondholders.

We now transfer our attention to a preloss analysis in order to determine whether insurance creates or destroys value for shareholders. This will be tackled in two parts. First, we will calculate the end of year values on the assumption that no loss occurs in the coming year. To do this, we continue to assume that all cash flows after the current year are discounted by shareholders at 12%. The earnings for the current year are assumed to accrue on the final day of the year. This permits calculation of end of year value of the equity and of the firm, as shown in Table 10-6. This table shows the effects of purchasing insurance protection for the coming year, future years being left to future decisions. Not surprisingly, the value of equity is higher if no insurance protection is purchased and no loss arises. However, we do not know whether a loss will arise or not. Thus the second stage is to derive the expected end of year values of equity and discount these to the present using a discount rate appropriate to the level of risk in each decision. If insurance is purchased, we assume that the discount rate will continue

TABLE 10-5
PAST GLORIES: END OF YEAR POSTLOSS ANALYSIS

	1 Insurance and reinvestment	2 Insurance and no reinvestment	3 No insurance and no reinvestment
EBIT	$100 million	0	0
Interest	$20 million	—	—
Earnings available for distribution (E)	$80 million	0	0
Equity capitalization rate (k_E)	0.12		
Market value of equity	$667 million	$950 million (proceeds of liquidation after discharge of debt)	0
Market value of debt	$250 million	$250 million (discharge debt)	0 (default on debt)
Total terminal value	$927 million	$1,200 million (insurance settlement)	0

279

TABLE 10-6
PAST GLORIES: END OF YEAR VALUES ASSUMING NO LOSS IN COMING YEAR
(Dollar Amounts in Millions)

	Insurance		No insurance	
	Current year*	**Future years**	**Current year***	**Future years**
EBIT	$100	$100	$100	$100
Interest	$20	$20	$20	$20
Insurance premium	$3.6	—	—	—
Earning available for distribution (E)	$76.4	$80	$80	$80
Equity capitalization rate (k_E)		0.12	—	0.12
Market value of equity (MVE)		$\frac{\$80}{0.12} = \$667$		$\frac{\$80}{0.12} = \$667$
	$\$76.4 + \frac{667}{1.12}$ $= \$672$		$\$80 + \frac{667}{1.12}$ $= \$676$	
Market value of firm (MVE + MVD)	$672 + 250$ $= 922$		$\$676 + \$250$ $= \$926$	

*These values accrue on the last day of the current year.

to be 12% for the current year. If no insurance is purchased, we assume that the cost of capital will rise to 12.1%. We would normally expect this difference to be fairly small for the reasons discussed earlier. These rates will be used to discount expected end of year values to the present. The expected end of year value can be calculated as follows:

$$P_{NL}V_{NL} + P_L V_L$$

where P_{NL} and P_L are the probabilities of no loss and loss, respectively, and V_{NL} and V_L are the end of year values of equity assuming no loss and loss, respectively.

The values of V_L are taken from Table 10-5 on the assumption that reinvestment will not be undertaken should a loss occur, since to do so would destroy value. V_{NL} values are taken from Table 10-6. Recalling that the probability of loss is 0.002, we have an expected end of year value with insurance of

$$0.998(\$672 \text{ million}) + 0.002(\$950 \text{ million}) = \$672.556 \text{ million}$$

and an expected end of year value without insurance of

$$0.998(\$676 \text{ million}) + 0.002(\$0) = \$674,648 \text{ million}$$

The appropriate present values of equity are therefore

$$\frac{672.556}{1 + 0.12} = 600.496 \qquad \text{with insurance}$$

and

$$\frac{674.648}{1 + 0.121} = 601.827 \qquad \text{without insurance}$$

In this example it appears that insurance is not justified. In general, we would expect this result to follow in many cases where firms currently operate with redundant assets. This is so because insurance effectively subsidizes bondholders who might otherwise carry the risk of default on their debt.

Thus although the cost of purchasing insurance is borne by the stockholders, part of the benefit of that protection is transferred to the holders of the firm's debt in the form of a reduction in default risk. If the firm is highly leveraged, and if prospective loss carries a high probability of corporate liquidation, then shareholders benefit little from insurance protection. Under these circumstances, insurance is not advisable, since little will be left of the insurance money to compensate the shareholders for their loss of equity. However, we cannot generalize this conclusion too far. Other possibilities may arise where leverage is low, the prospects of partial loss do not lead the firm into liquidation, or the beneficial effects of insurance on the cost of capital combine to create value from insurance.

Our conclusion is that insurance may be highly questionable when the q ratio for a firm is less than unity. However, this statement is intended to draw attention to the probability of a negative conclusion, not as a substitute for individual analysis.

SUMMARY AND CONCLUSION

The discussion of insurance admits various mechanisms by which insurance can affect the value of equity. Certainly, complete insurance protection will insulate equity values from the impact of a loss event, as seen in the postloss analysis. The preloss analysis focused on the effect of insurance and contingent losses on the current value of equity. The valuation framework used to compare alternative risk management strategies monitors the effect of insurance through its impact on a firm's expected level of earnings and through the rate at which these earnings are discounted to value the firm's equity. The loadings in the insurance premium often exceed the expected costs of alternative forms of financing (e.g., interest payments); thus expected earnings are usually negatively related to the level of insurance protection. In order to increase the value of equity, insurance must therefore reduce the cost of capital.

Insurance decisions can be analyzed and compared with alternative forms of financing in a preloss analysis comparable with that developed in the previous chapter. Under this approach, the expected value of the loss and the corresponding expected insurance payment together with the (certain) premium are used to derive estimates for future expected earnings. Earnings are discounted at a rate that impounds a risk premium which might be determined by the extent of insurance protection. This approach can be used to evaluate the effect of both direct loss protection and interruption insurance, although the latter will often fail to provide complete protection if there is a possibility of permanent interruption of earnings.

Under quite plausible assumptions, insurance may have no effect on the cost of capital, even if shareholders are risk-averse. If shareholders diversify away the riskiness inherent in contingent losses by adjusting their personal portfolios, the risk-reducing effects of insurance are redundant and should not be reflected by any increase in equity values. Moreover, as some evidence weakly suggests, the β values for risk management costs are approximately equal to zero, in which event, the systematic risk of the firm would be unaffected by insurance and the cost of capital would not change. Effects on the cost of capital require that loss distribution exhibit particular correlations with the market portfolio and/or that significant costs be associated with personal portfolio diversification. On the whole, we would expect that the effect of insurance on the cost of capital is either small (effects on systematic risk) or apply only to particular firms (those for which the costs of alternative forms of diversification are unusually high). In any case, we would expect any effects that are observed to be confined to those firms whose portfolios of in-house exposure units are not well diversified. Insurance can have little effect on the riskiness of earnings if the distribution of aggregate losses is already substantially risk-free.

The case for purchasing insurance may be strengthened by other factors, namely:

The provision of ancillary services
The availability of immediate financing
Reduction in expected bankruptcy costs
Contractual risk premiums paid by other claimholders
Agency costs

In contrast with earlier benefits, these factors operate on the expected earnings of a firm rather than on the cost of capital.

This chapter concludes with an examination of whether insurance will enhance corporate value when a firm's q ratio is negative. For such firms, major reinvestment following a loss will tend to destroy value and, therefore, is financially unsound. Under such circumstances, the purchase of insurance is unlikely to make much sense for two reasons. First, if reinvestment is not contemplated, there is no need for a source of financing. Second, if liquidation is contemplated following major loss, the proceeds of the insurance policy will go to subsidize those who have a prior claim on the firm's liquidation value.

QUESTIONS

1 From the following details calculate the impact of a major fire on the value of a firm's equity. The firm has an expected EBIT before loss of $25 million annually but, even though reinvestment is to be undertaken from the proceeds of a fire insurance policy, the firm expects

EBIT to be reduced to $23 million. A business interruption policy will cover the loss of earnings in the first year. The firm has no debt but has 2 million shares outstanding. The capitalization rate for equity before the fire was 15%; this is expected to rise to 15.5% since investors perceive that the fire will increase the riskiness of future cash flows. Show how the share price will change following the loss and describe the factors that give rise to this change.

2 A firm is considering the effects of its risk management strategy on the cost of capital. The firm has no existing debt. Earnings exclusive of risk management costs, E_N, have a beta of 1.3. Prospective losses are estimated to cause a displacement of earnings, E_L, having a beta of 0.5. Notice the sign of this beta; when the return on the market is high, the loss of earnings also is expected to be high. The values for E_N and E_L are $10 million and $0.5 million, respectively. The risk free rate is 0.1 and the expected return on the market portfolio 0.15. What will be the firm's cost of capital if:

a It insures?
b It does not insure and does not plan to reinvest?

3 The betas calculated in the previous question can be used in the following problem. The same firm must decide whether to purchase insurance or not. The alternative is to finance reinvestment with debt at 8% or not to reinvest at all. With debt financing the same equity capitalization rate can be used as in the no reinvestment case since the effect of prospective leverage is negligible. No interruption loss is expected. There are 1 million shares outstanding and the insurance premium is $1.5 million. The expected capital replacement cost for destroyed resources is $1.5 million. Which alternative should be chosen?

4 Using only incremental cash flows relating to the risk management decision, decide whether insurance is preferred to other financing methods such as new debt or equity. The following details are given:

Insurance premium	$3.2m
Expected loss	$3m
Loss beta	−0.3
$E(r_m)$	0.18
r_f	0.1
σ_m^2	0.02

Losses can be capitalized at 0.13 to determine their present value.
   Briefly outline the assumptions used for your calculation.

APPENDIX A: A Simplification
of the Insurance Decision Framework

To determine whether reinvestment should be undertaken and whether the reinvestment should be financed by insurance, debt, or some other means requires a comparison of the value of a firm under each alternative. This comparison is undertaken by identifying all corporate cash flows (not simply risk management flows) available to shareholders and capitalizing these at the cost of equity. Thus the risk manager must concern himself or herself with all corporate financial information and must be able to calculate the impact of the risk management strategy on the cost of capital. This process has two major disadvantages. Risk management decisions become incredibly complex, since the income statement for the whole firm must be reworked. Furthermore, there is a danger that the risk manager will ignore the cost-of-capital effects. We argued that the cost-of-capital effect from insurance is likely to be small. However, even a small change in the discount rate can lead to large absolute changes in value, since the rate is used to discount all corporate earnings, not just the risk management costs. The considerations suggest that it would be desirable to derive a decision framework that identifies changes in the value of equity solely on the basis of the risk management cash flows and the risk characteristics of these flows. Such a model would be much easier to use in practice. We will argue that this model can be derived by use of a market model such as the capital asset pricing model. The conclusion does not apply to small, concentrated-ownership firms.

In this appendix we will formally show that the value of a firm is simply the sum of the value added by risk management decisions and the value added by all other factors. This implies that, to maximize the value of equity, we need only to maximize the value added by the risk management decision. In the simplest terms, this leads to a familiar capital-budgeting decision rule. A risk management decision will add value if the net present value (NPV) of the risk management cash flows discounted at a suitable risk adjusted rate is positive, that is,

$$\text{NPV}_{RM} = \sum_i \frac{RM_i}{(1 + k_{RM})^i} > 0$$

where RM_i is the risk management cash flow for year i and k_{RM} is the discount rate appropriate for the systematic risk in RM_i.

Consider the model for valuing equity presented in Chapter 7:

$$\text{MVE} = A(1) + B(1) - I(1) + \frac{X(2) - B(1)(1 + k_D)}{1 + k} \qquad \text{(A-1)}$$

This is a two-period model in which $X(2)$ represents the output generated in period 2 from an investment of $I(1)$ dollars in period 1, recalling that $B(1)$ is period 1 borrowing and $A(1)$ represents initial equity.

Let us generalize this model to imply multiple periods and introduce losses by replacing $X(2)$ with the expression

$$E(f_2\{[I(1) - L(1)], k\}) = E(f_{2,A}) \qquad \text{(A-2)}$$

This expression represents the value of the firm at period 2. This value is the discounted value of future earnings for years 2, 3, . . . , etc.; thus it is shown to be a function of the discount rate k. However, output is also a function of the capital resources allocated to production, which is the difference between the initial investment $I(1)$ and any loss that might arise $L(1)$. We will assume that losses arise at the end of the year. Thus replacing $X(2)$ with equation (A-2), we have

$$\text{MVE} = A(1) + B(1) - I(1) + \frac{E(f_{2,A}) - B(1)(1 + k_D)}{1 + k} \qquad \text{(A-3)}$$

Notice that no reinvestment is contemplated in this specification. Now consider the purchase of insurance. This is secured by payment of a premium at the beginning of period 1 of $P[E(L)]$; that is, the premium is a function of the expected value of loss. Insurance is used to provide funds for reinvestment. Therefore, we can separate all the events that might arise at the end of the first period if a loss arises. First, an insurance payment will be made. Second, the insurance money will be reinvested. Third, the reinvested capital will increase the period 2 value $f_2(\cdot)$. Recognizing each of these effects, we can restate the period 1 cash flow and the period 2 value, respectively, as

$$C(1) = A(1) + B(1) - I(1) - P[E(L)] \qquad \text{(A-4)}$$

and labeling $f_2[I(1), k]$ as $f_{2,B}$, gives

$$E[V(2)] = [E(f_{2,A})] + [E(f_{2,B}) - E(f_{2,A})] + [E(L)] - [E(L)] - [B(1)(1 + k_D)] \qquad \text{(A-5)}$$

where $f_{2,A}$ = time 2 value without reinvestment
     $f_{2,B}$ = time 2 value with reinvestment

The five terms in $E[V(2)]$, each in brackets are, respectively,

1 Expected value without reinvestment
2 The expected increase in value from reinvestment
3 The expected value of the insurance payment, which is equal to
4 The expected reinvestment
5 Repayment of debt

The market value of equity with insurance, therefore is

$$\text{MVE} = C(1) + \frac{E[V(2)]}{1 + k} \qquad \text{(A-6)}$$

Now let us transfer our attention from cash flows to the cost of capital k. We will use the capital asset pricing model

$$k = r_f + \beta[E(r_M) - r_f] \qquad \text{(A-7)}$$

However, as shown in the text, the β value for the cash $V(2)$ depends on the β values for the individual components of the cash flow:

$$\beta = X_1\beta_B + X_2\beta_{RM} \qquad \text{(A-8)}$$

where X_i = weights
    B = nonrisk management activity
    RM = risk management activity

Thus,

$$\text{MVE} = C(1) + \frac{E[V(2)]}{1 + r_f + [X_1\beta_B + X_2\beta_{RM}][E(r_m) - r_f]} \qquad \text{(A-9)}$$

In other words, the period 2 value is discounted at a rate that reflects the level of systematic risk. Instead of adjusting for risk by modifying the discount rate, a dollar adjustment to the cash flow can be made in the numerator:

$$\text{MVE} = C(1) + \cfrac{E[V(2)] - [E(r_m) - r_f]\cfrac{\text{cov } [V(2), r_m]}{\sigma_m^2}}{1 + r_f} \qquad \text{(A-10)}$$

Using equation (A-5) to identify the components of $V(2)$, the covariance term can be expressed as the sum of the covariances of each of the components of the cash flow with r_m:

$$\begin{aligned} \text{cov } [V(2), r_m] = {} & \text{cov } (f_{2,A}, r_m) + \text{cov } (f_{2,B}, r_m) - \text{cov } (f_{2,A}, r_m) \\ & + \text{cov } (L, r_m) - \text{cov } (L, r_m) \end{aligned} \qquad \text{(A-11)}$$

Notice that since $B(1)$ and k_D are assumed to be nonrisky, there is no covariance term corresponding to the last expression in equation (A-5).

We now face the cumbersome task of stating the MVE with all components of $C(1)$ and $V(2)$ and all covariances shown. Taking a deep breath,

$$\begin{aligned} \text{MVE} = {} & A(1) + B(1) - I(1) - P[E(L)] \\ & + \frac{E(f_{2,A}) + E(f_{2,B}) - E(f_{2,A}) + E(L) - E(L) - B(1)(1 + k_D)}{1 + r_f} \\ & - \frac{\left[\dfrac{E(r_m) - r_f}{\sigma_m^2}\right]\left[\text{cov } (f_{2,A}, r_m) + \text{cov } (f_{2,B}, r_m) - \text{cov } (f_{2,A}, r_m) + \text{cov } (L, r_m) - \text{cov } (L, r_m)\right]}{1 + r_f} \end{aligned} \qquad \text{(A-12)}$$

which, with a little rearrangement, is

$$\begin{aligned} \text{MVE} = {} & \left\{A(1) + B(1) - I(1) + \frac{E(f_{2,A}) - B(1)(1 + k_D) - \left[\dfrac{E(r_m) - r_f}{\sigma_m^2}\right]\text{cov } (f_{2,A}, r_m)}{1 + r_f}\right\} \\ & + \left\{\frac{E(f_{2,B}) - E(f_{2,A}) - E(L) - \left[\dfrac{E(r_m) - r_f}{\sigma_m^2}\right]\left[\text{cov } (f_{2,B}, r_m) - \text{cov } (f_{2,A}, r_m) - \text{cov } (L, r_m)\right]}{1 + r_f}\right\} \\ & - \left\{P[E(L)] - \frac{E(L) - \left[\dfrac{E(r_m) - r_f}{\sigma_m^2}\right]\text{cov } (L, r_m)}{1 + r_f}\right\} \end{aligned} \qquad \text{(A-13)}$$

Thus the market value of the firm is the sum of three components, each of which can be given a clear economic interpretation. The first term in equation (A-13) is the value that the firm would have without a risk management strategy, i.e., without insurance and without contemplated reinvestment. The second term is the value added by contemplated reinvestment. The third term is the further value added by insurance. Since financing is necessary for reinvestment, and since insurance is the only source of financing considered, the reinvestment and insurance decisions are interconnected. Under such circumstances, the reinvestment should be undertaken (financed through insurance) if the sum of the second and third terms is positive. However, we can also examine whether it is worthwhile purchasing insurance if reinvestment is *not* contemplated. The purchase of insurance will add value to the firm if the third term is positive, irrespective of the sign of the second term. For a verbal interpretation of this condition, the firm should purchase insurance if the premium is less than the risk-adjusted present value of the expected loss. Given that insurers' premium loadings for expenses, commissions, and profit usually represent 25% or more of the expected loss (often between 50% and 100% of expected loss), the conditions for the third expression in equation (A-13) to be positive are unlikely to be met in practice. We would reinforce the conclusion of the section entitled "Insurance on Redundant Assets" that insurance on redundant assets is unlikely to add value to a firm; more likely, insurance will reduce value and should not be purchased.

Now suppose that a firm has other means for financing reinvestment. In this example we will assume that postloss debt is available at the same rate as initial debt k_D. Instead of paying premium $P[E(L)]$ at the beginning of period 1, the firm can increase debt at the end of the period to finance the loss. In a two-period model such as that being used, we can show the expected payback of debt as $B(1)(1 + k_D) + E(L)$. In this model, debt is repaid as soon as it is floated. Thus the payback $B(1)(1 + k_D) + E(L)$ may be considered to be the period 2 capitalized value of debt repayments. With debt repayment instead of insurance, the market value of equity is derived in the same manner as equation (A-13):

$$
\begin{aligned}
\text{MVE} = \Bigg\{ &A(1) + B(1) - I(1) + \frac{E(f_{2,A}) - B(1)(1 + k_D) - \left[\dfrac{E(r_m) - r_f}{\sigma_m^2}\right] \text{cov}(f_{2,A}, r_m)}{1 + r_f} \\
&+ \frac{\left[E(f_{2,B}) - E(f_{2,A}) - E(L) - \left[\dfrac{E(r_m) - r_f}{\sigma_m^2}\right]\right]\left[\text{cov}(f_{2,B}, r_m) - \text{cov}(f_{2,A}, r_m) - \text{cov}(L, r_m)\right]}{1 + r_f} \\
&+ \frac{\left[E(L) - E(L) - \left[\dfrac{E(r_m) - r_f}{\sigma_m^2}\right](1 - 1)\,\text{cov}(L, r_m)\right]}{1 + r_f} \Bigg\}
\end{aligned}
\tag{A-14}
$$

Notice that the first and second terms of equation (A-14) are identical to equation (A-13). The only thing that has changed is the final term, which relates to the form of reinvestment financing. Thus, assuming that the reinvestment decision is positive, the financing decision simply rests on which of the final terms in equations (A-13) or (A-14) is greater. However, notice that the final term in equation (A-14) is zero. Financing per se has a neutral effect on value (ignoring transaction cost), since the capitalized value of future debt-servicing payments is equal to the market value of the issue. Thus insurance will be preferred if

$$
\left\{ -P[E(L)] + \frac{E(L) - \left[\dfrac{E(r_m) - r_f}{\sigma_2 m}\right]\text{cov}(L, r_m)}{1 - r_f} \right\} > 0
\tag{A-15}
$$

That is, if the insurance premium is less than the risk-adjusted present value of the prospective loss payments to be made under the policy, insurance is preferred to debt financing. If the inequality is reversed, debt financing is preferred. Notice that the choice between insurance and debt (or any other form of financing) can be made independently of the reinvestment decision. Clearly, some form of financing is necessary to secure the value-creation effect of reinvestment, but the form of financing can be treated as a separate decision.

APPENDIX B: Estimation of Loss β Values

The expected earnings of a firm have been decomposed into that component E_N arising from non-risk management activity and that component E_L arising from risk management events, such that

$$E = E_N - E_L \tag{B-1}$$

The symbols $\tilde{R}$, $\tilde{N}$, and $\tilde{L}$ refer to actual earnings, the nonrisk management component, and the risk management component, respectively. Equation (B-2) now gives the counterpart of equation (B-1) shown in actual rather than expected values:

$$\tilde{R} = \tilde{N} - \tilde{L} \tag{B-2}$$

The value of a firm's equity can be calculated by capitalizing the earnings streams. Thus if expected earnings are constant in all future periods,

$$V = \frac{E}{k} = \frac{E_N}{k} - \frac{E_L}{k} = V_N - V_L \tag{B-3}$$

where k is the cost of capital. The two components on the right-hand side of the equation (B-3) show the respective contribution to equity value of the non-risk management activity ($V_N = E_N/k$) and the risk management activity ($V_L = E_L/k$).

The β value for a firm's rate of return on equity is defined as

$$\beta_S = \frac{\text{cov}(r, r_m)}{\sigma_m^2}$$
$$= \frac{\text{cov}(\tilde{R}/V, r_m)}{\sigma_m^2} \tag{B-4}$$

where $r = \tilde{R}/V$ is the rate of return on equity.

The component betas for non-risk management activity and risk management activity are

$$\beta_N = \frac{\text{cov}(\tilde{N}/V_N, r_m)}{\sigma_m^2} \tag{B-5}$$

and

$$\beta_{RM} = \frac{\text{cov}(\tilde{L}/V_L, r_m)}{\sigma_m^2} \tag{B-6}$$

Equations (B-5) and (B-6) can be rewritten in an alternative form:

$$\beta_N = \frac{\text{cov } (k\tilde{N}/E_N, r_m)}{\sigma_m^2} \tag{B-5a}$$

and

$$\beta_{RM} = \frac{\text{cov } (k\tilde{L}/E_L, r_m)}{\sigma_m^2} \tag{B-5b}$$

The relationship between a firm's β value and the β values of the component activities now emerges. From equation (B-4),

$$\begin{aligned}
\beta_S &= \frac{\text{cov } (\tilde{R}/V, r_m)}{\sigma_m^2} \\
&= \frac{\text{cov } \{[k(\tilde{N} - \tilde{L})/E], r_m\}}{\sigma_m^2} \\
&= \frac{E_N}{E} \frac{\text{cov } (k\tilde{N}/E_N, r_m)}{\sigma_m^2} - \frac{E_L}{E} \frac{\text{cov } (k\tilde{L}/E_L, r_m)}{\sigma_m^2} \\
&= \frac{E_N}{E} \beta_N - \frac{E_L}{E} \beta_{RM}
\end{aligned}$$

From these definitions, an example is constructed to show the calculation of the business and risk management β values. Consider the historical earnings data in Table B-1, suitably subdivided into risk management and non-risk management components.

Assuming a discount rate of 10%, the values V, V_N, and V_L can be constructed. Actually,

TABLE B-1
CASH FLOWS ON COMPONENT ACTIVITIES

Year	$\tilde{R}$ Total earnings	$\tilde{N}$ Earnings before deduction of risk management costs	$\tilde{L}$ Losses or risk management costs
1	70	80	10
2	70	70	0
3	70	80	10
4	90	90	0
5	80	80	0
6	40	70	30
7	70	80	10
8	90	90	0
9	80	90	10
10	70	70	0
Expected value	73	80	7

the discount rates used for capitalizing the different earnings streams would differ according to their systematic risk; thus the use of a single rate is a simplification:

$$V = \frac{73}{0.1} = 730$$

$$V_N = \frac{80}{0.1} = 800$$

$$V_L = \frac{7}{0.1} = 70$$

Therefore, $V = V_N - V_L = 800 - 70 = 730$. To calculate β values, we need to show the covariance of $\bar{R}/V$, $\bar{N}/V_N$, and $\bar{L}/V_L$, respectively, with the market portfolio. Details of the appropriate calculations, together with appropriate returns on the market portfolio, are shown in Table B-2.

The covariance with $\bar{r}_m$ are calculated in the usual way (remembering to divide by $n - 1$, since this is a sample):

$$\text{cov}\,(\bar{R}/V, r_m) = 0.003239$$
$$\text{cov}\,(\bar{N}/V, r_m) = 0.002583$$
$$\text{cov}\,(\bar{L}/V, r_m) = -0.004306$$

Given the variance of the market portfolio, that is,

$$\sigma_m^2 = 0.009$$

the β values are calculated as

$$\beta_S = 0.359$$
$$\beta_N = 0.281$$
$$\beta_{RM} = -0.478.$$

TABLE B-2
RATES OF RETURN ON COMPONENT
ACTIVITIES

Year	$\dfrac{\bar{R}}{V}$	$\dfrac{\bar{N}}{V_N}$	$\dfrac{\bar{L}}{V_L}$	$\bar{r}_m$
1	0.096	0.1	0.143	0.2
2	0.096	0.0875	0	0.1
3	0.096	0.1	0.143	0.2
4	0.123	0.1125	0	0.3
5	0.110	0.1	0	0.1
6	0.055	0.0875	0.429	0.0
7	0.096	0.1	0.143	0.1
8	0.123	0.1125	0	0.2
9	0.110	0.1125	0.143	0.3
10	0.096	0.0875	0	0.2

We can now verify that these results conform to the weighting defined by equation (10-7):

$$\beta_S = \frac{E_N}{E} \beta_N - \frac{E_L}{E}\beta_{RM} = \frac{80}{73} (0.281) - \frac{7}{73} (-0.478) = 0.354$$

In fact, there is a rounding of error in the calculation, but the calculations essentially are confirmed.

REFERENCES

Arrow K. J.: "Uncertainty and the Welfare Economics of Medical Care," *American Economic Review,* 52, 1963, pp. 941–973.

Biger, N. and Y. Kahane: "Risk Considerations in Insurance Ratemaking," *Journal of Risk and Insurance,* vol. 45, 1978, pp. 121–132.

Brealey, M., and S. Myers: *Principles of Corporate Finance,* McGraw-Hill, New York, 1981.

Cummins, J. D.: "Risk Management and the Theory of the Firm," *Journal of Risk and Insurance,* vol. 43, 1976, pp. 587–609.

————, and D. Nye: "The Stochastic Characteristics of Property Liability Insurance Company Underwriting Profits," *Journal of Risk and Insurance,* vol. 47, 1980, pp. 61–77.

————, and S. Harrington: "Property Liability Insurance Rate Regulation: Estimation of Underwriting Betas Using Quarterly Profit Data," *Journal of Risk and Insurance,* 1984.

Doherty, N. A., and H. Schlessinger: "The Optimal Deductible for an Insurance Policy when Initial Wealth is Random," *Journal of Business,* vol. 53, 1983, pp. 555–565.

————, and S. Tinic: "Reinsurance under Conditions of Capital Market Equilibrium: A Note," *Journal of Finance,* vol. 36, no. 4, 1981, pp. 949–953.

Fairley, W. B.: "Investment Income and Profit Margins in Property-Liability Insurance: Theory and Empirical Results," *Bell Journal of Economics,* vol. 10, 1979, pp. 192–210.

Greene, M. R. and O. N. Serbein: *"Risk Management: Text and Cases,"* 2d ed., Reston, Reston, Virginia, 1983.

Jensen, M., and W. Meckling: "Theory of the Firm: Managerial Behavior, Agency Costs, and Capital Structure," *Journal of Financial Economics,* vol. 3, 1976, pp. 305–360.

Lindenberg, E. B., and S. A. Ross: "Tobin's *q* Ratio and Industrial Organization," *Journal of Business,* vol. 54, 1981, pp. 1–32.

Mayers, D. and C. W. Smith, Jr.: "On the Corporate Demand for Insurance," *Journal of Business,* vol. 55, no. 2, 1982, pp. 281–296.

Mehr, R. I., and R. A. Hedges: *Risk Management: Concepts and Applications,* Irwin, Homewood, Ill., 1974.

Ross, S.: "The Economic Theory of Agency: The Principal's Problem," *American Economic Review,* vol. 63, 1973, pp. 134–139.

Smith, C. W., and J. B. Warner: "On Financial Contracting: An Analysis of Optimal Capital Structure," *Journal of Financial Economics,* vol. 7, 1978, pp. 117–161.

Warner, J. B.: "Bankruptcy Costs: Some Evidence," *Journal of Finance,* vol. 32, 1977, pp. 337–348.

Williams, C. A., Jr., and R. M. Heins: *Risk Management and Insurance,* McGraw-Hill, New York, 1964.

Vajda, S.: "Minimum Variance Reinsurance," *Astin Bulletin,* 1962.

CHAPTER 11

PRELOSS FINANCING: RETENTION FUNDING

Insurance is a mechanism for financing the investment demands generated by anticipated losses through a series of payments made prior to the period of exposure to loss. Another form of preloss financing arises with the establishment of an internal fund into which contributions are made periodically and from which withdrawals can be made following loss.

There is little current information on the extent of the practice of funding retained losses. A survey conducted in the 1960s by Goshay (1963) revealed that the majority of firms did not fund retained risk. Since then, changes in risk management practice cast doubt on whether this result is still valid. It is well known that retention levels have crept upward, in many cases beyond levels that can be easily financed from current liquidity. Higher retentions may require that more attention be given to loss financing. Furthermore, since Goshay's survey, the growth of captive insurers has been rapid. Although captives will be discussed separately, the issues of funding debated here do apply. Along with the dearth of information on funding, there appears to be no clear agreement as to the purpose of funding. Little academic literature exists on risk management funding, although there is a professional literature. In general, the literature appears to associate funding with financial stability and sound financial planning, yet these concepts are amorphous. In this chapter we will harden our understanding of risk properties and the economic functions of retention funds. This analysis will be conducted without reference to taxation issues, and the conclusions on funding are therefore tentative. In Chapter 15 we will examine taxation and modify some of our results.

ISSUES CONCERNING THE USE OF RETENTION FUNDS

In risk management parlance, it is usual to define losses as *retained* if they are not insured. This "definition by exception" is sometimes associated with self-insurance, although many would reserve the latter term to describe cases in which a firm mimics the operation of an insurance fund by a set of internal transactions. The firm sets up a fund into which contributions (quasi-premiums) are paid and from which the financial demands caused by loss events are met. The association of funding and self-insurance has led to the illusion that the funding of retained losses, like insurance, can remove risk for a firm. This misconception gains superficial support from the observation that any contingent loss will be exactly offset by a payment from the fund, leaving the firm immune from risk. However, a little deeper thought will reveal that such a firm does indeed lose value because the fund represents an asset of the firm and its value is depleted by the payment that follows the loss event. The negative cash flow caused by the loss is simply placed under a different accounting label. To avoid confusion, we will not use the term *self-insurance*. True insurance really does reduce or remove risk; self-insurance does not.

Funding is simply a means of providing financing for loss events. Unlike debt or equity financing, which were considered earlier, the opportunity costs for financing are incurred before a loss rather than after a loss. Thus contributions to a retention fund can be compared with the interest or dividend payments for postloss financing or, more directly, with insurance premiums. As with other forms of financing, our method of analysis rests on the effect that funding may have on the value of a firm's existing equity. If funding is able to generate higher value than other forms of financing, it is to be preferred.

To introduce the analysis of funding, we will develop an example using the tabular presentation of earlier chapters. In order to pursue the issues raised by the example, more formal analysis will then be applied.

EXAMPLE: SNODGRASS WEED CONTROL, INC.

Snodgrass Weed Control, Inc. has been presented with a risk management financing strategy by its new risk manager who is eager to impress the board with her modern approach. Losses can either be insured or financed through a funding/debt plan. Insurance on physical assets (value $60 million) costs $1.5 million per year. An alternative method of preloss financing has been presented to the board by the risk manager. This involves payment of an annual contribution of $1.2 million to a retention fund. Unless and until the assets of the fund reach $60 million, there will always be a nonzero probability that the fund will be inadequate to meet the reinvestment requirements following loss. The risk manager proposes that the surplus of any losses that exceed the value of the fund be financed by postloss debt at 8%. The expected value of these unfunded losses is $0.4 million; thus the expected annual interest burden from servicing debt on such contingent losses is $0.4(0.08) = $0.032 per year. The risk manager further informs the board that if outside funding is required, the firm will incur a transaction cost associated with the costs of floating the debt and the delays in obtaining outside funding. (This transaction cost is new to our analysis, and we will see later that it is important to explain why funding might be used. It will be explained in detail later.) Bearing in mind the probability that external funding will be required is fairly small, the risk manager estimates the expected value of this transaction cost to be $0.05 million.

The assets of the fund are to be kept liquid, and consequently, they are invested in Treasury bills yielding the risk-free rate of 6%. In valuing the equity of the firm with insurance financing, the risk manager estimates the cost of equity to be 10%. Whether correctly or not, the risk manager also proposes that equity should be capitalized at 10% under the funding/debt plan. Other relevant details are:

E_N	$12 million
Number of shares outstanding	2 million
Existing debt	Zero

To develop this example, we will consider only the immediate decision concerning the financing plan for the coming year. Strategies for subsequent years will be the subject of future decisions. Limiting the problem in this way allows us to focus on the cost and benefit of holding the fund for just the current year. Our solution is developed along the usual lines in Table 11-1. Consistent with our focus

TABLE 11-1
SNODGRASS WEED CONTROL, INC.: IMMATURE FUND

	Insurance financing		Funding	
	Year 1	**Subsequent years**	**Year 1**	**Subsequent years**
E_N	$12 million	$12 million	$12 million	$12 milion
Premium	$1.5 million	—	—	—
Contribution to retention fund	—	—	$1.2 million	—
Interest on expected unfunded loss	—	—	$0.032 million	$0.032 million
Expected transaction cost on debt	—	—	$0.05 million	—
Interest on retention fund	—	—	$0.072 million	—
Earnings available for distribution (E)	$10.5 million	$12 million	$10.79 million	$11.968 million
Number of shares (M)	2 million	2 million	2 million	2 million
Earnings per share (EPS = E/M)	$5.25	$6	$5.395	$5.984
Equity capitalization rate (k_E)	0.1	0.1	0.105	0.105
Price per share	$59.8	—	$56.97	—
Market value of equity	$119.6 million	—	$113.94 million	—

only on this year's decision, we show only the premium for the current year and the cost (contribution) and benefit (interest) of operating the fund for the current year. Next year, the fund may be dissolved or continued, but that must be decided at the appropriate time. The accumulation of interest reflects that the contribution is made in anticipation of loss. Allowance of one full year's interest implies that loss financing costs arise, on average, 1 year after payment of the fund contribution.

In this example, the insurance alternative is preferable to the funding/debt combination. This preference arises partly from differences in the expected value of earnings available to shareholders, but more importantly, from the difference in the equity capitalization rate.

This example raises some issues that are central to an understanding of the role of funding. First, it may be surmised that, if the firm reduced its contribution to the retention fund, the balance might tip in favor of the fund. However, such a reduction would shift the burden of financing more toward external debt, and the expected value of interest payments to service unfunded losses would increase. In addition, a lower contribution would increase the probability that a claim might arise above the fund's resources, thereby increasing the expected value of transaction costs. In addition, a reduction in the contribution would reduce the fund's assets and would correspondingly reduce the return on those assets. Whether or not these effects increase or reduce value depends on their respective size. Ideally, we would wish to be able to choose from an infinite number of possible alternative levels of fund coverage, selecting that contribution that maximizes value.

A second issue concerns the nature of the transaction costs. Setting up new external debt (or equity) will give rise to usual underwriting and issue costs. In addition, external issues are accomplished with some time delay, whereas internal funds might be liquidized immediately. This delay might be accompanied by loss of production and/or loss of revenue. Such a loss is also considered to be part of the transaction costs. We will show later that transaction costs are necessary to explain why funding might be sought. In the absence of transaction costs, the financial case for a retention fund is empty.

A third issue concerns the effect of a fund on the cost of capital. We have briefly stated earlier that funding does not reduce risk for a firm; rather, it merely shifts the cost to another accounting label. Accordingly, a firm is still exposed to the riskiness of the retained loss, and investors will discount the firm's cash flows at a rate determined by the systematic component of that risk. The loss β value is therefore important in determining the cost of equity, but we will also notice that a firm's cash flows are affected by the return on fund assets. Relevant risk in this return will influence the cost of equity.

A fourth issue concerns the maturity of the retention fund. What would the analysis look like if the fund had been in operation for a number of years and had been able to accumulate a balance that is inherited at the beginning of the year? Suppose that in recent years contributions to the fund have exceeded loss payments and that Snodgrass had started the year with an opening balance in the fund of $4 million. In addition, the fund accumulates by the annual contribution of $1.2 million made at the beginning of the year. Assuming that losses arise on average at the end of the year, the fund will accumulate 1 year's interest on $5.2 million. Since the fund's assets are larger than in the previous case, the probability that they will be insufficient to cover incurred losses is correspondingly smaller, the expected value of unfunded loss being $0.1 million. The expected annual interest burden from financing unfunded loss is $0.1(0.08) = $0.008 million. The expected transaction cost also is reduced.

The value of the firm under the mature funding system is now reworked in Table 11-2. The value is increased from $56.97 per share without the initial fund endowment to $57.211. This increase reflects the extra interest on fund assets as well as the lower expected interest burden from financing unfunded loss. However, is this value of equity accurate? In fact, there is a big open question. The fund inherits $4 million at the beginning of the year, but the total market value of the firm's equity only increases from $113.94 million to $114.422 million. Where has the extra value gone? It seems that the shareholders would have been better off receiving cash dividends of $4 million and starting the year with zero assets in the fund. Alternatively, if the firm had any existing debt, the money could have been used to redeem that debt. If such debt were costing the firm more in interest than it receives from investing the fund assets, there would appear to be little point in leaving the money in the retention fund. These problems arise because we have failed to account for the accumulated value of the fund when valuing the firm's equity and we have neglected the opportunity cost of maintaining the fund.

TABLE 11-2
SNODGRASS WEED CONTROL, INC.: MATURE RETENTION FUND

	Funding with $4 million initial endowment	
	Year 1	Subsequent years
E_N	$12 million	$12 milion
Premium	—	—
Contribution to retention fund	$1.2 million	—
Interest on expected unfunded loss	$0.008 million	$0.008 million
Expected transaction cost on debt	$0.04 million	—
Interest on retention fund	$0.312 million	—
Earnings available for distribution (E)	$11.064 million	$11.992 million
Number of shares (M)	2 million	2 million
Earnings per share (EPS $= E/M$)	$5.532	$5.996
Equity capitalization rate (k_E)	0.105	0.105
Price per share	$57.211	—
Market value of equity	$114.422 million	—

In order to be able to examine these issues and determine the optimal size for the risk management fund, the analysis will proceed with rather more formality. In particular, we use the capital asset pricing model (CAPM). To proceed with this examination, the reader should be familiar with the contents of Chapter 6. We also argue that the CAPM is used for illustration and the general conclusions also apply to multi-index models such as the arbitrage pricing model (APM).

RETENTION FUNDS WHEN ALTERNATIVE SOURCES OF FINANCE HAVE NO TRANSACTION COSTS

In order to simplify our analysis a little, we will discuss a firm that has no debt. This assumption enables us to look to the value of the firm rather than the value of equity to select the optimal strategy for retention funding. From earlier analyses, we know that the value of a firm is simply the sum of its earnings discounted at an appropriate risk-adjusted rate:

$$V(1) = \sum_{i=1}^{\infty} \frac{E(E_i)}{(1 + k)^i} = \sum_{i=1}^{\infty} \frac{E(E_i)}{(1 + r_f + \Pi)^i} \tag{11-1}$$

where $V(1)$ = present value

$E(E_i)$ = the expected earnings for year i

k = the risk-adjusted discount rate, which may be divided according to;

r_f = the risk-free rate

Π = the risk premium

This model can be reduced to two periods as follows:

$$V(1) = \frac{E[V(2)]}{(1 + r_f + \Pi)} \tag{11-2}$$

The equality of equations (11-1) and (11-2) is confirmed by noting that

$$V(2) = \frac{E[V(3)]}{1 + r_f + \Pi} \qquad V(3) = \frac{E[V(4)]}{1 + r_f + \Pi} \qquad \text{etc.}$$

Thus, by implication, all the individual cash flows E_i shown in equation (11-1) are represented in equation (11-2). Using the CAPM, the risk premium Π is

$$\Pi = \beta[E(r_m) - r_f] \tag{11-3}$$

By noting the usual formulation,

$$E(r) = r_f + \beta[E(r_m) - r_f] \tag{11-4}$$

Thus, from equations (11-2) and (11-3),

$$V(1) = \frac{E[V(2)]}{1 + r_f + \beta[E(r_m) - r_f]} \tag{11-5}$$

In this formulation, $V(1)$ is simply the expected value next year, discounted at a risk-adjusted rate. If β is positive and $E[V(2)]$ is positive, the risk adjustment will have the effect of reducing present value. The same effect is accomplished alternatively by treating the risk adjustment in the numerator rather than in the denominator. This practice is standard and is used in many texts (see Fama and Miller, 1972). Thus,

$$V(1) = \frac{E[V(2)] - [E(r_m) - r_f] \text{ cov } [V(2), r_m]/\sigma_m^2}{1 + r_f} \tag{11-6}$$

The risk premium is now the lengthy second term in the numerator, which represents a dollar adjustment to the expected value rather than an adjustment to the rate as shown in equation (11-5). However, the effect is identical.[1] It is seen that the risk premium is determined by the covariance between the cash flow and the market portfolio. Indeed, the term

$$\frac{\text{cov } [V(2), r_m]}{\sigma_m^2}$$

is simply a dollar-adjusted equivalent of β.

We will now use this valuation model to examine the effect that retention funding will have on the value of the firm, which, in this case, is equivalent to the value of equity because there is no debt. To accomplish this, we must first show how $E[V(2)]$ is determined in the face of risk management factors. First, suppose that no fund exists. The term $X(2)$ is used to denote value at time 2 before deduction of retained losses arising in period 2. If losses are partially insured, then $X(2)$ is specified net of the premium, and the term $L(2)$ refers to aggregate retained losses arising in period 2:

$$E[V(2)] = E[X(2)] - E[L(2)] \tag{11-7}$$

[1]To prove the equivalence, consider the following:
$$V(1) = \frac{E[V(2)] - [E(r_m) - r_f] \text{ cov } [V(2), r_m]/\sigma_m^2}{1 + r_f}$$

Noting that

$$\text{cov } [V(2), r_m] = \text{cov } \{[V(1)(1 + r)], r_m\} = V(1)[\text{cov } (r, r_m)] \quad \text{and} \quad \frac{\text{cov } (r, r_m)}{\sigma_m^2} = \beta$$

we have

$$V(1) = \frac{E[V(2)] - [E(r_m) - r_f]V(1)\beta}{1 + r_f}$$

Therefore,

$$V(1) = \frac{E[V(2)]}{1 + r_f + \beta[E(r_m) - r_f]}$$

This specification does allow for the financing of unfunded losses by external postloss methods, since the capitalized value of interest/dividend payments made to service new debt or equity will simply be the value of the new issue.[2] Now consider that the firm establishes (or inherits from the previous period) a retention fund with assets $F(1)$ at the beginning of the period. Any loss, and therefore any reinvestment following loss, is assumed to arise at the end of the period, so the value of the fund immediately before the end of the period will be

$$F(1)[1 + E(r_a)] \qquad (11\text{-}8)$$

where $E(r_a)$ is the expected rate of return on fund assets.

We now examine the cost of establishing such a fund. One approach is to consider that fund assets are competed away from alternative investment purposes within the firm (see Cummins, 1976). The opportunity cost is therefore the return that would have been yielded on those assets had they been allocated to alternative use (which is measured as the marginal productivity of investment). However, this approach implicitly assumes that the firm is denied access to capital markets to raise funds for both the alternative investment and the retention fund. If the investment yields a return in excess of the cost of capital, and if no capital constraints exist, then the firm will add value by raising new capital for the retention fund rather than diverting it from alternative investment. In such cases, the opportunity cost of the fund is measured by the cost of raising the capital, which is the weighted average cost of capital, denoted k. The expected value of the firm under these circumstances is

$$V(1) = E[X(2)] - F(1)(1 + k) + F(1)[1 + E(r_a)] - E[L(2)]$$
$$= E[X(2)] + F(1)[E(r_a) - k] - E[L(2)] \qquad (11\text{-}9)$$

Using equation (11-9) and the valuation equation (11-6), the value of the firm is specified as

$$V(1) = \frac{E[X(2)] + F(1)[E(r_a) - k] - E[L(2)] - \lambda\{\text{cov }[X(2) + F(1)(r_a - k) - L(2), r_m]\}}{1 + r_f}$$

$$(11\text{-}10)$$

where $\lambda = [E(r_m) - r_f]/\sigma_m^2$.

From this rather cumbersome formula, we will derive a principle that is important in financial economics and which has surprising implications for retention funding. The risk premium in the numerator of equation (11-10) can be disaggregated, noting that $F(1)$ is a given nonrisky value, as follows:

$$\text{cov }[X(2) + F(1)(r_a - k) - L(2), r_m] = \text{cov }[X(2), r_m]$$
$$+ F(1) \text{ cov }(r_a, r_m) - F(1) \text{ cov }(k, r_m) - \text{cov }[L(2), r_m] \qquad (11\text{-}11)$$

---

[2]This assumes that the expected cost of servicing new capital is the weighted average cost of capital.

Therefore, equation (11-10) can be respecified in terms of three components:

$$V(1) = \left\{ \frac{E[X(2)] - \lambda \operatorname{cov}[X(2), r_m]}{1 + r_f} \right\}$$
$$+ \left[\frac{F(1)E(r_a) - \lambda F(1) \operatorname{cov}(r_a, r_m)}{1 + r_f} - \frac{F(1)k - \lambda F(1) \operatorname{cov}(k, r_m)}{1 + r_f} \right]$$
$$- \left\{ \frac{E[L(2)] - \lambda \operatorname{cov}[L(2), r_m]}{1 + r_f} \right\} \qquad (11\text{-}12)$$

The value of the firm emerges as the sum of the commercial non-risk management activities (first set of braces), the value of the retention fund (the large term in brackets), and the (negative) value of the firm's loss exposure (the last term in braces). This seemingly innocuous result carries a very important implication for funding. It will be seen that the case for establishing a fund depends exclusively on the relationship between the risk-adjusted return on fund assets (the first expression in the second term, i.e., the term in brackets) and the risk-adjusted cost of the fund (the second expression in the same brackets). If the risk-adjusted return exceeds the risk-adjusted cost, the fund will add value to the firm; otherwise, it will reduce the value of the firm. *The case for establishing a fund is entirely independent of the firm's loss exposure.* In other words, *there is no risk management case for establishing a retention fund under these assumptions.* Certainly, the firm may choose to hold financial assets, such as might be held in a fund, but it will only be rational to hold such assets on the basis of the investment return on those assets.

This somewhat surprising result merits further discussion. Funding is usually understood to provide an orderly method for financing the capital demands induced by loss. Furthermore, the firm is not exposed to sudden financial demands caused by the occurrence of loss, and consequently, the fund is assumed to reduce financial risk. This perception ignores, or confuses, the economic costs and opportunities facing a firm. When a retention fund is established, a firm incurs an opportunity cost by diverting existing capital from other investment opportunities or by raising new capital to endow the fund. This cost continues while the fund is maintained, since at any time the fund could be dissolved, thereby releasing its resources for alternative investment or for the repurchase of outstanding debt/equity. If a loss arises, the fund's assets will be depleted and the firm will thereby loose the opportunity to divert fund assets to the repayment of capital or to alternative investment. Thus the fund does nothing to protect a firm from the random incidence of losses, and when such losses do arise, the firm will suffer loss of value. The result will be identical to an unfunded loss. This differs from insurance, which does protect a firm from loss of value following a loss.

When a firm has access to capital markets, losses can be financed by raising new capital. Whether such capital should be raised or not depends on the relationship between the rate of return on reinvestment and the cost of capital. If the former is higher than the latter, reinvestment will add value. Funding simply brings forward the date at which the firm goes to the market to raise funds. The firm can raise capital in anticipation of future losses, although the criterion for reinvestment is exactly the same as before. The only thing that has changed by switching from postloss financing to preloss funding is that the assets of the fund can be reinvested. Thus the case for bringing forward the date at which financing is raised rests on whether the investment of fund assets will yield a risk-adjusted return in excess of the cost of capital. If so, capital should be raised immediately to purchase the financial assets. However, the nature of this investment opportunity has nothing to do with risk management and the loss exposure. Even if there were no loss exposure, the firm would still have an opportunity to raise capital and use that capital to purchase financial assets. To bunch these assets together under the label of a risk management retention fund achieves nothing. In fact, allocation of the assets to the retention fund might even impose a cost on the firm, since the firm might be deterred from liquidizing the assets when the opportunity cost of continued holding of the funds becomes too high.

We have argued that no case for risk management retention funding exists when alternative financing has no transaction costs and when a firm has complete access to capital markets. We now examine whether the case for funding can be made by relaxing the assumption about access to capital markets. If a firm has no access to capital markets, it must raise capital for the fund from alternative internal sources, possibly with a high opportunity cost. Moreover, the firm cannot raise funds after loss for reinvestment. Under such circumstances, funding may be thought to be desirable because reinvestment would be denied from alternative postloss sources. However, insurance may still be available, and funding will only be justifiable if its costs are lower than the cost of insurance. Such a comparison should consider the true opportunity cost of the fund and, since alternative productive investments are sacrificed, this cost may be high.

For a firm to be denied access to capital markets for exploiting profitable investment opportunities is somewhat unusual. Capital markets are widely considered to be efficient in allocating funds to projects and to firms that promise attractive investment returns. If access is denied, or if financing is available only at very high cost, then either the market is inefficient for failing to endorse management's optimistic estimates of future returns or the market correctly assesses that the proposed use of the fund will yield low expected returns. For example, the risk manager may attempt to establish a case for funding by arguing that a fund can be set up now by raising new, cheap capital, but if a loss arises, new capital will be expensive or may not be available at all. However, the conditions under which a firm may raise new financing after a loss will reflect the market's estimate of the returns yielded by the firm. A high cost of capital reflects the market's judgment that reinvestments in a firm or project offers poor expected returns and probably should not be undertaken. Apparently, the argument over access to capital markets reflects differences in the estimates of future returns from reinvestment made by internal managers (including the risk manager) and external investors. Given the accumulation of evidence on market efficiency and the vested interests of managers, we contend that the burden of proof in presenting a case for funding on the grounds of inefficiencies in the capital market should be strong. Our general view is that capital markets are reasonably efficient in allocating funds. The case for funding based on capital market constraints of this sort is pretty weak, although we would hesitate to add nonexistent.

Having dismissed the widespread, but we think spurious, reasons for retention funding, we will now present a case for limited funding based on more sound financial reasoning.

RETENTION FUNDS WHEN ALTERNATIVE SOURCES OF FINANCE HAVE TRANSACTION COSTS

We have briefly discussed the possibility that external postloss sources of finance may have associated transaction costs, such as issue and underwriting fees, or cost stemming from the delays in structuring and marketing a new issue. As in the previous section, our initial analysis will be formal, and then we will present a discussion of the issues raised. The nontechnical reader may therefore choose to jump to the paragraph following equation (11-20).

The starting point is the valuation equation (11-6). As in the previous section, valuation requires a complete identification of the period 2 value $E[V(2)]$. The introduction of transaction costs can be accomplished by presenting a modified version of equation (11-9). Let us denote the value of the transaction costs from resorting to external financing as K. However, we do not know whether such a cost will be incurred. If a fund exists, losses below the value of the fund's assets can be met without resort to external financing, and therefore, the transaction costs will be avoided. Consequently, the expected value of transaction costs is

$$E(K) = R_n K$$

where R_n is the probability of ruin of the fund, defined as

$$R_n \equiv \Pr\left[L(2) > F(1)(1 + r_a)\right]$$

It is clear that the higher the value of the fund's assets, the smaller is the probability of ruin and the lower is the expected value of transaction costs. Thus R_n is a function of $F(2)$. It is also clear that the ruin probability depends on the size of loss. Thus, in functional form,

$$E(K) = R_n[F(2), L(2)]K \tag{11-13}$$

To make the notation less cumbersome, we will simply use R_n for the time being.

The expected year 2 value of the firm can now be represented as

$$E[V(2)] = E[X(2)] + F(1)[E(r_a) - k] - E[L(2)] - R_n K \tag{11-14}$$

and consequently, the present value of the firm is

$$V(1) = \frac{E[X(2)] + F(1)[E(r_a) - k] - E[L(2)] - R_n K}{1 + r_f}$$
$$- \frac{\lambda\{\text{cov } [X(2) + F(1)(r_a - k) - L(2) - R_n K, r_m]\}}{1 + r_f} \quad (11\text{-}15)$$

where λ is defined as before [following equation (11-10)].

Following the previous procedure, we will disaggregate value into the functional components. First, breaking down the covariance terms,

$$\text{cov } [X(2) + F(1)(r_a - k) - L(2) - R_n K, r_m] = \text{cov } [X(2), r_m]$$
$$+ F(1) \text{ cov } (r_a, r_m) - F(1) \text{ cov } (k, r_m) - \text{cov } [L(2), r_m] - K \text{ cov } (R_n, r_m)$$
$$(11\text{-}16)$$

Feeding equation (11-16) into equation (11-15) and disaggregating yields the value-additivity form

$$V(1) = \left\{ \frac{E[X(2)] - \lambda \text{ cov } [X(2), r_m]}{1 + r_f} \right\}$$
$$+ \left[\frac{F(1)E(r_a) - \lambda F(1) \text{ cov } (r_a, r_n)}{1 + r_f} - \frac{F(1)k + \lambda F(1) \text{ cov } (k, r_m)}{1 + r_f} \right]$$
$$- \left\{ \frac{E[L(2)] - \lambda \text{ cov } [L(2), r_m]}{1 + r_f} \right\}$$
$$- \left[\frac{R_n K - \lambda K \text{ cov } (R_n, r_m)}{1 + r_f} \right] \quad (11\text{-}17)$$

Comparing equation (11-17) with the no transaction costs case shown by equation (11-12), we notice an addition term. The components of equation (11-17) are, respectively, for each term enclosed either in braces or large brackets:

1 The value from commercial (nonrisk management) operations.
2 The value or cost from establishing a fund and investing its assets minus the cost of raising capital to finance the fund.
3 The (negative) value contributed by the loss exposure.
4 The (negative) contribution to value arising from the prospect of incurring transaction costs for unfunded losses.

In this formulation, *the value of the fund depends on the loss exposure.* This is evident from the last expression in equation (11-17), recalling from equation (11-13) that R_n is a function of both $F(2)$ and $L(2)$. *Thus we now have a risk management case for establishing a retention fund.* The argument may be verbalized in the following manner.

In the previous section, a case may or may not be made for raising capital to purchase financial assets. However, in the absence of transaction costs to alternative forms of financing, this case rested solely on the merit of the transaction as an investment activity. Even if transaction costs are present, the firm may still wish to pursue such investments in financial assets, although we can now develop the extended case for establishment of a retention fund. The demand for liquidity in a retention fund will usually require that the fund be invested in low-yielding assets, and as such, the investment may not be warranted on normal financial criteria. However, we have already developed the central theme of this book, which suggests that the need for loss financing rests on the satisfaction of the financial criteria for postloss reinvestment. Such reinvestment takes time; buildings may have to be reconstructed or repaired, equipment repurchased, inventories replaced, etc. Thus any major loss (and many minor losses) is often accompanied by some interruption loss. Interruption loss may be inevitable, although it will be minimized if financing is available to set the reinvestment in motion immediately. The establishment of a liquid fund specifically earmarked for reinvestment may facilitate the recovery. However, if external financing is needed, securing such financing may be more time consuming, thereby delaying recovery and increasing interruption loss. New debt from a bank may be secured fairly rapidly (immediately if a line of credit is available), although if larger values warrant a new bond issue, the flotation will take time. Similar arguments apply to new equity issues; a prospectus has to be drawn up and advertised, underwriting arrangements need to be negotiated, and the offer must be made. Furthermore, the firm will be conscious of the timing of the offer. If it follows immediately after a major loss, potential subscribers may be nervous and the terms of the issue and/or the value subscribed may not be satisfactory. Delay may lead to more orderly issue on more advantageous terms, but time is of the essence in recovering from the effects of a loss. With insurance, it is hoped that the payment required to finance reinvestment will be immediate. Certainly, if the insurer also carries the interruption loss, the insurer will benefit from rapid settlement. Nevertheless, insurance settlements often do follow lengthy negotiations and may not always be available as quickly as desired.

A case can be made for funding on risk management grounds if funding avoids the costs imposed by other forms of financing. Potential delays in securing alternative forms of finance may be considered to be a cost imposed on the firm as a result of those financing transactions. Another form of transaction cost is more direct. Negotiation of a loan or the raising of new equity often involves direct financing costs, such as issue expenses, underwriting costs, legal fees, etc. When internal funding is used, these expenses are avoided.

Transaction costs of the nature discussed arise when the loss exceeds the assets of the retention fund and the firm is driven to alternative sources of finance in order to undertake reinvestment. The larger the fund, the smaller the probability that an unfunded loss will arise and the smaller the probability that the firm will bear the transaction costs. However, the benefit of a large fund needs to be balanced against the opportunity costs of maintaining the fund. These opportunity costs probably rise roughly in proportion to the size of the fund. Such costs are represented by the second term in equation (11-17). It is likely that this term is negative, since such funds are usually invested in low-yielding assets that return less than the cost of capital. However, the transaction costs of raising funds from alternative external sources are unlikely to be proportional to the amount raised. Issue costs tend to be proportionately high for small issues, but proportionately low for large issues. In conjunction, these considerations imply that funding should only be undertaken on a limited basis, to cover those intermediate losses that cannot be financed routinely out of cash flow, but not those very large losses for which external financing would only give rise to proportionately modest transaction costs.

THE RUIN PROBABILITY OF A RETENTION FUND

The portfolio of exposure units for a noninsurance firm bears many similar characteristics to an insurance fund. Furthermore, many of the risk management choices facing a firm are analogous to choices facing an insurer. Among these are the optimal insurance strategy for a firm and the optimal reinsurance strategy for an insurer. Another parallel issue is the extent of funding for a firm and the size of reserves for an insurer. The behavior of insurer reserve funds has been studied extensively. In particular, collective risk theory, developed in the early years of this century by Lundberg, is a fairly complex branch of actuarial mathematics that analyzes the ruin probabilities of insurance reserves. The concept of ruin still dominates the actuarial literature, and the assumed objective of insurers is usually taken to be minimization of the probability of ruin. The mathematical sophistication of this approach is not matched by any economic sophistication, for it tends to ignore the capital market activities of insurers, the structure of ownership of the insurance company, and the economics of the market in which those ownership claims are traded. Yet, if risk theory has much to learn from modern financial economics, the reverse is also true.

For our immediate interest, risk theory provides a framework for analyzing how an insurer's reserves, or analogously, a risk management retention fund, will change over time, given premium inputs and random claims. The probability that the fund will be insufficient to meet random claims can be calculated for differing future periods, and the theory permits calculation of the contribution requirement to meet target ruin probabilities. For the risk manager, it is of interest to know how a retention fund will stand up in the face of random claim demands. We have argued that the most persuasive case for the establishment of a fund is to avoid the transaction costs associated with external funding. The only way to be sure to avoid these costs is to establish a fund equal to the maximum possible loss, but such a fund is financially inconceivable. Within this limit, the risk manager will wish to trade off the opportunity costs of operating a fund against the expected benefits, which is represented as a reduction in expected transaction costs from external financing. Expected transaction costs are directly determined by the ruin probability, and a study of the ruin process is essential to our understanding of retention funding. Our treatment of ruin will do little more than scratch the surface of collective risk theory, and our method of analysis is directed toward the financial framework developed in this book.

Ruin Probability: Single-Period Analysis

The *ruin probability* of a retention fund may be defined as the probability that the aggregate retained losses in a given period L_t exceed the value of the fund in that period F_t. Previously, we have defined the period to be of finite duration, e.g., 1 year, and have allowed the fund assets to earn an investment return from the beginning of the period (when the fund is established) to the end of the period (when claims are assumed to be paid). To be consistent, we will keep this notation. Our task is to establish whether the fund will be adequate at the time the claim is levied. In other words, we need to calculate the following probabilities:

$$\Pr\ [L(2) \geq F(1)(1 + r_a)] \tag{11-18}$$

or equivalently,

$$\Pr[F(1)(1 + r_a) - L(2) < 0]$$

In the previous discussion, both the return on fund assets r_a and the aggregate loss $L(2)$ were random variables. Thus failure might arise from an inadequate investment return and/or an excessively high aggregate loss. To start, we will assume that the fund is invested in assets yielding a known return, e.g., short-term federal bills. Such a strategy would provide appropriate liquidity. This assumption is very convenient, since the risk characteristics of the retention fund will simply echo the features of the loss distribution. This can be seen in Figure 11-1. A sample loss distribution is shown in Figure 11-1(*a*). The terminal value of the retention fund, after deduction of aggregate loss, is determined by $[F(1)(1 + r) - L(2)]$, which involves deduction of the distributional values in Figure 11-1(*a*) from the value of $F(1)(1 + r)$. This is shown in Figure 11-1(*b*); the spread, or standard deviation, is the same as in Figure 11-1(*a*), but the direction of skewness has been reversed.

Some preliminary analysis of ruin probability was given in Chapter 5. When a firm's portfolio of exposure units comprises a large number of independent risk units

FIGURE 11-1

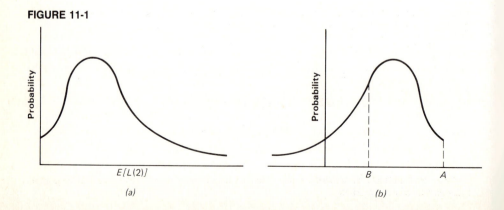

(a)

(b)

or, for some other reason, the distribution of aggregate loss can be considered to be approximately normal, the probability of ruin can be determined by the standard normal variate z, which is defined as

$$z = \frac{X^* - E(X)}{\sigma(X)} \tag{11-19}$$

where $X =$ the value of the fund after deduction of the aggregate loss, which is $F(1)(1 + r) - L(2)$

$X^* =$ the ruin value, which is assumed to be zero

$E(X) =$ the expected value of X

$\sigma(X) =$ the standard deviation of X

Using explicit values for X,

$$z = \frac{0 - E[F(1)(1 + r) - L(2)]}{\sigma[F(1)(1 + r) - L(2)]}$$
$$= \frac{E[L(2)] - F(1)(1 + r)}{\sigma[L(2)]} \tag{11-20}$$

since $L(2)$ is the only random variable.

EXAMPLE: RAINY DAY WEATHERWARE

To illustrate, consider a portfolio comprising a fleet of 100 vehicles each having a loss distribution with

$$E[L_i(2)] = 400$$
$$\sigma[L_i(2)] = 800$$
$$\sigma_{i,j} = 0$$

where the subscripts refer to individual risk units. The value of the fund at the beginning of the period is \$50,000, and it will earn a return of 8%.

Therefore,[3]

$$E[L(2)] = \sum_i E[L_i(2)] = 100(400) = 40,000$$
$$\sigma[L(2)] = \{\sum_i \sigma^2[L_i(2)] + \sum_{i \neq j}\sum 2\sigma_{i,j}\}^{1/2}$$
$$= [100(800)^2]^{1/2} = 8000$$

---

[3]In contrast to Chapter 5, our analysis is conducted here in terms of the aggregate values of the portfolio rather than in values per risk unit.

Consequently,

$$z = \frac{40{,}000 - 54{,}000}{8000} = -1.75$$

The negative sign merely indicates that we are identifying the probability below a critical value of X (that is, $X = 0$). However, the normal distribution is symmetrical, and we can find the ruin probability just by reading the absolute value of z from the tables for the standard normal variate (z tables). The solution is a ruin probability of 0.0401, a little over 4%.

This treatment of ruin is valid if the distribution of aggregate loss is approximately normal. However, for many risk management problems, this assumption is not met. Such a situation may be due to the small number of risk units within a firm's risk management portfolio, to independence between risk units, or to dominance of the portfolio by one or a small number of risk units. Individual risk exposures are usually distributed in a skewed manner (typically with a positive skewness), and without adequate diversification, this skewness does not disappear in a firm's distribution of aggregate portfolio loss if the preceding conditions are violated. The long righthand tail of a skewed distribution does not contain the same probability mass as a symmetrical distribution, and use of the standard normal variate z will produce unreliable estimates of ruin probability.

To produce reliable estimates of ruin probability, one must exactly specify the distribution of loss. In practice, the true form of the components' distributions is not known, but can only be hypothesized. Some considerable progress has been made in risk theory by postulating general forms, such as compound Poisson for the convolution, and methods such as the Esscher approximation can be used to give reasonable estimates of ruin probability. Our approach here is to use the normal power method, which adjusts for the skewness of the distribution. This method is simpler than the Esscher approximation and results in only slightly greater errors.

In Chapter 5, the Chebyshev method was used to show that conservative estimates can be provided for ruin probability that apply to all distributional forms. However, these estimates are so conservative that they are not of much practical value. The normal-power method provides much better estimates so long as the skewness is not too pronounced. To visualize the issue, Figure 11-2 shows a representative distribution of aggregate loss (the solid line).

The problem is to estimate the probability that losses will fall below some critical value, such as L^*. When using the normal approximation, we superimpose a normal distribution (shown by the dotted line) and calculate the probability in the tail of the normal distribution (as shown by the shaded area). This area is used as an estimate of the probability in the tail of the true distribution (shown by the solid line), which is clearly much larger. The problem is that the true distribution is skewed and, consequently, has a long tail with a different probability mass. The solution used with the normal-power approach is to modify the normal approximation to correct for

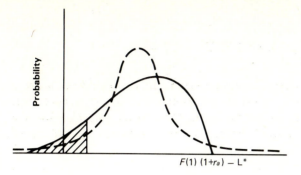

$F(1)\ (1+r_a) - L^*$ **FIGURE 11-2**

skewness. The measure of skewness used was introduced in Chapter 4. If the distribution is known, the skewness is measured by [equation (4-9)]:

$$\alpha_3(L) = \frac{\sum_i p_i[L_i - E(L_i)]^3}{[\sigma(L)]^3} \tag{11-21}$$

However, the distribution, and therefore the true values of $E(L)$ and $\sigma(L)$, will not be known. Rather, the risk manager will have a sample of observed loss data, and skewness must be estimated with the correction for sampling error [equation (4-12)]. Hence,

$$a_3(L) = \frac{\dfrac{n}{(n-1)(n-2)} \sum_{j=1}^{n} (L_j - \bar{L})^3}{[S(L)]^3} \tag{11-22}$$

where n is the number of data points and $S(L)$ is the sample standard error.

The normal-power approximation method uses the standard normal variate z, but in contrast to equation (11-19), the skewness correction is seen as the bracketed term on the lefthand side:

$$z + \left[\frac{1}{6}\alpha_3(X)(z^2 - 1)\right] = \frac{X^* - E(X)}{\sigma(X)} \tag{11-23}$$

It will be noticed that this equation is quadratic for z, and an explicit solution can be given for z by taking the positive root[4] of the usual solution:[5]

---

[4]See Beard et al., 1969, p. 43.
[5]That is,

$$\frac{-b \pm \sqrt{b^2 - 4ac}}{2a}$$

$$z = \frac{-1 + \sqrt{1 + 2\alpha_3(X)/3\ \{\alpha_3(X)/6 + [X^* - E(X)]/\sigma(X)\}}}{\alpha_3(X)/3} \tag{11-24}$$

Equations (11-23) and (11-24) are directly equivalent. If we wish to calculate the contribution to a retention fund that is required for a given ruin probability, we extract the appropriate z value for that ruin probability from the table and solve for X^*. However, if X^* is given and we wish to find the ruin probability, equation (11-24) is appropriate. To illustrate this equivalence, and to show the application of this method, we will develop an example using data from Table 4-1.

EXAMPLE: SUNSHINE SODAS

A retention fund is set up to finance reinvestment following loss. The initial contribution is equal to 150% of the estimated expected value of loss. The fund's assets are invested in federal bills yielding 10%. The loss distribution is not known, but some 20 years of loss experience is available. The loss data are shown in Table 4-1. These data are specified in constant dollars, and no growth in exposure has arisen over the period. Estimate the probability that this fund will be inadequate to meet first-year losses.

Solution

The sample mean is used to estimate the expected value of loss:

$$\bar{L} = \frac{1}{n}\sum_{j=1} L_j = \$118{,}800$$

The sample standard deviation and sample skewness are calculated, adjusting for sample size, to provide estimates of $\sigma(L)$ and $\alpha_3(L)$:

$$S(L) = \left[\frac{1}{n-1}\sum_{j=1}^{n}(L_j - \bar{L})^2\right]^{1/2} = \$160{,}360$$

$$a_3(L) = \frac{\dfrac{n}{(n-1)(n-2)}\sum_{j=1}^{n}(L_j - \bar{L})^3}{[S(L)]^3} = 2.162$$

These sample statistics will be used to estimate ruin probability. The contribution to the fund will be $1.5(118{,}800) = \$178{,}200$. The end-of-period value of the fund is given by

$$X = [F(1)(1 + r_a) - L(2)]$$

which has an expected value of

$$E(X) = \{F(1)(1 + r_a) - E[L(2)]\}$$
$$= \$178{,}200(1 + 0.1) - \$118{,}800 = \$77{,}220$$

The standard deviation of end value is simply the standard deviation of the loss distribution, since this is the only source of risk:

$$S(X) = \$160,360$$

The skewness is also taken from the loss distribution for the same reason. Since loss represents a deduction from wealth, the skewness is reversed; i.e., it is negative:

$$a_3(X) = -2.162$$

Since the task is to find the probability that $X < 0$, we use equation (11-27) with $X^* = 0$:

$$z = \frac{-1 + \sqrt{1 + 2\,(-2.162)/3\,(-2.162/6 - 77,220/160,360)}}{-2.162/3}$$
$$= -0.676814257 \text{ (or approximately } -0.68)$$

The negative sign indicates that we are finding the probability *below* the critical value zero. The answer is extracted using the absolute value of z. Using the z tables, the probability of ruin is 0.2483.

The decision might be posed in a different manner. The risk manager might wish to determine the contribution necessary to achieve some target ruin probability that is considered acceptable for the fund. To verify our calculation, suppose the target ruin probability is 0.2483. This problem is tackled with equation (11-23), which, with simple rearrangement, is

$$X^* = E(X) + \left[z + \frac{1}{6}a_3(X)(z^2 - 1)\right]\sigma(X) \qquad (11\text{-}25)$$

Since we are finding probability below X^*, the sign of z must be negative, that is,

$$X^* = 77,220 + \left\{(-0.68) + \frac{1}{6}(-2.162)[(-0.68)^2 - 1]\right\}160,360$$
$$= 77,220 - 77,980.6 = 760.6$$

The expected answer should be zero, since we know from the first part of the problem that the probability of ruin (Pr $x < 0$) is 0.2483. However, there is a rounding error. We established the ruin probability above by rounding the value for z (that is, 0.676814257) to 0.68 in order to use the z tables. To confirm that this error disappears, the reader should substitute into equation (11-25) the exact z value (that is, 0.676814257) to verify that $X^* = 0$. To find the required contribution, we find some value of loss $(-L^*)$ below which the actual loss will fall with the probability of 0.2483. This is accomplished by use of equation (11-25) again, but specifying in terms of losses:

$$L^* = E(L) + \left[z + \frac{1}{6}a_3(L)(z^2 - 1)\right]\sigma(L)$$
$$= 118,800 + \left\{0.68 + \frac{1}{6}(2.162)[(0.68)^2 - 1]\right\}160,360$$
$$= 196,781$$

Note that the final value of the fund is simply the difference between the value of the contribution (plus interest) and the loss, that is,

$$X^* = [F(1)(1 + r_a) - L^*] = 0$$

Therefore,

$$F(1) = \frac{0 + 196{,}781}{1 + 0.1} = 178{,}892 \ (\approx 178{,}200)$$

The difference between this value and the actual contribution required to produce the estimated 0.2483 probability of ruin is explained by the same rounding error. To verify this, the reader should recalculate L^*, using $z = 0.676814257$.

The normal-power method provides a correction for skewness. In the preceding example, the calculated ruin probability was 0.2483. Had this probability been estimated by the normal approximation, the calculated value[6] would be 0.3156. Generally, the normal-power method will provide more reliable estimates of ruin probabilities than the unadjusted normal approximation. However, it must be emphasized that the normal-power method provides approximate estimates, not exact answers. To obtain exact results, the functional form of the loss distribution must be known. When using normal-power approximations, we are forcing the sample values into a particular distributional shape, which is essentially a normal distribution into which a skewness error has been introduced. The approximate ruin probabilities estimated from the normal-power method are thought to be reasonably reliable if the distribution is not very highly skewed. As a rough rule of thumb, when the absolute value of the skewness coefficient α_3 is much greater than 2, the estimates are unreliable. In this example, the skewness is 2.162; thus one might conclude that the estimated ruin probability is on the border of acceptability. Certainly, the results would not be reliable if the skewness coefficient were significantly higher.

The preceding calculations of ruin probability had only to contend with a single source of risk arising from the loss distribution. Under these conditions, the terminal value of the retention fund will simply mirror the risk characteristics of the loss distribution. Whether such conditions are met depends on the investment strategy adopted for the fund's assets. Unless all assets are held in a risk-free form (e.g., cash or short-term Treasury bills), the analysis must be adapted to allow for investment risk. To proceed with the estimation with investment risk requires calculation of the expected value, standard deviation, and skewness of distribution of the terminal value of the fund. These parameters must be estimated from characteristics of the component distributions of investment yield and aggregate loss. We illustrate the nature of the

---

[6]This is easily verified:

$$z = \frac{X^* - E(X)}{\sigma(X)} = \frac{0 - 77{,}220}{160{,}360} = -0.48154$$

giving a ruin probability, extracted from the z table, of 0.3156.

problem in the text of this chapter using an example that ignores problems of skewness. In the appendix to this chapter we show how the normal power approximation method can be used with dual sources of risk, although the analysis is a little more complex.

In the first example of this section, the use of the normal approximation was illustrated with a single source of risk. To show the effects of dual risk, that example will be amended to reveal a nonzero standard deviation for the investment return.

EXAMPLE: RAINY DAY WEATHERWARE

The task is to establish

$$\Pr\,[F(1)(1 + r_a) - L(2)] < 0$$

when both r_a and $L(2)$ are risky. The given values are

$$E[(L(2)] = 40,000$$
$$\sigma[L(2)] = 8000$$
$$E(r_a) = 0.08$$
$$\sigma(r_a) = 0.15 \quad \text{(previously zero)}$$
$$\sigma_{RL} = 240 \quad \text{(previously zero)}$$
$$F(1) = 50,000$$

First, we must establish values for $E(X)$ and $\sigma(X)$ using the usual formulas:

$$E(X) = F(1)\,[1 + E(r_a)] - E[L(2)] = 14,000$$

$$\begin{aligned}
\sigma(X) &= \sigma[F(1)(1 + r_a) - L(2)] \\
&= \sigma[F(1)r_a - L(2)] \quad \text{[since $F(1)$ is constant]} \\
&= \{F(1)^2\sigma(r_a^2) + \sigma[L(2)]^2 - 2F(1)\sigma_{RL}\}^{1/2} \\
&= [50,000^2(0.15)^2 + 8000^2 - 2(50,000)(240)]^{1/2} \\
&= 12,010
\end{aligned}$$

Notice that the sign for covariance is negative because losses are deducted from the fund value. The probability of ruin is now calculated in the usual manner:

$$z = \frac{X^* - E(X)}{\sigma(X)} = \frac{0 - 14000}{12,010} = -1.17$$

which gives a ruin probability of 0.121.

The introduction of investment risk has increased the ruin probability from 0.0401 to 0.121. The newly introduced investment risk is substantial. Notice that the increased riskiness of the fund arises despite a favorable covariance between investment risk and loss risk. The covariance is positive, implying that large losses and large investment returns have some tendency to coincide, as have small losses and small investment returns. This stabilizing effect is too small to overwhelm the large variance of investment risk, and the total risk for the fund increases.

Ruin Probability: Multiperiod Analysis

Mathematical risk theory has addressed itself to the problem of determining how an insurance company's reserves will change over time given some model of premium determination and given the stochastic nature of claims made on the fund. If this process is described in discrete periods, e.g., years, the fund will grow during years in which premiums (net of expenses) exceed claims, and it will contract in periods for which claims exceed premiums. Due allowance should be made for investment income, although this feature has largely been ignored in actuarial literature. If we describe the behavior of a risk management retention fund in similar terms, the terminal value of the fund will change year to year in a random manner. Indeed, under some circumstances, the process is simply a random walk. We will now introduce some of the issues concerning the dynamic behavior of the retention fund. In particular, we will examine ruin probability. The mathematical complexity of this dynamic analysis soon outgrows the level prescribed for this book, and our analysis will be correspondingly brief. Happily, we do not see brevity as a major disadvantage, since we shall argue that the multiperiod approach does not fit well with our model of rational decision making. We do believe that some mention of the problem is important, since decision making may also reflect political considerations within the firm.

At the beginning of each year t, a contribution of $C(t)$ dollars is made to the retention fund. The fund earns an annual investment return at a rate r_a. Losses are realized at the end of each year, and the realized value for year t is $L(t)$. The value of the fund at the end of each year is denoted $F(t)$, and this value is inherited by the fund at the beginning value for year $t + 1$. Thus,

$$F(t) = [F(t - 1) + C(t)](1 + r_a) - L(t) \qquad (11\text{-}26)$$

and similarly, for the previous year,

$$F(t - 1) = [F(t - 2) + C(t - 1)] (1 + r_a) - L(t - 1) \qquad (11\text{-}27)$$

and so on. If the fund was established n years ago, its current value can be determined by successive substitutions of the set of equations represented by equations (11-26) and (11-27). Thus,

$$F(t) = \sum_{i=0}^{n} C(t - i)(1 + r_a)^{i+1} - \sum_{i=0}^{n} L(t - 1)(1 + r_a)^i \qquad (11\text{-}28)$$

The changing value of $F(t)$ can be illustrated as shown in Figure 11-3. The bottom section shows constant annual contributions made to the fund, but the losses deducted are random values. To simplify the illustration, the interest rate is assumed to be zero. The contributions are shown as positive values and the losses as negative values, the former occurring at beginning of year and the latter at year end. The fund develops as shown in the top segment, the value at each period reflecting the random effect of loss. In this particular example, the firm is fortunate because in the early years of the

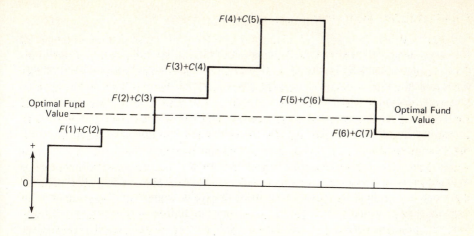

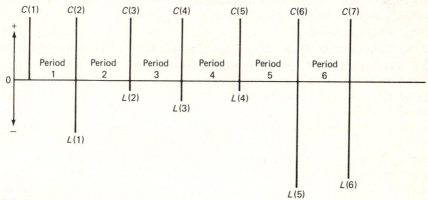

FIGURE 11-3

fund, the losses are less than the annual contributions, enabling the fund's value to increase up to period 5. The value at this time is sufficient that year 5 and year 6 losses, both of which exceed the contributions for those periods, can be met. However, it is easy to imagine that the sequence of losses might have been less favorable. If the heavy losses had arisen in the early years, the fund would have exhausted its value and correspondingly would have failed. Thus, for a fund to have a reasonable chance of surviving without ruin, it must have either good fortune in its early years or a large initial contribution.

In this dynamic setting, the terminal value of the fund at the end of each year is inherited at the beginning of the next year. This means that the fund starts each period with a randomly determined initial endowment. The ruin probability for each period is still identified by

$$Pr\ [F(t)(1 + r_a) - L(t)] < 0 \qquad\qquad (11\text{-}29)$$

However, since $F(t)$ will change from year to year, so too will the ruin probability. As an example, consider Figure 11-3. Here, $F(t)$ increases for four successive periods. Since contributions and expected losses are unchanged, the ruin probability has progressively declined. The heavy losses in years 5 and 6 reduce the fund. For each of these years, a smaller terminal value is transferred to the subsequent period, thereby increasing the ruin probability. Thus it seems that the ruin probability, together with the value of the fund, will vary in a random manner.

The problem of varying ruin probabilities arises because the retention fund is maintained as an independent financial entity from year to year. Other than the annual contribution, the fund is allowed to gain or lose value without further transfer to or from the fund. It would be easy to change this practice and stabilize the ruin probability. One way would be to transfer to the fund at the beginning of each period a contribution that is exactly equal to the previous year's aggregate loss. However, this contribution would have to be raised from alternative financial sources, and the effect would be exactly the same as if the loss itself were directly financed from those sources. The fund would, in effect, be an illusion. This example illustrates a fundamental problem with the multiperiod approach.

Earlier in this chapter we argued that the optimal size of a retention fund should be determined by balancing the opportunity costs of maintaining fund assets in a suitably liquid form with the benefit, which takes the form of a reduction in the expected value of transaction costs. Suppose that a fund is established in year t with an initial contribution that is equal to the optimal fund size and with provision for future contributions that are proportionate to the expected value of loss. The terminal value of the fund at the end of year t will be a random value that depends on the realized loss. At the beginning of period 2, the period 1 terminal value will be added to the fixed contribution to determine the value of the fund for the second period. However, there is no reason at all to suppose that this opening value is in any way optimal. Thus, over time, the value of a fund would simply wander away from its optimal value (or path) according to the random incidence of loss. During each period, the firm carries the opportunity cost of holding the fund in its current value. Therefore, the firm will maximize the value of its equity if it sets the fund value at the level that is currently optimal. For example, consider Figure 11-3. The contributions are constant, interest is ignored, and the optimal fund value is unchanging over time. The fund is established at a suboptimal level, but due to the capriciously random nature of losses, it builds to a level that is too high. During periods 3, 4, and 5, the opportunity costs of maintaining the fund outweigh any benefits that may accrue. The reverse side of this coin is revealed in periods 6 and 7, when the system is underfunded. Although this example does not allow for change, the same principles still arise even though optimal values may differ between periods.

Change in cost of capital and loss exposures may well cause the firm to reevaluate the optimal size of the fund. The value-maximizing strategy will be to release capital from the fund if it is too large (e.g., following years in which aggregate loss is small) and to extract new contributions sufficient to restore optimal value if the fund is too small. Two important implications flow from this financial approach:

1 The dynamic nature of fund values is of little interest to the risk manager. As a practical proposition, it seems useful to estimate the optimal fund value each year and to adjust to this value by means of a negative or positive contribution that depends on the inherited value from the previous period.

2 Since the firm is contributing to the fund each year at a level that is dictated largely by the previous period's loss, it is an illusion that the fund permits the firm to substitute a regular and predictable cash outflow for the random value arising from unfunded retained loss. *The fund has little or no stabilizing value. This conclusion reinforces our previous contention that the value of the fund lies in the provision of immediate liquidity that may help the firm to avoid the transaction costs associated with loss.*

CORPORATE LIQUIDITY AND COMPOSITE FUNDING

The ordinary operations of any firm will generate cash inflows and cash outflows. These flows arise from the income-generating activities of the firm and its need to pay bills. In the long run, profitability requires that the inflows dominate the outflows, but during any defined period, this may not be the case. Firms often have to pay bills before the receipt of income and will require capital to cover this delay. The problem is not restricted to one of financing the expected delay between cash payments and receipts. The timing of these flows is uncertain, and the firm requires additional liquidity to absorb unexpected fluctuations in the cash flows (such as delays in receipts) or to take advantage of speculative opportunities. The firm's liquidity may be viewed in similar light to a retention fund, the purpose being to constrain the probability that the net cash outflow will exceed corporate liquidity. However, liquidity has its cost, which is measured by the cost of raising the necessary capital. Since liquid resources must be held as cash or in a highly marketable form, the expected yield on these resources will most likely fall below the cost of capital. Thus the optimal level of liquidity involves a tradeoff between the cost of maintaining liquid resources and the benefits of avoiding cash embarrassment. The optimal tradeoff implies a particular probability of "ruin" for any given distribution of net cash flows, and this probability can be calculated, as described, for a retention fund.

Since the purpose of liquidity is to assist a firm over uncertainties, it may be used in the event of sudden unfunded risk management losses. This use of liquidity has been mentioned in the context of postloss sources of finance. However, since losses represent costs on the liquidity without corresponding inflows, liquidity will be gradually depleted by a series of small claims or suddenly depleted by a large loss. In order to maintain sufficient liquidity for normal operations, the fund must be restored to some appropriate level. This requires the raising of new capital, and in effect, the losses may be effectively postloss financed by new debt, equity, etc. The previous discussion does suggest that immediate use of available liquidity may have advantages over direct postloss financing with, say, debt. Immediate financing will help the firm in its postloss recovery by permitting rapid salvage operations, immediate reinvestment, immediate replacement of stocks to maintain continuity of sales, etc. In this sense, the availability of corporate liquidity implies a form of *de facto* risk management funding.

All firms wishing to maintain operations on a sound financial basis will try to preserve some desirable level of liquidity. Let us now address the question of whether such a firm should, in addition, maintain a retention fund that is specifically earmarked for risk management purposes. To address this issue, we return to the probability of ruin. Consider first that a firm that has a single pool of liquidity that is available for all purposes, including loss financing. Writing the two sources of corporate earnings as X (earnings before deduction of risk management costs) and L (risk management losses, which we assume to be uninsured), then earnings are

$$E = X - L \tag{11-30}$$

where X and L are both random variables. The net cash flows from the respective activities are

$$C = C_X + C_L \tag{11-31}$$

Here, C_X may be positive or negative, but C_L will always be negative. The cash flow relates to a specific period, and for simplicity, we can assume that all transactions are conducted on the last day of that period. What level of liquidity Q^* is required to ensure that the probability that $Q^* - C$ will fall below zero is kept at some acceptable low level, say, 0.05? To keep things simple, we assume that C is approximately normally distributed.[7] Our problem is to calculate Q^* such that

$$\Pr\,[C < -Q^*] = 0.05 \tag{11-32}$$

Note that from the usual portfolio formulas,

$$E(C) = E(C_X) + E(C_L) \tag{11-33}$$

and

$$\sigma(C) = [\sigma^2(C_X) + \sigma^2(C_L) + 2\sigma_{XL}]^{1/2} \tag{11-34}$$

Using the normal approximation method and noting that z will be negative (since we identify the lefthand tail of the distribution), we have

---

[7]To use the normal-power method, the mean, standard deviation, and skewness of total liquidity must be calculated from the characteristics of C_X and C_L together with the investment yield r_a. The difficulty lies in calculating skewness of aggregate liquidity, and this may be tackled in similar manner to that shown in the appendix to this chapter.

$$-z = \frac{-Q^* - E(C)}{\sigma(C)} = \frac{-Q^* - [E(C_X) + E(C_L)]}{[\sigma^2(C_X) + \sigma^2(C_L) + 2\sigma_{XL}]^{1/2}} \qquad (11\text{-}35)$$

EXAMPLE: PATTERNS WALLPAPERS

If the following values are selected, we calculate the required size of a composite fund;

$$E(C_X) = 10$$
$$E(C_L) = -7$$
$$\sigma(C_X) = 5$$
$$\sigma(C_L) = 12$$
$$\sigma_{XL} = 0$$

and $z_{0.05} = 1.64$, we have

$$-1.64 = \frac{-Q^* - [10 - 7]}{[5^2 + 12^2 + 2(0)]^{1/2}} = \frac{-Q^* - 3}{13}$$

Thus,

$$Q^* = 18.32$$

Now let the firm have a separate retention fund that is to be used exclusively for risk management purposes. In this case, we also assume that general liquidity is not to be used for risk management purposes. We label general liquidity as X^* and the retention fund assets as L^*. Not let us ask a comparable question. What total level of liquidity $X^* + L^*$ is needed to ensure that the probability of being able to meet cash demand from either or both sources is the same, that is, 0.05? More formally, what level of $X^* + L^*$ is required to ensure that

$$\left.\begin{array}{l} \Pr\,(C_X < X^*) \\ \Pr\,(C_L < L^*) \end{array}\right\} = 0.05 \qquad (11\text{-}36)$$

To solve this, we need a little probability theory. The probability of event A and/or event B happening is known as the probability of the union of two events. The appropriate formula is given in most basic statistics textbooks as

$$\Pr\,(A \text{ and/or } B) = P(A) + P(B) - P(A|B)P(B) \qquad (11\text{-}37)$$

$$
\begin{aligned}
\text{where } P(A) &= \text{probability of } A \\
P(B) &= \text{probability of } B \\
P(A|B) &= \text{probability of } A \text{ given} \\
&\quad\ \text{that } B \text{ has already occurred}
\end{aligned}
$$

Notice that information on the conditional probability $P(A|B)$ is required. However, in this case, the different cash flows are independent (zero covariance), and simplification is possible. In the special case where A and B are independent, equation (11-37) reduces to

$$
\text{Pr } (A \text{ and/or } B) = P(A) + P(B) - P(A)P(B) \tag{11-38}
$$

Therefore, if C_X and C_L are independent,

$$
\begin{aligned}
\text{Pr } [(C_X < -X^*) \text{ and/or } (C_L < -L^*)] = \text{Pr } (C_X < -X^*) \\
+ \text{Pr } (C_L < -L^*) - \text{Pr } (C_X < -X^*) \text{ Pr } (C_L < -L^*) \quad (11\text{-}39)
\end{aligned}
$$

EXAMPLE: PATTERNS WALLPAPERS

To compare the combined liquidity required with separate funds with the composite liquidity under a joint fund, we use similar values. From equation (11-39),

$$
0.05 = \text{Pr } (C_X < -X^*) + \text{Pr } (C_L < -L^*) - \text{Pr } (C_X < -X^*) \text{ Pr } (C_L < -L^*)
$$

Any number of values will satisfy this equation. Therefore, for our illustration, we will select a value of 0.02 for $\text{Pr } (C_X < -X^*)$ and derive the corresponding value for $\text{Pr } (C_L < -L^*)$ from equation (11-39), which, with rearrangement, is

$$
\begin{aligned}
\text{Pr } (C_L < -L^*) &= \frac{\text{Pr } [C_X < -X^*) \text{ and/or } (C_L < -L^*)] - \text{Pr } (C_X < -X^*)}{1 - \text{Pr } (C_X < -X^*)} \\
&= \frac{0.05 - 0.02}{1 - 0.02} = 0.03061
\end{aligned}
$$

Using these ruin values for general liquidity and the risk management retention fund, we can calculate the required fund sizes using the normal approximation method. For general liquidity,

$$
-z_{0.02} = \frac{-X^* - E(C_X)}{\sigma(C_X)}
$$

$$
-2.05 = \frac{-X^* - 10}{5}
$$

Therefore,

$$X^* = 0.25$$

For the retention fund,

$$-z_{0.03061} = \frac{-L^* - E(C_L)}{\sigma(C_L)}$$

$$-1.87 = \frac{-L^* - (-7)}{12}$$

Therefore,

$$L^* = 29.44$$

Thus the total liquidity requirement is $29.44 + 0.25 = 29.69$ compared with the required size for a combined fund of 18.32.

These comparative examples are simplified in order to use the straightforward normal approximation method. Further simplification is achieved by assuming the cash flows to be independent. However, these examples illustrate an important general principle: If separate funds are maintained to underwrite adverse fluctuations in different components of earnings, and if no transfers are permitted between the funds, then the funding requirement to maintain a given probability that either or both funds will be ruined is, in general, higher than the funding requirement to maintain a composite fund at the same probability of ruin. Consider the qualification *in general* in this statement. If separate funds are established of X^* and L^*, consider what will happen to the probability of ruin if they are subsequently combined into a joint fund with value $X^* + L^*$. It is obvious that the ruin probability cannot rise, since each opportunity that was available before the funds were brought together is still available. The combining of funds has only given additional opportunities for transfers. Therefore, the ruin probability must either stay the same or fall. In general, the ruin probability will fall.[8] This is equivalent to the earlier statement that, in general, higher funding is required to maintain separate funds than a combined fund at a comparable probability of ruin.

This analysis has very important implications for risk management retention funding. Earlier in this chapter we analyzed funding without reference to general corporate cash flow issues. The case for retention funding depended on the existence of transaction costs. Funding might permit a firm to recover from loss more quickly, since immediate

---

[8]The exception arises when C_X and C_L are perfectly negatively correlated. In this case, the ruin probabilities will be identical for separate and composite funds. In other words, the same level of funding is required to maintain any given ruin probability.

financing is available. Furthermore, retention funding may reduce transaction costs associated with the raising of external postloss financing. These advantages of liquidity are still present. However, now we would argue that any demand for liquidity should be met jointly with other demands for corporate liquidity. The establishment of a separate risk management retention fund makes no financial sense, since it merely adds constraints on the allocation of liquid resources over the many corporate needs. Segregation of corporate liquidity into separate risk management and nonrisk management pools merely increases the probability that one or another of the corporate cash flows will be unfunded. Instead, the risk manager should cooperate with other managers in jointly determining demands for corporate liquidity, and each should recognize the composite nature of demands on those liquid resources.

SUMMARY AND CONCLUSION

Losses that are not insured are, by definition, retained. A firm may choose to retain losses either because it proposes not to reinvest following a loss or because some other method of financing reinvestment is considered to be preferable. External sources of financing, such as new debt and equity, have been considered earlier together with available internal liquid resources. An alternative method is to establish an earmarked fund for retained losses.

In the absence of transaction costs, the risk management case for establishing a retention fund is somewhat tenuous. A fund only creates value for a firm if its assets yield a return in excess of the cost of capital. However, if such investment opportunities exist, they would be exploited by the value-maximizing firm independently of its risk management exposure. A risk management fund represents a use of capital, and consequently, a source of financing is required to meet the contributions to the fund. A limited case for funding may be established if the transaction costs of funding are lower than those prevailing for alternative sources of reinvestment financing. A fund may be envisioned that is designed only for intermediate losses. For such losses, the transaction costs of alternative preloss (insurance) or postloss (e.g., debt) financing may be disproportionately high yet they may be too high to finance from normal liquidity. Limited funding of this sort is considered again in the next chapter.

Since a limited financial case can be made for funding, it is useful to examine the properties of a retention fund. Of particular interest is the probability that the fund will be inadequate to meet the financing requirements following loss. Ruin probabilities are examined in the simple case in which losses follow a normal distribution. Corrections for skewness are later made using the normal-power method. Further adaptations of the model allow for multiple sources of risk, i.e., riskiness of loss and of investment earnings. This analysis is conducted for single periods at a time. The dynamic behavior of a fund has been examined extensively in the actuarial literature. However, we argue that this multiperiod analysis is not of great interest from an economic viewpoint because the value of the fund at each point in time represents a real opportunity cost to the firm. If the optimal size of the fund can be determined independently of the realized value of the past claims on the fund, the fund should be reconstituted each year at its optimal value.

The issue of funding may be seen as part of a firm's wider cash management decision process. Corporate liquidity is usually maintained at a level that is compatible with the firm's transaction needs and its desire to absorb unexpected fluctuations in its cash flow, including speculative opportunities and losses. Unless the risk management demands for liquidity and other business needs are perfectly correlated, the combined demand for liquidity will exhibit a portfolio effect. This effect can be seen by considering that a firm wishes to maintain a given probability that it will not run short of cash. The cash fund required to maintain this probability is lower if a pooled fund is used than if separate earmarked funds are maintained, one solely for risk management purposes and the other solely for remaining business needs. Thus, if retention funding is used, the amount of corporate liquidity to be maintained is best determined on joint business/risk management criteria, and the fund should not be earmarked for specific use.

The case for funding established in this chapter is rather qualified and somewhat limited. Funding does not necessarily displace other sources of finance, and composite financing may be required. This is our next topic.

QUESTIONS

1 Examine verbally the argument that a retention fund will stabilize the financial performance of a firm as compared with a nonfunded retention.

2 A firm establishes a reserve fund from which to pay the financing costs for future losses. The firm owns three exposure units with the following risk characteristics:

Unit	Expected loss	Standard deviation
1	10	20
2	50	60
3	40	30

Each of the loss distributions is normal. The fund assets will be invested at the risk free rate of 10%. Assuming that losses arise at the end of the year, what contribution must the firm make to the fund to maintain a probability of 0.9 that the fund assets will be adequate to meet losses? The correlation coefficients are:

$$r_{12} = 0.2$$
$$r_{23} = 0$$
$$r_{13} = -0.2$$

3 Calculate the ruin probability for a retention fund having the following features. Fund assets are invested risk free at 8%. The fund has an initial endowment of 50 and a beginning of year contribution of 200% of the expected loss. Losses are assumed to arise at the year-end and have the following distribution:

Loss	Probability
20	0.4
50	0.3
100	0.3

4 A risk manager is considering establishment of a reserve fund for (1) property losses and (2) liability losses. Separate funds or a composite fund can be established. Given the information below, calculate:

a The required contribution to a composite fund to maintain a ruin probability of 1%
b The required contributions to separate funds to maintain a 1% probability that either one or both funds will prove to be inadequate. You may fix the ruin probability for the property fund at $1/2\%$ for this exercise.

The losses from each source are normally distributed and losses are independent. The expected value of property loss is 20 and for liability loss, 40. The respective standard deviations are 25 and 60. What general idea is illustrated by these results?

APPENDIX: One-Period Ruin Probabilities When Losses and the Return of Fund Assets Are Both Risky

This appendix derives ruin probabilities for situations in which the retention fund has two sources of risk: interest-rate risk and loss-exposure risk. The sources of risk are both r and L in the distribution (tildes are used to emphasize sources of risk). Therefore,

$$\tilde{X} = [F(1)(1 + \tilde{r}_a) - \tilde{L}(2)] \tag{A-1}$$

In order to calculate ruin probabilities, calculations must be made of the expected value, standard deviation, and skewness of $\tilde{X}$. These values are determined by the properties of the distributions $\tilde{r}$ and $\tilde{L}$ and the interaction between these variables. The appropriate formulas are

$$E(X) = F(1)[1 + E(r_a)] - E[L(2)] \tag{A-2}$$

$$\begin{aligned}\sigma(X) &= \sigma[F(1)(1 + \tilde{r}_a) - \tilde{L}(2)] \\ &= \sigma[F(1)\tilde{r}_a - \tilde{L}(2)] \quad [\text{since } F(1) \text{ is not random}] \\ &= F(1)^2\sigma^2(r_a) + \sigma^2(L) - 2F(1)\sigma_{RL} \end{aligned} \tag{A-3}$$

where $\sigma^2(r_a)$ = variance of $\tilde{r}_a$
$\sigma^2(L)$ = variance of $\tilde{L}$
σ_{RL} = covariance between $\tilde{r}_a$ and $\tilde{L}$

$$\alpha_3(X) = \alpha_3[F(1)(1 + \bar{r}_a) - \hat{L}(2)]$$

$$= \alpha_3[F(1)\bar{r}_a - \hat{L}(2)] \qquad \text{[since } F(1) \text{ is not random]}$$

$$= \frac{F(1)^3\sigma^3(r_a) - \sigma^3(L) + 3F(1)[\sigma_{RLL} - F(1)\sigma_{RRL}]}{[\sigma(X)]^3} \qquad \text{(A-4)}$$

where $\sigma^3(r_a) = E[r_i - E(r)]^3$

$\sigma^3(L) = E[L_i - E(L)]^3$

$\sigma_{RLL} = E\{[r_i - E(r)][L_i - E(L)]^2\}$

$\sigma_{RRL} = E\{[r_i - E(r)]^2[L_i - E(L)]\}$

and $\sigma(X)$ is defined as in equation (A-3).

To illustrate application of the ruin problem, we will retain the data used for the example "Sunshine Sodas" earlier in this chapter and add information on the riskiness of $\bar{r}$ and its independence with $\hat{L}$. Therefore,

$$E(L) = 118,800$$
$$S(L) = 160,360$$
$$a_3(L) = 2.162$$
$$F(1) = 178,200$$
$$E(r_a) = 0.1$$
$$E(X) = 77,220$$

and the added data are

$$\sigma(r_a) = 0.2$$
$$\alpha_3(r_a) = 1.5$$
$$\sigma^3(r_a) = 0.012$$
$$\sigma^3(L) = 8.9146544 \ (10^{15})$$
$$\sigma_{RL} = 9500$$
$$\sigma_{RRL} = 6000$$
$$\sigma_{RLL} = 4,000,000,000$$

From equations (A-3) and (A-4), we can calculate the skewness of the terminal value of the retention fund as follows:

$$\sigma(X) = 153,622$$
$$\alpha_3(X) = \frac{-7.279943 \times 10^{15}}{3.6254406 \times 10^{15}} = -2.008$$

The positive correlation between the asset-investment yield (a positive value) and losses (wealth restriction) implies that there is some tendency for the fund to benefit from high investment yield during periods of heavy loss, and vice versa. This reduces the riskiness of the fund, thereby accounting for the reduction in standard deviation. (It will be recalled that with nonrisky investment returns, the standard deviation was $160,360.) The skewness also falls slightly from the value without investment risk of -2.162 to the value calculated above of -2.008.

We now use the calculated values to estimate the probability of loss. Before doing so, we will try to anticipate how the investment risk should affect the ruin probability. Since risk has been reduced by the offsetting effects of investment- and loss-related risk, we should find that the tail of the terminal-value distribution of the fund is smaller, and consequently, the probability of ruin will be small. The reduced skewness should reinforce this result. To verify these effects, we can use equation (11-24) to make the appropriate calculation:

$$z = \frac{-1 + \sqrt{1 + 2\alpha_3(X)/3 \{\alpha_3(X)/6 + [X^* - E(X)]/\sigma(X)\}}}{\alpha_3(X)/3}$$

$$= \frac{-1 + \sqrt{1 + 2(-2.008)/3 \, [(-2.008)/6 + (-77220)/153,622]}}{-2.008/3}$$

$$= -1.09829 \ (\approx -1.10)$$

From the z tables, the estimated ruin probability is 0.1357. (The answer calculated without investment risk was 0.2483.)

In the text to this chapter it was stated that the normal approximation method provided reasonable results when the measure of skewness was about 2 or less. In this example, the measure has an absolute value of about 2, and the results are probably fairly reliable.

REFERENCES

Beard, R. E., T. Pentikainen, and E. Personen: *Risk Theory,* Methuen, London, 1969.

Cummins, D.: "Risk Management and the Theory of the Firm," *Journal of Risk and Insurance,* vol. 43, 1976, pp. 587–609.

———: "Reply," *Journal of Risk and Insurance,* vol. 50, 1983, pp. 144–147.

Ehrlich, I., and G. S. Becker: "Market Insurance, Self-Insurance and Self-Protection," *Journal of Political Economy,* vol. 80, 1972, pp. 623–648.

Fama, E., and M. Miller: *The Theory of Finance,* Holt, Rinehart and Winston, New York, 1972.

Gerber, H. V.: *An Introduction to Mathematical Risk Theory* (Huebner Foundation Monograph No. 8), Richard D. Irwin, Homewood, Ill., 1979.

Goshay, R.: *"Corporate Self Insurance and Risk Retention Plans,"* Richard D. Irwin, Homewood, Ill., 1965.

Main, B.: "Risk Management and the Theory of the Firm, Comment," *Journal of Risk and Insurance,* vol. 50, 1983, pp. 140–144.

William, N. A. (ed.): *Risk Retention: Alternative Funding Methods.* The Society of C.P.C.U., Malvern, Pa., 1983.

CHAPTER **12**

COMPOSITE FINANCING STRATEGIES

For a variety of reasons, full insurance may not be desirable. The expenses incurred in settlement of small claims are usually disproportionately high, suggesting that small losses might be retained by a firm. Added to this is the "trading dollars" effects. Many medium or large firms will regularly and routinely suffer small losses; indeed, the regularity of such losses often permits a firm to accurately budget for their settlement. Such a firm would merely pay the premium in order that the insurer could later reimburse the predictable loss costs. The insured and the insurer are simply "trading dollars" for these small losses. The prospect of larger losses does present a firm with substantive risk (which may affect the cost of capital if this risk is of a systematic nature) and the attendant financing problems. One solution is to insure large losses but retain the routine small losses. A distinct, but related, argument is simply that insurance is costly and the insured should, rationally, balance the marginal cost and marginal benefit for each dollar of insurance that might be purchased. The tradeoff between the costs and benefits of protection may well lead to intermediate levels of insurance protection, and under some circumstances, such risk sharing can be shown to be "optimal" (see Mossin, 1968, and Smith, 1968).

If partial insurance is purchased, other sources of finance are required to fund reinvestment. The retained component of loss may, alternatively, be financed from internal sources (e.g., surplus cash) or from external sources, (e.g., new debt or equity). The purpose here is to examine composite financing strategies. These strategies may or may not involve insurance. However, it is important to consider the available forms of partial insurance before considering whether insurance should be included in any composite financing strategy. We first consider risk-sharing devices, and then we use the tabular model to compare partial insurance with alternative financing strategies.

327

More formalized decision models will then be developed to compare composite financing strategies more thoroughly.

FULL INSURANCE AND PARTIAL INSURANCE

Full insurance provides compensation for the full value of loss as defined within the insurance policy. Full insurance on property provides compensation for the cost of replacement or repair of destroyed or damaged property with similar materials and within reasonable time. For liability claims, full insurance implies that the full value of the liability settlement against the insured will be made good by the insurer together with associated legal costs incurred defending the claim. For interruption loss, the concept of full insurance is less clear. Methods of calculating loss follow rules of thumb designed to measure the reduction in profitability from the level that might have prevailed in the absence of loss. The difficulties in pinning down the precise reduction in profitability cast a haze on the measurement of full insurance in this case. In each of these applications, however, the insurance settlement is guided by the principle of indemnity, which asserts that the insurer will restore to the insured the financial loss arising from the insured event. To help give more concrete form to this principle, policies usually limit recovery to the "actual cash value" of the loss.

The meanings of *indemnity* and *actual cash value* are ultimately in the domain of judicial interpretation. While *actual cash value* is used to implement the principle of indemnity, it is not equivalent to the economic loss suffered by the owners of a firm. The actual cash value of property destroyed or damaged relates to the cost of restoring or replacing the property. The economic loss suffered by the owners relates to the loss in value of their equity as a result of the loss. This equity loss is not determined by the actual cash value of the property, but rather by its capacity for generating wealth in productive use. Similarly, with liability loss, the loss in equity value may be related to the cost of defending and satisfying litigation against the firm, but it is not the same thing. The result of, or even the fact of, litigation may affect a firm's ability to successfully market its product, compete in the labor market, raise capital, and so forth. Clearly, interruption insurance is targeted at the loss of wealth generated by active employment of capital, but the basis of settlement does not focus directly on the value of the ownership claims; rather, it is based on accounting definitions of profit and fixed costs. These considerations lead to a somewhat arbitrary relationship between loss in equity value and the actual cash value of the loss. Perhaps the reason for this lack of equivalence is that insurance policies fail to distinguish between the ownership claim of an individual on property (e.g., a home or automobile) and corporate ownership claims. The *actual cash value* may be an appropriate concept in measuring the direct ownership claim of an individual on his or her property, but the ownership claims of shareholders are less direct. These claims represent rights to the income generated from corporate investment and rights to share in the residual value of the firm. However, the valuation of these rights is determined by capital market activity, a fact not considered in the design of an insurance policy or, apparently, in the application of indemnity. In short, insurance policies appear to treat corporations as individuals.

The purpose of the foregoing discussion is to establish that full insurance for corporate risks is a somewhat arbitrary standard. It does not necessarily imply that shareholders are indifferent as to whether or not a loss arises, nor does it exactly compensate corporate owners for loss in the value of ownership claims. Nevertheless, full insurance does serve as a yardstick for identifying other financing strategies. Here, we refer to risk-sharing, or partial insurance, options. When full insurance is purchased, the insured acquires a probability distribution of contingent payments from the insurer. These payments represent the *actual cash value* of losses that may be suffered by the firm. This distribution of payments will be correlated with the loss in ownership values that will arise from insured events, but a perfect correlation will not arise in view of the lack of equivalence between actual cash value and loss in equity value. Partial insurance arises when the distribution is segmented in some predetermined way, with the insurer paying only some portion of the actual cash value according to a mutually acceptable formula.

Forms of Risk Sharing

To examine partial insurance, we shall use as our starting point the distribution of actual cash values (ACV). A specimen distribution of ACV is shown in Figure 12-1(*a*). This line represents the distribution of ACV suffered by a firm if no insurance is purchased. To aid our discussion of partial insurance strategies, we will assume that a battery of property, liability, and interruption policies is available to the firm and that, in aggregate, the ACV, as defined under these policies, is equal to the economic loss suffered by the firm's owners. The preceding discussion implies that this is not strictly true, but it may be held as an approximation if the ACV, as defined under the interruption policy, is included. With this assumption, we are able to segment the distribution in Figure 12-1 into the distribution of retained loss for the firm and the distribution of contingent payments made by the insurer.

   Various forms of risk sharing are commonly encountered in insurance contracts. (We concentrate on forms that are found in direct insurance contracts, although there are equivalent forms for reinsurance that are important for a firm that forms a captive insurer with direct access to the reinsurance markets.) The three most common forms are deductibles, coinsurance, and policy limits.

   Deductibles   A *deductible* is a provision for reducing the insurance settlement made on any loss by a specified sum. For example, private automobile policies often exclude the first, say, $100, of each loss. If the loss is less than $100, the insurer pays nothing; if it is above $100, the insurer pays the ACV minus $100. Deductibles may be arranged on a "per loss" basis or may be related to the accumulated losses within the period of the policy. If only one loss arises within the period, the effect is the same, but if more than one loss arises, the settlements will differ. Consider a fire insurance policy with a $10,000 deductible. The firm holding such a policy suffers three losses within a year, amounting to $6000, $23,000, and $62,000. The respective insurance settlements for each form of deductible are shown in Table 12-1. The per loss deductible is applied to each loss, in contrast with the cumulative deductible, which is applied to the annual total of losses.

   Per loss deductibles are more commonly encountered, although from a corporate financial planning viewpoint, cumulative deductibles are probably more useful. Cumulative deductibles permit a firm to establish a clear upper bound on its retained liability within any accounting period. We will focus attention more closely on cumulative deductibles in the following pages.

Deductibles are often used to avoid the disproportionately large settlement costs for small claims. Small claims often arise with regular frequency and easily can be budgeted for in a firm's cash flow plan. Small retentions for such routine small claims do not really imply any significant degree of risk bearing on the part of a firm. Depending on the interplay between the risk characteristics of higher retentions, the

FIGURE 12-1

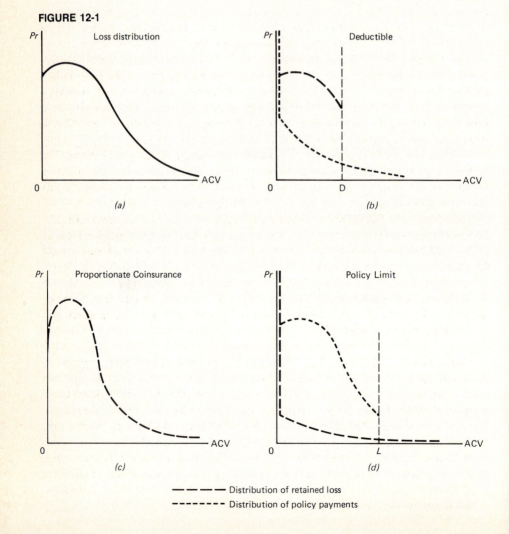

TABLE 12-1
COMPARISON OF "PER LOSS" AND "CUMULATIVE" DEDUCTIBLES

| Loss | Settlement under policy with $10,000 deductible | |
	Per loss deductible	Cumulative deductible
$6,000	$6,000 − $10,000 = 0	$6,000
$23,000	$23,000 − $10,000 = $13,000	$23,000
$62,000	$62,000 − $10,000 = $52,000	$62,000
		$91,000 ....$91,000
		Less deductible......$10,000
Total settlement	$65,000	$81,000

premium reduction from an increased deductible, and the costs of competing forms of financing, a firm may wish to consider very substantial deductibles that are well in excess of the "trading dollars" deductibles. Insurers traditionally have been reluctant to offer contracts with substantial deductibles. This may partly reflect the difficulties in pricing such contracts (which calls for an adequate estimation of the risky tail of the loss distribution) and a reluctance by insurers to loose a substantial portion of their revenue, which, in turn, is used to generate investment income. There may also have been little demand for such large deductibles, although various sources indicate that firms have been increasing retentions over recent years.[1]

Deductibles may be imposed by the insurer rather than selected by the insured. The deductible gives the insured a stake in prospective losses, thereby restoring incentive for the insured to undertake appropriate loss reduction/prevention measures. In this way, deductibles have some impact in offsetting moral hazard.

The effect of a deductible is illustrated in Figure 12-1(*b*). Losses below the deductible *D* are retained. Since all losses above *D* will elicit an insurance payment of ACV − *D*, there is a substantial probability that the firm will be left to bear exactly 0*D*. This is shown as the vertical line beginning at point *D*. The broken line represents the retained loss. In contrast, the dotted line shows the distribution of insurance payments for contingent losses. This distribution follows the vertical axis, showing the probability mass of zero insurance payments that arises if prospective losses turn out to be no greater than *D*.

Coinsurance Coinsurance has different meanings. In some coinsurance contracts, the insurer pays an agreed proportion of the ACV, leaving the insured to bear the residual proportion. The premium for proportionate coinsurance is usually scaled proportionately to the full insurance premium. Opportunities for partial insurance may be explored by balancing the systematic risk characteristics of the retained distribution, the premium reduction, and the costs of alternative financing methods.

A second meaning for coinsurance is associated with the coinsurance clause frequently encountered in property insurance contracts. The purpose of this clause is to

[1]See surveys by Hogue and Ohlson (1976) and the *The Cost of Risk*.

protect the insurer from making full payments for partial losses when there is clear underinsurance. The operation of the clause scales down payments for partial losses according to the degree of underinsurance. The clause may be represented by the following formula, which determines the maximum loss payment under the policy:

$$\frac{\text{Maximum}}{\text{payment}} = \text{loss} \times \frac{\text{amount of insurance carried}}{\text{actual cash value of property} \times \text{coinsurance percentage}}$$

A *coinsurance percentage* is a value selected by the insurer or negotiated between the parties to the contract that is between 0 and 100% (usually in the higher segment of this range). For example, consider a policy written on property valued at $10 million, for which a loss of $200,000 arises. The amount of insurance carried (and on which premium is based) is $6 million. Clearly, the insured has failed to fully insure the property, and it may be considered to be unfair to the insurer and/or other policyholders if a full settlement of the partial loss is made, even though this loss is far below the total value of insurance carried. The policy stipulates an 80% coinsurance percentage. The maximum payment is

$$\$200,000 \times \frac{6,000,000}{10,000,000(0.8)} = \$150,000$$

The formula cannot be used, for obvious reasons, to derive a settlement in excess of the value of loss or in excess of the $6 million amount of insurance carried. For example, had the coinsurance percentage been 50%, the loss payment would be $200,000, even though the formula gives a mechanical answer of $240,000.

It will be noticed that, if the coinsurance percentage is fixed at 100%, there is a strictly proportionate sharing of all losses in the sense understood in the first interpretation of coinsurance. If a firm explicitly negotiates a sharing arrangement in which the firm is considered to be its own insurer for part of each loss, the contract would normally operate on a strictly proportionate basis (implicitly, a 100% coinsurance percentage). The operation of the coinsurance clause with coinsurance percentages less than 100% is designed to provide some leeway for insureds who make fairly modest miscalculations in estimating the ACV of property or who, perhaps, fail to regularly upgrade the amount of insurance carried during a period of inflation.

The effect of coinsurance on the distribution of retained loss is illustrated in Figure 12-1(c). Coinsurance compresses the range of potential values of retained loss from those prevailing in Figure 12-1(a), in which all loss is retained. Thus the distribution of retained loss is compressed toward the vertical axis, as shown in Figure 12-1(c). The pattern illustrated represents proportionate coinsurance. The distribution of insurance payments is not shown, but this too would be compressed toward the vertical axis in the same fashion. If coinsurance were arranged with equal sharing on a proportionate basis (implicitly, the amount of insurance carried would be half the ACV of the property and the coinsurance percentage would be 100%), the distribution of insurance payments would be identical to the distribution of retained loss.

Policy Limits   For property insurance, the ACV of the property or, if lower, the amount of insurance carried on the property provides an upper limit to the insurance settlement. Sometimes the parties agree to exceptions to this procedure; one example would be replacement cost insurance that avoids reduction for depreciation. Nonetheless, there is usually a clear limit on the liability of the insurer, and this arises because the property itself has a limiting value. Liability suits brought against a firm are open-ended, and the insurer carrying the liability policy usually protects itself from assuming an equivalent open-ended claim payment. Thus the liability policy invariably will specify an upper limit to the settlement, although different types of limits are encountered. Limits are imposed on a per accident basis and a per person basis. For example, three people may be injured in one accident that arises from the insured's negligence. The policy contains a limit of $50,000 per occurrence and a limit of $20,000 for each person affected by the accident. The respective claims of the plaintiffs are $30,000, $40,000, and $14,000. The limit of policy liability is $50,000, as calculated in Table 12-2. Notice that the insured is left to carry an uninsured loss of $30,000.

Sometimes separate limits are applied for property damage and injury; other times they are combined. Many policies carry only a per occurrence limit with no per person limit. To establish an absolute limit on the total claims paid within a given period of insurance, many business liability policies carry a cumulative limit on all payments made in addition to a per occurrence limit.

Policy limits are generally considered to offer an unattractive form for risk sharing for the business firm because

1 The retained loss is open-ended and cannot be accommodated in a cash flow plan.

2 The uninsured component of the loss lies at the tail of the loss probability distribution. This tail is usually the most difficult part of the distribution to estimate because losses within this range are infrequent.

For the insurer, the policy limit is attractive for exactly the opposite reasons. The ceiling on liability makes for simpler calculation of loss reserves, and a reliable premium can be established from the fairly well defined lower segment of the prob-

TABLE 12-2
AN ILLUSTRATION OF THE EFFECT OF POLICY LIMITS

	Insured	Uninsured	Total Damages
Plaintiff A	$20,000	$10,000	$30,000
Plaintiff B	$20,000	$20,000	$40,000
Plaintiff C	$14,000	—	$14,000
Total	$54,000	$30,000	$84,000
Subject to limit of	$50,000		

ability distribution. Thus policy limits are typically imposed by the insurer rather than sought by the insured.

The impact of a policy limit on the distribution of retained loss and on the distribution of policy payments is illustrated in Figure 12-1(*d*). As with Figure 12-1(*b*) and (*c*), this is based on the distribution shown in Figure 12-1(*a*). The limit considered in this illustration is a cumulative limit on payments made within the policy period. The distribution of retained loss shows a substantial probability at zero, which is shown by the dotted line following the vertical axis. However, the open-ended nature of the loss is also shown. Notice that the distribution converges toward, but does not reach, the horizontal axis. The distribution of policy payments, in contrast, shows the limiting value of the insurer's payments of value 0*L*.

INSURANCE AND RISK REDUCTION

From the earlier analysis it should be clear that the ability of insurance to create value for a firm does not rest on its facility for reducing risk. Without reinvestment, insurance may be regarded simply as a financial asset. If it yields a return sufficient to compensate for the level of systematic risk, it will add value. Risk per se is not the issue, since this can largely be removed by investors in their personal portfolio management strategies. If reinvestment is contemplated, insurance may be viewed as one of a number of competing sources of finance; insurance is to be preferred if its cost is lower than the capitalized value of the cost of alternative sources.

Although risk reduction is not central to the issue of value creation, there are still good reasons why the risk manager may wish to estimate the risk-reduction effects of insurance. First, we have previously discussed factors other than direct value creation that might influence the purchase of insurance. Risk reduction is important to employers, managers, and creditors of a firm and will enter into the terms of their contracts with the firm. Second, for purposes of cash planning, a firm will need a forecast of demands on liquid funds and of the riskiness of such demands. Third, and subject to the reservations of Chapter 11, if a firm chooses to reserve for retained loss, it requires some estimate of ruin probabilities in order to estimate the optimal rate of buildup of reserve and to maintain the reserve at an acceptable level. For these reasons, we now show how partial insurance strategies affect the riskiness of corporate earnings. We compare the risk-reducing effects of coinsurance and deductibles.

Risk Reduction with Coinsurance

The expected earnings of a firm may be subdivided into the business component and the risk management component. For simplicity, any loss of assets, liability, etc. is treated as a deduction from earnings in the year of loss. That is,

$$E(E) = E(X) - E(R) \tag{12-1}$$

where $E(R)$ = expected value of loss from risk management factors

$E(X)$ = expected value of earnings before deduction of risk management loss

The calculation of X and R requires some estimates of their respective probability distributions. In both cases, this will probably be conducted, at least in part, from historical data. Methods for calculating distribution of aggregate losses L_j were discussed in Chapter 4. Thus,

$$E(X) = \sum_i P_i X_i \tag{12-2}$$

and

$$E(L) = \sum_j P_j L_j \tag{12-3}$$

where P_i and P_j represent the respective probability of X_i and L_j. The riskiness of the variables X_i and L_j can be measured by their standard deviations, although it is convenient first to define the respective variances:

$$\sigma_X^2 = \sum_i P_i [X_i - E(X)]^2 \tag{12-4}$$

and

$$\sigma_L^2 = \sum_j P_j [L_j - E(L)]^2 \tag{12-5}$$

The introduction of insurance will affect both $E(L)$ and σ_L^2. The form of these effects will depend on the premium paid for insurance, how much insurance is purchased, and in what forms (e.g., deductible or coinsurance). The simplest case arises when the policy covers an agreed proportion of all loss and the premium paid is simply scaled to the proportion of loss covered. The actual risk management cost $R_j(\alpha)$ is the sum of the retained or uninsured loss αL_j and the insurance premium $P(\alpha)$:

$$R_j(\alpha) = \alpha L_j + P(\alpha) \tag{12-6}$$

where α is the uninsured proportion of loss or $(1 - \alpha)$ is the proportion of loss insured. The expected risk management cost is therefore

$$E[R(\alpha)] = \alpha \sum_j P_j L_j + P(\alpha) = \alpha E(L) + P(\alpha) \tag{12-7}$$

$$[\sigma_R(\alpha)]^2 = \sum_j P_j \{[\alpha L_j + P(\alpha)] - [\alpha E(L) + P(\alpha)]\}^2 = \alpha^2 \sigma_L^2 \tag{12-8}$$

The premium will normally be calculated in relation to the expected value of claim payment. For example,

$$P(\alpha) = (1 - \alpha)(1 + f)E(L) + q \tag{12-9}$$

where f and q are positive constants to reflect the insurer's premium loadings. With this structure, we can rewrite $E[R(\alpha)]$ as follows:

$$E[R(\alpha)] = \alpha E(L) + (1 - \alpha)(1 + f)E(L) + q$$
$$= (1 + f - \alpha f)E(L) + q \qquad (12\text{-}10)$$

The various expressions can now be brought together to show the risk-return structure of the firm's earnings and how this is changed by insurance. We will use expected value and standard deviation as the appropriate measures. From equations (12-1) and (12-7), we show expected earnings $E(E)$ [or from equations (12-1) and (12-10) if the premium follows the form of equation (12-9)] as follows:

$$E(E) = E(X) - \alpha E(L) - P(\alpha) \qquad (12\text{-}11)$$

or

$$E(E) = E(X) - (1 + f - \alpha f)E(L) - q \qquad \text{[if equation (12-9) holds]} \quad (12\text{-}12)$$

Using the usual formula to calculate the standard deviation of the sum of random variables, we combine equations (12-4) and (12-8) to yield

$$\sigma_{E,\alpha} = \{\sigma_X^2 + [\sigma_L^2(\alpha)]^2 - 2 \text{ cov } [X, R(\alpha)]\}^{1/2}$$
$$= [\sigma_X^2 - \alpha^2 \sigma_L^2 - 2\alpha \text{ cov } (X,L)]^{1/2} \qquad (12\text{-}13)$$

where cov $[X, R(\alpha)]$ = the covariance between business earnings X and risk management cost $R(\alpha)$
    cov (X, L) = the covariance between business earnings X and uninsuranced losses L

The covariance term is deducted since the risk management term is negative.

The risk-return relationships can be illustrated graphically by considering the example based on the following value:

$$E(X) = 20 \qquad \sigma_X^2 = 100 \qquad \text{cov } (X, L) = -20 \qquad E(L) = 2 \qquad \sigma_L^2 = 20$$

The premium is defined by equation (12-9) with $f = 0.2$ and $q = 0.2$. Figure 12-2 shows the expected levels of earnings, together with the associated standard deviations, at different levels of insurance. The figure also shows the impact of insurance at different levels of covariance. Curve AB is calculated on the given values, which depict strong negative correlation. AC is derived with the covariance equal to -10. Two clear effects emerge:

1 The lower the covariance, the weaker the risk-reducing advantages of insurance. If covariance is negative, then large losses are likely to arise precisely at those times

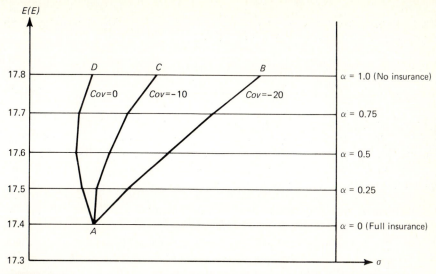

FIGURE 12-2

when earnings from business operations are low. The risks compound, and the distribution of earnings will be highly unstable. Under such circumstances, insurance does help to reduce risk, although there will still be a residual fluctuation in earnings.

Conversely, if there is positive correlation between the business and risk management components of earnings, there is a natural risk-offsetting effect that is disturbed by insurance. Positive covariance arises if losses have a high probability of assuming low values when earnings are low, and conversely they will tend to be high when earnings are high. Since the different elements tend to vary in opposing directions, the risks tend to cancel out, leaving the overall distribution fairly stable; i.e., variation in loss experience tends to remove the peaks and troughs from the sequence of annual earnings of the firm. Under such circumstances, insurance may *increase* risk in the overall earnings distribution.

Finally, there may be zero covariance. It is easily verified from equation (12-13) that the riskiness in earnings $\sigma_{E,\alpha}$ will always fall as the level of insurance increases. However, there is some diversification across the two random components of earnings, and the risk-reducing properties of insurance may not be as dramatic as appears at first sight. A simple illustration will demonstrate this point. Consider the impact on the "risk management risk" $\alpha^2\sigma_L^2$ when insurance protection is increased from 0 to 50% of losses using values given above:

$$[\alpha^2\sigma_L^2(\alpha)]^{1/2} = 4.472 \quad \text{when } \alpha = 1$$
$$= 2.236 \quad \text{when } \alpha = 0.5$$

However, the total riskiness of earnings falls, as follows from equation (12-13):

$$[\sigma_X^2 + \alpha^2\sigma_L^2]^{1/2} = 10.954 \qquad \text{when } \alpha = 1$$
$$= 10.247 \qquad \text{when } \alpha = 0.5$$

The reduction in total risk is much more modest, since "diversification" across the two risky variables X_i and L_j has already produced some risk-reducing benefit.

2 The second effect of insurance is also illustrated in Figure 12-2. Lines AB, AC, and AD are all concave from below. The implication is that there are diminishing returns to insurance protection. Consider curve AC. Position C is the no insurance position under the assumption that the covariance is zero. As insurance protection is increased from 0 to 25%, the level of expected earnings falls, but a significant reduction in risk is also achieved. As protection increases from 25 to 50%, the incremental change in expected earnings is the same, but the reduction in risk is notably smaller, and so on. Diminishing returns may lead to limited degrees of insurance protection. For example, with negative covariance, as illustrated by curve AD, insurance purchases up to $\alpha = 0.5$ would reduce risk, but increased protection beyond that point would increase risk. From a risk-reduction viewpoint, it would not be advisable to purchase beyond $\alpha = 0.5$, but remember that shareholders could still conceivably benefit if further reductions in the cost of capital occurred.

Diminishing returns and covariance are closely related. If the correlation between X_i and L_j is perfectly negative (that is, proportional changes in X_i are inversely associated with equal proportionate changes in L_j), then the insurance line will be linear, not concave.[2] Generally, the higher the covariance the more pronounced the tendency to diminishing returns.

This analysis of risk reduction has focused on the dollar earnings of a firm; the reason for this is that those claimholders most interested in risk reduction would probably focus closely on this variable. Whether risk is appropriately measured by the standard deviation (or variance) of earnings is a moot point. For some purposes it may be better to calculate the probability that earnings will fall below some critical level necessary for a firm's survival. This would provide a measure of the prospect of redundancy for the employee or manager and might be useful for cash flow planning. This measure is used elsewhere, but it should be noted here that the standard deviation is also a useful and convenient measure of risk:

1 It is much simpler to use. A study of all properties of the distribution of $(X_i + L_j)$ would take us to a level of complexity beyond that intended here.

2 Many relevant risks may be better measured by the standard deviation. One example is managerial or other compensation, which, formally, through bonus schemes or, informally, through bargaining stances may reflect earnings fluctuations. Similarly, the prospect of any individual becoming redundant may be better measured by standard deviation than by the probability of bankruptcy. All individuals will likely be redundant

---

[2]In other words, the correlation coefficient between X_i and L_j is equal to unity.

in the event of bankruptcy, but some may well be laid off with a smaller decline in earnings.

3 For most given distributions, the higher the standard deviation in earnings, the higher is the probability of bankruptcy.

Risk Reduction with Deductibles

Deductibles are generally held to be more efficient devices for reducing risk than proportionate sharing devices such as coinsurance or quota share reinsurance. This was first demonstrated by Vajda, but Arrow subsequently showed that a risk averter would prefer a policy with a deductible to another policy with the same expected payout but having risk divided between the insurer and the insured on a proportionate basis. Thus it would appear that use of a deductible is the preferred method of retaining some of the insurable risk, assuming that an adequate premium reduction is negotiated with the insurer.[3] We can now conduct similar, although slightly more complex, analyses of how insurance policies with deductibles after the riskiness of a firm's earnings.

The mean and variance of the "business" component of earnings have already been described by equations (12-1) and (12-3); that is,

$$E(X) = \sum_i P_i X_i$$

$$\sigma_X^2 = \sum_i P_i [X_i - E(X)]^2$$

If a firm purchases an insurance policy with a deductible δ for a premium $D(\delta)$, the actual risk management cost for the firm will be the random variable $R_j(\delta)$ as follows:

$$R_j(\delta) = \begin{cases} L_j + D(\delta & \text{if } L_j < \delta \\ \delta + D(\delta & \text{if } L_j \geq \delta \end{cases} \qquad (12\text{-}14)$$

The expected value of risk management costs and the standard deviation will be

$$\begin{aligned} E[R(\delta)] &= \sum_{L_j < \delta} P_j L_j + \delta \sum_{L_j > \delta} P_j + D(\delta) \\ &= E(L) - \sum_{L_j > \delta} P_j (L_j - \delta) + D(\delta) \end{aligned} \qquad (12\text{-}15)$$

---

[3]The result was derived for an individual under the assumption that all risk was insurable. In our case, there are two sources of risk: business risk and insurable risk. It can be shown that deductibles are still preferred if business and risk management risks are independent, but this result may fail when there is some interdependence (see Doherty and Schlesinger, 1983). Our general impression is that deductibles are likely to be preferred for most cases.

$$[\sigma_R(\delta)]^2 = \left(\sum_{L_j < \delta} P_j \{L_j + D(\delta) - E[R(\delta)]\}^2 \right.$$
$$\left. + \sum_{L_j \geqslant \delta} P_j \{\delta + D(\delta) - E[R(\delta)]\}^2 \right)^{1/2} \qquad (12\text{-}16)$$

The premium usually will be related to the expected value of the policy, which is, in fact, the middle term on the right side of equation (12-15). For example, the premium might be

$$D(\delta) = (1 + m) \sum_{L_j > \delta} P_j(L_j - \delta) + n \qquad (12\text{-}17)$$

We will now construct an example to show the effect of insurance on the risk and standard deviation of earnings.

Consider a firm facing the following loss distribution:

Probability	Loss ($)
0.5	0
0.3	100
0.1	1,000
0.08	10,000
0.02	20,000

This can be insured at a premium set as follows:

$$1.5 \sum_{L_j > \delta} P_j(L_j - \delta)$$

where the deductible δ can be set, at the insured's choice, at 0, 100, 1000, or 10,000. The firm's expected earnings (before deduction of risk management costs) are $15,000, with a standard deviation of $2000. Business and risk management components of earnings are uncorrelated.

The mean and standard deviation of earnings are derived from the business and risk management components as follows:

$$E(E) = E[R(\delta)] + E(X)$$

and

$$\sigma_E(\delta) = [\sigma_L(\delta)^2 + \sigma_X^2 + \text{covariance terms}]^{1/2}$$

Since the covariance terms are zero in this example, the standard deviation of earnings simplifies considerably. Calculation of $E(E)$ and $\sigma_E(\delta)$ requires prior calculation of $E[L(\delta)]$ and $\sigma_L(\delta)^2$. These are derived from equations (12-15) and (12-16), as shown in the solution table (Table 12-3). The graph of mean–standard deviation located at

TABLE 12-3
THE EFFECT OF DEDUCTIBLE ON EARNINGS

δ	$\sigma_R(\delta)$	1 $E(E)$	2 $\sigma_{E,\delta} = [\sigma_L(\delta)^2 + \sigma_R^2]^{1/2}$ since cov = 0	3 Premium $D(\delta)$	4 $E[R(\delta)]$, eq. (12-15)	5 $\sigma_R(\delta)^2$ eq. (12-17)
0	0	$15,000 - 1,995$ $= 13,005$	$[0^2 + 2000^2]^{1/2}$ $= 2000$	1995	$1330 - 1330 + 1995$ $= 1995$	$(0.5 + 0.3 + 0.1 + 0.08 + 0.02)(0 + 1995 - 1995)^2 = 0$
100	50	$15,000 - 1,970$ $= 13,030$	$[50^2 + 2000^2]^{1/2}$ $= 2001$	1920	$1330 - 1280 + 1920$ $= 1970$	$0.5(0 + 1920 - 1970)^2 + (0.3 + 0.1 + 0.08 + 0.02)(100 + 1920 - 1970)^2 = 2500$
1,000	387	$15,000 - 1,880$ $= 13,120$	$[387^2 + 2000^2]^{1/2}$ $= 2037$	1650	$1330 - 1100 + 1650$ $= 1880$	$0.5(0 + 1650 - 1880)^2 + 0.3(100 + 1650 - 1880)^2 = 150,100$
10,000	2,971	$15,000 - 1,430$ $= 13,570$	$[2971^2 + 2000^2]^{1/2}$ $= 3581$	300	$1330 - 200 + 300$ $= 1430$	$0.5(0 + 300 - 1430)^2 + 0.3(100 + 300 - 1430)^2 + 0.1(1000 + 300 - 1430)^2 + (0.08 + 0.02)(10,000 + 300 - 1430)^2 = 8,826,100$
20,000	3,786	$15,000 - 1,330$ $= 13,670$	$[3786^2 + 2000^2]^{1/2}$ $= 4282$	0	$1330 = 1330$	$0.5(0 + 0 - 1330)^2 + 0.3(100 + 0 - 1330)^2 + 0.1(1000 + 0 - 1330)^2 + 0.08(10,000 + 0 - 1330)^2 + 0.02(20,000 + 0 - 1330)^2 = 14,334,100$

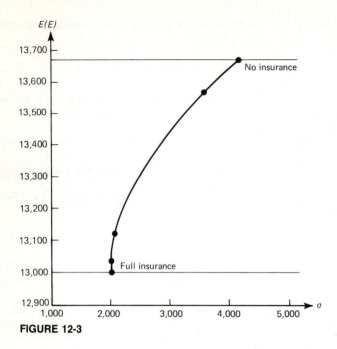

FIGURE 12-3

different levels of insurance shows the concave shape indicative of diminishing returns to insurance as shown in Figure 12-3. This again stresses that from a risk viewpoint, it may be advantageous to retain part of the risk by means of a deductible.

In the example shown, the premium structure was very simple; the expected value was subject to a proportionate loading. One advantage of a deductible is that it releases the insured and insurer from the disproportionately high administrative costs of filing and settling small claims. If this benefit is recognized, the parties to the insurance contract should be able to negotiate an attractive premium reduction for a deductible that eliminates these losses. From a risk-reduction viewpoint, however, the size of the deductible may well be much higher. This depends on the risk-return characteristics of the loss distribution and its correlation with business components of earnings.

DECISION ANALYSIS

Tabular Model and Capital Budgeting

The comparison of insurance with alternative methods of financing postloss reinvestment can be undertaken by calculating the aggregate value of a firm's equity under each alternative. This approach was adopted when full insurance solutions were compared, *inter alia*, with debt financing. There is no reason why the same approach cannot be adopted for intermediate solutions in which insurance is undertaken jointly with alternative financing. The advantage of this aggregate-value method is that the decision is measured directly against the adopted corporate objectives, that is, the maximization of corporate value. Furthermore, the method is appropriate when non-systematic risk is important. However, the method is cumbersome, since the risk manager is required to recalculate aggregate corporate value even though the proposed risk management decision may affect only a fraction of the firm's total resources. If a firm is valued solely on the basis of systematic risk, a simpler approach can be adopted that focuses only on the risk-adjusted present value of the risk management cash flows. This incremental cash flow approach uses only the cash flows affected by or induced by the decision. If the capitalized value of these is positive, the decision will add value to the firm. This alternative approach is familiar in capital budgeting and was presented earlier using full insurance decisions. An example will be used to illustrate partial insurance choices. This example is an extension of that for Rationality, Inc. considered in the Chapter 10.

EXAMPLE: RATIONALTY, INC.

In Chapter 10 we compared the choice facing this firm between preloss financing with insurance and postloss financing with debt. The insurance policy considered there covered all loss, but now an alternative policy is available that has a deductible of $200,000. The expected loss is $500,000, but this is now partitioned. If the deductible policy is chosen, the firm faces an expected retained loss of $150,000. The expected value of payments under the policy is the residual value, that is, $350,000. The premium for such a deductible policy is $450,000. Retained losses would be funded by debt at 9% as before. Other details are as follows:

Premium for full insurance: $650,000

Risk-free rate: 0.08

Expected return on market portfolio: 0.13

Beta value for losses: 0.3

Terms of debt: 5 years with balloon payment of principal at end

Losses are assumed to arise midyear. The solution is developed by summarizing the choices of full insurance and all-debt financing from the previous section.

Full Insurance

Risk-adjusted present value (RAPV): $650,000

All-Debt Financing

Expected value of loss: $500,000
Expected annual value of debt interest $500,000(0.09) = $45,000 per year
Capitalized value of expected debt repayment at expected time
of loss:

$$\sum_{i=1}^{5} \frac{45,000}{(1 + 0.08)^i} + \frac{500,000}{(1 + 0.08)^5} = \$519,964$$

Current RAPV of debt financing:

$$\frac{\$519{,}964}{1 + 0.0475} = \$496{,}386$$

Deductible Policy with Residual Debt Financing

The expected burden of debt repayment is calculated in similar fashion:

Expected value of retained loss: $150,000
Expected annual value of debt interest:

$$\$150{,}000(0.09) = \$13{,}500$$

Capitalized value of expected debt repayment at expected time of loss:

$$\sum_{i=1}^{5}\frac{13{,}500}{(1 + 0.08)^i} + \frac{150{,}000}{(1 + 0.08)^5} = \$155{,}989$$

Losses are expected to arise, on average, 6 months from the date of exposure. Therefore, this value must be discounted to a present RAPV using an appropriate risk-adjusted rate. The annual risk-adjusted rate was calculated with reference to the loss β value:

$$E(r_{RM}) = r_f + \beta_{RM}[E(r_m) - r_f]$$
$$= 0.08 + 0.3(0.13 - 0.08)$$
$$= 0.095$$

Using half this rate as an approximation for the 6-month period, we have

$$RAPV = \frac{155{,}989}{1 + 0.0475} = \$148{,}916$$

Adding the insurance premium, the total RAPV for this alternative is

$$\$148{,}916 + \$450{,}000 = \$598{,}916$$

Thus the three-way comparison reveals that debt financing is still preferred to both the insurance alternatives. However, the deductible policy is preferred to the full insurance policy.

Comparisons such as those shown in this example can be undertaken repeatedly, identifying each possible financing alternative and calculating the appropriate RAPV's. If there are many such alternatives, the decision process will become lengthy and complex. In order to confine the search for a preferred form of financing, we will probe somewhat deeper into the process by which financing creates value for a firm and into the relationship between reinvestment and loss financing. Our analysis is somewhat formal, following the approach adopted in the appendix to Chapter 10. The payoff to such a formal approach will be a heightened understanding of the financial role of corporate insurance. In pursuing the value-creation approach, we will develop more explicit criteria for partitioning the burden of financing between insurance and competing sources. We will show how risk-sharing devices, such as deductibles and policy limits, can be selected.

A Valuation Model without Transaction Costs

In earlier chapters we used a two-period valuation model to examine the impact of risk management decisions on the value of a firm's equity. This model was extended in the appendix to Chapter 10 to show that under given circumstances, the risk management decision can be separated from other financial decisions. We now use the same type of model. The current market value of equity is shown as the discounted value of the period 1 cash flow $C(1)$ and the expected value at time 2, that is, $E[V(2)]$. Instead of using a risk-adjusted discounted rate, we have made a dollar-value risk adjustment to the expected value at time 2 and have discounted the risk-adjusted value at the risk-free rate. The dollar risk adjustment takes account of the covariances between time 2 value and the return on the market index:

$$\text{MVE} = C(1) + \frac{E[V(2)] - [E(r_m) - r_f]\left\{\dfrac{\text{cov }[V(2),\, r_m]}{\sigma_m^2}\right\}}{1 + r_f} \tag{12-18}$$

where σ_m^2 is the variance of r_m, and other terms are defined in the usual manner. This formulation aggregates all sources of value creation for the firm, and these elements can be separated. As shown in the appendix to Chapter 10, this quality of separability permits us to choose between competing sources of financing. Thus we may compare sources of financing for reinvestment purely on the basis of the respective values created by each source. Suppose that the insurance policy covers a portion, say, $1 - \alpha$, of the loss, leaving the residual portion α to be raised from alternative sources. Writing the expected value of loss as $E(L)$, we can show the risk-adjusted present cost of insurance simply as the insurance premium, which is expressed as a function of the proportion of cover and of the expected value of loss, that is,

$$P = P[E(L),\, (1 - \alpha)] \tag{12-19}$$

With alternative financing, the risk-adjusted present cost is the capitalized value of the service payments, i.e., interest plus repayment of principal or dividends. The stream of service payments will have a capitalized value, at the time of issue, equal to the market value of the expected issue, which, ignoring transaction costs, will equal the expected sum to be raised $\alpha E(L)$. The time of issue will follow the loss. Therefore, the market value $\alpha E(L)$ must be adjusted to a present value after suitable adjustment for the riskiness inherent in the distribution of losses. The risk premium is represented as a dollar adjustment of the following form:

$$\frac{\alpha E(L) - [E(r_m) - r_f] \left[\dfrac{\text{cov } (\alpha L, \, r_m)}{\sigma_m^2}\right]}{1 + r_f}$$

$$= \alpha \left\{ \frac{E(L) - [E(r_m) - r_f] \left[\dfrac{\text{cov } (L, \, r_m)}{\sigma_m^2}\right]}{1 + r_f} \right\} \tag{12-20}$$

Comparison of equations (12-19) and (12-20) reveals that full insurance is preferred if

$$P[E(L)] < \frac{E(L) - [E(r_m) - r_f] \left[\dfrac{\text{cov } (L, \, r_m)}{\sigma_m^2}\right]}{1 + r_f} \tag{12-21}$$

That is, if the premium is less than the risk-adjusted present value of the cost of debt financing (which is equal to the present value of expected policy payments, since expected value of debt at the time of issue is equal to the expected value of loss). This condition is identical to that derived at the end of the appendix to Chapter 10. In practice, this condition is unlikely to be satisfied. The loading in the insurance premium is typically in the range of 25 to 75%.[4] Even ignoring discounting to allow for the time difference between premiums and claims and for the risk involved, equation (12-21) is unlikely to be satisified. This conclusion is a generalization. Since we are discussing expected values of losses, individual risk managers may have subjective expectations that exceed those used by the insurer for the purpose of premium calculation. In some cases, the risk manager's estimates may be more accurate. However, if insurers continuously and routinely underestimate loss probabilities, they will fail to survive. Thus satisfaction of equation (12-21) must be considered to be somewhat unusual. Accordingly, we are left without a strong explanation as to why firms might purchase full insurance.

Satisfaction of equation (12-21) is required to explain why a firm might choose to purchase full insurance. However, if the premium rate for full insurance fails to come close to satisfying this condition, it may also be that premiums for partial insurance are too high to justify insurance. This position would appear to be supported by the frequent complaints of risk managers that premium reductions for deductibles are

---

[4]These figures imply that the expected loss payment typically lies in the range 57 to 80% of the premium payment. *Ex post,* the loss payment sometimes exceeds the premium on an insurance portfolio. However, this is usually due to unforeseen loss records or abnormally poor investment performance. Insurers could not survive with planned ratios in excess of unity.

unrealistic and inadequate. For proportionate devices, the premium is usually scaled in proportion to the level of cover. If the condition suggested by equation (12-21) fails for full cover, it will also fail for proportionate cover. Thus we appear to be a long way from identifying conditions under which insurance will add value to a firm. This analysis appears to point strongly to other forms of financing that usually are associated with the investment activities and working capital needs of firms. The alternative forms include internal liquid funds and new issues of debt and equity. We will now look more closely at the cost structures of these alternative financing sources, and in so doing, we will identify a stronger, although somewhat restricted, case for the use of insurance to finance the reinvestment needs of a firm.

A Valuation Model with Transaction Costs

The treatment of the relative costs of insurance and competing methods of financing developed earlier was somewhat biased. The insurance premium was permitted to include transaction costs, such as management expenses, claim settlement expenses, agents' commissions, and a return on capital employed in the insurance industry. No such allowance was made for the transaction costs associated with other forms of financing. A firm would need to raise a value in excess of the sum required for reinvestment in order to cover the costs of raising such financing. The transaction costs include issue expenses and underwriting costs for new issues of debt and equity, commitment fees, compensating balances, etc. for other forms of debt, and perhaps the opportunity costs of maintaining internal liquid funds for risk management purposes. We will now modify our analysis to include such costs. In so doing, we assume that a firm must raise a residual sum to finance reinvestment (after insurance moneys are taken into account) that is equal to the cost of reinvestment plus the transaction costs of financing. Writing the transaction costs as C, we restate the condition for insurance purchase as

$$P[E(L)] < \frac{E(L + C) - [E(r_m) - r_f] \left\{ \dfrac{\text{cov } [(L + C), r_m]}{\sigma_m^2} \right\}}{1 + r_f} \quad (12\text{-}22)$$

The inclusion of transaction costs brings greater opportunity for satisfying the condition for insurance. In order to explore possibilities we will separate competing financing sources and consider the cost structure of each in more detail.

FINANCIAL LAYERING

An Illustration of Financial Layering

Cash flows that are regular and predictable can be managed within a firm in an orderly fashion without sudden recourse to outside funding and without the need to maintain large pools of cash and marketable securities that yield little or no return. Financing such losses from internal sources avoids the issue costs of external funding and the

TABLE 12-4
EXAMPLES OF FINANCING COST FROM DIFFERENT SOURCES

	Actual cost (AC)*	Present expected value (EC)*
1 Insurance	$(1 + a)E(\tilde{L})$	$(1 + a)E(\tilde{L})$
2 New Issue	$b + (1 + c)\tilde{L}$	$[P_{LA}b + (1 + c)E(\tilde{L})](1 + k_1)^{-1}$
3 Internal Liquid Resources	$\tilde{L}$	$E(\tilde{L})(1 + k_2)^{-1}$

*Where a, b, and c are positive constants with $a > c$, k_1 and k_2 are risk-adjusted discount rates, and P_{LA} is the probability that a loss will arise that is above some threshold level A.

premium loadings associated with insurance. The cost of financing any loss of size $\tilde{L}$ in this way is represented simply, as shown in Table 12-4. The insurance premium is represented by the form $(1 - a)E(\tilde{L})$, where $E(\tilde{L})$ is expected value of loss and a represents the markup or transaction costs. This form of premium is roughly implied by rating methods that allow calculation of the premium as a constant rate applied to some measure of exposure. Some parts of the premium loading are explicitly proportional to the premium, e.g., the commission. Other types of premium structures may be used, although the proportional structure is probably the best simple approximation. For new debt and equity, the main transaction costs are incurred with issue, although since issue costs typically increase modestly with the size of the issue, the cost of financing is represented in Table 12-4 as a linear function of the size of the loss, that is, $b + (1 + c)\tilde{L}$. Notice that $a > c$, which reveals the realistic case in which proportionate insurance transaction costs are high but variable costs of a new issue are low.

The present value of expected financing cost is also shown in Table 12-4. This results from simple discounting at some rate k_i that is appropriate to the riskiness of contingent financing costs. Since premiums are payable in advance, no discounting is required by insurance.

In Figure 12-4, the respective costs of each form of financing are represented. Each diagram shows the total actual present value of the cost of financing different levels of loss L, in each case assuming that all the loss is financed from a single source. It is evident that internal liquid resources represent the cheapest source for small losses,

FIGURE 12-4
Financing costs from alternative sources.

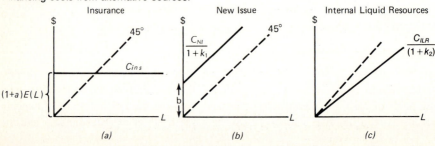

since no transaction costs are incurred. However, it is also clear that not all losses can be financed from this source. Only losses that are regular and predictable such that they can be accommodated within a cash management program without need for large liquid resources can adequately be financed in this way. We suppose that small losses below some value δ can be financed from internal liquid resources (we will calculate δ shortly), leaving larger losses to the remaining sources.

In Figure 12-5, we show some composite financing schemes in which two or more sources of financing are used. Since internal sources can be used up to value $L = δ$, we show a first *layer* of financing from this source. Losses above δ are funded by insurance (in which case δ is simply a deductible) or by new issue of debt or equity. If insurance is used, then the premium will be $1 + a$ times the expected value of the insured loss. Since the policy contains a deductible of δ, the premium can be represented as

$$(1 + a)E(L - δ) \qquad (12\text{-}23)$$

where $E(L - δ) = \displaystyle\int_{δ}^{\infty} (L - δ)f(L)dL$

FIGURE 12-5
Composite financing of losses: Alternative two-layer financing methods.

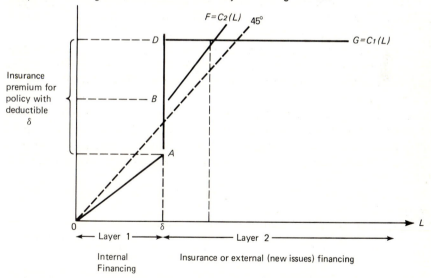

$OABF$ = Total cost function with small losses (0 - δ) financed by internal liquid resources and residual of larger losses financed by new issue

$OADG$ = Total cost function with small losses (0 - δ) financed by internal liquid resources and residual of larger losses financed by an insurance policy with deductible δ

This premium is represented by the value AD in Figure 12-5. The total cost for different values of loss is represented by the line $0ADG$.

Now consider a new issue to finance losses above δ. The fixed cost of the issue is shown as line AB. The total cost of financing by new issue is shown by the continuation along line BF, the difference in slope between BF and the 45° line representing the variable transaction cost. Thus the total financing costs, with small losses covered from internal sources and large losses from new issue, are represented by the line $0ABF$. Comparison between the two approaches may be undertaken by means of risk-adjusted present values.

We will presently mount an example to show how layering strategies might be derived. In constructing this example, we will follow this sequence:

1 Select a first layer to be financed by internal liquid resources. The size of this layer will be determined by its risk characteristics. More specifically, we will finance by this method only losses or portions of losses that arise with sufficient predictability that they can be accommodated within a cash budget. By first selecting this layer, we assume that internal financing has distinct cost advantages over external sources.

2 We then choose between insurance and new issues on the basis of the expected value of financing costs.

The method to be used in selecting the first layer may be developed using characteristics of the loss distribution that should now be familiar. The first layer will cover losses from values 0 to δ and will include a contribution of the sum δ to all losses exceeding δ. From equation (12-23), we show a value δ, for which the probability that loss L is less than δ is the selected value Θ:

$$\delta_\Theta = E(L) + [-z_\Theta + \frac{1}{6}\alpha_3(L)\,(-z_\Theta^2 - 1)]\sigma(L) \qquad (12\text{-}24)$$

where $E(L)$, $\sigma(L)$, and $\alpha_3(L)$ are the mean, standard deviation, and skewness of the distribution of aggregate loss, and z_Θ is the standard normal variate for probability Θ. Note that a negative sign is used because we wish to emphasize the probability below δ.

With Θ selected at some low value, say, 0.3, 0.2, or 0.1, the actual contribution of internal financing to aggregate annual loss will be δ in 70%, 80%, or 90% of years with values of less than δ in remaining years. By selecting a sufficiently low value for Θ, the demands placed on internal liquidity can be kept to an acceptable level of stability, such that this demand can be accommodated routinely within the firm's cash budget without holding a large pool of cash. The expected financing burden from internal funds (ILR) will be

$$E(C_{\text{ILR}}) = (P_{L>\delta})\delta + \sum_{i=0}^{\delta} P_i L_i \qquad (12\text{-}25)$$

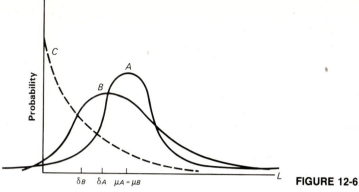

FIGURE 12-6

and the standard deviation of this financing burden will be

$$\sigma(C_{ILR}) = \left\{ P_{L>\delta}[\delta - E(C_{ILR})]^2 + \sum_{i=0}^{\delta} P_i[L_i - E(C_{ILR})]^2 \right\}^{1/2} \quad (12\text{-}26)$$

To illustrate how this method might work, consider two firms. Firm A has a well-diversified portfolio of loss exposure units, and the aggregate loss distribution is shown in Figure 12-6 as distribution A. Firm B is not well diversified; its aggregate loss distribution is shown as distribution B. These distributions are fairly representative of the respective circumstances. Each firm decides that it can provide an annual contribution of loss refinancing from internal funds up to some level δ, where δ is calculated such that the firm is 75% sure that the payment will be at this level. Should losses fall below this value, the firm will find itself with surplus cash, which is costly in terms of foregone investment earnings. However, by fixing Θ at 0.25, the probability of losses falling short of δ is constrained at the acceptable level of 25%. From Figure 12-6 it is seen that the more diversified firm, that is, firm A, is able to accept a higher level of δ while maintaining the same probability that losses will only fall below δ. This result arises in spite of the equality of the expected value of loss for the two firms.

Now for an example to illustrate layering.

EXAMPLE: WOODEN PUTTY PASTA

Wooden Putty Pasta manufacturers Italian and other ethnic foods. The risk manager is known for her creative risk management planning. She is charged with arranging a financing plan for reinvestment following loss. The finance director provides the following information:

The finance director can write into the cash budget a projected maximum contribution for loss reinvestment at some level δ. However, δ should not be fixed at such a high value that the firm will carry a large probability of being left with surplus cash. It is suggested that δ be fixed such that the probability that aggregate loss will be less than δ is 0.25.

New debt can be raised for reinvestment. The issue cost of new debt is estimated to be $15,000 plus $2^1/_2\%$ of the value of the issue.

The current risk-free rate is 10%, and the expected return on the market portfolio is 15%.

The risk manager's own staff provides the following information:

The β value for losses is estimated at 0.5.

The premium for insurance is estimated at 130% of the expected value of insured loss (that is, $a = 0.3$).

The estimated distribution of aggregate loss is given by the following table:

Loss (midpoints × $1000)	Probability	Cumulative probability
10	0.1	0.1
50	0.15	0.25
100	0.2	0.45
250	0.25	0.70
500	0.21	0.91
750	0.06	0.97
1000	0.0025	0.995
2000	0.005	1.00

The following summary data are calculated from the loss distribution:

$$E(L) = \$276,000$$
$$\sigma(L) = \$270,300$$
$$\alpha_3(L) = 1.99$$

Method 1

If the probability distribution is known, determination of various layers of financing can be undertaken by reading values directly from the loss distribution. This approach is appropriate if the distribution is assembled directly from aggregate annual loss payments and if such payments represent a reasonably large sample. If separate severity and frequency distributions are used, it is preferable to use some characterization of the aggregate loss distribution. Our approach based on the normal approximation method will be outlined presently (Method 2).

To calculate the first layer to be financed from internal liquid resources, we need simply determine δ such that the probability of L being less than δ is 0.25. Reading from the cumulative probability distribution, $\delta = \$50,000$. To see whether payments financed in this manner really are stable, we will determine the expected value and standard deviation of prospective payments from internal liquid resources using equations (12-25) and (12-26):

$$E(C_{ILR}) = 0.75(50,000) + 0.1(10,000) + 0.15(50,000)$$
$$= \$46,000$$
$$\sigma(C_{ILR}) = [0.75(50,000 - 46,000)^2 + 0.1(10,000 - 46,000)^2$$
$$+ 0.15(50,000 - 46,000)^2]^{1/2}$$
$$= \$12,000$$

To find the present value, the expected financing cost must be discounted at a risk-adjusted rate. Assuming both small and large losses have a β value of 0.5, the appropriate rate k_2 is calculated in the usual way. However,

$$
\begin{aligned}
k_2 &= r_f + \beta_L[E(r_m) - r_f] \\
&= 0.1 + 0.5(0.15 - 0.1) \\
&= 0.125
\end{aligned}
$$

Therefore,

$$
\frac{E(C_{ILR})}{1 + k_2} = \frac{46,000}{1.125} = \$40,889
$$

Now the second layer of financing must be decided on the basis of the respective risk-adjusted present costs of insurance and new issue.

Insurance: The insurance premium is calculated easily given the premium rate:

$$
C_{INS} = (1 + a)E(L)
$$

The expected insurance payment on the policy is calculated given a deductible δ. That is,

$$
\sum_{i=\delta}^{\infty} P_i(L_i - \delta)
$$

which (in thousands of dollars) is

$$
\begin{aligned}
& 0.2(100 - 50) + 0.25(250 - 50) + 0.21(500 - 50) + 0.06(750 - 50) \\
& + 0.025(1000 - 50) + 0.005(2000 - 50) = \$230,000
\end{aligned}
$$

Therefore,

$$
E_{INS} = (1 + 0.3 (\$230,000) = \$299,000
$$

New Debt Issue: The amount to be financed from this source is exactly equivalent to that required if insurance is purchased. The expected value is $230,000, calculated as earlier. However, there are transaction costs to the issue, and for comparison with insurance, a risk-adjusted present value is required. For simplicity we will use the rate used for internal financing. This may not be strictly correct, since large losses may exhibit different systematic risk characteristics than small losses and the task is slightly more complex here because of the fixed component of issue costs. However, the rate calculated from the overall loss β value gives a reasonable approximation. Using the formula from Table 12-4, we have

$$
\frac{E(C_{NI})}{(1 + k_2)} = \frac{0.75(15,000) + (1 + 0.025)(230,000)}{1.125} = \$219,556
$$

It turns out that the risk-adjusted cost of financing the second layer with a new debt issue is considerably cheaper than insurance. Thus the best two-layer financing strategy is

1 Finance the first $50,000 of losses with internal liquid resources.
2 Finance residual values with new debt issues.

Method 2

Normal-Power Method: Similar calculations can be undertaken using a "smoothed" version of the loss distribution. Our approach will be to reconstruct the probability distribution from its summary statistics in order to avoid the arbitrariness arising from the particular loss values fed into the original severity and frequency distributions (see Cummins and Friefelder, 1978/9, for a discussion). In reconstructing the distribution, cumulative loss probabilities can be assembled at any value of L. For convenience, we will keep with the original class midpoints, although, in addition, we calculate cumulative probability at $L = \$78,700$ for reasons that will become clear shortly.

To calculate cumulative probabilities at different values of L, equation (12-24) is rearranged to yield an explicit solution for z [see also equation (11-24)]

$$z_L = \frac{-1 \pm \sqrt{1 + 2\alpha_3(L)/3 \{\alpha_3(L)/6 + [L - E(L)]/\sigma(L)\}}}{\alpha_3(L)/3} \quad (12\text{-}27)$$

The higher value root is used for the solution. Calculation of z and substitution of the appropriate probability completes the reconstructed distribution shown. Some points to note are:

1 For $L = 10$, there is no real root for equation (12-27). The cumulative probability is interpreted as zero.
2 When z is negative, we identify the lefthand tail of the distribution, and the cumulative probability is read directly from the following z table:

Loss (in $1000)	z	Cumulative probability	Probability
10	—	—	—
50	−0.947	0.1711	0.1711
78.7	−0.677	0.2500	0.0789
100	−0.523	0.2981	0.0481
250	0.205	0.5832	0.2851
500	0.985	0.8389	0.2557
750	1.465	0.9292	0.0903
1000	2.065	0.9805	0.0513
2000	3.579	0.9991	0.0186

3 When z is positive, the area identified is the right-hand tail of the distribution, and the value in the z table must be subtracted from unity to give the cumulative probability.

The solution can now proceed in an identical fashion to the first method save only for use of the reconstructed probabilities.

Notice first that the first layer of financing from internal resources is calculated at a somewhat higher value, namely, $78,700. Therefore,

$$E(C_{ILR}) = 0.75(78,700) + 0.1711(50,000) + 0.0789(78,700) = \$73,789$$

and

$$\sigma(C_{ILR}) = [0.75(78,700 - 73,789)^2 + 0.1711(50,000 - 73,789)^2$$
$$+ 0.0789(78,700 - 73,789)^2]^{1/2} = \$10,808$$

The present value of the expected internal financing cost is therefore

$$\frac{\$73,789}{1.125} = \$65,590$$

The standard deviation is low in relation to the expected payment from internal liquid resources, probably indicating an acceptable level of stability for cash budgeting purposes.

The *insurance premium* is calculated in similar fashion:

$$C_{INS} = (1 + a)E(L)$$

where $E(L)$ is (in the thousands of dollars):

$$0.0481(100 - 78.7) + 0.2851(250 - 78.7) + 0.2557(500 - 78.7) +$$
$$0.903(750 - 78.7) + 0.0513(1000 - 78.7) + 0.0186(2000 - 78.7)$$
$$= \$301,206$$

Therefore,

$$C_{INS} = (1 + 0.3)(301,206) = \$371,568$$

For *new debt financing*,

$$\frac{E(C_{NI})}{(1 + k_2)} = \frac{0.75(15,000) + (1 + 0.025)(301,206)}{1.125} = \$284,432$$

As with the simple calculation, debt financing has a lower risk-adjusted expected cost than insurance. Thus the optimal two-layer financing scheme comprises a first layer of $78,700 financed from internal liquid resources with recourse to new debt issues for the residual financing requirements.

Layering: Some Qualifications and Further Discussion

The choice between Method 1 and Method 2 rests on the risk manager's judgment as to whether the raw distribution or the reconstructed distribution better represents the true distribution of loss probabilities. A further point is whether reconstruction is best undertaken by means of the normal-power approximation. The skewness parameter, which is less than 2 (just), indicates that normal-power approximation is not inappropriate, but it may also be important to consider the general shape of the distribution. The use of normal-power approximation assumes that the distribution has an "n" shape as shown by both A and B in Figure 12-6. These distributions are typical when the insured has a portfolio of risk units that exhibits some degree of diversification resulting in a positive-value modal loss. An example of such a distribution is the lognormal. For undiversified insureds having, say, a single risk unit or small number of risk units, the modal loss is often zero, as indicated by distribution C in Figure 12-6. An example of this type of distribution is the Pareto. When normal approximation is not appropriate, other techniques are required to reconstruct the form of the probability distribution. Curve-fitting techniques may be used in such circumstances, although those are beyond our scope here.

A second issue arising from this example is whether anything is lost by restricting the solution to two layers of financing. Since new issues involve heavy transaction costs, it may be preferable to reduce the probability δ that such transaction costs arise by having an intermediate level of insurance. This could be arranged with an insurance policy that has both a deductible of δ (calculated in the preceding fashion) and an upper limit of U. New debt will only be used for the residual of losses above value U, and the expected value of transaction costs is now reduced from $P_{L>\delta}b$ to $P_{L>U}b$. The potential benefit of a three-layer financing system is illustrated in Figure 12-7. The lines $0ABF$ and $0ADG$ are copied from Figure 12-5 in order to establish relationships with the two-layer strategies. An insurance policy is arranged to cover payments:

$$
\begin{array}{ll}
0 & \text{if } 0 \leq L \leq \delta \\
L - \delta & \text{if } \delta < L < U \\
U - \delta & \text{if } U < L < \infty
\end{array}
$$

Such a policy will normally have a lower premium than a policy with only a deductible δ. The premium for the "deductible only" policy is AD (also shown in Figure 12-5), which is now reduced to AD' in view of the upper limit. The transaction costs for debt comprise a fixed cost and a variable cost. The fixed cost was shown as AB in Figure 12-3 and is repeated here for reference. However, this cost will now arise only if losses exceed U. The upward shift HJ ($= AB$) shows the displacement for this cost. The segment JK shows the residual financing cost from a new issue. Thus the three-layer financing system reveals a cost function shown by the heavy line $0AD'HJK$. Over the most of its range, this line dominates the two-layer system represented by $0ABF$. However, to see which is preferred would require that we take expected values in a manner used in the example constructed for the two-layer system.

A third issue that should be addressed relates to insurance premiums. We assumed a particular functional form for insurance in which the expected value of insured loss was known and this value was multiplied by the constant $1 + a$ to derive the premium. In practice, the expected value of loss is never known with precision, and estimates may differ between the insured and insurer. For this reason, the premium savings from

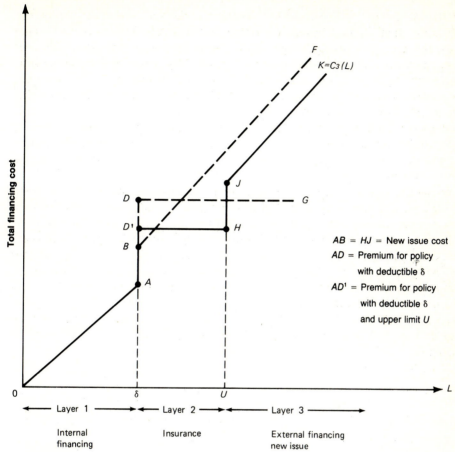

FIGURE 12-7
Illustration of three-layer financing.

deductibles may not be a constant multiple of expected loss or may not be perceived as such. A frequent complaint of risk managers is that, apart from very small deductibles that are often encouraged by insurers, premium savings for deductibles are often tiny in comparison to the risk assumed by the insured under the deductible. There is remarkably little evidence to affirm or negate this contention, but the issue does highlight the need for basing financing decisions on actual premium quotations from the insurer rather on simple formulas that attempt to anticipate the prices an insurer might charge. In the example presented earlier, we assumed that the premium change would be a constant multiple of the expected claim payment under the policy. This practice ensured some relationship between premium and expected claim payment, but actual premium quotations are preferable to such rough estimates.

OTHER OPTIMAL INSURANCE MODELS

Several types of insurance purchasing models have appeared in the literature. Perhaps the largest group of models is that using expected utility to derive the optimal level of coinsurance or the optimal deductible (examples include Smith, 1968, Mossin, 1968, Ehrlich and Becker, 1972, Gould, 1969, Raviv, 1979, Doherty, 1975, and Doherty and Schlesinger, 1983). These models typically take the following form. The problem is to maximize expected utility of wealth, where wealth depends both on loss experience, which is random, and the purchase of insurance, which is a decision. Therefore,

$$\text{Expected utility} = \sum_i P_i U[W_i(\text{INS})]$$

where W_i = decision maker's wealth if a loss of size L_i occurs [this wealth level is determined by the level of insurance (INS)]

P_i = probability that a loss of size L_i will arise

U = an index of the decision maker's utility

Using this type of model, various propositions concerning insurance buying have been derived; some of these were described in Chapter 3. These propositions apply to risk-averse decision makers. For example,

1 If the insurance premium is equal to (or less than) the expected value of loss, the rational decision maker will purchase insurance.

2 If the insurance premium is a constant multiple (greater than unity) of the expected value of the insured loss, the rational risk averter will retain part of the risk by means of a deductible or coinsurance.

3 Under the premium condition outlined in point 2, the preferred form of policy for a risk averter is a deductible rather than a proportionate coinsurance policy. The preference for the insurer is the reverse of that for the insured.

4 If individual A is "more risk averse" than B, he or she will purchase more insurance than B.

Although statements such as these are very useful in helping to identify broad choices consistent with aversion to risk and may even help to eliminate specific choices from a decision, they provide only limited guidance for risk management decisions. The value of the expected utility literature for risk management purposes is limited by the following:

1 To identify precise risk management strategies requires full identification of the decision maker's utility function. It is extremely doubtful if any corporate risk manager could persuade his or her board to articulate a utility function or a set of attitudes toward risk in a form that lends itself to the expected-utility decision models in the literature.

2 Even if the utility function could be articulated, it may not be necessary. Consistent with our financial approach to risk management, the appropriate utility is that of the owners, notably the firm's shareholders. The equity holdings of the shareholders are simply financial assets that are traded in a capital market according to market-determined risk-return relationships. Since risk is clearly priced in this market, it is consistent to impose the market price of risk on risk management decisions. This approach is clearly adopted in this chapter and elsewhere. If a firm is closely held and its equity is not traded, then risk preferences will not be measured by capital market activity, and conscious self-scrutiny to identify risk attitudes (i.e., identification of a utility function) is required. However, our focus is primarily on widely held firms.

3 A third problem is that virtually all the literature cited formulates the insurance decision as one in which insurable risk is the only source of risk. This has the effect of ignoring possible portfolio effects within a firm. Where noninsurable risk arising from ordinary commercial activities exhibits a low correlation with insurable risk, insurance has somewhat lower value than supposed by the usual specification of the expected-utility model. In the limit, the risk-reducing effects of insurance may lose all value if shareholders are able to diversify away this risk in their personal portfolio holdings. Such a position is broadly feasible where insurable losses exhibit low systematic risk. Recently, the expected utility approach has been modified by Doherty and Schlesinger (1983) and Turnbull (1983) to account for background wealth, although for corporate risk management decisions, an approach based on capital market valuation of risk offers more insight and guidance.

An interesting variation on the expected-utility model was developed by Cozzolino (1978), who shows a method for deriving the expected utility (or more specifically, the expected disutility, which he labels the *risk-adjusted cost*) of a loss distribution and how this is affected by insurance purchase. To simplify the problem of identifying risk preference, a specific form of (dis)utility function is assumed, namely, the exponential form. Use of this function requires only a single parameter to describe attitude toward risk. Such a single value might be easily inferred by the risk manager from statements of corporate objectives whereas inference of the whole utility function is unlikely. The second important advantage of using exponential utility lies in the separation of decisions. Within the utility-maximizing framework, the objective is to maximize expected utility from all operations under ownership of the decision maker. Thus, for a single insurance decision, we must calculate the total utility from all corporate activities rather than basing the decision solely on those factors directly related to insurable risk, such as the premium rate and the characteristics of the loss distribution. The use of exponential utility permits separation of decisions, since total utility is simply the sum of the separate utilities of individual activities. These advantages of the Cozzolino method are valuable, even if they are attained at the expense of restricting the form of utility. However, for firms with widely held equity, these advantages may be redundant. Risk measures can be inferred from capital market prices. Furthermore, the value-creation approach based on a market index pricing model such as the capital asset pricing model permits separation of decisions such that the risk management financing decision can be made without total calculation of corporate value. The Cozzolino method is potentially useful for small-business risk management.

A very different approach to retention and insurance relates to financial ratios. The emphasis on financial ratios appears to bring this approach in line with the financial methodology of this book, but this may or may not be the case. The financial ratio method is, in effect, a statement of adopted "rules of thumb" that relate a firm's retention level to key corporate accounting figures or financial ratios such as net operating income, liquidity ratios, and leverage ratios. The particular relationships are arbitrary. For example, "the retention limit on any one loss should not exceed $x\%$ of net operating income or $y\%$ of available cash and marketable securities." Such relationships may be important and may indeed prevail as a result of the financial modeling used in this text. However, when simply stated as arbitrary rules, there is no reasonable basis for deciding whether they really have much to do with value creation or whether a particular rule will stand up in a changing environment. For example, one such rule might permit risk management costs to vary only within limits that are defined independently of liquidity or borrowing capacity. Such a rule appears to make some sense if the objective of risk management is risk reduction, but we would claim that such an objective makes little sense when corporate equity is widely held. Another example might be that corporate retention must not exceed $y\%$ of cash/marketable securities. This is consistent with views on liquidity stressed in this text, but how can we determine the value of y. Furthermore, a given $y\%$ may work well when interest rates are low and the firm has extensive unused lines of credit, but with tighter capital markets, $y\%$ might expose the firm to totally unacceptable liquidity risk. In short, the derivation of such financial relationships should result from a proper formulation of corporate financial strategy rather than serving as a substitute for a more rigorous model.

One method that comes a little closer to our financial model is the often quoted Houston (1964) model. The purpose of the Houston approach is to determine whether insurance will add value to a firm, which is entirely consistent with the risk management objectives assumed in this book. Houston, in fact, uses net worth to measure value rather than market value, but since this term does not affect the value added by insurance, the distinction is not pertinent. To identify the value added by insurance, consider the "financial position" of a firm on the assumption that insurance is purchased FP_I and the "financial position" if no insurance is purchased FP_{NI}. Financial values FR are expressed as "end of year" values:

$$FP_I = NW - P + r(NW - P)$$

and

$$FP_{NI} = NW - L + r(NW - L - R) + iR$$

where NW = initial net worth

L = expected loss

P = the insurance premium

r = the marginal internal rate of return
on corporate investments
R = the firm's reserve to fund uninsured loss
i = the rate of return on fund investments

This presentation varies slightly, although not in significant detail, from the original. The value added by insurance is

$$VA_I = FP_I - FP_{NI} = R(r - i) - (1 + r)(P - L)$$

This expression tells us that the value added comprises two components. The first is the additional return to the firm from releasing funds that might otherwise have been tied up in a retention fund. If the firm has investment opportunities yielding returns in excess of those from fund investments (that is, $r > i$), this first term will represent a gain from insurance purchase. The second term represents the cost of insurance as a markup over the expected loss. Multiplying by $1 + r$ has the effect of expressing the markup as a terminal value, or "end of year" value, in accordance with the definition of FP.

This approach has the clear advantage of simplicity. However, this simplicity is achieved at a cost. Particularly,

1 The model does not address external or other internal sources of financing.

2 In the light of point 1, internal funding may not be an appropriate source of financing.

3 Even if funding is appropriate, it is arguable that its opportunity cost is measured by the cost of capital.

4 The model does not address any systematic risk effects of insurance purchase (such effect may in fact be small and it may be convenient to ignore in some circumstances).

5 The advantage of extreme simplicity is lost if one addresses the important issue of partial insurance purchase. The model may be scaled for proportionate coinsurance, but it is not easily adapted for consideration of deductibles.

6 The model assumes that reinvestment is desirable, and in consequence, financing is required.

The Houston model predates many of the interesting modern developments in finance that are incorporated in this book.

A more formal financial model was derived directly from the capital asset pricing model some years ago by Cummins (1976). This model again concentrates attention on value creation as an appropriate goal for risk management. However, Cummins himself apparently accepted, in concluding his paper, that the restrictive assumptions of the model limited its applicability. A very different approach was later adopted by Cummins in collaboration with Friefelder (1978). After showing how the distribution of aggregate loss could be assembled from component severity and frequency distributions, Cummins and Friefelder show that the concept of maximum probable loss (MPY) can be used to provide guidance on deductible selection. Implicitly, the purpose of selecting a deductible in this way would be to contain the riskiness of the retained risk at some acceptable level. Thus, in contrast to Cummins' earlier work, which focused on the systematic risk and its price as determined by capital market activity, the MPY approach relates to total risk reduction.

The method derived in this chapter has linkages with both the Cummins and the Cummins-Friefelder models, although its effect is very different. As with the earlier Cummins model, it is shown that insurance will add value if the premium rate is sufficiently low that it provides an abnormally high return for the attendant systematic risk. Such a condition is unlikely to be met. However, transaction costs are important, and the MPY approach, based on normal approximation, provides a useful method of calculating the expected value of transaction costs from competing sources of finance.

SUMMARY AND CONCLUSION

In earlier chapters we considered alternative sources of financing and derived a framework for selecting the form of financing to be used. In this chapter we considered the prospect that the optimal form of financing might require a package drawing on two or more competing sources, e.g., use of debt, internal liquidity, and insurance. For most sources, the difference between partial and full use of that source is simply a matter of scaling. For example, instead of raising all debt to finance reinvestment, we use 50% or so debt financing. However, partial use of insurance raises special issues.

Partial insurance can be arranged by means of proportionate devices such as coinsurance or nonproportionate devices such as deductibles or upper limits. The availability of these devices permits flexibility in deriving an appropriate composite financing package. If such composite packages are used, they can be evaluated using techniques derived earlier. A firm's earnings can be capitalized at appropriate risk-adjusted rates to derive alternative measures of corporate value for insurance financing, debt financing, equity financing, etc. or for any identified package of these financing methods.

Under reasonable assumptions, the components of value can be separated. This permits us to identify the contribution of each independent source of financing used in a financing package. Using the separation method, it is shown that the effects of different financing strategies on market value depend on the respective transaction costs. The transaction costs, typically, are not proportional to the sums to be raised from each source, and consequently, composite financing strategies are derived. These strategies involve "layering" the contingent reinvestment costs with different forms of financing allocated to different layers of the distribution. Examples of layers were given.

Many of the composite financing strategies involve insurance. In order to calculate the effects of layering, it is useful to see how different forms of insurance affect the distribution of retained loss. In particular, deductibles and coinsurance were compared, in each case considering the interaction of risk management and other forms of risk. Monitoring this total risk effect is also important if a firm wishes to consider the effect of insurance on its employees, managers, and other undiversified claimholders.

Finally, we compared other methodologies used for deriving optimal insurance strategies. The expected-utility model has received more attention, and it is very useful for conceptualizing the factors relevant to risky decision making. However, its value as a practical decision tool is limited by its subjective nature. Other models are also briefly mentioned.

In summary, this chapter shows that financing strategies can be packaged from the basic alternatives of debt, equity, insurance, funding, etc. Such composite packages often may be preferable to simple financing strategies and may permit a firm to lower its risk cost.

QUESTIONS

1 Consider the following loss distribution, L, and distribution of earnings, X:

Losses L			Earnings X	
Probability	L		Probability	X
0.3	3.33333*		0.2	100
0.4	10		0.4	300
0.2	30		0.2	500
0.1	50		0.2	700

Earnings and losses are uncorrelated. It is immediately apparent that a coinsurance policy covering 50% of all losses will have an actuarial value equal to 50% of the expected loss.
a What deductible will produce a policy having an actuarial value of 50% of the expected loss?
b Which policy will be more effective in stabilizing the earnings of the firm?
c Can you draw a general conclusion about the respective risk-reducing properties of coinsurance and deductible policies?

2 Compare the following three alternative financing methods:
a Full insurance at a premium of 500
b Partial insurance at a premium of 270 with residual financing by debt at 10% on a 10-year balloon. The policy is a 50% coinsurance arrangement.
c Total financing with debt on a 10-year balloon at 10.5%
The expected capital value of loss is 400 and the loss beta is 0.2. On average, losses arise half way through the year. The expected return on the market portfolio is 18% and the risk free rate 9%. Which package should be chosen?

3 Construct a layered risk financing solution for the following risk management issue. Aggregate losses are distributed as shown below. A retention fund is to be used for the first layer but the limit to this layer should be established such that the probability that the loss will exceed the value of the fund is 0.15. This layer will be supported either by a deductible policy or debt to cover losses in excess of the limit. The premium for the deductible policy is 110% of the expected value of insured loss whereas debt will be at 9% on a five year balloon. The loss beta is -0.2, the expected return on the market is 15% and the risk-free rate, 9%. Losses are assumed to arise at the end of the year. Fund assets will be invested risk free at 9%.

Aggregate loss	Probability
100	0.1
200	0.1
300	0.15
400	0.2
500	0.2
750	0.1
1,000	0.1
2,000	0.05

REFERENCES

Cozzolino, J. M.: "A Method for the Evaluation of Retained Risk," *Journal of Risk and Insurance,* vol. 45, 1978, pp. 449–471.

Cummins, J. D.: "Risk Management and the Theory of the Firm," *Journal of Risk and Insurance,* vol. 43, 1976, pp. 587–609.

———, and L. Friefelder: "Statistical Analysis in Risk Management," *Risk Management,* 1978–1979.

———, and L. Friefelder: "A Comparative Analysis of Maximum Probable Yearly Aggregate Loss Estimates," *Journal of Risk and Insurance,* vol. 45, 1978, pp. 27–52.

Doherty, N. A.: "Some Fundamental Theorems of Risk Management," *Journal of Risk and Insurance,* vol. 42, 1975, pp. 447–460.

———, and H. Schlesinger: "The Optimal Deductible for Insurance Policy when Initial Wealth Is Random," *Journal of Business,* vol. 56, 1983, pp. 555–565.

Ehrlich, I., and G. S. Becker: "Market Insurance, Self-Insurance and Self-Protection," *Journal of Political Economy,* vol. 80, 1972, pp. 623–648.

Gould, J. P.: "The Expected Utility Hypothesis and the Selection of Optimal Deductibles for a Given Insurance Policy," *Journal of Business,* vol. 42, pp. 143–151.

Hogue, M. E., and D. G. Olson: *Business Attitudes Toward Risk Management Insurance and Related Social Issues,* Dept. of Insurance, Wharton School, University of Pennsylvania, 1976.

Houston, D. R.: "Risk Insurance and Sampling," *Journal of Risk and Insurance,* 1964.

Mossin, J.: "Aspects of Rational Insurance Purchasing," *Journal of Political Economy,* vol. 76, 1968, pp. 553–568.

Raviv, A.: "The Design of an Optimal Insurance Policy," *American Economic Review,* vol. 69, 1979, pp. 223–239.

Smith, V.: "Optimal Insurance Coverage," *Journal of Political Economy,* vol. 68, 1968, pp. 68–77.

Turnbull, S. M.: "Additional Aspects of Rational Insurance Purchasing," *Journal of Business,* vol. 56, pp. 217–230.

CHAPTER 13

LOSS REDUCTION

More space is given in this text to the analysis of loss financing than to that of loss reduction. This emphasis does not reflect any priority ranking in the use of these techniques. Loss financing has not been well explored in the risk management literature, and its analysis requires more complex financial concepts than are necessary for analyzing loss reduction. However, the criteria for making loss-reduction decisions are the same as those used for loss financing. The common yardstick is the value of the firm; loss reduction decisions can be made according to their impact on the value of a firm's existing equity. In the appendix to Chapter 10 we considered the application of capital budgeting to loss financing decisions. Our conclusions there were somewhat guarded in view of the effects of nonsystematic risk on firm value. We will now review capital budgeting as our basic tool for analyzing loss-reduction decisions.

The term *loss reduction* is used for those activities which reduce the expected value of a firm's aggregate losses and/or which result in a reduction in the riskiness of the distribution of aggregate losses. The term *loss control* is also used. We feel that the word *control* is too general, since it could be construed to include loss financing activities. Accordingly, we prefer the greater descriptive content of *loss reduction*. The reduction in risk is assumed to be picked up by observing the change in the standard deviation or variance of the aggregate loss distribution in accordance with our mean-variance approach. The definition embraces the term *loss prevention* which is sometimes applied. Our construction of loss reduction is more general than that used by Mehr and Hedges (1974), who define loss reduction as a reduction in the frequency or severity of losses. In addition, we accept that loss-reduction programs may promote benefit in the form of reduction in the riskiness of the distribution. However, we do not envision such a tight definition of loss reduction that we are forced to include absurd examples. To illustrate one possibility, the uncertainty about future losses can be resolved by inducing an immediate loss. The expected value increases, but the variance of the aggregate distribution is dramatically reduced. Rather, we have in mind a more commonsense interpretation. In particular, we refer to those activities, such as the installation of safety devices, removal of sources of hazard, supervision of dangerous activities, product control, safety education, etc., which are meaningfully interpreted as loss reduction, safety, or loss prevention. Further, while our definition of loss reduction focuses on the aggregate loss of distribution, we do not mean to imply that the effects are confined to changes in this distribution. We shall argue that there are "spillover" or "external" effects that must also be considered in the decision process.

Loss reduction will usually entail direct expenditures in order to reap savings in the cost of future losses. In many cases, the bulk of cost is incurred at the inception of a loss prevention program, e.g., the installation of a sprinkler, the use of fireproof material for construction of a building, design changes to remove hazardous aspects of marketed products, reorganization of system of working, etc. These high initial costs may be followed by continued maintenance costs, e.g., inspection and repair of vehicles, periodic overhaul of a sprinkler system, or continuing costs of supervising a safety program. The benefits from loss reduction usually occur over an extended period of time. Fire-resistant construction in a building usually lasts the lifetime of the building; safety education may have a diminishing effect over time, with the need for "refresher" courses to reestablish awareness at periodic intervals. At the other extreme, some forms of loss reduction bring only immediate benefit, e.g., daily removal of flammable waste products from a factory or warehouse. In some cases, the benefits may be indirect and may not be monitored in terms of a change in the distribution of aggregate losses. For example, improved safety conditions on the work floor will produce a beneficial effect on the loss distribution. In addition, however, improved morale may affect productivity, and the safety program may be part of an employment compensation package in which direct wages are offset against improved working conditions. Such benefits do result from the safety program and should properly be credited to the program in the decision process. The benefits may be difficult to quantify, although the discipline of attempting estimation, even at the subjective level, will ensure that a reasonable weighting of these effects is achieved in the decision calculus. In some cases, the payback to loss reduction is compliance with the law, for example, the Occupational Safety and Health Act (OSHA). Our position here is judicial rather than economic. Rather than calculating the economic costs and benefits of compliance, our normative position is that compliance must be accepted as a constraint on the operations of the firm if it chooses to undertake an activity falling within the sphere of operation of the act.

Whatever the particular stream of economic cost and benefits, the use of discounted cash flow (DCF) techniques with appropriate discount rates will ensure that cash flows arising at different points in time are properly weighted in the decision process. By using the marginal cost of capital in the DCF analysis, the loss-reduction "investment" can be appraised in terms of the opportunity cost of capital used. This will ensure consistency in decision making not only between alternative loss-reduction investments, but also between loss reduction and competing investments in productive capacity, cost reduction, marketing, etc. To gain further insight into the temporal nature of loss-reduction investment, as well as into the sequential nature of decision making, the DCF approach will be supplemented by use of decision trees. First, however, we wish to identify and classify the various types of loss reduction and the benefits that might ensue.

CLASSIFICATIONS OF LOSS-REDUCTION PROGRAMS

Classification of types of loss prevention provides a convenient framework for searching for investment projects. Classification systems are arbitrary; the more useful systems provide an exhaustive categorization and focus on those variables which are important to the decision process. For example, variables used might relate to the subject of the loss, the stages of development of the loss, or the type of device used, as follows:

Subject of Loss	Development of loss	Reduction device
1 Human	1 Preconditions for loss	1 Physical
2 Physical capital	2 Prevention of loss	2 Procedural
3 Earnings	3 Early discovery of loss	3 Educational
	4 Limitation of loss/salvage	

The interaction of these variables gives $3 \times 4 \times 3 = 36$ different classes of loss prevention, as shown in Table 13-1. It is easy to expand this further by subdividing classes or by adding other variables for classification purposes. However, we will limit ourselves to an illustration in order that we may proceed with the development of our financial decision framework. This illustration is adapted from Doherty (in Carter and Doherty, 1974, Part 6.1) and uses development stage and device to form a 4×3 matrix.

LOSS REDUCTION AND THE DISTRIBUTION OF AGGREGATE LOSS

Consistent with the valuation approach to risk management, we are not interested in the effects of loss reduction on the distribution of aggregate loss per se. Rather, we are interested in the effect of loss reduction on the value of a firm, but analysis of the effect on the loss distribution will be instrumental in detecting the value effects.

Loss reduction may affect an individual exposure unit, several units, or all exposure units within a firm's portfolio. For example, sprinklers in one building will reduce loss expectancy in that building. However, there may also be some spillover effects to adjacent buildings. If a fire is controlled in the first location, it will not spread; thus conflagration hazard will be reduced. However, units that are distant from the original location may be entirely unaffected. In contrast, safety education may simultaneously affect all exposure units. In either case, our initial focus of attention is on the distribution of aggregate losses, and we must determine how changes in individual exposure units affect the aggregate distribution.

TABLE 13-1
SAMPLE CLASSIFICATION OF LOSS REDUCTION OPPORTUNITIES

Development of loss	1 Physical	2 Procedural	3 Educational
1 Preconditions	Isolation of hazardous processes Use of nonhazardous substitutes	Entry restrictions in hazardous areas Safety inspections	Courses in fire prevention/safety
2 Prevention	Overload switches, security locks Redundant systems	Notification of faults that could give rise to hazard	Courses in fire prevention/safety
3 Early discovery	Fire, burglar alarms	Security patrols Internal audits for embezzlement	Courses in fire prevention/safety
4 Limitation and salvage	Sprinkler systems First aid posts Replacement production facilities	High levels of inventory (interruption loss)	First aid training Evacuation drills

Recalling Chapter 4, the mean and standard deviation of the distribution of aggregate losses may be stated as follows:

$$E(L_p) = \sum_i E(L_i) \tag{13-1}$$

$$\sigma(L_p) = \left(\sum_i \sigma_i^2 + \sum_i \sum_{i \neq j} r_{i,j}\sigma_i\sigma_j \right)^{1/2} \tag{13-2}$$

where $E(L_i)$ = expected loss for unit i

σ_i = standard deviation for unit i

$r_{i,j}$ = correlation coefficient between units i and j

If an investment reduces the expected loss for one particular unit by some value $\Delta E(L_i)$, the expected value of the distribution of aggregate loss falls by the same value. This is easily shown by allowing the expected value of exposure unit 1 to fall by $\Delta E(L_1)$. The change in the expected value of the aggregate distribution $\Delta E(L_p)$ is

$$\Delta E(L_p) = \left[E(L_1) + \sum_{i=2}^{n} E(L_i) \right] - \left[E(L_1) - \Delta E(L_1) + \sum_{i=2}^{n} E(L_i) \right] \tag{13-3}$$

$$= \Delta E(L_1)$$

However, it should be clear from our study of the risk-reducing effects of diversification that the standard deviation of a portfolio is less than the "sum of the parts." Consequently, the fall in standard deviation will be less than the fall in the standard deviation of the individual exposure unit. Again, using the symbol Δ for "change in," we have

$$\Delta\sigma(L_p) = \left(\sigma_1^2 + 2\sum_{j=2}^{n} r_{1,j}\sigma_1\sigma_j + \sum_{i=2}^{n}\sum_{j=2}^{n} r_{i,j}\sigma_i\sigma_j \right)^{1/2}$$

$$- \left[(\sigma_1 - \Delta\sigma_1)^2 + 2\sum_{j=2}^{n} r_{1,j}(\sigma_1 - \Delta\sigma_1)\sigma_j + \sum_{i=2}^{n}\sum_{j=2}^{n} r_{i,j}\sigma_i\sigma_j \right]^{1/2} \qquad (13\text{-}4)$$

$$\neq \Delta\sigma_1 \qquad \text{if } r_{i,j} \neq 1$$

To illustrate these effects, consider a simple portfolio with three exposure units that have the following risk-return characteristics. A safety program in unit 1 changes the distribution for that unit as shown. Covariances are zero.

	Unit		
	1	2	3
Expected loss before safety program	20	30	10
Expected loss after safety program	10	30	10
Standard deviation before safety program	30	35	15
Standard deviation after safety program	20	35	15

Before loss, the portfolio mean and standard deviation, respectively, are

$$E(L_p) = 20 + 30 + 10 = 60$$
$$\sigma(L_p) = (30^2 + 35^2 + 15^2)^{1/2} = 48.48$$

And after the safety program, they are

$$E(L_p) = 10 + 30 + 10 = 50$$
$$\sigma(L_p) = (20^2 + 35^2 + 15^2)^{1/2} = 43.01$$

Thus the riskiness of the portfolio, as measured by the standard deviation, falls by less than that for the individual units affected.[1] This effect cautions us that if the risk-

---

[1]The reader may confirm that this statement does not hold if the correlation coefficients between individual risk units are unity. Using otherwise identical information, this is what happens:

Before: $\sigma(L_p) = [30^2 + 35^2 + 15^2 + 2(1)(30)(35) + 2(1)(30)(15) + 2(1)(35)(15)]^{1/2} = 80$

After: $\sigma(L_p) = [20^2 + 35^2 + 15^2 + 2(1)(20)(35) + 2(1)(20)(15) + 2(1)(35)(15)]^{1/2} = 70$

Therefore, $\Delta\sigma(L_p) = \Delta\sigma_i$.

reducing effects (as distinct from the reduction in expected value) is of benefit to a firm, the correct focus should be on the distribution of aggregate loss. By looking solely at the impact of the investment on the exposure unit concerned, we may overstate the reduction in risk. This problem does not arise when considering expected value.

In earlier analysis, the distribution of aggregate loss was compiled from separate distributions of loss frequency and loss severity. The data requirements for the assembly of these distributions included historical data both internal and external to the firm and perhaps subjective judgments reinforced by technical knowledge of the firm's operations and environment. It is helpful to consider the impact of loss reduction on the severity and frequency distributions and then to assemble these distributions into the aggregate distribution. Data for recording the impact of loss reduction may be available from a variety of sources. Examples are insurer records, safety organizations, academic research publications, and the publications of various government departments and agencies. Often these will permit the establishment of magnitude changes on the aggregate distribution or its component severity and frequency distributions. For example, it may be established that sprinklers reduce the expected value of loss by $x\%$. Such a reduction may be accompanied by any number of changes in the shape of the distribution, and judgments may have to be made. In other cases, the data sources on protected risks may permit direct estimation of the frequency and severity distributions, in which case, methods of convolution, curve fitting, simulation, etc. may be used to assemble the aggregate distribution. Sometimes no statistical data may be available, and subjective judgments must be made, hopefully reinforced by in-depth knowledge of the technological, economic, and legal factors involved. Documentation and analysis of data sources are of importance, although our main focus here is on the analysis of data and on financial decision making. We will therefore confine ourselves to an illustration of the potential effects of loss prevention.

EXAMPLE: RICE PAPER COMPANY

Rice Paper Company decided to install sprinklers. The loss frequency and security distributions before installation had been estimated from internal and external historical data and are shown below. Some industry data exist, and these, together with technical judgments, permit some estimates to be made of the loss distributions for the protected risk. The installation is not expected to influence the total number of fires, but it will cut down the frequency of medium to large fires. The revised distributions are also shown below.

Before Installation of Sprinklers

Loss frequency		Loss severity		
No. of losses	Probability	Severity range	Mean value	Probability
0	0.5	0–1,000	500	0.4
1	0.3	1,001–5,000	3,000	0.3
2	0.2	5,001–20,000	12,500	0.2
		20,001–50,000	35,000	0.1

After Installation of Sprinklers

Loss frequency		Loss severity		
No. of losses	**Probability**	**Severity range**	**Mean value**	**Probability**
0	0.5	0–1,000	500	0.6
1	0.3	1,001–5,000	3,000	0.23
2	0.2	5,001–20,000	12,500	0.13
		20,001–50,000	35,000	0.04

From these distributions, the distribution of aggregate losses is calculated using the convolution procedure described in Chapter 4. Also shown are summary statistics of the distribution.

Distribution of Aggregate Loss Before and After
Sprinkler Installation

Aggregate loss value	Probability	
	Before installation of sprinklers	**After installation of sprinklers**
0	0.5	0.5
500	0.12	0.18
1,000	0.032	0.072
3,000	0.09	0.069
3,500	0.048	0.0552
6,000	0.018	0.01058
12,500	0.06	0.039
13,000	0.032	0.0312
15,500	0.024	0.01196
25,000	0.008	0.00338
35,000	0.03	0.012
35,500	0.016	0.0096
38,000	0.012	0.00368
47,500	0.008	0.00208
70,000	0.002	0.00032
	1.0	1.0

Summary Statistics

	Before installation	After installation
Expected value (μ)	4,970	2,811
Standard deviation (σ)	10,249	6,973
Skewness (α_3)	2.717	3.820
Probability that loss exceeds value x^*		
0.1	$x = 21,052$	$x = 14,571$
0.05	$x = 29,620$	$x = 21,748$
0.01	$x = 49,405$	$x = 38,720$

*Using normal-power method (see Chapters 4 and 11). Since the skewness measure exceeds 2.0, these methods are unreliable.

The summary statistics show that the sprinkler installation reduces both the expected value of aggregate loss and the standard deviation. In this case, the skewness of the distribution (to the right) also increases. The combined impact is that the maximum probable loss estimates at the 90% level, 95% level, and 99% level all fall noticeably. Whereas previously the firm would be "90% confident" the losses would fall below $21,297, it is now "90% confident" that losses will be below $14,947, etc.

EARNINGS EFFECTS OF LOSS REDUCTION

Earnings Effects when Postloss Reinvestment Is Not Contemplated

The application of discounted cash flow techniques to loss-reduction decisions requires estimation of the impact of loss prevention on the expected cash flows generated by the firm and on the discount rate used for reducing cash flows to present values. Estimation of the loss-distribution changes is instrumental to this task. First, we consider the earnings effects when reinvestment is not contemplated. Here the firm will suffer a fall in earnings following loss, and the expected value of the fall in earnings must be calculated. The benefit of loss prevention will be a reduction in the expected value of lost earnings. It turns out that calculation of this value might be difficult, although we do outline the issues involved here.

The most direct effect of loss-reduction investment is to preserve resources that are used in the process of generating earnings for the firm. Loss reduction will reduce the probability that such resources will be depleted by a relevant peril, and/or it will reduce the severity of any loss that might occur. The most obvious measure of the annual expected value of this benefit is derived simply by taking the product of the expected reduction in aggregate loss and the estimated internal rate of return that would be foregone on those resources should they be destroyed. That is,

$$E(\Delta E) = [\Delta E(L_p)]\text{IRR}_{fg} \qquad (13\text{-}5)$$

where ΔE = change in earnings

IRR_{fg} = foregone internal rate of return

$E(L_p) = \sum_i p_i L_i$

This specification implicitly assumes that the foregone internal rate of return is constant across all possible sizes of loss. Such an assumption provides a convenient first approximation and may, indeed, be the only form of estimate that is permitted from available data. However, the foregone rate of return may be conditional on the size of the loss. If so, equation (13-5) will produce only a rough and ready approximation. Recalling the discussion of reinvestment criteria, it was accepted that the return foregone on lost resources may not be constant because of diminishing marginal productivity of investment or interdependency in the production process. To illustrate these effects, consider Figure 13-1. The curve *AB* represents the usual production transformation curve. The firm initially invests *AD*, which gives rise to 0*R* in period

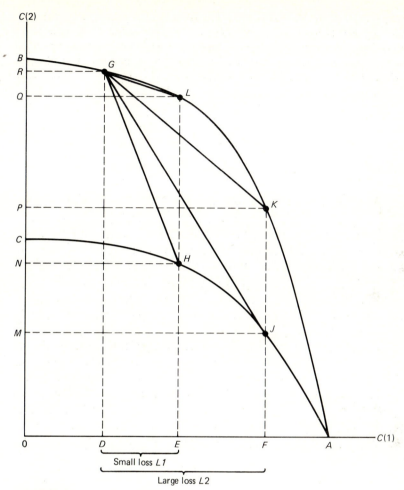

FIGURE 13-1

2 production. Now a loss occurs that destroys resources valued at DE on the horizontal axis (since we are not concerned here with measuring the value of equity, we will not bother to shift the curve horizontally to the left). If all resources are homogeneous, the production transformation curve will not change, but the production generated in period 2 will fall from $0R$ to $0Q$. The slope of the chord GL indicates the foregone rate of return on the lost capital resources. More precisely, the slope of GL (that is, S_1) equals

$$S_1 = -[1 + \text{IRR}_{fg}(L_1)] \tag{13-6}$$

where $\text{IRR}_{fg}(L_1)$ is the foregone internal rate of return on a loss of size L_1. Similarly, for a loss of size L_2, the foregone rate of return is shown by the slope of GK (that is, S_2) as follows:

$$S_2 = -[1 + IRR_{fg}(L_2)] \tag{13-7}$$

and so on. These foregone internal rates of return are not strictly marginal rates that are shown at different levels of investment by the slope of the transformation curve AB, but the chords do roughly estimate the shape of the curve over a given interval.

The expected loss of earnings can now be calculated as follows:

$$E(\Delta E) = \sum_{i=1}^{n} p_i(L_i)[IRR_{fg}(L_i)] \tag{13-8}$$

where p_i is the probability of loss of size L_i.

The problem is further complicated by the presence of production interdependencies. The loss not only affects the scale of activity, but also the mix of capital goods used in the production process. Now the production transformation curve shifts downward to AC. The production foregone on losses L_1 and L_2 is now RN and RM, respectively. The foregone internal rates of return for the expected losses are given by the negative of the slopes of GH and GJ. It turns out that, in this case, the slopes are reversed for the small and large losses, although this is not a general conclusion.

The benefit of loss-prevention activity is that the expected value of the loss of earnings will be reduced. The set of losses L_i will now have different probabilities as a result of the loss-reduction program. Thus the expected benefit of the loss-reduction program in terms of the savings in earnings loss is

$$\text{Expected annual benefit} = \sum_{i=1}^{n} \Delta p_i(L_i)[IRR_{fg}(L_i)] \tag{13-9}$$

The principles for calculating this value are reasonably straightforward, although, in practice, the data required may not be available. The risk manager will be doing well if he or she obtains a good estimate of the expected value of the reduction in aggregate loss, let alone the whole distribution. Furthermore, knowledge of the precise shape of the production transformation curve will rarely, if ever, be available. Use of the curve in this text has been to clarify ideas in order that we may begin to construct appropriate financial decision criteria. In reality, the information required to specify the curve would be very difficult to obtain because it would include precise knowledge of production possibilities at different levels of investment as well as complete knowledge of the demand for a firm's products. These considerations indicate that equation (13-5) provides the more feasible way of attributing value to the loss-prevention program, even if the estimate obtained is only an approximation.

Earnings Effects when Postloss Reinvestment Is Contemplated

When a firm is expected to reinvest following prospective future losses, the principle benefit of the loss-reduction program is the savings in expected financing costs. Ignoring interruption loss, the revenue of a firm will not directly suffer when a loss arises, since the firm will replace destroyed productive capacity. Therefore, a reduction in the expected value of loss will not affect the firm's earning potential. However, claims on earnings include the costs of financing such losses on a preloss or postloss basis, such as the payment of insurance premiums, interest payments on new debt, or the dilution effect of issuing new equity to finance the loss.

Consider the financing cost if debt is issued to finance the postloss reinvestment. Interest payment on that debt will reduce the earnings available to the shareholders. The stream of interest payments will reduce the value of the firm's equity, and according to our valuation approach, this is the ultimate burden of the loss. However, the increased leverage will also bid up the cost of equity. Thus the total effect arises from both the interest costs and the leverage effect, and we may consider these effects to be represented by the weighted average cost of capital rather than the interest rate. Conversely, financing the reinvestment by equity will reduce leverage, and the cost of equity will usually overstate the financing cost. Again, the cost can be represented by the weighted average cost of capital. Since the weighted average cost of capital is used to measure the postloss financing cost, and since it is the discount rate used to capitalize these costs, the financing cost is the value of the issue made to finance the reinvestment. This is equal to the replacement cost of the assets (ignoring transaction costs). Accordingly, if the loss-reduction program protects productive resources for a period of m years, the expected benefit of the program is the reduction in the expected value of loss (equal to the capitalized financing cost) for each year over the life of the project. This is formally stated as follows:

> With postloss financing, the expected benefit of loss reduction for year j is $\Delta E(L_j)$, for $j = 1, \ldots, m$. However, if the losses are insured, the expected annual benefit for each year j is simply the savings in the insurance premium, that is, expected benefit $= (\Delta P_j)$, for $j = 1, \ldots, m$, where p_j is the premium for year j.

The change in insurance premiums will depend on the type of premium structure operated by the insurer and on its procedures for collecting and using relevant information to measure loss probabilities. At one extreme, insurers may operate "schedule" rates, which specify reductions or additions to a base premium rate for features that affect the level of risk. Such a structure is typically used for fire insurance policies. If the loss reduction takes the form of a sprinkler installation or the installation of approved devices (such as fire doors), there will usually be a specified adjustment in the insurer's rating manual. In other cases, rate adjustment may depend on the technical judgment of an insurance surveyor based on an inspection. Conversely, the premium structure may fail to pick up all forms of loss reduction, either because the insurer does not recognize the benefit or because of the administrative simplicity of operating with a simple class rate that applies to large groups of insureds. For example, life insurance rates are based on age and sex such that a relevant change in occupation may not affect premiums. Normally, the benefit of loss reduction is a definite premium savings, which is not a contingent benefit but a certain reduction in the firm's costs. However, in some cases, the payback may be risky. A good example arises with workers' compensation insurance, which is usually rated on the loss experience of the firm. A loss-reduction program hopefully will improve loss experience, which will be rewarded by lower future premiums. This form of benefit is not certain, although it may be represented by its expected value. In addition to any savings in financing costs, loss reduction will bring further benefit if interruption loss is possible. The difficulties in placing a value on this benefit are usually severe. We will therefore avoid the complexities of the previous section and suggest that the expected benefit is roughly estimated as

$$\Delta E(E) = [\Delta E(L_j)]I/L_j \qquad j = 1, \ldots, m \qquad (13\text{-}10)$$

where I/L is the mean ratio of interruption loss to direct loss.

We are not aware of any reliable method by which the relationship between direct loss and interruption loss has been estimated. Ratios of I to L are sometimes encountered, and these are presumably based on insurers' claim payments. Taking into account the difficulties of estimating interruption claims on a "what might have been" basis and the further prospect that interruption losses from severe damage are rarely fully covered (inevitably so if interruption is permanent), it is clear that ratios that are encountered vary considerably. Consequently, the expected value of interruption loss, and how this might be reduced by loss-reduction programs, will be largely subjective.

LOSS REDUCTION AND THE COST OF CAPITAL

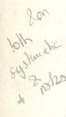

In addition to estimates of expected earnings, the application of discounted cash flow to loss-reductions decisions requires estimation of the effects of loss reduction on the cost of capital. This discussion parallels that of the effects of insurance on the cost of capital. Recall that we focused primarily on the effects of insurance on the systematic risk of a firm's earnings. This emphasis was dictated by the asset pricing model used to value a firm's securities. However, because of such inefficiencies as the transaction costs of diversification, unsystematic risk might also have some effect. Unsystematic risk is mainly of significance to firms whose ownership claims are highly concentrated in the hands of those having other interests in the firm (e.g., employment interest) and to firms whose securities have no clear secondary market. We shall concentrate attention on the systematic risk effects of loss reduction, having noted the special cases.

The β value, or systematic risk measure for a firm's earnings, is the weighted average of the β values of the component activities. Thus earnings E are defined in relation to the business and risk management components E_X and E_{RM}, respectively:

$$E = E_X + E_{RM} \qquad \text{where } E_{RM} \leq 0 \qquad (13\text{-}11)$$

and

$$\beta_E = \omega_X \beta_X + \omega_{RM} \beta_{RM} \qquad (13\text{-}12)$$

where the weights ω_i are defined as the proportion of total expected earnings represented by each component. Therefore,

$$\beta_E = \left(\frac{E_X}{E_X - E_{RM}}\right)\beta_X + \left(\frac{E_{RM}}{E_X - E_{RM}}\right)\beta_{RM} \qquad (13\text{-}13)$$

The cost of capital for a firm will be determined by the premiums that investors place on the levels of systematic risk in the firm's component activities. The systematic risk of the component activities combines to determine the riskiness of the firm's earnings. If we assume that the simple capital asset pricing model correctly describes security equilibrium prices, the following relationship determines the firm's cost of capital, which here is referred to as r_E:

$$E(r_E) = r_f + \beta_E[E(r_m) - r_f] \qquad (13\text{-}14)$$

where r_f = the risk-free rate

r_m = the return on the market portfolio

In addition, the components r_X and r_{RM} (which are discount rates appropriate to E_X and E_{RM}) are determined by the same relationship. That is,

$$E(r_{RM}) = r_f + \beta_{RM}[E(r_m) + r_f] \qquad (13\text{-}15)$$

Since earnings and discount rates can be broken down in this manner, we can isolate the loss-reduction decision. The risk-return characteristics of the loss-reduction program will add value to the firm if the added value of the cash flows, discounted at the rate r_{RM}, is positive. Alternatively, the risk management program will add value if its internal rate of return exceeds the rate appropriate to the activity's β value, that is, r_{RM}.

The values of β_{RM} and r_{RM} depend on the type of risk management program adopted. At the simplest level, if full insurance is purchased, the benefit will take the form of a known premium reduction. Accordingly, β will be 0, and the discount rate to be used will be the risk-free rate. Alternatively, if the loss is uninsured, the discount rate will be determined by the impact of losses on the earnings of the firm and on the systematic risk of those displaced earnings. We now discuss the application of capital budgeting techniques, and here we will elaborate on the discounting procedures appropriate to different risk management strategies.

A cautionary note is needed on the sign of the risk management β value before continuing. Suppose losses are not insured. The β value will be determined by the systematic risk of aggregate losses. If losses are positively correlated with the market portfolio, β will be positive. This feature is desirable for investors, because high losses will tend to offset otherwise high investment returns, and vice versa. This will smooth portfolio returns. However, we will need to be careful in deriving the respective discount rates from the loss β value because we must discount both positive and negative cash flows.

A CAPITAL BUDGETING FRAMEWORK
FOR LOSS-REDUCTION DECISIONS

The benefit from loss reduction includes indirect effects (such as reduction in prospective interruption loss and ancillary benefits to labor contracts) and the direct effects that arise from the preservation of productive resources. The direct benefits take the form of savings in the preloss or postloss financing costs for such losses or, if reinvestment is not contemplated, savings in the earnings flowing from the productive resources affected. First, we examine the use of capital budgeting analysis for the direct benefits. This is conducted for insured losses, postloss financing, and losses for which no reinvestment is contemplated, respectively. We then show how indirect benefits may be included.

Insured Losses

The capital budgeting framework to be used for loss-reduction decisions turns out to be a two-stage process in some cases. However, a simpler form is found when insurance is purchased. We will develop the framework without interruption loss, which will be introduced later. When insurance is purchased, the destroyed resources can be replaced from the proceeds of the policy. Consequently, destroyed resources can be replaced without loss of earnings. However, the insurance premium has to be paid, and the firm will benefit if the safety program causes the premium to fall. If the lifetime of the safety device is m years, the premium P should be reduced over a similar time period. The net present value (NPV) of the benefit of the loss-reduction program with insurance can be represented by the familiar discounting formula:

$$\text{NPV} = \sum_{j=1}^{m} \frac{\Delta P_j}{(1 + r)^j} \tag{13-16}$$

The discount rate to use is fairly straightforward. The premium normally is not a risky cash flow, and therefore, the reduction in premium also may be considered to be risk-free. Unless it can be argued that future premium reductions are uncertain for some reason, it is appropriate to use the risk-free rate of interest. A good example of uncertain premium reductions can be found in experience rating. Here, premiums are related to actual loss experience. Thus a loss-reduction program should, hopefully, improve loss experience, resulting in a potential premium reduction. However, claims do arise in a random fashion, and the premium reduction will therefore be risky. An appropriate risk-adjusted discount rate is now required. We will illustrate the riskless case here for simplicity.

EXAMPLE: SAFE HARBOR, INC.

Safe Harbor, Inc. fully insures its plant, which is used for manufacture of security equipment. The distribution of aggregate loss from fire and related perils is summarized by the following data:

$$\text{Expected loss } (\mu) = \$20,000$$
$$\text{Standard deviation } (\sigma) = \$30,000$$

The insurer is assumed to correctly estimate these values and calculates the premium P on the formula

$$P = 200 + 1.2\mu + 0.1\sigma$$

The firm must decide whether or not to undertake a loss-reduction program that would reduce both the expected loss and the standard deviation by 25%. The impact of the program on the premium will be recorded by the operation of the same formula. The cost of the program is $40,000, and it will have a lifetime of 10 years. The firm's weighted average cost of capital is 10%, and the risk-free rate is 7%.

Solution

The relevant cash flows comprise the initial cost of the program and the premium reductions over the project life. The premium reduction for each year is calculated by the following formula:

(Premium without loss reduction) $-$ (premium with loss reduction)
  $= [200 + 1.2(20,000) + 0.1(30,000)] - [200 + 1.2(15,000) + 0.1(22,500)] = \$6750$

Notice that the premium reduction exceeds the reduction in the expected value of the loss. This is so because the premium includes a loading related to both μ and σ.
  Since the premium reduction is riskless, it may be discounted at the 7% risk-free rate. Thus the NPV of the project is

$$\text{NPV} = -40,000 + \frac{6750}{1 + 0.7} + \frac{6750}{(1 + 0.7)^2} + \cdots + \frac{6750}{(1 + 0.7)^{10}}$$

Using the annuity table at the end of the book, an annuity of $1 per year for 10 years at 7% has a present value of $7.024. Therefore,

$$\text{NPV} = -40,000 + 6750(7.024) = \$7412$$

Since this value is positive, the firm should undertake the project.

In this example, the premium reduction was calculated from a mathematical rating formula. In practice, such a precise formula is not likely to be used and even less likely to be known by the insured. The purpose of using such a formula in this example was to show the impact of premium structures that incorporate a proportionate loading on the expected value of loss. The common use of target-loss ratios to set rates does imply the use of such structures, although, in fact, loss information is usually not of sufficient quality to allow use of a precise formula. In practice, the insured often will be quoted a premium reduction that broadly reflects collective experience over similar types of risk. In this case, the insured would simply be given a value of, say, $6750 for the premium reduction and would use this value in the calculation.

Losses for which Postloss Financing Is Contemplated

This case is more complicated than the insurance example. The earnings effects must take into account the effects of loss reduction on the incidence of losses and the flow of financing costs after the loss to service the debt or equity.

Stage 1 When a loss arises, a financing decision is invoked, since reinvestment is considered to be desirable. The burden of financing is spread over the years following the loss. However, the financing costs can be discounted backwards to give a capitalized value of the time of the loss. With either debt or equity, the appropriate discount rate is the weighted average cost of capital, as discussed earlier. Thus, at the time of loss, the financing costs have a capitalized value equal to the sum raised. In turn, this sum will be equal to the replacement costs of the destroyed assets. Therefore, loss reduction carries an expected benefit equal to the expected value of the reduction in the replacement costs of the lost assets for each year of the lifetime of the project.

Stage 2 We can therefore treat the cash flows as the savings in the expected value of the distribution of aggregate loss. However, loss incidence is risky and requires a discount rate that reflects the systematic risk of the loss distribution. For example, if losses are positively correlated with the market index, then loss-reduction devices have more to "bite on" when the market index is high. It would therefore be expected that the benefits of the reduction program also are positively correlated with the market index. An appropriate discount rate can be derived from the capital asset pricing model by first deriving the loss β value, that is, β_L. The appropriate model is

$$E(r_L) = r_f + \beta_L[E(r_m) - r_f] \tag{13-17}$$

where r_L = the discount rate for losses

r_f = the risk-free rate

$E(r_m)$ = the expected return on the market portfolio

The respective stages in the calculation of the NPV of loss reduction are shown schematically in Figure 13-2. The NPV of the benefit of the loss-reduction program is shown as the present value of the reductions in the annual expected value of aggregate loss discounted at the risk-adjusted rate appropriate for the loss β value.

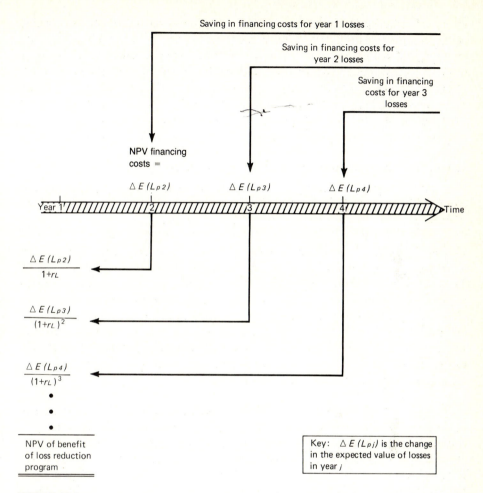

FIGURE 13-2

EXAMPLE: ANN TEAK COMPANY

Ann Teak Company manufactures hardwood furniture. The firm is one of a number of companies forming a diversified group and having common ownership. Group policy is to self-insure up to limits well beyond the value of AT's assets. Losses are to be financed by external financing. The aggregate loss distribution for relevant perils has an expected value and standard deviation of

$$\mu = \$75,000 \text{ per year}$$
$$\sigma = \$100,000 \text{ per year}$$

In view of the low existing level of leverage, reinvestment following loss will probably be financed by debt, the most likely scenario being 5-year debt at whatever rates are current at the time of loss.

A sprinkler system is contemplated, which, if installed, will reduce the expected value of losses from $75,000 to $30,000, with the standard deviation falling to $50,000. The systematic risk of the loss distribution is indicated by the β value, which is estimated to be 0.3. This positive β indicates that losses (which are a cost of the firm and consequently have a negative weight) are positively correlated with the market index. The risk-free rate is 8%, and the market portfolio is expected to deliver a 12% rate of return. The cost of the installation is $350,000. The life of the installation is expected to be 20 years. Should it be adopted?

Solution

The reduction in the expected financing costs for prospective losses may be equated with the value of the issues that will be raised to finance the losses. The target issue value will be the replacement cost of the destroyed assets. Thus the expected cash flows are the annual savings in the expected value of loss valued at replacement cost, that is, $45,000 per year for 20 years. The appropriate discount rate is determined by the systematic risk present in the distribution of losses. This is calculated as follows:

$$E(r_L) = r_f + \beta_L[E(r_m) - r_f]$$
$$= 008 + 0.3(0.12 - 0.08)$$
$$= 0.092$$

Thus the NPV of the program is

$$NPV = -\$350,000 + \sum_{i=1}^{20} \frac{45,000}{(1 + 0.092)^i}$$

The discounting table for annuities gives only values at percentage point intervals. Interpolating from the 9 and 10% values for an annuity of 20 years gives a value of 9.006. Therefore,

$$NPV = -\$350,000 + \$45,000(9.006) = \$55,270$$

The project should be undertaken.

Losses for which Reinvestment Is Not Contemplated

When reinvestment is not contemplated, the relevant cash flows are the earnings derived from the productive resources affected by the loss-reduction program. Since contingent losses will be fewer or less severe, the earnings from these resources are preserved. The calculation of this benefit again is a two-stage procedure that can be summarized as follows:

Stage 1   The loss-reduction program will affect the distribution of aggregate loss for each year in the lifetime of the project. This distribution is specified in terms of resource values. Thus we need to calculate the expected earnings flows that will arise from the resources affected by the program for each year in which an effect on the aggregate loss distribution is present. If $E(E_{j,k})$ is the expected earnings loss in year k resulting from an expected loss of resources $E(L_j)$ in year j, the earnings effects of loss prevention can be represented as follows:

$$\Delta E(L_1) \rightarrow [\Delta E(E_{1,1}), \Delta E(E_{1,2}), \ldots]$$
$$\Delta E(L_2) \rightarrow [\Delta E(E_{2,2}), \Delta E(E_{2,3}), \ldots]$$
$$\Delta E(L_j) \rightarrow [\Delta E(E_{j,j}), \Delta E(E_{j,j+1}), \ldots]$$

and so on until the end of the project life. These earnings will be subject to the usual business risks inherent in the market activity of the firm. Accordingly, they should be discounted at the rate appropriate for the firm's overall earnings risk, that is, the WACC. Thus for any future year j during the life time of the loss reduction project, the capitalized value of future earnings benefit will be

$$V_{E,j} = \sum_{k=1}^{p-j} \frac{\Delta E(E_{j,k})}{(1 + r_W)^k} = \sum_{k=1}^{p-j} \frac{\Delta E(L_j) \text{IRR}_{fg}}{(1 + r_W)^k} \qquad (13\text{-}18)$$

where r_W is the WACC. The expected productive life of the loss-reduction project is m years. This will normally be less than or equal to the life of the productive resources affected, which is denoted by p in equation (13-18). For example, a fire-resisting wall may last the lifetime of a building, but a burglar alarm system may have to be replaced and updated every few years. If the life of the productive resources exceeds that of the loss-reduction project, earnings benefits may still accrue after the safety device has ceased to afford protection. Losses that might otherwise have arisen within the life of the protective device would have given rise to earnings effects spreading beyond the life of the device.

Stage 2 This involves the discounting of the values $V_{E,j}$ to the present to derive the NPV of the project. The distribution of $V_{E,j}$ will reflect the stochastic incidence of losses. If there is systematic risk to the incidence of losses (i.e., the β value is not equal to zero), the discount rate should include an appropriate risk premium. The appropriate rate r_L was determined when looking at the effect of loss reduction on the assumption that postloss financing was not contemplated.

The two stages of the process are illustrated in Figure 13-3. The upper portion shows the capitalization of earnings at the years for which resource losses were affected. The appropriate discount rate, the WACC, reflects the risk inherent in these earnings. The lower segment shows further discounting from the years in which the distribution of aggregate loss will be affected by the program to give a net present value. The

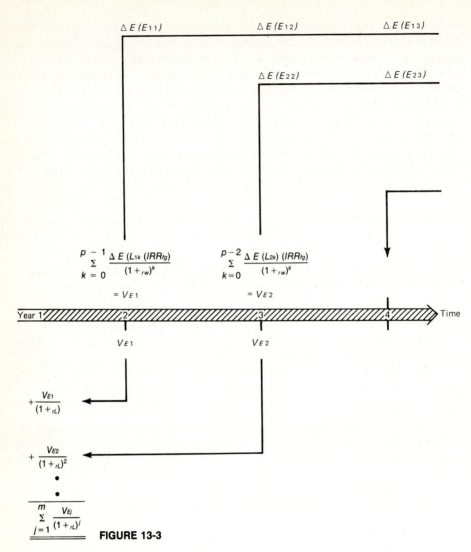

FIGURE 13-3

appropriate discount rate here reflects the systematic risk in the distribution of losses. The net present value of the loss-reduction program may therefore be stated as

$$\sum_{j=1}^{m} \frac{\sum_{k=0}^{p-j} [\Delta E(L_{j,k}) IRR_{fg}/(1 + r_W)^k]}{(1 + r_L)^j} \tag{13-19}$$

We have mentioned the difficulties in calculating the value of lost earnings because of the fact that the internal rate of return foregone on destroyed resources may not be constant. Equations (13-18) and (13-19) do simplify the issue by asssuming such a constant return. In view of the error built in by this simplifying assumption, it is useful to note that we can establish an upper boundary to this benefit by comparison with the postloss financing example. A firm would not choose to reinvest after loss if the present-value earnings generated from the reinvestment were less than the costs of reinvestment. Clearly, the expression in the numerator of equation (13-19) is the savings in earnings resulting from the protected resources. This cannot exceed the cost of reinvestment. Consequently, the benefit calculated for loss reduction under the assumption of no reinvestment cannot exceed that calculated under the assumption of reinvestment with postloss financing.

An example is now used to illustrate the calculation of the benefit of loss-reduction investment under conditions where postloss reinvestment is not comtemplated.

EXAMPLE: DYING EMBER FIREWORKS, INC.

Dying Ember Fireworks, Inc. has faced declining demand for its products over recent years. Owing to a large differential between the disposal value of its assets and the replacement costs, the company continues to operate but correctly assesses that replacement of assets following a major loss would be economically unsound. Nonetheless, the company still considers the prospect of further loss-reducing devices in view of the high degree of hazard involved. The cost of such protection is $6000, and this will reduce the expected value of losses to physical resources (measured at replacement cost) by $3000 per year for each of the next 10 years. The foregone internal rate of return on destroyed resources is estimated to be 8%, and the firm's weighted average cost of capital is 14%. Losses of physical capital are estimated to be uncorrelated with the market index (that is, $\beta_L = 0$). The risk-free rate is 8%, and the expected return on the market portfolio is 12%.

The first stage requires calculation of the earnings flows that are saved from the reduction in resource losses in each year of the project life. The appropriate discount rate is determined by the earnings risk, that is, the WACC, which is 14%. Therefore, since

$$V_{E,j} = \sum_{k=0}^{p-j} \frac{\Delta E(L_j)\text{IRR}_{fg}}{(1 + r_w)^k}$$

the following discounted earnings values at times 1 to 10 occur:

$$V_{E,1} = \sum_{j=0}^{9} \frac{3000(0.08)}{(1 + 0.14)^j} = 240(1 + 4.946) = 1427$$

$$V_{E,2} = \sum_{j=0}^{8} \frac{3000(0.08)}{(1 + 0.14)^j} = 240(1 + 4.639) = 1353$$

$$V_{E,3} = \sum_{j=0}^{7} \frac{3000(0.08)}{(1 + 0.14)^j} = 240(1 + 4.288) = 1269$$

$$V_{E,4} = \sum_{j=0}^{6} \frac{3000(0.08)}{(1 + 0.14)^j} = 240(1 + 3.889) = 1173$$

$$V_{E,5} = \sum_{j=0}^{5} \frac{3000(0.08)}{(1 + 0.14)^j} = 240(1 + 3.433) = 1064$$

$$V_{E,6} = \sum_{j=0}^{4} \frac{3000(0.08)}{(1 + 0.14)^j} = 240(1 + 2.914) = 939$$

$$V_{E,7} = \sum_{j=0}^{3} \frac{3000(0.08)}{(1 + 0.14)^j} = 240(1 + 2.322) = 797$$

$$V_{E,8} = \sum_{j=0}^{2} \frac{3000(0.08)}{(1 + 0.14)^j} = 240(1 + 1.647) = 635$$

$$V_{E,9} = \sum_{j=0}^{1} \frac{3000(0.08)}{(1 + 0.14)^j} = 240(1 + 0.877) = 450$$

$$V_{E,10} = \sum_{j=0}^{0} \frac{3000(0.08)}{(1 + 0.14)^j} = 240$$

Since these values are capitalized at times 1 to 10, they must be commonly discounted to the present time in order to value the project. The appropriate discount rate reflects the systematic risk inherent in the distribution of losses. Since systematic risk is zero, we can use the risk-free rate. Thus the NPV of the project is

$$-6000 + \frac{1427}{(1 + 0.08)} + \frac{1353}{(1 + 0.08)^2} + \frac{1269}{(1 + 0.08)^3} + \frac{1173}{(1 + 0.08)^4} + \frac{1064}{(1 + 0.08)^5}$$
$$+ \frac{939}{(1 + 0.08)^6} + \frac{797}{(1 + 0.08)^7} + \frac{635}{(1 + 0.08)^8} + \frac{450}{(1 + 0.08)^9} + \frac{240}{(1 + 0.08)^{10}} = 811$$

Therefore, the firm should proceed.

Indirect Benefits of Loss Reduction

Examples of indirect benefits mentioned earlier include improvement in labor productivity as a result of safety devices, improved bargaining over wage contracts because of safety, higher demand for the firm's product, and reductions in the expected value of interruption loss following the direct loss. The various benefits can be represented as cash flows that will arise during the life of the project (e.g., worker productivity may only improve while safety devices are in operation) or will spread beyond the life of the loss-reduction device (e.g., resource losses prevented during the life of the project will result in prospective interruption loss savings that may spread beyond the project life). The two-stage procedures discussed earlier can be used to value the indirect benefits:

Stage 1   The loss-reduction project has a life of m years. For each year j in which the project affects the distribution of aggregate loss, the capitalized value of these earnings benefits is calculated. The suggested discount rate is the WACC.

Stage 2   This stage involves the discounting of the stage 1 capitalized values using the rate r_L to give an NPV for the indirect benefits. The value derived from this process may be added to the NPV of direct benefits to provide an appropriate estimate of total benefits for the project.

Estimation of indirect benefits usually will pose problems. Data on which to base estimates will often be sparse and perhaps not directly relevant to the risk concerned. However, the failure to consider these benefits is equivalent to making the arbitrary assumption that they have zero value. This implied zero estimate does not resolve the uncertainty surrounding the value of these benefits. Indeed, the degree of estimation error will be lower with a "best guess" than with no guess at all, even though the best guess may be based largely on subjective judgment. We now show, by example, how such values may be incorporated into the decision framework.

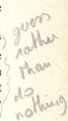
(margin annotation: guess rather than do nothing)

EXAMPLE: SOPORIFIC DRUG COMPANY

Soporific Drug Company is faced with a proposal to improve the quality control of its product. This involves replacement of equipment, new sampling and testing procedures for products taken off the line, and the purchase of new scanning equipment to detect faulty products. Direct productivity improvements are not expected. The motivation for this proposed investment is to guard againt potentially costly liability suits for defective products and against any fall in demand that might follow from the media exposure given to product defects. Given the competitive structure of the drug market, such interruption loss may well be severe, since rival firms may step up promotion of their own products to capture the market share of the distressed firm.

The project will reduce the expected value of liability losses by $22,000 per year. However, Soporific is insured for product defects with high liability limits, although there remains a possibility that a loss of catastrophic nature would exceed these limits. The direct benefits of the investment are estimated as follows:

1 Reduction in annual insurance premium quoted by insurer = $20,000
2 Reduction in the expected value of catastrophic losses that are self insured[2] = $1000

The uninsured losses are simply treated as a loss in equity value for the years in question. The direct benefits are expected to accrue for each of the 5 years of the project life.

Interruption loss may spread well beyond the life of the project. If a major loss were to arise, the adverse publicity would tarnish the consumer image of the product and the firm. Even if this effect is short-lived, competitors may increase their market share during the period following loss, causing a major shift in the structure of the industry. Such shifts may be permanent, and they may leave Soporific well down in the league table of competing drug manufacturers. The best guess for such an interruption loss is given as follows: For any loss in a future year j, the firm would suffer an expected loss of earnings of 0.02 of the value of the loss from that year forward, in perpetuity. We must consider such earnings consequences for each of the 5 years of expected life of the project. The consequences for each year j can be capitalized to that year using the WACC.

---

[2]The firm could not survive such losses and would be forced into liquidation. Consequently, the maximum liability to the owners is the value of their equity in view of the limited-liability nature of the company. This estimate is calculated by multiplying the probability of catastrophic loss by the value of equity.

The firm's WACC is 12% (reflecting an earnings β value of unity). The risk-free rate is 6%, and the return expected on the market portfolio is 12%. Historical data for the drug industry indicates a slight negative correlation between losses and the market index; the appropriate β value is 0.1. The cost of the protection system is $75,000.

The solution to this problem is complicated by the choice of discount rates. To capitalize the interruption loss to each of the 5 years in the life of the project, we can use a rate appropriate to the riskiness of those earnings. These capitalized values can then be reduced to a present value at a rate that reflects the systematic risk of losses. The uninsured catastrophic loss also poses a potential burden to the firm that exhibits the systematic risk of losses, and this too should be reduced to a present value at a rate determined by the loss β value. However, premium reductions are constant and may be discounted at the risk-free rate. These considerations imply that we should discount each effect separately.

Interruption Loss:

The capitalized values of earnings for each year of the project are denoted $I_{E,j}$, for $j = 1, \ldots,$ 5. Therefore,

$$I_{E,1} = \sum_{k=0}^{\infty} \frac{22,000(0.02)}{(1 + 0.12)^k} = 440 + \frac{440}{0.12} = 4107$$

$$I_{E,2} = \sum_{k=0}^{\infty} \frac{22,000(0.02)}{(1 + 0.12)^k} = 440 + \frac{440}{0.12} = 4107$$

$$I_{E,3} = \sum_{k=0}^{\infty} \frac{22,000(0.02)}{(1 + 0.12)^k} = 440 + \frac{440}{0.12} = 4107$$

$$I_{E,4} = \sum_{k=0}^{\infty} \frac{22,000(0.02)}{(1 + 0.12)^k} = 440 + \frac{440}{0.12} = 4107$$

$$I_{E,5} = \sum_{k=0}^{\infty} \frac{22,000(0.02)}{(1 + 0.12)^k} = 440 + \frac{440}{0.12} = 4107$$

To reduce these values to the present, we must calculate the risk-adjusted rate appropriate to the systematic risk of losses. That is,

$$E(r_L) = r_f + \beta_L[E(r_m) - r_f]$$
$$= 0.06 - 0.1[0.12 - 0.06] = 0.54$$

The NPV of interruption is

$$\sum_{j=1}^{5} \frac{4107}{(1 + 0.054)^j} = 4107(4.2822) = 17,587$$

(Since the discounting table only shows percentage points, we used interpolation.)

Uninsured Catastrophic Loss:

$$\sum_{j=1}^{5} \frac{1000}{(1 + 0.054)^j} = 1000(4.2822) = 4282$$

Premium Savings:

$$\sum_{j=1}^{5}\frac{20,000}{(1 + 0.06)^j} = 20,000(4.212) = 84,240$$

Thus, the net present value (NPV) of the project is

$$-75,000 + 17,587 + 4282 + 84,240 = 31,109$$

The firm should adopt the project.

Some Issues in Capital Budgeting

In using capital budgeting to analyze loss-reduction decisions, our main concern has been to concentrate on features that are peculiar to the loss-reduction decision. Attention has been focused on the two-stage framework, in which asset values are used only to derive earnings effects. We have superimposed this two-stage framework onto the net present value (NPV) formula without debate of the issues and controversies that surround the use of discounted cash flow. A full debate of these issues is not our purpose, and the reader is referred to works cited at the end of this chapter. However, it may be useful to refer to some of the main issues and problems which the interested reader can pursue as needed.

The generic discounted cash flow (DCF) methodology includes the NPV formulation and the internal rate of return (IRR). The IRR is defined as the implicit discount rate for which relevant cash flows have a zero net present value. In many cases, the use of IRR and NPV will give the same results. That is,

$$NPV > 0 \quad \text{implies that} \quad IRR > k$$

where k is the cost of capital. Consequently, there should be no ambiguity in making investment decisions. However, confusions and conflicts can arise. In some cases, the sequence of cash flows changes sign more than once. For example, consider the sequence $-4000, 25,000, -25,000$. This sequence has two internal rates of return, 25 and 400%. There is no consensus on how such problems should be tackled, except, perhaps, to avoid the problem by using NPV. Whether such problems are likely to arise with the loss-reduction investments contemplated here is an empirical issue. Typically, one might expect that loss-reduction investments involve an initial capital cost with subsequent cash flows (savings in earnings loss minus maintenance costs) being positive. However, one might also envision projects that have terminal costs of dismantling or demolition.

Another issue that can arise is that of conflicting rankings between NPV and IRR due to differences in the pattern of cash flows over time between two competing projects. Examples are common in basic business finance and capital budgeting texts.

This problem arises because of differences in the reinvestment assumptions used in the two methods. The use of NPV carries an implicit assumption that all cash flows generated by the project can be reinvested at the discount rate used for the calculation. In practice, this assumed reinvestment rate is probably conservative. In contrast, the IRR implicity assumes that generated cash flows can be reinvested at the internal rate of return derived. If the project is acceptable, this assumed reinvestment rate must be more ambitious than the cost-of-capital rate assumed with NPV. However, there is no general theory that tells us which rate is better. One way of avoiding the conflict is to use terminal values rather than present values and feed in explicit reinvestment assumptions.

A final issue worth noting here concerns real and nominal values. It is often easier to make forecasts in real terms. A forecast in nominal values involves joint prediction of real values and a rate of inflation; it is often simpler to attempt to forecast only the former. However, if expected cash flows are specified in real values, care must be taken to ensure that the discount rate used is also a real rate. The rates observed and quoted are usually nominal rates, and consequently, the inflation component must be extracted. The DCF methodology will, in fact, accommodate either nominal or real values, subject only to consistency. If cash flows are real, real discount rates should be used. If cash flows are nominal, nominal discount rates should be used.

In mentioning these complications, our purpose is simply to put the reader on guard. Certainly anyone wishing to use DCF should explore these issues in more depth.

DECISION TREES

Interdependent Decisions

From the capital budgeting analysis it is apparent that the benefits of loss reduction depend on the type of loss financing contemplated by a firm. As laid out, it appears that the financing decision may already have been made and that the firm must calculate the benefits of loss prevention given the financing decision. There is no intention to give either decision priority; they are interdependent. The financing decision can affect the loss reduction decision, and vice versa. One technique that might be used to some effect when decisions are interdependent is the decision tree. A decision tree can be used to lay out a sequence of interdependent decisions and to provide a visual presentation of the outcomes that might flow from different combinations of decisions. The decision tree will not introduce any new fundamental method, but it will provide a readily understood analysis of possible consequences.

Consider a simple decision to be made by a firm: whether or not to install a sprinkler system to protect its premises. The benefit of the sprinkler system is that if a fire arises, it may be effective in controlling and/or extinguishing the fire. Let us say that there are three possible outcomes: (1) no fire arises, (2) a fire occurs but is controlled by the sprinklers, and (3) a fire arises and it is not controlled. If the sprinkler system is not installed, there are two possible outcomes: (1) a fire does not arise, and (2) a fire does arise, but since there are no sprinklers, the fire causes major damage. Of course, we can generalize to consider multiple fires within any period, and we can

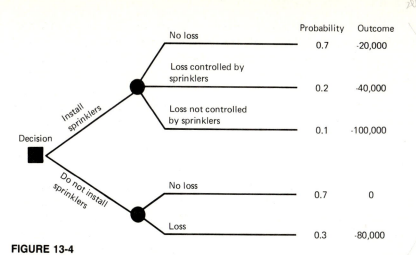

several years → more square + adjust with k if over several years

FIGURE 13-4

consider the effects over successive periods into the future. This set of consequences can be represented in a simple tree. The tree starts with a decision whether or not to install the sprinkler system. All decisions are represented by a square, and the one shown in Figure 13-4 has two branches leading off, which represent the two possible choices. Each branch ends in a circle, which represents a set of chance events or risky outcomes. The branches leading from the circle represent the possible outcomes. This gives a total of five possible outcomes depending both on the decision and on chance events. Each of the chance events may be given a probability and a value. The probabilities from each chance circle must sum to unity. In this case, the values are calculated by assuming that the installation costs $20,000 and that fires cost $20,000 if controlled and $80,000 if uncontrolled. Thus if sprinklers are chosen and a controlled fire ensues, the outcome is −($20,000 + $20,000) = −$40,000.

The framework is now extended to look at the joint decision concerning the installation of sprinklers and the form of loss financing (assuming that the firm will choose to reinvest). In addition, we extend the diagram to consider the impact of losses over a second period, and this is represented by a second set of circles to the right of the original set of risky outcomes. The new diagram is shown in Figure 13-5. The branches from the second set of squares (moving to the right) represent the possible decisions to be made:

1 Sprinklers and preloss financing
2 Sprinklers and postloss financing
3 No sprinklers and preloss financing
4 No sprinklers and postloss financing

We will now develop this example using probabilities, loss data, and the ideas on choice of discount rate developed earlier. The basic information is summarized as follows:

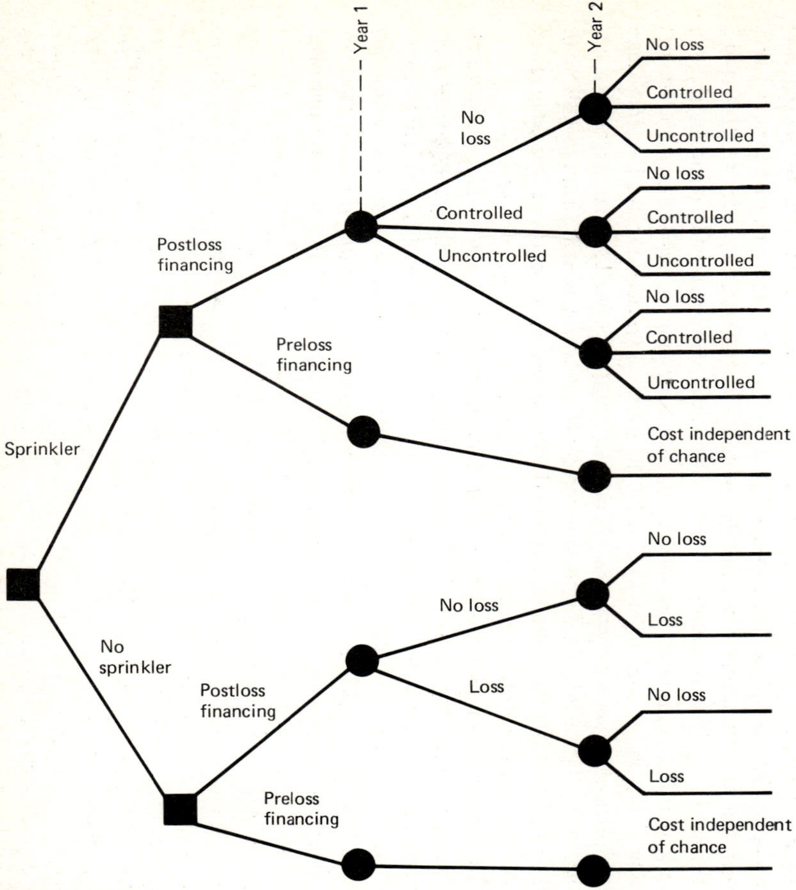

	PROBABILITY	NPV	(calculation)	Year 1 branch	Year 2 branch
	.49	-20,000	-20,000	No loss	No loss
	.14	-36,529	-20,000 -20,000/1.1^2	No loss	Controlled
	.07	-86,116	-20,000 -80,000/1.1^2	No loss	Uncontrolled
	.14	-38,182	-20,000 -20,000/1.1	Controlled	No loss
	.04	-54,711	-20,000 -20,000/1.1 -20,000/1.1^2	Controlled	Controlled
	.02	-104,298	-20,000 -20,000/1.1 -80,000/1.1^2	Controlled	Uncontrolled
	.07	-92,727	-20,000 -80,000/1.1	Uncontrolled	No loss
	.02	-109,257	-20,000 -80,000/1.1 -20,000/1.1^2	Uncontrolled	Controlled
Postloss financing	.01	-158,843	-20,000 -80,000/1.1 -80,000/1.1^2	Uncontrolled	Uncontrolled
	1.0	-40,827			
Preloss financing	1.0	-45,310	-20,000 -13,200 -13,200/1.09		Cost independent of chance
	.49	0		No loss	No loss
	.21	66,116	-80,000/1.1^2	No loss	Loss
	.21	72,727	-80,000/1.1	Loss	No loss
Postloss financing	.09	138,843	-80,000/1.1 -80,000/1.1^2	Loss	Loss
	1.0	-41,653			
Preloss financing	1.0	-50,620	-26,400 -26,400/1.09		Cost independent of chance

(Sprinkler / No sprinkler decision)

FIGURE 13-5

392

Cost of installation	20,000
Probability of loss (independent of protection) per year	0.3 per year
Probability that loss is controlled by sprinklers (if loss arises)	0.667
Probability that loss is not controlled (if loss arises)	0.333
Probability of no loss	0.7 per year
Cost of controlled loss	20,000
Cost of uncontrolled loss	80,000
Insurance premium without sprinklers	26,400
Insurance premium with sprinklers	13,200
Risk-free rate	0.09
Equilibrium rate for loss (assumes $\beta_L > 0$)	0.1

This problem is set in only two time periods, although, in reality, a sprinkler installation would last much longer. It may be imagined that by extending the time frame, the proliferation of branches becomes impressive. The explosion of possibilities can be handled easily by a computer, but the drawing of the tree rapidly becomes intricate. With the two-period model, we can first assign probabilities to the various terminal branches on the right. In so doing, we will make clear our assumption that the probable outcome in the second period is independent of what has happened previously. This means that for any branch, we can derive the final probability as the product of the probabilities of the branches leading to that final outcome. For example, the top branches represent the decisions (that is, install sprinklers and postloss financing) together with the chance events (that is, no loss in first year and no loss in second year). Since the probability of each chance event is 0.7, the combined probability is $0.7(0.7) = 0.49$. Filling in the remaining probabilities, it can be seen that the set of outcomes for each of the four main decision branches has a combined probability of unity. This must be true because we have included all possible outcomes.

The next step involves assignment of values to each of the terminal branches and, from these values, derivation of net present values for the risk management costs for each of the four decisions. The values feeding into each terminal branch are straightforward. For example, consider the sequence sprinklers, postloss financing, controlled loss in first year, and uncontrolled loss in second year. Total costs comprise the sprinklers ($20,000), a controlled loss in the first year ($20,000), and an uncontrolled loss in second year ($80,000). In deriving these values, we have recognized that the effect of loss on the earnings of a firm is measured by the capitalized value of the financing costs, which, in turn, is equal to the replacement costs of the destroyed resources. Consequently, we use the loss values given. To calculate the net present value for each decision, we need to discount these values. The choice of discount rate follows the logic used earlier. The set of choices relating to postloss financing decisions can be viewed as stage 2 of the capital budgeting process outlined earlier. The systematic risk inherent in the loss distribution calls for the corresponding risk-adjusted rate r_L. This rate is given as 10%, and the calculation of NPVs for each terminal branch is shown. This calculation assumes that losses arise at year end. By themselves, each of these values has little meaning, since the rate used acknowledges that each belongs to a set of risky outcomes. However, by weighting each by the probability values for that terminal branch and summing, we derive the NPV of the decision. Thus for the joint decision to install sprinklers and use postloss financing, the NPV is −$40,827. If sprinklers are not installed, but postloss financing is planned, the NPV is −$41,653.

The calculations for preloss financing with insurance use a different discounting assumption. Since insurance is purchased, final outcomes are risk-free, and the risk-free rate is used for discounting. Insurance premiums are assumed to be paid at the beginning of the year. The calculated values turn out to be higher than the corresponding NPVs under postloss financing. This result hinges on three factors. The insurance premium includes a 10% loading over the expected claim payment. This penalty for insurance is further enhanced by the prepayment of the premium, which, given the time value of money, increases the discounted cost of insurance. The third factor operating against insurance in this example is that the discount rate is less favorable than that used for the risky cash flows. In this case, the cash flows are all negative. Thus the lower the discount rate used, the lower is the present value of cash flows (i.e., the greater are the risk management losses). The positive β value for losses is an attractive feature to the investor, since it will tend to offset risk in an otherwise diversified portfolio. The positive β value for losses will lower the cost of capital for the firm and thereby increase its value. With insurance, risk-free cash flows result, and the risk-offsetting effect of uninsured losses is foregone. Had the loss β value been negative, insurance costs would have been discounted at a higher rate than uninsured cash flows and would have appeared to be less unfavorable.

Sequential and Conditional Decisions

Decision trees also may be useful when decisions have to be sequenced or when chance outcomes give rise to new opportunities or force new decisions. Consider a problem of loss reduction or safety investment. A decision can be made on a safety program now, but often the decision is delayed. Delay may change the magnitudes of the decision outcomes; that is, equipment may become cheaper or more expensive and losses may arise that could have been prevented had the safety program been undertaken earlier. Thus the delay may be accompanied by changing economic circumstances and by the occurrence of chance events. One way to approach the problem of delay is to present the decision process as a set of mutually exclusive outcomes as follows:

1 Install safety device in year 1.
2 Install safety device in year 2.
3 Install safety device in year 3.
And so on.

The decision tree presents an ideal framework for representing these choices. Before constructing such a tree, we will introduce a second decision problem that can be tackled simultaneously.

The background to all risk management problems is the uncertainty surrounding loss events. We have seen that this may be represented by branches stemming from chance circles, as shown in Figure 13-4. However, chance may provoke new decisions. One such possibility is that the firm may choose to liquidate its business operations should a large loss arise. Presumably, the rational firm will make this decision on the valuation basis discussed at length in this book. However, the outcome to this decision will affect the other decision currently facing the firm, i.e., whether to install the safety devices immediately. These decisions do involve interdependencies comparable with the decisions discussed earlier, i.e., sprinklers versus no sprinklers and preloss versus postloss financing. However, here the sequencing of decisions is essential to the problem.

In Figure 13-6 we trace out a simple two-period decision tree that captures both the delay and a potential liquidation decision if chance events turn out to be adverse. The immediate decision is whether or not to install a safety device. This decision is labeled 1. The chance event that follows this decision is whether or not a loss arises. Here we simply show a two-point distribution, namely, loss or no loss. However, the safety device may be expected to change the loss probabilities. The probabilities are noted against all chance branches. If the safety device is chosen, we proceed on the upper branch from decision 1. If no loss arises in the first period, no further decision is evoked and we simply await the period 2 loss experience. However, if a loss does arise, we face the further decision to continue in business or liquidate (decision 2). To evaluate the safety program, a correct solution to decision 2 must first be established. Suppose, for example, the liquidation value of the firm at the time of decision 2 is $5 million and the value of the firm if operations continue is 0.9($6 million) + 0.1($0) (discounted at a suitable risk-adjusted rate). It would benefit the firm to continue in operation. The liquidation branch from decision 2 can be ignored, thus permitting measurement of the present value of the safety program.

If the safety program is not adopted immediately, we may, depending on chance events, face further decisions on later installation and on liquidation should a loss arise. Thus decisions 3 and 4 have to be made before we can evaluate the negative option to decision 1. By taking present values for the two branches flowing from decision 3, we can select one branch. Similarly, we can eliminate two branches from decision 4. In this manner, the tree is simplified considerably, as shown by the heavy lines in Figure 13-6. Now there is only one decision to evaluate, represented by the following chance outcome:

Decision 1	Outcomes and probabilities
Install safety device	A(0.81), B(0.9), C(0.09), D(0.01)
Do not install safety device	F(0.49), G(0.21), N(0.3)

The usual discounting methods will permit this decision to be made.

This method of making sequential decisions from decision trees is called *rolling back*. Starting from the right, we work backward from the subsidiary branches to the first set of decisions we encounter. By taking (risk-adjusted) NPVs at these decision points, we can select alternatives and substitute the NPV of the most favored outcome

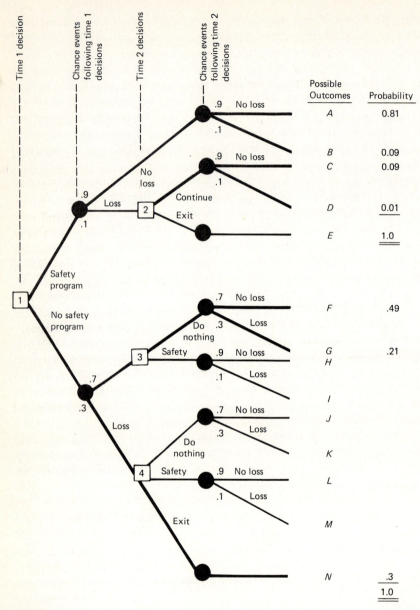

FIGURE 13-6

for the decision point. Thus at decision 2, the preferred outcome is "continue," which has an NPV of $5.4 million. The NPV of the installation of safety devices at decision point 1 can be established from the following outcomes and probabilities, together with appropriate discount rates:

Outcome	Probability
$5.4 million	0.1
A	0.9(0.9) = 0.81
B	0.9(0.1) = 0.09

Similar rolling back will solve decisions 3 and 4, permitting evaluation of the negative alternative to decision 1.

The proliferation of branches in a decision tree becomes impressive as the range of possible outcomes from each chance circle is increased, as more time periods are included, and as more decision options (sequential or simultaneous) are contemplated. Very soon, the visual impact of the tree will be lost within its intricate structure. However, the logic of the tree is still intact. The process of rolling back is still valid and will lead to consistent decisions. This logic can be put to good use with more complex problems by using a computer. The computer can be programmed to construct sequences of decisions and chance branches resulting in the final set of possible outcomes. Simple algorithms can accomplish the task of rolling back to make conditional decisions that are then fed into the dependent decision further to the left in the tree, finally arriving at the alternative present values relevant to the immediate decision. These values each embody an optimal sequence of conditional decisions.

Frequently, the proliferation of branches, the "combinatorial explosion," becomes unmanageable even for a computer. Consider a risk management problem that may seem to have quite reasonable dimensions. A fixed installation has a life of, say, 15 years, and we must decide whether to install now. The installation will affect the probabilities of losses within different size groups, and the risk manager has estimated such effects within a framework that includes 30 loss classes. Each year the firm faces another set of decisions that is then fed back into the first decision. These decisions might include further safety installations, removal of safety installations, abandonment of the enterprise altogether, or doing nothing. With four such choices every year, we have now determined the following set of decisions:

$$2(30^{15})(4^{15}) = 30,814,043,000,000,000,000,000,000,000,000$$

A simpler procedure is to use simulation. Here, the program will select loss experience in a random fashion for the sequence of years, given a certain set of decisions. Replicating this procedure many times, each with different random loss numbers, will give a distribution of possible results that can be summarized by their mean and variance. This can be repeated for a different set of decisions, and the summary can be compared with that for the first decision set. This process can be repeated for as many decision sets as required. Such programs are fairly straightforward to write, and, in fact, programs are currently available both for commercial and educational purposes. Their use is less expensive in computer time than programs that consider all possible permutations (if indeed this is feasible). The quality of programs does vary. It is important that a program accurately reflect corporate objectives in measuring outcomes (in our case, the emphasis should be on the effects of decision sets on equity value), as well as the economic structure of the firm. As expected, tailor-made programs are usually most suitable, although acceptable software packages are available.

SUMMARY AND CONCLUSION

Loss reduction refers to installation of devices, methods of work, or organizational practices designed to improve the characteristics of the distribution of aggregate losses facing a firm. Loss reduction may be compared with other investment activities of a firm; it requires a commitment of resources that may have other competing uses inside or outside the firm. Investment in loss reduction will reduce the expected cost to a firm of loss events. This is tantamount to a stream of positive cash flows.

Formation of a complete loss-reduction program requires that investment opportunities be identified and then evaluated. Classification of loss-reduction devices may help identify such opportunities, and one arbitrary classification was presented. However, our main purpose was to evaluate loss-reduction investments, and we began the task by considering the impact on the distribution of aggregte losses.

The valuation framework was that used for other investment decisions, that is, a captial budgeting system using discounted cash flow. To apply these techniques, we must estimate the effect of the loss-reduction program on the earnings of the firm and the effect of the program on the cost of capital. Earnings effects of loss reduction arise as a consequence of the change in the aggregate loss distribution. This distribution is specified in terms of set values or in terms of the direct liability costs of the loss event. Earnings effects include the earnings foregone on destroyed assets if reinvestment is not contemplated or the financing charges of financing reinvestment. These financing charges are a direct burden on earnings, and loss reduction will reduce their expected value.

Cost-of-capital effects of loss reduction are assumed to depend on the systematic risk of losses (although qualifications are drawn for firms with concentrated ownership). We argue that the appropriate discount rate is determined by the loss β value.

The capital budgeting framework derived requires a two-part calculation. Loss reduction will change the loss distribution over a future period of, say, m years. Each annual change in the distribution will induce a set of future earnings consequences, either in terms of earnings foregone or in terms of loss financing charges. These savings must be capitalized at the time they are induced, that is, at each of the m years of the project life. The relevant discount rate is the weighted average cost of capital. These capitalized values can then be discounted to a present value at a rate reflecting the loss β value.

This chapter concludes by looking at decision trees as an aid in making loss-reduction decisions that interact with other management decisions. Examples include simultaneous solution of loss-financing and loss-reduction decisions, sequential decisions that consider delays in implementation of the loss-reduction program, and further decisions that may be conditional on chance events. Even though the attractive visual presentation of the decision tree may be lost in complex multiperiod problems, the logic can be preserved in computer applications.

QUESTIONS

1 The earnings of a firm before consideration of risk management costs are:

$$\text{Expected earnings} \quad E(E_X) = 1000$$
$$\text{Standard deviation} \quad \sigma_X = 400$$

The distribution of earnings loss due to risk management perils is:

$$E(E_{RM}) = 100$$
$$\sigma_{RM} = 250$$

However, the installation of a safety device will reduce the latter values as follows:

$$E'(E_{RM}) = 50$$
$$\sigma'_{RM} = 125$$

Show the effect of the safety program on the final distribution of earnings, i.e., after deduction of risk management costs. Will the riskiness of final earnings decline by as much as that for E_{RM}?

2 A manufacturing company is contemplating installation of a quality control system that would reduce the probability of defective products and thereby save on potential liability suits. The saving is estimated to be a reduction in the expected loss from liability suits of $200,000 per year for each of the next 10 years. All losses that do arise will be fully financed from external sources (not insurance) and it is thought that losses will not affect earnings before interest and taxation. The loss beta is 0.25, the risk free rate is 0.11 and the expected return on the market portfolio is 0.19. The cost of the system is $1,000,000. Should it be installed?

3 Construct a decision tree to reflect the following decision/chance sequence. The fortunes of a firm depend upon two factors,

a whether a loss arises or not. The respective probabilities are 0.9 and 0.1.

b whether the demand for the firm's product is high or low. The respective probabilities are 0.6 and 0.4 and are independent of prior loss.

The firm has already decided to go ahead with its operations for this year but if a loss arises, it must decide whether or not it should reinvest. Reinvestment would be attractive if next year's demand turned out to be high but not if demand should be low. The firm can subsequently abandon its operations if demand does turn out to be low next year and indeed it may choose this option whether or not a loss arises. Next year's fortunes also will depend on loss experience. The probabilities of loss next year are the same as, and independent of, this year's loss probabilities if demand turns out to be high. But low demand would be associated with a doubling of the loss probability since morale and standards of workmanship would tend to decline.

Represent the choices and the possible outcomes in a decision tree showing the probabilities in each of the terminal branches.

REFERENCES

Ben Shahar, H., and F. M. Werner: "Multiperiod Capital Budgeting under Uncertainty: A Suggested Application," *Journal of Financial and Quantitative Analysis,* vol. 12, 1977, pp. 859–878.

Carter, R. L. and N. A. Doherty: *Handbook of Risk Management*, Kluwer Harrap, London, 1974.

Cozzolino, J. M.: "The Evaluation of Loss Control Options," *Journal of Risk and Insurance*, vol. 50, 1983, pp. 404–416.

Fama, E. F.: "Risk Adjusted Discount Rates and Capital Budgeting under Uncertainty," *Journal of Financial Economics*, vol. 5, 1977, pp. 3–24.

Hapern, J.: "Fire Loss Reduction: Fire Detectors vs. Fire Stations," *Management Science*, vol. 25, 1979, pp. 449–471.

Kalnneman, D., and A. Tversky: "Prospect Theory: An Analysis of Decisions under Risk," *Econometrica*, vol. 47, 1979, pp. 263–291.

Lewellen, W. G., and M. S. Long: "Simulation versus Single Value Estimates in Capital Budgeting Analysis," *Decision Sciences*, vol. 3, 1972.

Magee, J. F.: "How to Use Decision Trees in Capital Investment," *Harvard Business Review*, vol. 42, 1964, pp. 79–96.

Mehr, R. I., and B. A. Hedges: *Risk Management: Concepts and Applications*, Irwin, Homewood, Illinois, 1974.

Myers, S. C., and S. M. Turnbull: "Capital Budgeting and the Capital Asset Pricing Model," *Journal of Finance*, vol. 32, 1977, pp. 321–332.

Shpilberg, D., and R. De Neuville: "Use of Decision Analysis for Optimising Choice of Fire Protection and Insurance: An Airport Study," *Journal of Risk and Insurance*, vol. 42, 1975, pp. 133–149.

Weston, J. F.: "Investment Decisions Using the Capital Asset Pricing Model," *Financial Management*, vol. 2, 1973, pp. 25–33.

CHAPTER **14**

AN ANALYSIS
OF BUSINESS
INTERRUPTION

Property or casualty loss may cause a firm to suffer some temporary or permanent disruption in its trading pattern. Even if damaged capital is repaired or replaced and production capacity is restored to preloss levels, there will often be a temporary loss of production during the restoration period, with possible loss of revenue. More seriously, the disruption of trading during the restoration period and adverse publicity due to the loss may result in a fundamental restructuring of the industry in which the firm operates, with a resulting permanent loss of market share for the distressed firm. Here we consider those factors which determine the extent of interruption loss and the possible defensive strategies that permit a firm to limit interruption loss.

Interruption loss has been illustrated by showing a projection of the earnings of a firm from the level existing before loss under the assumption that the loss did not arise. The actual displacement of postloss earnings from this "no loss" growth path represents the interruption loss. This is shown in Figure 14-1 to set the stage for the discussion. The horizontal axis shows the timing of loss, which is assumed to disrupt production. Production is resumed at a later date. Actual earnings of the firm over time are shown as the solid line. The sudden loss of earnings at the time of the loss is partly made good when repair and/or replacement permits resumption of production. However, postloss earnings do not revert to the levels anticipated before loss. The shaded area represents the interruption loss, which is somewhat roughly divided between permanent and temporary losses. Implicitly, there would be no permanent interruption loss if the earnings returned to the preloss projected path at time 2 or shortly thereafter.

This analysis deals in what might have been. Since the level of earnings that might have prevailed in the absence of loss can never be known, the actual loss of earnings

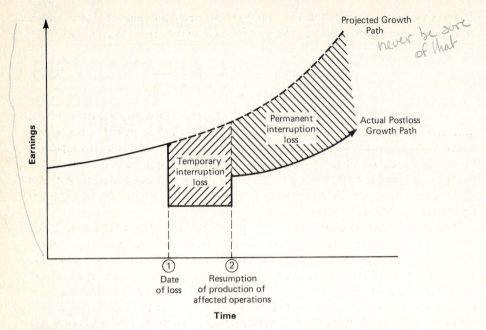

FIGURE 14-1

will never be known. However, estimates of the future earnings of a firm are impounded in stock prices. The model used for share valuation presents the current value V of equity as the capitalized value of the firm's expected earnings E. That is,

$$V = \sum_{i=0}^{\infty} \frac{E_i}{(1 + k)^i} \qquad (14\text{-}1)$$

If the projection of earnings is conducted by estimation of a rate of earnings growth g, the valuation model can be restated as follows:

$$V = \sum_{i=0}^{\infty} \frac{E_0(1 + g)^{i-1}}{(1 + k)^i} = \frac{E_0}{k - g} \qquad (14\text{-}2)$$

The valuation equation is still applicable after the loss, although investors may have very different earnings expectations (it is also possible that the capitalization rate will be changed, since postloss earnings may display a different level of systematic risk; this effect is not considered here). Using primes to denote postloss values, we have

$$V' = \sum_{i=0}^{\infty} \frac{E_i'}{(1 + k)^i} = \sum_{i=1}^{\infty} \frac{E_0(1 + g')^{i-1}}{(1 + k)^i} \qquad (14\text{-}3)$$

$$= \frac{E_0}{k - g'}$$

Comparison of equations (14-2) and (14-3) reveals that the change in V represents a capitalized value of the estimated effect of the loss on the firm's earnings. That is,

$$\Delta V = V - V' = E_0\left(\frac{1}{k - g} - \frac{1}{k - g'}\right) \qquad (14\text{-}4)$$

Any fall in stock prices following a loss will reflect investors' estimates of the interruption and, possibly, the effect of any underinsurance of capital losses. Given that all capital losses are fully insured and that destroyed resources are fully replaced, the fall in stock price, if any, will reflect the interruption loss. In fact, if the capital market is assumed to be efficient, the fall in share price will be an unbiased estimate of the interruption loss. Full insurance of interruption loss implies that stock prices should not respond to the loss.

In a study of the responses of stock prices to major loss, Sprecher and Pertl (1983) derive some instructive results from a sample of firms which suffered major losses. Their study considered major casualty losses in which the estimated loss of capital value was at least 10% of the firm's net worth. Using standard techniques for measuring the effect of sudden events on stock prices, Sprecher and Pertl show that the stock prices responded quickly. On the day of loss, stock prices fell an average of 3%, increasing to about 4% after 2 days. Unfortunately, the researchers did not have access to data on insurance coverage for such losses. Consequently, the results lead to various interpretations:

1 If capital loss had been fully insured but no interruption loss insurance was available, the 4% fall in stock price would probably reflect investors' estimate of the interruption loss.

2 If the firm had no insurance protection, the loss of 4% of value following capital losses representing at least 10% of the firm's net worth would probably indicate that the firm had excess capacity.

3 The most likely interpretation is probably a combination of the preceding. The combined effect of underinsurance on capital loss and interruption loss would cause equity values to fall, but this fall could have been moderated by any redundancy in the preloss capital in place.

After a loss, the value-maximizing strategy is that which minimizes the fall in share value. Before loss, the value-maximizing strategy focuses on current share value, which impounds expectations concerning the probabilities of capital loss and earnings interruption. Both *ex post* and *ex ante* value-maximizing strategies require some knowledge of the factors that give rise to interruption loss. We divide these between technical and organizational factors and economic factors.

TECHNICAL AND ORGANIZATIONAL FACTORS AFFECTING PRODUCTION LOSS

The technology of production and the organization of production and marketing activities have a close bearing on the potential severity of earnings interruption following a prospective loss. Some relevant issues include the following:

1 Investments that reduce the expected value of capital loss typically will reduce the expected value of interruption loss. Such investments may reduce the probability of some loss-causing event, with corresponding savings in the expected value of capital and interruption loss. Alternatively, the severity of capital loss may be reduced. Although there may be no tight relationship between severity of capital loss and severity of interruption loss, one would certainly expect any containment in the size of potential capital loss to produce some reduction in expected interruption loss.

2 The absence of a strong relationship between capital loss and interruption loss may be due, in part, to interdependencies in the production process. For example, a highly integrated plant in which certain processes represent bottlenecks in the flow of production may be especially vulnerable should damage arise at one such bottleneck. A fairly small loss may bring the whole production flow to a halt.

3 The technology of production may be easily replaceable or not. If standard machinery and plant are used, and if there is a ready market for such equipment, replacement may be quick and simple. But if technology is highly specialized or requires lengthy installation, the interruption loss may be serious. For example, a fire may not cause serious interruption for a small-scale manufacturer of clothing items. Production can quickly be relocated in a leased general-purpose building, and standard equipment can be purchased quickly. However, a manufacturer of electronic micro chips requires highly specialized equipment and a specialized environment, which, if damaged, may prove to be very time consuming to replace.

4 The consequences of direct loss of capital goods may be "exported" from one firm to another. Serious damage to the production facilities of a firm supplying inputs to another firm may cause serious business interruption to the latter, even though direct loss was sustained by the former. Most firms are at the center of a chain of suppliers and customers. Any concentration in their trading patterns may leave each firm vulnerable to the effects of external losses. A good example of such vulnerability would be a fertilizer manufacturer whose product includes a crucial ingredient for which there is only a single supplier. If that supplier is located abroad, the risk of disruption arises both from the usual "pure" risk events and from political disruption.

ECONOMIC FACTORS AFFECTING PRODUCTION LOSS

Although technical factors are important, the main emphasis here is on those economic factors which determine interruption loss and on the derivation of defensive strategies.

Market Structure

The competitive environment in which a firm operates may be very important in determining the possible extent of earnings loss following some loss event. The degree of competition will be particularly important in determining whether a firm is able to restore its preloss expected financial performance when preloss productive capacity is restored to its preloss level.

A firm may choose to exit from the industry following a loss that involves destruction of a substantial portion of its resources. The relevant issue is whether the firm can earn an expected return on its reinvestment that exceeds its cost of capital. In an aggressively competitive environment, prevailing rates of profits may be very low, and therefore, the incentive to reinvest will be small. Furthermore, in such an environment, the firm suffering a loss may find that rivals seek to capitalize on its distress by aggressively courting the firm's customers and seeking to absorb its market share. Such predatory practices make it difficult for a firm to recover and may even lead to its demise. However, the conditions that led to competition within the industry offer some ray of comfort for a firm suffering a major interruption in its production and trading.

Perhaps one of the most important factors determining market structure in an industry is the presence of *barriers to entry*. Competition may arise with most vigor in those industries in which entry is not deterred by high entry costs. This implies that reentry after a loss is not difficult. For example, ease of entry may be present where (1) capital investment is low, (2) consumer loyalty to brand name products is low, (3) markets are not geographically segmented, (4) technology is easily reproducible, and (5) technology is not protected by patents. Given such conditions, a distressed firm may find that its market evaporates during the temporary cessation of trading, but it is able to reestablish its market share with fairly modest capital and marketing investments when production capacity is restored.

The other extreme is the case of monopoly, where the industry is dominated by a single producer (in the limit, the industry comprises a single firm). Conditions of monopoly often exist when barriers to entry are substantial. Such conditions often permit the monopolist to earn an abnormally high return on its capital investment. Under such conditions, it would seem that a firm is afforded some protection in the event of disruption, for there are no immediate rivals to prey on its customers. However, this may prove to be a two-edged sword. The factors that deter new entrants may also result in lengthy disruption. For example, heavy capital investment and a lengthy construction period imply that reinvestment may absorb considerable time. The lengthy reinvestment period offers some protection for new entrants or for infant firms already in the industry. If these rivals gain a substantial foothold in the market, the factors that protected the monopolist before the loss may well serve to protect its rivals when the original market leader seeks to regain its dominant market share.

The effects of direct loss on the earnings of a firm are complex. Economists have modeled the effects of market structure on the pricing, marketing, and production decisions of a firm under the heading of the "theory of the firm." This theory provides a framework within which the manager can identify the types of market interactions that might arise from different pricing policies. The dynamics of competition are also relevant in determining how successfully a firm will recover from some serious "pure" loss. Consequently, the theory of the firm is a useful framework for the risk manager to identify likely reactions of rival firms in the event of serious loss and how such reactions will affect its recovery. Such market interactions differ according to market structure, and separate models are constructed for competitive, monopolistic, and oligopolistic markets. The appendix to this chapter presents an application of the principal theory of the firm models to the issue of business interruption.

Inventory

The market in which a firm operates may be taken as given in the short run. Certainly, strategic planning permits a firm to influence its choice of products as well as its relative market strength; thus risk management considerations may feed into a firm's strategic planning. In the short run, however, risk management decisions will probably have to be made against a given market environment. Another factor that may influence a firm's exposure to interruption loss, and which is amenable to short-term manipulation, is the level of inventory carried by the firm.

The inventory carried by a firm permits the firm to maintain short-term imbalances between the rate of production (or acquisition) of a product and the demand for (or use of) that product. Inventories can be useful at various stages in a firm's production and marketing activities:

1 The acquisition of raw materials may not be conducted on a regular basis. To take advantage of savings in bulk delivery, a firm may order batches of raw materials or other inputs that will serve the company for several days, weeks, or even months. Inventory has the further advantage that should some unexpected surge in production be required to meet unanticipated demand for a firm's output, production will not have to await the supply of new raw materials. In this way, inventory management may be used to control a firm's exposure to business risk. However, inventory may have a role to play in relation to "pure" risk management. A firm may find its source of supply eliminated should its supplier suffer some major loss that curtails production. The loss may be due to one of the usual risk management perils, but other causes might be political in nature. For example, a third world supplier might reevaluate its trading policy following a change in government. Inventory provides a breathing space during which a firm can seek alternative sources of supply.

2 In a similar fashion, inventories can be used to cover mismatch between supply and use at various stages of a vertically integrated production process. For example, in automobile production, there may well be a stock of engines, doors, electrical components, etc. from which the assembly plant draws as needed. These intermediate inventories are useful if certain processes are best undertaken in batch. In addition, however, they serve to protect the firm from complete shutdown should one specific process be interrupted. This interruption could be a machinery breakdown, a strike, or a fire.

3 Inventories of final products also may be kept. This strategy is useful if demand is irregular but production is best undertaken on a continuous basis, e.g., Christmas cards or snowmobiles. Alternatively, production may be irregular but demand continuous, as in the case of wine. Here again, inventories of final products serve a risk-protection purpose. Interruptions of production can be sustained without loss of revenue to a firm if it is able to meet demand from stockpiles.

In each of these situations, inventory can only provide a temporary cover for mismatched supply and demand. In this sense, inventory provides only temporary protection against business interruption following loss. However, temporary protection may have more enduring consequences. A temporary interruption of production can have long-term consequences if a firm is unable to fill orders and customers establish new trading relationships with competitors. This loss of customers can be prevented if orders are met from inventory. Thus inventory prevents short-term loss of revenue and gives the firm breathing space to restore its productive operations.

The inventory policy to be adopted by a firm may be determined jointly on business *and* risk management criteria. Inventory is costly. In addition to the direct carrying costs, such as breakage and protection, the value embodied in the inventory (purchase or production cost) represents a capital investment that must be financed, as must any other investment. Therefore, the relevant cost of holding inventory depends on the cost of capital. Such costs must be offset against benefits, some of which are risky. In the section entitled Use of Inventory to Mitigate Interruption Loss we present a decision procedure to evaluate whether inventory should be held and at what level. This procedure is based jointly on risk management and wider business considerations and is developed primarily for inventories of finished products. However, similar issues arise for inventories used at other stages of the production process.

Capacity

Most firms do not work continuously at full capacity. Firms that are in an industry undergoing a secular decline in demand usually operate with considerable surplus capacity. In contrast, new growth firms will often be pushing against the limits of their productive and marketing capacity. However, superimposed on the structural changes in the economy that give rise to declining and growing industries are shorter-term fluctuations often of a cyclical nature. The business cycle is associated with fluctuations in demand that affect all industries, although perhaps not all are affected to the same extent. The stages of the cycle are marked by significant differences in the utilization of productive capacity.

The level of capacity usage of a firm will affect its potential for interruption loss in two ways. Consider a firm that suffers physical destruction of productive resources at a time when operations are conducted well short of capacity, i.e., during recession. Since capital is not fully utilized and earnings are low, the potential for short-term loss of earnings while damage is repaired or the plant is replaced is correspondingly low. In the event of partial loss of productive capacity, it may be that production can be transferred from the damaged plant to another underutilized and undamaged plant. Whether this is possible depends on the degree of specialization in the firm's capital resources, but in general it appears that when business is slack, the potential for interruption loss is correspondingly diminished. In contrast, when capacity is fully utilized, any loss of capacity due to physical damage will lead to unfilled orders and lost sales. This interruption in earnings will prevail until production capacity is restored or until demand declines to a level compatible with the impaired capacity of the firm. In this way, the utilization of capacity influences interruption loss because it helps to determine the short-term earnings foregone when productive capital is destroyed or damaged.

Capacity utilization may also affect interruption loss in an indirect manner. In an earlier section (and more completely in the appendix), we examined the effects of market structure on potential interruption loss. In that analysis, we did not identify precisely how market conditions would affect vulnerability to interruption loss, but it was shown that different market structures tend to be associated with different forms of economic behavior. Should one firm suffer loss, incentives for rivals to respond to this loss in a competitive or cooperative way may be affected by market structure, although the final outcome is not easy to predict. When demand is high and capacity is fully utilized, rivals will be unable to expand production in the short term to take advantage of the firm's distress. Even if some firms do have surplus capacity, they may be able to increase sales and production by seeking new customers rather than by preying on the firm suffering loss. However, a situation of full capacity is not likely to induce rival firms to agree to supply the distressed firm on a subcontracting basis so that the firm may, in turn, supply its own customers. Cooperative subcontracting of this nature may be feasible during recession, when demand is low and capacity is underutilized. Indeed, rivals would be glad to pick up such orders to help cover their overhead costs. However, rivals may see an opportunity for bypassing the distressed firm and supplying the customers directly. This discussion does not point to any strong predictions about the behavior of rival firms and how such behavior is affected by capacity. However, it does point to issues that may become relevant in the individual case.

USE OF INVENTORY TO MITIGATE INTERRUPTION LOSS

If the demand for a firm's output is stable over time and production can be economically matched to the stable demand, then inventories are redundant. However, production and demand may not match because (1) production is not economically undertaken as a smooth process, (2) demand is uncertain over time, or (3) both production and demand are uncertain. There are many examples of discontinuous production. A bottling plant may sequentially bottle and label a batch of one brand of product before moving to another batch of a different brand rather than simultaneously maintaining production lines for each of a set of differentiated products. Similarly, a publisher may set type for batches of a book and run down inventories until a second printing is needed. Other forms of production are discontinuous for technical reasons, e.g., production of seasonal foodstuffs for which there is a year-round demand, such as corn, etc. Contrary to these examples, many manufactured goods, services, etc. are most conveniently provided by continuous production, thereby providing continuity of employment (avoiding expensive overtime, layoffs, and temporary workers) and full use of plant machinery, etc. We will focus on the case of continuous production, although we allow demand to fluctuate on a random basis.

Graphically, the production flow is denoted by the horizontal line AB and the demand over time is shown as line CD in Figure 14-2(a). If inventory is used to match the production and demand streams, the inventory will be run down during the periods indicated by vertical shading. Starting with an inventory level $0X$ in the third section of the figure, the level of inventory will follow the pattern shown. However, at time T, the inventory will be depleted by the excessive demand preceding that time. At time T, the firm will be unable to meet all its orders, and unless customers are willing to queue, business will be lost.

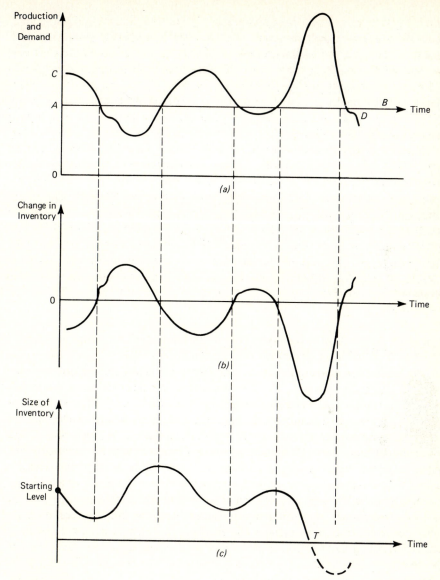

FIGURE 14-2

The same process can be seen in a risk sense. Consider that the demand per month follows the probability distribution shown in Figure 14-3. If demand is stable over time, it seems sensible to set long-term production to average the expected level of demand μ. However, to avoid costly changes in output month by month, it may be advantageous to increase production temporarily to build up inventories and then let production settle at μ. Taking a "snapshot" at a point in time, the firm will produce μ for the month and will have sufficient inventory to meet demand level $\mu + I$, where

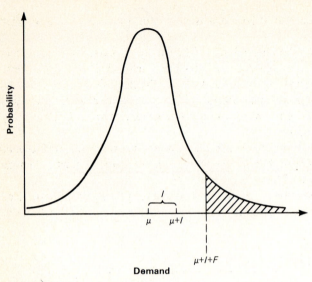

FIGURE 14-3

I represents the stock of inventory. If the inventory is depleted, some variation in production may be possible by overworking current resources (e.g., overtime), but such changes are restricted in the short term. Given this flexibility, the firm can meet demand up to level $\mu + I + F$. The shaded area in the righthand tail of the distribution represents the probability that orders will go unfilled.

To make a sensible inventory decision, the firm needs to estimate the probability of unsatisfied orders and the cost to the firm of these orders. To progress, we will assume initially that the demand distribution is normal (or approximately so). This enables us to estimate the adequacy of the inventory by the normal-approximation method. Suppose production is set at the expected level of demand, which is 1000 units per month. At the beginning of the month, inventory is 1200 units and production can be expanded by an extra 100 units if required. Thus the firm can meet orders of up to 2300 units in a given month. The standard deviation of monthly demand is estimated as 300 units. What is the probability that demand cannot be met? Using the formula

$$z = \frac{x - \bar{x}}{\sigma} = \frac{2300 - 1000}{300} = 4.33$$

where z = standard normal variate

$\quad x$ = maximum monthly supply

$\quad \bar{x}$ = mean monthly demand

$\quad \sigma$ = standard deviation

we see that $z_{4.33}$ equals less than 0.001, that is, less than $^1/_{10}$ of 1%, the true value being off the table.

Now we consider the probability of loss. When a loss occurs, we assume that production is halted completely (production is vertically integrated), but the severity of loss does vary by the period for which production is halted. We can now pose the question: What level of inventory is needed to hold the probability of interruption loss to some acceptable level? Alternatively, with given inventory, what is the probability that interruption loss will occur?

Using the preceding information, we add the prospect that there is a 10% chance that a loss will arise of sufficient severity to eliminate production for 1 month. Assume that demand and probability of loss are independent.

If a loss arises and production is halted, the firm will only be able to fill orders up to the level of inventory, that is, 1300 units. Thus *given a loss,* the probability of stockout is

$$z = \frac{1300 - 1000}{300} = 1 \qquad z_{1.00} = 0.1587$$

With a 10% chance of loss, the probability that an inventory of 1300 will be depleted *ex ante* is

$$0.1587(0.1) = 0.01587$$

The accuracy of this approach depends on how closely the demand distribution approaches normal. We now develop some further examples without using this assumption. The following table lists the probability distribution for demand, and we will read probabilities directly from this distribution:

Monthly demand	Probability	Probability that demand will exceed:		
200	0.1	200	is	0.9
800	0.2	800	is	0.7
1000	0.4	1000	is	0.3
1400	0.2	1400	is	0.1
1800	0.1	1800	is	0

The last column of the table is the reverse of the cumulative distribution. Reading off from the probability distribution, the probability that demand will exceed, say, 1000 is 0.3 (i.e., the sum of the probabilities that demand will be 1400 or 1800). Thus with production set at 1000 per month, the firm needs to carry 400 items in stock to restrict the stockout probability to 10% (assuming no losses). Now consider the following:

1 A 10% chance of complete loss of production for 1 month. What is the probability of stockout if inventory is held at 1000, that is, 1 month's supply? After loss, there is a probability of 0.3 that inventory will be insufficient. This value is derived from the final column (the probability of stockout given the loss) times the probability of loss, or $0.3(0.1) = 0.03$.

2 A 10% chance of complete loss of production for 1 month *plus* a 5% chance of a more severe loss resulting in 2 months of foregone production, i.e., the total probability of loss is 15%. Inventory is 1000. With the smaller loss (1 month), the probability of stockout *after* loss is 0.3 as before. With the larger loss, the probability of stockout is only slightly more complicated to calculate. A stockout will arise under the following circumstances; that is, the inventory of 1000 will be exhausted under the following circumstances (probabilities are calculated assuming that demand in successive months will be independent):

First month demand	Second month demand	Joint probability
1800	Any level	$0.1(1.0) = 0.1$
1400	Any level	$0.2(1.0) = 0.2$
1000	Any level	$0.4(1.0) = 0.4$
600	600 or greater	$0.2(0.9) = 0.18$
200	1000 or greater	$0.1(0.7) = \underline{0.07}$
		0.95

Therefore, total probability of stockout is the sum of the probabilities of stockout for the small and large losses. That is,

$$0.1(0.3) + 0.05(0.95) = 0.0505$$

Thus given the loss probabilities, there is a 5% chance that inventory will prove to be inadequate.

Now we ask questions about the "optimal" level of inventory to be held. Consider example 1 above, that is, a simple 10% chance of 1 month's loss. Also consider that the value of each unit produced is $2000 and that each unit not sold will result in the firm losing $500 profit. The total value of the inventory is now $2000 \times 1000 = $2 million. The firm's cost of capital is 12% (including risk premium), giving a monthly financing cost for inventory of about 1%. The dollar cost of financing the inventory per month is therefore $2 million $\times 0.01 = $20,000. There may also be holding costs, such as storage, protection, wastage, etc., but for this example, these costs are ignored. What is the benefit to the firm of holding this inventory, and does it justify the cost? To calculate this, we consider the cost of stockout with and without the inventory.

Without Inventory There is a 0.9 chance of no loss. In addition, we know that if there is no loss, there is a 0.3 chance that monthly production will be insufficient to meet demand. In addition, there is a 0.1 chance of a loss involving complete stoppage of production for the month. Without inventories, no sales will be made, leaving a total loss of monthly profit.

With Inventory If no loss arises, then production plus inventory will enable the firm to meet all demand. With a loss, demand for the first month can be met if it does not exceed 1000 units. Should demand exceed this value, the firm will lose surplus profit on the shortfall.

The calculations for no inventory proceed as follows:

Situation	a Demand	b Loss of profit	c Probability	b × c Cost ($)
No loss	1400	400 × 500 = 200,000	0.2	40,000
	1800	800 × 500 = 400,000	0.1	40,000
Expected loss of profit (no inventory, no loss)				= 80,000
Loss	200	200 × 500 = 100,000	0.1	10,000
	400	400 × 500 = 200,000	0.2	40,000
	1000	1000 × 500 = 500,000	0.4	200,000
	1400	1400 × 500 = 700,000	0.2	140,000
	1800	1800 × 500 = 900,000	0.1	90,000
Expected loss of profit (no inventory, loss)				= 480,000

Therefore, expected loss of profit with no inventory is

$$0.9(80,000) + 0.1(480,000) = \$120,000$$

Notice that this calculation is the probability that no loss will arise times the expected value of loss of profit in the event of no loss plus the probability of loss times the expected value of loss of profit following loss.

The calculations for an inventory of 1000 are as follows:

Situation	a Demand	b Loss of profit	c Probability	b × c Cost ($)
No loss	(Production plus inventory is sufficient to cover all levels of demand)			
Loss	1400	400 × 500 = 200,000	0.2	40,000
	1800	800 × 500 = 400,000	0.1	40,000
Expected loss of profit (inventory, loss)				= 80,000

Therefore, expected loss of profit with inventory is

$$0.9(0) + 0.1(80,000) = \$8000$$

The gain from holding inventory is the reduction in the expected loss of profit from $120,000 to $8000 per month. This gain is achieved by an investment with a monthly cost of only $20,000. The benefit of $102,000 clearly is well in excess of the cost, thereby justifying the investment. Alternatively, we could view the decision as requiring an investment of $2 million in inventories. The expected gain, considered on an annual basis, is $102,000 × 12 = $1,224,000, representing a 61.2% return on investment. The cost of capital is given at 12%, clearly indicating that the investment is profitable.

Some qualifications should be made to this analysis. First, the loss of profit in the example was calculated by attributing a dollar profit to each item and by multiplying this value by the number of items lost by the fire, etc. In practice, the temporary cost may well exceed this value, since many costs are fixed in the short run. With loss of production estimated at only 1 month, the firm might feel unable to release any workers because of the nature of its labor contracts or because it estimates the costs, in terms of adverse effects on labor relations, rehiring costs, etc., to be too high. Other costs, such as rents or leasing charges for equipment, may be fixed without discretion in the short run. The loss to the firm includes both the foregone profit and the continued payment of fixed costs. Thus estimated fixed costs should be included in the analysis. The second qualification relates to the dynamic nature of inventories. This was shown in Figure 14-2 and illustrated by example 2 above. The more severe the loss, the more likely it is that inventories will prove to be inadequate. Further, once an inventory has been depleted after a loss, the firm is vulnerable to further interruption loss until inventories are restored to a "safe" level. A third qualification is that the inventory of 1000 units is apparently preferred to no inventory, but we cannot conclude that 1000 units is the optimal inventory. Trial and error with alternative levels of stocks will reveal the optimal level of inventory.

The examples shown here are rather simple. The framework can be used to consider potential interruptions with multiple durations, holding costs, fixed costs, etc. Furthermore, similar analyses can be used to evaluate the effects of inventory held at different stages of production (inventory of raw materials and intermediate goods). However, the examples do show that inventory policy can be of significant value to a firm. Furthermore, this provides another example of why risk management strategies are best derived in conjunction with other aspects of financial decision making. The value created for a firm by holding inventory arises jointly from the effects of marketing with uncertain demand and from risk management effects.

INTERRUPTION LOSSES AND ABANDONMENT

The defensive action available to a firm to reduce potential interruption costs is not limited to preloss decisions. Several actions may help prevent major resource losses from developing into major interruption losses. Timely reconstruction, securing makeshift production facilities, subcontracting production, purchasing inventory, postloss marketing programs, etc., all may help a firm to return quickly to a normal trading pattern and may forestall permanent loss of market share. However, after a loss, a firm faces a more dramatic decision—whether to exit from the business.

We have already considered the prospect that a firm may choose not to reinvest after resource loss. The purpose here is simply to summarize the influence that interruption losses may have on such a decision. In the absence of loss, the decision to abandon will increase the value of equity if the exit value exceeds the market value. Indeed, if firms behaved rationally, their market value would not fall below their exit value, since exit would immediately be induced. Given limited liability, the exit value will not fall below zero; therefore, equity can never have a negative value.

In the absence of interruption losses, it is feasible that a major loss may induce a decision to abandon. Such a decision arises because the cost of replacing capital resources exceeds the disposal value of those resources before loss. Thus the decision to continue production before loss only required that the capitalized value of the cash flows exceed the disposal value. After loss, the capital value of the cash flows (which is unchanged, since we are assuming away interruption losses) must exceed the replacement value of destroyed resources (plus the disposal value of any undamaged resources). This hurdle is usually higher than that set up for the preloss decision to continue.

If a firm suffers interruption losses, by definition, its postloss cash flows will be less favorable than those estimated before the loss occurred. In addition to the temporary loss of revenue during periods of interrupted production not covered by inventory, there may be a permanent displacement of revenue from loss of market share. Even if the firm recovers market share by heavy advertising, the marketing costs themselves will serve to reduce the incremental cash flows. Thus a firm suffering major losses is penalized in its decision to continue in two ways: (1) the capital hurdle set up after loss (replacement cost) typically is higher than the capital hurdle before loss (disposal value), and (2) the loss itself may reduce the cash flows.

It may be argued that if a firm decided to liquidate after loss solely because of the higher capital hurdle imposed by replacement costs, it was already living on borrowed time. Sooner or later the capital resources would wear out or become too costly to maintain, and the exit decision would prevail. Thus without interruption losses, a major physical resource loss would probably only bring about the premature demise of a firm if it was already unhealthy. However, the shock waves of a major loss may result in severe interruption, which reorganizes the competitive structure of the market. Such dynamic effects can be far-reaching, and it is not inconceivable that firms that appeared to be in the bloom of economic health before a loss may rationally decide to liquidate after a loss.

The decision to liquidate after a loss is not affected by the presence of an insurance policy covering the full replacement costs of capital resources. If the capitalized value of the cash flows is below the replacement costs, the shareholders are better off receiving the insurance payment as a terminal dividend and winding up the firm. A qualification that is needed here is that the insurance payment is not conditional on actual replacement. Such a condition is not normally imposed. Interruption insurance may have a material effect on the abandonment decision, since the payment of insurance money implicitly appears to be conditional on continuity of operation. Interruption policies usually pay for the continued fixed costs (e.g., wages of workers not easily laid off) that are not covered from a firm's interrupted revenue. The issue is whether such costs are incurred in the event of liquidation and whether the liquidation would affect the insurer's liability to pay a claim on the interruption policy. This is a can of legal worms that is beyond our scope.

SUMMARY AND CONCLUSION

Interruption losses arise when a firm's revenue streams, and therefore its earnings, are disrupted as a consequence of some risk management loss. Such losses may only be temporary, and when destroyed resources are replaced, production and trading are restored to levels competitive with preloss expectations. However, an interruption in trading may cause some longer-term effects on the earnings of a firm. Customers may establish alternative sources of supply, and rival firms may cement these new trading relationships into a permanent realignment of relative market shares. Thus the firm may never fully recover from the effects of a major loss.

No clear relationship exists between the severity of direct losses and the severity of interruption losses. However, it is possible to identify some technical and economic factors upon which this relationship rests. When production flows through highly integrated and vertically interdependent stages, a firm is considerably at risk. A relatively small physical loss may be sufficient to provide a major interruption. In addition, firms that use highly specialized (custom-made) equipment are at risk because replacement may be very time consuming.

Economic factors also are important. The market structure in which a firm operates may be very important in determining the likely responses of customers and rival firms in the event of major loss. Rivals may engage in predatory behavior, seeking to take over the customers of the distressed firm. However, more cooperative actions may prevail as the distressed firm subcontracts part of its operations to the other firms. The analysis of these effects is complex, although a useful framework for addressing these issues has been developed by economists, i.e., the theory of the firm. Some issues are introduced and discussed in the appendix to this chapter.

Another economic factor that may influence a firm's exposure to interruption losses is its level of inventory. Inventory may help "see the firm through" a limited interruption of production by running down its stockpiles. If the stockpile is large, or if the loss of production is of short duration, a firm may be able to continue uninterrupted trading. This leads to the use of inventory as a risk management tool. Inventory levels may be chosen in order to absorb mismatches in production and demand caused by unexpected fluctuations in one or the other. Both risk management and normal business factors may lead to such fluctuations. For example, demand may be sensitive to economic conditions, and production may be affected by strikes or major physical damage. A simple decision procedure was derived to compare the risk-adjusted benefits for holding inventory with the holding costs. This procedure permits value-increasing inventory strategies to be formulated simultaneously on the basis of risk management and other business factors.

Finally, we examined the potential effects of interruption on the decision to continue operations or to liquidate. A previously unhealthy firm may rationally decide to liquidate if the threatened interruption from a recent loss is severe. Survival cannot be used as an obvious risk management objective. The value-maximizing decision may be presented with the usual discounted cash flow criteria.

QUESTIONS

1 ABC corporation recently suffered a major fire. Property damage is fully insured but no interruption policy is carried. The loss is expected to give rise to a major disruption of trading. The current year's expected earnings were estimated at $10 million before the loss, but this has been revised downwards to $6 million in light of the loss. The firm is expected to partially regain its market share; thus, its postloss expected growth of earnings is 6% compared with 5% estimated before the loss. The capitalization rate for equity of 10% is unaffected by the loss.

Calculate the effect of the loss on the value of the firm's equity. You may assume that all earnings are distributed as dividends.

2 The monthly demand for a firm's product is

Demand	Probability
1000 units	0.15
2000	0.7
3000	0.15

Each unit has a value of 150 and earns a profit of 10 upon sale. There is a 10% chance that an interruption from events such as fire, strike, etc., each month which would cause a complete loss of the month's production. Production is set at 2000 units per month and is not responsive to short term fluctuations in demand. The monthly cost of capital is 1%. Should the firm invest in:

a No inventory
b Inventory of 1000 units
c Inventory of 2000 units

3 Outline some of the factors that would determine the extent of potential interruption loss for a firm operating in an oligopolistic market structure.

APPENDIX: Theory of the Firm and Interruption Losses

The *theory of the firm* comprises a set of models that reveal the price and output decisions and their effects of profit under different competitive conditions. The general assumption used for such models is that a firm will seek to maximize its profit, which is defined in a single period. Using a diagrammatic approach, we can summarize the profit-maximizing decision as follows: The total revenue of a firm is shown in Figure 14-A1 along with a total cost curve. *Profit* is defined as the difference between revenue and cost and is maximized at the output level for which the curves are furthest appart, that is, at Q^*. At any other output level, the curves are either converging from left to right or they are diverging. At Q^*, they are parallel. An alternative way to describe the profit-maximizing position uses marginal cost and marginal revenue. *Marginal revenue* is defined as the rate at which total revenue changes with small changes in output. Thus marginal revenue is given by the slope of the total revenue curve. *Marginal cost* is similarly defined and is measured by the slope of the total cost curve. Since the slopes of total cost and total revenue are the same at Q^*, then marginal cost is equal to marginal revenue.

To add more intuition to the use of marginal cost and marginal revenue, consider the following. If an increase in quantity adds more to cost than to revenue, profit will fall and, by definition, marginal cost will exceed marginal revenue (that is, $MC > MR$). If $MR > MC$, an

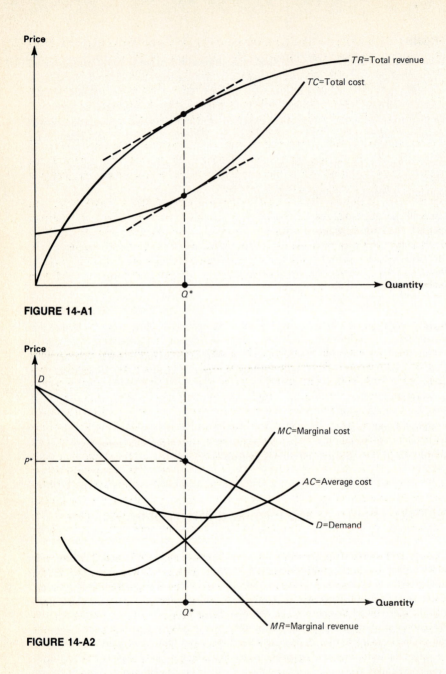

FIGURE 14-A1

FIGURE 14-A2

increase in quantity will increase profit. Therefore, to achieve a profit-maximizing level of output, a firm should increase output if $MR > MC$ until $MR = MC$. If $MC > MR$, then output should be reduced until $MR = MC$. Thus at the profit-maximizing level of output, marginal revenue equals marginal cost.

These concepts are redefined in Figure 14-A2. The line DD is the demand curve for the firm's product, and it displays the usual downward slope. This indicates higher demand at lower prices. The marginal revenue curve is shown as *MR*. Given the definition of marginal revenue, this must lie below the demand curve if the latter is falling. The demand curve shows what people will pay at different prices. However, if the same price is charged to all customers, that price must be the average revenue (quantity × price = total revenue, and total revenue ÷ quantity = average revenue; therefore, price = average revenue). Average revenue can only fall if increments to total revenue are below the average revenue. Thus if the average revenue (demand) curve is falling, marginal revenue must always lie below average revenue. This diminishing marginal revenue curve also corresponds with the total revenue curve in the upper segment, since increments are declining. Also shown are the average and marginal cost curves, their construction embodying similar reasoning.

In Figure 14-A1, profit is maximized at the position where the *TR* and *TC* curves are furthest apart. Thus in Figure 14-A2, the same position is identified where marginal revenue equals marginal cost. If output is increased beyond this point, *MC* will be greater than *MR*, implying that more is added to total cost than to total revenue, causing profit to decline. To reduce output below this point, profit must fall, since *MR* is greater than *MC*, implying that revenue will be reduced by more than cost. We now examine the effects of different market structures and show the probable impact of interruption losses.

PERFECT COMPETITION

A *perfectly competitive market* is characterized by a large number of buyers and sellers trading with a homogeneous product. Perfect information is available to consumers so that they may effectively shop around. With the additional assumption of no transport costs, there is perfect substitution between firms and consumers. Finally, there are no barriers to entry. The assumptions imply that the demand curve for a firm is horizontal, so that if a firm raises its price, it will lose all business to competitors. Since customers are indifferent as to which firm they purchase from, an equilibrium is reached at which no firm makes any abnormal profit. If firms were making abnormal profits, new entrants would come into the market, thereby increasing market supply and driving down the price. As long as excess profits persisted, this process would continue until an equilibrium was reached in which firms did not make excess profits. A further point of interest is that the prospects for concerted action on the part of sellers is small, since there are a large number of firms and each is small. Further, the demise of any particular firm would not have any perceptible effect on the market. The equilibrium is illustrated in Figure 14-A3.

Now consider a loss to a single firm resulting in a temporary halt in production. The combined assumptions imply that clients of this firm have no distinct preferences over sellers and that the supply would be met by rival firms. However, the same assumptions imply that the new trading patterns will be as fragile as the old, since there are no strong consumer preferences. When damage is repaired and production resumes, the firm should have no problem reestablishing its lost business. There are no barriers to entry, so no major effort or expenditure will be required to win back these customers. One further point can be detected. Since firms do not earn excess profits, there is no great incentive for a firm to reenter the industry after a total loss. In summary, this situation is one of "easy come, easy go." The ease of entry and reentry ensures that business will be lost, but it can also be won back easily.

Perfectly competitive conditions rarely, if ever, exist. Close examples that are sometimes given are the New York Stock Exchange and trade in grain. However, the framework does help us to identify the important factors. The market share of a firm is protected while it is out of business by

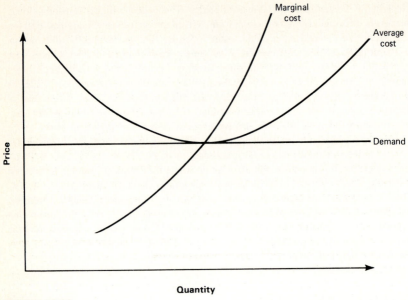

FIGURE 14-A3

1 Imperfect information about alternative suppliers or the quality of their products.
2 Additional transport costs of going to alternative suppliers.
3 Product differentiation that leads to definite consumer preference.
4 Barriers to entry, such as large initial investments or heavy promotional expenditures.

These factors make it difficult for clients of a distressed firm to secure suitable alternative supplies, and market share is not likely to be lost to rivals or new entrants in the short run. But this is a two-edged sword. The longer a firm is out of production, the more likely it becomes that obstacles can be overcome. Once new trading patterns do arise, these will afford the same protection to the new suppliers that was previously enjoyed by the distressed firm. The latter may therefore find that it is not able to regain its market share. Thus we find that a small firm in a highly competitive market will lose its market share rapidly in the event of a major loss of production, but it still may be able to come back, even if the disruption is protracted. Conversely, in a less competitive market, a firm may find its market intact after a fairly limited cessation of production, but if the interruption persists, it may find it difficult or impossible to reestablish its previous position or even resume trading at all.

MONOPOLY

A *monopolist* is strictly defined as a single supplier of a product for which there are no close substitutes. Since it is the only supplier, the demand curve for such a firm is the demand curve for the industry. The absence of competition gives the firm some choice over price, and it is able to restrict output and drive up prices thereby earning abnormal profits. The steeper the slope of the demand curve (i.e., the less elastic the curve), the greater is the potential for earning abnormal profits. Clearly, the profitability of the monopolist would tend to attract new entrants and new capital into the industry. Thus the monopolist's entrenched position endures only if there are barriers to entry, such as legal constraints to entry (patents), heavy capital expenditures (railroads, utilities), or control over some crucial raw material. The position of the monopolist is depicted in Figure 14-A4, with price and output labeled P_1 and Q_1. This position is derived by equating marginal cost and marginal revenue. The shaded area shows the profit earned.

Now consider a loss. If the loss involves only short-term loss of production, the firm may be able to retain its clients, since the entry barriers keep out new firms. Thus if the firm was supplying output Q_1 in Figure 14-A5 (derived from the preloss demand curve D_1), it should be able to return to this position. However, if loss of production is protracted, the existing inelastic market demand makes it both attractive and feasible for a new entrant to overcome the financial and organizational barriers to entry. If a new entrant appears, the existing firm will only be able to reenter with reduced demand. How much demand is lost will depend on the scale of operations of the new firm and how successful it has been in establishing customer loyalties. The new demand curve is shown as D_2. The effect of the interruption is a shift from the preloss position, shown as P_1Q_1, to lower output and prices, denoted as P_2Q_2. The firm may be able to shift D_2 back toward the orignal D_1 with a heavy marketing program, but this will be expensive and may not even increase sales at all if the new entrant responds in kind. Since the entrant has overcome the barriers to entry and lodged its foot in the door, the market may now be permanently divided between the two firms.

FIGURE 14-A4

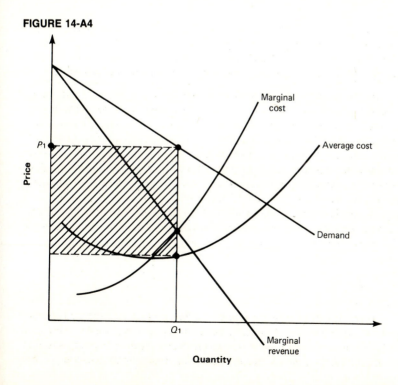

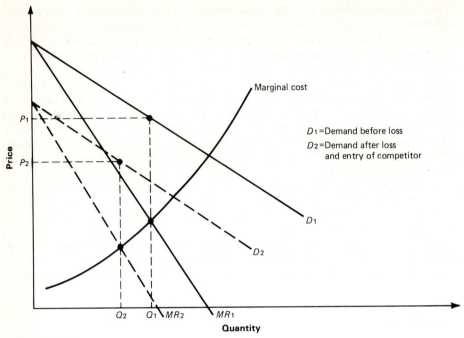

FIGURE 14-A5

OLIGOPOLY

Oligopoly is characterized by a small number of firms selling differentiated products for which there is some degree of substitution (e.g., brands of toothpaste or washing machines). Since there is a small number of suppliers, the fortune of each rests on the decision of each of the others, and each firm is likely to become acutely aware of this interdependence. This interdependence implies that a firm cannot predict the effects of its own price-output decisions unless it can predict the reactions of its rivals. If a firm raises its price, it may reap higher profit if the hike is not followed by rival firms who fear loss of market share. Alternatively, if a firm reduces its price to increase market share at the expense of rivals, it is only likely to be successful if others do not follow the lead.

Their interdependence is summarized by the kinked demand curve in Figure 14-A6. The firm may be considered to face two demand curves. Curve *DD* is based on the assumption that price changes will not be followed by rivals, but curve *dd* is based on the alternative assumption that rivals will follow suit. If firms are acutely aware of the nature of the interdependence and seek to protect their markets, each may assume that any price initiative on its own part will bring the least favorable response from rivals (since the firm itself would behave in such a manner if a rival changed its price). Thus the firm assumes that its demand curve is the hybrid of *DD* and *dd*. For price rises above the current price P_0, the relevant curve is *DD*. For price reductions, other firms are assumed to follow to protect their share of the market, and the relevant curve is *dd*. The hybrid curve is shown as the kinked line drawn in heavy ink, but the marginal revenue curve is also a hybrid of the respective *MR* curves for *DD* and *dd*. This is shown as the discontinuous line *MR*. Marginal cost cuts marginal revenue in the vertical section shown at the current quantity Q_0. This must be the case, since the firm has chosen the current output to equate marginal costs and revenue in order to maximize profit. The firm has no incentive to change price, for this would break the equality of MC and MR, thereby reducing profit. Even small changes in the marginal cost curve will not induce the firm to change prices, since these also will lead to intersections on the vertical section of the marginal revenue curve, as shown by MC_2 and MR.

Thus the oligopoly situation is characterized by interdependence, and this leads to price stability according to the kinked demand curve model. Other models of oligopoly have been derived, and these do differ in their predictions. The psychology of interdependence is rather like that of a poker game, and clearly, there can be no unique model. However, the observed tendency toward price stability has given the kinked demand curve model some general level of acceptability.

With the kinked demand curve model, there is a clear incentive to form cartels, but the model reveals the fragility of these cartels should they be formed. Firms will have an incentive to reduce price if they believe that rivals will not follow (i.e., they believe the downward section of demand to be DD), but in a cartel, there is an agreement not to indulge in price cutting. This is of advantage to all firms collectively, since a price war would leave all firms with lower profits. However, for any one firm, the agreement might be interpreted to imply that, if it broke away and cut its price, the remaining suppliers would stick to the existing cartel price. If the

FIGURE 14-A6

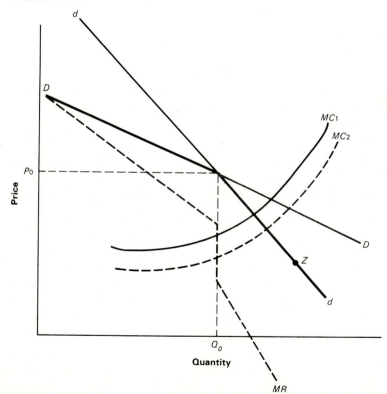

cartel remains intact despite this breakaway, the deviant firm would increase its demand along *DD*. This is tempting. However, if the cartel dissolves into a competitive "free for all," or if it remains intact but reduces the cartel price to match that of the deviating firm, the deviating firm will only move down the *dd* section of the kinked demand curve to some position such as Z. In this event, the deviant firm will be worse off: The original position Q_0 offered higher profits. Thus the cartel will remain intact as long as each firm resists the temptation to undercut the cartel in the fear that the cartel will dissolve or retaliate.

Similar logic is now applied to interruption losses. By analogy, there is an incentive for each firm to agree with all others that in the event of loss to any one, the others will refrain from predatory actions designed to capture its business. Further, there may be incentive for an agreement to undertake contractual production on behalf of the distressed firm should the remaining firms have the spare capacity. Such a reciprocal aid agreement would act as a form of insurance against interruption losses for all firms in the industry. Now let us suppose that no such agreement has been negotiated and one firm has a major fire that results in estimated stoppage of production for several months. There is now clear opportunity for the remaining firms to expand their respective market shares to absorb that of the incapacitated supplier. The more closely the products are substitutable, the easier it will be for the remaining firms to reap this harvest. An alternative strategy is for the rival firms to subcontract production facilities to the distressed firm. This action may be feasible, since each firm may believe that it would be similarly treated should it suffer a similar loss in the future. Whether the remaining firms would launch such a lifeboat depends on whether they trust their rivals sufficiently and on how probable, or improbable, they estimate a similar loss to themselves. No generalizations can be made here. Certainly there are collective advantages *ex ante* for such agreements. It may also be argued that such agreements are in the public interest, since a greater concentration of market power will result from the exit of the distressed firm, but whether such cooperation will arise depends on the level and nature of interaction between the competitors. Most insurers and loss adjusters will be able to cite examples either way.

Finally, it will be noted that the potential for interruption losses under oligopoly is severe. The concentration of market share into the hands of a few suppliers implies barriers to entry. The severity of these barriers suggests that there is relatively little danger of competition from new entrants, but it also suggests that a distressed firm may have great difficulty in winning back a market share that has devolved to competitors. The degree of differentiation of the product is also important. If the product trades under a well known brand name (toothpaste), or if there is limited substitution for technical reasons (after-sales service for automobiles), then short-term protection is afforded. Again, however, this is a two-edged sword. Once rivals break through the substitution barrier, the firm will find it difficult to reestablish itself.

CONCLUSION

The preceding analysis is based on one-period models of a firm and its position in the market. Profit was used as the objective function and was also used to define whether firms would survive. We have examined corporate objective in terms of the market value of a firm's equity. This was elaborated in a multiperiod framework. The economics approach and the investment approach are really two sides of the same coin, each looking at different aspects of a multidimensional problem. Thus the reduction in profit for a firm that loses its market share after a loss is equivalent to a downward revision in the expected earnings of the firm, and this will have a negative impact on the share value. We may also build into the theory of a firm some minimal profit level that is equivalent to the return required by investors to allocate capital funds to the firm. With a reduction in demand (market share captured by competitors) and the higher cost curves arising from loss financing not covered by insurance, a firm will, by definition, face a lower return on reinvested capital. The interruption losses analyzed in this section may be of sufficient magnitude to reduce the expected rate of return below the cost of capital. In this case, exit from the industry might be a reasonable and clear decision.

REFERENCES

Bierman, M., Jr., C. P. Bonini, and W. Hausman: *Quantitative Analysis for Business Decisions,* 5th ed., Chaps. 17–19, Irwin: Homewood, Ill., 1971.

Buffa, E. S., and W. H. Taubert: *Production-Inventory Systems: Planning and Control,* Irwin: Homewood, Ill., 1972.

Cohen, K. R., and R. M. Cyert: *Theory of the Firm: Resource Allocation in a Market Economy,* Prentice Hall: Englewood Cliffs, N.J., 1975.

Hausman, W. H., and A. Sanches-Bell: "The Stochastic Cash Balance Problem with Average Compensatory Balance Requirement," *Management Science,* vol. 21, 1975, pp. 849–857.

Hausman, W. H., and L. J. Thomas: "Inventory Control with Probabilistic Demand and Periodic Withdrawals," *Management Science,* vol. 18, 1972, pp. 265–275.

Henderson, J. M., and R. E. Quandt: *Microeconomic Theory: A Mathematical Approach,* McGraw-Hill: New York, 1971.

Mullins, D., and R. Homonoff: "Applications of Inventory Cash Management Models," in *Modern Developments in Financial Management,* (S. C. Myer, ed.), Praeger: New York, 1976.

Samuelson, P. A.: *Economics,* McGraw-Hill: New York, 1976.

Sprecher, C. R., and M. A. Pertl: "Large Losses, Risk Management and Stock Prices," *Journal of Risk and Insurance,* vol. XLX, 1983, pp. 107–117.

Stone, B. H.: "The Use of Forecasts and Smoothing in Control Limit Models for Cash Management," *Financial Management,* vol. 1, 1972, pp. 72–84.

CHAPTER 15

TAX ISSUES IN RISK MANAGEMENT

The treatment of taxation is included in a separate chapter for several reasons. First, the purpose of this book is to present a framework that ensures economic compatibility of risk management and other financial decisions. Taxation complicates cash flows and may change optimal decisions, but the decision framework is still intact. The only thing that needs to be altered is the calculation of cash flows to be fed into the framework. Thus tax has been excluded from previous chapters to simplify exposition while still preserving the main economic insights of the financial approach.

The second reason for deferring taxation to a separate chapter is that tax provisions are specific in time and place. Exclusion of taxation in previous chapters gives greater generality to the analysis. Specific tax provisions that apply in specific jurisdictions can be applied to calculate the tax flows to and from a firm in those jurisdictions. The treatment reserved for this chapter is illustrative of some of the effects of the U.S. Federal Tax Code. The provisions of that code are complex and are not considered in great detail. Furthermore, we do not include treatment of state corporate income taxes, which vary among states. The interested reader is referred to *Risk Management*, a magazine published monthly by the Risk and Insurance Management Society. This magazine contains special feature sections on issues of taxation that are relevant to risk management.

SOME GENERAL FEATURES OF CORPORATE INCOME TAX

Corporate income is subject to federal tax at a progressive rate and, in addition, is subject to state tax at rates determined by the individual states. Federal marginal tax rates effective from 1979 increase quickly to 46%, as shown in the following schedule:

Corporate income ($)	Marginal tax rate
0–25,000	17%
25,000–50,000	20%
50,000–75,000	30%
75,000–100,000	40%
100,000 and up	46%

The quick progression up the marginal tax rates ensures that larger corporations face an average tax rate approaching, but slightly less than, 46%. For example, on an income of, say, $10 million, the total tax is

$$
\begin{aligned}
& \$25,000 \times 0.17 \\
+\ & \$25,000 \times 0.2 \\
+\ & \$25,000 \times 0.3 \\
+\ & \$25,000 \times 0.4 \\
+\ & \$9,900,000 \times 0.46 = \$4,580,750
\end{aligned}
$$

which represents an average tax rate for the corporation of 45.8%. The following treatment of tax deals entirely with federal tax, and the reader should remember that state tax may also be levied.

Federal tax is imposed on corporate earnings, but a firm is permitted to deduct "ordinary and necessary" business expenses. The treatment of deductions has important implications for risk management purposes, since deductions do not carry neutral implications for the risk management choices facing a firm.

A useful broad distinction in examining tax deductions is between expenditures for the acquisition of capital assets having a useful life of multiple years and other expenditures. Expenditure on capital assets is not immediately deductible, but a firm may depreciate an asset over a number of years. Various depreciation schedules are permitted, i.e., straight line, units of production, sum-of-years digits, and declining balance. Some permit depreciation at a more rapid rate in early years; i.e., declining balance gives higher depreciation in early years than straight line. Given positive time preference, it is of advantage to write off assets as quickly as possible, since the bulk of tax benefit becomes available to the firm at an earlier date. Methods such as declining balance and sum-of-years digits are known as *accelerated* depreciation methods for this reason. On disposal of a capital asset, a firm may be subject to capital gains tax if the disposition yields a capital gain. This provision also has implications for disposition through casualty loss, as considered below.

The purchase of capital assets for investment also gives a firm an investment tax credit. Tax credits were introduced in 1962 and have been suspended and reinstated on occasions before becoming a permanent feature of the tax code. The provisions for tax credits were changed in 1978 and later in 1981. Clearly, this aspect of corporate taxation is volatile. The reason is that tax credits have been used as a major instrument of economic policy. Changes in the tax credit provisions have been used to stimulate new investment and, at times, to discourage investment.

The investment tax credit permits a firm undertaking new investment to count a stated portion of that investment expenditure as a credit toward its current tax liability. For example, consider a firm having a tax liability for the current year of $10 million. If the firm spends $20 million on new investment and the tax code provides a 10% tax credit, the firm can reduce its tax liability as follows:

Tax due before consideration of tax credit	$10 million
Tax credit 10% of $20 million	$ 2.0 million
Tax due	$ 8.0 million

Certain types of loss-reduction expenditures may count as capital investments for tax purposes and may thereby qualify for tax credit.

Expenditures other than those on capital assets may be deducted as they are incurred. Included as such expenditures are insurance premiums to external insurers (there are one or two exceptions, including premiums to some captives and premiums on capital assets under construction). However, other methods of financing reinvestment also are affected by tax provisions, as considered below.

Finally, the federal tax code incorporates a "carry forward–carry back" provision. Firms can carry losses (negative earnings) to prior or future years to reduce tax liability for years in which positive taxable earnings are made. This provision is extremely important in ensuring proper tax credit for large uninsured casualty or liability losses.

SOME RISK MANAGEMENT IMPLICATIONS

Financing Devices

It is recognized that insurance premiums constitute an ordinary and necessary business expense and are deductible as they are incurred, subject to the exceptions mentioned earlier. One of these exceptions, that for some captives, is considered again in Chapter 16. This provision reduces the net cost of purchasing insurance. However, other risk management financing devices also are affected by tax.

Interest payments on debt are deductible. Thus if debt is used to finance investment, the net cost is the after-tax interest payment. In contrast, dividend payments are not deductible. At face value, this asymmetry creates a bias in favor of debt financing rather than equity financing. However, the issue is further complicated by personal taxation. Furthermore, as pointed out by Miller (1977), the (after-tax) prices of debt and equity instruments in capital markets may well reflect their different tax treatment.

Premiums paid to captive insurers may or may not be deductible. If the captive provides a significant "shifting and distribution" of risk, the premium would appear to be deductible. This provision is reflected in the *Carnation* case discussed in Chapter 16. If a captive is wholly owned by a single parent and does not insure any external risk (i.e., risk for clients other than the parent), the premium is not deductible. What constitutes a significant "shifting and distribution" of risk is a matter for individual interpretation. Consistent with this distinction between captives that provide a meaningful risk-pooling function and those which do not is the treatment of retention funds not embodied in a captive. Contributions to a retention fund are not deductible.

Losses

The tax treatment of losses varies according to whether losses are insured and whether the loss represents a capital asset. In general, only uninsured losses are deductible. In the case of partial insurance, the deduction for loss is reduced by the insurance settlement. In other words, only the uninsured portion of the loss is deductible.

For property-casualty losses, a firm may deduct the lower of the following:

1 The difference between the fair market value before and after the loss, or
2 The adjusted (book) value of the property.

When total loss occurs, the deduction cannot exceed the book value of the property. In all cases, the amount of deduction is diminished by the insurance settlement. The insurance settlement can exceed the tax deduction, but this gives rise to the prospect of capital gains, and the treatment depends on whether the asset is classified as a capital asset and whether the insurance money is used for reinvestment or simply to increase the liquid resources of the firm. If reinvestment is not undertaken, tax may be levied at the capital gains rate or at the ordinary corporate rate for any gain resulting from an insurance settlement. A more detailed analysis of these provisions is given in Main (1983).

Liability losses are deductible to the amount of the settlement (whether litigation is involved or not) plus legal expenses, such as court fees, lawyers fees, expert witnesses, cost of securing evidence, etc. The deduction is, of course, reduced by the value of any insurance settlement. An exception to the deduction of liability awards is the case of punitive damages. Indeed, any such tax deduction for punitive damages may be considered to undermine the very purpose of such awards, which is to deter and/or punish the form of behavior that resulted in the loss event.

Loss Reduction   The tax treatment of loss-reduction expenditures depends on whether they are treated as capital assets or not. Some expenditures may be deducted immediately, such as the cost of safety education, the operating cost of a fire brigade, and the ongoing costs of inspecting goods for the purpose of quality control. However, other costs may represent the acquisition of capital assets. For example, the installation of a sprinkler system will have to be depreciated over its useful (multiyear) life. One useful loss-reduction device considered in Chapter 14 was inventory, which may be used to reduce business interruption following a loss. Inventory is not construed to be a capital asset and is not taxed as such.

REWORKING SELECTED PREVIOUS EXAMPLES

The remaining part of this chapter will comprise a selection of examples considered in previous chapters, but now reworked to include the main corporate tax effects. The examples will be reintroduced somewhat sparingly, and the reader is asked to refer to the earlier examples to obtain the relevant background and financial information specific to the case. On reworking, the firm will be subject to a flat 46% tax rate. This is an oversimplification, since the actual corporate rate is progressive. However, since the progression of marginal rates is rapid, the average tax rate for most larger corporations is very close to 46%. Further, I will assume that the carry forward–carry back provisions are not evoked. This simplification would have no effect if the carryover provisions were conducted at an appropriate discount rate. Since this is not so, some small distortion will arise. Each example will finish with a short discussion of the impact of taxation on the particular decision.

The examples are conducted to illustrate (1) how tax flows may be incorporated into the analysis, and (2) some of the material biases that taxation has on risk management decisions. Once again, the treatment is illustrative rather than detailed and exhaustive. The particular tax provisions and their applications to individual cases are complex, but sometimes they are matters of interpretation. The reader interested in a particular application is referred to the tax code and/or to a tax lawyer for specific provisions or advice.

H&RD Cheese (Chapter 9)

This example compared alternative postloss financing with debt and equity. The firm had already suffered a major flood loss that required a reinvestment of $2 million. New debt could be raised at 12%, or new shares could be issued at a price determined by investors' willingness to subscribe. In the "no-tax" example, debt financing was shown to be preferred. The fact that new debt was cheaper than equity more than offset the increase in the equity capitalization rate due to the increased leverage. With the introduction of tax, the choice between debt and equity will be further disturbed. Interest on the new (and for that matter, the old) debt is deductible for tax purposes. However, dividend payments are not deductible. We now rework Table 9-3 with this provision. All details, except for tax, are the same.

Reworking of H&RD Cheese with the capitalization rates originally used now reveals that debt is still preferred. The result of postloss debt financing will be a share price of $9.91 compared with $8.96 for equity financing. This is a wider margin and, therefore, a clearer choice in favor of debt than shown in the no tax case. Debt refinancing has gained extra advantage from the tax deductibility of debt.

This example has not considered the effects of personal taxation. One or two comments are in order, since the differential personal tax on dividends and interest may have some indirect effect on this decision via the equity capitalization rate. Generally speaking (and this is a fairly sweeping generalization), returns on equity receive more favorable tax treatment for individuals. It is difficult to be precise on this point, since much depends on the size and structure of the individual's income and whether the return on equity is delivered as a dividend or as a capital gain. However, accepting the proposition that equity returns are more favorably treated for individual tax, investors would be willing to accept a somewhat lower return on equity, relative to the return on debt, than considered in the no-tax example. For example, the equity

TABLE 15-1
H&RD CHEESE: EXAMPLE REWORKED WITH TAX

	1 Before loss	2 After loss with no reinvestment	After loss with reinvestment with:	
			Debt	Equity
EBIT	$2,000,000	$1,000,000	$2,000,000	$2,000,000
Interest	$200,000	$200,000	$440,000	$200,000
Taxable earnings	$1,800,000	$800,000	$1,560,000	$1,800,000
Tax	$828,000	$368,000	$717,600	$828,000
Earnings available for distribution (E)	$972,000	$432,000	$842,400	$972,000
No. of shares	500,000	500,000	500,000	723,214 (682,584)
Earnings per share (EPS)	$1.944	$0.864	$1.6848	$1.344 ($1.424)
Market capitalization rate (k_E)	0.15 (0.13)	0.17	0.17	0.15 (0.13)
Price per share (EPS/k_E)	$12.96 ($14.95)	$5.08	$9.91	$8.96 (10.95)
Market value of equity (E/k_E)	$6.48 million ($7.48 million)	$2.54 million	$4.96 million	$6.48 million ($7.48 million)

capitalization rate might be 13%, as opposed to the 15% considered in the no-tax case. The effect of refinancing with equity at 13% is shown in the parentheses alongside the prior figures in Table 15-1. Now the equity alternative turns out to be preferable to debt.

In summary, the main issues affecting the choice between postloss debt and equity are

1 Debt is usually cheaper than equity, favoring debt.

2 Debt financing increases leverage, thereby bidding up the cost of capital, favoring equity.

3 Tax deductibility of interest, but not dividends, is allowed on corporate accounts, favoring debt.

4 More favorable personal tax treatment of equity lowers cost of equity relative to debt, favoring equity.

No general conclusion can be drawn as to whether these conflicting effects will net out to favor debt or equity finance; it depends on individual circumstance.

Rationality, Inc. (Chapter 10)

This example was presented in Chapter 10 to show that the capital-budgeting framework could be used with incremental cash flows only. This saved the laborious recalculation of all the firm's cash flows for each decision. The incremental cash flow analysis is valid when the discount rate used relates to the systematic risk of the project. A positive decision is indicated when the net present value of the project is positive.

The Rationality, Inc. example required the risk manager to compare insurance purchase with the alternative of financing prospective future losses through postloss debt issue. The effects of introducing tax into this example are

1 Insurance premiums are tax deductible.
2 Interest payments on postloss debt are also deductible.
3 Uninsured casualty losses are deductible.

The net result of effects 1 and 3 should create a bias in favor of insurance, since the premium is deductible as it is incurred. Uninsured losses also are deductible as incurred, but since prospective losses are future events at the time of decision, positive discount rates would render the premium deduction more valuable. We assume here that losses typically lag the date of decision by 6 months. The tax bias in favor of insurance is further reinforced, since the tax benefit included deduction of the premium loading, whereas the expected deduction with uninsured losses is only the expected value of loss. Operating against these biases, interest payments on postloss debt are deductible.

The expected value of loss is $500,000; therefore, given 9% interest on postloss debt, the expected interest burden is $45,000 before tax. The expected present value of the repayment schedule before tax and at the time of loss is calculated using the risk-free discount rate, since repayments are assumed to be certain. Therefore,

$$D = \frac{45,000}{1 + 0.8} + \frac{45,000}{(1 + 0.8)^2} + \frac{45,000}{(1 + 0.8)^3} + \frac{45,000}{(1 + 0.8)^4} + \frac{45,000}{(1 + 0.8)^5}$$

$$+ \frac{500,000}{(1 + 0.8)^5} = \$519,964$$

This figure was shown in the previous example. Given tax deductibility of interest at 46%, the value of the stream is

$$D = \sum_{t=1}^{5} \frac{45,000(1 - 0.46)}{(1 + 0.8)^5} + \frac{500,000}{(1 + 0.8)^5}$$

$$= \$437,313$$

Since losses are assumed to arise in 6 months time, this cost may be considered to arise at that time. The discount rate used to discount over this period must reflect that losses are risky. This in no way contradicts the use of the risk-free rate earlier, since repayments following a given loss are not assumed to be risky. The appropriate risk-adjusted rate for the 6-month period is 4.75% (as in the previous example), reflecting systematic risk. However, also recall that the uninsured loss is deductible, the expected value of this benefit being 500,000(0.46) at the time the loss is assumed to arise. Since the loss is risky, the risk-adjusted rate is also used to discount to a present value at the time of decision.

The expected present value of financing contingent future losses by postloss debt, therefore, is

$$\text{RAPV debt} = \frac{\$437,313 - 500,000(0.46)}{1 + 0.475} = \$197,912$$

In contrast, the insurance premium is \$650,000. Tax deduction reduces the after-tax cost to $650,000(1 - 0.46) = \$351,000$.

In this example, the effects of tax make the decision in favor of debt financing over insurance even more pronounced. The after-tax risk-adjusted present value of debt is only 56% of that of insurance compared with 79% before consideration of tax. Despite the earlier tax benefit with insurance, debt is preferred because tax is deducted on both the uninsured loss and the interest payable on postloss financing.

Further issues that might be considered in this case are

1 The effect of increased leverage under the debt alternative on the weighted average of cost capital.

2 The prospect that losses will reduce corporate earnings to a negative value, thereby evoking the carry forward–carry back procedures.

3 The tax year ending can make a difference. Premiums and uninsured losses were deducted immediately. In practice, they would be deducted at the end of the current tax year. If the decision between insurance and debt is made at the beginning of the tax year, then prospective uninsured loss arising in 6 months would be deducted in the same tax year. If the decision is made at the end of the tax year, the prospective benefit from tax deductibility of uninsured losses would arise in future tax years. The problem should be adapted to the individual case.

Sunshine Sodas (Chapter 11)

This example did not compare financing costs, but considered the ruin probability for a retention fund set up to finance uninsured losses. The ruin probability will now be recalculated using the preceding tax provisions. In so doing, we will examine whether tax can have a material effect on the adequacy of a fund.

Before getting into this example, we will discuss the effect of taxation on the distribution of aggregate loss. Consider the values of the sample mean, standard deviation, and skewness measure before tax. The subscript B is used to indicate losses before tax. Thus we have

$$\bar{L}_B \qquad \text{and} \qquad S(L_B) \qquad \text{and} \qquad a_3(L_B)$$

as defined in equations (4-10), (4-11), and (4-12). Since the loss is tax deductible, we can define the equivalent values after tax using the subscript A as follows:

$$\bar{L}_A = \frac{1}{n}\sum_j(1 - t)L_{j,B} = (1 - t)\frac{1}{n}\sum_j L_{j,B}$$

$$= (1 - t)\bar{L}_B \tag{15-1}$$

$$S(L_A) = \left\{\frac{1}{n-1}\sum_j[(1 - t)L_{j,B} - (1 - t)\bar{L}_B]^2\right\}^{1/2}$$

$$= \left\{(1 - t)^2\left[\frac{1}{n-1}\sum_j(L_{j,B} - \bar{L}_B)\right]^2\right\}^{1/2}$$

$$= (1 - t)S(L_B) \tag{15-2}$$

$$a_3(L_A) = \frac{n/[(n - 1)(n - 2)]\sum_j[(1 - t)L_{j,B} - (1 - t)\bar{L}_B]^3}{[(1 - t)S(L_B)]^3}$$

$$= \frac{(1 - t)^3\{n/[(n - 1)(n - 2)]\sum_j(L_{j,B} - \bar{L}_B)^3\}}{(1 - t)^3[S(L_B)]^3}$$

$$= a_3(L_B) \tag{15-3}$$

For Sunshine Sodas, the before-tax values are restated and the after-tax values are calculated in accordance with the preceding formulas. Thus,

$$\bar{L}_B = \$118,800 \qquad \bar{L}_A = \$64,152$$
$$S(L_B) = \$160,360 \qquad S(L_A) = \$86,594$$
$$a_3(L_B) = 2.162 \qquad a_3(L_A) = 2.162$$

Since uninsured losses are tax deductible, only the after-tax loss represents a claim on the fund. Consequently, the example can proceed with the after-tax values summarizing the loss distribution. Other tax provisions also are relevant. The contribution to the fund is not tax deductible (although under some circumstances, it could be deductible if the fund was incorporated as a captive insurer; this is considered in Chapter 16). The fund is invested in interest-bearing securities, and the interest received is taxable (yields on equity investments would require different tax treatment).

Proceeding now with the example, the terminal value of the fund is

$$X_A = F(1)[1 + r_a(1 - t)] - (1 - t)L_B(2)$$

Setting $F(1)$ as 150% of the after-tax loss, we have

$$E(X_A) = 1.5(64,152)[1 + 0.1(0.54)] - 64,152 = \$37,272$$
$$\sigma(X_A) = 86,594$$
$$\alpha_3(X_A) = -2.162$$

Using equation (11-24) to calculate the ruin probability, we have

$$z = \frac{-1 + \sqrt{1 + 2(-2.162)/3 \,(-2.162/6 - 37{,}272/86{,}594)}}{-2.162/3}$$

$$= -0.6421634 \approx -0.64$$

Using the z tables, the probability of ruin is estimated to be 0.2611. Notice that this is very close to the ruin probability that was calculated in the no-tax example. Thus it seems that consideration of tax has had very little effect on the adequacy of the fund. Let us take a moment to reflect why this is so.

The effect of tax in this example is to reduce all claims on the retention fund to $(1 - t)$ times the before-tax value. However, the contribution was based on the after-tax expected loss, which was $(1 - t)$ times the before-tax expected loss. Under these circumstances, claims and contributions were reduced in equal proportion, thereby offsetting each other. In fact, these effects exactly offset each other given the method of calculating the fund contribution. The reader can verify this by reworking the example without imposing tax on the interest received from the investment. This calculation will result in the same ruin probability calculated in the no-tax case. It follows that the only material tax effect comes from the taxation of yields from fund investments. The effect turns out to be fairly small.

Ann Teak Company (Chapter 13)

The Ann Teak Company was facing the decision to install a sprinkler system. The existing profitability of the company suggested that, should a loss arise, reinvestment would be contemplated and such reinvestment would be undertaken from postloss financing sources. In the no-tax analysis, the sprinkler system was seen to be justified because the capital cost was lower than the capitalized value of the benefits. These benefits represented savings in the expected costs of reinvestment because the sprinkler system reduced the expected value of loss.

The principal tax implications of the case are

1 Ann Teak may depreciate its capital expenditure on the sprinkler system because it is considered to be a capital asset. For simplicity, we simply depreciate over a straight-line schedule over the life of the asset. In practice, the firm could depreciate at a more rapid rate, and this would prove advantageous given the time value of money.

2 Insofar as the loss-reduction expenditure represents capital investment, it will qualify for an investment tax credit. Thus the firm can use a given portion of the investment expenditure as an immediate credit against its tax liability. In this example, the investment tax credit is assumed to be 10%.

3 Since future losses are not insured, they are tax deductible as they arise. As long as the firm has sufficient earnings to pay the marginal tax rate, the expected tax benefit from the deduction is directly related to the expected value of loss. Since the sprinkler system will reduce the expected value of loss, it will correspondingly reduce the expected tax benefit on uninsured losses. For this example, the tax benefit on uninsured loss is simplified as the marginal tax rate t times the expected loss $E(L)$. Thus the expected loss of tax benefit is $t\Delta E(L)$.

4 There are also tax implications from postloss financing. Since the example did not specify the form of financing, we simplify the problem by assuming it away. The capitalized value of the financing costs at the time funds are raised is simply the value raised for reinvestment. Thus the expected capitalized value of financing costs is $75,000 if sprinklers are not installed and $30,000 if sprinklers are installed.

In addition, we continue to use a discount rate of 9.2% to represent the systematic risk of losses. Other details are as shown in Chapter 13.

The capital cost of the sprinkler system is represented as the sum of the before-tax cost, the capitalized value of depreciation allowances, and the tax credit. Depreciation allowances are considered to be risk-free and are discounted at the risk-free rate. Capital cost after tax K, therefore, is

$$K = -350,000 + \sum_{i=1}^{20} \frac{17,500}{(1 + 0.8)^i} + 350,000(0.1) = -\$143,183$$

The expected benefits are represented by the expected savings in financing costs over each year of the life of the system, that is, $45,000 per year. However, this benefit is reduced by the loss of tax benefit arising from the reduction in uninsured loss, that is, $0.46(\$45,000)$. Thus the net annual benefit is

$$(1 - 0.46)(\$45,000)$$

and its capitalized value using the rate appropriate to the systematic risk of loss, that is, 9.2%, is

$$B = \sum_{i=1}^{20} \frac{0.54(45,000)}{(1 + 0.092)^i}$$
$$= \$218,845$$

Thus the net present value of the sprinkler installation is

$$\text{NPV} = K + B = -143,183 + 218,845$$
$$= \$75,662$$

The sprinkler should still be installed.

In general, it is not obvious whether tax effects will encourage or discourage expenditures on loss reduction. However, tax lowers the net cost of investments in safety, thus encouraging the firm to spend more. Conversely, the net benefits of loss reduction are also reduced, since uninsured losses are partly absorbed by tax deductibility. How these conflicting effects balance out depends on the size of the depreciation allowances and tax credits. In this case, the net present value of the project has increased in absolute terms over the no-tax example (where the net present value was $55,270). This higher value appears despite the fact that the after-tax cost of the system is smaller.

SUMMARY AND CONCLUSION

Taxation may have a significant effect on risk management decisions. The purpose of this chapter has been to present very general details of the federal taxation system and to explore their potential implications for risk management by reworking selected examples from previous chapters.

Tax can influence the choice of risk management financing because it affects the various preloss and postloss sources in different ways. Insurance premiums are tax deductible, but so is the interest paid on debt. Dividends, in contrast, are not deductible, leading to the supposition that equity financing is penalized in the tax code. However, personal tax has not been considered, and this usually acts in favor of equity. The potential tax bias is further complicated by the treatment of losses. Although subject to various qualifications, the general effect of the tax code is to treat uninsured losses as tax deductible, thereby reducing the net cost of noninsurance financing devices. No general conclusion can be drawn as to how these various effects balance out: Much depends on the particular firm and its loss exposures and earnings prospects. In the limit, of course, a firm that has no expectation of paying tax will find its risk management decisions unaffected by the tax code.

Tax can also affect loss-reduction decisions, although effects differ depending on whether loss reduction involves acquisition of capital assets or not. Expenditures on loss prevention bring tax benefits in the form of depreciation write-offs or tax credits for capital assets and immediate deductions for other allowed expenditures. This reduces the net costs of loss reduction. However, the net benefit from deductibility of premiums or insured losses may partly be lost as these values are reduced by the loss-reduction program. The directional effect of tax on loss-reduction activity depends on the balance of net reductions in costs and net reductions in benefits. The overall effect is not predictable in general.

The reworked examples reveal some of these effects and illustrate how tax flows may be accommodated in the analysis. The examples are illustrative, and the reader is cautioned again about generalizing from these cases. Tax provisions are considerably more complex than considered by this brief introduction; they are subject to legislative change, and their application is often a matter of interpretation.

In the next chapter we turn our attention to a specialized risk management device that has received widespread attention in recent years—the captive insurance company. The emergence of this device may have much to do with taxes (although this is not beyond dispute), and we will therefore examine certain relevant tax features in some detail.

QUESTIONS

1 Discuss the following statement. The Internal Revenue Service acts as a coinsurer for uninsured casualty and liability losses.

2 Compare the following forms for post loss reinvestment:
  a *Insurance.* The premium is equal to 110% of the expected loss of capital resources.
  b *Post loss debt.* The interest rate is 12% and the debt is a 10-year balloon.
  Other information is:

Expected loss of capital resources	$3 million
Tax rate (assume this to be a flat rate)	0.46
Loss beta	0.2
Risk-free rate	0.12
Expected return on the market portfolio	0.18

Assume that the firm has sufficient taxable earnings in the current year to fully shield uninsured loss should the debt alternative be chosen. The expected timing of loss is 6 months from the present. The insurance premium is payable immediately.

3 A firm has in place a retention fund to finance postloss reinvestment. The relevant characteristics of the loss distribution are

$$E(L) = \$2 \text{ million} \qquad \sigma(L) = \$4 \text{ million} \qquad \alpha_3(L)1.5$$

The firm has initial reserves of $0.5 million and makes a beginning of year contribution to the fund of 1.5 million. Fund assets are invested in risk-free taxable bonds yielding 10%. The firm is subject to a 46% tax rate (assume a flat rate). What is the probability of ruin for the fund?

REFERENCES

DeAngelo, H., and R. W. Masulis: "Optimal Capital Structure under Corporate and Personal Taxation," *Journal of Financial Economics,* vol. 8, 1980, p. 3029.

Main, B. G. M.: "Corporate Insurance Purchases and Taxes," *Journal of Risk and Insurance,* vol. 50, 1983, pp. 197–223.

Mayers, D., and C. W. Smith: "On the Corporate Demand for Insurance," *Journal of Business,* vol. 55, 1982, pp. 281–296.

Miller, M. H.: "Debt and Taxes," *Journal of Finance,* vol. 32, 1977, pp. 266–278.

CHAPTER 16

CAPTIVE INSURANCE COMPANIES

Following a loss, a firm may or may not choose to replace destroyed resources. If an affirmative decision is reached, a source of contingent financing is required. Alternative sources of finance for reinvestment have been examined elsewhere, and a decision structure based on the existing value of equity has been developed. One solution to contingent financing is to set up a retention fund in anticipation of future losses, the assets of the fund being available for reinvestment purposes in the event of loss. However, the valuation model fails to establish a strong case for such a fund. A fund will add value to equity if its assets yield a return in excess of the cost of capital. However, such circumstances have little to do with risk management needs, and no value is gained for a firm by earmarking the fund for risk management purposes. A retention fund merely brings forward the date that a firm seeks funds. This negative conclusion on funding is revised in the face of transaction costs, since funding might help a firm to avoid the substantial transaction costs incurred on a hurried issue of new securities following loss. However, the general conclusion for the establishment of retention funds is weak, and this conclusion is further weakened by tax considerations, since loss reserves for retained risks are not tax deductible.

This summary of retention funds serves as a useful introduction to captive insurance companies. A *captive insurance company* is, in essence, a retention fund that is graced by having its own corporate identity as a subsidiary of a noninsurance parent firm. More succinctly, a captive insurance company is an insurance company that is owned by a noninsurance parent company or companies and which underwrites the insurance business of its parents either directly or by means of reinsurance. The "transfer" of risk to a corporate insurance subsidiary indicates that rating and reserving procedures are adopted in writing the parent's risks. Thus the "veneer" of insurance is present.

However, if the risk does not leave the corporate group, it may be argued that there has been no real transfer of risk at all. Thus it seems that establishing a captive insurance company is simply a fancy way of setting up a retention fund. Accordingly, the earlier conclusion about retention funds would appear to apply equally to captives. We shall soon see that this resemblance can be misleading. Captives can be treated very differently from retention funds for tax purposes. Furthermore, and not unrelated to the tax issue, the captive insurance subsidiary can also write external risks, a practice that can have material risk management effects. For all their apparent similarity with retention funds, captives turn out to be a different kettle of fish.

THE CAPTIVE INSURANCE INDUSTRY

The captive insurance industry is "big business." Some facts, estimates, and speculations about captives will help establish some appreciation of how pervasive this form of financing is:

1 In excess of 1800 captives exist, of which over half are domiciled in Bermuda (Kloman and Rosenbaum, 1982). Other popular locations are the Cayman Islands and Guernsey.

2 The industry is dominated by captives of U.S. parents.

3 Approximately 200 of the Fortune 500 companies have captive insurance companies (Loy and Pertl, 1982).

4 The largest captive is estimated to be Ancon, a subsidiary of Exxon. Ancon probably now has assets approaching $1 billion (Kloman and Rosenbaum, 1982). Only one U.S. reinsurer is larger.

5 In 1978, Bermuda captives had an estimated $2.3 billion in capital and surplus and $3/4 billion in premiums (Greene, 1979). By 1980, paid-in capital and surplus were estimated at $3.3 billion, and $5.6 billion to $6.8 billion was generated for investment (Porat, 1983). Currently (1985), premium income probably lies in the $4 billion to $5 billion range.

6 Total world premiums of captives were estimated at $6 billion to $7 billion in 1981 and growing rapidly (Kloman and Rosenbaum, 1982).

7 Some preliminary evidence by Cross, Thornton, and Davidson (1984) suggests that captive formation has indeed had a positive and significant effect on the value of some parent companies.

The captive concept is very old. An example of the enduring success of a group of captive insurance companies is given by the Factory Mutual System. These companies were established by factory owners seeking appropriate insurance rates for highly protected risks. Dismayed by the lack of recognition for high levels of loss protection from conventional insurers, groups of owners formed mutual insurance operations. Four such companies that share a common emphasis on loss reduction are affiliated through the Associated Factory Mutual Fire Insurance Companies. In essence, these are group captives owned jointly by the policyholders whose risks are insured. The growth of these companies has led to very considerable dilution of ownership, and correspondingly, the system is able to spread risk efficiently over a large number of risks.

(A much different and newer concept is the captive that is owned by a single parent and confines its underwriting activity to the risks of the parent company.) Any effective diversification of risk for this type of captive is limited by the properties of the portfolio of risk exposure units held by the parent) Clearly, this form of captive is very different from the mutual insurance company. Given such diversity, it clearly is useful for our analysis to be supported by some classification of captive insurance companies.

Building on a classification scheme presented by Kloman and Rosenbaum (1982), captives may be divided into the following categories:

1 *Pure captive*. This is a wholly owned or controlled subsidiary insurance company writing only, or predominantly, the risks of the parent. Kloman and Rosenbaum (1982) suggest that a pure captive is so characterized if 80% or more of its portfolio relates to risks of the parent. However, we shall decline to be so specific, since tax issues, which are of major concern, do not neatly follow the precise portfolio breakdowns used by Kloman and Rosenbaum to separate their categories of captive insurers.

2 *Senior captive*. This is a wholly owned or controlled subsidiary insurance company whose portfolio includes a significant, though not overwhelming, portion of external risks. Kloman and Rosenbaum suggest that this category is defined when the parent's risks represent between 25 and 75% of the captive's portfolio,[1] although we again prefer to be imprecise.

3 *Profit center captive*. For such captives, the parent's risks represent a small portion of total risks underwritten (Kloman and Rosenbaum suggest less than 25%).

4 *Group captive*. Unlike previous categories, group captives are jointly owned by two or more parents and underwrite the risks of those parents. Such group captives are usually designed to write only the risks of the parents, although it is useful not to impose this restriction if we wish to make our classification exhaustive. A mutual insurer is such a group captive, since policyholders acquire an equity interest in the firm. However, it is not our intention to consider those very widely based mutuals which offer policies generally to the public on a similar basis to stock insurers. Rather, our concern is with insurers owned on a stock or mutual basis by a small number of parents. No clear dividing line exists, although we would be more concerned with a captive formed by 20 or so oil companies to jointly write the risks of the respective parents than with mutual insurers, such as State Farm, that trade nationally.

These categories map out a range from the wholly owned pure captive to the national, or even international, mutual insurer. Within this range, insurers differ according to the spread of ownership and the degree to which the insurer concentrates on the risks of the owners. The capitve market broadly describes those insurers whose ownership is concentrated and in which the owners' risks constitute a significant portion of the insurer's portfolio.

This classification scheme directs attention to several important differences between

---

[1]Curiously leaving a missing 5% gap between the pure captive and the senior captive.

captives. However, another important distinction exists. A captive may directly insure the risks of a parent or it may insure the parent's risks in an indirect way. Direct insurance is straightforward; the parent pays a premium to its subsidiary, which, in turn, assumes a direct liability to the parent for future losses defined by the policy. A similar effect is achieved by the following transaction. The parent pays a premium to an unrelated insurer, which assumes a direct responsibility for the payment of claims. The unrelated insurer then reinsures the parent's risks with the parent's captive insurance company, which assumes a direct liability for claim payment to the unrelated insurer. (Note, however, that the captive is not directly responsible to the parent for claims, and should the captive default, the unrelated insurer is not relieved of its own contractual obligations.) Notice also that the unrelated insurer is a *front,* and this device is often referred to as *fronting*.

Why would the parent go to the trouble of fronting? In using the fronting device, regulations may be avoided and lower tax liabilities incurred. Most captives are located offshore, and premiums paid are subject to an excise tax. However, the rate of tax is 4% of gross premiums for direct policies but only 1% for reinsurance. Thus fronting gives an immediate 3% tax savings. This advantage may be absorbed partly by state taxes. A further reason is that in many locations, restrictive regulations apply to direct insurance but not to reinsurance. For example, some states and countries preclude unlicensed insureds from insuring domestic risks but permit licensed insurers to reinsure externally. These tax and regulatory issues will be discussed later.

SOME FEATURES OF CAPTIVE INSURANCE

We have seen that a captive insurance company can be viewed as a formalized self-insurance fund. Some writers perceive the reduction of risk through adequate reserving to be a valuable function. For example, Kloman and Rosenbaum (1982) suggest that "the second major factor which has fed the captive movement is the instability and unpredictability of modern economic life. . . . Within this environment, prudent managers seek to insulate the organization against the unexpected through larger contingent reserves" (p. 130). Such a statement may be accurate in describing the motivation of those forming captives. However, it is doubtful that such reasoning is valid for managers seeking to increase the value of a firm. This reasoning ignores the effect of diversification on the ultimate risk cost borne by equityholders; it ignores reinvestment decisions and other potential sources of finance for reinvestment. Earlier analysis established risk reduction to be a somewhat shallow motive for holding reserve funds for noninsured losses. In that analysis, the creation of value through reserve funding arose if it offered a savings in transaction costs over other forms of financing. In the case of captives, we will see that funding through formation of a subsidiary insurance company offers certain cost features that distinguish it from other sources.

Many of the papers cited in the References maintain that captives have certain advantages relative to conventional insurance. Somewhat representative is that by Lenrow et al. (1982), who suggest that captives offer the following advantages:

1 Investment income from reserve funds accrues to the parent rather than to an unrelated insurer.

2 Captives sometimes offer certain tax advantages over conventional insurance or other forms of retention.

3 Some types of cover may be difficult or expensive to obtain on the conventional insurance market because of general market conditions or poor underwriting experience.

4 The captive has access to the reinsurance market, which is often thought to be more competitive than the direct insurance market.

5 Underwriting costs are often lower than those offered by unrelated insurers, since commissions can be avoided as well as unrelated insurers' profit markup.

6 Incentives for effective loss control are stronger than under conventional insurance.

These points do give insights, but it appears that they address the disadvantages of conventional insurance rather more than the advantages of captives. If the terms of insurance are found to be unfavorable, several alternative forms of financing are available. The case for establishing a captive requires that it be shown to be preferable to all competing forms of postloss reinvestment financing rather than simply less costly than conventional insurance. From this more comprehensive comparison of sources of financing, the following comparative observations can be made on the issues identified by Lenrow et al.:

1 Investment income. To run a captive on established insurance principles requires that adequate premium rates be established, that reserves be established from which to pay outstanding claims and contingent claims from unearned premiums, and that the parent contributes adequate capital to maintain an acceptably low probability of ruin. Such practices may be imposed by the regulatory authority having jurisdiction in the domicile of the captive. Furthermore, if the parent is to have a chance to deduct premiums for tax purposes, the captive must be viewed as an insurance company by the Internal Revenue Service (IRS) and, presumably, must operate in an appropriate manner. Reserve funds and paid-in capital form a pool of investable funds, and the investment income serves to reduce the cost of operating the captive. If conventional insurance is purchased, comparable investment funds will accrue to the unrelated insurer. In a competitive market, this investment income will be reflected in premium rates. Therefore, direct access to this income with a captive does not represent a windfall gain over conventional insurance. However, the parent may secure some advantages, since

a Market imperfections may restrain conventional insurers from fully passing on investment income to insureds in the form of lower premium rates.

b Captives often are domiciled in offshore locations where investment regulations are more liberal. This may permit superior investment performances.

c Investment income from offshore locations often is treated more favorably for tax purposes than domestic investment income.

These points do suggest that consideration of investment income may bias the choice of captive over conventional insurance. However, this conclusion does rest on the captive having access to skilled and effective portfolio managers. Furthermore, our earlier conclusion—that reserving will only create value if it results in an after-tax yield in excess of the cost of capital—still holds. Favorable tax treatment will make the pursuit of attractive investment yields more worthwhile. Furthermore, we will now see that the favorable tax treatment of investments is only part of the story; under some circumstances, the parent can also deduct payment of premiums to the captive.

2 Under U.S. tax law, insurance premiums can be deducted from corporate income for purposes of calculating tax. If insurance is not purchased, the corporation can deduct uninsured losses as they are incurred. These provisions are not neutral in their impact on the decision to purchase insurance. Since the payment of premiums precedes the occurrence of losses, the tax benefit from premium payment arises earlier than the tax benefit from deduction of uninsured losses. Bringing forward the tax benefit in this way creates a bias in favor of insurance over other methods of financing loss. The IRS may or may not consider a captive to be an insurer for tax purposes. These circumstances will be examined in greater detail in a separate section, although, for the time being, we simplify the issue by stating that for IRS recognition as an insurance company, the captive must achieve a transfer and shifting of risk. This will be achieved if the captive underwrites a significant volume of insurance on risks unrelated to the parent or if ownership of the captive is widely spread. With IRS recognition, the parent is able to treat premiums paid to the captive as deductible in exactly the same manner as premiums to a conventional insurer. This removes the bias in the respective treatment of captive insurance and conventional insurance. However, it will be noted that a bias is still maintained in favor of (captive and conventional) insurance and against other forms of financing. Other tax effects may be pertinent, but these are somewhat more subtle in their operation and are discussed separately.

3 An argument frequently advanced in favor of captives is that the conventional market often fails to provide premiums that fairly reflect the insured's loss record. This argument may have some merit, but the reasoning is often seductively dangerous. In the first place, the excessive premiums do not necessarily favor captive insurance; they simply point toward the general class of noninsurance methods of financing, of which captive insurance is but one possibility. Second, it is tempting for any insured who has had recent favorable loss experience to argue that this is indicative of a low future loss probability and, consequently, the premium charged by the insurer is too high. However, losses follow a random process, and statistical inferences of this type can only be made within certain confidence limits. Frequently, the loss experience is based on a small statistical sample, and probability inference can only be drawn at low levels of confidence. Proper use of this reasoning requires some sophistication in the employment of statistical techniques, and casual inferences are likely to be quite misleading.

Despite such arguments, the rating methods adopted by conventional insurers are not perfect, and undoubtedly, some cross-subsidization or "averaging" does arise over different groups of insureds. The formation of a captive gives the firm the opportunity to use its own data and make its own rates rather than relying on those of unrelated insurers. This function is of value if a firm is able to produce a more reliable estimate of the probability distribution of future losses than that produced by the conventional market.

Similar arguments apply to the difficulties experienced in obtaining some types of cover on the conventional market. These difficulties point, in general, to noninsurance methods of financing, not particularly to captives. Second, such difficulties often indicate that loss expectancy is unusually high. It would be folly to form a captive without trying to "read the signs" given by such thin markets.

4 Many observers have noted that the insurance market is a dual market; direct insurance is written separately, although not independently of, reinsurance. Reinsurance is written by specialist firms or by direct writers wearing different hats. The nature and intensity of competition are quite different in the direct and reinsurance market for several reasons:

a Direct writing is usually subject to more intensive regulation than reinsurance. Regulation is aimed not simply at keeping prices low, but at protection from insolvency. Consequently, regulation may well serve to protect producers.[2] Reinsurance transactions have not received such regulatory attention since direct writers may be assumed to be more informed as purchasers of insurance protection than are direct insureds. Furthermore, the direct writer is not relieved of any direct liability to the insured by virtue of any reinsurance agreement.

b The relevant market for direct insurance services is statewide or nationwide in its dimensions. Reinsurance often is transacted on an international basis. The somewhat wider boundaries of the reinsurance market expose individual firms to more intensive competition.

c In selling direct insurance, insurers typically have incurred higher production and marketing costs than for reinsurance. Such costs typically are spread over the whole portfolio, although not necessarily in an even manner.

By forming a captive, a firm is not restricted to placing its insurance in the direct market; it also has access to the more competitive reinsurance market. Particular advantages of access to the reinsurance market that are often advanced are that the firm will have more flexibility in negotiating deductibles with adequate premium reduction. In the direct market, insurers are often reluctant to issue policies with high deductibles and/or to offer substantial premium reduction.

If access to reinsurance is the dominant motive for forming a captive, then the generic risk management financing strategy chosen is insurance; the captive is merely a fronting operation established to improve the conditions on which insurance is obtained.

5 Conventional insurance usually is expensive relative to the expected value of loss. In comparing alternative methods of financing reinvestment, the relative transaction costs of the various forms of financing play an important role. To establish comparison with conventional insurance costs, the expense ratios (ratios of expenses, including commission, to premium income) of captives are usually in the ballpark of 0.05 to 0.1 compared with comparable ratios of 0.3 or higher for conventional insurers (Kloman and Rosenbaum, 1982). Part of this savings arises from the exclusion of

---

[2]One of the more visible theories of regulation is that it serves the purpose of captivating market power for producers. See Stigler.

commission, marketing costs, and insurer profits for the captive. However, it must be borne in mind that insurers' expenses may, in part, reflect the provision of a service of value to the insured, e.g., loss prevention services, claim settlement services, etc. However, such services are usually tailor-made to meet underwriting needs rather than properly designed for the insured, and their value to the insured could be less than the cost of provision. Another point at issue here is that captives do not always avoid commissions. If the captives accept reinsurance on parent company risks from an unrelated fronting company, some commission typically will be paid to that insurer. Despite these qualifications, there is little doubt that expenses are distinctly lower for captives, reflecting mainly the absence of acquisition and marketing costs.

6 The final point raised by Lenrow et al. (1982) is related to more effective loss prevention. A loss survey is often undertaken by the insurer on underwriting a fire or liability risk. This survey often becomes the basis for offering the insured cost-prevention advice. Sometimes, acceptance of that advice is a precondition for insurance cover or it affects the terms and price of insurance. However, the main function of the survey is to provide appropriate underwriting information to the insurer so that it may determine whether to accept a proposed policy or on what conditions to accept such a proposal and at what rates of premium. Although insurer loss prevention advice may be of value to the insured, it is not designed primarily for the insured and may be less effective than an independent survey. The packaging of loss prevention survey costs into the insurance premium puts conventional insurance at a cost disadvantage in comparison with other forms of financing, including captives. This cost disadvantage is partly ameliorated to the extent that loss advice is of value to the insured. Note, however, that this potential disadvantage does not necessarily place captives at some advantage over other noninsurance methods of reinvestment financing.

A further relevant point concerning loss prevention also suggests that conventional insurance may be at a disadvantage in comparison with other forms of financing without indicating that captives secure any particular advantage. Insurance is thought to lead to moral hazard, since losses are transferred to a third party. The higher collective claim costs caused by moral hazard problems ultimately will be borne by policyholders as a group, if not by the specific policyholders that impose such costs. If the loss is not transferred to an unrelated insurer, this moral hazard cost is absent. Therefore, long-run risk management costs will be somewhat lower, other things being equal, if noninsurance financing methods are chosen. With a captive, there is no real transfer of risk, since it is retained within the parent's "family of companies." Accordingly, incentives to formulate effective loss control systems are preserved.

MOTIVATION FOR FORMING A CAPTIVE

The features described in the previous section may be crystallized into two broad motives for forming a captive:

1 *A captive may be formed with the purpose of obtaining insurance on more advantageous terms*. In this case, there is intention to seek meaningful preloss financing from an outside insurer. However, the formation of a captive permits acquisition of insurance on terms that are more favorable than could be acquired without the captive.

Stimulating this motive is the belief that the reinsurance market is a more favorable provider of insurance than the direct market. This belief is expressed with respect to

a More favorable reductions for large deductibles.

b More competitive pricing.

c Greater willingness to write unusual or "difficult to place" risks.

Such statements point to differences in the intensity of competition in the direct and reinsurance markets. As stated earlier, such statements are quite plausible, since direct markets are heavily regulated and reinsurance markets are not. Furthermore, direct markets are geographically segmented, permitting some exercise of local monopolistic power. In contrast, the reinsurance market is international in nature, exposing operators to a much wider range of competition. Thus the advantages of access to reinsurance are plausible. However, evidence to support this hypothesis appears to be entirely anecdotal; there is a dearth of serious scientific study.

This motive for captive formation may be partly supported by tax considerations. However, the main tax effect is likely to arise from deductibility of insurance premiums rather than deductibility of incurred losses, and this benefit may be conveyed equally to conventional insurance premiums and to the reinsurance premiums paid by the captive. In this respect, at least, tax is neutral, although other more complex tax effects can arise.

2 *A captive may represent a genuine alternative to insurance* in that there is intention to retain risk within the family of companies. (Under such circumstances, the captive is competing with alternative methods of reinvestment financing, such as internal funding, new debt, or new equity. Such a captive presumably will not be heavily reinsured.) If a captive is a meaningful alternative to insurance, tax effects are probably significant. Unlike other methods of retention, the captive may provide a vehicle for tax benefits if premiums of the parent are deductible. These tax effects are now discussed in more detail.

THE TAXATION OF CAPTIVE INSURERS

Transactions of the Parent

The taxation of captive insurance transactions is complex for several reasons. Tax law is imprecise in defining insurance and, therefore, the circumstances under which a captive insurer can be recognized as an insurance company for tax purposes. Second, captive insurance transactions are often international in nature, thus encroaching on the jurisdictions of more than one tax authority. Third, problems are enhanced by different forms of earned income in the family of companies, including the parent's trading income, the captive's underwriting income, and the captive's investment income. Our purpose here is not to provide an authoritative statement on the taxation of captives; this would probably absorb a whole book.[3] Rather, we simply wish to illustrate some of the main tax issues so that we can set up a suggested evaluation

---

[3]*Risk Management* magazine has maintained a stream of very useful articles on captive taxation over recent years. In addition to providing information on new developments, several of these papers have provided policy interpretations. Some recent papers are cited in the References.

procedure. Our focus will be a U.S. company examining whether to set up a captive. The first area of concern is the tax liability of the parent company with respect to premiums paid to the captive and losses incurred. These are domestic transactions, and we are concerned with U.S. tax law.

The second area of concern is with the taxation of the operations of the captive at its domicile, which may well be abroad. We will be very brief and illustrative, for there are many competing locations for captives, each with its own particular tax provisions. Since many locations are tax havens, these types of tax provisions may be very important to an actual decision, and the interested reader would be well advised to consult specific sources or experts.

A third area is that concerning the taxation of the profit yielded by the captive to the parent. Again, this is complex, since the captive may be located abroad. Our treatment here will also be somewhat brief and illustrative rather than authoritative.

If a U.S. firm pays insurance premiums to an unrelated insurer, the premiums are deductible for purposes of calculating corporate income tax. The premiums may be deducted for the period in which they were incurred. If losses are incurred, the firm may also deduct the value of loss (e.g., the depreciated value of a destroyed asset) minus any insurance settlement. Essentially, this means that any uninsured portion of loss is deductible. If the insurance payments exceed the depreciated value of the asset, a firm may be liable for capital gains tax. Losses are deductible at the time they are realized. The tax benefit from premium deduction normally is more valuable than the tax benefit from deducting uninsured loss, since (1) the premium usually exceeds the expected value of loss, and (2) the tax benefit on premium deduction occurs earlier than the tax benefit on deduction of uninsured loss. This inequality creates a tax bias in favor of insurance over the various noninsurance methods of reinvestment financing.

Under these tax circumstances a firm wishing not to transfer risk to an unrelated insurer would seem to reap the best of both worlds by forming a captive. The firm would, in essence, retain the risk but still get the attractive tax benefit of premium deduction. True, if all risks were written by the captive, the parent would not receive any tax benefit on incurred losses, but the tax benefit from premium deduction would more than compensate. Our task is to examine whether the parent can deduct captive premiums in this way, and the key to the issue lies in whether the IRS recognizes the captive as an insurance company.

The position of the IRS with respect to premium deductibility starts with the understanding that an insurance policy *per se* does not provide sufficient evidence of a meaningful insurance contract. An early tax ruling, Rev. Rul. 65-57, focuses on the *shifting* and *distribution* of risk. A risk is assumed to be shifted when it is transferred to an insurer. The distribution of risk is achieved when that insurer pools the risk with many similar coverages, thereby spreading or diversifying claim costs. Both conditions, shifting and distribution, are necessary for the IRS to accept premium deductibility. Later rulings have sought to apply this principle in the case of captive insurers; the most important ruling being Rev. Rul. 77-316. Here the IRS provided three captive examples as vehicles for interpreting the shift-distribution criteria:

1 A U.S. parent insures its property-liability risks directly with a foreign insurance subsidiary.

2 A U.S. parent insures with an unrelated insurer, who, in turn, reinsures 95% of the parent's risk with a foreign subsidiary.

3 A U.S. parent insures its risks with a foreign insurance subsidiary, which then reinsures 90% of these risks with an unrelated insurer.

The IRS held that there was no shifting and distribution of risk with respect to that portion of the parent's risk which was retained within the "economic family." Thus in example 2, the parent can deduct only the premium relating to the 5% retained by the unrelated insurer. In example 3, the parent can deduct only the premium for the 90% of risk reinsured with the unrelated insurer.[4] In example 1, the premium is not deductible at all.

When risk is retained within the economic family, the premium is treated as a capital contribution, and claim payments to the parent are treated as a dividend distribution. The effect is that loss to the parent that is not insured outside the economic family is deductible when it is incurred. This treatment is the same as that of uninsured losses. Thus, in effect, the IRS treats insurance contracts within the economic family as being uninsured. It must be pointed out that the foregoing is a description of the IRS's position and that this position is hotly disputed by many taxpayers. The ultimate interpretation is, of course, a perogative of the courts.

Despite this negative tax effect for captives, there are circumstances under which premiums to captives may be deductible:

1 If a captive is jointly owned by a group of parent companies and if the captive distributes risk in a meaningful way, the arrangement may be treated as a meaningful insurance arrangement. For example, the tax ruling, Rev. Rul. 78-338 held that a captive jointly owned by a group of oil companies and conducting its affairs in an independent insurance manner did qualify as an insurance company. Just how many parents, and what spread of risk are needed, is not entirely clear.

2 A wholly owned captive that writes a significant degree of unrelated risks (i.e., other than those of members of the economic family) may also qualify as an insurer for tax purposes. However, it is not clear how much unrelated risk is needed. The IRS has declined to be specific in this regard. In a technical advice memorandum (document no. 8215066, April 1982), the IRS conceded that "there is 'a large grey area' in the captive field between what is and what is not insurance," and that judgments ". . . must be based on the facts and circumstances and that such determination can better be made at the District Director level."

In summary, a captive may be treated as an insurer if it provides shifting and distribution of risk. Certainly, a wholly owned captive insuring only risks of the parent will not qualify. However, a wholly owned captive may qualify if it writes a "signif-

---

[4]In the case of Carnation, G. V. Commissioner, 71 T.C. No. 39 (1978), the tax court ruled on a case resembling example 2 in Rev. Rul. 77-316. In this case, the unrelated insurer had requested Carnation to give guarantees to ensure that its captive insurance subsidiary would not default on its reinsurance agreement with the unrelated insurer. Carnation refused, but instead provided greater security for the reinsurance agreement by increasing the capitalization of the captive. The court used this fact to demonstrate that there had not been a meaningful shifting and distribution of risk. On appeal, the decision was affirmed, but with additional arguments that the case resembled the example in Rev. Rul. 77-316.

icant" degree of unrelated risks, and a group captive may qualify if it achieves a "significant" shifting and distribution of risk over the various parent companies. However, there are no precise formulas for defining *significant,* and the IRS reserves the right to make individual judgments.

A further form of taxation that is relevant here is excise tax. If the captive is located offshore, an excise tax of 4% of the premium is due. However, for reinsurance transactions and life insurance, the excise tax is only 1%. This differential would appear to favor a fronting operation in which the parent's risks were placed with an unrelated insurer who then ceded to an offshore captive. However, the fronting insurer may well be liable to state premium taxes, which may reduce or remove this advantage. Consistent with the IRS position on premium deductibility, the IRS may take the view that such reinsurance premiums are effectively direct premiums attracting the 4% tax unless the fronting insurer actively participates in risk sharing.

Transactions of the Captive

A captive insurance company is subject to the taxation law at its domicile. Since captives are located in many different countries, a thorough treatment of captive taxation requires examination of the tax code applicable in each of the many captive locations. This is not possible here, and we will simply provide illustrations that will permit us to use the financial framework. Our concern is with the decision process, not the specific details of tax law.

Offshore locations for captives are sometimes chosen specifically because of a favorable tax environment, and many (e.g., Bermuda and the Cayman Islands) are indeed free of corporate and other income taxes. Despite the offshore location, a captive can be directly subject to U.S. federal tax. A captive doing regular and continuous business in the United States may become directly liable for U.S. federal income tax on its U.S. business. What level of U.S. activity is required for such categorization is a factual issue to be decided case by case. However, in Rev. Rul. 80-225, the IRS ruled that an offshore insurer having an independent U.S. agent with power to commit the insurer on covers and power to settle claims was indeed doing business in the United States. To avoid such implications, it would seem, at least, that activity and decision making must be located abroad. However, this may be insufficient to avoid U.S. tax, since it appears that the source of underwriting income, as determined by the location of the risk, may be the important factor [IRC 861(a)(7)].

U.S. federal taxation of captives domiciled in the United States is more straightforward if such captives are indeed recognized as insurance companies (see Transactions of the Parent). In such circumstances, the domestic captive is simply taxed as an insurance company. For stock insurers, federal corporate income tax is payable on the sum of underwriting and investment income.

Tax on Controlled Foreign Corporations (CFCs)

A U.S. parent may become responsible for U.S. federal tax on the earnings of its foreign captive if the latter is a CFC. In the case of captive insurers, a CFC exists if the captive receives more than 75% of its gross premium income from insuring risks located in the United States and if U.S. shareholders hold more than one-quarter of voting equity (the requirements for noninsurance CFCs are somewhat different). If the captive is designated a CFC, the parent is liable for U.S. income tax for that portion of its underwriting and investment earnings relating to U.S. risks, whether or not it repatriates any funds at all.

Tax: Some General Considerations

It is clear from the foregoing that captive taxation is complex and imprecise. Certainly, the preceding notes are not exhaustive, but they are sufficient to illustrate what appears to be the rationale of the IRS position. Tax rules permit deductibility of premiums or uninsured losses, but there is a tax bias in favor of insurance over retention, since the tax benefit accrues earlier. The assignment of risk to a captive is risk retention and will be treated as such for tax purposes unless it is shown that the captive provides for "significant" shifting and distribution of risk. However, the IRS has declined to give a precise interpretation of what is construed to be significant; rather it has left individual cases to the judgment of the local inspector. Accordingly, the tax issue is surrounded by a cloud of uncertainty, but certain general ideas do shine through. One interesting consequence of this uncertainty is that it may create some apparent confusion in reasons declared for establishing a captive. For example, in a survey by Greene (1979), the tax motive was relatively unimportant. Only 10% of respondents declared tax saving to be a "very important" objective in forming a captive. However, many respondents declared tax to be of little or no importance. Greene's surprise at this result is understandable. However, it is also understandable that risk managers would fail to admit to the importance of a tax motive when the IRS takes the position, in effect, that it will deny tax advantages when the captive amounts to little more than a tax-avoiding ploy. Some more meaningful testimony to the real importance of tax is given in Greene's survey by the fact that the great majority of respondents did deduct captive premiums for tax purposes. Further anecdotal evidence on the importance of taxes is noted by Kloman and Rosenbaum (1982, p. 146). In response to Rev. Rul. 77-136 and the subsequent *Carnation* case, captives appear to have engaged in a scramble to acquire unrelated business to qualify as *bona fide* insurers.

REGULATION

Like other insurance companies, captives are usually subject to some form of regulation in the jurisdiction in which they are domiciled. In some cases, the captive is treated like any other insurance company for tax purposes; however, parent firms will often seek out locations where such regulation is not burdensome. In other cases, captives receive less burdensome regulatory treatment than other insurers. This differential treatment is not in contradiction to the protection of consumer interests, since the parent and subsidiary presumably do not need protection from the monopolistic abuses of each other. Furthermore, the parent is well able to monitor the ruin probability of the captive.

The effect of regulation is felt in three areas:

1 Reporting. Most locations require reporting of annual accounts on some specified accounting basis.

2 Investment restrictions. Some regulatory authorities impose investment restrictions, whereas others do not. Some examples are given:

Bermuda. A distinction is made between listed and unlisted assets; the latter include some equities and advances to affiliates. At least 75% of assets must be listed.

Cayman Islands. There are no investment restrictions for appropriate captives.

Colorado. Same as for other Colorado insurers.

Vermont. None for appropriate captives.

3 Capital and surplus requirements. The paid-in capital and/or the surplus (effectively the net worth) are usually controlled. For example, the following minimum capital and surplus requirements apply:

Bermuda. For general business, $120,000; for long-term business, $250,000; for both classes, $370,000.

Cayman Islands. Specified in local currency, but similar to Bermuda at current exchange rates.

Colorado. $75,000 for wholly owned captives; $1 million for association captives.

Vermont. $250,000 for pure captives; $750,000 for association captives; and $500,000 for industrial association captives.

The burden of regulation is not accurately conveyed by the size of the capitalization requirement or the intensity of investment control. The burden is determined by the opportunity costs set up by these controls. Thus investment controls impose no cost on a firm that was going to invest in admitted assets in the absence of controls. For the firm whose behavior is affected by investment controls, the cost is determined by the differential return and risk between displaced and admitted investments.

In meeting capitalization requirements, the economic cost is also an opportunity cost. If the parent was able to raise funds at a cost of 10% and hold capital and surplus in assets bearing 10%, there is a zero opportunity cost of meeting the capitalization requirement. A positive cost arises when the capital and surplus are invested in assets that yield less than the cost of capital. However, by the same token, one might imagine that capitalization imposes a negative cost if it provides a vehicle for attractive financial investment. Sometimes investment regulation does restrict the form of financial assets that may be held. In some jurisdictions (e.g., Colorado and Vermont), the capitalization requirement may be met by means of a letter of credit. The capital cost of meeting this requirement is the opportunity cost of providing that letter, which may be a service fee to a bank or, perhaps, foregone yield on a compensatory balance held with the bank.

ANALYSIS OF CAPTIVE CASH FLOWS

The value created by a particular decision can be measured by identifying the expected cost flows pertinent to that decision, which are then discounted at a risk-adjusted rate to derive a net present value. This focus on incremental cash flows is valid when value of equity is measured by systematic risk alone. Under such circumstances, the total value of equity is simply the sum of the values of the component activities. In this section, an example will be presented to illustrate the calculation of incremental cash flows and the deviation of the net present value of captive formation. The resulting net present value provides a basis for comparison with competing methods of financing reinvestment, such as insurance or debt.

EXAMPLE: LONG TRADITION COMPANY

Long Tradition Company has, for as long as anyone can remember, financed its property and liability risks by means of insurance. A newly appointed risk manager, Mr. Shay Kitup, decides to explore the prospect of forming a captive, largely stimulated by the somewhat high financing costs associated with insurance. The proposed captive is to be located in Vermont. Currently, premiums paid to an unrelated insurer are $5.5 million annually although Mr. Kitup estimates expected losses to be $4 million.

Step 1

To set up his analysis of the captive, Mr. Kitup begins by identifying the components of the (proposed) captive's cash flow. First, losses are considered. During any year of exposure, incidents may arise that eventually give rise to loss payments. However, many losses take a considerable time to settle; thus not all claim payments are made in the year in which the loss is actually incurred. Mr. Kitup's estimate is that, from the current year of exposure, some $4 million in expected claim payments will be incurred. However, only $1 million of claim payments will be made in the current year, $2 million in the subsequent year, and a further $1 million in the year after that. At the end of the third year, all claim payments are expected to be complete. Claim payments by the captive are assumed to be made on the last day of the year. This pattern is stable over future years. The loss pattern is presented in Table 16-1. Notice that the total claims paid builds up over time as the captive matures.

A second aspect of the calculation relates to the reserves the captive must hold at any point in time to meet its outstanding liabilities to pay claims to the parent. At the end of the first year, the captive has been on cover for 1 year, but it can still expect claims to materialize even

TABLE 16-1
EXPECTED VALUE OF CLAIM PAYMENTS BY PROPOSED CAPTIVE ($000)

	Year claim paid			
	1	2	3	4
Year loss incurred:				
1	1000	2000	1000	—
2		1000	2000	1000
3			1000	2000
4				1000
Total claims paid	1000	3000	4000	4000
Reserve	3000	4000	4000	4000

TABLE 16-2
CALCULATIONS OF UNDERWRITING INCOME ON EARNED BASIS ($000)

	Year			
	1	2	3	4
Premiums earned	4000	4000	4000	4000
Expenses:				
Set up	(50)	—	—	—
Continuing	(500)	(500)	(500)	(500)
Incurred losses:				
Paid losses plus	(1000)	(3000)	(4000)	(4000)
Change in reserve	(3000)	(1000)	—	—
Underwriting income	(550)	(500)	(500)	(500)

though the cover has expired. For example, a worker injured by an industrial accident in year 1 may not receive a compensation settlement until the next year, when legal issues have been clarified and the extent of loss established.

At the end of the first year, the captive must hold sufficient reserves to meet the expected liabilities of $2 million in year 2 and $1 million in year 3. To err on the side of conservatism, these future expected losses are not discounted,[5] and the size of the reserve at the end of year 1 is $3 million. At the end of year 2, the firm must have sufficient reserves to meet the expected $1 million from losses incurred in year 1 that are expected to be paid in year 3, plus the liabilities for losses incurred in year 2 that have not been settled and which amount to $2 million (year 3) and $1 million (year 4). Thus the total reserves at the end of year 2 is $4 million. Similar calculations establish the values of the reserves for subsequent years.

Step 2

The second step involves calculation of the underwriting income of the captive. This step will be relevant for tax purposes. In calculating underwriting income for a given year, care must be taken to allocate losses to the relevant year of cover. Thus, for the first year, we assume that premiums are paid at the beginning of the year and the cover extends only over that year. Only $1 million in losses is incurred during that year, but the captive is holding $3 million in reserves to cover outstanding liabilities. Following this reasoning, underwriting earnings are defined as

Earned premiums − expenses paid − losses incurred

For any year, incurred losses differ from losses actually paid. Some paid losses relate to claims that originated in prior years; further, some losses incurred during the year will remain unsettled at the end of the year. However, incurred losses can be calculated quite simply as follows:

Incurred losses = paid losses + change in reserve

Table 16-2 shows the derivation of underwriting income on the assumption that a premium of $4 million is paid at the beginning of each year.

[5]The practice of not discounted cannot be defended on strictly financial criteria. However, failure to discount in calculating reserves is widespread in the insurance industry, and Mr. Kitup decides that the captive should follow normal industry procedures. There may be tax advantages to not discounting losses. Reserves will be increased, thereby reducing current taxable underwriting income. In this way, tax is deferred.

Step 3

This involves analysis of the cash flows of the captive, paying particular attention to the generation of investable funds and the tax liabilities. The first part of Table 16-3 simply shows the flow of funds into and out of the captive, with the stock of investable funds yielding a 12% return. The flow of funds into the captive includes an initial contribution of $2.5 million in surplus. Notice that this exceeds the Vermont requirements. The flow of funds out of the captive includes federal tax at 46% on the captive's earnings, defined as the sum of underwriting earnings and investment earnings. Also included is a premium tax of 1% of premiums.

Table 16-3 builds up year by year showing the beginning cash flows for year 1, which can be invested for the year, since claims are assumed to arise at year end. The fund is calculated at year end by adding in investment income and deducting losses. However, the captive also has to consider its tax liabilities, which are shown as the final part of the table. Thus the expected value of the captive at the end of the first year is $5,549,000. This value is carried forward to year 2, and similar calculations are undertaken.

Step 4

The penultimate step is to analyze the cash flows to the parent, and these will be used as a basis for calculating the net present value of the captive proposal. For purposes of calculating these cash flows, we will assume that premiums are deducted for tax purposes. Given previous comments, it is clear that some risk spreading is required, such as income from risks not owned within the group of companies. Such outside risks have not been shown in the example merely for simplicity. The reader who wishes to pursue this further may anticipate some unrelated income to the captive and rework Table 16-3. (In fact, the example given in Table 16-3 is OK if total unrelated earnings—underwriting plus investment—is zero.)

The calculation of the parent's cash flows is fairly straightforward. The parent pays premiums, contributes capital, and receives tax deductibility for premiums. However, one issue, which is a little more involved, relates to the time period over which the captive is to be evaluated. This time period will relate to the planning horizon of the firm. Suppose Mr. Kitup decides he can only plan as far as 4 years ahead because that is the extent of the firm's planning horizon. At the end of 4 years, the captive will still be in existence with current assets and liabilities. The assets of the firm at the end of year 4 comprise the value of the fund at that time, which is $7,566,000. However, against this fund, there are also liabilities for claims incurred in years 3 and 4 that are not all settled. In order to calculate the terminal value of these assets and liabilities, we must allow these claims to run out, bearing in mind that in running out, further investment income will accrue and this will be taxable. This run out is shown by extending Table 16-3 beyond year 4 but considering no further premium income. Table 16-3 shows that at the end of year 6, the fund will have a terminal value of $4,383,000 with no further liabilities. This value can be represented in the parent's cash flow.

This process of considering only a limited number of years does not tie the firm to holding the captive for 4 years. By implication, it suggests that the firm must make another decision in 4 year's time. The decision may turn out to be to continue the captive, in which case the net value of the fund and its liabilities at the end of year 4 represent an endowment that carries over to the new decision. However, the firm may wish to discontinue the captive, in which case the parent will realize the net terminal value of the fund as an actual cash flow. This device is used simply to recognize that the captive will accumulate value (which could be negative) and that this value must be considered in calculating the net present value of the captive project.

The cash flows of the parent are now shown in Table 16-4. The timing of cash flows within

TABLE 16-3
ANALYSIS OF CAPTIVE'S CASH FLOWS ($000)

	Year						
	1	2	3	4	5	6	7
Carried forward from:							
Previous year	—	5549	6825	7184	7566	5056	4383
Premiums	4000	4000	4000	4000	—	—	
Surplus	2500	—	—	—	—	—	
Expenses:							
Set up	(50)	—	—	—	—	—	
Continuing	(500)	(500)	(500)	(500)	—	—	
Investment funds at beginning of year	5950	9049	10,325	10,683	7566	5056	
Investment income (12%)	714	1086	1239	1282	908	607	
Losses paid	(1000)	(3000)	(4000)	(4000)	(3000)	(1000)	
Fund year end before tax	5664	7135	7564	7966	5474	4663	
Taxes:							
Earnings:							
Underwriting (Table 16-2)	(550)	(500)	(500)	(500)	—	—	
Investment	714	1086	1239	1282	908	607	
Total	164	586	739	782	908	607	
Tax (at 46%)	(74)	(270)	(340)	(360)	(418)	(208)	
Premium tax (1%)	(40)	(40)	(40)	(40)	—	—	
Total tax	(115)	(310)	(380)	(400)	(418)	(208)	
Fund year end after tax	5549	6825	7184	7566	5056	4383	

TABLE 16-4
CASH FLOWS OF PARENT: BEGINNING YEAR VALUES ($000)

	Year						
	1	**2**	**3**	**4**	**5**	**6**	**7**
Premium to captive	(4000)	(4000)	(4000)	(4000)	—	—	—
Surplus contribution	(2500)	—	—	—	—	—	—
Tax deductibility on premium	1840	1840	1840	1840	—	—	—
Terminal value of captive	—	—	—	—	—	—	4383
Total	(4660)	(2160)	(2160)	(2160)	—	—	4383

The cash flows of the parent are now shown in Table 16-4. The timing of cash flows within the year will be a matter of individual circumstance. However, we earlier assumed that premiums are payable at year beginning, as is the initial capital. Taxes also are assumed to be paid at this time. However, the terminal value of $4,383,000 relates to the end of year 6. To ensure that this value is properly discounted over year 6, the terminal value is shown at beginning year 7.

Step 5

The final step is to calculate a present value for the captive. To conduct this step, a discount rate is required, and its value will be determined by risk factors. The two major sources of risk in these cash flows derive from risky investment returns and from the random incidence of loss events. In most cases, the latter source of uncertainty will be the larger. For simplicity, we assume that losses are uncorrelated with market indices and are therefore free of systematic risk. Investment income exhibits systematic risk, and this will have the effect of pulling the discount rate up above the risk-free rate. The weighted average rate used for discounting is 10%, and the risk-free rate is 9%.

The present value of the parent's cash flow's discounted at the chosen rate represents the risk management costs for the captive insurance alternative. The calculation is as follows:

$$\text{NPV (\$000)} = -4660 - \frac{2160}{1 + 0.1} - \frac{2160}{(1 + 0.1)^2} - \frac{2160}{(1 + 0.1)^3} + \frac{4383}{(1 + 0.1)^6}$$

$$= -\$7558$$

This value may be compared with the cost of purchasing conventional insurance. Recalling the start of this example, the premium will be tax deductible, resulting in an annual net of tax cost of $5.5 million (0.54) = $2.97 million. The net present value of purchasing insurance is calculated using the risk-free rate, since external insurance has removed all risk:

$$\text{NPV (\$000)} = -2970 - \frac{2970}{1 + 0.09} - \frac{2970}{(1 + 0.09)^2} - \frac{2970}{(1 + 0.09)^3}$$

$$= -\$10,488$$

In this example, the captive is preferable to a conventional insurance arrangement.

DISCUSSION OF RELATED ISSUES

The example derived in the previous section was a special and rather uncomplex case. Some particular features of this example that are worthy of mention are

1 Tax deductibility of premiums
2 The correct size of surplus and premiums
3 Reinsurance of the captive's risk portfolio

Tax Deductibility of Premiums

Many of the issues surrounding tax deductibility have been debated. However, it is instructive to examine how much influence this assumption has on the decision to go captive. If premiums are not tax deductible because the IRS does not recognize the captive as a bona fide insurer, the parent is treated as if it were self-insuring. This means that losses are deductible as realized. For comparison, we assume that this means at the time of insurance claim settlement. We now examine the parent's cash flows with this assumption.

Table 16-5 shows a recalculation of the parent's cash flows without tax deductibility of premiums. The net present value of this cash flow discounting at 10% is

$$
\begin{aligned}
\text{NPV (\$000)} = {} & -6040 + \frac{-2620}{1 + 0.1} + \frac{-2160}{(1 + 0.1)^2} + \frac{-2160}{(1 + 0.1)^3} + \frac{1380}{(1 + 0.1)^4} \\
& + \frac{460}{(1 + 0.1)^5} + \frac{4383}{(1 + 0.1)^6} \\
= {} & \$8128
\end{aligned}
$$

TABLE 16-5
PARENT'S CASH FLOWS WITHOUT PREMIUM TAX DEDUCTIBILITY

	Year						
	1	2	3	4	5	6	7
Losses*	1000	3000	4000	4000	3000	1000	—
Tax deductibility	460	1380	1840	1840	1380	460	—
Premiums paid	(4000)	(4000)	(4000)	(4000)	—	—	—
Surplus	(2500)	—	—	—	—	—	—
Terminal value of captive	—	—	—	—	—	—	4383
Total	(6040)	(2620)	(2160)	(2160)	1380	460	4383

*Losses are shown only to calculate tax. They do not appear in the totals.

The difference between this value and the value calculated for the captive on the assumption of premium tax deductibility ($-$$7558$) represents the value created by bringing forward the tax benefit as a premium deduction rather than as a loss deduction. Notice that for this example, the captive is still preferable to external insurance with an unrelated insurer, although the margin of advantage has narrowed.

The Correct Level of Surplus and Premiums

If the parent wishes to create a captive with a low ruin probability, the paid-in capital and premiums act as substitutes for each other. A low value of initial capital can be compensated for by paying higher premiums (in relation to the expected value of loss) to build up the surplus. There may be some tax advantages in going this route if premiums paid to the captive are tax deductible. However, the surplus will take time to accumulate, and additional reinsurance protection may be needed for the captive during its early years.

If the captive is located in a favorable tax environment, it may be tempting for the parent to pay excessive premiums. However, since the IRS retains considerable discretion in deciding whether the captive is a bona fide insurer, this tactic may induce the IRS to disallow tax deduction of the parent's premiums on the grounds that the captive is merely a device for tax arbitrage.

If the captive is located in the United States, the tax effects of excessive premiums are probably neutral. The premium deduction will be increased, but so too will the underwriting profit of the captive, which will be subject to U.S. federal tax. There will be a dollar-for-dollar offset within the same accounting period. Similar considerations apply if the captive is a controlled foreign corporation insuring U.S. risks for U.S. shareholders.

Thus it seems that there is little fiscal advantage in channeling excessive premiums to the captive, except for the purpose of building up surplus to desired levels. In fact, it seems that most Bermuda captives do maintain rather high levels of surplus relative to premium income. In Porat's (1982) study, most captives operated well within a ratio of $2 in net written premiums to $1 in surplus. (This ratio is known as the *exposure ratio*.) However, Porat's data do reveal that larger captives tend to have larger exposure ratios. This pattern may be explicable if larger insurers have a more efficient spread of risk, thereby permitting them to maintain a given ruin probability on a larger exposure ratio than smaller captives who may well be less diversified. The relative size of premiums and surplus may be important in attracting high-quality unrelated business to the captives and thereby securing IRS blessing for premium tax deductibility.

Reinsurance of the Captive's Risk Portfolio

Most captives protect their liability portfolio with reinsurance. Indeed, access to the reinsurance market is probably one of the dominant attractions of forming a captive, as discussed earlier. The reinsurance transactions can be embodied in the preceding discounted cash flow analysis quite routinely. The captive will cede part of its premium income to the reinsurer. In return, part of the claim liability will be offset by payment from the reinsurer. These cash flows require insertion in the analysis together with any commission paid to the captive by the reinsurer.

In a similar vein, fronting with an unrelated insurer can be represented by appropriate cash flows.

SUMMARY AND CONCLUSION

Captive insurance companies are insurers formed primarily to insure the risks of their owners. Such a definition also covers mutual insurance companies, although here our main concern was with captives that have a restricted spread of ownership, including ownership by a single parent company.

The captive insurance industry has been one of the major growth industries of the past two decades. Most captives of U.S. parent companies are located abroad, particularly in Bermuda, the Cayman Islands, and other locations that offer tax advantages. Captives may be classified by various criteria. One such classification separates captives according to that portion of the portfolio which is accounted for by the parent's risks. A pure captive insurer only insures risks of the parent, a senior captive insures a small amount of outside risk, but a profit center captive insures mainly outside risks. Another useful distinction is made between the captive that acts as a direct insurer of its parent's risks and the captive that acts as reinsurer to an unrelated fronting company that underwrites the parent's risk. With both devices, risk of the parent is retained by the subsidiary, although in each case the captive may seek its own reinsurance protection.

Various reasons for captive formation have been presented, but these appear to boil down to two. Some captives are simply devices for obtaining insurance on more advantageous terms. The captive gives the parent access to the reinsurance market, which, apparently, is more competitive than the direct insurance market. Such captives are heavily reinsured; thus there is still a large transfer of risk. Other captives that are not heavily reinsured represent a genuine alternative to external insurance. The captive, subject to the blessing of the IRS, may offer the tax advantages of insurance while avoiding the high cost of insurance financing.

Tax considerations of captives are complex largely because captives are usually located offshore. One important issue is whether the parent can deduct premiums paid to the captive from corporate income. Deductibility is allowed if the captive offers significant shifting and distribution of risk. Although the IRS determines this on a case-by-case basis, it appears that captives must either insure the risks of a spread of owners or underwrite a significant number of risks outside the corporate family.

Captives are regulated in a similar fashion to regular insurers; however, regulation of captives is usually much lighter. Regulation includes specified minimal levels of capital and surplus and control over investments.

A case study illustrating a cash flow analysis of captive cash flows is developed. The cash flows to the parent permit estimation of the net present value of this device, and this can be used as a basis for comparison with other reinvestment financing alternatives.

QUESTIONS

1 A firm is setting up a captive insurance company. The following is the expected loss development pattern for the captive's loss exposure.

Losses settled in year incurred (i.e., year 0)	30
Losses settled in year 1	25
Losses settled in year 2	10
Losses settled in year 3	5

The firm's expected loss distribution is expected to be stable over time. Calculate the reserves required in subsequent years following inception of the captive:

a Assuming that liabilities for future loss are not discounted

b Assuming that such liabilities are discounted at 10%

2 Rework the example of the calculation of the net present value of captive formation given in this chapter under the alternative assumption that the captive cedes 60% of all premiums and losses to a reinsurer on a proportionate basis. You should go through the five steps of analysis shown in the chapter making clear any assumptions you have to make to proceed with your answer.

REFERENCES

Cross M., J. Thornton, and D. Davidson: "Impact of the Captive Insurance Company's Foundation on the Parent Firm's Value," paper to American Risk and Insurance Association, Minneapolis, 1984.

Davey, P. J.: "Managing Risks through Captive Insurance Companies," Conference Board Research Report no. 768, Risk and Insurance Management Society, 1980.

Glenn, E. M., and R. W. Cooper: "The Use of Captives in Risk Management," in John D. Long (ed.), *Issues in Insurance*, vol. 2, American Institute for Property and Liability Underwriters, Malvern, Pa., 1978.

Greene, M. R.: "Analyzing Captives—How, and What are They Doing," *Risk Management*, December 1979, pp. 13–20.

Johnson, J. F., J. J. Sarchio, and R. E. Beane: "Captive Insurance Companies: The Vermont Alternative," *Risk Management*, June 1981, pp. 20–25.

Kloman, M. F., and D. H. Rosenbaum: "The Captive Insurance Phenomenon: A Cautionary Tale," *The Geneva Papers in Risk and Insurance*, vol. 7, no. 23, 1982, pp. 129–151.

Lenrow, G. I., J. H. Brainerd, J. Hall, and M. S. Heitz: "Captive Insurers: Pitfalls and Practicabilities," *Best's Review*, vol. 82, #12, 1982.

Loy, D., and M. Pertl: "Why Do Fortune 500 Companies Form Captives," *Risk Management*, January 1982, pp. 32–36.

Pine, S. R., A. M. Stanger, and P. B. Wright: "IRS Revenue Ruling 77-316: Avoiding Its Consequences," *Risk Management*, April 1978, pp. 10–23.

———, and P. B. Wright: "The Carnation Case: How Will Captives Be Affected," *Risk Management*, March 1979, pp. 37–44.

———, and ———: "Captive Insurer Premium Deductibility: Trying to Illuminate the Grey Area," *Risk Management*, August 1982, pp. 34–40.

Porat, M. M.: "Bermuda Captive Insurers: An Analysis of Underwriting Exposure Ratios," *CPCU Journal*, vol. 35, no. 2, 1982, pp. 95–99.

————: "Bermuda Captives: Investments, Instrument, Rates of Return," *CPCU Journal,* vol. 36, no. 1, 1983, pp. 21–30.

Stigler, G.: "The Theory of Economic Regulation," *Bell Journal of Economic and Management Science,* vol. 2, no. 1, 1971, pp. 3–21.

Wright, P. B.: "Domestic vs. Offshore: Captive Insurer Domiciles," *Risk Management,* June 1982, pp. 24–31.

CHAPTER 17

TEN QUESTIONS

In the design and construction of this book, I have tried to make a final summary and conclusion unnecessary. The framework of the book is described in the early chapters, and each chapter concludes with a summary. The closing pages will be used to reflect on the methodology used. This is undertaken by posing a set of questions designed to focus on the strengths and weaknesses of the financial economics methodology used and its application to risk management. The purpose is not to provide firm answers, but to illustrate the foundations of the financial economic methodology.

1 IS VALUE MAXIMIZATION THE APPROPRIATE OBJECTIVE FOR RISK MANAGEMENT?

This may be an empty question; the relevant issue is whether value maximization is the appropriate objective for a firm. Throughout this book, the motivating objective for risk management has simply been that adopted for the firm as a whole. It may be expedient to set operational goals for the risk manager that are designed to provide clearer direction than a remote reference to share prices (e.g., a directive on the amount of retention and on the procedures to be used for capitalizing cash flows). These should not be confused with the corporate goals from which such internal rules are derived.

Lest a concentration on shareholder welfare be thought to be too narrow given the diverse interest groups in a firm, it should be remembered that share prices are not independent of the risk costs imposed on other claimants. When corporate decisions affect employees, managers, creditors, customers, etc., these effects will tend to be reflected in the contracts the firm is able to negotiate. In turn, these contracts will affect earnings and, thereby, share values.

2 SHOULD A FIRM REINVEST IN THE REPLACEMENT OF DESTROYED CAPITAL RESOURCES?

To my mind, this issue more than any other separates this book from its predecessors. In much of the literature, insurance is seen as the main pillar of risk management, around which all other devices are defined. This often is supported by an explicit objective of corporate survival. This framework leaves little opportunity to query the continuity of productive operations following major loss. The view adopted here is that this question is not trivial and should not be assumed away.

The reinvestment decision helps focus attention on a classification scheme for risk management devices. In this scheme, decisions are made on the sources and uses of funds with a view toward maximizing equity value (corporate finance is structured in this way). Attention is now directed to the financing function of insurance and to other mechanisms such as debt and equity that fill the same function.

3 IS LOSS FINANCING CONTINGENT UPON REINVESTMENT?

It would be curious indeed to raise new debt without having in mind some proposed use for the funds raised; e.g., after loss, debt might be raised to finance reinvestment. Thus the question should refer to reinvestment financing rather than loss financing. Now consider insurance purchase. Traditionally, insurance is viewed as a device for reducing risk. With attention directed to the financing role of insurance, it would appear that insurance is redundant unless reinvestment is contemplated. The financing role of insurance is promoted here, but insurance may also be viewed as a financial asset having a purchase price and a stochastic payoff that is contingent upon loss. Whether insurance can be justified without reinvestment depends on the rate of return yielded on its purchase. In view of loadings, commissions, and expenses included in the premium, insurance probably will yield an unattractive negative return. However, this is an empirical issue, and analysis of the relevant cash flows is required.

4 IS RISK ADDITIVE?

Risk is used here to refer to the variability of a firm's cash flows. Adopting the usual mathematical conventions for measuring risk, the riskiness of a portfolio is usually less than the sum of its parts. Unless there is perfect correlation, some risk will be diversified away in the portfolio. Accordingly, the corporate decision maker cannot measure the risk of a particular project and assume that an equivalent degree of extra risk will be absorbed by the firm's owners if the project is accepted. The risk manager might well reflect that some risk will be diversified away within the portfolio of risk management exposures, some risk will be diversified away in combining in firm's risk management exposures with its other risky cash flows, and still more risk can be diversified away by the firm's owners in the management of their personal portfolios. Such considerations suggest that decisions should be based on the incremental risk (and return) contributed by a particular decision rather than on the total risk of the project. This approach is adopted by asset pricing models such as the capital asset pricing model.

5 ARE DECISIONS SEPARABLE?

The preceding comments on risk suggest that risk management decisions, and indeed all corporate decisions, are interdependent. The apparent implication would appear to be that for each decision, the entire cash flows of the firm require identification and capitalization in order to see whether the decision adds value. However, discounted cash flow analysis can be used with only the incremental cash flows from the decision. This is made possible by using a risk adjustment that excludes diversifiable risk. One such approach uses the β value of the cash flows to derive an appropriate discount rate. Using this methodology, the risk manager will base decisions on loss exposures not on their level of total risk, but only on systematic risk.

6 DOES SHARE PRICE MONITOR ACTUAL AND PROSPECTIVE LOSS COSTS?

Share prices appear to fluctuate in a somewhat random fashion. In some instances, a sudden jump in the stock value can be attributed, *ex post,* to an observable event. However, there is a lot of random "noise," and the effects of less significant events or decisions with relatively small cash flows will be lost in the spray. Thus there is little doubt that a major, uninsured casualty or liability loss will produce a perceptible effect on share price. However, decisions on prospective losses may not have a discernible influence on the share value, since the expected value of these losses is small relative to the total value of the firm. Thus, the argument goes, share value is an insensitive and therefore inappropriate barometer of risk management decisions. However, if this argument is valid, one must also reject the use of capital budgeting for all "small" decisions, since one can never be sure that the effects of the decision will be discernible in the "white noise." The use of capital budgeting is based on a theoretical model of share valuation, as is the risk management methodology of this book. This earnings valuation model does receive widespread support, and its validity is assumed in this book.

Subject to the qualifications just mentioned, the share price provides a comprehensive monitor of loss costs. The effect of prospective and actual earnings loss will be recorded in the share value. Only under very restrictive assumptions will share value provide an accurate measure of the capital loss. More generally, share prices pick up the effects of capital loss on the earnings of a firm and include the investors' estimated projections of indirect effects such as interruption loss.

7 IS CORPORATE INSURANCE REDUNDANT?

The traditional rationale for insurance purchase is that the buyer, be it an individual or a firm, is risk-averse and that insurance reduces risk. This reasoning is far too simplistic. In fact, a counterargument can be made that corporate insurance is redundant. If insurable losses are diversifiable, shareholders can duplicate the effects of insurance in their personal portfolio management; therefore, corporate insurance is redundant. An alternative rationale for insurance can be provided that operates on a firm's expected cash flows rather than on the riskiness of its earnings. Insurance may permit a firm to negotiate more advantageous contracts with its employees, customers, bondholders, etc. In addition, there may be positive tax benefits from insurance purchase, as well as a reduction in the expected costs of bankruptcy. More central to the theme of the book, insurance will add value if it offers provision of financing for reinvestment at a cost that is lower than that available from other sources.

8 DOES RETENTION FUNDING ADD VALUE?

By funding retained losses, the argument goes, fluctuations in value can be absorbed, thereby stabilizing earnings. This argument is spurious. The fund will lose value on payment of a loss, and since the fund is an asset of the firm, the firm will lose value correspondingly. We claimed that the risk management case for funding was weak, resting largely on the lowering of transaction costs.

9 ARE INSURANCE AND LOSS REDUCTION SUBSTITUTES?

It has become customary to present loss reduction as an alternative risk management device to insurance. Whether *alternative* means "substitute" is unclear, although the comparison does appear to mix chalk and cheese. Insurance provides funds to support the reinvestment decision. Loss reduction represents an investment in its own terms that will require a source of financing. Certainly, decisions of this sort may be interdependent. Insurance rates usually depend on insurer's estimates of expected loss, which will depend on the insured's observable efforts to reduce loss expectancy. To present these devices as alternatives confuses their very different functions. Had this text tackled risk management as an exercise simply in reducing risk, insurance and loss reduction might well have been presented as alternative methods of achieving the same goal. However, with the financial management approach, they only become mutually exclusive alternatives if severe capital rationing prevents a firm from paying the insurance premium and installing the sprinkler system.

10 IS THE METHODOLOGY OF RISK MANAGEMENT PROPERLY DERIVED FROM FINANCIAL ECONOMICS?

Two historians may well see the unfolding of a sequence of events as determined by quite different mechanisms. For example, the industrial revolution in eighteenth century Europe may be viewed as the product of economic structure and of the behavioral incentives and opportunities it provided. Alternatively, the same process may be seen to result from the changing philosophical underpinning of the societies with the rediscovery of Greek mathematics, the emergence of the Protestant ethic, and the restructuring of political power between monarchies and elected assemblies. The search for a prime mover might be quite futile. Both views enrich our knowledge and understanding of historical change.

The view presented here is not that the financial economic approach to risk management is the only valid perspective. As discussed at the beginning of the book, the risk manager may be viewed as a safety engineer, an insurance technician, or a manager with a more diverse function involving the control of scarce resources and the management of people. The financial economics presented here cannot help the risk manager assess the probability that an electrical wire will short circuit or that a given drug will produce damaging side effects, nor will it make the risk manager a better negotiator or people manager; all of these functions are important for the successful risk manager. However, these functions are not the "be all and end all" of risk management. A firm still has to allocate scarce and expensive resources to risk management activities, and these uses compete with other projects available to the firm. Some methodology is required to ensure that competing projects are appraised in a manner that is consistent across uses and which ensures satisfaction of corporate objectives. Such methodology does not flow naturally from a study of safety engineering, nor has it emerged in the behavioral/managerial approaches to risk management that characterize the literature.

The "firms are risk-averse; therefore, purchase of insurance is prudent . . . Q.E.D." school has largely been replaced by a newer breed of risk managers that recognize the scarcity problem. This book addresses the scarcity issue. Value maximization is a market-based criterion for ensuring consistency in decision making. It provides a framework in which the conflicting interests of those having claims on a firm can be resolved.

An apology for the use of financial economic methodology does not undervalue the engineering or managerial skills of the risk manager or his or her knowledge of relevant institutions, but it often does conflict with views of risk management presented elsewhere. Where such conflict exists, I have tried to be consistent in the application of finance methodology rather than attempting to accommodate alternative perspectives. To borrow from my friend Robert I. Mehr, I should thank those previous writers on risk management who have made this book not only possible, but necessary.

STATISTICAL AND PRESENT VALUE TABLES

TABLE A
STANDARD NORMAL (TABLE SHOWS SHADED AREA) DISTRIBUTION, THREE VALUES

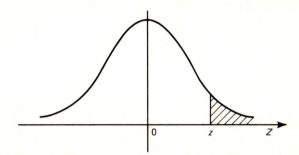

z	.00	.01	.02	.03	.04	.05	.06	.07	.08	.09
0.0	.5000	.4960	.4920	.4880	.4840	.4801	.4761	.4721	.4681	.4641
0.1	.4602	.4562	.4522	.4483	.4443	.4404	.4364	.4325	.4286	.4247
0.2	.4207	.4168	.4129	.4090	.4052	.4013	.3974	.3936	.3897	.3859
0.3	.3821	.3783	.3745	.3707	.3669	.3632	.3594	.3557	.3520	.3483
0.4	.3446	.3409	.3372	.3336	.3300	.3264	.3228	.3192	.3156	.3121
0.5	.3085	.3050	.3015	.2981	.2946	.2912	.2877	.2843	.2810	.2776
0.6	.2743	.2709	.2676	.2643	.2611	.2578	.2546	.2514	.2483	.2451
0.7	.2420	.2389	.2358	.2327	.2296	.2266	.2236	.2206	.2177	.2148
0.8	.2119	.2090	.2061	.2033	.2005	.1977	.1949	.1922	.1894	.1867
0.9	.1841	.1814	.1788	.1762	.1736	.1711	.1685	.1660	.1635	.1611
1.0	.1587	.1562	.1539	.1515	.1492	.1469	.1446	.1423	.1401	.1379
1.1	.1357	.1335	.1314	.1292	.1271	.1251	.1230	.1210	.1190	.1170
1.2	.1151	.1131	.1112	.1093	.1075	.1056	.1038	.1020	.1003	.0985
1.3	.0968	.0951	.0934	.0918	.0901	.0885	.0869	.0853	.0838	.0823
1.4	.0808	.0793	.0778	.0764	.0749	.0735	.0721	.0708	.0694	.0681
1.5	.0668	.0655	.0643	.0630	.0618	.0606	.0594	.0582	.0571	.0559
1.6	.0548	.0537	.0526	.0516	.0505	.0495	.0485	.0475	.0465	.0455
1.7	.0446	.0436	.0427	.0418	.0409	.0401	.0392	.0384	.0375	.0367
1.8	.0359	.0351	.0344	.0336	.0329	.0322	.0314	.0307	.0301	.0294
1.9	.0287	.0281	.0274	.0268	.0262	.0256	.0250	.0244	.0239	.0233
2.0	.0228	.0222	.0217	.0212	.0207	.0202	.0197	.0192	.0188	.0183
2.1	.0179	.0174	.0170	.0166	.0162	.0158	.0154	.0150	.0146	.0143
2.2	.0139	.0136	.0132	.0129	.0125	.0122	.0119	.0116	.0113	.0110
2.3	.0107	.0104	.0102	.0099	.0096	.0094	.0091	.0089	.0087	.0084
2.4	.0082	.0080	.0078	.0075	.0073	.0071	.0069	.0068	.0066	.0064
2.5	.0062	.0060	.0059	.0057	.0055	.0054	.0052	.0051	.0049	.0048
2.6	.0047	.0045	.0044	.0043	.0041	.0040	.0039	.0038	.0037	.0036
2.7	.0035	.0034	.0033	.0032	.0031	.0030	.0029	.0028	.0027	.0026
2.8	.0026	.0025	.0024	.0023	.0023	.0022	.0021	.0021	.0020	.0019
2.9	.0019	.0018	.0018	.0017	.0016	.0016	.0015	.0015	.0014	.0014
3.0	.0013	.0013	.0013	.0012	.0012	.0011	.0011	.0011	.0010	.0010

TABLE B
HOTELLING-PABST TEST STATISTIC

n	$p = .001$	.005	.010	.025	.050	.100	$\frac{1}{3}n(n^2 - 1)$
4					2	2	20
5			2	2	4	6	40
6		2	4	6	8	14	70
7	2	6	8	14	18	26	112
8	6	12	16	24	32	42	168
9	12	22	28	38	50	64	240
10	22	36	44	60	74	92	330
11	36	56	66	86	104	128	440
12	52	78	94	120	144	172	572
13	76	110	130	162	190	226	728
14	106	148	172	212	246	290	910
15	142	194	224	270	312	364	1120
16	186	250	284	340	390	450	1360
17	238	314	356	420	480	550	1632
18	300	390	438	512	582	664	1938
19	372	476	532	618	696	790	2280
20	454	574	638	738	826	934	2660
21	546	686	758	870	972	1092	3080
22	652	810	892	1020	1134	1270	3542
23	772	950	1042	1184	1312	1464	4048
24	904	1104	1208	1366	1510	1678	4600
25	1050	1274	1390	1566	1726	1912	5200
26	1212	1462	1590	1786	1960	2168	5850
27	1390	1666	1808	2024	2216	2444	6552
28	1586	1890	2046	2284	2494	2744	7308
29	1800	2134	2306	2564	2796	3068	8120
30	2032	2398	2584	2868	3120	3416	8990

TABLE C
PRESENT VALUE OF $1

Year	1%	2%	3%	4%	5%	6%	7%	8%	9%	10%	12%	14%	15%
1	.990	.980	.971	.962	.952	.943	.935	.926	.917	.909	.893	.877	.870
2	.980	.961	.943	.925	.907	.890	.873	.857	.842	.826	.797	.769	.756
3	.971	.942	.915	.889	.864	.840	.816	.794	.772	.751	.712	.675	.658
4	.961	.924	.889	.855	.823	.792	.763	.735	.708	.683	.636	.592	.572
5	.951	.906	.863	.822	.784	.747	.713	.681	.650	.621	.567	.519	.497
6	.942	.888	.838	.790	.746	.705	.666	.630	.596	.564	.507	.456	.432
7	.933	.871	.813	.760	.711	.665	.623	.583	.547	.513	.452	.400	.376
8	.923	.853	.789	.731	.677	.627	.582	.540	.502	.467	.404	.351	.327
9	.914	.837	.766	.703	.645	.592	.544	.500	.460	.424	.361	.308	.284
10	.905	.820	.744	.676	.614	.558	.508	.463	.422	.386	.322	.270	.247
11	.896	.804	.722	.650	.585	.527	.475	.429	.388	.350	.287	.237	.215
12	.887	.788	.701	.625	.557	.497	.444	.397	.356	.319	.257	.208	.187
13	.879	.773	.681	.601	.530	.469	.415	.368	.326	.290	.229	.182	.163
14	.870	.758	.661	.577	.505	.442	.388	.340	.299	.263	.205	.160	.141
15	.861	.743	.642	.555	.481	.417	.362	.315	.275	.239	.183	.140	.123
16	.853	.728	.623	.534	.458	.394	.339	.292	.252	.218	.163	.123	.107
17	.844	.714	.605	.513	.436	.371	.317	.270	.231	.198	.146	.108	.093
18	.836	.700	.587	.494	.416	.350	.296	.250	.212	.180	.130	.095	.081
19	.828	.686	.570	.475	.396	.331	.276	.232	.194	.164	.116	.083	.070
20	.820	.673	.554	.456	.377	.312	.258	.215	.178	.149	.104	.073	.061
25	.780	.610	.478	.375	.295	.233	.184	.146	.116	.092	.059	.038	.030
30	.742	.552	.412	.308	.231	.174	.131	.099	.075	.057	.033	.020	.015

Year	16%	18%	20%	24%	28%	32%	36%	40%	50%	60%	70%	80%	90%
1	.862	.847	.833	.806	.781	.758	.735	.714	.667	.625	.588	.556	.526
2	.743	.718	.694	.650	.610	.574	.541	.510	.444	.391	.346	.309	.277
3	.641	.609	.579	.524	.477	.435	.398	.364	.296	.244	.204	.171	.146
4	.552	.516	.482	.423	.373	.329	.292	.260	.198	.153	.120	.095	.077
5	.476	.437	.402	.341	.291	.250	.215	.186	.132	.095	.070	.053	.040
6	.410	.370	.335	.275	.227	.189	.158	.133	.088	.060	.041	.029	.021
7	.354	.314	.279	.222	.178	.143	.116	.095	.059	.037	.024	.016	.011
8	.305	.266	.233	.179	.139	.108	.085	.068	.039	.023	.014	.009	.006
9	.263	.226	.194	.144	.108	.082	.063	.048	.026	.015	.008	.005	.003
10	.227	.191	.162	.116	.085	.062	.046	.035	.017	.009	.005	.003	.002
11	.195	.162	.135	.094	.066	.047	.034	.025	.012	.006	.003	.002	.001
12	.168	.137	.112	.076	.052	.036	.025	.018	.008	.004	.002	.001	.001
13	.145	.116	.093	.061	.040	.027	.018	.013	.005	.002	.001	.001	.000
14	.125	.099	.078	.049	.032	.021	.014	.009	.003	.001	.001	.000	.000
15	.108	.084	.065	.040	.025	.016	.010	.006	.002	.001	.000	.000	
16	.093	.071	.054	.032	.019	.012	.007	.005	.002	.001	.000		
17	.080	.060	.045	.026	.015	.009	.005	.003	.001	.000			
18	.069	.051	.038	.021	.012	.007	.004	.002	.001	.000			
19	.060	.043	.031	.017	.009	.005	.003	.002	.000				
20	.051	.037	.026	.014	.007	.004	.002	.001	.000				
25	.024	.016	.010	.005	.002	.001	.000	.000					
30	.012	.007	.004	.002	.001	.000	.000						

TABLE D
PRESENT VALUE OF AN ANNUITY OF $1

Year	1%	2%	3%	4%	5%	6%	7%	8%	9%	10%
1	0.990	0.980	0.971	0.962	0.952	0.943	0.935	0.926	0.917	0.909
2	1.970	1.942	1.913	1.866	1.859	1.833	1.808	1.783	1.759	1.736
3	2.941	2.884	2.829	2.775	2.723	2.673	2.624	2.577	2.531	2.487
4	3.902	3.808	3.717	3.630	3.546	3.465	3.387	3.312	3.240	3.170
5	4.853	4.713	4.580	4.452	4.329	4.212	4.100	3.993	3.890	3.791
6	5.795	5.601	5.417	5.242	5.076	4.917	4.766	4.623	4.486	4.355
7	6.728	6.472	6.230	6.002	5.786	5.582	5.389	5.206	5.033	4.868
8	7.652	7.325	7.020	6.733	6.463	6.210	5.971	5.747	5.535	5.335
9	8.566	8.162	7.786	7.435	7.108	6.802	6.515	6.247	5.985	5.759
10	9.471	8.983	8.530	8.111	7.722	7.360	7.024	6.710	6.418	6.145
11	10.368	9.787	9.253	8.760	8.306	7.887	7.499	7.139	6.805	6.495
12	11.255	10.575	9.954	9.385	8.863	8.384	7.943	7.536	7.161	6.814
13	12.134	11.348	10.635	9.986	9.394	8.853	8.358	7.904	7.487	7.103
14	13.004	12.106	11.296	10.563	9.899	9.295	8.745	8.244	7.786	7.367
15	13.865	12.849	11.938	11.118	10.380	9.712	9.108	8.559	8.060	7.606
16	14.718	13.578	12.561	11.652	10.838	10.106	9.447	8.851	8.312	7.824
17	15.562	14.292	13.166	12.166	11.274	10.477	9.763	9.122	8.544	8.022
18	16.398	14.992	13.754	12.659	11.690	10.828	10.059	9.372	8.756	8.201
19	17.226	15.678	14.324	13.134	12.085	11.158	10.336	9.604	8.950	8.365
20	18.046	16.351	14.877	13.590	12.462	11.470	10.594	9.818	9.128	8.514
25	22.023	19.523	17.413	15.622	14.094	12.783	11.654	10.675	9.823	9.077
30	25.808	22.397	19.600	17.292	15.373	13.765	12.409	11.258	10.274	9.427

Year	12%	14%	16%	18%	20%	24%	28%	32%	36%
1	0.893	0.877	0.862	0.847	0.833	0.806	0.781	0.758	0.735
2	1.690	1.647	1.605	1.566	1.528	1.457	1.392	1.332	1.276
3	2.402	2.322	2.246	2.174	2.106	1.981	1.868	1.766	1.674
4	3.037	2.914	2.798	2.690	2.589	2.404	2.241	2.096	1.966
5	3.605	3.433	3.274	3.127	2.991	2.745	2.532	2.345	2.181
6	4.111	3.889	3.685	3.498	3.326	3.020	2.759	2.534	2.339
7	4.564	4.288	4.039	3.812	3.605	3.242	2.937	2.678	2.455
8	4.968	4.639	4.344	4.078	3.837	3.421	3.076	2.786	2.540
9	5.328	4.946	4.607	4.303	4.031	3.566	3.184	2.868	2.603
10	5.650	5.216	4.833	4.494	4.193	3.682	3.269	2.930	2.650
11	5.988	5.453	5.029	4.656	4.327	3.776	3.335	2.978	2.683
12	6.194	5.660	5.197	4.793	4.439	3.851	3.387	3.013	2.708
13	6.424	5.842	5.342	4.910	4.533	3.912	3.427	3.040	2.727
14	6.628	6.002	5.468	5.008	4.611	3.962	3.459	3.061	2.740
15	6.811	6.142	5.575	5.092	4.675	4.001	3.483	3.076	2.750
16	6.974	6.265	5.669	5.162	4.730	4.033	3.503	3.088	2.758
17	7.120	6.373	5.749	5.222	4.775	4.059	3.518	3.097	2.763
18	7.250	6.467	5.818	5.273	4.812	4.080	3.529	3.104	2.767
19	7.366	6.550	5.877	5.316	4.844	4.097	3.539	3.109	2.770
20	7.469	6.623	5.929	5.353	4.870	4.110	3.546	3.113	2.772
25	7.843	6.873	6.097	5.467	4.948	4.147	3.564	3.122	2.776
30	8.055	7.003	6.177	5.517	4.979	4.160	3.569	3.124	2.778

TABLE E
SELECTED PERCENTILES OF THE "t" DISTRIBUTION

ν	$1 - \alpha$				
	.90	.95	.975	.99	.995
1	3.078	6.314	12.706	31.821	63.657
2	1.886	2.920	4.303	6.965	9.925
3	1.638	2.353	3.182	4.451	5.841
4	1.533	2.132	2.776	3.747	4.604
5	1.476	2.015	2.571	3.365	4.032
6	1.440	1.943	2.447	3.143	3.707
7	1.415	1.895	2.365	2.998	3.499
8	1.397	1.860	2.306	2.896	3.355
9	1.383	1.833	2.262	2.821	3.250
10	1.372	1.812	2.228	2.764	3.169
11	1.363	1.796	2.201	2.718	3.106
12	1.356	1.782	2.179	2.681	3.055
13	1.350	1.771	2.160	2.650	3.012
14	1.345	1.761	2.145	2.624	2.977
15	1.341	1.753	2.131	2.602	2.947
16	1.337	1.746	2.120	2.583	2.921
17	1.333	1.740	2.110	2.567	2.898
18	1.330	1.734	2.101	2.552	2.878
19	1.328	1.729	2.093	2.539	2.861
20	1.325	1.725	2.086	2.528	2.845
21	1.323	1.721	2.080	2.518	2.831
22	1.321	1.717	2.074	2.508	2.819
23	1.319	1.714	2.069	2.500	2.807
24	1.318	1.711	2.064	2.492	2.797
25	1.316	1,708	2.060	2.485	2.787
30	1.310	1.697	2.042	2.457	2.750
40	1.303	1.684	2.021	2.423	2.704
60	1.296	1.671	2.000	2.390	2.660
120	1.289	1.658	1.980	2.358	2.617
∞	1.282	1.645	1.960	2.326	2.576

INDEX

INDEX